This edition of El
Professor Gerald

ABOUT THE AUTHOR

Stephen D. Umans   is a graduate of the Massachusetts Institute of Technology, from which he received the S.B., S.M., E.E., and Sc.D. degrees, all in electrical engineering. He is currently engaged as an independent consultant, having previously held the position of Principal Research Engineer in the MIT Electromechanical Systems Laboratory and lecturer in the MIT Department of Electrical Engineering and Computer Science. He is a member of the US National Academy of Engineering, a Fellow of the IEEE and a recipient of the Cyril Veinott Electromechanical Energy Conversion Award from the IEEE Power Engineering Society.

BRIEF CONTENTS

v

CONTENTS

Since Professors Fitzgerald & Kingsley first published the first edition in 1952, a consistent theme of ELECTRIC MACHINERY has been an emphasis on the development of both physical insight into the characteristics of electric machinery as well as facility with the analytical techniques used to describe their performance. Much has changed since the publication of the first edition; the development of lower-loss electrical steels, rare-earth permanent-magnet materials, improvements in manufacturing techniques, and the advent of power-electronic control and drive systems. The net result is that modern electric machines achieve higher efficiency and are found in an ever-increasing number of applications.

However, the basic principles which govern the performance of electric machinery remain unchanged. The long-standing reputation of ELECTRIC MACHINERY stems in great part from the emphasis on these fundamentals principles. The challenge in producing each new edition is to appropriately "modernize" the treatment while retaining this basic focus. Modernization in previous editions has included an introduction of rare-earth permanent-magnet materials, the inclusion of permanent-magnet ac machines, variable-reluctance machines, and stepping motors as well as a discussion of field-oriented control algorithms.

A significant addition to the sixth edition was the introduction of MATLAB® for use in examples and practice problems as well as in end-of-chapter problems. MATLAB[1] is widely used in many universities and is available in a student version[2]. Although very little in the way of sophisticated mathematics is required of the reader of ELECTRIC MACHINERY, the mathematics can get somewhat messy and tedious. This is especially true in the analysis of ac machines in which there is a significant amount of algebra involving complex numbers. Analytic tools such as MATLAB can relieve the student of having to perform lengthy calculations which in themselves do little to enhance understanding.

Consider: At the time of the publication of the first edition, the chief computational tool available to students was the slide rule. Using only a slide rule, calculating the performance of an induction motor at a single load point, which involves solving equations with complex arguments, is a significant task which can be quite time consuming and which leaves many opportunities for calculation error.

Fast forward to 2013. A MATLAB script to solve the same problem can be easily written and debugged in a matter of minutes, with the solution then obtained essentially instantaneously. With only a slight modification, the same script can be

---

[1] MATLAB and Simulink are registered trademarks of The MathWorks, Inc., 3 Apple Hill Drive, Natick, MA 01760 (http://www.mathworks.com).

[2] The MATLAB Student Version is published and distributed by The MathWorks, Inc. (http://www.mathworks.com).

used to calculate, plot and investigate the performance of the motor over its complete operating range as well as to study the effects of parameter changes, etc.; a task which, if performed with a slide rule (or even a calculator), would require the repeated calculation of many operating points, with each calculation as time consuming as the first.

It should be emphasized that although MATLAB has been chosen for ELECTRIC MACHINERY, equivalent alternative numerical-analysis programs, of which there are many, can be used with equal effectiveness. The key point is that the use of such programs immensely reduces the computational burden on the student and thus significantly increases his/her ability to focus on the principles under consideration.

Note that, even in cases where it is not specifically suggested, most of the end-of-chapter problems in the book can be worked using MATLAB or an equivalent program. Thus, students who are comfortable using such tools should be encouraged to do so to save themselves the need to grind through messy calculations by hand. When solving homework problems, students should still of course be required to show on paper how they formulated their solution, since it is the formulation of the solution that is key to understanding the material. However, once a problem is properly formulated, there is typically little additional to be learned from the number crunching itself. The value of working examples and end-of-chapter problems is derived primarily from the process of formulating the solution and from examining the results.

In addition, at the time the revision of the sixth edition was underway, topics related to energy conversion were being re-introduced into a number of engineering curricula. Feedback from faculty involved in these programs led to the inclusion of a chapter which covered the basic principles of power electronics with an emphasis on their application to electric machines. The power-electronics chapter was of course not intended to be a substitute for a full-fledged course in power electronics. At this time, such courses exist in many engineering programs. Faculty members surveyed in advance of this seventh edition indicated that there is no longer a need for the power-electronics chapter. As a result, it has been removed from the seventh edition and moved to the seventh-edition website.

In considering this revision, there was no question of any change in the focus on fundamental physical principles underlying the performance of electric machines which has been the strength of ELECTRIC MACHINERY since the first edition. In addition, a survey of current adopters of the sixth edition indicated that, with the exception of elimination of the chapter on power electronics, there was no need to revise the range of topics covered. On the other hand, elimination of the power-electronics chapter resulted in space for expansion. Thus, the key features of this revision are:

■   The presentation of all material in the book has been carefully reviewed, revised and/or expanded as needed for additional clarity. One such example is the expanded treatment of permanent-magnet ac machines in Chapter 5. Similarly, the dc-machine presentation of Chapter 7 has been reorganized for added clarity.

- 15 new examples have been added to this edition, bringing the total number of examples in the book to 111, and in addition, some of the examples from the previous edition have been revised.

- Of the total of 371 end-of-chapter problems in this edition, 96 are new problems. Almost all of the remaining problems, although retained in form from the previous edition, have been altered either in substance or numerically such that previous solutions are no longer valid.

- The use of MATLAB has been considerably expanded in the seventh edition, in examples, in practice problems and in end-of-chapter problems.

- New to this edition is a list of variables and their definitions included at the end of each chapter.

- The seventh edition introduces some simple examples of electric-machinery dynamics and includes a few MATLAB/Simulink® examples and problems.

- The majority of photographs from the previous edition have been updated.

As has been the case with past editions, it is highly likely that there is simply too much material in this edition of ELECTRIC MACHINERY for a single introductory course. The material has been organized so that instructors can pick and choose material appropriate to the topics which they wish to cover. The first two chapters introduce basic concepts of magnetic circuits, magnetic materials and transformers. The third chapter introduces the basic concept of electromechanical energy conversion. The fourth chapter then provides an overview of, and introduction to, the various machine types. Some instructors may choose to omit all or most of the material in Chapter 3 from an introductory course. This can be done without significantly impacting the presentation of the material in the remainder of the book.

The next five chapters provide a more in-depth discussion of the various machine types: synchronous machines in Chapter 5, induction machines in Chapter 6, dc machines in Chapter 7, variable-reluctance machines in Chapter 8 and single/two-phase machines in Chapter 9. Since the chapters are relatively independent (with the exception of the material in Chapter 9 which builds upon the polyphase-induction-motor discussion of Chapter 6), the order of these chapters can be changed and/or an instructor can choose to focus on only one or two machine types and not to cover the material in all five of these chapters.

Finally, instructors may wish to select topics from the control material of Chapter 10 rather than include it all. The material on speed control is a relatively straightforward extension of the material found in earlier chapters on the individual machine types. The material on field-oriented control requires a somewhat more sophisticated understanding and builds upon the dq0 transformation found in Appendix C. It would certainly be reasonable to omit this material in an introductory course and to delay it for a more advanced course where sufficient time is available to devote to it.

I would like to specifically acknowledge Prof. Charles Brice of the University of South Carolina and Prof. Gerald Brown of Cedarville University who carefully reviewed various sections of the draft and caught a number of typos and numerical errors. I also wish to thank the many other reviewers who provided feedback during the planning process of this revision.

Mukhtar Ahmad – *Aligarh Muslim University*
Said Ahmed-Zaid – *Boise State University*
Steven Barrett – *University of Wyoming*
Tapas Kumar Bhattacharya – *Indian Institute of Technology Kharagpur*
Kalpana Chaudhary – *Indian Institute of Technology, Banaras Hindu University, Varanasi*
Nagamani Chilakapati – *National Institute of Technology Tiruchirapalli*
S. Arul Daniel – *National Institute of Technology Tiruchirapalli*
Jora M. Gonda – *National Institute of Technology Surathkal*
N. Ammasai Gounden – *National Institute of Technology Tiruchirapalli*
Alan Harris – *University of North Florida*
R.K. Jarial – *National Institute of Technology Hamirpur*
Urmila Kar – *National Institute of Technical Teachers' Training and Research, Kolkata*
M. Rizwan Khan – *Aligarh Muslim University*
Jonathan Kimball – *Missouri University of Science and Technology*
Dave Krispinsky – *Rochester Institute of Technology*
Prabhat Kumar – *Aligarh Muslim University*
Praveen Kumar – *Indian Institute of Technology Guwahati*
N. Kumaresan – *National Institute of Technology Tiruchirapalli*
Eng Gee Lim – *Xi'an Jiaotong-Liverpool University*
Timothy Little – *Dalhousie University*
S. N. Mahendra – *Indian Institute of Technology, Banaras Hindu University, Varanasi*
Yongkui Man – *Northeastern University, China*
David McDonald – *Lake Superior State University*
Shafique S. Mirza – *New Jersey Institute of Technology*
Medhat M. Morcos – *Kansas State University*
G. Narayanan – *Indian Institute of Science, Bangalore*
Adel Nasiri – *University of Wisconsin-Milwaukee*
Sudarshan R. Nelatury – *Penn State*
Sanjoy K. Parida – *Indian Institute of Technology Patna*
Amit N. Patel – *Nirma University*
Peter W. Sauer – *University of Illinois at Urbana-Champaign*
Hesham Shaalan – *US Merchant Marine Academy*
Karma Sonam Sherpa – *Sikkim-Manipal Institute of Technology*
Ajay Srivastava – *G.B. Pant University of Agriculture & Technology*
Murry Stocking – *Ferris State University*
A. Subramanian – *V.R.S College of Engineering and Technology*
Wayne Weaver – *Michigan Technological University*
Jin Zhong – *University of Hong Kong*

Visit the textbook website at **www.mhhe.com/umans7e**. The sixth edition Power Electronics chapter has been posted to the website. For instructors, a downloadable version of the solutions manual, PowerPoint slides of figures from the book, and PowerPoint lecture outlines are posted to the Instructor Edition. Copies of the MATLAB and Simulink files for the various examples used in the book are available for students and instructors.

My mother, Nettie Umans, passed away during the time of this revision. I had looked forward to sharing the seventh edition with her; she would have been excited to see it. She is deeply missed.

Stephen D. Umans
Belmont, MA
2013

Craft your teaching resources to match the way you teach! With McGraw-Hill Create, you can easily rearrange chapters, combine material from other content sources, and quickly upload content you have written like your course syllabus or teaching notes. Find the content you need in Create by searching through thousands of leading McGraw-Hill textbooks. Arrange your book to fit your teaching style. Create even allows you to personalize your book's appearance by selecting the cover and adding your name, school, and course information. Order a Create book and you'll receive a complimentary print review copy in 3-5 business days or a complimentary electronic review copy (eComp) via email in minutes. Go to www.mcgrawhillcreate.com today and register to experience how McGraw-Hill Create empowers you to teach your students your way.

Electronic Textbook Option

This text is offered through CourseSmart for both instructors and students. CourseSmart is an online resource where students can purchase the complete text online at almost half the cost of a traditional text. Purchasing the eTextbook allows students to take advantage of CourseSmart's web tools for learning, which include full text search, notes and highlighting, and email tools for sharing notes between classmates. To learn more about CourseSmart options, contact your sales representative or visit www.CourseSmart.com.

CHAPTER 1

Magnetic Circuits and Magnetic Materials

The objective of this book is to study the devices used in the interconversion of electric and mechanical energy. Emphasis is placed on electromagnetic rotating machinery, by means of which the bulk of this energy conversion takes place. However, the techniques developed are generally applicable to a wide range of additional devices including linear machines, actuators, and sensors.

Although not an electromechanical-energy-conversion device, the transformer is an important component of the overall energy-conversion process and is discussed in Chapter 2. As with the majority of electromechanical-energy-conversion devices discussed in this book, magnetically coupled windings are at the heart of transformer performance. Hence, the techniques developed for transformer analysis form the basis for the ensuing discussion of electric machinery.

Practically all transformers and electric machinery use ferro-magnetic material for shaping and directing the magnetic fields which act as the medium for transferring and converting energy. Permanent-magnet materials are also widely used in electric machinery. Without these materials, practical implementations of most familiar electromechanical-energy-conversion devices would not be possible. The ability to analyze and describe systems containing these materials is essential for designing and understanding these devices.

This chapter will develop some basic tools for the analysis of magnetic field systems and will provide a brief introduction to the properties of practical magnetic materials. In Chapter 2, these techniques will be applied to the analysis of transformers. In later chapters they will be used in the analysis of rotating machinery.

In this book it is assumed that the reader has basic knowledge of magnetic and electric field theory such as is found in a basic physics course for engineering students. Some readers may have had a course on electromagnetic field theory based on Maxwell's equations, but an in-depth understanding of Maxwell's equations is not a prerequisite for mastery of the material of this book. The techniques of magnetic-circuit analysis which provide algebraic approximations to exact field-theory solutions are widely used in the study of electromechanical-energy-conversion devices and form the basis for most of the analyses presented here.

1.1 INTRODUCTION TO MAGNETIC CIRCUITS

The complete, detailed solution for magnetic fields in most situations of practical engineering interest involves the solution of Maxwell's equations and requires a set of constitutive relationships to describe material properties. Although in practice exact solutions are often unattainable, various simplifying assumptions permit the attainment of useful engineering solutions.[1]

We begin with the assumption that, for the systems treated in this book, the frequencies and sizes involved are such that the displacement-current term in Maxwell's equations can be neglected. This term accounts for magnetic fields being produced in space by time-varying electric fields and is associated with electromagnetic radiation. Neglecting this term results in the magneto-quasi-static form of the relevant Maxwell's equations which relate magnetic fields to the currents which produce them.

$$\oint_C \mathbf{Hdl} = \int_S \mathbf{J} \cdot \mathbf{da} \tag{1.1}$$

$$\oint_S \mathbf{B} \cdot \mathbf{da} = 0 \tag{1.2}$$

Equation 1.1, frequently referred to as *Ampere's Law*, states that the line integral of the tangential component of the *magnetic field intensity* **H** around a closed contour *C* is equal to the total current passing through any surface *S* linking that contour. From Eq. 1.1 we see that the source of **H** is the *current density* **J**. Eq. 1.2, frequently referred to as *Gauss' Law for magnetic fields*, states that *magnetic flux density* **B** is conserved, i.e., that no net flux enters or leaves a closed surface (this is equivalent to saying that there exist no monopolar sources of magnetic fields). From these equations we see that the magnetic field quantities can be determined solely from the instantaneous values of the source currents and hence that time variations of the magnetic fields follow directly from time variations of the sources.

A second simplifying assumption involves the concept of a *magnetic circuit*. It is extremely difficult to obtain the general solution for the magnetic field intensity **H** and the magnetic flux density **B** in a structure of complex geometry. However, in many practical applications, including the analysis of many types of electric machines, a three-dimensional field problem can often be approximated by what is essentially

---

[1] Computer-based numerical solutions based upon the finite-element method form the basis for a number of commercial programs and have become indispensable tools for analysis and design. Such tools are typically best used to refine initial analyses based upon analytical techniques such as are found in this book. Because such techniques contribute little to a fundamental understanding of the principles and basic performance of electric machines, they are not discussed in this book.

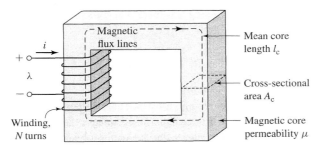

Figure 1.1 Simple magnetic circuit. λ is the winding flux linkage as defined in Section 1.2.

$$\mu_0 = 4\pi \times 10^{-7}\, \frac{H}{m}$$

a one-dimensional circuit equivalent, yielding solutions of acceptable engineering accuracy.

A magnetic circuit consists of a structure composed for the most part of high-permeability magnetic material.[2] The presence of high-permeability material tends to cause magnetic flux to be confined to the paths defined by the structure, much as currents are confined to the conductors of an electric circuit. Use of this concept of the magnetic circuit is illustrated in this section and will be seen to apply quite well to many situations in this book.[3]

A simple example of a magnetic circuit is shown in Fig. 1.1. The core is assumed to be composed of magnetic material whose *magnetic permeability* μ is much greater than that of the surrounding air ($\mu \gg \mu_0$) where $\mu_0 = 4\pi \times 10^{-7}$ H/m is the magnetic permeability of free space. The core is of uniform cross section and is excited by a winding of N turns carrying a current of i amperes. This winding produces a magnetic field in the core, as shown in the figure.

Because of the high permeability of the magnetic core, an exact solution would show that the magnetic flux is confined almost entirely to the core, with the field lines following the path defined by the core, and that the flux density is essentially uniform over a cross section because the cross-sectional area is uniform. The magnetic field can be visualized in terms of flux lines which form closed loops interlinked with the winding.

As applied to the magnetic circuit of Fig. 1.1, the source of the magnetic field in the core is the ampere-turn product Ni. In magnetic circuit terminology Ni is the *magnetomotive force* (mmf) $\mathcal{F}$ acting on the magnetic circuit. Although Fig. 1.1 shows only a single winding, transformers and most rotating machines typically have at least two windings, and Ni must be replaced by the algebraic sum of the ampere-turns of all the windings.

---

[2] In its simplest definition, magnetic permeability can be thought of as the ratio of the magnitude of the magnetic flux density B to the magnetic field intensity H.

[3] For a more extensive treatment of magnetic circuits see A.E. Fitzgerald, D.E. Higgenbotham, and A. Grabel, *Basic Electrical Engineering*, 5th ed., McGraw-Hill, 1981, chap. 13; also E.E. Staff, M.I.T., *Magnetic Circuits and Transformers*, M.I.T. Press, 1965, chaps. 1 to 3.

The net *magnetic flux* ϕ crossing a surface S is the surface integral of the normal component of **B**; thus

$$\phi = \int_S \mathbf{B} \cdot \mathbf{da} \tag{1.3}$$

In SI units, the unit of ϕ is the *weber* (Wb).

Equation 1.2 states that the net magnetic flux entering or leaving a closed surface (equal to the surface integral of **B** over that closed surface) is zero. This is equivalent to saying that all the flux which enters the surface enclosing a volume must leave that volume over some other portion of that surface because magnetic flux lines form closed loops. Because little flux "leaks" out the sides of the magnetic circuit of Fig. 1.1, this result shows that the net flux is the same through each cross section of the core.

For a magnetic circuit of this type, it is common to assume that the magnetic flux density (and correspondingly the magnetic field intensity) is uniform across the cross section and throughout the core. In this case Eq. 1.3 reduces to the simple scalar equation

$$\phi_c = B_c A_c \tag{1.4}$$

where

$$\phi_c = \text{core flux}$$
$$B_c = \text{core flux density}$$
$$A_c = \text{core cross-sectional area}$$

From Eq. 1.1, the relationship between the mmf acting on a magnetic circuit and the magnetic field intensity in that circuit is.[4]

$$\mathcal{F} = Ni = \oint \mathbf{Hdl} \tag{1.5}$$

The core dimensions are such that the path length of any flux line is close to the mean core length l_c. As a result, the line integral of Eq. 1.5 becomes simply the scalar product $H_c l_c$ of the magnitude of **H** and the mean flux path length l_c. Thus, the relationship between the mmf and the magnetic field intensity can be written in magnetic circuit terminology as

$$\mathcal{F} = Ni = H_c l_c \tag{1.6}$$

where H_c is average magnitude of **H** in the core.

The direction of H_c in the core can be found from the *right-hand rule*, which can be stated in two equivalent ways. (1) Imagine a current-carrying conductor held in the right hand with the thumb pointing in the direction of current flow; the fingers then point in the direction of the magnetic field created by that current. (2) Equivalently, if the coil in Fig. 1.1 is grasped in the right hand (figuratively speaking) with the fingers

---

[4] In general, the mmf drop across any segment of a magnetic circuit can be calculated as $\int \mathbf{Hdl}$ over that portion of the magnetic circuit.

pointing in the direction of the current, the thumb will point in the direction of the magnetic fields.

The relationship between the magnetic field intensity **H** and the magnetic flux density **B** is a property of the material in which the field exists. It is common to assume a linear relationship; thus

$$\mathbf{B} = \mu \mathbf{H} \qquad (1.7)$$

where μ is the material's magnetic permeability. In SI units, **H** is measured in units of *amperes per meter*, **B** is in *webers per square meter*, also known as *teslas* (T), and μ is in *webers per ampere-turn-meter*, or equivalently *henrys per meter*. In SI units the permeability of free space is $\mu_0 = 4\pi \times 10^{-7}$ henrys per meter. The permeability of linear magnetic material can be expressed in terms of its *relative permeability* μ_r, its value relative to that of free space; $\mu = \mu_r \mu_0$. Typical values of μ_r range from 2,000 to 80,000 for materials used in transformers and rotating machines. The characteristics of ferromagnetic materials are described in Sections 1.3 and 1.4. For the present we assume that μ_r is a known constant, although it actually varies appreciably with the magnitude of the magnetic flux density.

Transformers are wound on closed cores like that of Fig. 1.1. However, energy conversion devices which incorporate a moving element must have air gaps in their magnetic circuits. A magnetic circuit with an air gap is shown in Fig. 1.2. When the air-gap length g is much smaller than the dimensions of the adjacent core faces, the core flux ϕ_c will follow the path defined by the core and the air gap and the techniques of magnetic-circuit analysis can be used. If the air-gap length becomes excessively large, the flux will be observed to "leak out" of the sides of the air gap and the techniques of magnetic-circuit analysis will no longer be strictly applicable.

Thus, provided the air-gap length g is sufficiently small, the configuration of Fig. 1.2 can be analyzed as a magnetic circuit with two series components both carrying the same flux ϕ: a magnetic core of permeability μ, cross-sectional area A_c and mean length l_c, and an air gap of permeability μ_0, cross-sectional area A_g and length g. In the core

$$B_c = \frac{\phi}{A_c} \qquad (1.8)$$

Figure 1.2 Magnetic circuit with air gap.

and in the air gap

$$B_g = \frac{\phi}{A_c} \tag{1.9}$$

Application of Eq. 1.5 to this magnetic circuit yields

$$\mathcal{F} = H_c l_c + H_g g \tag{1.10}$$

and using the linear *B-H* relationship of Eq. 1.7 gives

$$\mathcal{F} = \frac{B_c}{\mu} l_c + \frac{B_g}{\mu_0} g \tag{1.11}$$

Here the $\mathcal{F} = Ni$ is the mmf applied to the magnetic circuit. From Eq. 1.10 we see that a portion of the mmf, $\mathcal{F}_c = H_c l_c$, is required to produce magnetic field in the core while the remainder, $\mathcal{F}_g = H_g g$ produces magnetic field in the air gap.

For practical magnetic materials (as is discussed in Sections 1.3 and 1.4), B_c and H_c are not simply related by a known constant permeability μ as described by Eq. 1.7. In fact, B_c is often a nonlinear, multi-valued function of H_c. Thus, although Eq. 1.10 continues to hold, it does not lead directly to a simple expression relating the mmf and the flux densities, such as that of Eq. 1.11. Instead the specifics of the nonlinear B_c-H_c relation must be used, either graphically or analytically. However, in many cases, the concept of constant material permeability gives results of acceptable engineering accuracy and is frequently used.

From Eqs. 1.8 and 1.9, Eq. 1.11 can be rewritten in terms of the flux ϕ_c as

$$\mathcal{F} = \phi \left(\frac{l_c}{\mu A_c} + \frac{g}{\mu_0 A_g} \right) \tag{1.12}$$

The terms that multiply the flux in this equation are known as the *reluctance* ($\mathcal{R}$) of the core and air gap, respectively,

$$\mathcal{R}_c = \frac{l_c}{\mu A_c} \tag{1.13}$$

$$\mathcal{R}_g = \frac{g}{\mu_0 A_g} \tag{1.14}$$

and thus

$$\mathcal{F} = \phi(\mathcal{R}_c + \mathcal{R}_g) \tag{1.15}$$

Finally, Eq. 1.15 can be inverted to solve for the flux

$$\phi = \frac{\mathcal{F}}{\mathcal{R}_c + \mathcal{R}_g} \tag{1.16}$$

or

$$\phi = \frac{\mathcal{F}}{\frac{l_c}{\mu A_c} + \frac{g}{\mu_0 A_g}} \tag{1.17}$$

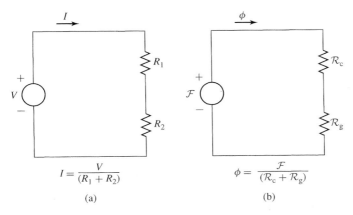

Figure 1.3 Analogy between electric and magnetic circuits.
(a) Electric circuit. (b) Magnetic circuit.

In general, for any magnetic circuit of total reluctance $\mathcal{R}_{\text{tot}}$, the flux can be found as

$$\phi = \frac{\mathcal{F}}{\mathcal{R}_{\text{tot}}} \tag{1.18}$$

The term which multiplies the mmf is known as the *permeance* $\mathcal{P}$ and is the inverse of the reluctance; thus, for example, the total permeance of a magnetic circuit is

$$\mathcal{P}_{\text{tot}} = \frac{1}{\mathcal{R}_{\text{tot}}} \tag{1.19}$$

Note that Eqs. 1.15 and 1.16 are analogous to the relationships between the current and voltage in an electric circuit. This analogy is illustrated in Fig. 1.3. Figure 1.3a shows an electric circuit in which a voltage V drives a current I through resistors R_1 and R_2. Figure 1.3b shows the schematic equivalent representation of the magnetic circuit of Fig. 1.2 . Here we see that the mmf $\mathcal{F}$ (analogous to voltage in the electric circuit) drives a flux ϕ (analogous to the current in the electric circuit) through the combination of the reluctances of the core $\mathcal{R}_c$ and the air gap $\mathcal{R}_g$. This analogy between the solution of electric and magnetic circuits can often be exploited to produce simple solutions for the fluxes in magnetic circuits of considerable complexity.

The fraction of the mmf required to drive flux through each portion of the magnetic circuit, commonly referred to as the *mmf drop* across that portion of the magnetic circuit, varies in proportion to its reluctance (directly analogous to the voltage drop across a resistive element in an electric circuit). Consider the magnetic circuit of Fig. 1.2. From Eq. 1.13 we see that high material permeability can result in low core reluctance, which can often be made much smaller than that of the air gap; i.e., for $(\mu A_c / l_c) \gg (\mu_0 A_g / g)$, $\mathcal{R}_c \ll \mathcal{R}_g$ and thus $\mathcal{R}_{\text{tot}} \approx \mathcal{R}_g$. In this case, the reluctance of the core can be neglected and the flux can be found from Eq. 1.16 in terms of $\mathcal{F}$ and the air-gap properties alone:

$$\phi \approx \frac{\mathcal{F}}{\mathcal{R}_g} = \frac{\mathcal{F} \mu_0 A_g}{g} = Ni \frac{\mu_0 A_g}{g} \tag{1.20}$$

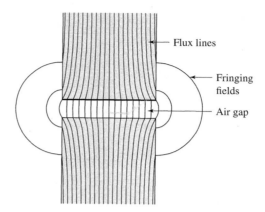

Figure 1.4 Air-gap fringing fields.

As will be seen in Section 1.3, practical magnetic materials have permeabilities which are not constant but vary with the flux level. From Eqs. 1.13 to 1.16 we see that as long as this permeability remains sufficiently large, its variation will not significantly affect the performance of a magnetic circuit in which the dominant reluctance is that of an air gap.

In practical systems, the magnetic field lines "fringe" outward somewhat as they cross the air gap, as illustrated in Fig. 1.4. Provided this fringing effect is not excessive, the magnetic-circuit concept remains applicable. The effect of these *fringing fields* is to increase the effective cross-sectional area A_g of the air gap. Various empirical methods have been developed to account for this effect. A correction for such fringing fields in short air gaps can be made by adding the gap length to each of the two dimensions making up its cross-sectional area. In this book the effect of fringing fields is usually ignored. If fringing is neglected, $A_g = A_c$.

In general, magnetic circuits can consist of multiple elements in series and parallel. To complete the analogy between electric and magnetic circuits, we can generalize Eq. 1.5 as

$$\mathcal{F} = \oint \mathbf{Hdl} = \sum_k \mathcal{F}_k = \sum_k H_k l_k \tag{1.21}$$

where $\mathcal{F}$ is the mmf (total ampere-turns) acting to drive flux through a closed loop of a magnetic circuit, and $\mathcal{F}_k = H_k l_k$ is the *mmf drop* across the k'th element of that loop. This is directly analogous to Kirchoff's voltage law for electric circuits consisting of voltage sources and resistors

$$V = \sum_k R_k i_k \tag{1.22}$$

where V is the source voltage driving current around a loop and $R_k i_k$ is the voltage drop across the k'th resistive element of that loop.

Similarly, the analogy to Kirchoff's current law

$$\sum_n i_n = 0 \tag{1.23}$$

which says that the net current, i.e. the sum of the currents, into a node in an electric circuit equals zero is

$$\sum_n \phi_n = 0 \tag{1.24}$$

which states that the net flux into a node in a magnetic circuit is zero.

We have now described the basic principles for reducing a magneto-quasi-static field problem with simple geometry to a *magnetic circuit model*. Our limited purpose in this section is to introduce some of the concepts and terminology used by engineers in solving practical design problems. We must emphasize that this type of thinking depends quite heavily on engineering judgment and intuition. For example, we have tacitly assumed that the permeability of the "iron" parts of the magnetic circuit is a constant known quantity, although this is not true in general (see Section 1.3), and that the magnetic field is confined solely to the core and its air gaps. Although this is a good assumption in many situations, it is also true that the winding currents produce magnetic fields outside the core. As we shall see, when two or more windings are placed on a magnetic circuit, as happens in the case of both transformers and rotating machines, these fields outside the core, referred to as *leakage fields*, cannot be ignored and may significantly affect the performance of the device.

EXAMPLE 1.1

The magnetic circuit shown in Fig. 1.2 has dimensions $A_c = A_g = 9$ cm^2, $g = 0.050$ cm, $l_c = 30$ cm, and $N = 500$ turns. Assume the value $\mu_r = 70{,}000$ for core material. (a) Find the reluctances $\mathcal{R}_c$ and $\mathcal{R}_g$. For the condition that the magnetic circuit is operating with $B_c = 1.0$ T, find (b) the flux ϕ and (c) the current i.

■ **Solution**

a. The reluctances can be found from Eqs. 1.13 and 1.14:

$$\mathcal{R}_c = \frac{l_c}{\mu_r \mu_0 A_c} = \frac{0.3}{70{,}000 \,(4\pi \times 10^{-7})(9 \times 10^{-4})} = 3.79 \times 10^3 \ \frac{A \cdot \text{turns}}{Wb}$$

$$\mathcal{R}_g = \frac{g}{\mu_0 A_g} = \frac{5 \times 10^{-4}}{(4\pi \times 10^{-7})(9 \times 10^{-4})} = 4.42 \times 10^5 \ \frac{A \cdot \text{turns}}{Wb}$$

b. From Eq. 1.4,

$$\phi = B_c A_c = 1.0(9 \times 10^{-4}) = 9 \times 10^{-4} \ \text{Wb}$$

c. From Eqs. 1.6 and 1.15,

$$i = \frac{\mathcal{F}}{N} = \frac{\phi(\mathcal{R}_c + \mathcal{R}_g)}{N} = \frac{9 \times 10^{-4}(4.46 \times 10^5)}{500} = 0.80 \ \text{A}$$

Practice Problem 1.1

Find the flux ϕ and current for Example 1.1 if (a) the number of turns is doubled to $N = 1000$ turns while the circuit dimensions remain the same and (b) if the number of turns is equal to $N = 500$ and the gap is reduced to 0.040 cm.

Solution

    a. $\phi = 9 \times 10^{-4}$ Wb and $i = 0.40$ A
    b. $\phi = 9 \times 10^{-4}$ Wb and $i = 0.64$ A

EXAMPLE 1.2

The magnetic structure of a synchronous machine is shown schematically in Fig. 1.5. Assuming that rotor and stator iron have infinite permeability ($\mu \rightarrow \infty$), find the air-gap flux ϕ and flux density B_g. For this example $I = 10$ A, $N = 1{,}000$ turns, $g = 1$ cm, and $A_g = 200$ cm^2.

■ Solution

Notice that there are two air gaps in series, of total length $2g$, and that by symmetry the flux density in each is equal. Since the iron permeability is assumed to be infinite, its reluctance is negligible and Eq. 1.20 (with g replaced by the total gap length $2g$) can be used to find the flux

$$\phi = \frac{NI\mu_0 A_g}{2g} = \frac{1000(10)(4\pi \times 10^{-7})(0.02)}{0.02} = 12.6 \text{ m Wb}$$

and

$$B_g = \frac{\phi}{A_g} = \frac{0.0126}{0.02} = 0.630 \text{ T}$$

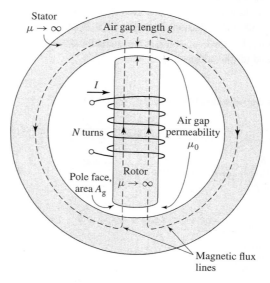

Figure 1.5 Simple synchronous machine.

For the magnetic structure of Fig. 1.5 with the dimensions as given in Example 1.2, the air-gap flux density is observed to be $B_g = 0.9$ T. Find the air-gap flux ϕ and, for a coil of $N = 500$ turns, the current required to produce this level of air-gap flux.

Solution

$\phi = 0.018$ Wb and $i = 28.6$ A.

1.2 FLUX LINKAGE, INDUCTANCE, AND ENERGY

When a magnetic field varies with time, an electric field is produced in space as determined by another of Maxwell's equations referred to as *Faraday's law*:

$$\oint_C \mathbf{E} \cdot \mathbf{ds} = -\frac{d}{dt} \int_S \mathbf{B} \cdot \mathbf{da} \qquad (1.25)$$

Equation 1.25 states that the line integral of the *electric field intensity* $\mathbf{E}$ around a closed contour C is equal to the time rate of change of the magnetic flux linking (i.e., passing through) that contour. In magnetic structures with windings of high electrical conductivity, such as in Fig. 1.2, it can be shown that the $\mathbf{E}$ field in the wire is extremely small and can be neglected, so that the left-hand side of Eq. 1.25 reduces to the negative of the *induced voltage*[5] e at the winding terminals. In addition, the flux on the right-hand side of Eq. 1.25 is dominated by the core flux ϕ. Since the winding (and hence the contour C) links the core flux N times, Eq. 1.25 reduces to

$$e = N\frac{d\varphi}{dt} = \frac{d\lambda}{dt} \qquad (1.26)$$

where λ is the *flux linkage* of the winding and is defined as

$$\lambda = N\varphi \qquad (1.27)$$

Flux linkage is measured in units of webers (or equivalently weber-turns). Note that we have chosen the symbol φ to indicate the instantaneous value of a time-varying flux.

In general the flux linkage of a coil is equal to the surface integral of the normal component of the magnetic flux density integrated over any surface spanned by that coil. Note that the direction of the induced voltage e is defined by Eq. 1.25 so that if the winding terminals were short-circuited, a current would flow in such a direction as to oppose the change of flux linkage.

For a magnetic circuit composed of magnetic material of constant magnetic permeability or which includes a dominating air gap, the relationship between λ

---

[5] The term *electromotive force* (emf) is often used instead of induced voltage to represent that component of voltage due to a time-varying flux linkage.

and i will be linear and we can define the *inductance L* as

$$L = \frac{\lambda}{i} \tag{1.28}$$

Substitution of Eqs. 1.5, 1.18 and 1.27 into Eq. 1.28 gives

$$L = \frac{N^2}{\mathcal{R}_{\text{tot}}} \tag{1.29}$$

from which we see that the inductance of a winding in a magnetic circuit is proportional to the square of the turns and inversely proportional to the reluctance of the magnetic circuit associated with that winding.

For example, from Eq. 1.20, under the assumption that the reluctance of the core is negligible as compared to that of the air gap, the inductance of the winding in Fig. 1.2 is equal to

$$L = \frac{N^2}{(g/\mu_0 A_{\text{g}})} = \frac{N^2 \mu_0 A_{\text{g}}}{g} \tag{1.30}$$

Inductance is measured in *henrys* (H) or *weber-turns per ampere*. Equation 1.30 shows the dimensional form of expressions for inductance; inductance is proportional to the square of the number of turns, to a magnetic permeability and to a cross-sectional area and is inversely proportional to a length. It must be emphasized that strictly speaking, the concept of inductance requires a linear relationship between flux and mmf. Thus, it cannot be rigorously applied in situations where the non-linear characteristics of magnetic materials, as is discussed in Sections 1.3 and 1.4, dominate the performance of the magnetic system. However, in many situations of practical interest, the reluctance of the system is dominated by that of an air gap (which is of course linear) and the non-linear effects of the magnetic material can be ignored. In other cases it may be perfectly acceptable to assume an average value of magnetic permeability for the core material and to calculate a corresponding average inductance which can be used for calculations of reasonable engineering accuracy. Example 1.3 illustrates the former situation and Example 1.4 the latter.

EXAMPLE 1.3

The magnetic circuit of Fig. 1.6a consists of an N-turn winding on a magnetic core of infinite permeability with two parallel air gaps of lengths g_1 and g_2 and areas A_1 and A_2, respectively.

Find (a) the inductance of the winding and (b) the flux density B_1 in gap 1 when the winding is carrying a current i. Neglect fringing effects at the air gap.

■ Solution

a. The equivalent circuit of Fig. 1.6b shows that the total reluctance is equal to the parallel combination of the two gap reluctances. Thus

$$\phi = \frac{Ni}{\frac{\mathcal{R}_1 \mathcal{R}_2}{\mathcal{R}_1 + \mathcal{R}_2}}$$

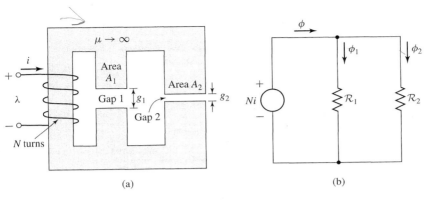

Figure 1.6 (a) Magnetic circuit and (b) equivalent circuit for Example 1.3.

where

$$\mathcal{R}_1 = \frac{g_1}{\mu_0 A_1} \qquad \mathcal{R}_2 = \frac{g_2}{\mu_0 A_2}$$

From Eq. 1.28,

$$L = \frac{\lambda}{i} = \frac{N\phi}{i} = \frac{N^2(\mathcal{R}_1 + \mathcal{R}_2)}{\mathcal{R}_1 \mathcal{R}_2}$$

$$= \mu_0 N^2 \left(\frac{A_1}{g_1} + \frac{A_2}{g_2} \right)$$

b. From the equivalent circuit, one can see that

$$\phi_1 = \frac{Ni}{\mathcal{R}_1} = \frac{\mu_0 A_1 Ni}{g_1}$$

and thus

$$B_1 = \frac{\phi_1}{A_1} = \frac{\mu_0 Ni}{g_1}$$

EXAMPLE 1.4

In Example 1.1, the relative permeability of the core material for the magnetic circuit of Fig. 1.2 is assumed to be $\mu_r = 70,000$ at a flux density of 1.0 T.

a. In a practical device, the core would be constructed from electrical steel such as M-5 electrical steel which is discussed in Section 1.3. This material is highly nonlinear and its relative permeability (defined for the purposes of this example as the ratio B/H) varies from a value of approximately $\mu_r = 72,300$ at a flux density of $B = 1.0$ T to a value of on the order of $\mu_r = 2,900$ as the flux density is raised to 1.8 T. Calculate the inductance under the assumption that the relative permeability of the core steel is 72,300.

b. Calculate the inductance under the assumption that the relative permeability is equal to 2,900.

■ Solution

a. From Eqs. 1.13 and 1.14 and based upon the dimensions given in Example 1.1,

$$\mathcal{R}_c = \frac{l_c}{\mu_r \mu_0 A_c} = \frac{0.3}{72{,}300 \, (4\pi \times 10^{-7})(9 \times 10^{-4})} = 3.67 \times 10^3 \, \frac{A \cdot turns}{Wb}$$

while $\mathcal{R}_g$ remains unchanged from the value calculated in Example 1.1 as $\mathcal{R}_g = 4.42 \times 10^5$ A·turns/Wb.

Thus the total reluctance of the core and gap is

$$\mathcal{R}_{tot} = \mathcal{R}_c + \mathcal{R}_g = 4.46 \times 10^5 \, \frac{A \cdot turns}{Wb}$$

and hence from Eq. 1.29

$$L = \frac{N^2}{\mathcal{R}_{tot}} = \frac{500^2}{4.46 \times 10^5} = 0.561 \, H$$

b. For $\mu_r = 2{,}900$, the reluctance of the core increases from a value of 3.79×10^3 A · turns / Wb to a value of

$$\mathcal{R}_c = \frac{l_c}{\mu_r \mu_0 A_c} = \frac{0.3}{2{,}900 \, (4\pi \times 10^{-7})(9 \times 10^{-4})} = 9.15 \times 10^4 \, \frac{A \cdot turns}{Wb}$$

and hence the total reluctance increases from 4.46×10^5 A · turns / Wb to 5.34×10^5 A · turns / Wb. Thus from Eq. 1.29 the inductance decreases from 0.561 H to

$$L = \frac{N^2}{\mathcal{R}_{tot}} = \frac{500^2}{5.34 \times 10^5} = 0.468 \, H$$

This example illustrates the linearizing effect of a dominating air gap in a magnetic circuit. In spite of a reduction in the permeablity of the iron by a factor of 72,300/2,900 = 25, the inductance decreases only by a factor of 0.468/0.561 = 0.83 simply because the reluctance of the air gap is significantly larger than that of the core. In many situations, it is common to assume the inductance to be constant at a value corresponding to a finite, constant value of core permeability (or in many cases it is assumed simply that $\mu_r \rightarrow \infty$). Analyses based upon such a representation for the inductor will often lead to results which are well within the range of acceptable engineering accuracy and which avoid the immense complication associated with modeling the non-linearity of the core material.

Practice Problem 1.3

Repeat the inductance calculation of Example 1.4 for a relative permeability $\mu_r = 30{,}000$.

Solution
$L = 0.554 \, H$

EXAMPLE 1.5

Using MATLAB,[6] plot the inductance of the magnetic circuit of Example 1.1 and Fig. 1.2 as a function of core permeability over the range $100 \leq \mu_r \leq 100{,}000$.

---

[6] "MATLAB" ia a registered trademarks of The MathWorks, Inc., 3 Apple Hill Drive, Natick, MA 01760, http://www.mathworks.com. A student edition of Matlab is available.

■ Solution

Here is the MATLAB script:

Important
for Lab

```
clc
clear

% Permeability of free space
mu0 = pi*4.e-7;

%All dimensions expressed in meters
Ac = 9e-4; Ag = 9e-4; g = 5e-4; lc = 0.3;
N = 500;

%Reluctance of air gap
Rg = g/(mu0*Ag);

mur = 1:100:100000;
Rc = lc./(mur*mu0*Ac);
Rtot = Rg+Rc;
L = N^2./Rtot;

plot(mur,L)
xlabel('Core relative permeability')
ylabel('Inductance [H]')
```

The resultant plot is shown in Fig. 1.7. Note that the figure clearly confirms that, for the magnetic circuit of this example, the inductance is quite insensitive to relative permeability

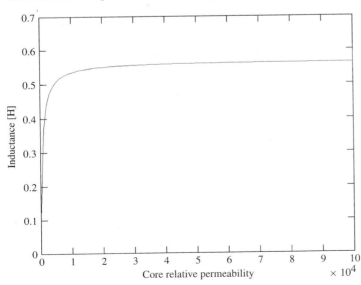

Figure 1.7 MATLAB plot of inductance vs. relative permeability for Example 1.5.

until the relative permeability drops to on the order of 1,000. Thus, as long as the effective relative permeability of the core is "large" (in this case greater than 1,000), any non-linearities in the properties of the core material will have little effect on the terminal properties of the inductor.

Write a MATLAB script to plot the inductance of the magnetic circuit of Example 1.1 with $\mu_r = 70,000$ as a function of air-gap length as the the air gap is varied from 0.01 cm to 0.10 cm.

Figure 1.8 shows a magnetic circuit with an air gap and two windings. In this case note that the mmf acting on the magnetic circuit is given by the *total ampere-turns* acting on the magnetic circuit (i.e., the net ampere-turns of both windings) and that the reference directions for the currents have been chosen to produce flux in the same direction. The total mmf is therefore

$$\mathcal{F} = N_1 i_1 + N_2 i_2 \tag{1.31}$$

and from Eq. 1.20, with the reluctance of the core neglected and assuming that $A_c = A_g$, the core flux ϕ is

$$\phi = (N_1 i_1 + N_2 i_2) \frac{\mu_0 A_c}{g} \tag{1.32}$$

In Eq. 1.32, ϕ is the *resultant core flux* produced by the total mmf of the two windings. It is this resultant ϕ which determines the operating point of the core material.

If Eq. 1.32 is broken up into terms attributable to the individual currents, the resultant flux linkages of coil 1 can be expressed as

$$\lambda_1 = N_1 \phi = N_1{}^2 \left(\frac{\mu_0 A_c}{g} \right) i_1 + N_1 N_2 \left(\frac{\mu_0 A_c}{g} \right) i_2 \tag{1.33}$$

which can be written

$$\lambda_1 = L_{11} i_1 + L_{12} i_2 \tag{1.34}$$

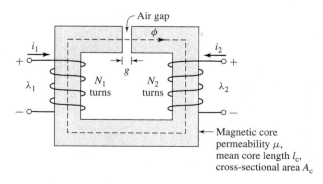

Figure 1.8   Magnetic circuit with two windings.

where

$$L_{11} = N_1{}^2 \frac{\mu_0 A_c}{g} \qquad (1.35)$$

is the *self-inductance* of coil 1 and $L_{11}i_1$ is the flux linkage of coil 1 due to its own current i_1. The *mutual inductance* between coils 1 and 2 is

$$L_{12} = N_1 N_2 \frac{\mu_0 A_c}{g} \qquad (1.36)$$

and $L_{12}i_2$ is the flux linkage of coil 1 due to current i_2 in the other coil. Similarly, the flux linkage of coil 2 is

$$\lambda_2 = N_2\phi = N_1 N_2 \left(\frac{\mu_0 A_c}{g}\right) i_1 + N_2{}^2 \left(\frac{\mu_0 A_c}{g}\right) i_2 \qquad (1.37)$$

or

$$\lambda_2 = L_{21}i_1 + L_{22}i_2 \qquad (1.38)$$

where $L_{21} = L_{12}$ is the mutual inductance and

$$L_{22} = N_2{}^2 \frac{\mu_0 A_c}{g} \qquad (1.39)$$

is the self-inductance of coil 2.

It is important to note that the resolution of the resultant flux linkages into the components produced by i_1 and i_2 is based on superposition of the individual effects and therefore implies a linear flux-mmf relationship (characteristic of materials of constant permeability).

Substitution of Eq. 1.28 in Eq. 1.26 yields

$$e = \frac{d}{dt}(Li) \qquad (1.40)$$

for a magnetic circuit with a single winding. For a static magnetic circuit, the inductance is fixed (assuming that material nonlinearities do not cause the inductance to vary), and this equation reduces to the familiar circuit-theory form

$$e = L\frac{di}{dt} \qquad (1.41)$$

However, in electromechanical energy conversion devices, inductances are often time-varying, and Eq. 1.40 must be written as

$$e = L\frac{di}{dt} + i\frac{dL}{dt} \qquad (1.42)$$

Note that in situations with multiple windings, the total flux linkage of each winding must be used in Eq. 1.26 to find the winding-terminal voltage.

The power at the terminals of a winding on a magnetic circuit is a measure of the rate of energy flow into the circuit through that particular winding. The *power, p,* is determined from the product of the voltage and the current

$$p = ie = i\frac{d\lambda}{dt} \qquad (1.43)$$

and its unit is *watts* (W), or *joules per second*. Thus the change in *magnetic stored energy* ΔW in the magnetic circuit in the time interval t_1 to t_2 is

$$\Delta W = \int_{t_1}^{t_2} p \, dt = \int_{\lambda_1}^{\lambda_2} i \, d\lambda \tag{1.44}$$

In SI units, the magnetic stored energy W is measured in *joules* (J).

For a single-winding system of constant inductance, the change in magnetic stored energy as the flux level is changed from λ_1 to λ_2 can be written as

$$\Delta W = \int_{\lambda_1}^{\lambda_2} i \, d\lambda = \int_{\lambda_1}^{\lambda_2} \frac{\lambda}{L} \, d\lambda = \frac{1}{2L}(\lambda_2^2 - \lambda_1^2) \tag{1.45}$$

The total magnetic stored energy at any given value of λ can be found from setting λ_1 equal to zero:

$$W = \frac{1}{2L}\lambda^2 = \frac{L}{2}i^2 \tag{1.46}$$

EXAMPLE 1.6

For the magnetic circuit of Example 1.1 (Fig. 1.2), find (a) the inductance L, (b) the magnetic stored energy W for $B_c = 1.0$ T, and (c) the induced voltage e for a 60-Hz time-varying core flux of the form $B_c = 1.0 \sin \omega t$ T where $\omega = (2\pi)(60) = 377$.

■ Solution

a. From Eqs. 1.16 and 1.28 and Example 1.1,

$$L = \frac{\lambda}{i} = \frac{N\phi}{i} = \frac{N^2}{\mathcal{R}_c + \mathcal{R}_g}$$

$$= \frac{500^2}{4.46 \times 10^5} = 0.56 \text{ H}$$

Note that the core reluctance is much smaller than that of the gap ($\mathcal{R}_c \ll \mathcal{R}_g$). Thus to a good approximation the inductance is dominated by the gap reluctance, i.e.,

$$L \approx \frac{N^2}{\mathcal{R}_g} = 0.57 \text{ H}$$

b. In Example 1.1 we found that when $B_c = 1.0$ T, $i = 0.80$ A. Thus from Eq. 1.46,

$$W = \frac{1}{2}Li^2 = \frac{1}{2}(0.56)(0.80)^2 = 0.18 \text{ J}$$

c. From Eq. 1.26 and Example 1.1,

$$e = \frac{d\lambda}{dt} = N\frac{d\varphi}{dt} = NA_c\frac{dB_c}{dt}$$

$$= 500 \times (9 \times 10^{-4}) \times (377 \times 1.0 \cos{(377t)})$$

$$= 170 \cos{(377t)} \quad V$$

Repeat Example 1.6 for $B_c = 0.8$ T and assuming the core flux varies at 50 Hz instead of 60 Hz.

Solution

    a. The inductance L is unchanged.

    b. $W = 0.115$ J

    c. $e = 113 \cos(314t)$ V

1.3 PROPERTIES OF MAGNETIC MATERIALS

In the context of electromechanical-energy-conversion devices, the importance of magnetic materials is twofold. Through their use it is possible to obtain large magnetic flux densities with relatively low levels of magnetizing force. Since magnetic forces and energy density increase with increasing flux density, this effect plays a large role in the performance of energy-conversion devices.

In addition, magnetic materials can be used to constrain and direct magnetic fields in well-defined paths. In a transformer they are used to maximize the coupling between the windings as well as to lower the excitation current required for transformer operation. In electric machinery magnetic materials are used to shape the fields to obtain desired torque-production and electrical terminal characteristics. Thus a knowledgeable designer can use magnetic materials to achieve specific desirable device characteristics.

Ferromagnetic materials, typically composed of iron and alloys of iron with cobalt, tungsten, nickel, aluminum, and other metals, are by far the most common magnetic materials. Although these materials are characterized by a wide range of properties, the basic phenomena responsible for their properties are common to them all.

Ferromagnetic materials are found to be composed of a large number of domains, i.e., regions in which the magnetic moments of all the atoms are parallel, giving rise to a net magnetic moment for that domain. In an unmagnetized sample of material, the domain magnetic moments are randomly oriented, and the net resulting magnetic flux in the material is zero.

When an external magnetizing force is applied to this material, the domain magnetic moments tend to align with the applied magnetic field. As a result, the domain magnetic moments add to the applied field, producing a much larger value of flux density than would exist due to the magnetizing force alone. Thus the *effective permeability* μ, equal to the ratio of the total magnetic flux density to the applied magnetic-field intensity, is large compared with the permeability of free space μ_0. As the magnetizing force is increased, this behavior continues until all the magnetic moments are aligned with the applied field; at this point they can no longer contribute to increasing the magnetic flux density, and the material is said to be fully *saturated*.

In the absence of an externally applied magnetizing force, the domain magnetic moments naturally align along certain directions associated with the crystal structure of the domain, known as axes of easy magnetization. Thus if the applied magnetizing

Figure 1.9 *B-H* loops for M-5 grain-oriented electrical steel 0.012 in thick. Only the top halves of the loops are shown here. (Armco Inc)

force is reduced, the domain magnetic moments relax to the direction of easy magnetism nearest to that of the applied field. As a result, when the applied field is reduced to zero, although they will tend to relax towards their initial orientation, the magnetic dipole moments will no longer be totally random in their orientation; they will retain a net magnetization component along the applied field direction. It is this effect which is responsible for the phenomenon known as *magnetic hysteresis*.

Due to this hysteresis effect, the relationship between B and H for a ferromagnetic material is both nonlinear and multivalued. In general, the characteristics of the material cannot be described analytically. They are commonly presented in graphical form as a set of empirically determined curves based on test samples of the material using methods prescribed by the American Society for Testing and Materials (ASTM).[7]

The most common curve used to describe a magnetic material is the *B-H curve* or *hysteresis loop*. The first and second quadrants (corresponding to $B \geq 0$) of a set of hysteresis loops are shown in Fig. 1.9 for M-5 steel, a typical grain-oriented

---

[7] Numerical data on a wide variety of magnetic materials are available from material manufacturers. One problem in using such data arises from the various systems of units employed. For example, magnetization may be given in oersteds or in ampere-turns per meter and the magnetic flux density in gauss, kilogauss, or teslas. A few useful conversion factors are given in Appendix D. The reader is reminded that the equations in this book are based upon SI units.

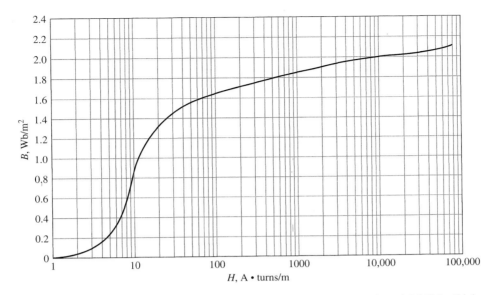

Figure 1.10 Dc magnetization curve for M-5 grain-oriented electrical steel 0.012 in. thick. (Armco Inc.)

electrical steel used in electric equipment. These loops show the relationship between the magnetic flux density B and the magnetizing force H. Each curve is obtained while cyclically varying the applied magnetizing force between equal positive and negative values of fixed magnitude. Hysteresis causes these curves to be multivalued. After several cycles the B-H curves form closed loops as shown. The arrows show the paths followed by B with increasing and decreasing H. Notice that with increasing magnitude of H the curves begin to flatten out as the material tends toward saturation. At a flux density of about 1.7 T this material can be seen to be heavily saturated.

Notice also that as H is decreased from its maximum value to zero, the flux density decreases but not to zero. This is the result of the relaxation of the orientation of the magnetic moments of the domains as described above. The result is that there remains a *remanent magnetization* when H is zero.

Fortunately, for many engineering applications, it is sufficient to describe the material by a single-valued curve obtained by plotting the locus of the maximum values of B and H at the tips of the hysteresis loops; this is known as a *dc* or *normal magnetization curve*. A dc magnetization curve for M-5 grain-oriented electrical steel is shown in Fig. 1.10. The dc magnetization curve neglects the hysteretic nature of the material but clearly displays its nonlinear characteristics.

EXAMPLE 1.7

Assume that the core material in Example 1.1 is M-5 electrical steel, which has the dc magnetization curve of Fig. 1.10. Find the current i required to produce $B_c = 1$ T.

■ Solution

The value of H_c for $B_c = 1$ T is read from Fig. 1.10 as

$$H_c = 11 \text{ A} \cdot \text{turns/m}$$

The mmf drop for the core path is

$$\mathcal{F}_c = H_c l_c = 11(0.3) = 3.3 \text{ A} \cdot \text{turns}$$

Neglecting fringing, $B_g = B_c$ and the mmf drop across the air gap is

$$\mathcal{F}_g = H_g g = \frac{B_g g}{\mu_0} = \frac{1(5 \times 10^{-4})}{4\pi \times 10^{-7}} = 396 \text{ A} \cdot \text{turns}$$

The required current is

$$i = \frac{\mathcal{F}_c + \mathcal{F}_g}{N} = \frac{399}{500} = 0.80 \text{ A}$$

Practice Problem 1.6

Repeat Example 1.7 but find the current i for $B_c = 1.6$ T. By what factor does the current have to be increased to result in this factor of 1.6 increase in flux density?

Solution

The current i can be shown to be 1.302 A. Thus, the current must be increased by a factor of $1.302/0.8 = 1.63$. Because of the dominance of the air-gap reluctance, this is just slightly in excess of the fractional increase in flux density in spite of the fact that the core is beginning to significantly saturate at a flux density of 1.6 T.

1.4 AC EXCITATION

In ac power systems, the waveforms of voltage and flux closely approximate sinusoidal functions of time. This section describes the excitation characteristics and losses associated with steady-state ac operation of magnetic materials under such operating conditions. We use as our model a closed-core magnetic circuit, i.e., with no air gap, such as that shown in Fig. 1.1. The magnetic path length is l_c, and the cross-sectional area is A_c throughout the length of the core. We further assume a sinusoidal variation of the core flux $\varphi(t)$; thus

$$\varphi(t) = \phi_{max} \sin \omega t = A_c B_{max} \sin \omega t \tag{1.47}$$

where

$$\phi_{max} = \text{amplitude of core flux } \varphi \text{ in webers}$$
$$B_{max} = \text{amplitude of flux density } B_c \text{ in teslas}$$
$$\omega = \text{angular frequency} = 2\pi f$$
$$f = \text{frequency in Hz}$$

From Eq. 1.26, the voltage induced in the N-turn winding is

$$e(t) = \omega N \phi_{max} \cos(\omega t) = E_{max} \cos \omega t \tag{1.48}$$

where

$$E_{max} = \omega N \phi_{max} = 2\pi f N A_c B_{max} \tag{1.49}$$

In steady-state ac operation, we are usually more interested in the *root-mean-square* or *rms* values of voltages and currents than in instantaneous or maximum values. In general, the rms value of a periodic function of time, $f(t)$, of period T is defined as

$$F_{rms} = \sqrt{\left(\frac{1}{T} \int_0^T f^2(t)\, dt\right)} \tag{1.50}$$

From Eq. 1.50, the rms value of a sine wave can be shown to be $1/\sqrt{2}$ times its peak value. Thus the rms value of the induced voltage is

$$E_{rms} = \frac{2\pi}{\sqrt{2}} f N A_c B_{max} = \sqrt{2}\,\pi f N A_c B_{max} \tag{1.51}$$

An *excitation current* i_φ, corresponding to an excitation mmf $N i_\varphi(t)$, is required to produce the flux $\varphi(t)$ in the core.[8] Because of the nonlinear magnetic properties of the core, the excitation current corresponding to a sinusoidal core flux will be non sinusoidal. A curve of the exciting current as a function of time can be found graphically from the magnetic characteristics of the core material, as illustrated in Fig. 1.11a. Since B_c and H_c are related to φ and i_φ by known geometric constants, the ac hysteresis loop of Fig. 1.11b has been drawn in terms of $\varphi = B_c A_c$ and is $i_\varphi = H_c l_c / N$. Sine waves of induced voltage, e, and flux, φ, in accordance with Eqs. 1.47 and 1.48, are shown in Fig. 1.11a.

At any given time, the value of i_φ corresponding to the given value of flux can be found directly from the hysteresis loop. For example, at time t' the flux is φ' and the current is i_φ'; at time t'' the corresponding values are φ'' and i_φ''. Notice that since the hysteresis loop is multivalued, it is necessary to be careful to pick the rising-flux values (φ' in the figure) from the rising-flux portion of the hysteresis loop; similarly the falling-flux portion of the hysteresis loop must be selected for the falling-flux values (φ'' in the figure).

Notice that, because the hysteresis loop "flattens out" due to saturation effects, the waveform of the exciting current is sharply peaked. Its rms value $I_{\varphi,rms}$ is defined by Eq. 1.50, where T is the period of a cycle. It is related to the corresponding rms value H_{rms} of H_c by the relationship

$$I_{\varphi,rms} = \frac{l_c H_{rms}}{N} \tag{1.52}$$

The ac excitation characteristics of core materials are often described in terms of rms voltamperes rather than a magnetization curve relating B and H. The theory

---

[8] More generally, for a system with multiple windings, the exciting mmf is the net ampere-turns acting to produce flux in the magnetic circuit.

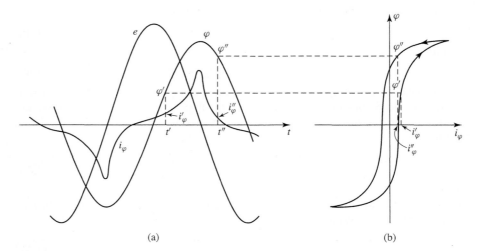

Figure 1.11 Excitation phenomena. (a) Voltage, flux, and exciting current;
(b) corresponding hysteresis loop.

behind this representation can be explained by combining Eqs. 1.51 and 1.52. From
Eqs. 1.51 and 1.52, the rms voltamperes required to excite the core of Fig. 1.1 to a
specified flux density is equal to

$$E_{rms} I_{\varphi,rms} = \sqrt{2}\, \pi f N A_c B_{max} \frac{l_c H_{rms}}{N}$$

$$= \sqrt{2}\, \pi f B_{max} H_{rms} (A_c l_c) \tag{1.53}$$

In Eq. 1.53, the product $A_c l_c$ can be seen to be equal to the volume of the core and
hence the rms exciting voltamperes required to excite the core with sinusoidal can be
seen to be proportional to the frequency of excitation, the core volume and the product
of the peak flux density, and the rms magnetic field intensity. For a magnetic material
of mass density ρ_c, the mass of the core is $A_c l_c \rho_c$ and the *exciting rms voltamperes
per unit mass*, S_a, can be expressed as

$$S_a = \frac{E_{rms} I_{\varphi,rms}}{mass} = \sqrt{2}\, \pi f \left(\frac{B_{max} H_{rms}}{\rho_c} \right) \tag{1.54}$$

Note that, normalized in this fashion, the rms exciting voltamperes depends only
on the frequency and B_{max} because H_{rms} is a unique function of B_{max} as determined by
the shape of the material hysteresis loop at any given frequency f. As a result, the ac
excitation requirements for a magnetic material are often supplied by manufacturers
in terms of rms voltamperes per unit mass as determined by laboratory tests on
closed-core samples of the material. These results are illustrated in Fig. 1.12 for M-5
grain-oriented electrical steel.

The exciting current supplies the mmf required to produce the core flux and the
power input associated with the energy in the magnetic field in the core. Part of this

Figure 1.12   Exciting rms voltamperes per kilogram at 60 Hz for M-5 grain-oriented electrical steel 0.012 in. thick. (Armco Inc.)

energy is dissipated as losses and results in heating of the core. The rest appears as reactive power associated with energy storage in the magnetic field. This reactive power is not dissipated in the core; it is cyclically supplied and absorbed by the excitation source.

Two loss mechanisms are associated with time-varying fluxes in magnetic materials. The first is due to the hysteretic nature of magnetic material. As has been discussed, in a magnetic circuit like that of Fig. 1.1, a time-varying excitation will cause the magnetic material to undergo a cyclic variation described by a hysteresis loop such as that shown in Fig. 1.13.

Equation 1.44 can be used to calculate the energy input W to the magnetic core of Fig. 1.1 as the material undergoes a single cycle

$$W = \oint i_\varphi \, d\lambda = \oint \left(\frac{H_c l_c}{N} \right) (A_c N \, dB_c) = A_c l_c \oint H_c \, dB_c \qquad (1.55)$$

Recognizing that $A_c l_c$ is the volume of the core and that the integral is the area of the ac hysteresis loop, we see that each time the magnetic material undergoes a cycle, there is a net energy input into the material. This energy is required to move around the magnetic dipoles in the material and is dissipated as heat in the material. Thus for a given flux level, the corresponding *hysteresis losses* are proportional to the area of the hysteresis loop and to the total volume of material. Since there is an energy loss per cycle, hysteresis power loss is proportional to the frequency of the applied excitation.

The second loss mechanism is ohmic heating, associated with induced currents in the core material. From Faraday's law (Eq. 1.25) we see that time-varying magnetic

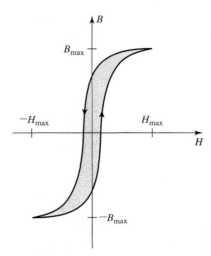

Figure 1.13 Hysteresis loop; hysteresis loss is proportional to the loop area (shaded).

fields give rise to electric fields. In magnetic materials these electric fields result in induced currents, commonly referred to as *eddy currents*, which circulate in the core material and oppose changes in flux density in the material. To counteract the corresponding demagnetizing effect, the current in the exciting winding must increase. Thus the resultant "dynamic" *B-H* loop under ac operation is somewhat "fatter" than the hysteresis loop for slowly varying conditions and this effect increases as the excitation frequency is increased. It is for this reason that the charactersitics of electrical steels vary with frequency and hence manufacturers typically supply characteristics over the expected operating frequency range of a particular electrical steel. Note for example that the exciting rms voltamperes of Fig. 1.12 are specified at a frequency of 60 Hz.

To reduce the effects of eddy currents, magnetic structures are usually built with thin sheets or *laminations* of magnetic material. These laminations, which are aligned in the direction of the field lines, are insulated from each other by an oxide layer on their surfaces or by a thin coat of insulating enamel or varnish. This greatly reduces the magnitude of the eddy currents since the layers of insulation interrupt the current paths; the thinner the laminations, the lower the losses. In general, as a first approximation, eddy-current loss can be considered to increase as the square of the excitation frequency and also as the square of the peak flux density.

In general, core losses depend on the metallurgy of the material as well as the flux density and frequency. Information on core loss is typically presented in graphical form. It is plotted in terms of watts per unit mass as a function of flux density; often a family of curves for different frequencies is given. Figure 1.14 shows the core loss density P_c for M-5 grain-oriented electrical steel at 60 Hz.

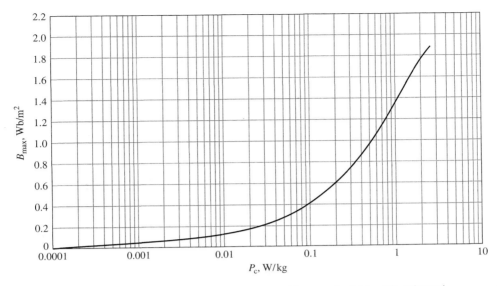

Figure 1.14 Core loss density at 60 Hz in watts per kilogram for M-5 grain-oriented electrical steel 0.012 in. thick. (Armco Inc.)

Nearly all transformers and certain components of electric machines use sheet-steel material that has highly favorable directions of magnetization along which the core loss is low and the permeability is high. This material is termed *grain-oriented steel*. The reason for this property lies in the atomic structure of a crystal of the silicon-iron alloy, which is a body-centered cube; each cube has an atom at each corner as well as one in the center of the cube. In the cube, the easiest axis of magnetization is the cube edge; the diagonal across the cube face is more difficult, and the diagonal through the cube is the most difficult. By suitable manufacturing techniques most of the crystalline cube edges are aligned in the rolling direction to make it the favorable direction of magnetization. The behavior in this direction is superior in core loss and permeability to *nonoriented steels* in which the crystals are randomly oriented to produce a material with characteristics which are uniform in all directions. As a result, oriented steels can be operated at higher flux densities than the nonoriented grades.

Nonoriented electrical steels are used in applications where the flux does not follow a path which can be oriented with the rolling direction or where low cost is of importance. In these steels the losses are somewhat higher and the permeability is very much lower than in grain-oriented steels.

EXAMPLE 1.8

The magnetic core in Fig. 1.15 is made from laminations of M-5 grain-oriented electrical steel. The winding is excited with a 60-Hz voltage to produce a flux density in the steel of $B = 1.5 \sin \omega t$ T, where $\omega = 2\pi 60 \approx 377$ rad/sec. The steel occupies 0.94 of the core cross-sectional area. The mass-density of the steel is 7.65 g/cm³. Find (a) the applied voltage, (b) the peak current, (c) the rms exciting current, and (d) the core loss.

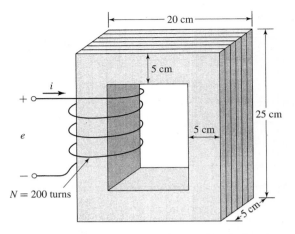

Figure 1.15 Laminated steel core with winding for Example 1.8.

■ Solution

a. From Eq. 1.26 the voltage is

$$e = N\frac{d\varphi}{dt} = NA_c\frac{dB}{dt}$$

$$= 200 \times 25 \text{ cm}^2 \times 0.94 \times 1.5 \times 377 \cos{(377t)}$$

$$= 266 \cos{(377t)} \text{ V}$$

b. The magnetic field intensity corresponding to $B_{max} = 1.5$ T is given in Fig. 1.10 as $H_{max} = 36$ A turns/m. Notice that, as expected, the relative permeability $\mu_r = B_{max}/(\mu_0 H_{max}) = 33{,}000$ at the flux level of 1.5 T is lower than the value of $\mu_r = 72{,}300$ found in Example 1.4 corresponding to a flux level of 1.0 T, yet significantly larger than the value of 2,900 corresponding to a flux level of 1.8 T.

$$l_c = (15 + 15 + 20 + 20) \text{ cm} = 0.70 \text{ m}$$

The peak current is

$$I = \frac{H_{max}l_c}{N} = \frac{36 \times 0.70}{200} = 0.13 \text{ A}$$

c. The rms current is obtained from the value of S_a of Fig. 1.12 for $B_{max} = 1.5$ T.

$$S_a = 1.5 \text{ VA/kg}$$

The core volume and mass are

$$\text{Vol}_c = 25 \text{ cm}^2 \times 0.94 \times 70 \text{ cm} = 1645 \text{ cm}^3$$

$$M_c = 1645 \text{ cm}^3 \times \left(\frac{7.65 \text{ g}}{1.0 \text{ cm}^3}\right) = 12.6 \text{ kg}$$

The total rms voltamperes and current are

$$S = 1.5 \text{ VA/kg} \times 12.6 \text{ kg} = 18.9 \text{ VA}$$

$$I_{\varphi,\text{rms}} = \frac{S}{E_{\text{rms}}} = \frac{18.9}{266/\sqrt{2}} = 0.10 \text{ A}$$

d. The core-loss density is obtained from Fig. 1.14 as $P_c = 1.2$ W/kg. The total core loss is

$$P_{\text{core}} = 1.2 \text{ W/kg} \times 12.6 \text{ kg} = 15.1 \text{ W}$$

Practice Problem 1.7

Repeat Example 1.8 for a 60-Hz voltage of $B = 1.0 \sin \omega t$ T.

Solution

a. $V = 177 \cos 377t$ V
b. $I = 0.042$ A
c. $I_\varphi = 0.041$ A
d. $P = 6.5$ W

1.5 PERMANENT MAGNETS

Figure 1.16a shows the second quadrant of a hysteresis loop for Alnico 5, a typical permanent-magnet material, while Fig. 1.16b shows the second quadrant of a hysteresis loop for M-5 steel.[9] Notice that the curves are similar in nature. However, the hysteresis loop of Alnico 5 is characterized by a large value of *residual* or *remanent magnetization*, B_r, (approximately 1.22 T) as well as a large value of *coercivity*, H_c, (approximately -49 kA/m).

The residual magnetization, B_r, corresponds to the flux density which would remain in a section of the material if the applied mmf (and hence the magnetic field intensity H) were reduced to zero. However, although the M-5 electrical steel also has a large value of residual magnetization (approximately 1.4 T), it has a much smaller value of coercivity (approximately -6 A/m, smaller by a factor of over 7500). The coercivity H_c is the value of magnetic field intensity (which is proportional to the mmf) required to reduce the material flux density to zero. As we will see, the lower the coercivity of a given magnetic material, the easier it is to demagnetize it.

The significance of residual magnetization is that it can produce magnetic flux in a magnetic circuit in the absence of external excitation such as is produced by winding currents. This is a familiar phenomenon to anyone who has afixed notes to a refrigerator with small magnets and is widely used in devices such as loudspeakers and permanent-magnet motors.

---

[9] To obtain the largest value of residual magnetization, the hysteresis loops of Fig. 1.16 are those which would be obtained if the materials were excited by sufficient mmf to ensure that they were driven heavily into saturation. This is discussed further in Section 1.6.

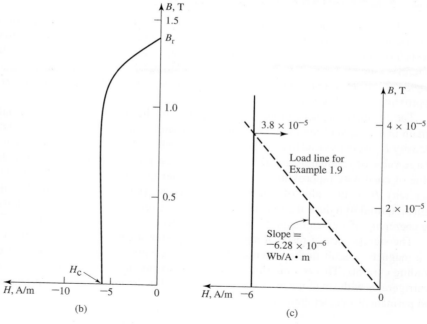

Figure 1.16 (a) Second quadrant of hysteresis loop for Alnico 5; (b) second quadrant of hysteresis loop for M-5 electrical steel; (c) hysteresis loop for M-5 electrical steel expanded for small *B*. (Armco Inc.)

From Fig. 1.16, it would appear that both Alnico 5 and M-5 electrical steel would be useful in producing flux in unexcited magnetic circuits since they both have large values of residual magnetization. That this is not the case can be best illustrated by an example.

EXAMPLE 1.9

As shown in Fig. 1.17, a magnetic circuit consists of a core of high permeability ($\mu \to \infty$), an air gap of length $g = 0.2$ cm, and a section of magnetic material of length $l_m = 1.0$ cm. The cross-sectional area of the core and gap is equal to $A_m = A_g = 4$ cm^2. Calculate the flux density B_g in the air gap if the magnetic material is (a) Alnico 5 and (b) M-5 electrical steel.

■ **Solution**

a. Since the core permeability is assumed infinite, H in the core is negligible (otherwise a finite H would produce an infinite B). Recognizing that there is zero mmf acting on the magnetic circuit of Fig. 1.17, we can write

$$\mathcal{F} = 0 = H_g g + H_m l_m$$

or

$$H_g = -\left(\frac{l_m}{g}\right) H_m$$

where H_g and H_m are the magnetic field intensities in the air gap and the magnetic material, respectively.

Since the flux must be continuous through the magnetic circuit,

$$\phi = A_g B_g = A_m B_m$$

or

$$B_g = \left(\frac{A_m}{A_g}\right) B_m$$

where B_g and B_m are the magnetic flux densities in the air gap and the magnetic material, respectively.

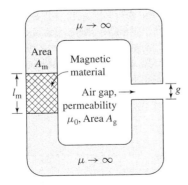

Figure 1.17 Magnetic circuit for Example 1.9.

These equations can be solved to yield a linear relationship for B_m in terms of H_m

$$B_m = -\mu_0 \left(\frac{A_g}{A_m}\right)\left(\frac{l_m}{g}\right) H_m = -5\,\mu_0\,H_m = -6.28 \times 10^{-6}\,H_m$$

To solve for B_m we recognize that for Alnico 5, B_m and H_m are also related by the curve of Fig. 1.16a. Thus this linear relationship, commonly referred to as a *load line*, can be plotted on Fig. 1.16a and the solution obtained graphically, resulting in

$$B_g = B_m = 0.30\,\text{T} = 3{,}000\,\text{gauss}$$

b. The solution for M-5 electrical steel proceeds exactly as in part (a). The load line is the same as that of part (a) because it is determined only by the permeability of the air gap and the geometries of the magnet and the air gap. Hence from Fig. 1.16c

$$B_g = 3.8 \times 10^{-5}\,\text{T} = 0.38\,\text{gauss}$$

which is much less than the value obtained with Alnico 5 and is essentially negligible.

Example 1.9 shows that there is an immense difference between permanent-magnet materials (often referred to as *hard magnetic materials*) such as Alnico 5 and *soft magnetic materials* such as M-5 electrical steel. This difference is characterized in large part by the immense difference in their coercivities H_c. The coercivity is a measure of the magnitude of the mmf required to reduce the material flux density to zero. As seen from Example 1.9, it is also a measure of the capability of the material to produce flux in a magnetic circuit which includes an air gap. Thus we see that materials which make good permanent magnets are characterized by large values of coercivity H_c (considerably in excess of 1 kA/m).

A useful measure of the capability of permanent-magnet material is known as its *maximum energy product*. This corresponds to the largest magnitude of the *B-H* product $(B \cdot H)_{max}$ found in the second quadrant of that material's hysteresis loop. As can be seen from Eq. 1.55, the product of B and H has the dimensions of energy density (joules per cubic meter). We now show that operation of a given permanent-magnet material in a magnetic circuit at this point will result in the smallest volume of that material required to produce a given flux density in an air gap.

In Example 1.9, we found an expression for the flux density in the air gap of the magnetic circuit of Fig. 1.17:

$$B_g = \frac{A_m}{A_g} B_m \tag{1.56}$$

We also found that

$$H_g = -\left(\frac{l_m}{g}\right) H_m \tag{1.57}$$

Equation 1.57 can be multiplied by μ_0 to obtain $B_g = \mu_0 H_g$. Multiplying by Eq. 1.56 yields

$$B_g^2 = \mu_0 \left(\frac{l_m A_m}{g A_g} \right) (-H_m B_m)$$

$$= \mu_0 \left(\frac{\text{Vol}_{\text{mag}}}{\text{Vol}_{\text{air gap}}} \right) (-H_m B_m) \tag{1.58}$$

where Vol_{mag} is the volume of the magnet, $\text{Vol}_{\text{air gap}}$ is the air-gap volume, and the minus sign arises because, at the operating point of the magnetic circuit, H in the magnet (H_m) is negative.

Solving Eq. 1.58 gives

$$\text{Vol}_{\text{mag}} = \frac{\text{Vol}_{\text{air gap}} B_g^2}{\mu_0(-H_m B_m)} \tag{1.59}$$

which is the desired result. It indicates that to achieve a desired flux density in the air gap, the required volume of the magnet can be minimized by operating the magnet at the point of the largest possible value of the B-H product $H_m B_m$, i.e., at the point of maximum energy product. Furthermore, the larger the value of this product, the smaller the size of the magnet required to produce the desired flux density. Hence the maximum energy product is a useful performance measure for a magnetic material and it is often found as a tabulated "figure of merit" on data sheets for permanent-magnet materials. As a practical matter, this result applies to many practical engineering applications where the use of a permanent-magnet material with the largest available maximum energy product will result in the smallest required magnet volume.

Equation 1.58 appears to indicate that one can achieve an arbitrarily large air-gap flux density simply by reducing the air-gap volume. This is not true in practice because a reduction in air-gap length will increase the flux density in the magnetic circuit and as the flux density in the magnetic circuit increases, a point will be reached at which the magnetic core material will begin to saturate and the assumption of infinite permeability will no longer be valid, thus invalidating the derivation leading to Eq. 1.58.

EXAMPLE 1.10

The magnetic circuit of Fig. 1.17 is modified so that the air-gap area is reduced to $A_g = 2.0\,\text{cm}^2$, as shown in Fig. 1.18. Find the minimum magnet volume required to achieve an air-gap flux density of 0.8 T.

■ **Solution**

Note that a curve of constant B-H product is a hyperbola. A set of such hyperbolas for different values of the B-H product is plotted in Fig. 1.16a. From these curves, we see that the maximum energy product for Alnico 5 is 40 kJ/m^3 and that this occurs at the point $B = 1.0$ T and $H = -40$ kA/m. The smallest magnet volume will be achieved with the magnet operating at this point.

Figure 1.18   Magnetic circuit for Example 1.10.

Thus from Eq. 1.56,

$$A_m = A_g \left(\frac{B_g}{B_m} \right)$$

$$= 2 \text{ cm}^2 \left(\frac{0.8}{1.0} \right) = 1.6 \text{ cm}^2$$

and from Eq. 1.57

$$l_m = -g \left(\frac{H_g}{H_m} \right) = -g \left(\frac{B_g}{\mu_0 H_m} \right)$$

$$= -0.2 \text{ cm} \left(\frac{0.8}{(4\pi \times 10^{-7})(-40 \times 10^3)} \right)$$

$$= 3.18 \text{ cm}$$

Thus the minimum magnet volume is equal to $1.6 \text{ cm}^2 \times 3.18 \text{ cm} = 5.09 \text{ cm}^3$.

Practice Problem 1.8

Repeat Example 1.10 assuming the air-gap area is further reduced to $A_g = 1.8 \text{ cm}^2$ and that the desired air-gap flux density is 0.6 T.

Solution

Minimum magnet volume = 2.58 cm^3.

1.6   APPLICATION OF PERMANENT-MAGNET MATERIALS

Examples 1.9 and 1.10 consider the operation of permanent-magnetic materials under the assumption that the operating point can be determined simply from a knowledge of the geometry of the magnetic circuit and the properties of the various magnetic

Figure 1.19 Magnetization curves for common permanent-magnet materials.

materials involved. In fact, in practical engineering devices, the situation is often more complex.[10] This section will expand upon these issues.

Figure 1.19 shows the magnetization characteristics for a few common permanent-magnet materials. These curves are simply the second-quadrant characteristics of the hysteresis loops for each material obtained when the material is driven heavily into saturation. Alnico 5 is a widely-used alloy of iron, nickel, aluminum, and cobalt originally discovered in 1931. It has a relatively large residual flux density. Alnico 8 has a lower residual flux density and a higher coercivity than Alnico 5. It is hence less subject to demagnetization than Alnico 5. Disadvantages of the Alnico materials are their relatively low coercivity and their mechanical brittleness.

Ceramic permanent-magnet materials (also known as *ferrite magnets*) are made from iron-oxide and barium- or strontium-carbonate powders and have lower residual flux densities than Alnico materials but significantly higher coercivities. As a result, they are much less prone to demagnetization. One such material, Ceramic 7, is shown in Fig. 1.19, where its magnetization characteristic is almost a straight line. Ceramic magnets have good mechanical characteristics and are inexpensive to manufacture.

---

[10]For a further discussion of permanent magnets and their application, see P. Campbell, *Permanent Magnet Materials and Their Application*, Cambridge University Press, 1994; R.J. Parker, *Advances in Permanent Magnetism*, John Wiley & Sons, 1990; R.C. O'Handley, *Modern Magnetic Materials: Principles and Applications*, John Wiley & Sons, 2000; and E.P. Ferlani, *Permanent Magnet and Electromechanical Devices*, Academic Press, 2001.

Samarium-cobalt represents a significant advance in permanent-magnet technology which began in the 1960s with the discovery of rare-earth permanent-magnet materials. From Fig. 1.19 it can be seen to have a high residual flux density such as is found with the Alnico materials, while at the same time having a much higher coercivity and maximum energy product.

The newest of the rare-earth magnetic materials is the family of neodymium-iron-boron materials. They feature even larger residual flux density, coercivity, and maximum energy product than does samarium-cobalt. The development of neodymium-iron-boron magnets has had a tremendous impact in the area of rotating machines and as a result permanent-magnet motors with increasingly large ratings are being developed by manufacturers around the world.

Note that in Fig. 1.19 the hysteretic nature of the magnetization characteristics of Alnico 5 and Alnico 8 is readily apparent while the magnetization characteristics of the remaining materials appear to be essentially straight lines. This straight-line characteristic is deceiving; in each case the material characteristic bends sharply downward just as does that of the Alnico materials. However, unlike the Alnico materials, this bend, commonly referred to as the *knee* of the magnetization curve, occurs in the third quadrant and hence does not appear in Fig. 1.19.

Consider the magnetic circuit of Fig. 1.20. This includes a section of hard magnetic material in a core of highly permeable soft magnetic material as well as an N-turn excitation winding. With reference to Fig. 1.21, we assume that the hard magnetic material is initially unmagnetized (corresponding to point (a) of the figure) and consider what happens as current is applied to the excitation winding. Because the core is assumed to be of infinite permeability, the horizontal axis of Fig. 1.21 can be considered to be both a measure of the applied current $i = Hl_\mathrm{m}/N$ as well as a measure of H in the magnetic material.

As the current i is increased to its maximum value, the B-H trajectory rises from point (a) in Fig. 1.21 toward its maximum value at point (b). To fully magnetize the material, we assume that the current has been increased to a value i_max sufficiently large

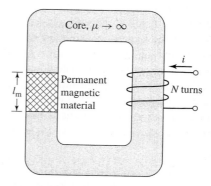

Figure 1.20 Magnetic circuit including both a permanent magnet and an excitation winding.

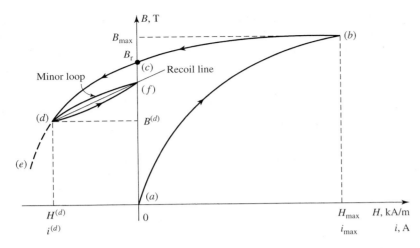

Figure 1.21 Portion of a *B-H* characteristic showing a minor loop and a recoil line.

that the material has been driven well into saturation at point (b). When the current is then decreased to zero, the *B-H* characteristic will begin to form a hysteresis loop, arriving at point (c) at zero current. At point (c), notice that H in the material is zero but B is at its remanent value B_r.

As the current then goes negative, the *B-H* characteristic continues to trace out a hysteresis loop. In Fig. 1.21, this is seen as the trajectory between points (c) and (d). If the current is then maintained at the value $i^{(d)}$, the operating point of the magnet will be that of point (d). Note that, as in Example 1.9, this same operating point would be reached if the material were to start at point (c) and, with the excitation held at zero, an air gap of length $g = l_m(A_g/A_m)(-\mu_0 H^{(d)}/B^{(d)})$ were then inserted in the core.

Should the current then be made more negative, the trajectory would continue tracing out the hysteresis loop toward point (e). However, if instead the current is returned to zero, the trajectory does not in general retrace the hysteresis loop toward point (c). Rather it begins to trace out a *minor hysteresis loop*, reaching point (f) when the current reaches zero. If the current is then varied between zero and $i^{(d)}$, the *B-H* characteristic will trace out the minor loop as shown.

As can be seen from Fig. 1.21, the *B-H* trajectory between points (d) and (f) can be represented by a straight line, known as the *recoil line*. The slope of this line is called the *recoil permeability* μ_R. We see that once this material has been demagnetized to point (d), the effective residual magnetization of the magnetic material is that of point (f) which is less than the residual magnetization B_r which would be expected based on the hysteresis loop. Note that should the demagnetization be decreased past point (d), for example, to point (e) of Fig. 1.21, a new minor loop will be created, with a new recoil line and recoil permeability.

The demagnetization effects of negative excitation which have just been discussed are equivalent to those of an air gap in the magnetic circuit. For example, clearly the magnetic circuit of Fig. 1.20 could be used as a system to magnetize hard magnetic materials. The process would simply require that a large excitation be applied to the winding and then reduced to zero, leaving the material at a residual magnetization B_r (point (c) in Fig. 1.21).

Following this magnetization process, if the material were removed from the core, this would be equivalent to opening a large air gap in the magnetic circuit, demagnetizing the material in a fashion similar to that seen in Example 1.9. At this point, the magnet has been effectively weakened, since if it were again inserted in the magnetic core, it would follow a recoil line and return to a residual magnetization somewhat less than B_r. As a result, hard magnetic materials, such as the Alnico materials of Fig. 1.19, often do not operate stably in situations with varying mmf and geometry, and there is often the risk that improper operation can significantly demagnetize them.

At the expense of a reduction in value of the residual magnetization, hard magnetic materials such as Alnico 5 can be stabilized to operate over a specified region. This procedure, based on the recoil trajectory shown in Fig. 1.21, can best be illustrated by an example.

EXAMPLE 1.11

Figure 1.22 shows a magnetic circuit containing hard magnetic material, a core and plunger of high (assumed infinite) permeability, and a 100-turn winding which will be used to magnetize the hard magnetic material. The winding will be removed after the system is magnetized. The plunger moves in the x direction as indicated, with the result that the air-gap area varies over the range $2 \text{ cm}^2 \leq A_g \leq 4 \text{ cm}^2$. Assuming that the hard magnetic material is Alnico 5 and that the system is initially magnetized with $A_g = 2$ cm, (a) find the magnet length l_m such that the system will operate on a recoil line which intersects the maximum B-H product point on the magnetization curve for Alnico 5, (b) devise a procedure for magnetizing the magnet, and (c) calculate the flux density B_g in the air gap as the plunger moves back and forth and the air gap varies between these two limits.

Figure 1.22   Magnetic circuit for Example 1.11.

■ Solution

a. Figure 1.23a shows the magnetization curve for Alnico 5 and two load lines corresponding to the two extremes of the air gap, $A_g = 2$ cm^2 and $A_g = 4$ cm^2. We see that the system will operate on the desired recoil line if the load line for $A_g = 2$ cm^2 intersects the B-H characteristic at the maximum energy product point (labeled point (a) in Fig. 1.23a), $B_m^{(a)} = 1.0$ T and $H_m^{(a)} = -40$ kA/m.

From Eqs. 1.56 and 1.57, we see that the slope of the required load line is given by

$$\frac{B_m^{(a)}}{-H_m^{(a)}} = \frac{B_g}{H_g}\frac{A_g}{A_m}\frac{l_m}{g}$$

and thus

$$l_m = g\left(\frac{A_m}{A_g}\right)\left(\frac{B_m^{(a)}}{-\mu_0 H_m^{(a)}}\right)$$

$$= 0.2 \text{ cm} \left(\frac{2}{2}\right)\left(\frac{1.0}{4\pi \times 10^{-7} \times 4 \times 10^4}\right) = 3.98 \text{ cm}$$

b. Figure 1.23b shows a series of load lines for the system with $A_g = 2$ cm^2 and with current i applied to the excitation winding. The general equation for these load lines can be readily derived since from Eq. 1.5

$$Ni = H_m l_m + H_g g$$

and from Eqs. 1.3 and 1.7

$$B_m A_m = B_g A_g = \mu_0 H_g A_g$$

Thus

$$B_m = -\mu_0\left(\frac{A_g}{A_m}\right)\left(\frac{l_m}{g}\right)H_m + \frac{\mu_0 N}{g}\left(\frac{A_g}{A_m}\right)i$$

$$= \mu_0\left[-\left(\frac{2}{2}\right)\left(\frac{3.98}{0.2}\right)H_m + \frac{100}{2 \times 10^{-3}}\left(\frac{2}{2}\right)i\right]$$

$$= -2.50 \times 10^{-5} H_m + 6.28 \times 10^{-2} i$$

From this equation and Fig. 1.23b, we see that to drive the magnetic material into saturation to the point (H_{max}, B_{max}), the current in the magnetizing winding must be increased to the value i_{max} where

$$i_{max} = \frac{B_{max} + 2.50 \times 10^{-5} H_{max}}{6.28 \times 10^{-2}} \quad \text{A}$$

In this case, we do not have a complete hysteresis loop for Alnico 5, and hence we will have to estimate B_{max} and H_{max}. Linearly extrapolating the B-H curve at $H = 0$ back to 4 times the coercivity, that is, $H_{max} = 4 \times 50 = 200$ kA/m, yields $B_{max} = 2.1$ T. This value is undoubtedly extreme and will overestimate the required current somewhat. However, using $B_{max} = 2.1$ T and $H_{max} = 200$ kA/m yields $i_{max} = 113$ A.

Thus with the air-gap area set to 2 cm^2, increasing the current to 113 A and then reducing it to zero will achieve the desired magnetization.

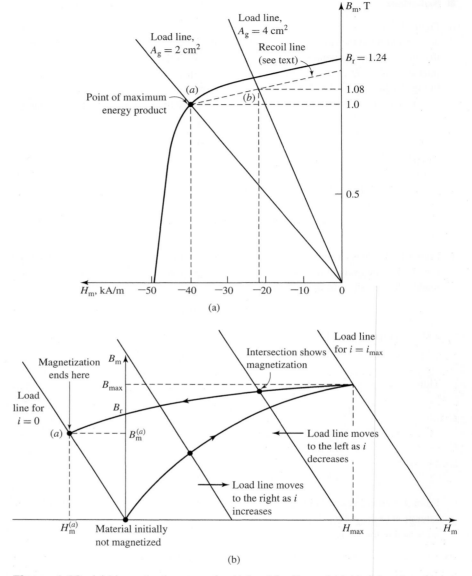

Figure 1.23   (a) Magnetization curve for Alnico 5 for Example 1.11; (b) series of load lines for $A_g = 2\ cm^2$ and varying values of i showing the magnetization procedure for Example 1.11.

c. Because we do not have specific information about the slope of the recoil line, we shall assume that its slope is the same as that of the B-H characteristic at the point $H = 0$, $B = B_r$. From Fig. 1.23a, with the recoil line drawn with this slope, we see that as the air-gap area varies between 2 and 4 cm^2, the magnet flux density B_m varies between 1.00

and 1.08 T. Since the air-gap flux density equals A_m/A_g times this value, the air-gap flux density will equal $(2/2)1.00 = 1.0$ T when $A_g = 2.0 \text{cm}^2$ and $(2/4)1.08 = 0.54$ T when $A_g = 4.0 \text{ cm}^2$. Note from Fig. 1.23a that, when operated with these air-gap variations, the magnet appears to have an effective residual flux density of 1.17 T instead of the initial value of 1.24 T. As long as the air-gap variations limited to the range considered here, the system will continue to operate on the line labeled "Recoil line" in Fig. 1.23a and the magnet can be said to be *stabilized*.

As has been discussed, hard magnetic materials such as Alnico 5 can be subject to demagnetization, should their operating point be varied excessively. As shown in Example 1.11, these materials can be stabilized with some loss in effective residual magnetization. However, this procedure does not guarantee absolute stability of operation. For example, if the material in Example 1.11 were subjected to an air-gap area smaller than 2 cm^2 or to excessive demagnetizing current, the effect of the stabilization would be erased and the material would be found to operate on a new recoil line with further reduced magnetization.

However, many materials, such as samarium-cobalt, Ceramic 7, and neodymium-iron-boron (see Fig. 1.19), which have large values of coercivity, tend to have very low values of recoil permeability, and the recoil line is essentially tangent to the *B-H* characteristic for a large portion of the useful operating region. For example, this can be seen in Fig. 1.19, which shows the dc magnetization curve for neodymium-iron-boron, from which we see that this material has a residual magnetization of 1.25 T and a coercivity of -940 kA/m. The portion of the curve between these points is a straight line with a slope equal to $1.06\mu_0$, which is the same as the slope of its recoil line. As long as these materials are operated on this low-incremental-permeability portion of their *B-H* characteristic, they do not require stabilization, provided they are not excessively demagnetized.

For these materials, it is often convenient to assume that their dc magnetization curve is linear over their useful operating range with a slope equal to the recoil permeability μ_R. Under this assumption, the dc magnetization curve for these materials can be written in the form

$$B = \mu_R(H - H'_c) = B_r + \mu_R H \qquad (1.60)$$

Here, H'_c is the *apparent coercivity* associated with this linear representation. As can be seen from Fig. 1.19, the apparent coercivity is typically somewhat larger in magnitude (i.e. a larger negative value) than the material coercivity H_c because the dc magnetization characteristic tends to bend downward for low values of flux density.

A significant (and somewhat unfortunate) characteristic of permanent-magnet materials is that their properties are temperature dependent. For example, the residual magnetization and coercivity of neodymium-iron-boron and samarium-cobalt magnets decrease as the temperature increases, although samarium-cobalt is much less temperature sensitive than neodymium-iron-boron.

Figure 1.24 shows magnetization curves for a high-temperature grade of neodymium-boron-iron at various temperatures. We see that the residual magnetism

Figure 1.24   Second-quadrant magnetization curves for neodymium-iron-boron material showing their temperature dependence.

drops from around 1.14 T at a temperature of 20 C to around 0.85 T at a temperature of 180 C. Table 1.1 gives a more complete listing of the residual flux density as a function of temperature for this material, which has a recoil permeability $\mu_R = 1.04\mu_0$.

Interestingly, unlike rare-earth magnets, although ceramic magnets exhibit a decrease in residual magnetism with temperature, they exhibit a corresponding increase in coercivity. Figure 1.25 shows the general nature of the temperature dependence of the magnetization characteristic of a typical ceramic magnet material.

Although these permanent magnet materials display a reduction in magnetization with increasing temperature, this decrease in magnetization is often reversible. Provided the operating point of the magnet material, which will vary as the magnet temperature changes, remains in the linear portion of the magnetization characteristic,

Table 1.1   Residual flux density as a function of temperature for the magnetization curves of Fig. 1.24.

Temperature	B_r [T]	Temperature	B_r [T]
20 C	1.15	150 C	0.99
80 C	1.08	180 C	0.94
120 C	1.03	210 C	0.89

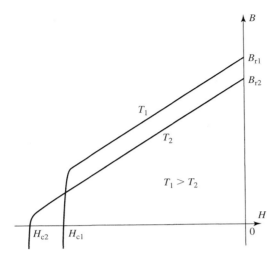

Figure 1.25 General form of the temperature dependence of the magnetization characteristics of a typical ceramic magnetic material.

it will fully recover its magnetization with a decrease in temperature. However, if the temperature is increased to a value known as the *Curie Temperature*, the material will become fully demagnetized and magnetism will not be restored by a reduction in temperature.[11]

Consider a magnetic circuit containing a permanent magnet and a winding such as that which is shown in Fig. 1.26. Fig. 1.24 includes a zero-excitation load line, corresponding to zero-winding-current operation of this magnetic circuit. As the temperature varies between 20 C and 120 C, the operating point varies between points (a) and (c). Each operating point over this temperature range lies on a portion on the material hysteresis loop which is linear in the second quadrant. As we have seen, operation on this linear portion of the magnetization characteristic is stabilized and as the winding current is varied, the magnetic will continue to operate on the linear portion of its magnetization characteristic as long as the operation remains in the second quadrant.[12] The material will not be permanently demagnetized and it will recover any temperature-induced loss of magnetization as the temperature is reduced.

As the temperature is further increased, a temperature will be reached for which the downward bend appears in the second quadrant of the magnetization characteristic.

---

[11]The Curie temperature of neodymium-boron-iron is on the order of 350 C and that of samarium-cobalt and Alnico is on the order of 700 C.

[12]Note that the magnet will be permanently demagnetized if its operating point is driven into the third quadrant past the point at which the magnetization characteristic ceases to be linear and begins to bend downward.

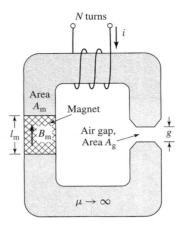

Figure 1.26 Magnetic circuit with a permanent magnet, an air gap and an excitation winding.

This can be seen in the curves for 180 C and 210 C in Fig. 1.24. In the case of the 180 C characteristic, the winding current can be varied without demagnetizing the magnet as long as the magnet flux density does not drop below the point where the magnetization characteristic becomes non linear. Operation below this point is analogous to the operation of Alnico 5 as discussed with reference to the minor loop and recoil line of Fig. 1.21. Thus, if sufficient winding current is applied to drive the magnet below this point and the current is then reduced, a minor loop will be created and the magnet will be somewhat demagnetized. If the magnet temperature is reduced, the magnet will be found to be partially demagnetized. In the case of the 210 C characteristic, we see that the zero-excitation operating point falls in the non-linear portion of the magnetization current. As a result, any winding current which causes an increase in magnet flux density will demagnetize the magnet.

EXAMPLE 1.12

A magnetic circuit similar to that of Fig. 1.26 has a 200-turn winding ($N = 200$) and includes a neodymium-boron-iron magnet of length $l_m = 3$ cm and cross-sectional area $A_m = 2.5$ cm². The airgap has an effective area of $A_g = 0.259$ cm² and an effective length of $g = 0.9$ cm.

a. Derive an expression for the load-line of this magnetic circuit as a function of winding current i and show that it coincides with the zero-excitation load line of Fig. 1.24 when the winding current is equal to zero.

b. The magnetic circuit is excited by a sinusoidal winding current of peak amplitude I_{peak}. In order to avoid the possibility of demagnetizing the magnet, it is desirable to limit I_{peak} to a value such that the magnet flux density B_m remains positive. Calculate the maximum amplitude of I_{peak} for magnet operating temperatures of 20 C and 120 C.

■ Solution

a. This magnetic circuit is essentially identical to that of Example 1.11 and Fig. 1.22. Hence the equation for the load line is identical to that derived in that example. Specifically,

$$B_m = -\mu_0 \left(\frac{A_g}{A_m}\right)\left(\frac{l_m}{g}\right)H_m + \frac{\mu_0 N}{g}\left(\frac{A_g}{A_m}\right)i$$

$$= \mu_0 \left[-\left(\frac{0.259}{2.5}\right)\left(\frac{3}{0.9}\right)H_m + \frac{200}{9 \times 10^{-3}}\left(\frac{0.259}{2.5}\right)i\right]$$

$$= -4.34 \times 10^{-7} H_m + 2.89 \times 10^{-3} i$$

With $i = 0$, when $H_m = -600$ kA/m, this equation gives $B_m = 0.26$ T which closely coincides with the zero-excitation load line of Fig 1.24.

b. From Eq.1.60, over the linear operating region the relationship between B_M and H_m in the magnet is given by

$$B_m = B_r + \mu_R H_m$$

Combining this expression with the equation for the load-line of part (a) gives

$$B_m = \frac{\mu_R N i + l_m B_r}{l_m + g\left(\frac{\mu_R}{\mu_0}\right)\left(\frac{A_m}{A_g}\right)} = 2.17 \times 10^{-3} i + 0.249 B_r$$

For a sinusoidal current of peak amplitude I_{peak}, B_m will remain positive as long as

$$I_{peak} = \frac{l_m B_r}{\mu_R N} = 114.8 B_r$$

For a temperature of 80 C, from Table 1.1 $B_r = 1.15$ T and thus the maximum value of I_{peak} is 132 A. Similarly, for a temperature of 120 C, $B_r = 1.03$ and the maximum value of I_{peak} is 118 A.

1.7 SUMMARY

Electromechanical devices which employ magnetic fields often use ferromagnetic materials for guiding and concentrating these fields. Because the magnetic permeability of ferromagnetic materials can be large (up to tens of thousands times that of the surrounding space), most of the magnetic flux is confined to fairly well-defined paths determined by the geometry of the magnetic material. In addition, often the frequencies of interest are low enough to permit the magnetic fields to be considered quasi-static, and hence they can be determined simply from a knowledge of the net mmf acting on the magnetic structure.

As a result, the solution for the magnetic fields in these structures can be obtained in a straightforward fashion by using the techniques of magnetic-circuit analysis. These techniques can be used to reduce a complex three-dimensional magnetic field solution to what is essentially a one-dimensional problem. As in all engineering solutions, a certain amount of experience and judgment is required, but the technique gives useful results in many situations of practical engineering interest.

Ferromagnetic materials are available with a wide variety of characteristics. In general, their behavior is nonlinear, and their *B-H* characteristics are often represented in the form of a family of hysteresis (*B-H*) loops. Losses, both hysteretic and eddy-current, are functions of the flux level and frequency of operation as well as the material composition and the manufacturing process used. A basic understanding of the nature of these phenomena is extremely useful in the application of these materials in practical devices. Typically, important properties are available in the form of curves supplied by the material manufacturers.

Certain magnetic materials, commonly known as hard or permanent-magnet materials, are characterized by large values of residual magnetization and coercivity. These materials produce significant magnetic flux even in magnetic circuits with air gaps. With proper design they can be made to operate stably in situations which subject them to a wide range of mmfs and temperature variations. Permanent magnets find application in many small devices, including loudspeakers, ac and dc motors, microphones, and analog electric meters.

1.8 CHAPTER 1 VARIABLES

μ	Magnetic permeability [H/m]
μ_0	Permeability of free space $= 4\pi \times 10^{-7}$ [H/m]
μ_r	Relative permeability
μ_R	Recoil permeability [H/m]
$\phi, \varphi, \phi_{max}$	Magnetic flux [Wb]
ω	Angular frequency [rad/sec]
ρ	Mass density [kg/m^3]
A	Cross-sectional area [m^2]
B, B	Magnetic flux density [T]
B_r	Residual/remanent magnetization [T]
e	Electromotive force [V]
e, E	Voltage [V]
E	Electric field intensity [V/m]
f	Frequency [Hz]
$\mathcal{F}$	Magnetomotive force [A]
g	Gap length [m]
H, H, H_{rms}	Magnetic field intensity [A/m]
H_c	Coercivity [A/m]
i, I	Current [A]
$i_\varphi, I_{\phi,rms}$	Exciting current [A]
J	Current density [A/m^2]
l	Linear dimension [m]
L	Inductance [H]
N	Number of turns
P	Power [W]
P_{core}	Core loss [W]
P_a	Exciting rms voltamperes per unit mass [W/kg]

P_c	Core loss density [W/kg]
$\mathcal{P}$	Permeance [H]
R	Resistance [Ω]
$\mathcal{R}$	Reluctance [H^{-1}]
S	Exciting rms voltamperes [VA]
S_a	Exciting rms voltamperes per mass [VA/kg]
t	Time [sec]
T	Period [sec]
T	Temperature [C]
V	Voltage [V]
Vol	Volume [m^3]
W	Energy [J]

Subscripts:

c	Core
g	Gap
m, mag	Magnet
max	Maximum
rms	Root mean square
tot	Total

1.9 PROBLEMS

1.1 A magnetic circuit with a single air gap is shown in Fig. 1.27. The core dimensions are

Cross-sectional Area $A_c = 3.5$ cm^2
Mean core length $l_c = 25$ cm
Gap length $g = 2.4$ mm
$N = 95$ turns

Assume that the core is of infinite permeability ($\mu \rightarrow \infty$) and neglect the effects of fringing fields at the air gap and leakage flux. (a) Calculate the reluctance of the core $\mathcal{R}_c$ and that of the gap $\mathcal{R}_g$. For a current of $i = 1.4$ A, calculate (b) the total flux ϕ, (c) the flux linkages λ of the coil, and (d) the coil inductance L.

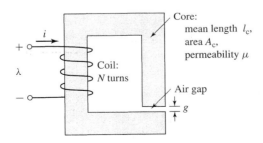

Figure 1.27 Magnetic circuit for Problem 1.1.

1.2 Repeat Problem 1.1 for a finite core permeability of $\mu = 2350\ \mu_0$.

1.3 Consider the magnetic circuit of Fig. 1.27 with the dimensions of Problem 1.1. Assuming infinite core permeability, calculate (a) the number of turns required to achieve an inductance of 15 mH and (b) the inductor current which will result in a core flux density of 1.15 T.

1.4 Repeat Problem 1.3 for a core permeability of $\mu = 1700\ \mu_0$.

1.5 The magnetic circuit of Problem 1.1 has a non-linear core material whose permeability as a function of B_m is given by

$$\mu = \mu_0 \left(1 + \frac{2153}{\sqrt{1 + 0.43(B_m)^{12.1}}} \right)$$

where B_m is the material flux density.

   a. Using MATLAB, plot a dc magnetization curve for this material (B_m vs. H_m) over the range $0 \le B_m \le 2.1$ T.

   b. Find the current required to achieve a flux density of 2.1 T in the air gap.

   c. Again using MATLAB, plot the coil flux linkages as a function of coil current as the current is varied from 0 to the value found in part (b).

1.6 The magnetic circuit of Fig. 1.28 consists of a core and a moveable plunger of width l_p, each of permeability μ. The core has cross sectional area A_c and mean length l_c. The overlap area of the two air gaps A_g is a function of the plunger position x and can be assumed to vary as

$$A_g = A_c \left(1 - \frac{x}{X_0} \right)$$

You may neglect any fringing fields at the air gap and use approximations consistent with magnetic-circuit analysis.

   a. Assuming that $\mu \to \infty$, derive an expression for the magnetic flux density in the air gap B_g as a function of the winding current i and the plunger position x (assume x is limited to the range $0 \le x \le 0.5\ X_0$). Write an expression for the corresponding flux density in the core?

   b. Repeat part (a) for a finite permeability μ.

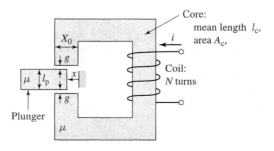

Figure 1.28   Magnetic circuit for Problem 1.6.

1.7 The magnetic circuit of Fig. 1.28 has 125 turns and the following dimension:

$$l_c = 50 \text{ cm} \qquad l_p = 4 \text{ cm}$$
$$g = 0.25 \text{ cm} \qquad A_c = 100 \text{ cm}^2$$
$$X_0 = 10 \text{ cm}$$

With $x = 0.5 \, X_0$, the measured inductance is 52 mH. Using reasonable approximations, calculate the relative permeability μ_r of the core and plunger material.

1.8 Figure 1.29 shows an inductor made up of two C-cores. Each core as area A_c and mean length l_c. There are two air gaps, each of length g and effective area A_g. Finally, there are two N-turn coils, one on each of the C-cores. Assuming infinite core permeability and for cores of dimensions

Cross-sectional area: $A_c = A_g = 38.7 \text{ cm}^2$
Core-length: $l_c = 45 \text{ cm}$
Gap length: $g = 0.12 \text{ cm}$

a. Calculate the number of turns required to achieve an inductance of 12.2 mH, assuming infinite core permeability and that the coils are connected in series. Since the number of turns must be an integer, your answer must be rounded to the nearest integer. Calculated the actual inductance value based upon the resultant number of turns.

b. The inductance can be fine-tuned by adjusting the air-gap length to achieve the desired inductance. Based upon the number of turns found in part (a), calculate the air-gap length required to achieve the desired inductance of 12.2 mH.

c. Based upon this final inductor design, calculate the inductor current which will produce a core flux density of 1.5 T.

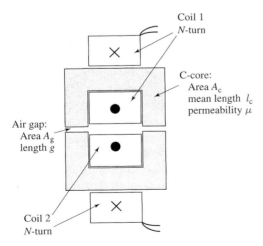

Figure 1.29 C-core inductor for problem 1.8.

1.9 Assuming that the coils are connected in parallel, repeat Problem 1.8.

1.10 Repeat Problem 1.8 assuming that the core has a permeability of 1800 μ_0.

1.11 The magnetic circuit of Fig. 1.28 and Problem 1.6 has the following dimensions:

$$
\begin{array}{ll}
A_c = 9.3 \text{ cm}^2 & l_c = 27 \text{ cm} \\
l_p = 2.7 \text{ cm} & g = 0.6 \text{ mm} \\
X_0 = 2.3 \text{ cm} & N = 480 \text{ turns}
\end{array}
$$

    a. Assuming a constant permeability of $\mu = 3150 \, \mu_0$, calculate the current required to achieve a flux density of 1.25 T in the air gap when the plunger is fully retracted ($x = 0$).

    b. Repeat the calculation of part (a) for the case in which the core and plunger are composed of a a non-linear material whose permeability is given by

$$
\mu = \mu_0 \left(1 + \frac{1065}{\sqrt{1 + 0.038 |B_m|^9}} \right)
$$

    where B_m is the magnetic flux density in the material.

    c. For the non-linear material of part (b), use MATLAB to plot the air-gap flux density as a function of winding current for $x = 0$ and $x = 0.5 X_0$.

1.12 An inductor of the form of Fig. 1.27 has dimensions

    Cross-sectional area $A_c = 3.8 \text{ cm}^2$

    Mean core length $l_c = 19 \text{ cm}$

    $N = 122 \text{ turns}$

Assuming a core permeability of $\mu = 3240 \, \mu_0$ and neglecting the effects of leakage flux and fringing fields, calculate the air-gap length required to achieve an inductance of 6.0 mH.

1.13 The magnetic circuit of Fig. 1.30 consists of rings of magnetic material in a stack of height h. The rings have inner radius R_i and outer radius R_o. Assume that the iron is of infinite permeability ($\mu \to \infty$) and neglect the effects of

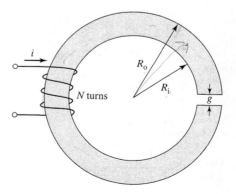

Figure 1.30 Magnetic circuit for Problem 1.13.

magnetic leakage and fringing. For

$$R_i = 3.2 \text{ cm}$$
$$R_o = 4.1 \text{ cm}$$
$$h = 1.8 \text{ cm}$$
$$g = 0.15 \text{ cm}$$

calculate:

a. The mean core length l_c and the core cross-sectional area A_c

b. The reluctance of the core $\mathcal{R}_c$ and that of the gap $\mathcal{R}_g$

For $N = 72$ turns, calculate

c. The inductance L

d. Current i required to operate at an air-gap flux density of $B_g = 1.25\text{T}$

e. The corresponding flux linkages λ of the coil

1.14 Repeat Problem 1.13 for a core permeability of $\mu = 750\ \mu_0$.

1.15 Using MATLAB, plot the inductance of the inductor of Problem 1.13 as a function of relative core permeability as the core permeability varies from $\mu_r = 100$ to $\mu_r = 10{,}000$. (Hint: Plot the inductance versus the log of the relative permeability.) What is the minimum relative core permeability required to insure that the inductance is within 5 percent of the value calculated assuming that the core permeability is infinite?

1.16 The inductor of Fig. 1.31 has a core of uniform circular cross-section of area A_c, mean length l_c and relative permeability μ_r, and an N-turn winding. Write an expression for the inductance L.

1.17 The inductor of Fig. 1.31 has the following dimensions.

$$A_c = 1.1\text{cm}^2$$
$$l_c = 12 \text{ cm}$$
$$g = 0.9 \text{ mm}$$
$$N = 520 \text{ turns}$$

a. Neglecting leakage and fringing and assuming $\mu_r = 1{,}000$, calculate the inductance.

b. Calculate the core flux density and the inductor flux linkages for a winding current of 1.2 A.

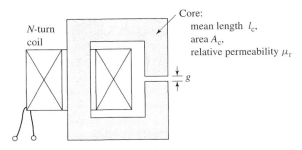

Figure 1.31 Inductor for Problem 1.16.

1.18 The inductor of Problem 1.17 is to be operated from a 60-Hz voltage source.
(a) Assuming negligible coil resistance, calculate the rms inductor voltage
corresponding to a peak core flux density of 1.5 T. (b) Under this operating
condition, calculate the rms current and the peak stored energy.

1.19 Assume the core material of the inductor of Problem 1.17 has the permeability
given in Problem 1.5. Write a MATLAB script to calculate the core flux
density and the inductor flux linkages at a current of 1.2 A.

1.20 Consider the cylindrical magnetic circuit of Fig. 1.32. This structure, known
as a pot-core, is typically made in two halves. The N-turn coil is wound on a
cylindrical bobbin and can be easily inserted over the central post of the core
as the two halves are assembled. Because the air gap is internal to the core,
provided the core is not driven excessively into saturation, relatively little
magnetic flux will "leak" from the core, making this a particularly attractive
configuration for a wide variety of applications, both for inductors such as that
of Fig. 1.31 and transformers.

Assume the core permeability to be $\mu = 2,300\,\mu_0$ and $N = 180$ turns. The
following dimensions are specified:

$$R_1 = 1.6\ \text{cm} \quad R_2 = 4.2\ \text{cm} \quad l = 2.8\ \text{cm}$$

$$h = 0.78\ \text{cm} \quad g = 0.45\ \text{mm}$$

a. Although the flux density in the radial sections of the core (the sections of
thickness h) actually decreases with radius, assume that the flux density
remains uniform. Find the value of the radius R_3 such that the average
flux density in the outer wall of the core is equal to that within the central
cylinder.

b. Write an expression for the coil inductance and evaluate it for the given
dimensions.

Figure 1.32 Pot-core inductor for
Problem 1.20.

c.   The core is to be operated at a peak flux density of 0.6 T at a frequency of 60 Hz. Find (i) the corresponding rms value of the voltage induced in the winding, (ii) the rms coil current, and (iii) the peak stored energy.

d.   Repeat part (c) for a frequency of 50 Hz.

1.21 A square voltage wave having a fundamental frequency of 60 Hz and equal positive and negative half cycles of amplitude E is applied to a 575-turn winding surrounding a closed iron core of cross sectional area $A_c = 9$ cm^2 and of length $l_c = 35$ cm. Neglect both the winding resistance and any effects of leakage flux.

a.   Sketch the voltage, the winding flux linkage, and the core flux as a function of time.

b.   Find the maximum permissible value of E if the maximum flux density is not to exceed 0.95 T.

c.   Calculate the peak winding current if the core has a magnetic permeability of 1,000 μ_0.

1.22 Assume that iron core of Problem 1.21 can be described by a magnetic permeability given by

$$\mu = \mu_0 \left(1 + \frac{1210}{\sqrt{1 + 0.04 \ |B|^{8.5}}} \right)$$

where B is the core flux density.

a.   Plot the core-material B-H curve for flux densities in the range -1.8 T $\leq B \leq 1.8$ T.

b.   A 110 V rms, 60-Hz sinusoidal voltage is applied to the winding. Using MATLAB, plot one cycle of the resultant winding current as a function of time. What is the peak current?

c.   The voltage of part (b) is doubled to 220 V rms. Add a plot of the resultant current as a function of time to the plot of part (b). What is the peak current for this case?

1.23 Repeat parts (b) and (c) of Problem 1.22 if a 10 mm air gap is inserted in the magnetic core.

1.24 An inductor is to be designed using a magnetic core of the form of that of Fig. 1.31. The core is of uniform cross-sectional area $A_c = 6.0$ cm^2 and of mean length $l_c = 28$ cm.

a.   Calculate the air-gap length g and the number of turns N such that the inductance is 23 mH and so that the inductor can operate at peak currents of 10 A without saturating. Assume that saturation occurs when the peak flux density in the core exceeds 1.7 T and that, below saturation, the core has permeability $\mu = 2700 \ \mu_0$.

b.   For an inductor current of 10 A, use Eq. 3.21 to calculate (i) the magnetic stored energy in the air gap and (ii) the magnetic stored energy in the core. Show that the total magnetic stored energy is given by Eq. 1.46.

1.25 Write a MATLAB script to design inductors based upon the magnetic core of Fig. 1.31. Assume the core has a cross-sectional area of 10.0 cm^2, a length of 35 cm and a relative magnetic permeability of 1,700. The inductor is to be operated with a sinusoidal current at 50-Hz and it must be designed such that the peak core flux density will be equal to 1.4 T when the peak inductor current is equal to 7.5 A.

Write a simple design program in the form of a MATLAB script to calculate the number of turns and air-gap length as a function of the desired inductance. The script should be written to request a value of inductance (in mH) from the user, with the output being the air-gap length in mm and the number of turns. Write your script to reject as unacceptable any designs for which the gap length is out of the range of 0.05 mm to 6.0 mm or for which the number of turns drops below 10.

Using your program, find (a) the minimum and (b) the maximum inductances (to the nearest mH) which will satisfy the the given constraints. For each of these values, find the required air-gap length and the number of turns as well as the rms voltage corresponding to the peak core flux.

1.26 Consider an inductor composed of two C-cores as shown in Fig. 1.29. Each C-core has cross-sectional area $A_c = 105$ cm^2 and a mean length $l_c = 48$ cm.

a. Assuming the coils are connected in parallel, calculate the number of turns N per coil and the air-gap length g such that the inductance is 350 mH and such that the inductor current can be increased to 6.0 A without exceeding a core flux density of 1.2 T, thus avoiding saturation of the core. You may neglect the reluctance of the core and the effects of fringing at the air gap.

b. Repeat part a) assuming the coils are connected in series.

1.27 Assuming the C-cores of Problem 1.26 have a magnetic permeability of $\mu = 3,500 \, \mu_0$, repeat Problem 1.26.

1.28 Write a MATLAB script to automate the calculations of Problem 1.26 and 1.27. The inputs to your script should be the core area, mean core length, the core permeability and the winding connection (parallel or series) as well as the desired inductance and maximum core flux density and current. Exercise your script to design an inductor of 220 mH with cores of cross-sectional area of 40 cm^2 and mean length 35 cm. The inductor should be able to carry a current of up to 9.0 A at a flux density not to exceed 1.1 T.

1.29 A proposed energy storage mechanism consists of an N-turn coil wound around a large non-magnetic ($\mu = \mu_0$) toroidal form as shown in Fig. 1.33. As can be seen from the figure, the toroidal form has a circular cross section of radius a and toroidal radius r, measured to the center of the cross section. The geometry of this device is such that the magnetic field can be considered to be zero everywhere outside the toroid. Under the assumption that $a \ll r$, the H field inside the toroid can be considered to be directed around the toroid and of uniform magnitude

$$H = \frac{Ni}{2\pi r}$$

Figure 1.33 Toroidal winding for Problem 1.29.

For a coil with $N = 12,000$ turns, $r = 9$ m and $a = 0.55$ m:

a. Calculate the coil inductance L.

b. The coil is to be charged to a magnetic flux density of 1.80 T. Calculate the total stored magnetic energy in the torus when this flux density is achieved.

c. If the coil is to be charged at a uniform rate (i.e. $di/dt = \text{constant}$), calculate the terminal voltage required to achieve the required flux density in 40 s. Assume the coil resistance to be negligible.

1.30 Figure 1.34 shows an inductor wound on a laminated iron core of rectangular cross section. Assume that the permeability of the iron is infinite. Neglect magnetic leakage and fringing in the two air gaps (total gap length $= g$). The N-turn winding is insulated copper wire whose resistivity is $\rho \, \Omega \cdot$m. Assume that the fraction f_w of the winding space is available for copper; the rest of the space being used for insulation.

a. Calculate the cross-sectional area and volume of the copper in the winding space.

b. Write an expression for the flux density B in the inductor in terms of the current density J_{cu} in the copper winding.

c. Write an expression for the copper current density J_{cu} in terms of the coil current I, the number of turns N and the coil geometry.

d. Derive an expression for the electric power dissipation in the coil in terms of the current density J_{cu}.

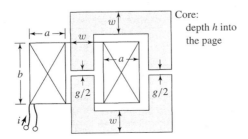

Figure 1.34 Iron-core inductor for Problem 1.30.

e. Derive an expression for the magnetic stored energy in the inductor in terms of the applied current density J_{cu}.

f. From parts (d) and (e) derive an expression for the L/R time constant of the inductor. Note that this expression is independent of the number of turns in the coil and hence does not change as the inductance and coil resistance are changed by varying the number of turns.

1.31 The inductor of Fig. 1.34 has the following dimensions:

$$a = h = w = 1.8 \text{ cm} \quad b = 2.2 \text{ cm} \quad g = 0.18 \text{ cm}$$

The winding factor (i.e. the fraction of the total winding area occupied by conductor) is $f_w = 0.55$. The resistivity of copper is $1.73 \times 10^{-8}\,\Omega\cdot\text{m}$. When the coil is operated with a constant dc applied voltage of 40 V, the air-gap flux density is measured to be 1.3 T. Find the power dissipated in the coil, coil current, number of turns, coil resistance, inductance, time constant, and wire size to the nearest standard size. (Hint: Wire size can be found from the expression

$$AWG = 36 - 4.312 \ln \left(\frac{A_{\text{wire}}}{1.267 \times 10^{-8}} \right)$$

where AWG is the wire size, expressed in terms of the American Wire Gage, and A_{wire} is the conductor cross-sectional area measured in m^2.)

1.32 The magnetic circuit of Fig. 1.35 has two windings and two air gaps. The core can be assumed to be of infinite permeability. The core dimensions are indicated in the figure.

a. Assuming coil 1 to be carrying a current I_1 and the current in coil 2 to be zero, calculate (i) the magnetic flux density in each of the air gaps, (ii) the flux linkage of winding 1, and (iii) the flux linkage of winding 2.

b. Repeat part (a), assuming zero current in winding 1 and a current I_2 in winding 2.

c. Repeat part (a), assuming the current in winding 1 to be I_1 and the current in winding 2 to be I_2.

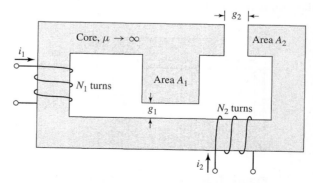

Figure 1.35   Magnetic circuit for Problem 1.32.

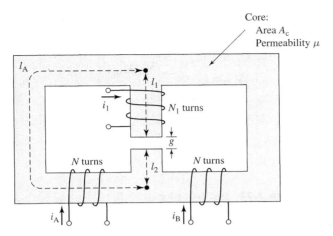

Figure 1.36 Symmetric magnetic circuit for Problem 1.33.

d. Find the self-inductances of windings 1 and 2 and the mutual inductance between the windings.

1.33 The symmetric magnetic circuit of Fig. 1.36 has three windings. Windings A and B each have N turns and are wound on the two bottom legs of the core. The core dimensions are indicated in the figure.

a. Find the self-inductances of each of the windings.

b. Find the mutual inductances between the three pairs of windings.

c. Find the voltage induced in winding 1 by time-varying currents $i_A(t)$ and $i_B(t)$ in windings A and B. Show that this voltage can be used to measure the imbalance between two sinusoidal currents of the same frequency.

1.34 The reciprocating generator of Fig. 1.37 has a movable plunger (position x) which is supported so that it can slide in and out of the magnetic yoke while maintaining a constant air gap of length g on each side adjacent to the yoke. Both the yoke and the plunger can be considered to be of infinite permeability. The motion of the plunger is constrained such that its position is limited to $0 \le x \le w$.

There are two windings on this magnetic circuit. The first has N_1 turns and carries a constant dc current I_0. The second, which has N_2 turns, is open-circuited and can be connected to a load.

a. Neglecting any fringing effects, find the mutual inductance between windings 1 and 2 as a function of the plunger position x.

b. The plunger is driven by an external source so that its motion is given by

$$x(t) = \frac{w(1 + \epsilon \sin \omega t)}{2}$$

where $\epsilon \le 1$. Find an expression for the sinusoidal voltage which is generated as a result of this motion.

Figure 1.37 Reciprocating generator for Problem 1.34.

1.35 Figure 1.38 shows a configuration that can be used to measure the magnetic characteristics of electrical steel. The material to be tested is cut or punched into circular laminations which are then stacked (with interspersed insulation to avoid eddy-current formation). Two windings are wound over this stack of laminations: the first, with N_l turns, is used to excite a magnetic field in the lamination stack; the second, with N_2 turns, is used to sense the resultant magnetic flux.

The accuracy of the results requires that the magnetic flux density be uniform within the laminations. This can be accomplished if the lamination width $w = R_o - R_i$ is much smaller than the lamination radius and if the excitation winding is wound uniformly around the lamination stack. For the

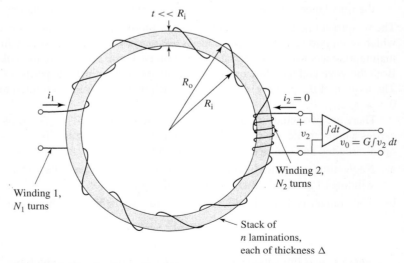

Figure 1.38 Configuration for measurement of magnetic properties of electrical steel.

purposes of this analysis, assume there are n laminations, each of thickness Δ. Also assume that winding 1 is excited by a current $i_1 = I_0 \sin \omega t$.

a. Find the relationship between the magnetic field intensity H in the laminations and current i_1 in winding 1.

b. Find the relationship between the voltage v_2 and the time rate of change of the flux density B in the laminations.

c. Find the relationship between the voltage $v_0 = G \int v_2 dt$ and the flux density.

In this problem, we have shown that the magnetic field intensity H and the magnetic flux density B in the laminations are proportional to the current i_1 and the voltage v_0 by known constants. Thus, B and H in the magnetic steel can be measured directly, and the B-H characteristics as discussed in Arts. 1.3 and 1.4 can be determined.

1.36 From the dc magnetization curve of Fig. 1.10 it is possible to calculate the relative permeability $\mu_r = B_c/(\mu_0 H_c)$ for M-5 electrical steel as a function of the flux level B_c. Assuming the core of Fig. 1.2 to be made of M-5 electrical steel with the dimensions given in Example 1.1, calculate the range of flux densities for which the reluctance of the core never exceeds 5 percent of the reluctance of the total magnetic circuit.

1.37 In order to test the properties of a sample of electrical steel, a set of laminations of the form of Fig. 1.38 have been stamped out of a sheet of the electrical steel of thickness 3.0 mm. The radii of the laminations are $R_i = 80$ mm and $R_o = 90$ mm. They have been assembled in a stack of 15 laminations (separated by appropriate insulation to eliminate eddy currents) for the purposes of testing the magnetic properties at a frequency of 50 Hz.

a. The flux in the lamination stack will be excited from a variable-amplitude, 50-Hz voltage source whose peak amplitude is 20 V. Ignoring any voltage drop across the winding resistance, calculate the number of turns N_1 for the excitation winding required to insure that the lamination stack can be excited up to a peak flux density of 1.8 T.

b. With a secondary winding of $N_2 = 10$ turns and an integrator gain $G = 1,000$, the output of the integrator is observed to be 7.5 V peak. Calculate (i) the corresponding peak flux in the lamination stack and (ii) the corresponding amplitude of the voltage applied to the excitation winding.

1.38 The coils of the magnetic circuit shown in Fig. 1.39 are connected in series so that the mmfs of paths A and B both tend to set up flux in the center leg C in the same direction. The coils are wound with equal turns, $N_1 = N_2 = 120$. The dimensions are:

Cross-section area of A and B legs $= 8$ cm^2
Cross-section area of C leg $= 16$ cm^2
Length of A path $= 17$ cm
Length of B path $= 17$ cm

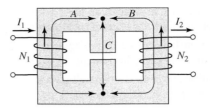

Figure 1.39 Magnetic circuit for Problem 1.38.

Length of C path $= 5.5$ cm
Air gap length $= 0.35$ cm

The material is M-5 grade, 0.012-in steel. Neglect fringing and leakage.

a. How many amperes are required to produce a flux density of 1.3 T in the air gap?

b. Under the condition of part (a), how many joules of energy are stored in the magnetic field in the air gap and in the core? Based upon this stored energy, calculate the inductance of this series-connected winding.

c. Calculate the inductance of this system assuming the core to be of infinite permeability. Compare your inductance with the value calculated in part (b).

1.39 The following table includes data for the top half of a symmetric 60-Hz hysteresis loop for a specimen of magnetic steel:

B, T	0	0.2	0.4	0.6	0.7	0.8	0.9	1.0	0.95	0.9	0.8	0.7	0.6	0.4	0.2	0
H, A·turns/m	48	52	58	73	85	103	135	193	80	42	2	−18	−29	−40	−45	−48

Using MATLAB, (a) plot this data, (b) calculate the area of the hysterises loop in joules, and (c) calculate the corresponding 60-Hz core loss density in Watts/kg. Assume the density of the steel is 7.65 g/cm^3.

1.40 A magnetic circuit of the form of Fig. 1.27 has dimension

Cross-sectional Area $A_c = 27$ cm^2
Mean core length $l_c = 70$ cm
Gap length $g = 2.4$ mm
$N = 95$ turns

and is made up of M-5 electrical steel with the properties described in Figs. 1.10, 1.12, and 1.14. Assume the core to be operating with a 60-Hz sinusoidal flux density of the rms flux density of 1.1 T. Neglect the winding resistance and leakage inductance. Find the winding voltage, rms winding current, and core loss for this operating condition. The density of M-5 steel is 7.65 g/cm^3.

1.41 Repeat Example 1.8 under the assumption that all the core dimensions are doubled.

Figure 1.40 Magnetic circuit for the loudspeaker of Problem 1.44 (voice coil not shown).

1.42 Using the magnetization characteristics for samarium cobalt given in Fig. 1.19, find the point of maximum-energy product and the corresponding flux density and magnetic field intensity. Using these values, repeat Example 1.10 with the Alnico 5 magnet replaced by a samarium-cobalt magnet. By what factor does this reduce the magnet volume required to achieve the desired air-gap flux density?

1.43 Using the magnetization characteristics for neodymium-iron-boron given in Fig. 1.19, find the point of maximum energy product and the corresponding flux density and magnetic field intensity. Using these values, repeat Example 1.10 with the Alnico 5 magnet replaced by a neodymium-iron-boron magnet. By what factor does this reduce the magnet volume required to achieve the desired air-gap flux density?

1.44 Figure 1.40 shows the magnetic circuit for a permanent-magnet loudspeaker. The voice coil (not shown) is in the form of a circular cylindrical coil which fits in the air gap. A samarium-cobalt magnet is used to create the air-gap dc magnetic field which interacts with the voice coil currents to produce the motion of the voice coil. The designer has determined that the air gap must have radius $R = 2.2$ cm, length $g = 0.1$ cm, and height $h = 1.1$ cm.

Assuming that the yoke and pole piece are of infinite magnetic permeability ($\mu \to \infty$), find the magnet height h_m and the magnet radius R_m that will result in an air-gap magnetic flux density of 1.3 T and require the smallest magnet volume.

(Hint: Refer to Example 1.10 and to Fig. 1.19 to find the point of maximum energy product for samarium cobalt.)

1.45 Repeat Problem 1.44 replacing the samarium-cobalt magnet with a neodymium-iron-boron magnet assuming the magnetization characteristics of Fig. 1.19.

1.46 Based upon the characteristics of the neodymium-iron-boron material of Fig. 1.24 and Table 1.1, calculate the maximum-energy product of this grade of neodymium-iron-boron magnet material at each of the temperatures of

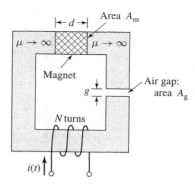

Figure 1.41   Magnetic circuit for Prob 1.47.

Table 1.1 and the corresponding values of H and B. (Hint: Write an analytic expression for the maximum energy product in terms of H using the fact that the recoil permeability is $1.04\ \mu_0$.)

1.47 It is desired to achieve a time-varying magnetic flux density in the air gap of the magnetic circuit of Fig. 1.41 of the form

$$B_g = B_0 + B_1 \sin \omega t$$

where $B_0 = 0.6$ T and $B_1 = 0.20$ T. The dc field B_0 is to be created by a neodymium-iron-boron magnet with magnetization characteristic of Fig. 1.19, whereas the time-varying field is to be created by a time-varying current. For $A_g = 7\ \text{cm}^2$, $g = 0.35$ cm, and $N = 175$ turns, and based upon the neodymium-iron-boron characteristics of Fig. 1.19, find:

a. the magnet length d and the magnet area A_m that will achieve the desired dc air-gap flux density and minimize the magnet volume and

b. the amplitude of the time-varying current required to achieve the desired time-variation of the air-gap flux density.

1.48 A magnetic circuit of the form of Fig. 1.41 is to be designed using neodymium-iron-boron material with the characteristics of Fig. 1.24 and Table 1.1.

The magnetic circuit core will have cross-sectional area $A_g = 9\ \text{cm}^2$ and the air-gap length will be $g = 0.32$ cm. The circuit is designed to be operated at temperatures up to 180 C.

a. Find the magnet length d and the magnet area A_m corresponding to the minimum magnet volume that will produce a magnetic flux density of 0.8 T with the system operating at a temperature of 180 C.

b. For the magnet of part (a), find the flux density in the air-gap when the operating temperature is 60 C.

CHAPTER 2

Transformers

Before we proceed with a study of electric machinery, it is desirable to discuss certain aspects of the theory of magnetically coupled circuits, with emphasis on transformer action. Although the static transformer is not an energy conversion device, it is an indispensable component in many energy conversion systems. A significant component of ac power systems, it makes possible electric generation at the most economical generator voltage, power transfer at the most economical transmission voltage, and power utilization at the most suitable voltage for the particular utilization device. The transformer is also widely used in low-power, low-current electronic and control circuits for performing such functions as matching the impedances of a source and its load for maximum power transfer, isolating one circuit from another, or isolating direct current while maintaining ac continuity between two circuits.

The transformer is one of the simpler devices comprising two or more electric circuits coupled by a common magnetic circuit. Its analysis involves many of the principles essential to the study of electric machinery. Thus, our study of the transformer will serve as a bridge between the introduction to magnetic-circuit analysis of Chapter 1 and the more detailed study of electric machinery to follow.

2.1 INTRODUCTION TO TRANSFORMERS

Essentially, a transformer consists of two or more windings coupled by mutual magnetic flux. If one of these windings, the *primary*, is connected to an alternating-voltage source, an alternating flux will be produced whose amplitude will depend on the primary voltage, the frequency of the applied voltage, and the number of turns. A portion of this flux, referred to as *mutual flux*, will link a second winding, the *secondary*,[1] and

---

[1] It is conventional to think of the "input" to the transformer as the primary and the "output" as the secondary. However, in many applications, power can flow either way and the concept of primary and secondary windings can become confusing. An alternate terminology, which refers to the windings as "high-voltage" and "low-voltage," is often used and eliminates this confusion.

will induce a voltage in it whose value will depend on the number of secondary turns as well as the magnitude of the mutual flux and the frequency. The *voltage ratio,* or *ratio of transformation,* between the two windings can be varied by proportioning the number of primary and secondary turns.

The essence of transformer action requires only the existence of time-varying mutual flux linking two windings. Such action can occur for two windings coupled through air. However, coupling between the windings can be made much more effective through the use of a core of iron or other ferromagnetic material because most of the flux will be confined to a definite, high-permeability path linking the windings. Such a transformer is commonly called an *iron-core transformer.* Most transformers are of this type. The following discussion is concerned almost wholly with iron-core transformers.

As discussed in Section 1.4, to reduce the losses caused by eddy currents in the core, the magnetic circuit in a transformer usually consists of a stack of thin laminations. Two common types of construction are shown schematically in Fig. 2.1. In the *core type* (Fig. 2.1a) the windings are wound around two legs of a rectangular magnetic core; in the *shell type* (Fig. 2.1b) the windings are wound around the center leg of a three-legged core. Silicon-steel laminations of thickness 0.014 in (0.55 mm) are commonly used for transformers operating at frequencies below a few hundred hertz. Silicon steel has the desirable properties of low cost, low core loss, and high permeability at high flux density. The cores of small transformers used in communication circuits at high frequencies and low energy levels are sometimes made of compressed powdered ferromagnetic alloys known as *ferrites.*

In each of these configurations, most of the flux is confined to the core and therefore links both windings. The windings also produce additional flux, known as

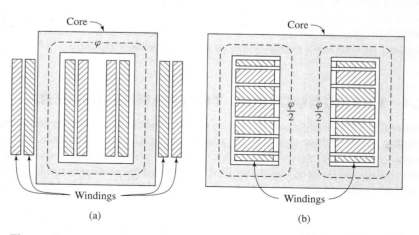

Figure 2.1   Schematic views of (a) core-type and (b) shell-type transformers.

Figure 2.2 A self-protected distribution transformer typical of sizes 2 to 25 kVA, 7200:240/120 V. Only one high-voltage insulator and lightning arrester are needed because one side of the 7200-V line and one side of the primary are grounded.

leakage flux, which links one winding without linking the other. Although leakage flux is a small fraction of the total flux, it plays an important role in determining the behavior of the transformer. In practical transformers, leakage is reduced by subdividing the windings into sections placed as close together as possible. In the core-type construction, each winding consists of two sections, one section on each of the two legs of the core, the primary and secondary windings being concentric coils. In the shell-type construction, variations of the concentric-winding arrangement may be used or the windings may consist of a number of thin "pancake" coils assembled in a stack with primary and secondary coils interleaved.

Figure 2.2 shows the internal construction of a *distribution transformer* such as is used in public utility systems to provide the appropriate voltage for use by residential consumers. A large power transformer is shown in Fig. 2.3.

2.2 NO-LOAD CONDITIONS

Figure 2.4 shows in schematic form a transformer with its secondary circuit open and an alternating voltage v_1 applied to its primary terminals. To simplify the drawings, it is common on schematic diagrams of transformers to show the primary and secondary windings as if they were on separate legs of the core, as in Fig. 2.4, even though the windings are actually interleaved in practice. As discussed in Section 1.4, a small steady-state current i_φ, called the *exciting current,* flows in the primary and establishes

Figure 2.3 A 230 kV Y - 115 kV Y, 100/133/167 MVA Autotransformer. (*Photo courtesy of SPX Transformer Solutions, Inc.*)

Figure 2.4 Transformer with open secondary.

an alternating flux in the magnetic circuit.[2] This flux induces an emf[3] e_1 in the primary equal to

Induced Voltage Given

$$e_1 = \frac{d\lambda_1}{dt} = N_1 \frac{d\varphi}{dt} \tag{2.1}$$

---

[2] In general, the exciting current corresponds to the net ampere-turns (mmf) acting to produce the flux in the magnetic circuit and it is not possible to distinguish whether it flows in the primary or secondary winding or partially in each winding.

[3] As discussed in Chapter 1, the term emf (electromotive force) is often used instead of induced voltage to represent that component of voltage due to a time-varying flux linkage.

where

$\lambda_1 = $ flux linkage of the primary winding

$\varphi = $ flux in the core linking both windings

$N_1 = $ number of turns in the primary winding

The voltage e_1 is in volts when φ is in webers. This emf, together with the voltage drop in the *primary resistance* R_1 (shown schematically as a series resistance in Fig. 2.4), must balance the applied voltage v_1; thus

$$v_1 = R_1 i_\varphi + e_1 \tag{2.2}$$

Note that for the purposes of the current discussion, we are neglecting the effects of primary leakage flux, which will add an additional induced-emf term in Eq. 2.2. In typical transformers, this flux is a small percentage of the core flux, and it is quite justifiable to neglect it for our current purposes. It does, however, play an important role in the behavior of transformers and is discussed in some detail in Section 2.4.

In most large transformers, the no-load resistance drop is very small indeed, and the induced emf e_1 very nearly equals the applied voltage v_1. Furthermore, the waveforms of voltage and flux are very nearly sinusoidal. The analysis can then be greatly simplified, as we have shown in Section 1.4. Thus, if the instantaneous flux φ is

$$\varphi = \phi_{max} \sin \omega t \tag{2.3}$$

the induced voltage e_1 is

$$e_1 = N_1 \frac{d\varphi}{dt} = \omega N_1 \phi_{max} \cos \omega t \tag{2.4}$$

where ϕ_{max} is the maximum value of the flux and $\omega = 2\pi f$, the frequency being f Hz. For the current and voltage reference directions shown in Fig. 2.4, the induced emf leads the flux by 90°. The rms value of the induced emf e_1 is

$$E_1 = \frac{2\pi}{\sqrt{2}} f N_1 \phi_{max} = \sqrt{2}\,\pi f N_1 \phi_{max} \tag{2.5}$$

As can be seen from Eq. 2.2, if the resistive voltage drop is negligible, the counter emf equals the applied voltage. Under these conditions, if a sinusoidal voltage is applied to a winding, a sinusoidally varying core flux must be established whose maximum value ϕ_{max} satisfies the requirement that E_1 in Eq. 2.5 equal the rms value V_1 of the applied voltage; thus

$$\phi_{max} = \frac{V_1}{\sqrt{2}\pi f N_1} \tag{2.6}$$

Under these conditions, the core flux is determined solely by the applied voltage, its frequency, and the number of turns in the winding. This important relation applies not only to transformers but also to any device operated with a sinusoidally-alternating impressed voltage, as long as the resistance and leakage-inductance voltage drops are negligible. The core flux is fixed by the applied voltage, and the required exciting current is determined by the magnetic properties of the core; the exciting current must adjust itself so as to produce the mmf required to create the flux demanded by Eq. 2.6.

The importance and utility of this concept cannot be over-emphasized. It is often extremely useful in the analysis of electric machines which are supplied from single or poly-phase voltage sources. To a first approximation, the winding resistance can often be neglected and, in spite of additional windings (for example the shorted windings on the rotor of induction machines as will be seen in Chapter 6), the flux in the machine will be determined by the applied voltage and the winding currents must adjust to produce the corresponding mmf.

Because of the nonlinear magnetic properties of iron, the waveform of the exciting current differs from the waveform of the flux; the exciting current for a sinusoidal flux waveform will not be sinusoidal. This effect is especially pronounced in closed magnetic circuits such as are found in transformers. In magnetic circuits where the reluctance is dominated by an air gap with its linear magnetic characteristic, such as is the case in many electric machines, the relationship between the net flux and the applied mmf is relatively linear and the exciting current will be much more sinusoidal.

In the case of a closed magnetic circuit, a curve of the exciting current as a function of time can be found graphically from the ac hysteresis loop, as is discussed in Section 1.4 and shown in Fig. 1.11. If the exciting current is analyzed by Fourier-series methods, it is found to consist of a fundamental component and a series of odd harmonics. The fundamental component can, in turn, be resolved into two components, one in phase with the counter emf and the other lagging the counter emf by 90°. The in-phase component supplies the power absorbed by hysteresis and eddy-current losses in the core. It is referred to as *core-loss component* of the exciting current. When the core-loss component is subtracted from the total exciting current, the remainder is called the *magnetizing current*. It comprises a fundamental component lagging the counter emf by 90°, together with all the harmonics. The principal harmonic is the third. For typical power transformers, the third harmonic is usually about 40 percent of the exciting current.

Except in problems concerned directly with the effects of harmonic currents, the peculiarities of the exciting-current waveform usually need not be taken into account, because the exciting current itself is small, especially in large transformers. For example, the exciting current of a typical power transformer is about 1 to 2 percent of full-load current. Consequently the effects of harmonics are usually swamped out by the sinusoidal-currents supplied to other linear elements in the circuit. The exciting current can then be represented by an equivalent sinusoidal current which has the same rms value and frequency and produces the same average power as the actual exciting current.

Such a representation is essential to the construction of a *phasor diagram,* which represents the phase relationship between the various voltages and currents in a system in vector form. Each signal is represented by a phasor whose length is proportional to the amplitude of the signal and whose angle is equal to the phase angle of that signal as measured with respect to a chosen reference signal. In Fig. 2.5, the phasors $\hat{E}_1$

Figure 2.5 No-load phasor diagram.

and $\hat{\Phi}$ respectively, represent the complex amplitudes of the rms-induced emf and the flux. The phasor $\hat{I}_\varphi$ represents the complex amplitude of the rms equivalent sinusoidal exciting current. It lags the induced emf $\hat{E}_1$ by a phase angle θ_c. Also shown in the figure is the phasor $\hat{I}_c$, in phase with $\hat{E}_1$, which is the core-loss component of the exciting current, The component $\hat{I}_m$, in phase with the flux, represents an equivalent sine wave current having the same rms value as the magnetizing current.

The core loss P_{core}, equal to the product of the in-phase components of $\hat{E}_1$ and $\hat{I}_\varphi$, is given by

$$P_{core} = E_1 I_\varphi \cos \theta_c = E_1 I_c \tag{2.7}$$

Typical exciting volt-ampere and core-loss characteristics of high-quality silicon steel used for power and distribution transformer laminations are shown in Figs. 1.12 and 1.14.

EXAMPLE 2.1

In Example 1.8 the core loss and exciting voltamperes for the core of Fig. 1.15 at $B_{max} = 1.5$ T and 60 Hz were found to be

$$P_{core} = 16 \text{ W} \qquad (VI)_{rms} = 20 \text{ VA}$$

and the induced voltage was $V = 274/\sqrt{2} = 194$ V rms when the winding had 200 turns.

Find the power factor, the core-loss current I_c, and the magnetizing current I_m.

■ **Solution**

Power factor: $\cos \theta_c = \frac{16}{20} = 0.80$ (lag) thus $\theta_c = -36.9°$

Note that we know that the power factor is lagging because the system is inductive.

Exciting current: $I_\varphi = \frac{(VI)_{rms}}{V} = 0.10$ A rms

Core-loss component: $I_c = \frac{P_{core}}{V} = 0.082$ A rms

Magnetizing component: $I_m = I_\varphi \times \sin \theta_c = 0.060$ A rms

2.3 EFFECT OF SECONDARY CURRENT; IDEAL TRANSFORMER

As a first approximation to a quantitative theory, consider a transformer with a primary winding of N_1 turns and a secondary winding of N_2 turns, as shown schematically in Fig. 2.6. Notice that the secondary current is defined as positive out of the winding; thus positive secondary current produces an mmf in the opposite direction from that created by positive primary current. Let the properties of this transformer be idealized under the assumption that winding resistances are negligible, that all the flux is confined to the core and fully links both windings (i.e., leakage flux is assumed negligible), that there are no losses in the core, and that the permeability of the core is so high that only a negligible exciting mmf is required to establish the flux. These properties are closely approached but never actually attained in practical transformers. A hypothetical transformer having these properties is often called an *ideal transformer*.

Under the above assumptions, when a time-varying voltage v_1 is impressed on the primary terminals, a core flux φ must be established such that the counter emf e_1 equals the impressed voltage v_1. Thus

$$v_1 = e_1 = N_1 \frac{d\varphi}{dt} \tag{2.8}$$

The core flux also links the secondary and produces an induced emf e_2, and an equal secondary terminal voltage v_2, given by

$$v_2 = e_2 = N_2 \frac{d\varphi}{dt} \tag{2.9}$$

From the ratio of Eqs. 2.8 and 2.9,

$$\frac{v_1}{v_2} = \frac{N_1}{N_2} \tag{2.10}$$

Thus an ideal transformer transforms voltages in the direct ratio of the turns in its windings.

Now let a load which draws a current i_2 be connected to the secondary. The load current thus produces an mmf $N_2 i_2$ in the secondary. Since the impressed primary voltage sets the core flux as specified by Eq. 2.8, the core flux is unchanged by the presence of a load on the secondary. Furthermore, since the net exciting mmf acting

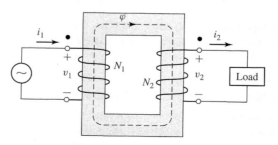

Figure 2.6   Ideal transformer and load.

on the core (equal to $N_1 i_1 - N_2 i_2$) must remain negligible, the primary and secondary currents must satisfy the relationship

$$N_1 i_1 - N_2 i_2 = 0 \tag{2.11}$$

From Eq. 2.11 we see that a compensating primary mmf must result to cancel that of the secondary. Hence

$$N_1 i_1 = N_2 i_2 \tag{2.12}$$

From this discussion, we see that the requirement that the core flux and hence the corresponding net mmf remain unchanged is the means by which the primary "knows" of the presence of load current in the secondary; any change in mmf flowing in the secondary as the result of a load must be accompanied by a corresponding change in the primary mmf. Note that for the reference directions shown in Fig. 2.6 the mmfs of i_1 and i_2 are in opposite directions and therefore compensate.

From Eq. 2.12

$$\frac{i_1}{i_2} = \frac{N_2}{N_1} \tag{2.13}$$

Thus an ideal transformer transforms currents in the inverse ratio of the turns in its windings.

Also notice from Eqs. 2.10 and 2.13 that

$$v_1 i_1 = v_2 i_2 \tag{2.14}$$

i.e., the instantaneous power input to the primary equals the instantaneous power output from the secondary, a necessary condition because all dissipative and energy storage mechanisms in the transformer have been neglected.

An additional property of the ideal transformer can be seen by considering the case of a sinusoidal applied voltage and an impedance load. The circuit is shown in simplified form in Fig. 2.7a, in which the dot-marked terminals of the transformer correspond to the similarly marked terminals in Fig. 2.6. Because all the voltages and currents are sinusoidal, the voltages and currents are represented by their complex amplitudes. The dot markings indicate terminals of corresponding polarity; i.e., if

(a)   (b)   (c)

Figure 2.7 Three circuits which are identical at the terminal a-b when the transformer is ideal.

one follows through the primary and secondary windings of Fig. 2.6, beginning at their dot-marked terminals, one will find that both windings encircle the core in the same direction with respect to the flux. Therefore, if one compares the voltages of the two windings, the voltages from a dot-marked to an unmarked terminal will be of the same instantaneous polarity for primary and secondary. In other words, the voltages $\hat{V}_1$ and $\hat{V}_2$ in Fig. 2.7a are in phase. Also currents $\hat{I}_1$ and $\hat{I}_2$ are in phase as seen from Eq. 2.12. Note again that the polarity of $\hat{I}_1$ is defined as into the dotted terminal and the polarity of $\hat{I}_2$ is defined as out of the dotted terminal.

The circuits of Fig. 2.7 let us investigate the impedance transformation properties of the ideal transformer. In phasor form, Eqs. 2.10 and 2.13 can be expressed as

$$\hat{V}_1 = \frac{N_1}{N_2} \hat{V}_2 \quad \text{and} \quad \hat{V}_2 = \frac{N_2}{N_1} \hat{V}_1 \tag{2.15}$$

$$\hat{I}_1 = \frac{N_2}{N_1} \hat{I}_2 \quad \text{and} \quad \hat{I}_2 = \frac{N_1}{N_2} \hat{I}_1 \tag{2.16}$$

From these equations

$$\frac{\hat{V}_1}{\hat{I}_1} = \left(\frac{N_1}{N_2}\right)^2 \frac{\hat{V}_2}{\hat{I}_2} \tag{2.17}$$

We note that the load impedance Z_2 is related to the secondary voltages and currents as

$$Z_2 = \frac{\hat{V}_2}{\hat{I}_2} \tag{2.18}$$

where Z_2 is the complex impedance of the load. Thus, from Eqs. 2.17 and 2.18, we see that the impedance Z_1 seen at the terminals a-b is equal to

$$Z_1 = \frac{\hat{V}_1}{\hat{I}_1} = \left(\frac{N_1}{N_2}\right)^2 Z_2 \tag{2.19}$$

and consequently we see that from the primary terminals a-b, an impedance Z_2 in the secondary circuit can be replaced by an equivalent impedance Z_1 in the primary circuit satisfying the relationship

$$Z_1 = \left(\frac{N_1}{N_2}\right)^2 Z_2 \tag{2.20}$$

The three circuits of Fig. 2.7 are indistinguishable as far as their performance viewed from terminals a-b is concerned. Transferring an impedance from one side of a transformer to the other in this fashion is called *referring the impedance* to the other side; impedances transform as the square of the turns ratio. In a similar manner, voltages and currents can be *referred* to one side or the other by using Eqs. 2.15 and 2.16 to evaluate the equivalent voltage and current on that side.

To summarize, *in an ideal transformer, voltages are transformed by the direct ratio of turns, currents by the inverse ratio, impedances by square of the turns-ratio and power and voltamperes are unchanged.*

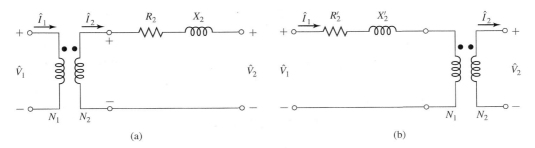

Figure 2.8 Equivalent circuits for Example 2.2. (a) Impedance in series with the secondary. (b) Impedance referred to the primary.

EXAMPLE 2.2

The equivalent circuit of Fig. 2.8a shows an ideal transformer with an impedance $R_2 + jX_2 = 1 + j4\ \Omega$ connected in series with the secondary. The turns ratio $N_1/N_2 = 5:1$. (a) Draw an equivalent circuit with the series impedance referred to the primary side. (b) For a primary voltage of 120 V rms and a short connected across the secondary terminals $(V_2 = 0)$, calculate the primary current and the current flowing in the short.

■ **Solution**

a. The new equivalent is shown in Fig. 2.8b. The secondary impedance is referred to the primary by the turns ratio squared. Thus

$$R_2' + jX_2' = \left(\frac{N_1}{N_2}\right)^2 (R_2 + jX_2)$$

$$= 25 + j100\ \Omega$$

b. From Eq. 2.20, a short at terminals A-B will appear as a short at the primary of the ideal transformer in Fig. 2.8b since the zero voltage of the short is reflected by the turns ratio N_1/N_2 to the primary. Hence the primary current will be given by

$$\hat{I}_1 = \frac{\hat{V}_1}{R_2' + jX_2'} = \frac{120}{25 + j100} = 0.28 - j1.13\ \text{A rms}$$

corresponding to a magnitude of 1.16 A rms. From Eq. 2.13, the secondary current will equal $N_1/N_2 = 5$ times that of the current in the primary. Thus the current in the short will have a magnitude of $5(1.16) = 5.8$ A rms.

Practice Problem 2.1

Repeat part (b) of Example 2.2 for a series impedance $R_2 + jX_2 = 0.05 + j0.97\ \Omega$ and a turns ratio of 14:1.

Solution

The primary current is $0.03 - j0.63$ A rms, corresponding to a magnitude of 0.63 A rms. The current in the short will be 14 times larger and thus will be of magnitude 8.82 A rms.

2.4 TRANSFORMER REACTANCES AND EQUIVALENT CIRCUITS

The departures of an actual transformer from those of an ideal transformer must be included to a greater or lesser degree in most analyses of transformer performance. A more complete model must take into account the effects of winding resistances, leakage fluxes, and finite exciting current due to the finite (and indeed nonlinear) permeability of the core. In some cases, the capacitances of the windings also have important effects, notably in problems involving transformer behavior at frequencies above the audio range or during rapidly changing transient conditions such as those encountered in power system transformers as a result of voltage surges caused by lightning or switching transients. The analysis of these high-frequency problems is beyond the scope of the present treatment however, and accordingly capacitances of the windings will be neglected.

Two methods of analysis by which departures from the ideal can be taken into account are (1) an equivalent-circuit technique based on physical reasoning and (2) a mathematical approach based on the classical theory of magnetically coupled circuits. Both methods are in everyday use, and both have very close parallels in the theories of rotating machines. Because it offers an excellent example of the thought process involved in translating physical concepts to a quantitative theory, the equivalent-circuit technique is presented here.

To begin the development of a transformer equivalent circuit, we first consider the primary winding. The total flux linking the primary winding can be divided into two components: the resultant mutual flux, confined essentially to the iron core and produced by the combined mmfs of the primary and secondary currents, and the primary leakage flux, which links only the primary. These components are identified in the schematic transformer shown in Fig. 2.9, where for simplicity the primary and

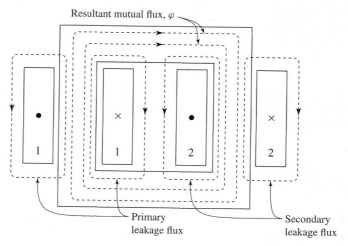

Figure 2.9 Schematic view of mutual and leakage fluxes in a transformer. The "X" and the dot indicate current directions in the various coils.

secondary windings are shown on opposite legs of the core. In an actual transformer with interleaved windings, the details of the flux distribution are more complicated, but the essential features remain the same.

The leakage flux induces voltage in the primary winding which adds to that produced by the mutual flux. Because the leakage path is largely in air, this flux and the voltage induced by it vary linearly with primary current $\hat{I}_1$. It can therefore be represented by a *primary leakage inductance* L_{l_1} (equal to the leakage-flux linkages with the primary per unit of primary current). The corresponding *primary leakage reactance* X_{l_1} is found as

$$X_{l_1} = 2\pi f L_{l_1} \tag{2.21}$$

In addition, there will be a voltage drop in the *primary resistance* R_1 (not shown in Fig. 2.9).

We now see that the primary terminal voltage $\hat{V}_1$ consists of three components: the $\hat{I}_1 R_1$ drop in the primary resistance, the $j\hat{I}_1 X_{l_1}$ drop arising from primary leakage flux, and the emf $\hat{E}_1$ induced in the primary by the resultant mutual flux. Fig. 2.10a shows an equivalent circuit for the primary winding which includes each of these voltages.

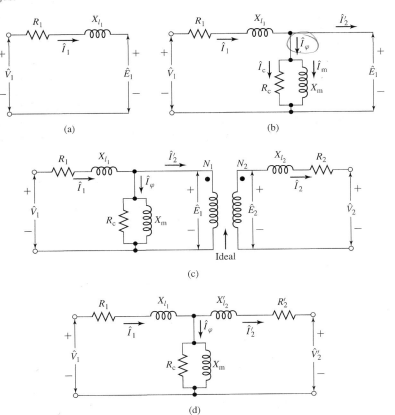

Figure 2.10 Steps in the development of the transformer equivalent circuit.

The resultant mutual flux links both the primary and secondary windings and is created by their combined mmfs. It is convenient to treat these mmfs by considering that the primary current must meet two requirements of the magnetic circuit: It must not only produce the mmf required to produce the resultant mutual flux, but it must also counteract the effect of the secondary mmf which acts to demagnetize the core. An alternative viewpoint is that the primary current must not only magnetize the core, it must also supply current to the load connected to the secondary. According to this picture, it is convenient to resolve the primary current into two components: an exciting component and a load component. The *exciting component* $\hat{I}_\varphi$ is defined as the additional primary current required to produce the resultant mutual flux. It is a nonsinusoidal current of the nature described in Section 2.2.[4] The *load component* $\hat{I}'_2$ is defined as the component current in the primary which would exactly counteract the mmf of secondary current $\hat{I}_2$.

Since it is the exciting component which produces the core flux, the net mmf must equal $N_1\hat{I}_\varphi$ and thus we see that

$$N_1\hat{I}_\varphi = N_1\hat{I}_1 - N_2\hat{I}_2$$
$$= N_1(\hat{I}_\varphi + \hat{I}'_2) - N_2\hat{I}_2 \qquad (2.22)$$

and from Eq. 2.22 we see that

$$\hat{I}'_2 = \frac{N_2}{N_1}\hat{I}_2 \qquad (2.23)$$

From Eq. 2.23, we see that the load component of the primary current equals the secondary current referred to the primary as in an ideal transformer.

The exciting current can be treated as an equivalent sinusoidal current $\hat{I}_\varphi$, in the manner described in Section 2.2, and can be resolved into a core-loss component $\hat{I}_c$ in phase with the emf $\hat{E}_1$ and a magnetizing component $\hat{I}_m$ lagging $\hat{E}_1$ by 90°. In the equivalent circuit of Fig. 2.10b the equivalent sinusoidal exciting current is accounted for by means of a shunt branch connected across $\hat{E}_1$, comprising a *core-loss resistance* R_c in parallel with a *magnetizing inductance* L_m whose reactance, known as the *magnetizing reactance*, is given by

$$X_m = 2\pi f L_m \qquad (2.24)$$

In the equivalent circuit of Fig. 2.10b the power E_1^2/R_c accounts for the core loss due to the resultant mutual flux. R_c, also referred to as the *magnetizing resistance*, together with X_m forms the *excitation branch* of the equivalent circuit, and we will refer to the parallel combination of R_c and X_m as the *magnetizing impedance* Z_φ. When R_c is assumed constant, the core loss is thereby assumed to vary as E_1^2. Strictly speaking, the magnetizing reactance X_m varies with the saturation of the iron. However, X_m is often assumed constant and the magnetizing current is thereby assumed to be independent of frequency and directly proportional to the resultant mutual flux.

---

[4] In fact, the exciting current corresponds to the net mmf acting on the transformer core and cannot, in general, be considered to flow in the primary alone. However, for the purposes of this discussion, this distinction is not significant.

Both R_c and X_m are usually determined at rated voltage and frequency; they are then assumed to remain constant for the small departures from rated values associated with normal operation.

We will next add to our equivalent circuit a representation of the secondary winding. We begin by recognizing that the resultant mutual flux $\hat{\Phi}$ induces an emf $\hat{E}_2$ in the secondary, and since this flux links both windings, the induced-emf ratio must equal the winding turns ratio, i.e.,

$$\frac{\hat{E}_1}{\hat{E}_2} = \frac{N_1}{N_2} \tag{2.25}$$

just as in an ideal transformer. This voltage transformation and the current transformation of Eq. 2.23 can be accounted for by introducing an ideal transformer in the equivalent circuit, as in Fig. 2.10c. Just as is the case for the primary winding, the emf $\hat{E}_2$ is not the secondary terminal voltage because of the *secondary resistance R_2* and because the secondary current $\hat{I}_2$ creates secondary leakage flux (see Fig. 2.9). The secondary terminal voltage $\hat{V}_2$ differs from the induced voltage $\hat{E}_2$ by the voltage drops due to secondary resistance R_2 and *secondary leakage reactance X_{l_2}* (corresponding to the *secondary leakage inductance L_{l_2}*) as in the portion of the complete transformer equivalent circuit (Fig. 2.10c) to the right of $\hat{E}_2$.

From the equivalent circuit of Fig. 2.10, the actual transformer therefore can be seen to be equivalent to an ideal transformer plus external impedances. By referring all quantities to the primary or secondary, the ideal transformer in Fig. 2.10c can be moved out to the right or left, respectively, of the equivalent circuit. This is almost invariably done, and the equivalent circuit is usually drawn as in Fig. 2.10d, with the ideal transformer not shown and all voltages, currents, and impedances referred to either the primary or secondary winding. Specifically, for Fig. 2.10d,

$$X'_{l_2} = \left(\frac{N_1}{N_2}\right)^2 X_{l_2} \tag{2.26}$$

$$R'_2 = \left(\frac{N_1}{N_2}\right)^2 R_2 \tag{2.27}$$

and

$$V'_2 = \frac{N_1}{N_2} V_2 \tag{2.28}$$

The circuit of Fig. 2.10d is called the *equivalent-T circuit* for a transformer.

In Fig. 2.10d, in which the secondary quantities are referred to the primary, the referred secondary values are indicated with primes, for example, X'_{l_2} and R'_2, to distinguish them from the actual values of Fig. 2.10c. In the discussion that follows we almost always deal with referred values, and the primes will be omitted. One must simply keep in mind the side of the transformers to which all quantities have been referred.

EXAMPLE 2.3

A 50-kVA 2400:240-V 60-Hz distribution transformer has a leakage impedance of $0.72 + j0.92 \, \Omega$ in the high-voltage winding and $0.0070 + j0.0090 \, \Omega$ in the low-voltage winding. At rated voltage and frequency, the impedance Z_φ of the shunt branch (equal to the impedance of

Figure 2.11   Equivalent circuits for transformer of Example 2.3 referred to (a) the high-voltage side and (b) the low-voltage side.

R_c and jX_m in parallel) accounting for the exciting current is $6.32 + j43.7\ \Omega$ when viewed from the low-voltage side. Draw the equivalent circuit referred to (a) the high-voltage side and (b) the low-voltage side, and label the impedances numerically.

■ **Solution**

The circuits are given in Fig. 2.11a and b, respectively, with the high-voltage side numbered 1 and the low-voltage side numbered 2. The voltages given on the nameplate of a power system transformer are based on the turns ratio and neglect the small leakage-impedance voltage drops under load. Since this is a 10-to-1 transformer, impedances are referred by multiplying or dividing by 100; for example, the value of an impedance referred to the high-voltage side is greater by a factor of 100 than its value referred to the low-voltage side.

The ideal transformer may be explicitly drawn, as shown dotted in Fig. 2.11, or it may be omitted in the diagram and remembered mentally, making the unprimed letters the terminals. If this is done, one must of course remember to refer all connected impedances and sources to be consistent with the omission of the ideal transformer.

Practice Problem 2.2

If 2,400 V rms is applied to the high-voltage side of the transformer of Example 2.3, calculate the magnitude of the current into the magnetizing impedance Z_φ in Figs. 2.11a and b respectively.

Solution

The current through Z_φ is 0.543 A rms when it is referred to the high-voltage side as in Fig. 2.11a and 5.43 A rms when it is referred to the low-voltage side.

2.5   ENGINEERING ASPECTS OF TRANSFORMER ANALYSIS

In engineering analyses involving the transformer as a circuit element, it is customary to adopt one of several approximate forms of the equivalent circuit of Fig. 2.10 rather than the full circuit. The approximations chosen in a particular case depend largely on physical reasoning based on orders of magnitude of the neglected quantities. The

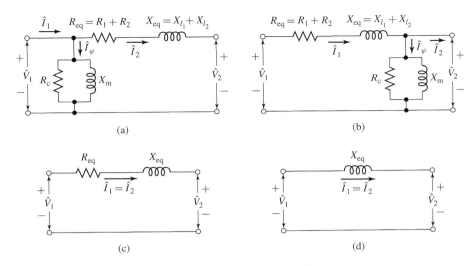

Figure 2.12 Approximate transformer equivalent circuits.

more common approximations are presented in this section. In addition, test methods are given for determining the transformer constants.

The approximate equivalent circuits commonly used for constant-frequency power transformer analyses are summarized for comparison in Fig. 2.12. All quantities in these circuits are referred to either the primary or the secondary, and the ideal transformer is not shown.

Computations can often be greatly simplified by moving the shunt branch representing the exciting current out from the middle of the T circuit to either the primary or the secondary terminals, as in Fig. 2.12a and b. These forms of the equivalent circuit are referred to as *cantilever circuits*. The series branch is the combined resistance and leakage reactance of the primary and secondary, referred to the same side. This impedance is sometimes called the *equivalent series impedance* and its components the *equivalent series resistance* R_{eq} and *equivalent series reactance* X_{eq}, as shown in Fig. 2.12a and b.

As compared to the equivalent-T circuit of Fig. 2.10d, the cantilever circuit is in error in that it neglects the voltage drop in the primary or secondary leakage impedance caused by the exciting current. Because the impedance of the exciting branch is typically quite large in large power transformers, the corresponding exciting current is quite small. This error is insignificant in most situations involving large transformers.

EXAMPLE 2.4

Consider the equivalent-T circuit of Fig. 2.11a of the 50-kVA 2400:240 V distribution transformer of Example 2.3 in which the impedances are referred to the high-voltage side. (a) Draw the cantilever equivalent circuit with the shunt branch at the high-voltage terminal. Calculate

Figure 2.13 Cantilever equivalent circuit for Example 2.4.

and label R_{eq} and X_{eq}. (b) With the low-voltage terminal open-circuit and 2400 V applied to the high-voltage terminal, calculate the voltage at the low-voltage terminal as predicted by each equivalent circuit.

■ **Solution**

a. The cantilever equivalent circuit is shown in Fig. 2.13. R_{eq} and X_{eq} are found simply as the sum of the high- and low-voltage winding series impedances of Fig. 2.11a

$$R_{eq} = 0.72 + 0.70 = 1.42 \ \Omega$$

$$X_{eq} = 0.92 + 0.90 = 1.82 \ \Omega$$

b. For the equivalent-T circuit of Fig. 2.11a, the voltage at the terminal labeled c′-d′ will be given by

$$\hat{V}_{c'\text{-}d'} = 2400 \left(\frac{Z_\varphi}{Z_\varphi + Z_{l_1}} \right) = 2399 + j0.3 \ \text{V}$$

with an rms magnitude of 2399 V. Reflected to the low-voltage terminals by the low- to high-voltage turns ratio, this in turn corresponds to a voltage of 239.9 V.

Because the magnetizing impedance is connected directly across the high-voltage terminals in the cantilever equivalent circuit of Fig. 2.13, there will be no voltage drop across any series leakage impedance and the predicted secondary voltage will be 240 V. These two solutions differ by 0.025 percent, well within reasonable engineering accuracy and clearly justifying the use of the cantilever equivalent circuit for analysis of this transformer.

Further analytical simplification results from neglecting the exciting current entirely, as in Fig. 2.12c, in which the transformer is represented as an equivalent series impedance. If the transformer is large (several hundred kilovoltamperes or more), the equivalent resistance R_{eq} is small compared with the equivalent reactance X_{eq} and can frequently be neglected, giving the equivalent circuit of Fig. 2.12d. The circuits of Fig. 2.12c and d are sufficiently accurate for most ordinary power-system problems and are used in all but the most detailed analyses. Finally, in situations where the currents and voltages are determined almost wholly by components external to the transformer or when a high degree of accuracy is not required, the entire transformer impedance can be neglected and the transformer considered to be ideal, as in Section 2.3.

The circuits of Fig. 2.12 have the additional advantage that the total equivalent resistance R_{eq} and equivalent reactance X_{eq} can be found from a very simple test in which one terminal is short-circuited. On the other hand, the process of determining the individual leakage reactances X_{l_1} and X_{l_2} and a complete set of parameters for the equivalent-T circuit of Fig. 2.10c is more difficult. Example 2.4 illustrates that, due to the voltage drop across leakage impedances, the ratio of the measured voltages of a transformer will not be identically equal to the idealized voltage ratio which would be measured if the transformer were ideal. In fact, without some apriori knowledge of the turns ratio (based for example upon knowledge of the internal construction of the transformer), it is not possible to make a set of measurements which uniquely determine the turns ratio, the magnetizing inductance, and the individual leakage impedances.

It can be shown that, with respect to terminal measurements, neither the turns ratio, the magnetizing reactance, or the leakage reactances are unique characteristics of a transformer equivalent circuit. For example, the turns ratio can be chosen arbitrarily and for each choice of turns ratio, there will be a corresponding set of values for the leakage and magnetizing reactances which matches the measured characteristic. Each of the resultant equivalent circuits will have the same electrical terminal characteristics, a fact which has the fortunate consequence that any self-consistent set of empirically determined parameters will adequately represent the transformer.

EXAMPLE 2.5

The 50-kVA 2400:240-V transformer whose parameters are given in Example 2.3 is used to step down the voltage at the load end of a feeder whose impedance is $0.30 + j1.60\ \Omega$. The voltage V_s at the sending (primary) end of the feeder is 2400 V.

Find the voltage at the secondary terminals of the transformer when the load connected to its secondary draws rated current from the transformer and the power factor of the load is 0.80 lagging. Neglect the voltage drops in the transformer and feeder caused by the exciting current.

■ Solution

The equivalent circuit with all quantities referred to the high-voltage (primary) side of the transformer is shown in Fig. 2.14a, where the transformer is represented by its equivalent impedance, as in Fig. 2.12c. From Fig. 2.11a, the value of the equivalent impedance is $Z_{eq} = 1.42 + j1.82\ \Omega$ and the combined impedance of the feeder and transformer in series is $Z = 1.72 + j3.42\ \Omega$. From the transformer rating, the load current referred to the high-voltage side is $I = 50{,}000/2400 = 20.8$ A.

Note that the power factor is defined at the load side of the transformer and hence defines the phase angle θ between the load current $\hat{I}$ and the voltage $\hat{V}_2$ where

$$\theta = -\cos^{-1}(0.80) = -36.87°$$

Thus

$$\hat{I} = 20.8\, e^{-j36.87°}\ \text{A}$$

Figure 2.14   (a) Equivalent circuit and (b) phasor diagram for Example 2.5.

From the equivalent-circuit of Fig. 2.11 we see that

$$\hat{V}_2 = \hat{V}_s - Z\hat{I} = 2400 - (1.72 + j3.42) \times 20.8\, e^{-j36.87°}$$

$$= 2329\, e^{-j0.87°}\ \text{V}$$

Although an algebraic solution of the complex equation is often the simplest and most direct way to obtain a solution, it is sometimes useful to solve these type of problems with the aid of a phasor diagram. We will illustrate this with a phasor diagram referred to the high-voltage side as shown in Fig. 2.14b. From the phasor diagram

$$Ob = \sqrt{V_s^2 - (bc)^2} \quad \text{and} \quad V_2 = Ob - ab$$

Note that

$$bc = IX\cos\theta - IR\sin\theta \quad ab = IR\cos\theta + IX\sin\theta$$

where R and X are the combined transformer and feeder resistance and reactance, respectively. Thus

$$bc = 20.8(3.42)(0.80) - 20.8(1.72)(0.60) = 35.5\ \text{V}$$

$$ab = 20.8(1.72)(0.80) + 20.8(3.42)(0.60) = 71.4\ \text{V}$$

Substitution of numerical values shows that $V_2 = 2329$ V, referred to the high-voltage side. The actual voltage at the secondary terminals is 2329/10, or

$$V_2 = 233\ \text{V}$$

Practice Problem 2.3

Repeat Example 2.5 for a load which draws rated current from the transformer with a power factor of 0.8 leading.

Solution

$$V_2 = 239\ \text{V}$$

Two very simple tests serve to determine the parameters of the equivalent circuits of Fig. 2.10 and 2.12. These consist of measuring the input voltage, current, and power at one side of the transformer, first with the second side short-circuited and then with

Figure 2.15 Equivalent circuit with short-circuited secondary. (a) Complete equivalent circuit. (b) Cantilever equivalent circuit with the exciting branch at the transformer secondary.

the second side open-circuited. Note that, following common practice, the transformer voltage ratio is used as the turns ratio when referring parameters from side to side for the purposes of parameter determination.

Short-Circuit Test The *short-circuit test* can be used to find the equivalent series impedance $R_{eq} + jX_{eq}$. Although the choice of winding to short-circuit is arbitrary, for the sake of this discussion we will consider the short circuit to be applied to the transformer secondary and voltage applied to primary. For convenience, the high-voltage side is usually taken as the primary in this test. Because the equivalent series impedance in a typical transformer is relatively small, typically an applied primary voltage on the order of 10 to 15 percent or less of the rated value will result in rated current.

Figure 2.15a shows the equivalent circuit with transformer secondary impedance referred to the primary side and a short circuit applied to the secondary. The short-circuit impedance Z_{sc} looking into the primary under these conditions is

$$Z_{sc} = R_1 + jX_{l_1} + \left(\frac{Z_\varphi(R_2 + jX_{l_2})}{Z_\varphi + R_2 + jX_{l_2}} \right) \quad (2.29)$$

Because the impedance Z_φ of the exciting branch is much larger than that of the secondary leakage impedance (which will be true unless the core is heavily saturated by excessive voltage applied to the primary; certainly not the case here), the short-circuit impedance can be approximated as

$$Z_{sc} \approx R_1 + jX_{l_1} + R_2 + jX_{l_2} = R_{eq} + jX_{eq} \quad (2.30)$$

Note that the approximation made here is equivalent to the approximation made in reducing the equivalent-T circuit to the cantilever equivalent. This can be seen from Fig. 2.15b; the impedance seen at the input of this equivalent circuit is clearly $Z_{sc} = Z_{eq} = R_{eq} + jX_{eq}$ since the exciting branch is directly shorted out by the short on the secondary.

Typically the instrumentation used for this test will measure the rms magnitude of the applied voltage V_{sc}, the short-circuit current I_{sc}, and the power P_{sc}. Based upon these three measurements, the equivalent resistance and reactance (referred to the primary) can be found from

$$|Z_{\text{eq}}| = |Z_{\text{sc}}| = \frac{V_{\text{sc}}}{I_{\text{sc}}} \qquad (2.31)$$

$$R_{\text{eq}} = R_{\text{sc}} = \frac{P_{\text{sc}}}{I_{\text{sc}}^2} \qquad (2.32)$$

$$X_{\text{eq}} = X_{\text{sc}} = \sqrt{|Z_{\text{sc}}|^2 - R_{\text{sc}}^2} \qquad (2.33)$$

where the notation | | indicates the magnitude of the enclosed complex quantity. The equivalent impedance can, of course, be referred from one side to the other in the usual manner.

Note that the short-circuit test does not provide sufficient information to determine the individual leakages impedances of the primary and secondary windings. On the occasions when the equivalent-T circuit in Fig. 2.10d must be used, approximate values of the individual primary and secondary resistances and leakage reactances can be obtained by assuming that $R_1 = R_2 = 0.5R_{\text{eq}}$ and $X_{1_1} = X_{1_2} = 0.5X_{\text{eq}}$ when all impedances are referred to the same side. Strictly speaking, of course, it is possible to measure R_1 and R_2 directly by a dc resistance measurement on each winding (and then referring one or the other to the other side of the ideal transformer). However, as has been discussed, no such simple test exists for the leakage reactances X_{l_1} and X_{l_2}.

Open-Circuit Test　The *open-circuit test* is performed with the secondary open-circuited and a voltage impressed on the primary. Under this condition an exciting current of a few percent of full-load current (less on large transformers and more on smaller ones) is obtained. Typically, the test is conducted at rated voltage to insure that the core, and hence the magnetizing reactance, will be operating at a flux level close to that which will exist under normal operating conditions. If the transformer is to be used at other than its rated voltage, the test should be done at that voltage. For convenience, the low-voltage side is usually taken as the primary in this test. If the primary is chosen to be the opposite winding from that of the short-circuit test, one must of course be careful to refer the various measured impedances to the same side of the transformer in order to obtain a self-consistent set of parameter values.

Figure 2.16a shows the equivalent circuit with the transformer secondary impedance referred to the primary side and with the secondary open-circuited. The open-circuit impedance Z_{oc} looking into the primary under these conditions is

$$Z_{\text{oc}} = R_1 + jX_{l_1} + Z_{\varphi} = R_1 + jX_{l_1} + \frac{R_{\text{c}}\,(jX_{\text{m}})}{R_{\text{c}} + jX_{\text{m}}} \qquad (2.34)$$

Because the impedance of the exciting branch is quite large, the voltage drop in the primary leakage impedance caused by the exciting current is typically negligible, and the primary impressed voltage $\hat{V}_{\text{oc}}$ very nearly equals the emf $\hat{E}_{\text{oc}}$ induced by the resultant core flux. Similarly, the primary $I_{\text{oc}}^2 R_1$ loss caused by the exciting current is negligible, so that the power input P_{oc} very nearly equals the core loss $E_{\text{oc}}^2/R_{\text{c}}$. As a result, it is common to ignore the primary leakage impedance and to approximate the

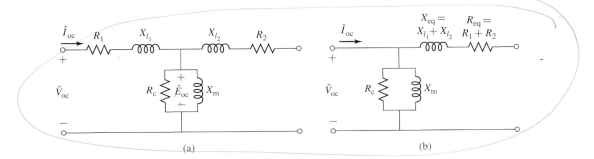

Figure 2.16 Equivalent circuit with open-circuited secondary. (a) Complete equivalent circuit. (b) Cantilever equivalent circuit with the exciting branch at the transformer primary.

open-circuit impedance as being equal to the magnetizing impedance

$$Z_{oc} \approx Z_\varphi = \frac{R_c(jX_m)}{R_c + jX_m} \tag{2.35}$$

Note that the approximation made here is equivalent to the approximation made in reducing the equivalent-T circuit to the cantilever equivalent circuit of Fig. 2.16b; the impedance seen at the input of this equivalent circuit is clearly Z_φ since no current will flow in the open-circuited secondary.

As with the short-circuit test, typically the instrumentation used for this test will measure the rms magnitude of the applied voltage, V_{oc}, the open-circuit current I_{oc}, and the power P_{oc}. Neglecting the primarily leakage impedance and based upon these three measurements, the magnetizing resistance and reactance (referred to the primary) can be found from

$$R_c = \frac{V_{oc}^2}{P_{oc}} \tag{2.36}$$

$$|Z_\varphi| = \frac{V_{oc}}{I_{oc}} \tag{2.37}$$

$$X_m = \frac{1}{\sqrt{(1/|Z_\varphi|)^2 - (1/R_c)^2}} \tag{2.38}$$

The values obtained are, of course, referred to the side used as the primary in this test.

The open-circuit test can be used to obtain the core loss for efficiency computations and to check the magnitude of the exciting current. Sometimes the voltage at the terminals of the open-circuited secondary is measured as a check on the turns ratio.

Note that, if desired, a slightly more accurate calculation of X_m and R_c can be found by retaining the measurements of R_1 and X_{l_1} obtained from the short-circuit test (referred to the proper side of the transformer) and basing the derivation on Eq. 2.34. However, such additional effort is rarely necessary for the purposes of engineering accuracy.

EXAMPLE 2.6

With the instruments located on the high-voltage side and with the low-voltage side short-circuited, the short-circuit test readings for the 50-kVA 2400:240-V transformer of Example 2.3 are 48 V, 20.8 A, and 617 W. An open-circuit test with the low-voltage side energized gives instrument readings on that side of 240 V, 5.41 A, and 186 W. Determine the efficiency and the voltage regulation of the transformer operating at full load, 0.80 power factor lagging.

■ **Solution**

From the short-circuit test, the magnitude of the equivalent impedance, the equivalent resistance, and the equivalent reactance of the transformer (referred to the high-voltage side as denoted by the subscript H) are

$$|Z_{eq,H}| = \frac{48}{20.8} = 2.31 \ \Omega \quad R_{eq,H} = \frac{617}{20.8^2} = 1.42 \ \Omega$$

$$X_{eq,H} = \sqrt{2.31^2 - 1.42^2} = 1.82 \ \Omega$$

Operation at full-load, 0.80 power factor lagging corresponds to a current of

$$I_H = \frac{50000}{2400} = 20.8 \text{ A}$$

and an output power

$$P_{output} = P_{load} = (0.8)50000 = 40000 \text{ W}$$

Note that the short-circuit test was conducted at rated current and hence the full-load $I^2 R$ loss will equal that of the short-circuit test. Similarly, the open-circuit test was conducted at rated voltage and hence the full-load core loss is equal to that of the open-circuit test. As a result, the total loss under this operating condition is equal to the sum of the winding loss

$$P_{winding} = I_H^2 R_{eq,H} = 20.8^2(1.42) = 617 \text{ W}$$

and the open-circuit core loss

$$P_{core} = 186 \text{ W}$$

Thus

$$P_{loss} = P_{winding} + P_{core} = 803 \text{ W}$$

and the power input to the transformer is

$$P_{input} = P_{output} + P_{loss} = 40803 \text{ W}$$

The *efficiency* of a power conversion device is defined as

$$\text{efficiency} = \frac{P_{output}}{P_{input}} = \frac{P_{input} - P_{loss}}{P_{input}} = 1 - \frac{P_{loss}}{P_{input}}$$

which can be expressed in percent by multiplying by 100 percent. Hence, for this operating condition

$$\text{efficiency} = 100\% \left(\frac{P_{output}}{P_{input}} \right) = 100\% \left(\frac{40000}{40000 + 803} \right) = 98.0\%$$

The *voltage regulation* of a transformer is defined as the change in secondary terminal voltage from no load to full load and is usually expressed as a percentage of the full-load value. In power systems applications, regulation is one figure of merit for a transformer; a low value indicates that load variations on the secondary of that transformer will not significantly affect the magnitude of the voltage being supplied to the load. It is calculated under the assumption that the primary voltage remains constant as the load is removed from the transformer secondary.

The equivalent circuit of Fig. 2.12c will be used with all quantities referred to the high-voltage side. The primary voltage is assumed to be adjusted so that the secondary terminal voltage has its rated value at full load, or $V_{2\text{H}} = 2400$ V. For a load of rated value and 0.8 power factor lagging (corresponding to a power-factor angle $\theta = -\cos^{-1}(0.8) = -36.9°$), the load current will be

$$\hat{I}_\text{H} = \left(\frac{50 \times 10^3}{2400}\right) e^{-j36.9°} = 20.8\ e^{-j36.9°} = 16.6 - j12.5\ \text{A}$$

The required value of the primary voltage $V_{1\text{H}}$ can be calculated as

$$\hat{V}_{1\text{H}} = \hat{V}_{2\text{H}} + \hat{I}_\text{H}(R_{\text{eq,H}} + jX_{\text{eq,H}})$$
$$= 2400 + (16.6 - j12.5)\ (1.42 + j1.82)$$
$$= 2446\ e^{j0.29°}\ \text{V}$$

The magnitude of $\hat{V}_{1\text{H}}$ is 2446 V. If this voltage were held constant and the load removed, the secondary voltage on open circuit would rise to 2446 V referred to the high-voltage side. Then

$$\text{Regulation} = \left(\frac{2446 - 2400}{2400}\right) \times 100\% = 1.92\%$$

Practice Problem 2.4

Repeat the voltage-regulation calculation of Example 2.6 for a load of 50 kW (rated load, unity power factor).

Solution

$$\text{Regulation} = 1.24\%$$

2.6 AUTOTRANSFORMERS; MULTIWINDING TRANSFORMERS

The principles discussed in previous sections have been developed with specific reference to two-winding transformers. They are also applicable to transformers with other winding configurations. Aspects relating to autotransformers and multiwinding transformers are considered in this section.

2.6.1 Autotransformers

In Fig. 2.17a, a two-winding transformer is shown with N_1 and N_2 turns on the primary and secondary windings respectively. Substantially the same transformation effect on voltages, currents, and impedances can be obtained when these windings are connected as shown in Fig. 2.17b. However, note that in Fig. 2.17b, winding bc is

Figure 2.17 (a) Two-winding transformer.
(b) Connection as an autotransformer.

common to both the primary and secondary circuits. This type of transformer is called an *autotransformer*. It is similar to a normal transformer connected in a special way, with the exception that the windings must be appropriately insulated for the operating operating voltage.

One important difference between the two-winding transformer and the auto-transformer is that the windings of the two-winding transformer are electrically iso-lated whereas those of the autotransformer are connected directly together. Also, in the autotransformer connection, winding *ab* must be provided with extra insulation since it must be insulated against the full maximum voltage of the autotransformer. Autotransformers have lower leakage reactances, lower losses, and smaller exciting current and cost less than two-winding transformers when the voltage ratio does not differ too greatly from 1:1.

The following example illustrates the benefits of an autotransformer for those situations where electrical isolation between the primary and secondary windings is not an important consideration.

EXAMPLE 2.7

The 2400:240-V 50-kVA transformer of Example 2.6 is connected as an autotransformer, as shown in Fig. 2.18a, in which ab is the 240-V winding and bc is the 2400-V winding. (It is assumed that the 240-V winding has enough insulation to withstand a voltage of 2640 V to ground.)

a. Compute the voltage ratings V_H and V_X of the high- and low-voltage sides, respectively, for this autotransformer connection.
b. Compute the kVA rating as an autotransformer.
c. Data with respect to the losses are given in Example 2.6. Compute the full-load efficiency as an autotransformer operating with a rated load of 0.80 power factor lagging.

■ **Solution**

a. Since the 2400-V winding bc is connected to the low-voltage circuit, $V_L = 2400$ V. When $V_{bc} = 2400$ V, a voltage $V_{ab} = 240$ V in phase with V_{bc} will be induced in winding ab

Figure 2.18 (a) Autotransformer connection for Example 2.7. (b) Currents under rated load.

(leakage-impedance voltage drops being neglected). The voltage of the high-voltage side therefore is

$$V_H = V_{ab} + V_{bc} = 2640 \text{ V}$$

b. From the rating of 50 kVA as a normal two-winding transformer, the rated current of the 240-V winding is $50,000/240 = 208$ A. Since the high-voltage lead of the autotransformer is connected to the 240-V winding, the rated current I_H at the high-voltage side of the autotransformer is equal to the rated current of the 240-V winding or 208 A. The kVA rating as an autotransformer therefore is

$$\frac{V_H I_H}{1000} = \frac{2640 \times 208}{1000} = 550 \text{ kVA}$$

Note that, in this connection, the autotransformer has an equivalent turns ratio of 2640/2400. Thus the rated current at the low-voltage winding (the 2400-V winding in this connection) must be

$$I_L = \left(\frac{2640}{2400} \right) 208 \text{ A} = 229 \text{ A}$$

At first, this seems rather unsettling since the 2400-V winding of the transformer has a rated current of 50 kVA/2400 V = 20.8 A. Further puzzling is that fact that this transformer, whose rating as a normal two-winding transformer is 50 kVA, is capable of handling 550 kVA as an autotransformer.

The higher rating as an autotransformer is a consequence of the fact that not all the 550 kVA has to be transformed by electromagnetic induction. In fact, all that the transformer has to do is to boost a current of 208 A through a potential rise of 240 V, corresponding to a power transformation capacity of 50 kVA. This fact is perhaps best illustrated by Fig. 2.18b which shows the currents in the autotransformer under rated conditions. Note that the windings carry only their rated currents in spite of higher rating of the transformer.

c. When it is connected as an autotransformer with the currents and voltages shown in Fig. 2.18, the losses are the same as in Example 2.6, namely 803 W. But the output as an autotransformer at full load, 0.80 power factor is $0.80 \times 550,000 = 440,000$ W. The efficiency therefore is

$$\left(1 - \frac{803}{440,803}\right)100\% = 99.82\%$$

The efficiency is so high because the losses are those corresponding to transforming only 50 kVA.

Practice Problem 2.5

A 450-kVA, 460-V:7.97-kV transformer has an efficiency of 97.8 percent when supplying a rated load of unity power factor. If it is connected as a 7.97:8.43-kV autotransformer, calculate its rated terminal currents, rated kVA, and efficiency when supplying a unity-power-factor load.

Solution

The rated current at the 8.43-kV terminal is 978 A, at the 7.97-kV terminal is 1034 A and the transformer rating is 8.25 MVA. Its efficiency supplying a rated, unity-power-factor load is 99.88 percent.

From Example 2.7, we see that when a transformer is connected as an autotransformer as shown in Fig. 2.17, the rated voltages of the autotransformer can be expressed in terms of those of the two-winding transformer as

Low-voltage:

$$V_{L_{\text{rated}}} = V_{1_{\text{rated}}} \tag{2.39}$$

High-voltage:

$$V_{H_{\text{rated}}} = V_{1_{\text{rated}}} + V_{2_{\text{rated}}} = \left(\frac{N_1 + N_2}{N_1}\right)V_{L_{\text{rated}}} \tag{2.40}$$

The effective turns ratio of the autotransformer is thus $(N_1 + N_2)/N_1$. In addition, the power rating of the autotransformer is equal to $(N_1 + N_2)/N_2$ times that of the two-winding transformer, although the actual power processed by the transformer will not increase over that of the standard two-winding connection.

2.6.2   Multiwinding Transformers

Transformers having three or more windings, known as *multiwinding* or *multicircuit transformers,* are often used to interconnect three or more circuits which may have different voltages. For these purposes a multiwinding transformer costs less and is more efficient than an equivalent number of two-winding transformers. Transformers having a primary and multiple secondaries are frequently found in multiple-output dc power supplies for electronic applications. Distribution transformers used to supply power for domestic purposes usually have two 120-V secondaries connected in series.

Circuits for lighting and low-power applications are connected across each of the 120-V windings, while electric ranges, domestic hot-water heaters, clothes-dryers, and other high-power loads are supplied with 240-V power from the series-connected secondaries.

Similarly, a large distribution system may be supplied through a three-phase bank of multiwinding transformers from two or more transmission systems having different voltages. In addition, the three-phase transformer banks used to interconnect two transmission systems of different voltages often have a third, or tertiary, set of windings to provide voltage for auxiliary power purposes in substations or to supply a local distribution system. Static capacitors or synchronous condensers may be connected to the tertiary windings for power factor correction or voltage regulation. Sometimes Δ-connected tertiary windings are put on three-phase banks to provide a low-impedance path for third harmonic components of the exciting current to reduce third-harmonic components of the neutral voltage.

Some of the issues arising in the use of multiwinding transformers are associated with the effects of leakage impedances on voltage regulation, short-circuit currents, and division of load among circuits. These problems can be solved by an equivalent-circuit technique similar to that used in dealing with two-circuit transformers.

The equivalent circuits of multiwinding transformers are more complicated than in the two-winding case because they must take into account the leakage impedances associated with each pair of windings. Typically, in these equivalent circuits, all quantities are referred to a common base, either by use of the appropriate turns ratios as referring factors or by expressing all quantities in per unit. The exciting current usually is neglected.

2.7 TRANSFORMERS IN THREE-PHASE CIRCUITS

Three single-phase transformers can be connected to form a *three-phase transformer bank* in any of the four ways shown in Fig. 2.19. In all four parts of this figure, the windings at the left are the primaries, those at the right are the secondaries, and each primary winding in one transformer corresponds to the secondary winding drawn parallel to it. Also shown are the voltages and currents resulting from balanced impressed primary line-to-line voltages V and line currents I when the ratio of primary-to-secondary turns $N_1/N_2 = a$ and ideal transformers are assumed.[5] Note that the rated voltage and current at the primary and secondary of the three-phase transformer bank depend upon the connection used but that the rated kVA of the three-phase bank is three times that of the individual single-phase transformers, regardless of the connection.

The Y-Δ connection is commonly used in stepping down from a high voltage to a medium or low voltage. One reason is that a neutral is thereby provided for grounding on the high-voltage side, a procedure which can be shown to be desirable in many cases. Conversely, the Δ-Y connection is commonly used for stepping up to

---

[5] The relationship between three-phase and single-phase quantities is discussed in Appendix A.

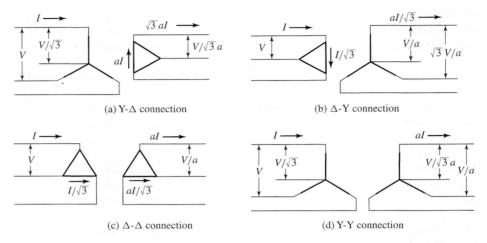

Figure 2.19 Common three-phase transformer connections; the transformer windings are indicated by the heavy lines.

a high voltage. The Δ-Δ connection has the advantage that one transformer can be removed for repair or maintenance while the remaining two continue to function as a three-phase bank with the rating reduced to 58 percent of that of the original bank; this is known as the *open-delta,* or *V,* connection. The Y-Y connection is seldom used because of difficulties with exciting-current phenomena.[6]

Instead of three single-phase transformers, a three-phase bank may consist of one *three-phase transformer* having all six windings on a common multi-legged core and contained in a single tank. Advantages of three-phase transformers over connections of three single-phase transformers are that they cost less, weigh less, require less floor space, and have somewhat higher efficiency. A photograph of the internal parts of a three-phase transformer is shown in Fig. 2.20.

Circuit computations involving three-phase transformer banks under balanced conditions can be made by dealing with only one of the transformers or phases and recognizing that conditions are the same in the other two phases except for the phase displacements associated with a three-phase system. It is usually convenient to carry out the computations on a single-phase (per-phase-Y, line-to-neutral) basis, since transformer impedances can then be added directly in series with transmission line impedances. The impedances of transmission lines can be referred from one side of the transformer bank to the other by use of the square of the ideal line-to-line voltage ratio of the bank. In dealing with Y-Δ or Δ-Y banks, all quantities can be referred to the Y-connected side. In dealing with Δ-Δ banks in series with transmission lines, it is convenient to replace the Δ-connected impedances of the transformers by equivalent Y-connected impedances. It can be shown that a balanced Δ-connected circuit of

---

[6] Because there is no neutral connection to carry harmonics of the exciting current, harmonic voltages are produced which significantly distort the transformer voltages.

Figure 2.20 Internal view of a three-phase, 480V-Y/208V-Δ, 112-kVA transformer.

Z_Δ Ω/phase is equivalent to a balanced Y-connected circuit of Z_Y Ω/phase if

$$Z_Y = \frac{1}{3}Z_\Delta \tag{2.41}$$

EXAMPLE 2.8

Three single-phase, 50-kVA 2400:240-V transformers, each identical with that of Example 2.6, are connected Y-Δ in a three-phase 150-kVA bank to step down the voltage at the load end of a feeder whose impedance is $0.15 + j1.00$ Ω/phase. The voltage at the sending end of the feeder is 4160 V line-to-line. On their secondary sides, the transformers supply a balanced three-phase load through a feeder whose impedance is $0.0005 + j0.0020$ Ω/phase. Find the line-to-line voltage at the load when the load draws rated current from the transformers at a power factor of 0.80 lagging.

■ Solution

For the given connection, the rated line-line voltage at the high-voltage terminals of the three-phase transformer bank will $\sqrt{3}\,2400 \approx 4160$ V. Thus, the transformer bank will have an rated turns ratio of 4160/240. The computations can be made on a single-phase basis by referring everything to the high-voltage, Y-connected side of the transformer bank. The voltage at the sending end of the feeder is equivalent to a source voltage V_s of

$$V_s = \frac{4160}{\sqrt{3}} \approx 2400 \text{ V line-to-neutral}$$

From the transformer rating, the rated current on the high-voltage side is 20.8 A/phase Y. The low-voltage feeder impedance referred to the high voltage side by means of the square of the rated turns ratio

$$Z_{lv,H} = \left(\frac{4160}{240}\right)^2 (0.0005 + j0.0020) = 0.15 + j0.60 \text{ Ω}$$

and the combined series impedance of the high- and low-voltage feeders referred to the high-voltage side is thus

$$Z_{\text{feeder,H}} = 0.30 + j1.60 \ \Omega/\text{phase Y}$$

Because the transformer bank is Y-connected on its high-voltage side, its equivalent single-phase series impedance is equal to the single-phase series impedance of each single-phase transformer as referred to its high-voltage side. This impedance was originally calculated in Example 2.4 as

$$Z_{\text{eq,H}} = 1.42 + j1.82 \ \Omega/\text{phase Y}$$

Due to the choice of values selected for this example, the single-phase equivalent circuit for the complete system is identical to that of Example 2.5, as can been seen with specific reference to Fig. 2.14a. In fact, the solution on a per-phase basis is exactly the same as the solution to Example 2.5, whence the load voltage referred to the high-voltage side is 2329 V to neutral. The actual line-neutral load voltage can then be calculated by referring this value to the low-voltage side of the transformer bank as

$$V_{\text{load}} = 2329 \left(\frac{240}{4160} \right) = 134 \ \text{V line-to-neutral}$$

which can be expressed as a line-to-line voltage by multiplying by $\sqrt{3}$

$$V_{\text{load}} = 134\sqrt{3} = 233 \ \text{V line-to-line}$$

Note that this line-line voltage is equal to the line-neutral load voltage calculated in Example 2.5 because in this case the transformers are delta connected on their low-voltage side and hence the line-line voltage on the low-voltage side is equal to the low-voltage terminal voltage of the transformers.

Practice Problem 2.6

Repeat Example 2.8 with the transformers connected Y-Y and all other aspects of the problem statement remaining unchanged.

Solution
405 V line-line

EXAMPLE 2.9

The three transformers of Example 2.8 are reconnected Δ-Δ and supplied with power through a 2400-V (line-to-line) three-phase feeder whose reactance is 0.80 Ω/phase as shown in Fig. 2.21. At its sending end, the feeder is connected to the secondary terminals of a three-phase Y-Δ-connected transformer whose rating is 500 kVA, 24 kV:2400 V (line-to-line). The equivalent series impedance of the sending-end transformer is $0.17 + j0.92 \ \Omega$/phase referred to the 2400-V side. The voltage applied to the primary terminals of the sending-end transformer is 24.0 kV line-to-line.

A three-phase short circuit occurs at the 240-V terminals of the receiving-end transformers. Compute the steady-state short-circuit current in the 2400-V feeder phase wires, in the primary and secondary windings of the receiving-end transformers, and at the 240-V terminals.

Figure 2.21 One-line diagram for Example 2.9 .

■ Solution

The computations will be made on an equivalent line-to-neutral basis with all quantities referred to the 2400-V feeder. The source voltage then is

$$\frac{2400}{\sqrt{3}} = 1385 \text{ V line-to-neutral}$$

From Eq. 2.41, the single-phase-equivalent series impedance of the Δ-Δ transformer seen at its 2400-V side is

$$Z_{eq} = R_{eq} + j X_{eq} = \frac{1.42 + j1.82}{3} = 0.47 + j0.61 \text{ Ω/phase}$$

The total series impedance to the short circuit is then the sum of this impedance, that of sending-end transformer and the reactance of the feeder

$$Z_{tot} = (0.47 + j0.61) + (0.17 + j0.92) + j0.80 = 0.64 + j2.33 \text{ Ω/phase}$$

which has a magnitude of

$$|Z_{tot}| = 2.42 \text{ Ω/phase}$$

The magnitude of the phase current in the 2400-V feeder can now simply be calculated as the line-neutral voltage divided by the magnitude of the series impedance

$$\text{Current in 2400-V feeder} = \frac{1385}{2.42} = 572 \text{ A}$$

and, as is shown in Fig. 2.19c, the winding current in the 2400-V winding of the receiving-end transformer is equal to the phase current divided by $\sqrt{3}$ or

$$\text{Current in 2400-V windings} = \frac{572}{\sqrt{3}} = 330 \text{ A}$$

while the current in the 240-V windings is 10 times this value

$$\text{Current in 240-V windings} = 10 \times 330 = 3300 \text{ A}$$

Finally, again with reference to Fig. 2.19c, the phase current at the 240-V terminals into the short circuit is given by

$$\text{Current at the 240-V terminals} = 3300\sqrt{3} = 5720 \text{ A}$$

Note of course that this same result could have been computed simply by recognizing that the turns ratio of the Δ-Δ transformer bank is equal to 10:1 and hence, under balanced-three-phase conditions, the phase current on the low voltage side will be 10 times that on the high-voltage side.

Repeat Example 2.9 under the condition that the three transformers are connected Δ-Y instead of Δ-Δ such that the short low-voltage side of the three-phase transformer is rated 416 V line-to-line.

Solution

$$\text{Current in 2400-V feeder} = 572 \text{ A}$$

$$\text{Current in 2400-V windings} = 330 \text{ A}$$

$$\text{Current in 416-V windings} = 3300 \text{ A}$$

$$\text{Current at the 416-V terminals} = 3300 \text{A}$$

2.8 VOLTAGE AND CURRENT TRANSFORMERS

Transformers are often used in instrumentation applications to match the magnitude of a voltage or current to the range of a meter or other instrumentation. For example, most 60-Hz power-systems' instrumentation is based upon voltages in the range of 0-120 V rms and currents in the range of 0–5 A rms. Since power system voltages range up to 765-kV line-to-line and currents can be 10s of kA, some method of supplying an accurate, low-level representation of these signals to the instrumentation is required.

One common technique is through the use of specialized transformers known as *potential transformers* or *PTs* and *current transformers* or *CTs*. If constructed with a turns ratio of $N_1:N_2$, an ideal potential transformer would have a secondary voltage equal in magnitude to N_2/N_1 times that of the primary and identical in phase. Similarly, an ideal current transformer would have a secondary output current equal to N_1/N_2 times the current input to the primary, again identical in phase. In other words, potential and current transformers (also referred to as *instrumentation transformers*) are designed to approximate ideal transformers as closely as is practically possible.

The equivalent circuit of Fig. 2.22 shows a transformer loaded with an impedance $Z_b = R_b + j X_b$ at its secondary. For the sake of this discussion, the core-loss resistance R_c has been neglected; if desired, the analysis presented here can be easily expanded to include its effect. Following conventional terminology, the load on an instrumentation transformer is frequently referred to as the *burden* on that transformer, hence the subscript 'b'. To simplify our discussion, we have chosen to refer all the secondary quantities to the primary side of the ideal transformer.

Consider first a potential transformer. Ideally it should accurately measure voltage while appearing as an open circuit to the system under measurement, i.e., drawing negligible current and power. Thus, its load impedance should be "large" in a sense we will now quantify.

Figure 2.22 Equivalent circuit for an instrumentation transformer.

First, let us assume that the transformer secondary is open-circuited (i.e., $|Z_b| = \infty$). In this case we can write that

$$\frac{\hat{V}_2}{\hat{V}_1} = \left(\frac{N_2}{N_1}\right) \frac{jX_m}{R_1 + j(X_1 + X_m)} \tag{2.42}$$

From this equation, we see that a potential transformer with an open-circuited secondary has an inherent error (in both magnitude and phase) due to the voltage drop of the magnetizing current through the primary resistance and leakage reactance. To the extent that the primary resistance and leakage reactance can be made small compared to the magnetizing reactance, this inherent error can be made quite small.

The situation is worsened by the presence of a finite burden. Including the effect of the burden impedance, Eq. 2.42 becomes

$$\frac{\hat{V}_2}{\hat{V}_1} = \left(\frac{N_2}{N_1}\right) \frac{Z_{eq} Z'_b}{(R_1 + jX_1)(Z_{eq} + Z'_b + R'_2 + jX'_2)} \tag{2.43}$$

where

$$Z_{eq} = \frac{jX_m(R_1 + jX_1)}{R_1 + j(X_m + X_1)} \tag{2.44}$$

and

$$Z'_b = \left(\frac{N_1}{N_2}\right)^2 Z_b \tag{2.45}$$

is the burden impedance referred to the transformer primary.

From these equations, it can be seen that the characteristics of an accurate potential transformer include a large magnetizing reactance (more accurately, a large magnetizing impedance since the effects of core loss, although neglected in the analysis presented here, must also be minimized) and relatively small winding resistances and leakage reactances. Finally, as will be seen in Example 2.10, the burden impedance must be kept above a minimum value to avoid introducing excessive errors in the magnitude and phase angle of the measured voltage.

EXAMPLE 2.10

A 2400:120-V, 60-Hz potential transformer has the following parameter values (referred to the 2400-V winding):

$$X_1 = 143\ \Omega \qquad X'_2 = 164\ \Omega \qquad X_m = 163\ \text{k}\Omega$$

$$R_1 = 128\ \Omega \qquad R'_2 = 141\ \Omega$$

(a) Assuming a 2400-V input, which ideally should produce a voltage of 120 V at the low-voltage winding, calculate the magnitude and relative phase-angle errors of the secondary voltage if the secondary winding is open-circuited. (b) Assuming the burden impedance to be purely resistive ($Z_b = R_b$), calculate the minimum resistance (maximum burden) that can be applied to the secondary such that the magnitude error is less than 0.5 percent. (c) Repeat part (b) but find the minimum resistance such that the phase-angle error is less than 1.0 degree.

■ Solution

a. This problem is most easily solved using MATLAB.[†] From Eq. 2.42 with $\hat{V}_1 = 2400$ V, the following MATLAB script gives

$$\hat{V}_2 = 119.90 \angle 0.045° \text{ V}$$

which corresponds to a magnitude error of less than 0.1% and a phase angle error of 0.045°.

Here is the MATLAB script:

```
clc
clear

%PT parameters
R1 = 128;
X1 = 143;
Xm = 163e3;
N1 = 2400;
N2 = 120;
N = N1/N2;

%Primary voltage
V1 = 2400;

%Secondary voltage
V2 = V1*(N2/N1)*(j*Xm/(R1+ j*(X1+Xm)));
magV2 = abs(V2);
phaseV2 = 180*angle(V2)/pi;

fprintf('\nMagnitude of V2 = %g [V]',magV2)
fprintf('\n    and angle = %g [degrees]\n\n',phaseV2)
```

b. Here, again, it is relatively straight forward to write a MATLAB script to implement Eq. 2.43 and to calculate the percentage error in the magnitude of voltage $\hat{V}_2$ as compared to the 120 Volts that would be measured if the PT were ideal. The resistive burden R_b can be initialized to a large value and then reduced until the magnitude error reaches

---

[†] MATLAB is a registered trademark of The MathWorks, Inc.

0.5 percent. The result of such an analysis would show that the minimum resistance is 162.5 Ω, corresponding to a magnitude error of 0.50 percent and a phase angle of 0.22°. (Note that this appears as a resistance of 65 kΩ when referred to the primary.)

c. The MATLAB script of part (b) can be modified to search for the minimum resistive burden that will keep the phase angle error less than 1.0 degrees. The result would show that the minimum resistance is 41.4 Ω, corresponding to a phase angle of 1.00° and a magnitude error of 1.70 percent.

Practice Problem 2.8

Using MATLAB, repeat parts (b) and (c) of Example 2.10 assuming the burden impedance is purely reactive $(Z_b = jX_b)$ and finding the corresponding minimum impedance X_b in each case.

Solution

The minimum burden reactance which results in a secondary voltage magnitude within 0.5 percent of the expected 120 V is $X_b = 185.4$ Ω, for which the phase angle is 0.25°. The minimum burden reactance which results in a secondary voltage phase-angle of within 1.0° of that of the primary voltage is $X_b = 39.5$ Ω, for which the voltage-magnitude error is 2.0 percent.

Consider next a current transformer. An ideal current transformer would accurately measure current while appearing as a short circuit to the system under measurement, i.e., developing negligible voltage drop and drawing negligible power. Thus, its load impedance should be "small" in a sense we will now quantify.

Let us begin with the assumption that the transformer secondary is short-circuited (i.e., $|Z_b| = 0$). In this case we can write that

$$\frac{\hat{I}_2}{\hat{I}_1} = \left(\frac{N_1}{N_2}\right) \frac{jX_m}{R_2' + j(X_2' + X_m)} \tag{2.46}$$

Based upon an argument similar to that used in the discussion of a potential transformer, Eq. 2.46 shows that a current transformer with a shorted secondary has an inherent error (in both magnitude and phase) due to the fact that some of the primary current is shunted through the magnetizing reactance and does not reach the secondary. To the extent that the magnetizing reactance can be made large in comparison to the secondary resistance and leakage reactance, this error can be made quite small.

A finite burden appears in series with the secondary impedance and increases the error. Including the effect of the burden impedance, Eq. 2.46 becomes

$$\frac{\hat{I}_2}{\hat{I}_1} = \left(\frac{N_1}{N_2}\right) \frac{jX_m}{Z_b' + R_2' + j(X_2' + X_m)} \tag{2.47}$$

From these equations, it can be seen that an accurate current transformer should have a large magnetizing impedance and relatively small winding resistances and leakage reactances. In addition, as is seen in Example 2.11, the burden impedance on a current transformer must be kept below a maximum value to avoid introducing excessive additional magnitude and phase errors in the measured current.

EXAMPLE 2.11

A 800:5-A, 60-Hz current transformer has the following parameter values (referred to the 800-A winding):

$$X_1 = 44.8 \ \mu\Omega \quad X_2' = 54.3 \ \mu\Omega \quad X_m = 17.7 \ m\Omega$$

$$R_1 = 10.3 \ \mu\Omega \quad R_2' = 9.6 \ \mu\Omega$$

Assuming that the high-current winding is carrying a current of 800 amperes, calculate the magnitude and relative phase of the current in the low-current winding if the load impedance is purely resistive with $R_b = 2.5 \ \Omega$.

■ **Solution**

The secondary current can be found from Eq. 2.47 by setting $\hat{I}_1 = 800$ A and $R_b' = (N_1/N_2)^2 R_b = 0.097$ mΩ. The following MATLAB script gives

$$\hat{I}_2 = 4.98 \ \angle 0.346° \ A$$

Here is the MATLAB script:

```
clc
clear

%CT parameters
R_2p = 9.6e-6;
X_2p = 54.3e-6;
X_m = 17.7e-3;

N_1 = 5;
N_2 = 800;
N = N_1/N_2;

%Load impedance
R_b = 2.5;
X_b = 0;
Z_bp = N\^{}2*(R_b + j * X_b);

% Primary current
I1 = 800;

%Secondary current
I2 = I1*N*j*X_m/(Z_bp + R_2p + j*(X_2p + X_m));

magI2 = abs(I2);
phaseI2 = 180*angle(I2)/pi;

fprintf('\nSecondary current magnitude = %g [A]',magI2)
fprintf('\n    and phase angle = \%g [degrees]\n$\n',phaseI2)
```

For the current transformer of Example 2.11, find the maximum purely reactive burden $Z_b = jX_b$ such that, for 800 A flowing in the transformer primary, the secondary current will be greater than 4.95 A (i.e., there will be at most a 1.0 percent error in current magnitude).

Solution

X_b must be less than 3.19 Ω

2.9 THE PER-UNIT SYSTEM

Electric power systems typically consist of the interconnection of a large number of generators, transformers, transmission lines and loads (a large fraction of which include electric motors). The characteristics of these components vary over a large range; with voltages ranging from hundreds of volts to hundreds of kilovolts and power ratings ranging from kilowatts to hundreds of megawatts. Power-system analyses, and indeed analyses of individual power-system components are often carried out in *per-unit* form, i.e., with all pertinent quantities expressed as decimal fractions of appropriately chosen *base values*. All the usual computations are then carried out in these per-unit values instead of the familiar volts, amperes, ohms, and so on.

There are a number of advantages to the use of the per-unit system. One is that, when expressed in per-unit based upon their rating, the parameter values of machines and transformers typically fall in a reasonably narrow numerical range. This both permits a quick "sanity check" of parameter values as well enables "back-of-the en-velope" estimates of parameter values which are otherwise not available. A second advantage is that when transformer equivalent-circuit parameters are converted to their per-unit values, the ideal transformer turns ratio becomes 1:1 and hence the ideal trans-former can be eliminated from the equivalent circuit. This greatly simplifies analyses since it eliminates the need to refer impedances to one side or the other of transformers.

Quantities such as voltage V, current I, power P, reactive power Q, voltamperes VA, resistance R, reactance X, impedance Z, conductance G, susceptance B, and admittance Y can be translated to and from per-unit form as follows:

$$\text{Quantity in per unit} = \frac{\text{Actual quantity}}{\text{Base value of quantity}} \qquad (2.48)$$

where "Actual quantity" refers to the value in volts, amperes, ohms, and so on. To a certain extent, base values can be chosen arbitrarily, but certain relations between them must be observed for the normal electrical laws to hold in the per-unit system. Thus, for a single-phase system, the power base (total, real and reactive power) is related to the base voltage and base current as

$$VA_{\text{base}} \ (P_{\text{base}}, Q_{\text{base}}) = V_{\text{base}} \times I_{\text{base}} \qquad (2.49)$$

and the impedance base (complex, real and reactive) is related to the base voltage and base current as

$$Z_{\text{base}} \ (R_{\text{base}}, X_{\text{base}}) = \frac{V_{\text{base}}}{I_{\text{base}}} \qquad (2.50)$$

The net result is that *only two independent base quantities can be chosen arbitrarily;* the remaining quantities are determined by the relationships of Eqs. 2.49 and 2.50. In typical usage, values of VA_{base} and V_{base} are chosen first; values of I_{base} and all other quantities in Eqs. 2.49 and 2.50 are then uniquely established.

The value of VA_{base} must be the same over the entire system under analysis. As can be seen with reference to the equivalent circuit of Fig. 2.10c, if the base voltages of the primary and secondary are chosen to be in the ratio of the turns of the ideal transformer, the per-unit ideal transformer will have a unity turns ratio and hence can be eliminated. Usually the rated or nominal voltages of the respective sides are chosen as the base values. Although, as we have seen, transformer equivalent-circuit parameters values vary by the square of the turns ratio as they are reflected from one side of the transformer to the other, the per-unit impedances will be the same independent of the side of the transformer from which they are initially calculated. This is consistent with the unity-turns-ratio per-unit ideal transformer and is automatically accounted for by using Eqs. 2.49 and 2.50 to determine the per-unit values.

If these rules are followed, the procedure for performing system analyses in per-unit can be summarized as follows:

1.   Select a *VA* base and a base voltage at some point in the system.
2.   Convert all quantities to per unit on the chosen *VA* base and with a voltage base that transforms as the turns ratio of any transformer which is encountered as one moves through the system.
3.   Perform a standard electrical analysis on the resultant electric circuit with all quantities in per unit.
4.   When the analysis is completed, all quantities can be converted back to real units (e.g., volts, amperes, watts, etc.) by multiplying their per-unit values by their corresponding base values.

When only one electric device, such as a transformer, is involved, the device's own rating is generally used for the volt-ampere base. When their parameters are expressed in per-unit on their rating as a base, the characteristics of power and distribution transformers do not vary much over a wide range of ratings. For example, the exciting current is often between 0.02 and 0.06 per unit (2 percent to 6 percent of rated current) or less on the largest transformers, the equivalent resistance is usually between 0.005 and 0.02 per unit (the smaller values applying to large transformers), and the equivalent reactance is usually between 0.05 and 0.10 per unit (with the larger values applying to large high-voltage transformers as required to limit short-circuit currents). Similarly, the per-unit values of synchronous- and induction-machine parameters fall within a relatively narrow range. The reason for this is that the physics behind each type of device is the same and, in a crude sense, they can each be considered to be simply scaled versions of the same basic device. As a result, when normalized to their own rating, the effect of the scaling is eliminated and the result is a set of per-unit parameter values which is quite similar over the whole size range of that device.

Often, manufacturers supply device parameters in per unit on the device base. When several devices are involved, however, an arbitrary choice of volt-ampere base must usually be made, and that value must then be used for the overall system. As a result, when performing a system analysis, it may be necessary to convert the supplied per-unit parameter values to per-unit values on the base chosen for the analysis. The following relations can be used to convert per-unit (pu) values from one base to another:

$$(P, Q, VA)_{\text{pu on base 2}} = (P, Q, VA)_{\text{pu on base 1}} \left[\frac{VA_{\text{base 1}}}{VA_{\text{base 2}}} \right] \tag{2.51}$$

$$(R, X, Z)_{\text{pu on base 2}} = (R, X, Z)_{\text{pu on base 1}} \left[\frac{(V_{\text{base 1}})^2 VA_{\text{base 2}}}{(V_{\text{base 2}})^2 VA_{\text{base 1}}} \right] \tag{2.52}$$

$$V_{\text{pu on base 2}} = V_{\text{pu on base 1}} \left[\frac{V_{\text{base 1}}}{V_{\text{base 2}}} \right] \tag{2.53}$$

$$I_{\text{pu on base 2}} = I_{\text{pu on base 1}} \left[\frac{V_{\text{base 2}} VA_{\text{base 1}}}{V_{\text{base 1}} VA_{\text{base 2}}} \right] \tag{2.54}$$

EXAMPLE 2.12

The equivalent circuit for a 100-MVA, 7.97-kV:79.7-kV transformer is shown in Fig. 2.23a. The equivalent-circuit parameters are:

$$X_L = 0.040 \ \Omega \quad X_H = 3.75 \ \Omega \quad X_m = 114 \ \Omega$$

$$R_L = 0.76 \ \text{m}\Omega \quad R_H = 0.085 \ \Omega$$

Note that the magnetizing inductance has been referred to the low-voltage side of the equivalent circuit. Convert the equivalent circuit parameters to per unit using the transformer rating as base.

■ Solution

The base quantities for the transformer are:

Low-voltage side:

$$VA_{\text{base}} = 100 \ \text{MVA} \quad V_{\text{base}} = 7.97 \ \text{kV}$$

and from Eqs. 2.49 and 2.50

$$R_{\text{base}} = X_{\text{base}} = \frac{V_{\text{base}}^2}{VA_{\text{base}}} = 0.635 \ \Omega$$

High-voltage side:

$$VA_{\text{base}} = 100 \ \text{MVA} \quad V_{\text{base}} = 79.7 \ \text{kV}$$

and from Eqs. 2.49 and 2.50

$$R_{\text{base}} = X_{\text{base}} = \frac{V_{\text{base}}^2}{VA_{\text{base}}} = 63.5 \ \Omega$$

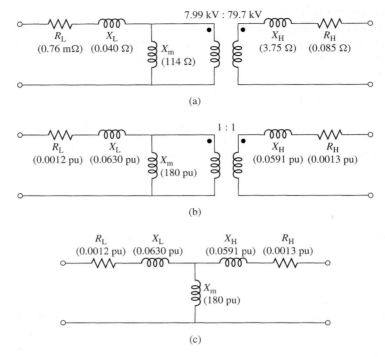

Figure 2.23 Transformer equivalent circuits for Example 2.12.
(a) Equivalent circuit in actual units. (b) Per-unit equivalent circuit with
1:1 ideal transformer. (c) Per-unit equivalent circuit following
elimination of the ideal transformer.

The per-unit values of the transformer parameters can now be calculated by division by
their corresponding base quantities.

$$X_L = \frac{0.040}{0.635} = 0.0630 \text{ per unit}$$

$$X_H = \frac{3.75}{63.5} = 0.0591 \text{ per unit}$$

$$X_m = \frac{114}{0.635} = 180 \text{ per unit}$$

$$R_L = \frac{7.6 \times 10^{-4}}{0.635} = 0.0012 \text{ per unit}$$

$$R_H = \frac{0.085}{63.5} = 0.0013 \text{ per unit}$$

Finally, the voltages representing the turns ratio of the ideal transformer must each be divided by the base voltage on that side of the transformer. Thus the turns ratio of 7.97-kV:79.7-kV

becomes in per unit

$$\text{Per-unit turns ratio} = \left(\frac{7.97 \text{ kV}}{7.97 \text{ kV}}\right) : \left(\frac{79.7 \text{ kV}}{79.7 \text{ kV}}\right) = 1 : 1$$

The resultant per-unit equivalent circuit is shown in Fig. 2.23b. Because it has unity turns ratio, there is no need to keep the ideal transformer and hence this equivalent circuit can be reduced to the form of Fig. 2.23c.

EXAMPLE 2.13

The exciting current measured on the low-voltage side of a 50-kVA, 2400:240-V transformer is 5.41 A. Its equivalent impedance referred to the high-voltage side is $1.42 + j1.82 \ \Omega$. Using the transformer rating as the base, express in per unit on the low- and high-voltage sides (a) the exciting current and (b) the equivalent impedance.

■ Solution

The base values of voltages and currents are

$$V_{\text{base,H}} = 2400 \text{ V} \quad V_{\text{base,L}} = 240 \text{ V} \quad I_{\text{base,H}} = 20.8 \text{ A} \quad I_{\text{base,L}} = 208 \text{ A}$$

where subscripts H and L indicate the high- and low-voltage sides, respectively.

From Eq. 2.50

$$Z_{\text{base,H}} = \frac{2400}{20.8} = 115.2 \ \Omega \quad Z_{\text{base,L}} = \frac{240}{208} = 1.152 \ \Omega$$

a. From Eq. 2.48, the exciting current in per unit referred to the low-voltage side can be calculated as:

$$I_{\varphi,\text{L}} = \frac{5.41}{208} = 0.0260 \text{ per unit}$$

The exciting current referred to the high-voltage side is 0.541 A. Its per-unit value is

$$I_{\varphi,\text{H}} = \frac{0.541}{20.8} = 0.0260 \text{ per unit}$$

Note that, as expected, the per-unit values are the same referred to either side, corresponding to a unity turns ratio for the ideal transformer in the per-unit transformer. This is a direct consequence of the choice of base voltages in the ratio of the transformer turns ratio and the choice of a constant volt-ampere base.

b. From Eq. 2.48 and the value for Z_{base}

$$Z_{\text{eq,H}} = \frac{1.42 + j1.82}{115.2} = 0.0123 + j0.0158 \text{ per unit}$$

The equivalent impedance referred to the low-voltage side is $0.0142 + j0.0182 \Omega$. Its per-unit value is

$$Z_{\text{eq,L}} = \frac{0.142 + 0.0182}{1.152} = 0.0123 + j0.0158 \text{ per unit}$$

The per-unit values referred to the high- and low-voltage sides are the same, the transformer turns ratio being accounted for in per unit by the base values. Note again that this is consistent with a unity turns ratio of the ideal transformer in the per-unit transformer equivalent circuit.

A 15-kVA 120:460-V transformer has an equivalent series impedance of $0.018 + j0.042$ per unit. Calculate the equivalent series impedance in ohms (a) referred to the low-voltage side and (b) referred to the high-voltage side.

Solution

$$Z_{eq,L} = 0.017 + j0.040 \ \Omega \quad \text{and} \quad Z_{eq,H} = 0.25 + j0.60 \ \Omega$$

When they are applied to the analysis of three-phase systems, the base values for the per-unit system are chosen so that the relations for a balanced three-phase system hold between them:

$$(P_{base}, Q_{base}, VA_{base})_{3-phase} = 3VA_{base, \ per \ phase} \tag{2.55}$$

In dealing with three-phase systems, $VA_{base, \ 3-phase}$, the three-phase volt-ampere base, and $V_{base, \ 3-phase} = V_{base, \ 1-1}$, the line-to-line voltage base are usually chosen first. The base values for the phase (line-to-neutral) voltage then follows as

$$V_{base, \ 1-n} = \frac{1}{\sqrt{3}} V_{base, \ 1-1} \tag{2.56}$$

Note that the base current for three-phase systems is equal to the phase current, which is the same as the base current for a single-phase (per-phase) analysis. Hence

$$I_{base, \ 3-phase} = I_{base, \ per \ phase} = \frac{VA_{base, \ 3-phase}}{\sqrt{3} \ V_{base, \ 3-phase}} \tag{2.57}$$

Finally, the three-phase base impedance is chosen to the be the single-phase base impedance. Thus

$$Z_{base, \ 3-phase} = Z_{base, \ per \ phase}$$
$$= \frac{V_{base, \ 1-n}}{I_{base, \ per \ phase}}$$
$$= \frac{V_{base, \ 3-phase}}{\sqrt{3} I_{base, \ 3-phase}}$$
$$= \frac{(V_{base, \ 3-phase})^2}{VA_{base, \ 3-phase}} \tag{2.58}$$

The equations for conversion from base to base, Eqs. 2.51 through 2.54, apply equally to three-phase base conversion. Note that the factors of $\sqrt{3}$ and 3 relating Δ to Y quantities of volts, amperes, and ohms in a balanced three-phase system are automatically taken care of in per unit by the base values. Three-phase problems can thus be solved in per unit as if they were single-phase problems and the details of transformer (Y vs Δ on the primary and secondary of the transformer) and impedance (Y vs Δ) connections disappear, except in translating volt, ampere, and ohm values into and out of the per-unit system.

EXAMPLE 2.14

Rework Example 2.9 in per unit, specifically calculating the short-circuit phase currents which will flow in the feeder and at the 240-V terminals of the receiving-end transformer bank. Perform the calculations in per unit on the three-phase, 150-kVA, rated-voltage base of the receiving-end transformer.

■ **Solution**

We start by converting all the impedances to per unit. The impedance of the 500-kVA, 24 kV:2400 V sending end transformer is $0.17 + j0.92$ Ω/phase as referred to the 2400-V side. From Eq. 2.58, the base impedance corresponding to a 2400-V, 150-kVA base is

$$Z_{base} = \frac{2400^2}{150 \times 10^3} = 38.4 \ \Omega$$

From Example 2.9, the total series impedance is equal to $Z_{tot} = 0.64 + j2.33$ Ω/phase and thus in per unit it is equal to

$$Z_{tot} = \frac{0.64 + j2.33}{38.4} = 0.0167 + j0.0607 \text{ per unit}$$

which is of magnitude

$$|Z_{tot}| = 0.0629 \text{ per unit}$$

The voltage applied to the high-voltage side of the sending-end transformer is $V_s = 24.0$ kV $= 1.0$ per unit on a rated-voltage base and hence the short-circuit current will equal

$$I_{sc} = \frac{V_s}{|Z_{tot}|} = \frac{1.0}{0.0629} = 15.9 \text{ per unit}$$

To calculate the phase currents in amperes, it is simply necessary to multiply the per-unit short-circuit current by the appropriate base current. Thus, at the 2400-V feeder the base current is

$$I_{base, \ 2400-V} = \frac{150 \times 10^3}{\sqrt{3} \ 2400} = 36.1 \text{ A}$$

and hence the feeder current will be

$$I_{feeder} = 15.9 \times 36.1 = 574 \text{ A}$$

The base current at the 240-V secondary of the receiving-end transformers is

$$I_{base, \ 240-V} = \frac{150 \times 10^3}{\sqrt{3} \ 240} = 361 \text{ A}$$

and hence the short-circuit current is

$$I_{240-V \ secondary} = 15.9 \times 361 = 5.74 \text{ kA}$$

As expected, these values are equivalent within numerical accuracy to those calculated in Example 2.9.

Calculate the magnitude of the short-circuit current in the feeder of Example 2.9 if the 2400-V feeder is replaced by a feeder with an impedance of $0.07 + j0.68 \ \Omega$/phase. Perform this calculation on the 500-kVA, rated-voltage base of the sending-end transformer and express your solution both in per unit and in amperes per phase.

Solution

Short-circuit current $= 5.20$ per unit $= 636$ A

EXAMPLE 2.15

A three-phase load is supplied from a 2.4-kV:460-V, 250-kVA transformer whose equivalent series impedance is $0.026 + j0.12$ per unit on its own base. The load voltage is observed to be 438 V line-line, and it is drawing 95 kW at unity power factor. Calculate the voltage at the high-voltage side of the transformer. Perform the calculations on a 460-V, 100-kVA base.

■ **Solution**

The 460-V side base impedance for the transformer is

$$Z_{\text{base, transformer}} = \frac{460^2}{250 \times 10^3} = 0.846 \ \Omega$$

while that based upon a 100-kVA base is

$$Z_{\text{base, 100-kVA}} = \frac{460^2}{100 \times 10^3} = 2.12 \ \Omega$$

Thus, from Eq. 2.52 the per-unit transformer impedance on a 100-kVA base is

$$Z_{\text{transformer}} = (0.026 + j0.12) \left(\frac{0.864}{2.12} \right) = 0.0106 + j.0489 \text{ per unit}$$

The per-unit load voltage is

$$\hat{V}_{\text{load}} = \frac{438}{460} = 0.952 \ \angle 0° \text{ per unit}$$

where the load voltage has been chosen as the reference for phase-angle calculations.

The per-unit load power is

$$P_{\text{load}} = \frac{95}{100} = 0.95 \text{ per unit}$$

and hence the per-unit load current, which is in phase with the load voltage because the load is operating at unity power factor, is

$$\hat{I}_{\text{load}} = \frac{P_{\text{load}}}{V_{\text{load}}} = \frac{0.95}{0.952} = 0.998 \ \angle 0° \text{ per unit}$$

Thus we can now calculate the high-side voltage of the transformer

$$\hat{V}_{\text{H}} = \hat{V}_{\text{load}} + \hat{I}_{\text{load}} \ Z_{\text{transformer}}$$

$$= 0.952 + 0.998 \times (0.0106 + j0.0489)$$

$$= 0.963 + j0.0488 = 0.964 \ \angle 29.0° \text{ per unit}$$

Thus the high-side voltage is equal to 0.964×2400 V $= 2313$ V (line-line).

Repeat Example 2.15 if the 250-kV three-phase transformer is replaced by a 150-kV transformer also rated at 2.4-kV:460-V and whose equivalent series impedance is $0.038 + j0.135$ per unit on its own base. Perform the calculations on a 460-V, 100-kVA base.

Solution

$$\text{High-side voltage} = 0.982 \text{ per unit} = 2357 \text{ V (line-line)}$$

2.10 SUMMARY

Although not an electromechanical device, the transformer is a common and indispensable component of ac systems where it is used to transform voltages, currents, and impedances to appropriate levels for optimal use. For the purposes of our study of electromechanical systems, transformers serve as valuable examples of the analysis techniques which will be employed. They offer us opportunities to investigate the properties of magnetic circuits, including the concepts of mmf, magnetizing current, and magnetizing, mutual, and leakage fluxes and their associated inductances.

In both transformers and rotating machines, a magnetic field is created by the combined action of the currents in the windings. In an iron-core transformer, most of this flux is confined to the core and links all the windings. This resultant mutual flux induces voltages in the windings proportional to their number of turns and is responsible for the voltage-changing property of a transformer. In rotating machines, the situation is similar, although there is an air gap which separates the rotating and stationary components of the machine. Directly analogous to the manner in which transformer core flux links the various windings on a transformer core, the mutual flux in rotating machines crosses the air gap, linking the windings on the rotor and stator. As in a transformer, the mutual flux induces voltages in these windings proportional to the number of turns and the time rate of change of the flux.

A significant difference between transformers and rotating machines is that in rotating machines there is relative motion between the windings on the rotor and stator. This relative motion produces an additional component of the time rate of change of the various winding flux linkages. As will be discussed in Chapter 3, the resultant voltage component, known as the *speed voltage,* is characteristic of the process of electromechanical energy conversion. In a static transformer, however, the time variation of flux linkages is caused simply by the time variation of winding currents; no mechanical motion is involved, and no electromechanical energy conversion takes place.

The resultant core flux in a transformer induces a counter emf in the primary which, together with the primary resistance and leakage-reactance voltage drops, must balance the applied voltage. Since the resistance and leakage-reactance voltage drops usually are small, the counter emf must approximately equal the applied voltage and the core flux must adjust itself accordingly. Exactly similar phenomena must take place in the armature windings of an ac motor; the resultant air-gap flux wave must adjust itself to generate a counter emf approximately equal to the applied voltage. In both transformers and rotating machines, the net mmf produced by all of the currents must accordingly adjust itself to create the resultant flux required by this voltage balance.

In a transformer, the secondary current is determined by the voltage induced in the secondary, the secondary leakage impedance, and the electric load. As we will see, in an induction motor, the secondary (rotor) current is determined by the voltage induced in the secondary, the secondary leakage impedance, and the mechanical load on its shaft. Essentially the same phenomena take place in the primary winding of the transformer and in the armature (stator) windings of induction and synchronous motors. In all three the story remains the same; the primary, or armature, current must adjust itself so that the combined mmf of all currents creates the flux required by the applied voltage and as a result, a change in the load current will result in a corresponding change in the primary current.

In addition to the useful mutual fluxes, in both transformers and rotating machines there are leakage fluxes which link individual windings without linking others. Although the detailed picture of the leakage fluxes in rotating machines is more complicated than that in transformers, their effects are essentially the same. In both, leakage fluxes produce leakage-reactance voltage drops in the windings and typically reduce the mutual flux below the level which would otherwise be produced by the applied voltage. In both, the reluctances of the leakage-flux paths are dominated by that of a path through air, and hence the leakage fluxes are nearly linearly proportional to the currents producing them. Leakage reactances therefore are often assumed to be constant, independent of the degree of saturation of the main magnetic circuit.

Further examples of the basic similarities between transformers and rotating machines can be cited. Except for friction and windage, the losses in transformers and rotating machines are essentially the same. Tests for determining the losses and equivalent circuit parameters are similar: an open-circuit, or no-load, test gives information regarding the excitation requirements and core losses (along with friction and windage losses in rotating machines), while a short-circuit test together with dc resistance measurements gives information regarding leakage reactances and winding resistances. Modeling of the effects of magnetic saturation is another example: In both transformers and ac rotating machines, the leakage reactances are usually assumed to be unaffected by saturation, and the saturation of the main magnetic circuit is assumed to be determined by the resultant mutual or air-gap flux.

2.11 CHAPTER 2 VARIABLES

λ	Flux linkages [Wb]
ω	Angular frequency [rad/sec]
φ, ϕ_{max}	Magnetic flux [Wb]
$\hat{\Phi}$	Magnetic flux, complex amplitude [Wb]
θ	Phase angle [rad]
B_{max}	Peak flux density [T]

e	Electromotive force (emf), induced voltage [V]
E	Voltage [V]
$\hat{E}$	EMF, voltage, complex amplitude [V]
f	Frequency [Hz]
i, I	Current [A]
i_φ	Exciting current [A]
$\hat{I}$	Current, complex amplitude [A]
$\hat{I}_c$	Core-loss component of exciting current, complex amplitude [A]
$\hat{I}_m$	Magnetizing current, complex amplitude [A]
$\hat{I}_\varphi$	Exciting current, complex amplitude [A]
L	Inductance [H]
N	Number of turns
Q	Reactive power [VAR]
R	Resistance [Ω]
R_{base}	Base resistance [Ω]
t	Time [sec]
v, V	Voltage [V]
V_{base}	Base voltage [V]
$\hat{V}$	Voltage, complex amplitude [V]
$VA =$	Voltamperes [VA]
X	Reactance [Ω]
Z	Impedance [Ω]
Z_Δ	Delta-equivalent line-neutral impedance [Ω/phase]
Z_φ	Exciting impedance [Ω]
Z_Y	Y-equivalent line-neutral impedance [Ω/phase]

Subscripts:

ϕ	Exciting
b	Burden
base	Base quantity
c	Core
eq	Equivalent
H	High-voltage side
l	Leakage
l-n	Line-to-neutral
L	Low-voltage side
m	Magnetizing
max	Maximum
oc	Open circuit
pu	Per unit
rms	Root mean square
s	Sending
sc	Short circuit
tot	Total

2.12 PROBLEMS

2.1 A transformer is made up of a 1150-turn primary coil and an open-circuited 80-turn secondary coil wound around a closed core of cross-sectional area 56 cm^2. The core material can be considered to saturate when the rms applied flux density reaches 1.45 T. What maximum 60-Hz rms primary voltage is possible without reaching this saturation level? What is the corresponding secondary voltage? How are these values modified if the applied frequency is lowered to 50 Hz?

2.2 A magnetic circuit with a cross-sectional area of 20 cm^2 is to be operated at 60 Hz from a 115-V rms supply. Calculate the number of turns such that the peak core magnetic flux density is 1.6 T.

2.3 A transformer is to be used to transform the impedance of a 75-Ω resistor to an impedance of 300 Ω. Calculate the required turns ratio, assuming the transformer to be ideal.

2.4 A 150 Ω resistor is connected to the secondary of a transformer with a turns ratio of 1:4 (primary to secondary). A 12 V rms, 1 kHz voltage source is connected to the primary. (a) Assuming the transformer to be ideal, calculate the primary current and the resistor voltage and power. (b) Repeat this calculation assuming that the transformer has a leakage inductance of 340 μH as referred to the primary.

2.5 A load consisting of a 5 Ω resistor in series with a 2.5 mH inductor is connected to the low-voltage winding of a 20:120 V transformer. A 110 V rms, 50-Hz supply is connected to the high-voltage winding. Assuming the transformer to be ideal, calculate the rms load current and the rms current which will be drawn from the supply.

2.6 A source which can be represented by a 12 V rms voltage source in series with a resistance of 1.5 kΩ is connected to a 75-Ω load resistance through an ideal transformer. Calculate the value of turns ratio for which maximum power is supplied to the load and the corresponding load power? Using MATLAB, plot the the power in milliwatts supplied to the load as a function of the transformer ratio, covering ratios from 1.0 to 10.0.

2.7 Repeat the calculations of Problem 2.6 with the source resistance replaced by a 1.5 kΩ inductive reactance.

2.8 A single-phase 60-Hz transformer has a nameplate voltage rating of 7.97 kV:120 V based on its known winding turns ratio. The manufacturer calculates that the primary (7.97-kV) leakage inductance is 193 mH and the primary magnetizing inductance is 167 H. For an applied primary voltage of 7970 V at 60 Hz, calculate the resultant open-circuit secondary voltage.

2.9 The manufacturer calculates that the transformer of Problem 2.8 has a secondary leakage inductance of 44 μH.

   a. Calculate the magnetizing inductance as referred to the secondary side.

   b. A voltage of 120 V, 60 Hz is applied to the secondary. Calculate (i) the resultant open-circuit primary voltage and (ii) the secondary current which would result if the primary were short-circuited.

2.10 A 230-V:6.6-kV, 50-Hz, 45 kVA transformer has a magnetizing reactance (as measured from the 230-V terminals) of 46.2 Ω. The 230-V winding has a leakage reactance of 27.8 mΩ and the 6.6-kV winding has a leakage reactance of 25.3 Ω.

   a. With the secondary open-circuited and 230 V applied to the primary (230-V) winding, calculate the primary current and the secondary voltage.

   b. With the secondary short-circuited, calculate the primary voltage which will result in rated current in the primary winding. Calculate the corresponding current in the secondary winding.

2.11 The transformer of Problem 2.10 is to be used on a 60-Hz system.

   a. Calculate the magnetizing reactance referred to the low-voltage winding and the leakage reactance of each winding.

   b. With 240 V applied to the low-voltage (primary) winding and with the secondary winding open-circuited, calculate the primary-winding current and the secondary voltage.

2.12 A 460-V:2400-V transformer has a series leakage reactance of 39.3 Ω as referred to the high-voltage side. A load connected to the low voltage side is observed to draw 42 kW at unity power factor and the voltage is measured to be 447 V. Calculate the corresponding voltage and power factor as measured at the high-voltage terminals.

2.13 The 460-V:2400-V transformer of Problem 2.12 is to be operated from a 50-Hz source. A unity-power-factor load connected to the low-voltage side is observed to draw 34.5 kW, unity-power-factor load at a voltage of 362 V. Calculate the voltage applied to the transformer high-voltage winding.

2.14 The resistances and leakage reactances of a 40-kVA 60-Hz 7.97-kV-V:240-V single-phase distribution transformer are

$$R_1 = 41.6\ \Omega \quad R_2 = 37.2\ \text{m}\Omega$$

$$X_{l_1} = 42.1\ \Omega \quad X_{l_2} = 39.8\ \text{m}\Omega$$

where subscript 1 denotes the 7.97-kV winding and subscript 2 denotes the 240-V winding. Each quantity is referred to its own side of the transformer.

   a. Draw the equivalent circuit referred to (i) the high- and (ii) the low-voltage sides. Label the impedances numerically.

   b. Consider the transformer to deliver its rated kVA to a load on the low-voltage side with 240 V across the load. (i) Find the high-side terminal voltage for a load power factor of 0.87 power factor lagging. (ii) Find the high-side terminal voltage for a load power factor of 0.87 power factor leading.

   c. Consider a rated-kVA load connected at the low-voltage terminals. Assuming the load voltage to remain constant at 240 V, use MATLAB to plot the high-side terminal voltage as a function of the power-factor angle as the load power factor varies from 0.6 leading through unity power factor to 0.6 lagging.

2.15 Repeat the calculations of Problem 2.14 for a 75-kVA, 50-Hz, 3.81-kV:230-V single-phase distribution transformer whose resistances and leakage reactances are

$$R_1 = 4.85 \ \Omega \quad R_2 = 16.2 \ \text{m}\Omega$$

$$X_{1_1} = 4.13 \ \Omega \quad X_{1_2} = 16.9 \ \text{m}\Omega$$

where subscript 1 denotes the 3.81-kV winding and subscript 2 denotes the 230-V winding. Each quantity is referred to its own side of the transformer. The load in parts (b) and (c) should be assumed to be operating at a voltage of 230 V.

2.16 A single-phase load is supplied through a 35-kV feeder whose impedance is $90 + j320 \ \Omega$ and a 35-kV: 2400-V transformer whose equivalent series impedance is $0.21 + j1.33 \ \Omega$ referred to its low-voltage side. The load is 135 kW at 0.78 leading power factor and 2385 V.

   a. Compute the voltage at the high-voltage terminals of the transformer.

   b. Compute the voltage at the sending end of the feeder.

   c. Compute the power and reactive power input at the sending end of the feeder.

2.17 Write a MATLAB script to (a) repeat the calculations of Problem 2.16 for power factors of 0.78 leading, unity and 0.78 lagging assuming the load power remains constant at 135 kW and the load voltage remains constant at 2385 V. (b) Use your MATLAB script to plot (versus power factor angle) the sending-end voltage required to maintain a load voltage of 2385 V as the power factor varies from 0.7 leading through unity to 0.7 lagging.

2.18 Repeat Example 2.6 with the transformer operating at full load and unity power factor.

2.19 A 450-kVA 50-Hz single-phase transformer with a 11-kV primary winding draws 0.33 A and 2700 W at no load, rated voltage and frequency. Another transformer has a core with all its linear dimensions $\sqrt{2}$ times as large as the corresponding dimensions of the first transformer. The core material and lamination thickness are the same in both transformers. (a) If the primary windings of both transformers have the same number of turns, what impressed primary voltage will result in the same flux density in the core. (b) With the primary excited by the voltage found in part (a), calculate the primary current and power.

2.20 The nameplate on a 25-MVA, 60-Hz single-phase transformer indicates that it has a voltage rating of 8.0-kV:78-kV. A short-circuit test from the high-voltage side (low-voltage winding short circuited) gives readings of 4.53 kV, 321 A, and 77.5 kW. An open-circuit test is conducted from the low-voltage side and the corresponding instrument readings are 8.0 kV, 39.6 A, and 86.2 kW.

   a. Calculate the equivalent series impedance of the transformer as referred to the high-voltage terminals.

   b. Calculate the equivalent series impedance of the transformer as referred to the low-voltage terminals.

c. Making appropriate approximations, draw a T equivalent circuit for the transformer.

2.21 Perform the calculations of Problem 2.20 for a 175-kVA, 50-Hz single-phase transformer with a voltage rating of 3.8-kV:6.4-kV. An open-circuit test is conducted from the low-voltage side and the corresponding instrument readings are 3.8 kV, 0.58 A, and 603 W. Similarly, a short-circuit test from the high-voltage side (low-voltage winding short-circuited) gives readings of 372 V, 27.3 A, and 543 W.

2.22 A voltage of 7.96 kV is applied to the low-voltage winding of a 7.96 kV:39.8 kV, 60 Hz, 10 MVA single-phase transformer with the high-voltage winding open-circuited and the resultant current is 17.3 A and power is 48.0 kW. The low-voltage winding is then short-circuited and a voltage of 1.92 kV applied to the high-voltage winding results in a current of current of 252 A and a power of 60.3 kW.

 a. Calculate the parameters of the cantilever equivalent circuits of Figs. 2.12a and b as referred to the transformer high-voltage winding.

 b. Calculate the cantilever equivalent-circuit parameters as referred to the transformer low-voltage winding.

 c. With the transformer carrying rated load and rated voltage at its low-voltage terminal, calculate the power dissipated in the transformer.

2.23 The following data were obtained on a 2.5 MVA, 50-Hz, 19.1-kV:3.81-kV single-phase transformer tested at 50 Hz:

	Voltage, V	Current, A	Power, kW
LV winding with HV terminals open-circuited	3810	9.86	8.14
HV winding with LV terminals short-circuited	920	141	10.3

 a. Calculate the parameters of the cantilever equivalent circuits of Figs. 2.12a and b as referred to the transformer high-voltage winding.

 b. Calculate the cantilever equivalent-circuit parameters as referred to the transformer low-voltage winding.

 c. With the transformer carrying rated load and rated voltage at its low-voltage terminal, calculate the power dissipated in the transformer.

2.24 Write a MATLAB script to calculate the parameters for the cantilever transformer equivalent circuits of Figs. 2.12a and b with the parameters referred to the high-voltage winding based upon the following test data:

 ■ Voltage, current and power from an open-circuit test conducted from the low-voltage winding (high-voltage winding open-circuited).

 ■ Voltage, current and power from a short-circuit test conducted from the low-voltage winding (high-voltage winding short-circuited).

Test your script on the measurements made on the transformer of Problem 2.22.

2.25 The high-voltage winding of the transformer of Problem 2.22 is replaced by an otherwise identical winding of twice the number of turns with wire of half the cross-sectional area.

   a.   Calculate the rated voltage and power of this modified transformer.

   b.   With the high-voltage winding open-circuited and with rated voltage applied to the low-voltage winding, calculate the current and power supplied to the low-voltage winding.

   c.   With the low-voltage winding short-circuited, calculate the voltage applied to the high-voltage winding that will result in a short-circuit power dissipation of 60.3 kW.

   d.   Calculate the cantilever-equivalent-circuit parameters of this transformer referred to (i) the low-voltage side and (ii) the high-voltage side.

2.26 (a) Determine the efficiency and voltage regulation of the transformer of Problem 2.20 if it is supplying rated load (unity power factor) at rated voltage at its low-voltage terminals. (b) Repeat part (a), assuming the load to be at 0.9 power factor leading.

2.27 Assume the transformer of Problem 2.23 to be operating at rated voltage and with a load that draws rated current at its low-voltage terminals. Write a MATLAB script to plot (a) the efficiency and (b) the voltage regulation of the transformer as the as a function of the load power-factor as the power factor varies from 0.75 lagging through unity through 0.75 leading.

2.28 The following data were obtained for a 25-kVA, 60-Hz, 2400:240-V distribution transformer tested at 60 Hz:

	Voltage, V	Current, A	Power, W
LV winding with HV terminals open-circuited	240	1.37	139
HV winding with LV terminals short-circuited	67.8	10.1	174

   a.   Compute the transformer efficiency when the tranformer is operating at rated terminal voltage with an 0.85 power-factor (lagging) load at its secondary terminal that draws full-load current.

   b.   The transformer is observed to be operating with rated voltage at both its primary and secondary terminals and supplying a load at its secondary terminals which draws rated current. Calculate the power factor of the load. (HINT: Use MATLAB to search for the solution).

2.29 A 150-kVA, 240-V:7970-V, 60-Hz single-phase distribution transformer has the following parameters referred to the high-voltage side:

$$R_1 = 2.81 \ \Omega \quad X_1 = 21.8 \ \Omega$$

$$R_2 = 2.24 \ \Omega \quad X_2 = 20.3 \ \Omega$$

$$R_c = 127 \ \text{k}\Omega \quad X_m = 58.3 \ \text{k}\Omega$$

Assume that the transformer is supplying its rated kVA at its low-voltage terminals. Write a MATLAB script to determine the efficiency and regulation of the transformer for any specified load power-factor (leading or lagging). You may use reasonable engineering approximations to simplify your analysis. Use your MATLAB script to determine the efficiency and regulation for a load power-factor of 0.92 leading.

2.30 A 45-kVA, 120-V:280-V single-phase transformer is to be connected as a 280-V:400-V autotransformer. Determine the voltage ratings of the high- and low-voltage windings for this connection and the kVA rating of the autotransformer connection.

2.31 A 120:480-V, 10-kVA single-phase transformer is to be used as an autotransformer to supply a 480-V circuit from a 600-V source. When it is tested as a two-winding transformer at rated load, unity power factor, its efficiency is 0.982.

    a.   Make a diagram of connections as an autotransformer.

    b.   Determine its kVA rating as an autotransformer.

    c.   Find its efficiency as an autotransformer when operating with a load of rated kVA and 0.93 power factor leading and 480 V connected to the low-voltage winding.

2.32 Consider the 8-kV:78-kV, 25-MVA transformer of Problem 2.20 connected as a 78-kV:86-kV autotransformer.

    a.   Determine the voltage ratings of the high-and low-voltage windings for this connection and the MVA rating of the autotransformer connection.

    b.   Calculate the efficiency of the transformer in this connection when it is supplying its rated load at unity power factor.

2.33 Write a MATLAB script whose inputs are the rating (voltage and kVA) and rated-load, unity-power-factor efficiency of a single-phase transformer and whose output is the transformer rating and rated-load, unity-power-factor efficiency when connected as an autotransformer. Exercise your program on the autotransformer of Problem 2.32.

2.34 The high-voltage terminals of a three-phase transformer bank of three single-phase transformers are supplied from a three-wire, three-phase 13.8-kV (line-to-line) system. The low-voltage terminals are to be connected to a three-wire, three-phase substation load drawing up to 4500 kVA at 2300 V line to line. Specify the required voltage, current, and kVA ratings of each transformer (both high- and low-voltage windings) for the following connections:

	High-voltage Windings	Low-voltage Windings
a.	Y	Δ
b.	Δ	Y
c.	Y	Y
d.	Δ	Δ

2.35 Three 75-MVA single-phase transformers, rated at 39.8-kV:133-kV, are to be connected in a three-phase bank. Each transformer has a series impedance of $0.97 + j11.3\,\Omega$ referred to its 133-kV winding.

   a. If the transformers are connected Y-Y, calculate (i) the voltage and power rating of the three-phase connection, (ii) the equivalent impedance as referred to its low-voltage terminals, and (iii) the equivalent impedance as referred to its high-voltage terminals.

   b. Repeat part (a) if the transformer is connected Y on its low-voltage side and Δ on its high-voltage side.

2.36 Repeat the calculations of Problem 2.35 for three 225-kVA, 277-V:7.97-kV transformers whose series impedances is $3.1 + j21.5\,\text{m}\Omega$ referred to its low-voltage winding.

2.37 Repeat Example 2.8 for a load drawing rated current from the transformers at unity power factor.

2.38 A three-phase Y-Y transformer is rated at 25 MVA, 13.8-kV:69-kV and has a single-phase equivalent series impedance $62 + j388\,\text{m}\Omega$ referred to the low-voltage winding.

   a. A three-phase short circuit is applied to the low-voltage winding. Calculate the voltage applied to the high-voltage winding which will result in rated current into the short circuit.

   b. The short circuit is removed and a three-phase load is connected to the low-voltage winding. With rated voltage applied to the high-voltage winding, the input power to the transformer is observed to be 18 MW at 0.75 power-factor lagging. Calculate the line-line terminal voltage at the load.

2.39 A three-phase Y-Δ transformer is rated 225-kV:24-kV, 400 MVA and has a single-phase equivalent series reactance of $6.08\,\Omega$ as referred to its high-voltage terminals. The transformer is supplying a load of 375 MVA at 0.89 power factor leading at a voltage of 24 kV (line to line) on its low-voltage side. It is supplied from a feeder whose impedance is $0.17 + j2.2\,\Omega$ connected to its high-voltage terminals. For these conditions, calculate (a) the line-to-line voltage at the high-voltage terminals of the transformer and (b) the line-to-line voltage at the sending end of the feeder.

2.40 Assume the apparent power of the load in the system of Problem 2.39 to remain constant at 375 MVA. Write a MATLAB script to calculate the line-to-line voltage which must be applied to the sending end of the feeder to maintain the load voltage at 24 kV line-to-line as a function of the load power factor. Plot the sending-end voltage as a function of power factor angle for power factors in range from 0.3 lagging to unity to 0.3 leading.

2.41 A Δ-Y connected bank of three identical 150-kVA, 2400-V:120-V, 60-Hz transformers is supplied at its high-voltage terminals through a feeder whose impedance is $6.4 + j154\,\text{m}\Omega$ per phase. The voltage at the sending end of the feeder is held constant at 2400 V line to line. The results of a single-phase short-circuit test on one of the transformers with its low-voltage terminals short-circuited are

$$V_H = 131 \text{ V} \quad I_H = 62.5 \text{ A} \quad P = 1335 \text{ W}$$

a. Calculate the series impedance of this three-phase transformer bank as referred to its high-voltage terminal.

b. Determine the line-to-line voltage supplied to the feeder when the transformer bank delivers rated current at rated voltage to a balanced three-phase unity power factor load at its low-voltage terminal.

2.42 A 13.8-kV:120-V 60-Hz potential transformer has the following parameters as seen from the high-voltage (primary) winding:

$$X_1 = 6.88 \text{ k}\Omega \quad X_2' = 7.59 \text{ k}\Omega \quad X_m = 6.13 \text{ M}\Omega$$

$$R_1 = 5.51 \text{ k}\Omega \quad R_2' = 6.41 \text{ k}\Omega$$

a. Assuming that the secondary is open-circuited and that the primary is connected to a 13.8-kV source, calculate the magnitude and phase angle (with respect to the high-voltage source) of the voltage at the secondary terminals.

b. Calculate the magnitude and phase angle of the secondary voltage if a 750 Ω resistive load is connected to the secondary terminals.

c. Repeat part (b) if the burden is changed to a 750 Ω reactance.

2.43 For the potential transformer of Problem 2.42, find the maximum reactive burden (minimum reactance) which can be applied at the secondary terminals such that the voltage magnitude error does not exceed 0.75 percent.

2.44 Consider the potential transformer of Problem 2.42 with connected to a 13.8 kV source.

a. Use MATLAB to plot the percentage error in voltage magnitude as a function of the magnitude of the burden impedance (i) for a resistive burden of 100 Ω ≤ R_b ≤ 2000 Ω and (ii) for a reactive burden of 100 Ω ≤ X_b ≤ 2000 Ω. Plot these curves on the same axis.

b. Next plot the phase error in degrees as a function of the magnitude of the burden impedance (i) for a resistive burden of 100 Ω ≤ R_b ≤ 2000 Ω and (ii) for a reactive burden of 100 Ω ≤ X_b ≤ 2000 Ω. Again, plot these curves on the same axis.

2.45 A 150-A:5-A, 60-Hz current transformer has the following parameters as seen from the 150-A (primary) winding:

$$X_1 = 1.70 \text{ m}\Omega \quad X_2' = 1.84 \text{ m}\Omega \quad X_m = 1728 \text{ m}\Omega$$

$$R_1 = 306 \text{ }\mu\Omega \quad R_2' = 291 \text{ }\mu\Omega$$

   a.   Assuming a current of 150 A in the primary and that the secondary is
        short-circuited, find the magnitude and phase angle of the secondary
        current.

   b.   Repeat the calculation of part (a) if the CT is shorted through a 0.1-mΩ
        burden.

2.46   Consider the current transformer of Problem 2.45.

   a.   Use MATLAB to plot the percentage error in current magnitude as a
        function of the magnitude of the burden impedance (i) for a resistive
        burden of 50 $\mu\Omega \leq R_b \leq$ 200 $\mu\Omega$ and (ii) for a reactive burden of
        50 $\mu\Omega \leq X_b \leq$ 200 $\mu\Omega$. Plot these curves on the same axis.

   b.   Next plot the phase error in degrees as a function of the magnitude of the
        burden impedance (i) for a resistive burden of 50 $\mu\Omega \leq R_b \leq$ 200 $\mu\Omega$ and
        (ii) for a reactive burden of burden of 50 $\mu\Omega \leq X_b \leq$ 200 $\mu\Omega$. Again, plot
        these curves on the same axis.

2.47   A 15-kV:175-kV, 225-MVA, 60-Hz single-phase transformer has primary and
        secondary impedances of $0.0029 + j0.023$ per unit each. The magnetizing
        impedance is $j172$ per unit. All quantities are in per unit on the transformer
        base. Calculate the primary and secondary resistances and reactances and the
        magnetizing reactance in ohms (referred to the low-voltage side).

2.48   Calculate the per-unit parameters for a cantilever equivalent circuit for the
        transformer of Problem 2.20.

2.49   Calculate the per-unit parameters for a cantilever equivalent circuit for the
        transformer of Problem 2.23.

2.50   The nameplate on a 7.97-kV:266-V, 25-kVA single-phase transformer
        indicates that it has a series reactance of 7.5 percent (0.075 per unit).

   a.   Calculate the series reactance in ohms as referred to (i) the low-voltage
        terminal and (ii) the high-voltage terminal.

   b.   If three of these transformers are connected in a three-phase Y-Y
        connection, calculate (i) the three-phase voltage and power rating, (ii) the
        per unit impedance of the transformer bank, (iii) the series reactance in
        ohms as referred to the high-voltage terminal and (iv) the series reactance
        in ohms as referred to the low-voltage terminal.

   c.   Repeat part (b) if the three transformers are connected in Y on their HV
        side and Δ on their low-voltage side.

2.51 a.   Consider the Y-Y transformer connection of Problem 2.50, part (b). If a
        line-line voltage of 500 V is applied to the high-voltage terminals and the
        three low-voltage terminals are short-circuited, calculate the magnitude of
        the phase current in per unit and in amperes on (i) the high-voltage side
        and (ii) the low-voltage side.

   b.   Repeat this calculation for the Y-Δ connection of Problem 2.50, part (c).

2.52   A three-phase generator step-up transformer is rated 26-kV:345-kV, 850 MVA
        and has a series impedance of $0.0025 + j0.057$ per unit on this base. It is
        connected to a 26-kV 800-MVA generator, which can be represented as a

voltage source in series with a reactance of $j1.28$ per unit on the generator base.

a. Convert the per unit generator reactance to the step-up transformer base.

b. The system is supplying 750 MW at 345 kV and 0.90 power factor leading to the system at the transformer terminals. Draw a phasor diagram for this condition, using the transformer high-side voltage as the reference phasor.

c. Calculate the generator terminal voltage and internal voltage behind its reactance in kV for the conditions of part (b). Find the generator output power in MW and the power factor.

3 CHAPTER

Electromechanical-Energy-Conversion Principles

I n this chapter we discuss the electromechanical-energy-conversion process which takes place through the medium of the electric or magnetic field of the conversion device. Although the various conversion devices operate on similar principles, their structures depend on their function. Devices for measurement and control are frequently referred to as *transducers;* they generally operate under linear input-output conditions and with relatively small signals. The many examples include microphones, pickups, sensors, and loudspeakers. A second category of devices encompasses *force-producing devices* and includes solenoids, relays, and electromagnets. A third category includes *continuous energy-conversion equipment* such as motors and generators.

This chapter is devoted to the basic principles of electromechanical energy conversion and the analysis of the devices which accomplish this function. Emphasis is placed on the analysis of systems which use magnetic fields as the conversion medium since the remaining chapters of the book deal with such devices. However, the analytical techniques for electric field systems are quite similar.

The purpose of such analysis is threefold: (1) to aid in understanding how energy conversion takes place, (2) to provide techniques for designing and optimizing the devices for specific requirements, and (3) to develop models of electromechanical-energy-conversion devices that can be used in analyzing their performance as components in engineering systems. Transducers and force-producing devices are treated in this chapter; continuous energy-conversion devices in the form of rotating electric machinery are treated in the rest of the book.

The concepts and techniques presented in this chapter are quite powerful and can be applied to a wide range of engineering situations involving electromechanical energy conversion. Sections 3.1 and 3.2 present a quantitative discussion of the forces in electromechanical systems and an overview of the energy method which forms the basis for the derivations presented here. Based upon the energy method, the remainder of the chapter develops expressions for forces and torques in magnetic-field-based electromechanical systems.

3.1 FORCES AND TORQUES IN MAGNETIC-FIELD SYSTEMS

The *Lorentz Force Law*

$$\mathbf{F} = q(\mathbf{E} + \mathbf{v} \times \mathbf{B}) \tag{3.1}$$

gives the force $\mathbf{F}$ on a particle of charge q in the presence of electric and magnetic fields. In SI units, $\mathbf{F}$ is in *newtons* and q is in *coulombs*. The electric-field intensity $\mathbf{E}$ is in *volts per meter*, the magnetic flux density $\mathbf{B}$ is in *teslas* and v, which is the velocity of the particle relative to the magnetic field, is in *meters per second*.

Thus, in a pure electric-field system ($\mathbf{B} = \mathbf{0}$), the force is determined simply by the charge on the particle and the electric field

$$\mathbf{F} = q\mathbf{E} \tag{3.2}$$

The force acts in the direction of the electric field and is independent of any particle motion.

In pure magnetic-field systems ($\mathbf{E} = 0$), the situation is somewhat more complex. Here the force

$$\mathbf{F} = q(\mathbf{v} \times \mathbf{B}) \tag{3.3}$$

is determined by the magnitude of the charge on the particle and the magnitude of the $\mathbf{B}$ field as well as the velocity of the particle. In fact, the direction of the force is always perpendicular to the direction of both the particle motion and that of the magnetic field. Mathematically, this is indicated by the vector cross product $\mathbf{v} \times \mathbf{B}$ in Eq. 3.3. The magnitude of this cross product is equal to the product of the magnitudes of $\mathbf{v}$ and $\mathbf{B}$ and the sine of the angle between them; its direction can be found from the right-hand rule, which states that when the thumb of the right hand points in the direction of $\mathbf{v}$ and the index finger points in the direction of $\mathbf{B}$, the force, which is perpendicular to the directions of both $\mathbf{B}$ and $\mathbf{v}$, points in the direction normal to the palm of the hand, as shown in Fig. 3.1.

For situations where large numbers of charged particles are in motion, it is convenient to rewrite Eq. 3.1 in terms of the *charge density* ρ (measured in units of *coulombs per cubic meter*) as

$$\mathbf{F}_v = \rho(\mathbf{E} + \mathbf{v} \times \mathbf{B}) \tag{3.4}$$

where the subscript v indicates that $\mathbf{F}_v$ is a *force density* (force per unit volume) which in SI units is measured in *newtons per cubic meter*.

The product $\rho\mathbf{v}$ is known as the *current density*

$$\mathbf{J} = \rho\mathbf{v} \tag{3.5}$$

Figure 3.1 Right-hand rule for determining the direction magnetic-field component of the Lorentz force $\mathbf{F} = q(\mathbf{v} \times \mathbf{B})$.

which has the units of *amperes per square meter*. The magnetic-system force density corresponding to Eq. 3.3 can then be written as

$$\mathbf{F}_v = \mathbf{J} \times \mathbf{B} \tag{3.6}$$

For currents flowing in conducting media, Eq. 3.6 can be used to find the force density acting on the material itself. Note that a considerable amount of physics is hidden in this seemingly simple statement, since the mechanism by which the force is transferred from the moving charges to the conducting medium is a complex one.

EXAMPLE 3.1

A non-magnetic cylindrical rotor (mounted on a shaft at its center) containing a single-turn coil is placed in a uniform magnetic field of magnitude B_0, as shown in Fig. 3.2. The coil sides are

Figure 3.2 Single-coil rotor for Example 3.1.

at radius R and the wire carries current I as indicated. Find the θ-directed torque as a function of rotor position α when $I = 10$ A, $B_0 = 0.02$ T and $R = 0.05$ m. Assume that the rotor is of length $l = 0.3$ m.

■ **Solution**

The net current I in a wire is equal to the integral of the current density J over the cross-sectional area of the wire.

$$I = \int_{wire} \mathbf{J} \cdot d\mathbf{A}$$

Similarly, the net force per unit length on a wire in a uniform magnetic field B can be found from integrating Eq. 3.6 over the cross sectional area of the wire. Hence

$$\mathbf{F} = \left(\int_{wire} \mathbf{J} \cdot d\mathbf{A} \right) \times \mathbf{B} = \mathbf{I} \times \mathbf{B}$$

Thus, for wire 1 carrying current I into the paper, the θ-directed force is given by

$$F_{1_\theta} = -I B_0 l \sin \alpha$$

and for wire 2 (which carries current in the opposite direction and is located $180°$ away from wire 1)

$$F_{2_\theta} = -L B_0 l \sin \alpha$$

where l is the length of the rotor. The torque T acting on the rotor is given by the sum of the force-moment-arm products for each wire

$$T = -2I B_0 R l \sin \alpha = -2(10)(0.02)(0.05)(0.3) \sin \alpha = -0.006 \sin \alpha \quad \text{N} \cdot \text{m}$$

Practice Problem 3.1

Repeat Example 3.1 for the situation in which the uniform magnetic field points to the right instead of vertically upward as in Fig. 3.2.

Solution

$T = -0.006 \cos \alpha \quad \text{N} \cdot \text{m}$

For situations in which the forces act only on current-carrying elements and which are of simple geometry (such as that of Example 3.1), Eq. 3.6 is generally the simplest and easiest way to calculate the forces acting on the system. Unfortunately, very few practical situations fall into this class. In fact, as discussed in Chapter 1, most electromechanical-energy-conversion devices contain magnetic material; in these systems, forces act directly on the magnetic material and clearly cannot be calculated from Eq. 3.6. Techniques for calculating forces and torques in these systems are discussed in the next section.

3.2 ENERGY BALANCE AND THE ENERGY METHOD

Techniques for calculating the detailed, localized forces acting in sytems with magnetic materials are extremely complex and require detailed knowledge of the field distribution throughout the structure. Fortunately, most electromechanical-energy-conversion devices are constructed of rigid, non-deforming structures. The performance of these devices is typically determined by the net force, or torque, acting on the moving component and it is rarely necessary to calculate the details of the internal force distribution. For example, in a properly designed motor, the motor characteristics are determined by the net accelerating torque acting on the rotor; accompanying forces, which act to squash or deform the rotor, play no significant role in the performance of the motor and generally are not calculated.

Thus, to understand the behavior of rotating machinery, a simple physical picture is quite useful. Associated with the rotor structure is a magnetic field (produced in many machines by currents in windings on the rotor) and similarly with the stator; one can picture them as a set of north and south magnetic poles associated with each structure. Just as a compass needle tries to align with the earth's magnetic field, these two sets of fields attempt to align, and torque is associated with their displacement from alignment. In a motor, the stator magnetic field rotates ahead of that of the rotor, pulling on it and performing work. The opposite is true for a generator, in which the rotor does work on the stator.

We begin with the principle of *conservation of energy* which states that energy is neither created nor destroyed; it is merely changed in form. For example, a golf ball leaves the tee with a certain amount of kinetic energy; this energy is eventually dissipated as heat due to air friction or rolling friction by the time the ball comes to rest on the fairway. Similarly, the kinetic energy of a hammer is eventually dissipated as heat as a nail is driven into a piece of wood. For isolated systems with clearly identifiable boundaries, this fact permits us to keep track of energy in a simple fashion: the net flow of energy into the system across its boundary is equal to the sum of the time rate of change of energy stored in the system.

The technique for calculating forces and torques in the electromechanical-energy-conversion process developed in this chapter and used throughout the book is known as the *energy method* and is based on the principle of conservation of energy. This result, which is a statement of the first law of thermodynamics, is quite general. We apply it in this chapter to electromechanical systems whose predominant energy-storage mechanism is in magnetic fields. In such systems, one can account for energy transfer as

$$\begin{pmatrix} \text{Energy input} \\ \text{from electric} \\ \text{sources} \end{pmatrix} = \begin{pmatrix} \text{Mechanical} \\ \text{energy} \\ \text{output} \end{pmatrix} + \begin{pmatrix} \text{Increase in energy} \\ \text{stored in magnetic} \\ \text{field} \end{pmatrix} + \begin{pmatrix} \text{Energy} \\ \text{converted} \\ \text{into heat} \end{pmatrix}$$

$$(3.7)$$

Equation 3.7 is written so that, in the case of a motor, both the electric and mechanical energy terms have positive values; i.e. electric input power is converted

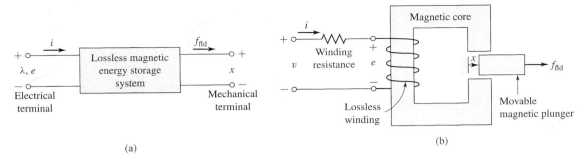

(a)

(b)

Figure 3.3 (a) Schematic magnetic-field electromechanical-energy-conversion device; (b) simple force-producing device.

into mechanical output power. In the case of a generator, in which mechanical input power is converted to electrical output power, both of these terms are negative. In either case, the sign of the heat generation term is such that heat generation within the system results in a flow of thermal energy out of the system.

In the systems which we consider here, the conversion of energy into heat occurs by mechanisms such as ohmic heating due to current flow in the windings of the electric terminals and mechanical friction due to the motion of the system components forming the mechanical terminals. In these systems, it is generally possible to mathematically separate these loss mechanisms from the energy-storage mechanism. In such cases, the interaction between the electric and mechanical terminals, i.e., the electromechanical energy conversion, occurs through the medium of the magnetic stored energy and the device can be represented as a lossless energy-storage system with electric and mechanical terminals as shown in Fig. 3.3a. In systems which can be modeled in this fashion, loss mechanisms can be represented by external elements connected to these terminals: resistances to the electric terminals, and mechanical dampers to the mechanical terminals, and the losses do not need to be considered in calculations involving the electromechanical-energy-conversion process. Figure 3.3b shows an example of such a system; a simple force-producing device with a single coil forming the electric terminal, and a movable plunger serving as the mechanical terminal.

Figure 3.3a can be readily generalized to situations with any number of electric or mechanical terminals. Note that Fig. 3.3a represents a system in which there is stored magnetic energy and the magnetic field serves as the coupling medium between the electric and mechanical terminals. This discussion can be applied equally well to a system with stored electric energy.

The ability to identify a lossless-energy-storage system is the essence of the energy method. It is important to recognize that this is done mathematically as part of the modeling process. It is not possible, of course, to take the resistance out of windings or the friction out of bearings. Instead we are making use of the fact that a model in which this is done is a valid representation of the physical system.

For a lossless energy-storage system, Eq. 3.7 can be written as

$$P_{\text{elec}} = P_{\text{mech}} + \frac{dW_{\text{fld}}}{dt} \tag{3.8}$$

where

$$P_{\text{elec}} = \text{Electric input power}$$

$$P_{\text{mech}} = \text{Mechanical output power}$$

$$\frac{dW_{\text{fld}}}{dt} = \text{Time rate-of-change of the magnetic stored energy}$$

In Fig. 3.3a, the electric terminal has two terminal variables, a voltage e and a current i, and the mechanical terminal also has two terminal variables, a force f_{fld} and a position x. The electrical input power can be written as the product of the voltage e and the current i

$$\frac{dW_{\text{elec}}}{dt} = ei \tag{3.9}$$

and the mechanical output power can be written as the product of the force f_{fld} and the velocity (the time derivative of the position x) as

$$P_{\text{mech}} = f_{\text{fld}} \frac{dx}{dt} \tag{3.10}$$

Re-arranging Eq. 3.8 and substituting Eqs. 3.9 and 3.10 gives

$$\frac{dW_{\text{fld}}}{dt} = ei - f_{\text{fld}} \frac{dx}{dt} \tag{3.11}$$

For a magnetic-energy-storage system, the electrical terminal typically represents a winding such as that shown in Fig. 3.3b. Recognizing that, from Eq. 1.26, the voltage at the terminals of a lossless winding is given by the time-derivative of the winding flux linkages

$$e = \frac{d\lambda}{dt} \tag{3.12}$$

Substitution into Eq. 3.11 and multiplying by dt gives

$$dW_{\text{fld}} = i\,d\lambda - f_{\text{fld}}\,dx \tag{3.13}$$

As shown in Section 3.4, Eq. 3.13 permits us to solve for the force simply as a function of the flux linkage λ and the mechanical terminal position x. Note again that this result comes about as a consequence of our assumption that it is possible to separate the losses out of the physical problem, resulting in a lossless energy-storage system, as in Fig. 3.3a.

Equations 3.11 and 3.13 form the basis for the energy method. This technique is quite powerful in its ability to calculate forces and torques in complex electromechanical-energy-conversion systems. The reader should recognize that this power comes at the expense of a detailed picture of the force-producing mechanism. The forces themselves are produced by such well-known physical phenomena as the

Lorentz force on current carrying elements, described by Eq. 3.6, and the interaction of the magnetic fields with the dipoles in the magnetic material.

3.3 ENERGY IN SINGLY EXCITED MAGNETIC-FIELD SYSTEMS

In Chapters 1 and 2 we were concerned primarily with fixed-geometry magnetic circuits such as those used for transformers and inductors. Energy in those devices is stored in the leakage fields and to some extent in the core itself. However, the stored energy does not enter directly into the transformation process. In this chapter we are dealing with energy-conversion systems; the magnetic circuits have air gaps between the stationary and moving members in which considerable energy is stored in the magnetic field. This field acts as the energy-conversion medium, and its energy is the reservoir between the electric and mechanical systems.

[margin note: energy-conversion medium]

Consider the electromagnetic relay shown schematically in Fig. 3.4. The resistance of the excitation coil is shown as an external resistance R and the mechanical terminal variables are shown as a force f_{fld} produced by the magnetic field directed from the relay to the external mechanical system and a displacement x; mechanical losses can be included as external elements connected to the mechanical terminal. Similarly, the moving armature is shown as being massless; its mass represents mechanical energy storage and can be included as an external mass connected to the mechanical terminal. As a result, the magnetic core and armature constitute a lossless magnetic-energy-storage system as is represented schematically in Fig. 3.3a.

[margin note: example of a magnetic-energy-storage system.]

This relay structure is essentially the same as the magnetic structures analyzed in Chapter 1 in which we saw that the magnetic circuit of Fig. 3.4 can be described by an inductance L which is a function of the geometry of the magnetic structure and the magnetic permeabilities of the various system components. Electromechanical-energy-conversion devices contain air gaps in their magnetic circuits to separate the moving parts and, as discussed in Section 1.1, in most such cases the reluctance of the air gap is much larger than that of the magnetic material. Thus the predominant

[margin note: explaining how this relates to Ch. 1]

Figure 3.4 Schematic of an electromagnetic relay.

energy storage occurs in the air gap, and the properties of the magnetic circuit are determined by the dimensions of the air gap.

Because of the simplicity of the resulting relations, magnetic nonlinearity and core losses are often neglected in the analysis of practical devices. The final results of such approximate analyses can, if necessary, be corrected for the effects of these neglected factors by semi-empirical methods. Consequently, analyses are carried out under the assumption that the mmf and flux are directly proportional for the entire magnetic circuit. Thus the flux linkages λ and current i are considered to be linearly related by an inductance which depends solely on the geometry and hence on the armature position x.

$$\lambda = L(x)i \tag{3.14}$$

where the explicit dependence of L on x has been indicated.

Since the magnetic energy storage system is lossless, it is a *conservative system* and the value of W_{fld} is uniquely specified by the values of λ and x; λ and x are thus referred to as *state variables* since their values uniquely determine the state of the system. Since the magnetic force f_{fld} has been defined as acting from the relay upon the external mechanical system, P_{mech} is defined as the mechanical energy output of the relay, consistent with the derivations of Section 3.2 and Eq. 3.13, which is repeated here showing explicitly the dependence of W_{fld} on λ and x.

$$dW_{\text{fld}}(\lambda, x) = i\, d\lambda - f_{\text{fld}}\, dx \tag{3.15}$$

From this discussion we see that the stored energy W_{fld}, being uniquely determined by the values of λ and x, *is the same regardless of how λ and x are brought to their final values.* Consider Fig. 3.5, in which two separate paths are shown over which Eq. 3.15 can be integrated to find W_{fld} at the point (λ_0, x_0). Path 1 is the general case and is difficult to integrate unless both i and f_{fld} are known explicitly as a function of λ and x. However, because the integration of Eq. 3.15 is path independent, path 2

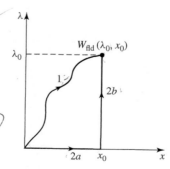

Figure 3.5 Integration paths for W_{fld}.

[handwritten margin notes:]

neglect non-linearity

mmf & flux are directly proportional

How this circuit is dependant on λ and x.

λ and x are state variables that determine P_{mech}

• Easier to determine through path 2 because it is path independent gives the same result and is much easier to integrate. From Eq. 3.15

$$W_{fld}(\lambda_0, x_0) = \int_{path\ 2a} dW_{fld} + \int_{path\ 2b} dW_{fld} \qquad (3.16)$$

Notice that on path 2a, $d\lambda = 0$ and $f_{fld} = 0$ (since $\lambda = 0$ and there can be no magnetic force in the absence of magnetic fields). Thus from Eq. 3.15, $dW_{fld} = 0$ on path 2a. On path 2b, $dx = 0$, and, thus, from Eq. 3.15, Eq. 3.16 reduces to the integral of $i\ d\lambda$ over path 2b (for which $x = x_0$).

$$W_{fld}(\lambda_0, x_0) = \int_0^{\lambda_0} i(\lambda, x_0)\ d\lambda \qquad (3.17)$$

For a linear system in which λ is proportional to i, as in Eq. 3.14, Eq. 3.17 gives

$$W_{fld}(\lambda_0, x_0) = \int_0^{\lambda_0} i(\lambda, x_0)\ d\lambda = \int_0^{\lambda_0} \frac{\lambda}{L(x_0)}\ d\lambda = \frac{1}{2}\frac{\lambda_0^2}{L(x_0)} \qquad (3.18)$$

Note that the point (λ_0, x_0) is arbitrary; the expression for W_{fld} of Eq. 3.18 is valid for all points (λ, x). To emphasize this point, Eq. 3.18 can be re-written as

$$W_{fld}(\lambda, x) = \frac{1}{2}\frac{\lambda^2}{L(x)} \qquad (3.19)$$

It can be shown that the magnetic stored energy can also be expressed in terms of the energy density of the magnetic field integrated over the volume V of the magnetic field. In this case

$$W_{fld} = \int_V \left(\int_0^B \mathbf{H} \cdot d\mathbf{B}' \right) dV \qquad (3.20)$$

For soft magnetic material of constant permeability ($\mathbf{B} = \mu\mathbf{H}$), this reduces to

$$W_{fld} = \int_V \left(\frac{B^2}{2\mu} \right) dV \qquad (3.21)$$

EXAMPLE 3.2

The relay shown in Fig. 3.6a is made from infinitely-permeable magnetic material with a movable plunger, also of infinitely-permeable material. The height of the plunger is much greater than the air-gap length ($h \gg g$). Calculate the magnetic stored energy W_{fld} as a function of plunger position ($0 < x < d$) for $N = 1000$ turns, $g = 2.0$ mm, $d = 0.15$ m, $l = 0.1$ m, and $i = 10$ A.

■ **Solution**

Equation 3.19 can be used to solve for W_{fld} when λ is known. For this situation, i is held constant, and thus it would be useful to have an expression for W_{fld} as a function of i and x. This can be obtained quite simply by substituting Eq. 3.14 into Eq. 3.19, with the result

$$W_{fld} = \frac{1}{2}L(x)i^2$$

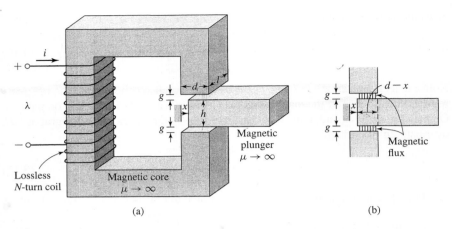

Figure 3.6 (a) Relay with movable plunger for Example 3.2. (b) Detail showing air-gap configuration with the plunger partially removed.

The inductance is given by

$$L(x) = \frac{\mu_0 N^2 A_{gap}}{2g}$$

where A_{gap} is the gap cross-sectional area. From Fig. 3.6b, A_{gap} can be seen to be

$$A_{gap} = l(d - x) = ld\left(1 - \frac{x}{d}\right)$$

Thus

$$L(x) = \frac{\mu_0 N^2 ld(1 - x/d)}{2g}$$

and

$$\begin{aligned}
W_{fld} &= \frac{1}{2}\frac{N^2 \mu_0 ld(1 - x/d)}{2g} i^2 \\
&= \frac{1}{2}\frac{(1000^2)(4\pi \times 10^{-7})(0.1)(0.15)}{2(0.002)} \times 10^2 \left(1 - \frac{x}{d}\right) \\
&= 236\left(1 - \frac{x}{d}\right) \text{ J}
\end{aligned}$$

Practice Problem 3.2

The relay of Fig. 3.6 is modified in such a fashion that the air gaps surrounding the plunger are no longer uniform. The top air-gap length is increased to $g_{top} = 3.5$ mm and that of the bottom gap is increased to $g_{bot} = 2.5$ mm. The number of turns is increased to $N = 1500$. Calculate the stored energy as a function of plunger position ($0 < x < d$) for a current of $i = 5$ A.

Solution

$$W_{fld} = 88.5\left(1 - \frac{x}{d}\right) \text{ J}$$

In this section we have seen the relationship between the magnetic stored energy and the electric and mechanical terminal variables for a system which can be represented in terms of a lossless-magnetic-energy-storage element. If we had chosen for our example a device with a rotating mechanical terminal instead of a linearly displacing one, the results would have been identical except that force would be replaced by torque and linear displacement by angular displacement. In Section 3.4 we see how knowledge of the magnetic stored energy permits us to solve for the mechanical force and torque.

3.4 DETERMINATION OF MAGNETIC FORCE AND TORQUE FROM ENERGY

As discussed in Section 3.3, for a lossless magnetic-energy-storage system, the magnetic stored energy W_{fld} is a *state function*, determined uniquely by the values of the independent state variables λ and x. This is shown explicitly by Eq. 3.15, repeated here

$$dW_{fld}(\lambda, x) = i\, d\lambda - f_{fld}\, dx \qquad (3.22)$$

For any state function of two independent variables, e.g., $F(x_1, x_2)$, the total differential of F with respect to the two state variables x_1 and x_2 can be written

$$dF(x_1, x_2) = \frac{\partial F}{\partial x_1}\bigg|_{x_2} dx_1 + \frac{\partial F}{\partial x_2}\bigg|_{x_1} dx_2 \qquad (3.23)$$

It is extremely important to recognize that the partial derivatives in Eq. 3.23 are each taken by holding the opposite state variable constant.

Equation 3.23 is valid for any state function F and hence it is certainly valid for W_{fld}; thus

$$dW_{fld}(\lambda, x) = \frac{\partial W_{fld}}{\partial \lambda}\bigg|_{x} d\lambda + \frac{\partial W_{fld}}{dx}\bigg|_{\lambda} dx \qquad (3.24)$$

Since λ and x are independent variables, Eqs. 3.22 and 3.24 must be equal for all values of $d\lambda$ and dx, and so, equating terms, we see that

$$i = \frac{\partial W_{fld}(\lambda, x)}{\partial \lambda}\bigg|_{x} \qquad (3.25)$$

where the partial derivative is taken while holding x constant and

$$f_{fld} = -\frac{\partial W_{fld}(\lambda, x)}{\partial x}\bigg|_{\lambda} \qquad (3.26)$$

in this case holding λ constant while taking the partial derivative.

This is the result we have been seeking. Once we know W_{fld} as a function of λ and x, Eq. 3.25 can be used to solve for $i(\lambda, x)$. More importantly, Eq. 3.26 can be used to solve for the mechanical force $f_{fld}(\lambda, x)$. It cannot be over-emphasized that *the partial derivative of Eq. 3.26 is taken while holding the flux linkages λ constant.* This is easily done provided W_{fld} is a known function of λ and x. Note that this is purely a mathematical requirement and has nothing to do with whether λ is held constant when operating the actual device.

The force f_{fld} is determined from Eq. 3.26 directly in terms of the electrical state variable λ. If we then want to express the force as a function of i, we can do so by substituting the appropriate expression for λ as a function of i into the expression for f_{fld} that is obtained by using Eq. 3.26. Note that this substitution must be done only after the partial derivative is taken.

For linear magnetic systems for which $\lambda = L(x)i$, the energy is expressed by Eq. 3.19 and the force can be found by direct substitution in Eq. 3.26

$$f_{fld} = -\frac{\partial}{\partial x}\left(\frac{1}{2}\frac{\lambda^2}{L(x)}\right)\Bigg|_{\lambda} = \frac{\lambda^2}{2L(x)^2}\frac{dL(x)}{dx} \tag{3.27}$$

At this point, the force can be expressed in terms of the current i simply by substitution of $\lambda = L(x)i$

$$f_{fld} = \frac{i^2}{2}\frac{dL(x)}{dx} \tag{3.28}$$

EXAMPLE 3.3

Table 3.1 contains data from an experiment in which the inductance of a solenoid was measured as a function of position x, where $x = 0$ corresponds to the solenoid being fully retracted.

Table 3.1   Data for Example 3.3.

x [cm]	0	0.2	0.4	0.6	0.8	1.0	1.2	1.4	1.6	1.8	2.0
L [mH]	2.8	2.26	1.78	1.52	1.34	1.26	1.20	1.16	1.13	1.11	1.10

Plot the solenoid force as a function of position for a current of 0.75 A over the range $0.2 \leq x \leq 1.8$ cm.

■ Solution

The solution is most easily obtained using MATLAB. First, a fourth-order polynomial fit of the inductance as a function of x is obtained using the MATLAB function *polyfit*. The result is of the form

$$L(x) = a(1)\,x^4 + a(2)\,x^3 + a(3)\,x^2 + a(4)\,x + a(5)$$

Figure 3.7a shows a plot of the data points along with the results of the polynomial fit.

Once this fit has been obtained, it is a straightforward matter to calculate the force from Eq. 3.28.

$$f_{fld} = \frac{i^2}{2}\frac{dL(x)}{dx} = \frac{i^2}{2}(4a(1)\,x^3 + 3a(2)\,x^2 + 2a(3)\,x + a(4))$$

This force is plotted in Figure 3.7b. Note that the force is negative, which means that it is acting in such a direction as to pull the solenoid inwards towards $x = 0$.

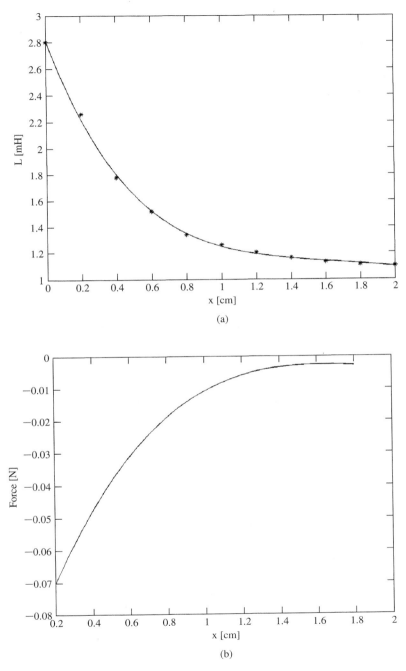

Figure 3.7 Example 3.3. (a) Polynomial curve fit of inductance. (b) Force as a function of position x for $i = 0.75$ A.

Here is the MATLAB script:

```
clc
clear

% Here is the data:  x in cm, L in mH
xdata = [0 0.2 0.4 0.6 0.8 1.0 1.2 1.4 1.6 1.8 2.0];
Ldata = [2.8 2.26 1.78 1.52 1.34 1.26 1.20 1.16 1.13 1.11 1.10];

%Convert to SI units
x = xdata*1.e-2;
L = Ldata*1.e-3;

len = length(x);
xmax = x(len);

% Use polyfit to perform a 4'rd order fit of L to x.  Store
% the polynomial coefficients in vector a. The fit will be
% of the form:
%
%          Lfit = a(1)*x^4 + a(2)*x^3 + a(3)*x^2 + a(4)*x + a(5);
%

a = polyfit(x,L,4);

% Let's check the fit

n = 1:101;
xfit = xmax*(n-1)/100;
   Lfit = a(1)*xfit.^4 + a(2)*xfit.^3 + a(3)*xfit.^2 ...
   + a(4)*xfit + a(5);

% Plot the data and then the fit to compare (convert xfit to cm and
% Lfit to mH)

plot(xdata,Ldata,'*')
hold
plot(xfit*100,Lfit*1000)
hold
xlabel('x [cm]')
ylabel('L [mH]')

fprintf('\n Paused.  Hit any key to plot the force.\n')
pause;
% Now plot the force.  The force will be given by
%
```

```
%     i^2      dL       i^2
%     ---   *  ----  =  ---  ( 4*a(1)*x^3 + 3*a(2)*x^2+ 2*a(3)*x + a(4))
%      2       dx        2

%Set current to 0.75 A
I = 0.75;

n = 1:101;
xfit = 0.002+ .016*(n-1)/100;
F = 4*a(1)*xfit.^3 + 3* a(2)*xfit.^2 + 2*a(3)*xfit + a(4);
F = (I^2/2)*F;

plot(xfit*100,F)
xlabel('x [cm]')
ylabel('Force [N]')
```

An external controller is connected to the solenoid of Example 3.3 which maintains the coil flux linkages constant at $\lambda = 1.5$ mWb. Plot the resultant solenoid force over the range $0.2 \leq x \leq 1.8$ cm.

Solution

The resultant force is plotted in Fig. 3.8.

Figure 3.8 Practice problem 3.3. Plot of force vs. x for $\lambda = 1.5$ mWb.

Rotation
has Torge and θ
rotating
instead of
λ and i

For a system with a rotating mechanical terminal, the mechanical terminal variables become the angular displacement θ and the torque T_{fld}. In this case, Eq. 3.22 becomes

Rotating Systems

$$dW_{\text{fld}}(\lambda, \theta) = i\, d\lambda - T_{\text{fld}}\, d\theta \qquad (3.29)$$

where the explicit dependence of W_{fld} on state variables λ and θ has been indicated.

By analogy to the development that led to Eq. 3.26, the torque can be found from the negative of the partial derivative of the energy with respect to θ taken holding λ constant

How we
can determine
torque given
the points
we have.

$$T_{\text{fld}} = -\frac{\partial W_{\text{fld}}(\lambda, \theta)}{\partial \theta}\bigg|_{\lambda} \qquad (3.30)$$

For linear magnetic systems for which $\lambda = L(\theta)i$, by analogy to Eq. 3.19 the energy is given by

$$W_{\text{fld}}(\lambda, \theta) = \frac{1}{2}\frac{\lambda^2}{L(\theta)} \qquad (3.31)$$

The torque is therefore given by

$$T_{\text{fld}} = -\frac{\partial}{\partial \theta}\left(\frac{1}{2}\frac{\lambda^2}{L(\theta)}\right)\bigg|_{\lambda} = \frac{1}{2}\frac{\lambda^2}{L(\theta)^2}\frac{dL(\theta)}{d\theta} \qquad (3.32)$$

which can be expressed indirectly in terms of the current i as

$$T_{\text{fld}} = \frac{i^2}{2}\frac{dL(\theta)}{d\theta} \qquad (3.33)$$

EXAMPLE 3.4

The magnetic circuit of Fig. 3.9 consists of a single-coil stator and an oval rotor. Because the air-gap is nonuniform, the coil inductance varies with rotor angular position, measured between the magnetic axis of the stator coil and the major axis of the rotor, as

$$L(\theta) = L_0 + L_2\cos(2\theta)$$

where $L_0 = 10.6$ mH and $L_2 = 2.7$ mH. Note the second-harmonic variation of inductance with rotor angle θ. This is consistent with the fact that the inductance is unchanged if the rotor is rotated through an angle of $180°$.

Finding
torque
given
angular
position.

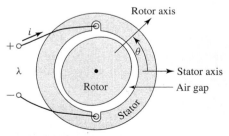

Figure 3.9   Magnetic circuit for Example 3.4.

Find the torque as a function of θ for a coil current of 2 A.

■ Solution

From Eq. 3.33

$$T_{\text{fld}}(\theta) = \frac{i^2}{2} \frac{dL(\theta)}{d\theta} = \frac{i^2}{2} \left(-2L_2 \sin(2\theta) \right)$$

Numerical substitution gives

$$T_{\text{fld}}(\theta) = -(1.08 \times 10^{-2}) \sin(2\theta) \quad \text{N} \cdot \text{m}$$

Note that in this case the torque acts in such a direction as to pull the rotor axis in alignment with the coil axis and hence to maximize the coil inductance.

Practice Problem 3.4

The inductance of a coil on a magnetic circuit similar to that of Fig. 3.9 is found to vary with rotor position as

$$L(\theta) = L_0 + L_2 \cos(2\theta) + L_4 \sin(4\theta)$$

where $L_0 = 25.4$ mH, $L_2 = 8.3$ mH and $L_4 = 1.8$ mH. (a) Find the torque as a function of θ for a winding current of 3.5 A. (b) Find a rotor position θ_{max} that produces the largest negative torque.

Solution

a. $T_{\text{fld}}(\theta) = -0.1017 \sin(2\theta) + 0.044 \cos(4\theta) \quad \text{N} \cdot \text{m}$

b. The largest negative torque occurs when $\theta = 45°$ and $\theta = 225°$. This can be determined analytically, but it is helpful to plot the torque using MATLAB.

3.5 DETERMINATION OF MAGNETIC FORCE AND TORQUE FROM COENERGY

A mathematical manipulation of Eq. 3.22 can be used to define a new state function, known as the *coenergy*, from which the force can be obtained directly as a function of the current. The selection of energy or coenergy as the state function is purely a matter of convenience; they both give the same result, but one or the other may be simpler analytically, depending on the desired result and the characteristics of the system being analyzed.

The coenergy W_{fld}' is defined as a function of i and x such that

$$W_{\text{fld}}'(i, x) = i\lambda - W_{\text{fld}}(\lambda, x) \tag{3.34}$$

The desired derivation is carried out by using the differential of $i\lambda$

$$d(i\lambda) = i \, d\lambda + \lambda \, di \tag{3.35}$$

and the differential of $dW_{\text{fld}}(\lambda, x)$ from Eq. 3.22. From Eq. 3.34

$$dW_{\text{fld}}'(i, x) = d(i\lambda) - dW_{\text{fld}}(\lambda, x) \tag{3.36}$$

[handwritten margin note: derivation to come up with Co-energy of a as Force to a function of current]

Substitution of Eqs. 3.22 and 3.35 into Eq. 3.36 results in

$$dW'_{fld}(i, x) = \lambda \, di + f_{fld} \, dx \tag{3.37}$$

From Eq. 3.37, the coenergy $W'_{fld}(i, x)$ can be seen to be a state function of the two independent variables i and x. Thus, its differential can be expressed as

$$dW'_{fld}(i, x) = \left. \frac{\partial W'_{fld}}{\partial i} \right|_x di + \left. \frac{\partial W'_{fld}}{\partial x} \right|_i dx \tag{3.38}$$

Equations 3.37 and 3.38 must be equal for all values of di and dx; thus

$$\lambda = \left. \frac{\partial W'_{fld}(i, x)}{\partial i} \right|_x \tag{3.39}$$

$$f_{fld} = \left. \frac{\partial W'_{fld}(i, x)}{\partial x} \right|_i \tag{3.40}$$

Equation 3.40 gives the mechanical force directly in terms of i and x. Note that *the partial derivative in Eq. 3.40 is taken while holding i constant;* thus W'_{fld} must be a known function of i and x. For any given system, Eqs. 3.26 and 3.40 will give the same result; the choice as to which to use to calculate the force is dictated by user preference and convenience.

By analogy to the derivation of Eq. 3.17, the coenergy can be found from the integral of $\lambda \, di$

$$W'_{fld}(i, x) = \int_0^i \lambda(i', x) \, di' \tag{3.41}$$

For linear magnetic systems for which $\lambda = L(x)i$, the coenergy is therefore given by

$$W'_{fld}(i, x) = \frac{1}{2}L(x)i^2 \tag{3.42}$$

and the force can be found from Eq. 3.40

$$f_{fld} = \frac{i^2}{2}\frac{dL(x)}{dx} \tag{3.43}$$

which, as expected, is identical to the expression given by Eq. 3.28.

Note that for linear systems, substitution of $L(x)i$ for λ in Eq. 3.19 shows that numerically, $W'_{fld} = W_{fld}$. This fact is in fact used to solve for W_{fld} in Example 3.2. However, it is important to recognize that when calculating force from energy using Eq. 3.26, the energy must be expressed explicitly in terms of λ in the form of Eq. 3.19. Similarly, when calculating force from coenergy using Eq. 3.40, the energy must be expressed explicitly in terms of i in the form of Eq. 3.42.

For a system with a rotating mechanical displacement, the coenergy can be expressed in terms of the current and the angular displacement θ

$$W'_{fld}(i, \theta) = \int_0^i \lambda(i', \theta) \, di' \tag{3.44}$$

and the torque is given by

$$T_{\text{fld}} = \left. \frac{\partial W'_{\text{fld}}(i, \theta)}{\partial \theta} \right|_i \tag{3.45}$$

[handwritten: angular displacement, Torque, coenergy]

If the system is magnetically linear,

$$W'_{\text{fld}}(i, \theta) = \frac{1}{2} L(\theta) i^2 \tag{3.46}$$

and

$$T_{\text{fld}} = \frac{i^2}{2} \frac{dL(\theta)}{d\theta} \tag{3.47}$$

which is identical to Eq. 3.33.

In field-theory terms, for soft magnetic materials (for which $\mathbf{B} = 0$ when $\mathbf{H} = 0$), it can be shown that

$$W'_{\text{fld}} = \int_V \left(\int_0^{H_0} \mathbf{B} \cdot d\mathbf{H} \right) dV \tag{3.48}$$

[handwritten: soft magnetic material]

For soft magnetic material with constant permeability ($\mathbf{B} = \mu \mathbf{H}$), this reduces to

$$W'_{\text{fld}} = \int_V \frac{\mu H^2}{2} \, dV \tag{3.49}$$

[handwritten: constant "]

For permanent-magnet (hard) materials such as those which are discussed in Chapter 1 (for which $B = 0$ when $H = H_c$), the energy and coenergy are equal to zero when $B = 0$ and hence when $H = H_c$. Thus, although Eq. 3.20 still applies for calculating the energy, Eq. 3.48 must be modified to the form

$$W'_{\text{fld}} = \int_V \left(\int_{H_c}^{H_0} \mathbf{B} \cdot d\mathbf{H} \right) dV \tag{3.50}$$

[handwritten: Hard]

Note that Eq. 3.50 can be considered to apply in general since soft magnetic materials can be considered to be simply hard magnetic materials with $H_c = 0$, in which case Eq. 3.50 reduces to Eq. 3.48.

In some cases, magnetic circuit representations may be difficult to realize or may not yield solutions of the desired accuracy. Often such situations are characterized by complex geometries and/or magnetic materials driven deeply into saturation. In such situations, numerical techniques can be used to evaluate the system energy using Eq. 3.20 or the coenergy using either Eqs. 3.48 or 3.50.

[handwritten: when to use these equations]

One such technique, known as the *finite-element method*,[1] has become widely used. For example, such programs, which are available commercially from a number of vendors, can be used to calculate the system coenergy for various values of the displacement x of a linear-displacement actuator (making sure to hold the current constant as x is varied). The force can then be obtained from Eq. 3.40, with the derivative of coenergy with respect to x being calculated numerically from the results of the finite-element analysis.

---

[1] See, for example, P. P. Sylvester and R. L. Ferrari, *Finite Elements for Electrical Engineers,* Cambridge University Press, New York, 1983.

EXAMPLE 3.5

For the relay of Example 3.2, find the force on the plunger as a function of x when the coil is driven by a controller which produces a current as a function of x of the form

$$i(x) = I_0 \left(\frac{x}{d}\right) \text{ A}$$

■ **Solution**

From Example 3.2

$$L(x) = \frac{\mu_0 N^2 l d (1 - x/d)}{2g}$$

This is a magnetically-linear system for which the force can be calculated from Eq. 3.43 as

$$f_{\text{fld}} = \frac{i^2}{2} \frac{dL(x)}{dx} = -\frac{i^2}{2} \left(\frac{\mu_0 N^2 l}{2g}\right)$$

Substituting for $i(x)$, the expression for the force as a function of x can be determined as

$$f_{\text{fld}} = -\frac{I_0^2 \mu_0 N^2 l}{4g} \left(\frac{x}{d}\right)^2$$

Note that from Eq. 3.42, the coenergy for this system is equal to

$$W'_{\text{fld}}(i, x) = \frac{i^2}{2} L(x) = \frac{i^2}{2} \frac{N^2 \mu_0 l d (1 - x/d)}{2g}$$

and the derivative of this expression with respect to x gives the expected expression for the force in terms of the current i.

In this example, one might be tempted to introduce the expression for $i(x)$ directly into the coenergy expression, in which case the coenergy would be given by

$$W'_{\text{fld}}(i, x) = \frac{I_0^2 N^2 \mu_0 l d (1 - x/d)}{4g} \left(\frac{x}{d}\right)^2$$

Although this is a perfectly correct expression for the coenergy as a function of x under the specified operating conditions, if one were to attempt to calculate the force from taking the partial derivative of this expression for W'_{fld} with respect to x, the resultant expression would not give the correct expression for the force. The reason for this is quite simple: As seen from Eq. 3.40, the partial derivative must be taken holding the current constant. Having substituted the expression for $i(x)$ to obtain this equation for the coenergy, the current is no longer a constant and this requirement cannot be met. This illustrates the problems that can arise if the various force and torque expressions developed here are misapplied.

Practice Problem 3.5

Consider a plunger whose inductance varies as

$$L(x) = L_0(1 - (x/d)^2)$$

Find the force on the plunger as a function of x when the coil is driven by a controller which produces a current as a function of x of the form

$$i(x) = I_0 \left(\frac{x}{d}\right)^2 \text{ A}$$

Solution

$$f_{\text{fld}} = -\left(\frac{L_0 I_0^2}{d}\right)\left(\frac{x}{d}\right)^5$$

For a magnetically linear system, the energy and coenergy are numerically equal: $\frac{1}{2}\lambda^2/L = \frac{1}{2}Li^2$. The same is true for the energy and coenergy densities: $\frac{1}{2}B^2/\mu = \frac{1}{2}\mu H^2$. For a nonlinear system in which λ and i or B and H are not linearly proportional, the two functions are not even numerically equal. A graphical interpretation of the energy and coenergy for a nonlinear system is shown in Fig. 3.10. The area between the $\lambda - i$ curve and the vertical axis, equal to the integral of $i\,d\lambda$, is the energy. The area to the horizontal axis given by the integral of $\lambda\,di$ is the coenergy. For this singly-excited system, the sum of the energy and coenergy is, by definition (see Eq. 3.34),

$$W_{\text{fld}} + W'_{\text{fld}} = \lambda i \tag{3.51}$$

The force produced by the magnetic field in a device such as that of Fig. 3.4 for some particular value of x and i or λ cannot, of course, depend upon whether it is calculated from the energy or coenergy. A graphical illustration will demonstrate that both methods must give the same result.

Assume that the relay armature of Fig. 3.4 is at position x so that the device is operating at point a in Fig. 3.11a. The partial derivative of Eq. 3.26 can be interpreted as the limit of $-\Delta W_{\text{fld}}/\Delta x$ with λ constant as $\Delta x \to 0$. If we allow a change Δx, the change $-\Delta W_{\text{fld}}$ is shown by the shaded area in Fig. 3.11a. Hence, the force $f_{\text{fld}} = (\text{shaded area})/\Delta x$ as $\Delta x \to 0$. On the other hand, the partial derivative of Eq. 3.40 can

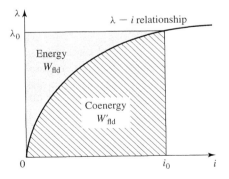

Figure 3.10 Graphical interpretation of energy and coenergy in a singly excited system.

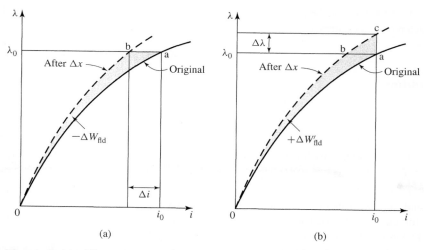

Figure 3.11 Effect of Δx on the energy and coenergy of a singly-excited device: (a) change of energy with λ held constant; (b) change of coenergy with i held constant.

be interpreted as the limit of $\Delta W'_{fld}/\Delta x$ with i constant as $\Delta x \rightarrow 0$. This perturbation of the device is shown in Fig. 3.11b; the force $f_{fld} = $ (shaded area)$/\Delta x$ as $\Delta x \rightarrow 0$. The shaded areas differ only by the small triangle abc of sides Δi and $\Delta \lambda$, so that in the limit the shaded areas resulting from Δx at constant λ or at constant i are equal. Thus the force produced by the magnetic field is independent of whether the determination is made with energy or coenergy.

Equations 3.26 and 3.40 express the mechanical force of electrical origin in terms of partial derivatives of the energy and coenergy functions $W_{fld}(\lambda, x)$ and $W'_{fld}(i, x)$. It is important to note two things about them: the variables in terms of which they must be expressed and their algebraic signs. Physically, of course, the force depends on the dimension x and the magnetic field. The field (and hence the energy or coenergy) can be specified in terms of flux linkage λ, or current i, or related variables. We again emphasize that the selection of the energy or coenergy function as a basis for analysis is a matter of convenience.

The algebraic signs in Eqs. 3.26 and 3.40 show that the force acts in a direction to decrease the magnetic field stored energy at constant flux or to increase the coenergy at constant current. In a singly-excited device, the force acts to increase the inductance by pulling on members so as to reduce the reluctance of the magnetic path linking the winding.

EXAMPLE 3.6

The magnetic circuit shown in Fig. 3.12 is made of high-permeability electrical steel. The rotor is free to turn about a vertical axis. The dimensions are shown in the figure.

a. Derive an expression for the torque acting on the rotor in terms of the dimensions and the magnetic field in the two air gaps. Assume the reluctance of the steel to be negligible (i.e., $\mu \rightarrow \infty$) and neglect the effects of fringing.

Figure 3.12 Magnetic system of Example 3.6.

b. The maximum flux density in the overlapping portions of the air gaps is to be limited to 1.65 T to avoid excessive saturation of the steel. Compute the maximum torque for $r_1 = 2.5$ cm, $h = 1.8$ cm, and $g = 3$ mm.

■ **Solution**

a. There are two air gaps in series, each of length g, and hence because the permeability of the steel is assumed infinite, the air-gap field intensity H_{ag} is equal to

$$H_{ag} = \frac{Ni}{2g}$$

B_{steel} must remain finite and because $\mu \rightarrow \infty$, $H_{steel} = B_{steel}/\mu$ and and the coenergy density (Eq. 3.49) in the steel are zero ($\mu H_{steel}^2/2 = B_{steel}^2/2\mu = 0$). Hence the system coenergy is equal to that of the air gaps. The air-gap coenergy density in the is $\mu_0 H_{ag}^2/2$ and the volume of the two overlapping air gaps is $2gh(r_1 + 0.5g)\theta$. Thus, the coenergy is equal to the product of the air-gap coenergy density and the air-gap volume

$$W'_{ag} = \left(\frac{\mu_0 H_{ag}^2}{2}\right)\left(2gh(r_1 + 0.5g)\theta\right) = \frac{\mu_0(Ni)^2 h(r_1 + 0.5g)\theta}{4g}$$

and thus, from Eq. 3.40

$$T_{fld} = \left.\frac{\partial W'_{ag}(i, \theta)}{\partial \theta}\right|_i = \frac{\mu_0(Ni)^2 h(r_1 + 0.5g)}{4g}$$

The sign of the torque is positive, hence acting in the direction to increase the overlap angle θ and thus to align the rotor with the stator pole faces.

b. For $B_{ag} = 1.65$ T,

$$H_{ag} = \frac{B_{ag}}{\mu_0} = \frac{1.65}{4\pi \times 10^{-7}} = 1.31 \times 10^6 \text{ A/m}$$

and thus

$$Ni = 2g H_{ag} = 2(3 \times 10^{-3})(1.31 \times 10^6) = 7860 \text{ A-turns}$$

T_{fld} can now be calculated as

$$T_{fld} = \frac{4\pi \times 10^{-7}(7860)^2(1.8 \times 10^{-2})(2.5 \times 10^{-2} + 0.5(3 \times 10^{-3}))}{4(3 \times 10^{-3})}$$

$$= 3.09 \text{ N} \cdot \text{m}$$

<hr>

Practice Problem 3.6

a. Write an expression for the inductance of the magnetic circuit of Fig. 3.12 as a function of θ.

b. Using this expression, derive an expression for the torque acting on the rotor as a function of the winding current i and the rotor angle θ.

Solution

a.

$$L(\theta) = \frac{\mu_0 N^2 h(r_1 + 0.5g)\theta}{2g}$$

b.

$$T_{fld} = \frac{i^2}{2}\frac{dL(\theta)}{d\theta} = \frac{i^2}{2}\left(\frac{\mu_0 N^2 h(r_1 + 0.5g)}{2g}\right)$$

<hr>

3.6 MULTIPLY EXCITED MAGNETIC-FIELD SYSTEMS

Many electromechanical devices have multiple electrical terminals. In measurement systems it is often desirable to obtain torques proportional to two electric signals; a meter which determines power as the product of voltage and current is one example. Similarly, most electromechanical-energy-conversion devices consist of multiply excited magnetic-field systems.

Analysis of these systems follows directly from the techniques discussed in previous sections. This section illustrates these techniques based on a system with two electric terminals. A schematic representation of a simple system with two electrical terminals and one mechanical terminal is shown in Fig. 3.13. In this case it represents a system with rotary motion, and the mechanical terminal variables are torque T_{fld} and angular displacement θ. Since there are three terminals, the system must be described in terms of three independent variables; these can be the mechanical angle θ along with the flux linkages λ_1 and λ_2, currents i_1 and i_2, or a hybrid set including one current and one flux.[2]

<hr>

[2] See, for example, H. H. Woodson and J. R. Melcher, *Electromechanical Dynamics,* Wiley, New York, 1968, Pt. I, Chap. 3.

Figure 3.13 Multiply excited magnetic energy storage system.

When the fluxes are used, the differential energy function $dW_{fld}(\lambda_1, \lambda_2, \theta)$ cor-responding to Eq. 3.29 is

Just add additional to eq. 3.29

$$dW_{fld}(\lambda_1, \lambda_2, \theta) = i_1\, d\lambda_1 + i_2\, d\lambda_2 - T_{fld}\, d\theta \tag{3.52}$$

and in direct analogy to the previous development for a singly-excited system

$$i_1 = \left.\frac{\partial W_{fld}(\lambda_1, \lambda_2, \theta)}{\partial \lambda_1}\right|_{\lambda_2, \theta} \tag{3.53}$$

$$i_2 = \left.\frac{\partial W_{fld}(\lambda_1, \lambda_2, \theta)}{\partial \lambda_2}\right|_{\lambda_1, \theta} \tag{3.54}$$

and

$$T_{fld} = -\left.\frac{\partial W_{fld}(\lambda_1, \lambda_2, \theta)}{\partial \theta}\right|_{\lambda_1, \lambda_2} \tag{3.55}$$

multiple electric sources

Note that in each of these equations, *the partial derivative with respect to each independent variable must be taken holding the other two independent variables constant.*

The energy W_{fld} can be found by integrating Eq. 3.52. As in the singly-excited case, although the energy at any given point is independent of the integration path, this integration is most conveniently done by holding λ_1 and λ_2 fixed at zero and integrating first over θ; under these conditions, T_{fld} is zero, and thus this integral is zero. One can then integrate over λ_2 (while holding λ_1 zero) and finally over λ_1. Thus

finding the energy:

$$W_{fld}(\lambda_{1_0}, \lambda_{2_0}, \theta_0) = \int_0^{\lambda_{2_0}} i_2(\lambda_1 = 0, \lambda_2, \theta = \theta_0)\, d\lambda_2$$

$$+ \int_0^{\lambda_{1_0}} i_1(\lambda_1, \lambda_2 = \lambda_{2_0}, \theta = \theta_0)\, d\lambda_1 \tag{3.56}$$

This path of integration is illustrated in Fig. 3.14 and is directly analogous to that of Fig. 3.5. One could, of course, interchange the order of integration for λ_2 and λ_1. It is extremely important to recognize however that, for the expression of Eq. 3.56, the state variables are integrated over a specific path over which only one state variable is varied at a time; for example, λ_1 is maintained initially at zero while integrating over λ_2. This is explicitly indicated in Eq. 3.56 and can also be seen from Fig. 3.14. Failure to observe the constraints imposed by a chosen integration path is one of the most common errors made in analyzing such systems.

make sure you integrate in the correct order

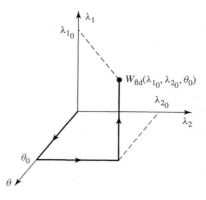

Figure 3.14 Integration path to obtain $W_{fld}(\lambda_{1_0}, \lambda_{2_0}, \theta_0)$.

In a magnetically-linear system, the relationships between λ and i can be specified in terms of inductances as is discussed in Section 1.2

$$\lambda_1 = L_{11}i_1 + L_{12}i_2 \tag{3.57}$$

$$\lambda_2 = L_{21}i_1 + L_{22}i_2 \tag{3.58}$$

where

$$L_{12} = L_{21} \tag{3.59}$$

Here the inductances are, in general, functions of angular position θ.

These equations can be inverted to obtain expressions for the is as a function of the θs

$$i_1 = \frac{L_{22}\lambda_1 - L_{12}\lambda_2}{D} \tag{3.60}$$

[handwritten: Determinant]

$$i_2 = \frac{-L_{21}\lambda_1 + L_{11}\lambda_2}{D} \tag{3.61}$$

where

$$D = L_{11}L_{22} - L_{12}L_{21} \tag{3.62}$$

The energy for this linear system can be found from Eq. 3.56

$$
\begin{aligned}
W_{fld}(\lambda_{1_0}, \lambda_{2_0}, \theta_0) &= \int_0^{\lambda_{2_0}} \frac{L_{11}(\theta_0)\lambda_2}{D(\theta_0)} \, d\lambda_2 \\
&\quad + \int_0^{\lambda_{1_0}} \frac{(L_{22}(\theta_0)\lambda_1 - L_{12}(\theta_0)\lambda_{2_0})}{D(\theta_0)} \, d\lambda_1 \\
&= \frac{1}{2D(\theta_0)}L_{11}(\theta_0)\lambda_{2_0}^2 + \frac{1}{2D(\theta_0)}L_{22}(\theta_0)\lambda_{1_0}^2 \\
&\quad - \frac{L_{12}(\theta_0)}{D(\theta_0)}\lambda_{1_0}\lambda_{2_0}
\end{aligned}
\tag{3.63}
$$

[handwritten margin note: different for uses for the current and λ and inductance]

where the dependence of the inductances and the determinant $D(\theta)$ on the angular displacement θ has been explicitly indicated.

In Section 3.5, the coenergy function was defined to permit determination of force and torque directly in terms of the current for a single-winding system. A similar coenergy function can be defined in the case of systems with two windings as

$$W'_{\text{fld}}(i_1, i_2, \theta) = \lambda_1 i_1 + \lambda_2 i_2 - W_{\text{fld}} \qquad (3.64)$$

It is a state function of the two terminal currents and the mechanical displacement. Its differential, following substitution of Eq. 3.52, is given by

$$dW'_{\text{fld}}(i_1, i_2, \theta) = \lambda_1 \, di_1 + \lambda_2 \, di_2 + T_{\text{fld}} \, d\theta \qquad (3.65)$$

From Eq. 3.65 we see that

$$\lambda_1 = \left. \frac{\partial W'_{\text{fld}}(i_1, i_2, \theta)}{\partial i_1} \right|_{i_2, \theta} \qquad (3.66)$$

$$\lambda_2 = \left. \frac{\partial W'_{\text{fld}}(i_1, i_2, \theta)}{\partial i_2} \right|_{i_1, \theta} \qquad (3.67)$$

(handwritten: Co-energy)

Most significantly, the torque can now be determined directly in terms of the currents as

$$T_{\text{fld}} = \left. \frac{\partial W'_{\text{fld}}(i_1, i_2, \theta)}{\partial \theta} \right|_{i_1, i_2} \qquad (3.68)$$

(handwritten: — Torque)

Analogous to Eq. 3.56, the coenergy can be found as

$$W'_{\text{fld}}(i_{1_0}, i_{2_0}, \theta_0) = \int_0^{i_{2_0}} \lambda_2(i_1 = 0, i_2, \theta = \theta_0) \, di_2$$

$$+ \int_0^{i_{1_0}} \lambda_1(i_1, i_2 = i_{2_0}, \theta = \theta_0) \, di_1 \qquad (3.69)$$

For the linear system of Eqs. 3.57 to 3.59

$$W'_{\text{fld}}(i_1, i_2, \theta) = \frac{1}{2} L_{11}(\theta) i_1^2 + \frac{1}{2} L_{22}(\theta) i_2^2 + L_{12}(\theta) i_1 i_2 \qquad (3.70)$$

(handwritten: — Linear system)

For such a linear system, the torque can be found either from the energy of Eq. 3.63 using Eq. 3.55 or from the coenergy of Eq. 3.70 using Eq. 3.68. It is at this point that the utility of the coenergy function becomes apparent. The energy expression of Eq. 3.63 is a complex function of displacement, and its derivative is even more so. Alternatively, the coenergy function is a relatively simple function of displacement, and from its derivative a straightforward expression for torque can be determined as a function of the winding currents i_1 and i_2 as

$$T_{\text{fld}} = \left. \frac{\partial W'_{\text{fld}}(i_1, i_2, \theta)}{\partial \theta} \right|_{i_1, i_2}$$

$$= \frac{i_1^2}{2} \left(\frac{dL_{11}(\theta)}{d\theta} \right) + \frac{i_2^2}{2} \left(\frac{dL_{22}(\theta)}{d\theta} \right) + i_1 i_2 \left(\frac{dL_{12}(\theta)}{d\theta} \right) \qquad (3.71)$$

Systems with more than two electrical terminals are handled in analogous fashion. As with the two-terminal-pair system above, the use of a coenergy function of the terminal currents greatly simplifies the determination of torque or force.

EXAMPLE 3.7

In the system shown in Fig. 3.15, the inductances in henrys are given as $L_{11} = (3 + \cos 2\theta) \times 10^{-3}$; $L_{12} = 0.3 \cos \theta$; $L_{22} = 30 + 10 \cos 2\theta$. Find and plot the torque $T_{fld}(\theta)$ for current $i_1 = 0.8$ A and $i_2 = 0.01$ A.

■ **Solution**

The torque can be determined from Eq. 3.71.

$$T_{fld} = \frac{i_1^2}{2}\left(\frac{dL_{11}(\theta)}{d\theta}\right) + \frac{i_2^2}{2}\left(\frac{dL_{22}(\theta)}{d\theta}\right) + i_1 i_2\left(\frac{dL_{12}(\theta)}{d\theta}\right)$$

$$= \frac{i_1^2}{2}(-2 \times 10^{-3}) \sin 2\theta + \frac{i_2^2}{2}(-20 \sin 2\theta) - i_1 i_2 (0.3) \sin \theta$$

For $i_1 = 0.8$ A and $i_2 = 0.01$ A, the torque is

$$T_{fld} = -1.64 \times 10^{-3} \sin 2\theta - 2.4 \times 10^{-3} \sin \theta$$

Notice that the torque expression consists of terms of two types. One term, proportional to $i_1 i_2 \sin \theta$, is due to the mutual interaction between the rotor and stator currents; it acts in a direction to align the rotor and stator so as to maximize their mutual inductance. Alternately, it can be thought of as being due to the tendency of two magnetic fields (in this case those of the rotor and stator) to align.

The torque expression also has terms proportional to $\sin 2\theta$ and to the square of the individual coil currents. These terms are due to the action of the individual winding currents alone and correspond to the torques one sees in singly-excited systems. Here each torque

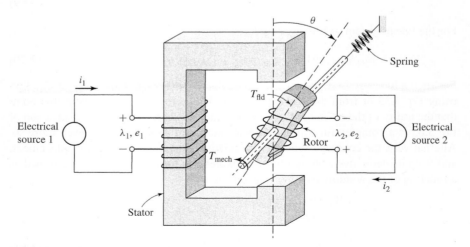

Figure 3.15 Multiply excited magnetic system for Example 3.7.

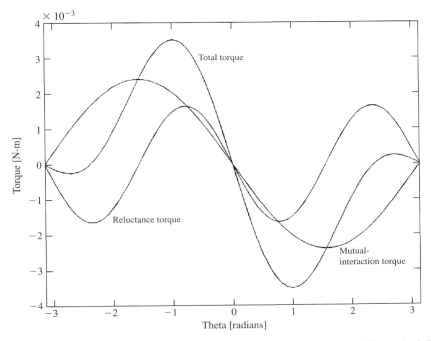

Figure 3.16 Plot of torque components for the multiply excited system of Example 3.7.

component acts in a direction to maximize its corresponding inductance so as to maximize the coenergy. The 2θ torque variation is due to the 2θ variation in the self inductances (exactly as was seen previously in Example 3.4), which in turn is due to the variation of the air-gap reluctance; notice that rotating the rotor by $180°$ from any given position gives the same air-gap reluctance (hence the twice-angle variation). This torque component is known as the *reluctance torque*. The two torque components (mutual and reluctance), along with the total torque, are plotted with MATLAB in Fig. 3.16.

Practice Problem 3.7

Find an expression for the torque of a symmetrical two-winding system whose inductances vary as

$$L_{11} = L_{22} = 0.8 + 0.27 \cos 4\theta$$

$$L_{12} = 0.65 \cos 2\theta$$

for the condition that $i_1 = -i_2 = 0.37$ A.

Solution

$$T_{\text{fld}} = -0.148 \sin (4\theta) + 0.178 \sin (2\theta)$$

The derivation presented above for angular displacement can be repeated in an analogous fashion for the systems with linear displacement. If this is done, the expressions for energy and coenergy will be found to be

$$W_{\text{fld}}(\lambda_{1_0}, \lambda_{2_0}, x_0) = \int_0^{\lambda_{2_0}} i_2(\lambda_1 = 0, \lambda_2, x = x_0)\, d\lambda_2$$

$$+ \int_0^{\lambda_{1_0}} i_1(\lambda_1, \lambda_2 = \lambda_{2_0}, x = x_0)\, d\lambda_1 \tag{3.72}$$

$$W'_{\text{fld}}(i_{1_0}, i_{2_0}, x_0) = \int_0^{i_{2_0}} \lambda_2(i_1 = 0, i_2, x = x_0)\, di_2$$

$$+ \int_0^{i_{1_0}} \lambda_1(i_1, i_2 = i_{2_0}, x = x_0)\, di_1 \tag{3.73}$$

Similarly the force can be found from

$$f_{\text{fld}} = -\left.\frac{\partial W_{\text{fld}}(\lambda_1, \lambda_2, x)}{\partial x}\right|_{\lambda_1, \lambda_2} \tag{3.74}$$

or

$$f_{\text{fld}} = \left.\frac{\partial W'_{\text{fld}}(i_1, i_2, x)}{\partial x}\right|_{i_1, i_2} \tag{3.75}$$

For a magnetically linear system, the coenergy expression of Eq. 3.70 becomes

$$W'_{\text{fld}}(i_1, i_2, x) = \frac{1}{2} L_{11}(x) i_1^2 + \frac{1}{2} L_{22}(x) i_2^2 + L_{12}(x) i_1 i_2 \tag{3.76}$$

and the force is thus given by

$$f_{\text{fld}} = \frac{i_1^2}{2}\left(\frac{dL_{11}(x)}{dx}\right) + \frac{i_2^2}{2}\left(\frac{dL_{22}(x)}{dx}\right) + i_1 i_2 \left(\frac{dL_{12}(x)}{dx}\right) \tag{3.77}$$

3.7 FORCES AND TORQUES IN SYSTEMS WITH PERMANENT MAGNETS

The derivations of the force and torque expressions of Sections 3.4 through 3.6 focus on systems in which the magnetic fields are produced by the electrical excitation of specific windings in the system. However, in Section 3.5, it is seen that special care must be taken when considering systems which contain permanent magnets (also referred to as *hard* magnetic materials). Specifically, the discussion associated with the derivation of the coenergy expression of Eq. 3.50 points out that in such systems the magnetic flux density is zero when $H = H_c$, not when $H = 0$.

For this reason, the derivation of the expressions for force and torque in Sections 3.4 through 3.6 must be modified for systems which contain permanent magnets. Consider for example that the derivation of Eq. 3.17 depends on the fact that in Eq. 3.16 the force can be assumed zero when integrating over path $2a$ because there is no electrical excitation in the system. A similar argument applies in the derivation of the coenergy expressions of Eqs. 3.41 and 3.69.

In systems with permanent magnets, these derivations must be carefully revisited. In some cases, such systems have no windings at all; their magnetic fields are due solely to the presence of permanent-magnet material, and it is not possible to base a derivation purely upon winding fluxes and currents. In other cases, magnetic fields may be produced by a combination of permanent magnets and windings.

A modification of the techniques presented in the previous sections can be used in systems which contain permanent magnets. Although the derivation presented here applies specifically to systems in which the magnet appears as an element of a magnetic circuit with a uniform internal field, it can be generalized to more complex situations; in the most general case, the field theory expressions for energy (Eq. 3.20) and coenergy (Eq. 3.50) can be used.

The essence of this technique is to consider the system as having an additional *fictitious winding* acting upon the same portion of the magnetic circuit as does the permanent magnet. Under normal operating conditions, the fictitious winding carries zero current. Its function is simply that of a mathematical crutch which can be used to accomplish the required analysis. The current in this winding can be adjusted to cancel the magnetic fields produced by the permanent magnet in order to achieve the "zero-force" starting point for the analyses such as that leading from Eq. 3.16 to Eq. 3.17.

For the purpose of calculating the energy and coenergy of the system, this winding is treated as any other winding, with its own set of current and flux linkages. As a result, energy and coenergy expressions can be obtained as a function of all the winding flux linkages or currents, including those of the fictitious winding. Since under normal operating conditions the current in this winding will be set equal to zero, it is useful to derive the expression for the force from the system coenergy since the winding currents are explicitly expressed in this representation.

Figure 3.17a shows a magnetic circuit with a permanent magnet and a movable plunger. To find the force on the plunger as a function of the plunger position, we assume that there is a fictitious winding of N_f turns carrying a current i_f wound so as to produce flux through the permanent magnet, as shown in Fig. 3.17b.

Figure 3.17 (a) Magnetic circuit with permanent magnet and movable plunger; (b) fictitious winding added.

Writing your equation to include the fictitious winding

Setting current to zero

For this single-winding system we can write the expression for the differential in coenergy from Eq. 3.37 as

$$dW'_{fld}(i_f, x) = \lambda_f \, di_f + f_{fld} \, dx \qquad (3.78)$$

where the subscript 'f' indicates the fictitious winding. Corresponding to Eq. 3.40, the force in this system can be written as

$$f_{fld} = \left. \frac{\partial W'_{fld}(i_f = 0, x)}{\partial x} \right|_{i_f} \qquad (3.79)$$

where the partial derivative is taken while holding i_f constant at $i_f = 0$ as is explicitly indicated in Eq 3.79. As we have seen, holding i_f constant for the derivative in Eq. 3.79 is a requirement of the energy method. In this case it must be set equal to zero to properly calculate the force due to the magnet alone so as not to include a force component from current in the fictitious winding.

To calculate the coenergy $W'_{fld}(i_f = 0, x)$ in this system, it is necessary to integrate Eq. 3.78. Since W'_{fld} is a state function of i_f and x, we are free to choose any integration path we wish. Figure 3.18 illustrates a path over which this integration is particularly simple. For this path we can write the expression for coenergy in this system as

$$W'_{fld}(i_f = 0, x) = \int_{\text{path 1a}} dW'_{fld} + \int_{\text{path 1b}} dW'_{fld}$$

$$= \int_0^x f_{fld}(i_f = I_{f0}, x') \, dx' + \int_{I_{f0}}^0 \lambda_f(i_f, x) \, di_f \qquad (3.80)$$

which corresponds directly to the analogous expression for energy found in Eq. 3.16.

Note that the integration is initially over x with the current i_f held fixed at $i_f = I_{f0}$. This is a very specific current, equal to that fictitious-winding current which reduces the magnetic flux in the system to zero. In other words, the current I_{f0} is that current in the fictitious winding which totally counteracts the magnetic field produced by the permanent magnet. Thus, the force f_{fld} is zero at point A in Fig. 3.18 and remains so

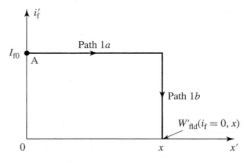

Figure 3.18 Integration path for calculating $W_{fld}(i_f = 0, x)$ in the permanent magnet system of Fig. 3.17.

for the integral over x of path $1a$. Hence the integral over path $1a$ in Eq. 3.80 is zero, and Eq. 3.80 reduces to

$$W'_{fld}(i_f = 0, x) = \int_{I_{f0}}^{0} \lambda_f(i_f, x)\, di_f \qquad (3.81)$$

It should be emphasized that Eq. 3.81 is perfectly general and does not require either the permanent magnet or the magnetic material in the magnetic circuit to be linear. Once Eq. 3.81 has been evaluated, the force at a given plunger position x can be readily found from Eq. 3.79.

EXAMPLE 3.8

The magnetic circuit of Fig. 3.19 is excited by a samarium-cobalt permanent magnet and includes a movable plunger. Also shown is the fictitious winding of N_f turns carrying a current i_f which is included here for the sake of the analysis. The dimensions are:

$$W_m = 2.0\text{ cm} \quad W_g = 3.0\text{ cm} \quad W_0 = 2.0\text{ cm}$$
$$d = 2.0\text{ cm} \quad g = 0.2\text{ cm} \quad D = 3.0\text{ cm}$$

Find (a) an expression for the coenergy of the system as a function of plunger position x and (b) an expression for the force on the plunger as a function of x. Finally, (c) calculate the force at $x = 0$ and $x = 0.5$ cm. Neglect any effects of fringing fluxes in this calculation.

■ **Solution**

a. Because it is quite linear over most of its useful operating range, the dc magnetization curve for samarium-cobalt can be represented as a straight line of the form of Eq. 1.60

$$B_m = \mu_R(H_m - H'_c) = \mu_R H_m + B_r$$

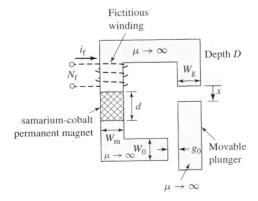

Figure 3.19 Magnetic circuit for Example 3.8.

where the subscript "m" is used here to refer specifically to the fields within the samarium-cobalt magnet and

$$\mu_R = 1.05\mu_0$$

$$H'_c = -712 \text{ kA/m}$$

$$B_r = 0.94 \text{ T}$$

Note from Fig. 1.19 that the DC magnetization curve for samarium-cobalt is not completely linear; it bends slightly downward for low flux densities. Hence, in the linearized B-H characteristic given above, the apparent coercivity H'_c is somewhat larger than the actual coercivity of samarium-cobalt.

From Eq. 1.5 we can write

$$N_f i_f = H_m d + H_g x + H_0 g_0$$

where the subscript "g" refers to the variable gap of length x and the subscript "0" refers to the fixed gap of length g_0. Similarly from the continuity of flux condition, Eq. 1.3, we can write

$$B_m W_m D = B_g W_g D = B_0 W_0 D$$

Recognizing that in the air gaps $B_g = \mu_0 H_g$ and $B_0 = \mu_0 H_0$, we can solve the above equations for B_m:

$$B_m = \frac{\mu_R (N_f i_f - H'_c d)}{d + W_m \left(\dfrac{\mu_R}{\mu_0}\right)\left(\dfrac{x}{W_g} + \dfrac{g_0}{W_0}\right)}$$

Finally we can solve for the flux linkages λ_f of the fictitious winding as

$$\lambda_f = N_f W_m D B_m = \frac{N_f W_m D \mu_R (N_f i_f - H'_c d)}{d + W_m \left(\dfrac{\mu_R}{\mu_0}\right)\left(\dfrac{x}{W_g} + \dfrac{g_0}{W_0}\right)}$$

Thus we see that the flux linkages λ_f will be zero when $i_f = I_{f0}$ where

$$I_{f0} = \frac{H'_c d}{N_f} = \frac{-B_r d}{\mu_R N_f}$$

and from Eq. 3.81 we can find the coenergy as

$$W'_{fld}(x) = \int_{H'_c d/N_f}^{0} \left[\frac{N_f W_m D \mu_R (N_f i_f - H'_c d)}{d + W_m \left(\dfrac{\mu_R}{\mu_0}\right)\left(\dfrac{x}{W_g} + \dfrac{g_0}{W_0}\right)} \right] di_f$$

$$= \frac{W_m D (B_r d)^2}{2\mu_R \left[d + W_m \left(\dfrac{\mu_R}{\mu_0}\right)\left(\dfrac{x}{W_g} + \dfrac{g_0}{W_0}\right)\right]}$$

Note that the answer does not depend upon N_f or i_f, which is as we would expect since the fictitious winding does not actually exist in this system.

b. Once the coenergy has been found, the force can be found from Eq. 3.79 as

$$f_{fld} = -\frac{W_m^2 D(B_r d)^2}{2\mu_0 W_g \left[d + W_m \left(\dfrac{\mu_R}{\mu_0} \right) \left(\dfrac{x}{W_g} + \dfrac{g_0}{W_0} \right) \right]^2}$$

Notice that the force is negative, indicating that the force is acting in the direction to decrease x, that is to pull the plunger in the direction which decreases the gap.

c. Finally, substitution into the force expression yields

$$f_{fld} = \begin{cases} -115 \text{ N} & \text{at } x = 0 \text{ cm} \\ -85.8 \text{ N} & \text{at } x = 0.5 \text{ cm} \end{cases}$$

Practice Problem 3.8

a. Derive an expression for the coenergy in the magnetic circuit of Fig. 3.20 as a function of the plunger position x.
b. Derive an expression for the x-directed force on the plunger and evaluate it at $x = W_g/2$. Neglect any effects of fringing fluxes.

The dimensions are:

$$W_m = 2.0 \text{ cm} \quad W_g = 2.5 \text{ cm} \quad D = 3.0 \text{ cm}$$
$$d = 1.0 \text{ cm} \quad g = 0.2 \text{ cm}$$

Figure 3.20 Magnetic circuit for Practice Problem 3.8.

Solution

a.
$$W'_{fld} = \frac{W_m D(B_r d)^2}{2\mu_R \left[d + \left(\dfrac{\mu_R}{\mu_0} \right) \left(\dfrac{2g W_m}{(W_g - x)} \right) \right]}$$

b.
$$f_{fld} = -\frac{\mu_0 g D(W_m B_r d)^2}{(2\mu_R g W_m + \mu_0 d(W_g - x))^2}$$

At $x = W_g/2$, $f_{fld} = -38.6$ N.

Consider the schematic magnetic circuit of Fig. 3.21a. It consists of a section of linear, hard magnetic material ($B_m = \mu_R(H_m - H'_c)$) of area A and length d. It is connected in series with an external magnetic circuit of mmf $\mathcal{F}_e$.

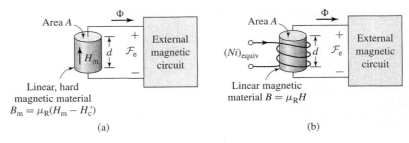

Figure 3.21   (a) Generic magnetic circuit containing a section of linear, permanent-magnet material. (b) Generic magnetic circuit in which the permanent-magnet material has been replaced by a section of linear magnetic material and a fictitious winding.

From Eq. 1.21, since there are no additional ampere-turns acting on this magnetic circuit,

$$H_m d + \mathcal{F}_e = 0 \tag{3.82}$$

The flux produced in the external magnetic circuit by the permanent magnet is given by

$$\Phi = A B_m = \mu_R A (H_m - H'_c) \tag{3.83}$$

Substitution for H_m from Eq. 3.82 in Eq. 3.83 gives

$$\Phi = \mu_R A \left(-H'_c - \frac{\mathcal{F}_e}{d} \right) \tag{3.84}$$

Now consider the schematic magnetic circuit of Fig. 3.21b in which the linear, hard magnetic material of Fig. 3.21a has been replaced by soft, linear magnetic material of the same permeability ($B = \mu_R H$) and of the same dimensions, length d and area A. In addition, a winding carrying $(Ni)_{equiv}$ ampere-turns has been included.

For this magnetic circuit, the flux can be shown to be given by

$$\Phi = \mu_R A \left(\frac{(Ni)_{equiv}}{d} - \frac{\mathcal{F}_e}{d} \right) \tag{3.85}$$

Comparing Eqs. 3.84 and 3.85, we see that the same flux is produced in the external magnetic circuit if the ampere-turns, $(Ni)_{equiv}$, in the winding of Fig. 3.21b is equal to $-H'_c d$.

This is a useful result for analyzing magnetic-circuit structures which contain linear, permanent-magnet materials whose B-H characteristic can be represented in the form of Eq. 1.60. In such cases, replacing the permanent-magnet section with a section of linear-magnetic material of the same permeability μ_R and geometry and an equivalent winding of ampere-turns

$$(Ni)_{equiv} = -H'_c d \tag{3.86}$$

results in the same flux in the external magnetic circuit. As a result, both the linear permanent magnet and the combination of the linear magnetic material and the winding are indistinguishable with regard to the production of magnetic fields in the external magnetic circuit, and hence they produce identical forces. Thus, the analysis of such systems may be simplified by this substitution, as is shown in Example 3.9. This technique is especially useful in the analysis of magnetic circuits containing both a permanent magnetic and one or more windings.

EXAMPLE 3.9

Figure 3.22a shows an actuator consisting of an infinitely-permeable yoke and plunger, excited by a section of neodymium-iron-boron magnet and an excitation winding of $N_1 = 1500$ turns. The dimensions are:

$$W = 4.0 \text{ cm} \quad W_1 = 4.5 \text{ cm} \quad D = 3.5 \text{ cm}$$
$$d = 8 \text{ mm} \quad g_0 = 1 \text{ mm}$$

Find (a) the x-directed force on the plunger when the current in the excitation winding is zero and $x = 3$ mm. (b) Calculate the current in the excitation winding required to reduce the plunger force to zero.

■ **Solution**

a. As discussed in Section 1.6, the dc-magnetization characteristic of neodymium-iron-boron can be represented by a linear relationship of the form

$$B = \mu_R(H - H_c') = B_r + \mu_R H$$

where $\mu_R = 1.06\mu_0$, $H_c' = -940$ kA/m and $B_r = 1.25$ T. As discussed in this section, we can replace the magnet by a section of linear material of permeability μ_R and an equivalent winding of ampere-turns

$$(Ni)_{equiv} = -H_c'd = -(-9.4 \times 10^5)(8 \times 10^{-3}) = 7520 \text{ ampere-turns}$$

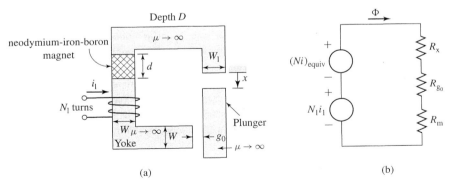

(a) (b)

Figure 3.22 (a) Actuator for Example 3.9. (b) Equivalent circuit for the actuator with the permanent magnet replaced by linear material and an equivalent winding carrying $(Ni)_{equiv}$ ampere-turns.

Based upon this substitution, the equivalent circuit for the system becomes that of Fig. 3.22b. There are two sources of mmf in series with three reluctances: the variable gap $\mathcal{R}_x$, the fixed gap $\mathcal{R}_0$, and the magnet $\mathcal{R}_m$.

$$\mathcal{R}_x = \frac{x}{\mu_0 W_1 D}$$

$$\mathcal{R}_0 = \frac{g_0}{\mu_0 W D}$$

$$\mathcal{R}_m = \frac{d}{\mu_R W D}$$

With $i_1 = 0$, the actuator is equivalent to a single-winding system whose coenergy is given by

$$W'_{\text{fld}} = \frac{1}{2} L i_1^2 = \frac{1}{2} \left(\frac{(Ni)^2_{\text{equiv}}}{\mathcal{R}_x + \mathcal{R}_0 + \mathcal{R}_m} \right)$$

The force on the plunger can then be found from

$$f_{\text{fld}} = \left. \frac{\partial W'_{\text{fld}}}{\partial x} \right|_{i_{\text{equiv}}} = -\frac{(Ni)^2_{\text{equiv}}}{(\mathcal{R}_x + \mathcal{R}_0 + \mathcal{R}_m)^2} \left(\frac{d\mathcal{R}_x}{dx} \right)$$

$$= -\frac{(Ni)^2_{\text{equiv}}}{\mu_0 W_1 D (\mathcal{R}_x + \mathcal{R}_0 + \mathcal{R}_m)^2}$$

Substituting the given values gives $f_{\text{fld}} = -703$ N, where the minus sign indicates that the force acts in the direction to reduce x (i.e., to close the gap).

b. The flux in the actuator is proportional to the total effective ampere-turns $(Ni)_{\text{equiv}} + N_1 i_1$ acting on the magnetic circuit. Thus, the force will be zero when the net ampere-turns is equal to zero or when

$$i_1 = \frac{(Ni)_{\text{equiv}}}{N_1} = \frac{7520}{1500} = 5.01 \text{ A}$$

Note however that the sign of the current (i.e., in which direction it should be applied to the excitation winding) cannot be determined from the information given here since we do not know the direction of magnetization of the magnet. Since the force depends upon the square of the magnetic flux density, the magnet can be oriented to produce flux either upward or downward in the left-hand leg of the magnetic circuit, and the force calculated in part (a) will be the same. To reduce the force to zero, the excitation winding current of 5.01 amperes must be applied in such a direction as to reduce the flux to zero; if the opposite current is applied, the flux density will increase, as will the force.

Practice Problem 3.9

Practice Problem 3.8 is to be reworked replacing the samarium-cobalt magnet by a section of linear material and an equivalent winding. Write (a) expressions for $\mathcal{R}_m$, the reluctance of the section of linear material; $\mathcal{R}_g$, the reluctance of the air gap; and $(Ni)_{\text{equiv}}$, the ampere-turns of the equivalent winding; and (b) an expression for the inductance of the equivalent winding and the coenergy.

$$W_{\mathrm{m}} = 2.0 \text{ cm} \quad W_{\mathrm{g}} = 2.5 \text{ cm} \quad D = 3.0 \text{ cm}$$
$$d = 1.0 \text{ cm} \quad g_0 = 0.2 \text{ cm}$$

Solution

a.
$$\mathcal{R}_{\mathrm{m}} = \frac{d}{\mu_{\mathrm{R}} W_{\mathrm{m}} D}$$

$$\mathcal{R}_{\mathrm{g}} = \frac{2g}{\mu_0 (W_{\mathrm{g}} - x) D}$$

$$(Ni)_{\text{equiv}} = -H_{\mathrm{c}}' d = \frac{(B_{\mathrm{r}} d)}{\mu_{\mathrm{R}}}$$

b.
$$L = \frac{N_{\text{equiv}}^2}{(\mathcal{R}_{\mathrm{m}} + \mathcal{R}_{\mathrm{g}})}$$

$$W_{\mathrm{fld}}' = \frac{L i_{\text{equiv}}^2}{2} = \frac{(B_{\mathrm{r}} d)^2}{2\mu_{\mathrm{R}}^2 (\mathcal{R}_{\mathrm{m}} + \mathcal{R}_{\mathrm{g}})} = \frac{W_{\mathrm{m}} D (B_{\mathrm{r}} d)^2}{2\mu_{\mathrm{R}} \left[d + \left(\dfrac{\mu_{\mathrm{R}}}{\mu_0} \right) \left(\dfrac{2g W_{\mathrm{m}}}{(W_{\mathrm{g}} - x)} \right) \right]}$$

Clearly the methods described in this chapter can be extended to handle situations in which there are permanent magnets and multiple current-carrying windings. In many devices of practical interest, the geometry is sufficiently complex, independent of the number of windings and/or permanent magnets, that magnetic-circuit analysis is not necessarily applicable, and analytical solutions can be expected to be inaccurate, if they can be found at all. In these cases, numerical techniques, such as the finite-element method discussed previously, can be employed. Using this method, the coenergy of Eq. 3.48, or Eq. 3.50 if permanent magnets are involved, can be evaluated numerically at constant winding currents and for varying values of displacement.

3.8 DYNAMIC EQUATIONS

We have derived expressions for the forces and torques produced in electro-mechanical-energy-conversion devices as functions of electrical terminal variables and mechanical displacement. These expressions were derived for conservative energy-conversion systems for which it can be assumed that losses can be assigned to external electrical and mechanical elements connected to the terminals of the energy-conversion system. Such energy-conversion devices are intended to operate as a coupling means between electric and mechanical systems. Hence, we are ulti-mately interested in the operation of the complete electromechanical system and not just of the electromechanical-energy-conversion system around which it is built.

The model of a simple electromechanical system shown in Fig. 3.23 shows the basic system components, the details of which may vary from system to sys-tem. The system shown consists of three parts: an external electric system, the electromechanical-energy-conversion system, and an external mechanical system.

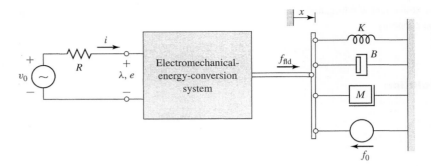

Figure 3.23 Model of a singly excited electromechanical system.

The electric system is represented by a voltage source v_0 and resistance R; the source could alternatively be represented by a current source and a parallel conductance G.

Note that all the electrical losses in the system, including those which are inherent to the electromechanical-energy-conversion system are assigned to the resistance R in this model. For example, if the voltage source has an equivalent resistance R_s and the winding resistance of the electromechanical-energy-conversion system is R_w, the resistance R would equal the sum of these two resistances; $R = R_s + R_w$.

The electric equation for this model is

$$v_0 = iR + e = iR + \frac{d\lambda}{dt} \tag{3.87}$$

If the flux linkage λ can be expressed as $\lambda = L(x)i$, the external equation becomes

$$v_0 = iR + L(x)\frac{di}{dt} + i\frac{dL(x)}{dx}\frac{dx}{dt} \tag{3.88}$$

The second term on the right, $L(di/dt)$, is the self-inductance voltage term. The third term $i(dL/dx)(dx/dt)$ includes the multiplier dx/dt. This is the speed of the mechanical terminal and thus the third term is often called simply the *speed voltage*. A speed-voltage term is common to all electromechanical-energy-conversion systems and represents the mechanism by which energy is transferred to and from the mechanical system by the electrical system.

For a multiply-excited system, electric equations corresponding to Eq. 3.87 are written for each input pair. If the expressions for the λ's are to be expanded in terms of inductances, as in Eq. 3.88, both self- and mutual-inductance terms will be required.

The mechanical system of Fig. 3.23 includes the representation for a spring (spring constant K), a damper (damping constant B), a mass M, and an external mechanical excitation force f_0. Here, as for the electrical system, the damper represents the losses both of the external mechanical system as well as any mechanical losses of the electromechanical-energy-conversion system.

The x-directed forces and displacement x are related as follows:

Spring:

$$f_K = -K(x - x_0) \tag{3.89}$$

Damper:

$$f_D = -B\frac{dx}{dt} \tag{3.90}$$

Mass:

$$f_M = -M\frac{d^2x}{dt^2} \tag{3.91}$$

where x_0 is the value of x with the spring normally unstretched. Force equilibrium thus requires that

$$f_{fld} + f_K + f_D + f_M - f_0 = f_{fld} - K(x - x_0) - B\frac{dx}{dt} - M\frac{d^2x}{dt^2} - f_0 = 0 \tag{3.92}$$

Combining Eqs. 3.88 and 3.92, the differential equations for the overall system of Fig. 3.23 for arbitrary inputs $v_0(t)$ and $f_0(t)$ are thus

$$v_0(t) = iR + L(x)\frac{di}{dt} + i\frac{dL(x)}{dx} \tag{3.93}$$

$$f_0(t) = -M\frac{d^2x}{dt^2} - B\frac{dx}{dt} - K(x - x_0) + f_{fld}(x, i) \tag{3.94}$$

The functions $L(x)$ and $f_{fld}(x, i)$ depend on the properties of the electromechanical-energy-conversion system and are calculated as previously discussed.

EXAMPLE 3.10

Figure 3.24 shows in cross section a cylindrical solenoid magnet in which the cylindrical plunger of mass M moves vertically in brass guide rings of thickness g and mean diameter d. The permeability of brass is the same as that of free space and is $\mu_0 = 4\pi \times 10^{-7}$ H/m in SI units. The plunger is supported by a spring whose spring constant is K. Its unstretched length is l_0. A mechanical load force f_t is applied to the plunger from the mechanical system connected to it, as shown in Fig. 3.24. Assume that frictional force is linearly proportional to the velocity and that the coefficient of friction is B. The coil has N turns and resistance R. Its terminal voltage is v_t and its current is i. The effects of magnetic leakage and reluctance of the steel are negligible.

Derive the dynamic equations of motion of the electromechanical system, i.e., the differential equations relating the dependent variables i and x in terms of v_t, f_t, and the given constants and dimensions.

■ **Solution**

We begin by expressing the inductance as functions of x. The coupling terms, i.e., the magnetic force f_{fld} and induced emf e, can then be expressed in terms of x and i and these relations substituted in the equations for the mechanical and electric systems.

The reluctance of the magnetic circuit is that of the two guide rings in series, with the flux directed radially through them, as shown by the dashed flux lines φ in Fig. 3.24. Because $g \ll d$, the flux density in the guide rings is very nearly constant with respect to the radial distance. In a region where the flux density is constant, the reluctance is

$$\frac{\text{Length of flux path in direction of field}}{\mu \text{ (area of flux path perpendicular to field)}}$$

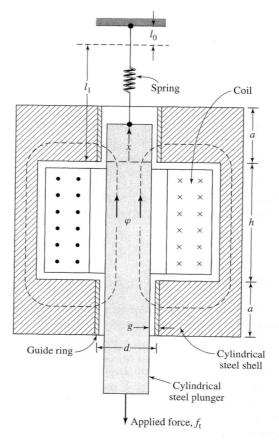

Figure 3.24 Solenoid magnet for Example 3.10.

The reluctance of the upper gap is

$$\mathcal{R}_1 = \frac{g}{\mu_0 \pi x d}$$

in which it is assumed that the field is concentrated in the area between the upper end of the plunger and the lower end of the upper guide ring. Similarly, the reluctance of the lower gap is

$$\mathcal{R}_2 = \frac{g}{\mu_0 \pi a d}$$

The total reluctance is

$$\mathcal{R} = \mathcal{R}_1 + \mathcal{R}_2 = \frac{g}{\mu_0 \pi d} \left(\frac{1}{x} + \frac{1}{a} \right) = \frac{g}{\mu_0 \pi a d} \left(\frac{a+x}{x} \right)$$

Hence, the inductance is

$$L(x) = \frac{N^2}{\mathcal{R}} = \frac{\mu_0 \pi a d N^2}{g} \left(\frac{x}{a+x} \right) = L' \left(\frac{x}{a+x} \right)$$

where

$$L' = \frac{\mu_0 \pi a d N^2}{g}$$

The magnetic force acting upward on the plunger in the positive x direction is

$$f_{\text{fld}} = \left. \frac{\partial W'_{\text{fld}}(i, x)}{\partial x} \right|_i = \frac{i^2}{2} \frac{dL}{dx} = \frac{i^2}{2} \frac{aL'}{(a+x)^2}$$

The induced emf in the coil is

$$e = \frac{d}{dt}(Li) = L\frac{di}{dt} + i\frac{dL}{dx}\frac{dx}{dt}$$

or

$$e = L' \left(\frac{x}{a+x} \right) \frac{di}{dt} + L' \left(\frac{ai}{(a+x)^2} \right) \frac{dx}{dt}$$

Substitution of the magnetic force in the differential equation of motion of the mechanical system (Eq. 3.94) gives

$$f_t = -M\frac{d^2 x}{dt^2} - B\frac{dx}{dt} - K(x - l_0) + \frac{1}{2} L' \frac{ai^2}{(a+x)^2}$$

The voltage equation for the electric system is (from Eq. 3.93)

$$v_t = iR + L' \left(\frac{x}{a+x} \right) \frac{di}{dt} + iL' \left(\frac{a}{(a+x)^2} \right) \frac{dx}{dt}$$

These last two equations are the desired results. They are valid only as long as the upper end of the plunger is well within the upper guide ring, say, between the limits $0.1a < x < 0.9a$. This is the normal working range of the solenoid.

3.9 ANALYTICAL TECHNIQUES

We have described relatively simple devices in this chapter. These devices have one or two electrical terminals and one mechanical terminal, which is usually constrained to incremental motion. More complicated devices capable of continuous energy conversion are treated in the following chapters. We have discussed analytic techniques in the context of simple devices, but the principles are equally applicable to more complex devices.

Devices such as those described in this chapter are often used to produce gross motion, such as in the case of relays and solenoids, where the devices operate under essentially "on" and "off" conditions. Techniques described in this chapter can be used to determine force as a function of displacement and reaction on the electric source. If the details of the motion, such as the displacement as a function of time after the device is energized, are required, often non-linear differential equations of the form of Eqs. 3.93 and 3.94 must be solved.

In contrast to gross-motion devices, other devices such as loudspeakers, pickups, and transducers of various kinds are intended to operate with relatively small displacements and to produce a linear relationship between electrical signals and mechanical motion, and vice versa. The relationship between the electrical and mechanical variables is made linear either by the design of the device or by restricting the excursion of the signals to a linear range. In either case the differential equations are linear and can be solved using standard techniques for transient response, frequency response, and so forth, as required.

3.9.1   Gross Motion

The differential equations for a singly excited device as derived in Example 3.10 are of the form

$$\frac{1}{2} L' \left(\frac{ai^2}{(a+x)^2} \right) = M \frac{d^2x}{dt^2} + B \frac{dx}{dt} + K(x - l_0) + f_t \tag{3.95}$$

$$v_t = iR + L' \left(\frac{x}{a+x} \right) \frac{di}{dt} + L' \left(\frac{ai}{(a+x)^2} \right) \frac{dx}{dt} \tag{3.96}$$

A typical problem using these differential equations is to find the excursion $x(t)$ when a prescribed voltage $v_t = V_0$ is applied at $t = 0$. There is no general analytical solution for these differential equations; they are non-linear, involving products and powers of the variables x and i and their derivatives. Typically, a solution is most easily obtained through the use of computer-based numerical-integration techniques.

A number of commercial packages are available to expedite the analysis of these systems. One such package is the MATLAB/Simulink package.[3] Using Simulink, equations such as Eq. 3.95 and 3.96 can be readily solved by reformulating them as integral equations which are then numerically integrated. Specifically, Simulink solves such problems in the form of a set of first-order, non-linear integral equations.

Eqs. 3.95 and 3.96 can be formulated in the required form by defining a third variable x_1 such

$$x_1 = \frac{dx}{dt} \tag{3.97}$$

which, when combined with Eqs. 3.95 and 3.96 results in a set of three first-order, non-linear differential equations.

$$\frac{dx}{dt} = x_1 \tag{3.98}$$

$$\frac{dx_1}{dt} = \frac{1}{M} \left[\frac{1}{2} L' \left(\frac{ai^2}{(a+x)^2} \right) - Bx_1 - K(x - l_0) - f_t \right] \tag{3.99}$$

$$\frac{di}{dt} = \left(\frac{a+x}{x} \right) \left[v_t - iR - L' \left(\frac{ai}{(a+x)^2} \right) x_1 \right] \tag{3.100}$$

---

[3] "MATLAB" and "Simulink" are registered trademarks of The MathWorks, Inc., 3 Apple Hill Drive, Natick, MA 01760, http://www.mathworks.com. Both Matlab and Simulink are avalailable in a Student Edition.

In integral form these become

$$x = \int_0^t \{x_1\} dt \tag{3.101}$$

$$x_1 = \int_0^t \left\{ \frac{1}{M} \left[\frac{1}{2} L' \left(\frac{ai^2}{(a+x)^2} \right) - Bx_1 - K(x - l_0) - f_t \right] \right\} dt \tag{3.102}$$

$$i = \int_0^t \left\{ \left(\frac{a+x}{x} \right) \left[v_t - iR - L' \left(\frac{ai}{(a+x)^2} \right) x_1 \right] \right\} dt \tag{3.103}$$

EXAMPLE 3.11

The plunger system of Ex. 3.10 has the following characteristics:

$$
\begin{array}{ll}
M = 0.5 \text{ kg} & K = 60 \text{ N/m} \\
B = 1 \text{ kg/sec} & l_o = 5 \text{ cm} \\
a = 2.5 \text{ cm} & L' = 46.8 \text{ mH} \\
R = 5 \ \Omega &
\end{array}
$$

The system is initial at rest with $v_t = 0$ and $f_t = 0$. Use Simulink to calculate and plot the plunger position x and current i if the voltage v_t is switched to 10 V at time $t = 0.5$ sec.

■ **Solution**
Figure 3.25 shows the Simulink model. As can be seen, there are three integrators, corresponding to each of the three integral equations, Eqs. 3.101 - 3.103. The model includes two subsystems which implement Eqs. 3.102 and 3.103. The details of these implementations are shown in Fig. 3.26.

Figure 3.27 shows the results of the simulation. Note that the current settles out to a steady value in approximately 0.5 sec to the expected value of $V_t/R = 2$ A with a response which appears to be essentially first order. On the other hand, the transient in x is essentially second order and which damps out in approximately 4.5 seconds. Not surprisingly, increasing the value of the damping constant B and re-running the simulation will result in a response which damps out more rapidly.

Frequently, a gross-motion problem can be simplified. Some cases permit solution by analytic methods, thus eliminating the necessity of a setting up and solving a numerical simulation. In many cases, such simplification provides important insight into the behavior of the system and the physical mechanisms which determine this behavior. For example, when the winding of the system of Example 3.10 has a relatively large resistance, the iR term may dominate the right-hand side of Eq. 3.96 as compared with the di/dt self-inductance voltage term and the dx/dt speed-voltage term. The current i can then be assumed equal to v_t/R and inserted directly into Eq. 3.95. Similarly, in cases where the current is supplied directly from electronic circuitry, the supplied current waveform can also be inserted directly into Eq. 3.95.

Figure 3.25 Simulink model for Example 3.11.

3.9.2 Linearization

Often times, although the behavior of electro-mechanical devices is inherently non-linear, the devices are intended to provide linear response to input signals. In other cases, these devices are designed to operate at fixed operating points and their stability at these operating points can be investigated by examining their behavior for small deviations for these operating points. For example, when used as transducers, devices characterized by non-linear differential equations such as Eqs. 3.95 and 3.96 will in general yield non-linear responses to arbitrary input signals. To obtain linear behavior, such devices must be restricted to small excursions of displacement and electrical signals about their equilibrium values. For example, the equilibrium point in a given system might be determined by a bias mmf produced by a dc winding (or equivalently a permanent magnet) acting against a spring. In another system, it might be determined by a pair of windings producing mmfs whose forces cancel at the equilibrium point. In either case, the equilibrium point must be stable; the transducer should return to the equilibrium position following a small disturbance.

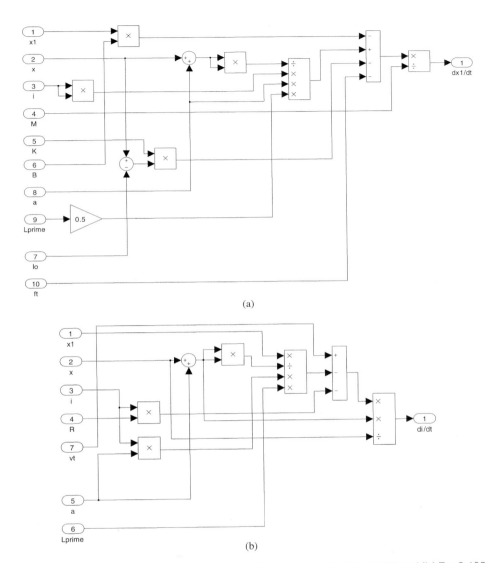

(a)

(b)

Figure 3.26 Simulink subsystems which implement (a) Eq. 3.102 and (b) Eq. 3.103.

Consider the system of Example 3.10. With the voltage and applied force set equal to their equilibrium values, V_{t_0} and F_{t_0} respectively, equations for the equilibrium displacement X_0 and current I_0 can be determined for the system described from Eqs. 3.95 and 3.96 by setting the time derivatives equal to zero. Thus

$$\frac{1}{2} L' \left(\frac{a I_0^2}{(a + X_0)^2} \right) = K(X_0 - l_0) + F_{t_0} \tag{3.104}$$

$$V_{t_0} = I_0 R \tag{3.105}$$

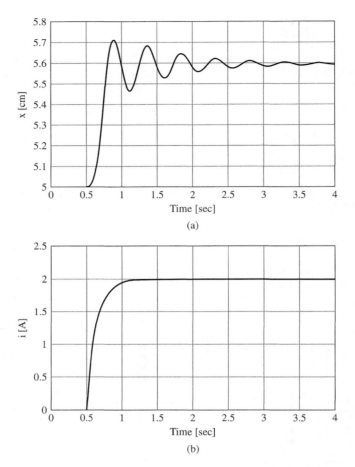

Figure 3.27 Plots of (a) x and (b) i for Example 3.11.

The incremental operation can be described by expressing each variable as the sum of its equilibrium and incremental values; thus $i = I_0 + i'$, $f_t = F_{t_0} + f'$, $v_t = V_{t_0} + v'$, and $x = X_0 + x'$. Equations 3.95 and 3.96 are then linearized by canceling any products of increments as being of second order. Thus

$$\frac{L'a(I_0 + i')^2}{2(a + X_0 + x')^2} = M\frac{d^2x'}{dt^2} + B\frac{dx'}{dt} + K(X_0 + x' - l_0) + F_{t_0} + f' \qquad (3.106)$$

and

$$V_0 + v' = (I_0 + i')R + \left(\frac{L'(X_0 + x')}{a + X_0 + x'}\right)\frac{di'}{dt} + \left(\frac{L'a(I_0 + i')}{(a + X_0 + x')^2}\right)\frac{dx'}{dt} \qquad (3.107)$$

The equilibrium terms cancel, and retaining only first-order incremental terms yields a set of linear differential equations.

$$\frac{L'aI_0}{(a + X_0)^2}\, i' = M\frac{d^2x'}{dt^2} + B\frac{dx'}{dt} + \left[K + \frac{L'aI_0^2}{(a + X_0)^3} \right] x' + f' \qquad (3.108)$$

$$v' = i'R + \left(\frac{L'X_0}{a + X_0} \right) \frac{di'}{dt} + \left(\frac{L'aI_0}{(a + X_0)^2} \right) \frac{dx'}{dt} \qquad (3.109)$$

Standard techniques, including numerical integration, can be used to solve for the time response of this set of linear differential equations. Alternatively, as is frequently done when designing control systems and/or investigating system stability, sinusoidal-steady-state operation can be assumed, and Eqs. 3.108 and 3.109 can be converted to a set of linear, complex algebraic equations and solved in the frequency domain.

3.10 SUMMARY

In electromechanical systems, energy is stored in magnetic and electric fields. When the energy in the field is influenced by the configuration of the mechanical parts constituting the boundaries of the field, mechanical forces are created which tend to move the mechanical elements so that energy is transferred from the field to the mechanical system.

Singly-excited magnetic systems are considered first in Section 3.3. By removing electric and mechanical loss elements from the electromechanical-energy-conversion system (and incorporating them as loss elements in the external electrical and mechanical systems), the energy conversion device can be modeled as a conservative system. Its energy then becomes a state function, determined by the state variables λ and x. Section 3.4 derives expressions for determining the force and torque as the negative of partial derivative of the energy with respect to the displacement, taken while holding the flux-linkage λ constant.

In Section 3.5 the state function coenergy, with state variables i and x or θ, is introduced. The force and torque are then shown to be given by the partial derivative of the coenergy with respect to displacement, taken while holding the current i constant.

These concepts are extended in Section 3.6 to include systems with multiple windings. Section 3.7 further extends the development to include systems in which permanent magnets are included among the sources of the magnetic energy storage.

Energy conversion devices operate between electric and mechanical systems. Their behavior is described by differential equations which include the coupling terms between the systems, as discussed in Section 3.8. These equations are usually non-linear and can be solved by numerical methods if necessary. As discussed in Section 3.9, in some cases approximations can be made to simplify the equations. For example, in many cases, linearized analyses can provide useful insight, both with respect to device design and performance.

This chapter has been concerned with basic principles applying broadly to the electromechanical-energy-conversion process, with emphasis on magnetic-field systems. Basically, rotating machines and linear-motion transducers work in the same way. The remainder of this text is devoted almost entirely to rotating machines. Rotating machines typically include multiple windings and may include permanent magnets. Their performance can be analyzed by using the techniques and principles developed in this chapter.

3.11 CHAPTER 3 VARIABLES

α, θ	Angular position [rad]
λ	Flux linkages [Wb]
ρ	Charge density [Coulomb/m^3]
μ	Magnetic permeability [H/m]
μ_0	Permeability of free space $= 4\pi \times 10^{-7}$ [H/m]
μ_R	Recoil permeability [H/m]
Φ	Magnetic flux [Wb]
a, h, l, d, D, W	Linear dimension [m]
A	Area [m^2]
$B, \mathbf{B}$	Flux density [T]
B	Damping coefficient [N/(m/sec)]
B_r	Residual/remanent magnetization [T]
e, v	Voltage [V]
$\mathbf{E}$	Electric field intensity [V/m]
$f, f_{fld}, F, \mathbf{F}$	Force [N]
$\mathbf{F}_v$	Force density [N/m^3]
$\mathcal{F}$	Magnetomotive force [A]
g	Gap length [m]
$\mathbf{H}$	Magnetic field intensity [A/m]
H_c	Coercivity [A/m]
$i, I, \mathbf{I}$	Current [A]
$\mathbf{J}$	Current density [A/m^2]
K	Spring constant [N/m]
L	Inductance [H]
M	Mass [kg]
N	Number of turns
Ni_{equiv}	Equivalent ampere-turns [A]
P_{elec}	Electrical input power [W]
P_{mech}	Mechanical output power [W]
q	Electric charge [Coulomb]
r	Radius [m]
R	Resistance [Ω]
$\mathcal{R}$	Reluctance [H^{-1}]
t	Time [sec]
T, T_{fld}	Torque [N· m]
$\mathbf{v}$	Velocity [m/sec]
W_{fld}	Magnetic stored [J]

W'_{fld}	Coenergy [J]
x, X	Position [m]

Subscripts:

e	External
equiv	Equivalent
f	Field
gap, ag	Air gap
m	Magnet

3.12 PROBLEMS

3.1 The rotor of Fig. 3.28 is similar to that of Fig. 3.2 (Example 3.1) except that it has two coils instead of one. The rotor is nonmagnetic and is placed in a uniform magnetic field of magnitude B_0. The coil sides are of radius R and are uniformly spaced around the rotor surface. The first coil is carrying a current I_1 and the second coil is carrying a current I_2.

Assuming that the rotor is 0.32 m long, $R = 0.13$ m, and $B_0 = 0.87$ T, find the θ-directed torque as a function of rotor position α for (a) $I_1 = 0$ A and $I_2 = 5$ A, (b) $I_1 = 5$ A and $I_2 = 0$ A, and (c) $I_1 = 8$ A and $I_2 = 8$ A.

3.2 The winding currents of the rotor of Problem 3.1 are controlled as a function of rotor angle α such that

$$I_1 = 8 \sin \alpha \quad \text{A} \qquad \text{and} \qquad I_2 = 8 \cos \alpha \quad \text{A}$$

Write an expression for the rotor torque as a function of the rotor position α.

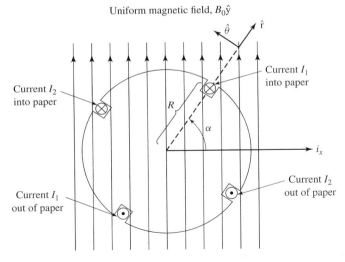

Figure 3.28 Two-coil rotor for Problem 3.1.

3.3 Consider the magnetic circuit of Example 1.2. For the stated operating
condition (a) find the magnetic stored energy from Eq. 3.21 and (b) Find
(i) the inductance of the N-turn winding, (ii) the winding flux linkages and
(iii) the magnetic stored energy from Eq. 3.19.

3.4 An inductor has an inductance which is found experimentally to be of the form

$$L = \frac{2L_0}{1 + \frac{x}{x_0}}$$

where $L_0 = 70$ mH, $x_0 = 1.20$ mm, and x is the displacement of a movable
element. Its winding resistance is measured and found to equal 135 mΩ.

a. The displacement x is held constant at 1.30 mm, and the current is
    increased from 0 to 7.0 A. Find the resultant magnetic stored energy in the
    inductor.

b. The current is then held constant at 7.0 A, and the displacement is
    increased to 2.5 mm. Find the corresponding change in magnetic stored
    energy.

3.5 The inductor of Problem 3.4 is driven by a sinusoidal current source of the
form

$$i(t) = I_0 \sin \omega t$$

where $I_0 = 7.0$ A and $\omega = 120\pi$ (60 Hz). With the displacement held fixed at
$x = x_0$, calculate (a) the time-averaged magnetic stored energy (W_{fld}) in the
inductor and (b) the time-averaged power dissipated in the winding
resistance.

3.6 An actuator with a rotating vane is shown in Fig. 3.29. You may assume that
the permeability of both the core and the vane are infinite ($\mu \rightarrow \infty$). The total

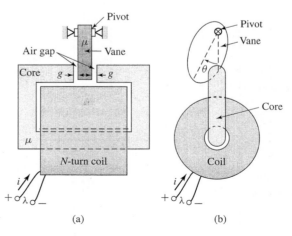

Figure 3.29 Actuator with rotating vane for
Problem 3.6. (a) Side view. (b) End view.

Figure 3.30   An RC circuit for Problem 3.8.

air-gap length is $2g$ and shape of the vane is such that the effective area of the air gap can be assumed to be of the form

$$A_g = A_0 \left(1 - \left(\frac{4\theta}{\pi} \right)^2 \right)$$

(valid only in the range $|\theta| \leq \pi/6$).

a. Find the inductance $L(\theta)$.

b. For $g = 0.9$ mm, $A_0 = 5.0$ mm^2, and $N = 450$ turns, and $i = 5$ A, use MATLAB to plot the magnetic stored energy in the actuator as a function of angle θ for $|\theta| \leq \pi/6$.

3.7 The inductor of Problem 3.6 is connected to a controller which maintains constant winding flux linkage. The winding current is observed to be 5 A when $\theta = 0$. Using MATLAB, plot the magnetic stored energy in the actuator as a function of angle θ for $|\theta| \leq \pi/6$.

3.8 An RC circuit is connected to a battery, as shown in Fig. 3.30. Switch S is initially closed and is opened at time $t = 0$.

a. Find the capacitor voltage $v_C(t)$ for $t \geq 0$

b. What are the initial and final ($t = \infty$) values of the stored energy in the capacitor? (Hint: $W_{\mathrm{fld}} = \frac{1}{2}q^2/C$, where $q = Cv_c$.) What is the energy stored in the capacitor as a function of time?

c. What is the power dissipated in the resistor as a function of time? What is the total energy dissipated in the resistor?

3.9 An RL circuit is connected to a battery, as shown in Fig. 3.31. Switch S is initially closed and is opened at time $t = 0$.

a. Find the inductor current $i_L(t)$ for $t \geq 0$. (Hint: Note that while the switch is closed, the diode is reverse-biased and can be assumed to be an open circuit. Immediately after the switch is opened, the diode becomes forward-biased and can be assumed to be a short circuit.)

b. What are the initial and final ($t = \infty$) values of the stored energy in the inductor? What is the energy stored in the inductor as a function of time?

c. What is the power dissipated in the resistor as a function of time? What is the total energy dissipated in the resistor?

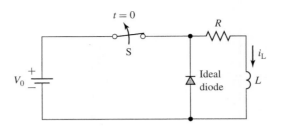

Figure 3.31   An RL circuit for Problem 3.9.

3.10   The L/R time constant of the field winding of a 500-MVA synchronous generator is 4.8 s. At normal operating conditions, the field winding is known to be dissipating 1.3 MW. (a) Calculate the magnetic stored energy under this condition. (b) If the field-winding terminal voltage is suddenly reduced to 70 percent of the value of part (a), calculate the magnetic stored energy as a function of time.

3.11   Over its normal operating range, the inductance of an actuator which operates an electric bell is measured to be of the form

$$L(x) = \frac{L_0}{(x/X_0)^2}$$

over the operating range $0.5 X_0 \leq x \leq 2 X_0$.

a.   Find the magnetic stored energy $W_{\text{fld}}(\lambda, x)$.

b.   Find an expression for the force on the actuator as a function of λ and x.

c.   Find an expression for the force as a function of x assuming the actuator current is held constant at $i = I_0$. Does the force act to increase or decrease x?

3.12   The inductance of a phase winding of a three-phase salient-pole motor is measured to be of the form

$$L(\theta_{\text{m}}) = L_0 + L_2 \cos 2\theta_{\text{m}}$$

where θ_{m} is the angular position of the rotor.

a.   How many poles are on the rotor of this motor?

b.   Assuming that all other winding currents are zero and that this phase is excited by a constant current I_0, find the torque $T_{\text{fld}}(\theta)$ acting on the rotor.

3.13   A magnetic field system includes a single coil and a rotor such that the coil inductance varies with rotor angle θ_{m} as

$$L(\theta_{\text{m}}) = L_0 + L_6 \sin 6\theta_{\text{m}}$$

The coil is supplied by a power supply which uses feedback to maintain a constant current I_0.

a.   Find an expression for the magnetic torque T_{fld} acting on the rotor as a function of its position θ_{m}.

N-turn
winding

$\mu \rightarrow \infty$

Electromagnet,
cross-sectional
area A_c

g g

Iron slab, mass M

Figure 3.32 Electromagnet lifting an iron slab
(Problem 3.14).

b. If the rotor is driven at a constant angular velocity such that $\theta_m = \omega_m t$,
find an expression the instantaneous power $p(t)$ which must be supplied
to the coil by the power supply.

3.14 As shown in Fig. 3.32, an N-turn electromagnet is to be used to lift a slab
of iron of mass M. The surface roughness of the iron is such that when the
iron and the electromagnet are in contact, there is an effective air gap of
$g_{min} = 0.31$ mm in each leg. The electromagnet cross-sectional area
$A_c = 32$ cm^2 and the 475-turn coil has a resistance of 2.3 Ω. Calculate the
minimum coil voltage which must be used to lift a slab of mass 12 kg against
the force of gravity. Neglect the reluctance of the flux path through the
iron.

3.15 Cylindrical iron-clad solenoid actuators of the form shown in Fig. 3.33 are
used for tripping circuit breakers, for operating valves, and in other
applications in which a relatively large force is applied to a member which
moves a relatively short distance. When the coil current is zero, the plunger
drops against a stop such that the gap g is at a maximum value g_{max}. When the
coil is energized by a direct current of sufficient magnitude, the plunger is
raised until it hits another stop set so that g is equal to g_{min}. The plunger is
supported so that it can move freely in the vertical direction.

For the purposes of this problem, you may neglect magnetic fringing in the
air gaps and assume that the mmf drop in the iron can be neglected.

a. Derive an expression for the flux density B_g in the variable air gap as a
function of the gap length g and the coil current i.

b. Derive an expression for the coil flux linkage λ and inductance L as a
function of the current gap length g and the coil current i.

c. Derive an expression for the magnetic coenergy W'_{fld} in the actuator as a
function of the current gap length g and the coil current i.

d. Derive an expression for the force on the plunger as a function of the gap
length g and the coil current i. If i is held constant, does the force act to
increase or decrease g?

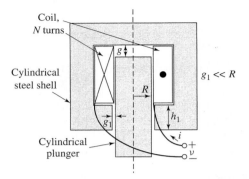

Figure 3.33 Cylindrical plunger actuator for Problem 3.15.

3.16 Consider the plunger actuator of Problem 3.15 and Fig. 3.33 with the following characteristics

$R = 6$ cm	$h_1 = 3$ cm
$g_{min} = 0.15$ cm	$g_{max} = 2.2$ cm
$g_1 = 0.6$ mm	$N = 2500$ turns
Coil resistance $= 2.9$ Ω	

a. The actuator gap g is set equal to its minimum value g_{min} and a current source is used to adjust the coil current such that the flux density in the variable gap is equal to 0.8 T. Calculate the coil current I_0.

b. With the coil current held constant at I_0, an external force is applied to the plunger and it is pulled open to its maximum position g_{max}. Use MATLAB to plot the external force f_{ext} required to move the plunger as the gap varies from g_{min} to g_{max}.

c. As the variable gap varies from from g_{min} to g_{max} in part (b), calculate

  i. the change in magnetic stored energy ΔW_{fld},

  ii. the total energy supplied to the actuator by the external system E_{ext} and

  iii. the total energy E_{gen} supplied to the current source. Hint: Use conservation of energy. Since the coil current is constant, the power dissipated in the coil resistance is also constant and does not need to be considered in this calculation.

3.17 Figure 3.34 shows a schematic view of a cylindrically symmetric shaker system which can be used to excite low-frequency oscillations in a system under test. There is an N-turn coil of resistance R_c. The plunger is of radius R and separated from the core by a small fixed air gap of length $g \ll R$ on its sides and by a variable gap of length δ on the bottom. Both the core and plunger can be assumed to be of infinite permeability.

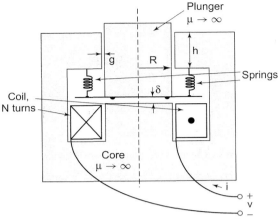

Figure 3.34 Low-frequency shaker system for Problem 3.17.

The plunger is supported by a set of springs with combined spring constant K which produces a net force on the plunger of

$$f_K = K(\delta_0 - \delta)$$

Mechanical stops on the plunger limit the minimum value of δ to 1 mm. For the purposes of this problem, you may neglect any effects of fringing fields.

$$R = 4 \text{ cm} \qquad h = 3 \text{ cm}$$
$$g = 0.5 \text{ mm} \qquad K = 4.5 \text{ N/mm}$$
$$N = 1000 \text{ turns} \qquad \delta_0 = 5 \text{ mm}$$
$$R_c = 35 \text{ m}\Omega$$

a. Write an expression for the inductance of the coil as a function of δ.

b. Find an expression for the magnetic force on the plunger as a function of the plunger position δ and (i) the coil flux linkages λ and (ii) the coil current i. In each case, indicate whether the force act in a direction to increase or decrease δ.

c. Using MATLAB, plot the net force on the plunger over the range $1 \text{ mm} \leq \delta \leq \delta_0$ for a current of 150 mA. Find the corresponding equilibrium position for the plunger.

3.18 The inductor of Fig. 3.35 is made up of two C-cores, each of cross-sectional area A_c and mean length l_c. There are two air gaps, each of length g and two series-connected coils, each of N turns. Assume the core to be of infinite permeability and neglect any fringing at the air gaps.

$$A_c = 9.7 \text{ cm}^2 \qquad l_c = 15 \text{ cm}$$
$$g = 5 \text{ mm} \qquad N = 450 \text{ turns}$$

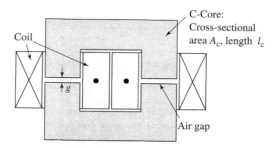

Figure 3.35   C-core inductor for Problem 3.18.

a. Calculate the inductance.

b. The air gaps are each held open by 5 mm spacers. Calculate the magnetic flux density in the air gap and the force in N and pressure in N/cm² acting to crush each spacer if the coils are carrying a current of 15 A.

3.19 The results of a set of measurements of the dc magnetization characteristics of an electrical steel are presented in the following table:

H [A/m]	B[T]	H [A/m]	B[T]
0	0	1100	1.689
68	0.733	1500	1.703
135	1.205	2500	1.724
203	1.424	4000	1.731
271	1.517	5000	1.738
338	1.560	9000	1.761
406	1.588	12000	1.770
474	1.617	20000	1.80
542	1.631	25000	1.816
609	1.646		

Electrical-steel *B-H* data for Problem 3.19.

a. Use MATLAB to plot the *B-H* curve for this material.
    Consider the inductor of Problem 3.18 and Fig. 3.35 with C-cores made up of this material.

b. For a range of gap and core flux densities up to 1.8 T, plot the flux density as a function of the required coil current. (Hint: Use the MATLAB "spline" function to solve for the value of *H* for a given value of *B*. This can then be used to solve for the mmf drop at that value of *B*.) Over the same range of current, plot the core flux density that would result if the C-core were of infinite permeability. Up to what flux density and coil current can the core be approximated as being of infinite magnetic permeability?

c. Calculate the force and pressure acting to crush each spacer if the coil is carrying a current of 10 A.

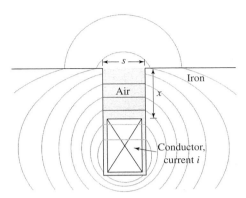

Figure 3.36 Conductor in a slot
(Problem 3.21).

   d. Calculate the force and pressure acting to crush each spacer if the coil is carrying a current of 20 A. (Hint: Use MATLAB to calculate the co-energy W'_{fld} for a coil current of 20 A and gap lengths of 5 mm and 5.01 mm.)

3.20 An inductor is made up of a 480-turn coil on a core of 15-cm^2 cross-sectional area and gap length 0.14 mm. The coil is connected directly to a 120-V rms, 60-Hz voltage source. Neglect the coil resistance and leakage inductance. Assuming the core reluctance to be negligible, calculate the time-averaged force acting on the core tending to close the air gap. How would this force vary if the air-gap length were doubled?

3.21 Figure 3.36 shows the general nature of the slot leakage flux produced by current i in a rectangular conductor seated in a rectangular slot in iron. Assume that the iron reluctance is negligible and that the slot leakage flux goes straight across the slot in the region between the top of the conductor and the top of the slot.

   a. Derive an expression for the flux density B_s in the region between the top of the conductor and the top of the slot.

   b. Find an expression for the coenergy stored in the region of the slot above the conductor per meter of slot length as a function of the net current i and the dimensions s amd x.

   c. Find an expression for the force x-directed force per meter, f_x, on the conductor from the coenergy of part (b) using Eq. 3.40. Note that although there is additional coenergy associated with flux within the conductor, this coenergy remains constant independent of the position of the conductor in the slot and hence its derivative with respect to x is zero and it does not play a role in the force calculation. In what direction does the force act?

   d. When the conductor current is 900 A, compute the force per meter on a conductor in a slot 5.0 cm wide.

Figure 3.37
Solenoid coil
(Problem 3.22).

3.22 A long, thin solenoid of radius r_0 and height h is shown in Fig. 3.37. The magnetic field inside such a solenoid is axially directed, essentially uniform and equal to $H = Ni/h$. The magnetic field outside the solenoid can be shown to be negligible. Derive an expression for the radial pressure in newtons per square meter acting on the sides of the solenoid for constant coil current $i = I_0$.

3.23 An electromechanical system in which electric energy storage is in electric fields that can be analyzed by techniques directly analogous to those derived in this chapter for magnetic field systems. Consider such a system in which it is possible to separate the loss mechanism mathematically from those of energy storage in electric fields. Then the system can be represented as in Fig. 3.38. For a single electric terminal, Eq. 3.8 applies, where

$$dW_{\text{elec}} = vi\, dt = v\, dq$$

where v is the electric terminal voltage and q is the net charge associated with electric energy storage. Thus, by analogy to Eq. 3.15,

$$dW_{\text{fld}} = v\, dq - f_{\text{fld}}\, dx$$

a. Derive an expression for the electric stored energy $W_{\text{fld}}(q, x)$ analogous to that for the magnetic stored energy in Eq. 3.17.

Figure 3.38 Lossless electric energy storage system.

Figure 3.39 Capacitor plates (Problem 3.24).

b. Derive an expression for the force of electric origin f_{fld} analogous to that of Eq. 3.26. State clearly which variable must be held constant when the derivative is taken.

c. By analogy to the derivation of Eqs. 3.34 to 3.41, derive an expression for the coenergy $W'_{\text{fld}}(v, x)$ and the corresponding force of electric origin.

3.24 A capacitor (Fig. 3.39) is made of two conducting plates of area A separated in air by a spacing x. The terminal voltage is v, and the charge on the plates is q. The capacitance C, defined as the ratio of charge to voltage, is

$$C = \frac{q}{v} = \frac{\epsilon_0 A}{x}$$

where ϵ_0 is the dielectric constant of free space (in SI units $\epsilon_0 = 8.85 \times 10^{-12}$ F/m).

a. Using the results of Problem 3.23, derive expressions for the energy $W_{\text{fld}}(q, x)$ and the coenergy $W'_{\text{fld}}(v, x)$.

b. The terminals of the capacitor are connected to a source of constant voltage V_0. Derive an expression for the force required to maintain the plates separated by a constant spacing $x = \delta$.

3.25 Figure 3.40 shows in schematic form an *electrostatic voltmeter*, a capacitive system consisting of a fixed electrode and a moveable electrode. The

Figure 3.40 Schematic electrostatic voltmeter (Problem 3.25).

moveable electrode is connected to a vane which rotates on a pivot such that the air gap between the two electrodes remains fixed as the vane rotates. The capacitance of this system is given by

$$C(\theta) = \frac{\epsilon_0 R d(\alpha - |\theta|)}{g} \quad (|\theta| \leq \alpha)$$

A torsional spring is connected to the moveable vane, producing a torque

$$T_{\text{spring}} = -K(\theta - \theta_0)$$

a. For $0 \leq \theta \leq \alpha$, using the results of Problem 3.23, derive an expression for the electromagnetic torque T_{fld} in terms of the applied voltage V_{dc}.

b. Find an expression for the angular position of the moveable vane as a function of the applied voltage V_{dc}.

c. For a system with

$$R = 13 \text{ cm}, \qquad d = 3.8 \text{ cm}, \qquad g = 0.2 \text{ mm}$$
$$\alpha = \pi/3 \text{ rad}, \qquad \theta_0 = 0 \text{ rad}, \qquad K = 4.15 \text{ N} \cdot \text{m/rad}$$

Plot the vane position in degrees as a function of applied voltage for $0 \leq V_{\text{dc}} \leq 1800$ V.

3.26 The two-winding magnetic circuit of Fig. 3.41 has a winding on a fixed yoke and a second winding on a moveable element. The moveable element is constrained to motion such that the lengths g of both air gaps remain equal.

a. Find the self-inductances of windings 1 and 2 in terms of the core dimensions and the number of turns.

b. Find the mutual inductance between the two windings.

c. Find the coenergy $W'_{\text{fld}}(i_1, i_2)$.

d. Find an expression for the force acting on the moveable element as a function of the winding currents.

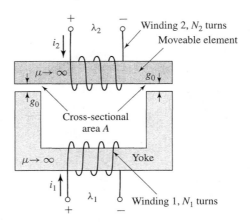

Figure 3.41 Two-winding magnetic circuit for Problem 3.26.

3.27 Two coils, one mounted on a stator and the other on a rotor, have self- and mutual inductances of

$$L_{11} = 5.3 \text{ mH} \quad L_{22} = 2.7 \text{ mH} \quad L_{12} = 3.1 \cos \theta \text{ mH}$$

where θ, the angle between the axes of the coils, is constrained to the range $0 \le \theta \le 90°$. The coils are connected in series and carry a current

$$i = \sqrt{2}I \sin \omega t$$

a. Derive an expression for the instantaneous torque T on the rotor as a function of the angular position θ.

b. Find an expression for the time-averaged torque T_{avg} as a function of θ.

c. Compute the numerical value of T_{avg} for $I = 10$ A and $\theta = 90°$.

d. Sketch curves of T_{avg} versus θ for currents $I = 5, 7.07$, and 10 A.

e. A helical restraining spring which tends to hold the rotor at $\theta = 90°$ is now attached to the rotor. The restraining torque of the spring is proportional to the angular deflection from $\theta = 90°$ and is -0.1 N · m when the rotor is turned to $\theta = 0°$. Show on the curves of part (d) how you could find the angular position of the rotor-plus-spring combination for coil currents $I = 5, 7.07$, and 10 A. From your curves, estimate the rotor angle for each of these currents.

f. Write a MATLAB script to plot the angular position of the rotor as a function of rms current for $0 \le I \le 10$ A.

(Note that this problem illustrates the principles of the dynamometer-type ac ammeter.)

3.28 Two windings, one mounted on a stator and the other on a rotor, have self- and mutual inductances of

$$L_{11} = 7.3 \text{ H} \quad L_{22} = 4.7 \text{ H} \quad L_{12} = 5.6 \cos \theta \text{ H}$$

where θ is the angle between the axes of the windings. The resistances of the windings may be neglected. Winding 2 is short-circuited, and the current in winding 1 as a function of time is $i_1 = \sqrt{2} I_0 \sin \omega t$ A. Plot the time-averaged torque versus θ for $I_0 = 10$ A for $0 \le \theta \le 180°$.

3.29 A loudspeaker is made of a magnetic core of infinite permeability and circular symmetry, as shown in Figs. 3.42a and b. The air-gap length g is much less than the radius r_0 of the central core. The voice coil is constrained to move only in the x direction and is attached to the speaker cone, which is not shown in the figure. A constant radial magnetic field is produced in the air gap by a direct current in coil 1, $i_1 = I_1$. An audio-frequency signal $i_2(t)$ is then applied to the voice coil. Assume the voice coil to be of negligible thickness and composed of N_2 turns uniformly distributed over its height h. Also assume that its displacement x is such that it remains in the air gap $(0 \le x \le l - h)$.

a. Derive an expression for the force on the voice coil, using the Lorentz Force Law (Eq. 3.1) in terms of the voice-coil displacement x and current i_2.

Figure 3.42 Loudspeaker for Problem 3.29.

b. Derive expressions for the self-inductance of each coil.

c. Derive an expression for the mutual inductance between the coils. (Hint: Assume that current is applied to the voice coil, and calculate the flux linkages of coil 1. Note that these flux linkages vary with the displacement x.)

d. Derive an expression for the system coenergy W'_{fld} and the force on the voice coil as a function of the voice-coil displacement and current i_2.

3.30 Repeat Example 3.8 with the samarium-cobalt magnet replaced by a neodymium-iron-boron magnet.

3.31 The magnetic structure of Fig. 3.43 is a schematic view of a system designed to support a block of magnetic material ($\mu \to \infty$) of mass M against the force of gravity. The system includes a permanent magnet and a winding. Under normal conditions, the force is supplied by the permanent magnet alone. The

Figure 3.43 Magnetic support system for Problem 3.31.

function of the winding is to counteract the field produced by the magnet so
that the mass can be removed from the device. The system is designed such
that the air gaps at each side of the mass remain constant at length $g_0/2$.

Assume that the permanent magnet can be represented by a linear
characteristic of the form

$$B_m = \mu_R(H_m - H_c)$$

and that the winding direction is such that positive winding current reduces
the air-gap flux produced by the permanent magnet. Neglect the effects of
magnetic fringing.

a. Assume the winding current to be zero.

    i. Find the force $f_{fld}(x)$ acting on the mass due to the permanent magnet
alone $((0 \leq x \leq h))$.

    ii. Find the maximum mass M_{max} that can be supported against gravity.

b. For $M = M_{max}/2$, find the minimum current I_{min} required to cause the
mass to fall out of the system when the current is applied.

3.32 Winding 1 in the loudspeaker of Problem 3.29 (Fig. 3.42) is replaced by a
permanent magnet as shown in Fig. 3.44. The magnet can be represented by
the linear characteristic $B_m = \mu_R(H_m - H_c)$.

a. Assuming the voice coil current to be zero, ($i_2 = 0$), derive and
expression for the magnetic flux density in the air gap.

b. Derive an expression for the flux linkage of the voice coil due to the
permanent magnet as a function of the displacement x.

c. Derive an expression for the system coenergy $W'_{fld}(i_2, x)$ assuming that
the voice coil current is sufficiently small so that the component of W'_{fld}
due to the voice coil self inductance can be ignored.

d. Based upon the coenergy expression of part (c), derive an expression for
the force on the voice coil.

Figure 3.44 Core of loudspeaker of
Fig. 3.42 with winding 1 replaced by a
permanent magnet (Problem 3.32).

Figure 3.45 Permanent-magnet system for Problem 3.33.

3.33 Figure 3.45 shows a circularly symmetric system in which a moveable plunger (constrained to move only in the vertical direction) is supported by a spring of spring constant K. The system is excited by a samarium-cobalt permanent-magnet in the shape of a washer of outer radius R_3, inner radius R_2, and thickness t_m. The system dimensions are:

$$R_1 = 2.1 \text{ cm}, \quad R_2 = 4 \text{ cm}, \quad R_3 = 4.5 \text{ cm}$$
$$h = 1 \text{ cm}, \quad g = 1 \text{ mm}, \quad t_m = 3 \text{ mm}$$

The equilibrium position of the plunger is observed to be $X_0 = 0.5$ mm.

a. Find the magnetic flux density B_g in the fixed gap and B_x in the variable gap.

b. Calculate the x-directed magnetic force pulling down on the plunger.

c. Plot the magnetic force on the plunger over the range $0 \le x \le X_0$.

d. Find the minimum value of the spring constant K in N/cm that will guarantee that the plunger will return to this stable equilibrium point if the plunger is depressed so that $x = 0$ and then released.

3.34 The plunger of a solenoid is connected to a spring. The inductance of the solenoid is of the form $L = L_0(1 - x/X_0)$, and its winding resistance is R_c. The spring force is given by $f_{\text{spring}} = K_0 (0.5 X_0 - x)$, where x is the air-gap length. The plunger is initially stationary at position $x = 0.5X_0$ when a dc voltage of magnitude V_0 is applied to the solenoid.

a. Find an expression for the force as a function of time required to hold the plunger at position $X_0/2$.

b. If the plunger is then released and allowed to come to equilibrium, find the equilibrium position x_0. You may assume that K_0 is sufficiently large that x_0 falls in the range $0 \le x_0 \le X_0$.

3.35 Consider the single-coil rotor of Example 3.1. Assume the rotor winding to be carrying a constant current of $I = 8$ A and the rotor to have a moment of inertia $J = 0.0175$ kg $\cdot$ m^2.

a. Find the equilibrium position of the rotor. Is it stable?

b. Write the dynamic equations for the system.

c. Find the natural frequency in hertz for incremental rotor motion around this equilibrium position.

3.36 Consider a solenoid magnet similar to that of Example 3.10 (Fig. 3.24) except that the length of the cylindrical plunger is reduced to $a + h$. The plunger is initially set to position $x = X_0 = a/2$ and the coil is then connected to a supply which maintains constant flux linkages, $\lambda = \lambda_0$. Calculate the force on the plunger as a function of x. You may assume that the plunger remains well within the core, e.g. $a/4 \le x \le 3a/4$.

3.37 Consider the solenoid system of Problem 3.34. Assume the following parameter values:

$$L_0 = 6.2 \, \text{mH} \quad X_0 = 2.4 \, \text{cm} \quad R_c = 1.6 \, \Omega \quad K_0 = 4.1 \, \text{N/cm}$$

Assume the coil to be connected to a dc voltage source of magnitude 4.0 V.

a. Find the equilibrium displacement x_0.

b. The plunger has mass M. Write the dynamic equations of motion for the system.

c. For $M = 0.2$ kg, assuming that the current remains constant at its steady-state value, calculate the frequency of oscillation of the plunger should it be perturbed from its equilibrium position x_0.

d. Simulate the system response using Simulink. Assume that the system is initially at rest with zero applied voltage and that the 4.0 V dc source is suddenly applied at time $t = 1.0$ sec. Plot

  i. the resultant motion of the plunger as a function of time, and

  ii. the corresponding time-varying component of the coil current.

3.38 Consider the shaker system of Problem 3.17. Assuming the plunger is initially at rest with zero coil current, use Simulink to solve for the motion of the plunger $\delta(t)$ if a dc voltage of 0.1 V is suddenly applied to the coil.

4 CHAPTER

Introduction to Rotating Machines

The object of this chapter is to introduce and discuss some of the principles underlying the performance of electric machinery. As will be seen, these principles are common to both ac and dc machines. Various techniques and approximations involved in reducing a physical machine to simple mathematical models, sufficient to illustrate the basic principles, will be developed.

4.1 ELEMENTARY CONCEPTS

Equation 1.26, $e = d\lambda/dt$, can be used to determine the voltages induced by time-varying magnetic fields. Electromagnetic energy conversion occurs when changes in the flux linkage λ result from mechanical motion. In rotating machines, voltages are generated in windings or groups of coils by rotating these windings mechanically through a magnetic field, by mechanically rotating a magnetic field past the winding, or by designing the magnetic circuit so that the reluctance varies with rotation of the rotor. By any of these methods, the flux linking a specific coil is changed cyclically, and a time-varying voltage is generated.

A set of such coils connected together is typically referred to as an *armature winding*. In general, the term armature winding is used to refer to a winding or a set of windings on a rotating machine which carry ac currents. In *ac machines* such as synchronous or induction machines, the armature winding is typically on the stationary portion of the motor referred to as the *stator,* in which case these windings may also be referred to as *stator windings*. Figure 4.1 shows the stator winding of a large, three-phase synchronous generator under construction.

In a *dc machine,* the armature winding is found on the rotating member, referred to as the *rotor*. Figure 4.2 shows a dc-machine rotor. As we will see, the armature winding of a dc machine consists of many coils connected together to form a closed loop. A rotating mechanical contact is used to supply current to the armature winding as the rotor rotates.

Figure 4.1 Stator of a 100-MVA three-phase air-cooled synchronous generator under construction.(*Photo courtesy of General Electric Company.*)

Figure 4.2 Armature of a dc motor. (*Photo courtesy of Baldor Electric/ABB*)

Synchronous and dc machines typically include a second winding (or set of windings) which carry dc current and which are used to produce the main operating flux in the machine. Such a winding is typically referred to as *field winding*. The field winding on a dc machine is found on the stator, while that on a synchronous machine is found on the rotor, in which case current is typically supplied to the field winding via a rotating mechanical contact, with the exception being machines for which a rotating excitation system supplies the field current. As we have seen, permanent magnets also produce dc magnetic flux and are used in the place of field windings in

Figure 4.3 Field winding installation on the rotor of a 200-MW, 2-pole synchronous generator. (*Photo courtesy of General Electric Company.*)

some machines. Figure 4.3 shows the field winding being installed on the rotor of a large, 200-MW, 4-pole synchronous generator.

In most rotating machines, the stator and rotor are made of electrical steel, and the windings are inserted in slots on these structures. As is discussed in Chapter 1, the use of such high-permeability material maximizes the coupling between the coils and increases the magnetic energy density associated with the electromechanical interaction. It also enables the machine designer to shape and distribute the magnetic fields according to the requirements of each particular machine design. The time-varying flux present in the armature structures of these machines tends to induce currents, known as *eddy currents,* in the electrical steel. Eddy currents can be a large source of loss in such machines and can significantly reduce machine performance. In order to minimize the effects of eddy currents, the armature structure is typically built from thin laminations of electrical steel which are insulated from each other.

In some machines, such as *variable reluctance machines* and *stepper motors,* there are no windings on the rotor. Operation of these machines depends on the non-uniformity of air-gap reluctance associated with variations in rotor position in conjunction with time-varying currents applied to their stator windings. In such machines, both the stator and rotor structures are subjected to time-varying magnetic flux and, as a result, both may require lamination to reduce eddy-current losses.

Rotating electric machines take many forms and are known by many names: dc, synchronous, permanent-magnet, induction, variable reluctance, hysteresis, brushless, and so on. Although these machines appear to be quite dissimilar, the physical principles governing their behavior are quite similar, and it is often helpful to think of them in terms of the same physical picture. For example, analysis of a dc machine shows that associated with both the rotor and the stator are magnetic flux distributions which are fixed in space and that the torque-producing characteristic of the dc machine stems from the tendency of these flux distributions to align. An induction machine, in spite of many fundamental differences, works on exactly the same principle; one can identify flux distributions associated with the rotor and stator. Although they are not stationary but rather rotate in synchronism, just as in a dc motor they are displaced by a constant angular separation, and torque is produced by the tendency of these flux distribution to align.

Analytically-based models are essential to the analysis and design of electric machines, and such models will be derived throughout this book. However, it is also important to recognize that physical insight into the performance of these devices is equally useful. One objective of this and subsequent chapters is to guide the reader in the development of such insight.

Vocabulary

4.2 INTRODUCTION TO AC AND DC MACHINES

4.2.1 AC machines

Traditional ac machines fall into one of two categories: *synchronous* and *induction*. In synchronous machines, rotor-winding currents are supplied directly from the stationary frame through a rotating contact. In induction machines, rotor currents are induced in the rotor windings by a combination of the time-variation of the stator currents and the motion of the rotor relative to the stator.

Synchronous Machines   A preliminary picture of synchronous-machine performance can be gained by discussing the voltage induced in the armature of the very much simplified *salient-pole* ac synchronous generator shown schematically in Fig. 4.4. The field-winding of this machine produces a single pair of magnetic poles (similar to that of a bar magnet), and hence this machine is referred to as a *two-pole* machine.

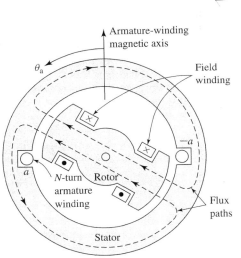

Notes

Figure 4.4 Schematic view of a simple, two-pole, single-phase synchronous generator.

With rare exceptions, the armature winding of a synchronous machine is on the stator, and the field winding is on the rotor, as is true for the simplified machine of Fig. 4.4. The field winding is excited by direct current, typically conducted to it by means of stationary carbon *brushes* which contact rotating *slip rings* or *collector rings* although in some cases the field winding may be supplied from a rotating excitation system, typically referred to as a *brushless excitation system*. Practical factors usually dictate this orientation of the two windings: It is advantageous to have the single, low-power field winding on the rotor while having the high-power, typically multiple-phase, armature winding on the stator.

The armature winding, consisting here of only a single coil of N turns, is indicated in cross section by the two coil sides a and $-a$ placed in diametrically opposite narrow slots on the inner periphery of the stator of Fig. 4.4. The conductors forming these coil sides are parallel to the shaft of the machine and are connected in series by end connections (not shown in the figure). The rotor is turned at a constant speed by a source of mechanical power connected to its shaft. The armature winding is assumed to be open-circuited and hence the flux in this machine is produced by the field winding alone. Flux paths are shown schematically by dashed lines in Fig. 4.4.

A highly idealized analysis of this machine would assume a sinusoidal distribution of magnetic flux in the air gap. The resultant idealized radial distribution of air-gap flux density B is shown in Fig. 4.5a as a function of the spatial angle θ_a (measured with respect to the magnetic axis of the armature winding) around the rotor periphery. In practice, the air-gap flux-density of practical salient-pole machines can be made to approximate a sinusoidal distribution by properly shaping the pole faces.

As the rotor rotates, the flux-linkages of the armature winding change with time. Under the assumption of a sinusoidal flux distribution and constant rotor speed, the resulting coil voltage will be sinusoidal in time as shown in Fig. 4.5b. The coil voltage passes through a complete cycle for each revolution of the two-pole machine of Fig. 4.4. Its frequency in cycles per second (Hz) is the same as the speed of the rotor in revolutions per second: the electric frequency of the generated voltage is synchronized with the mechanical speed, and this is the reason for the designation "synchronous" machine. Thus a two-pole synchronous machine must revolve at 3600 revolutions per minute to produce a 60-Hz voltage.

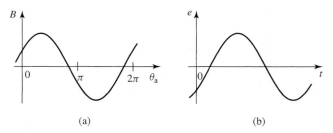

(a)   (b)

Figure 4.5   (a) Idealized sinusoidal space distribution of the air-gap radial flux density and (b) corresponding waveform of the generated voltage for the single-phase generator of Fig. 4.4.

Figure 4.6 Schematic view of a simple, four-pole, single-phase synchronous generator.

A great many synchronous machines have more than two poles. As a specific example, Fig. 4.6 shows in schematic form a *four-pole* single-phase generator. The field coils are connected so that the poles are of alternate polarity. There are two complete wavelengths, or cycles, in the flux distribution around the periphery, as shown in Fig. 4.7. The armature winding now consists of two coils a_1, $-a_1$ and a_2, $-a_2$ which can be connected either in series or parallel. The span of each coil is one wavelength of flux. The generated voltage now goes through two complete cycles per revolution of the rotor. The frequency in hertz will thus be twice the speed in revolutions per second.

When a machine has more than two poles, it is convenient to concentrate on a single pair of poles and to recognize that the electric, magnetic, and mechanical conditions associated with every other pole pair are repetitions of those for the pair under consideration. For this reason it is convenient to express angles in *electrical degrees* or *electrical radians* rather than in physical units. One pair of poles in a multipole machine or one cycle of flux distribution corresponds to 360 electrical degrees

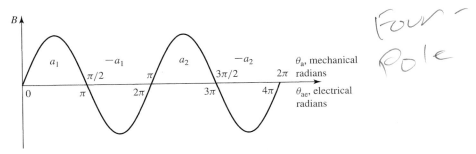

Figure 4.7 Space distribution of the air-gap flux density in an idealized, four-pole synchronous generator.

or 2π electrical radians. Since there are poles/2 complete wavelengths, or cycles, in one complete revolution, it follows, for example, that

$$\theta_{ae} = \left(\frac{\text{poles}}{2}\right)\theta_a \tag{4.1}$$

where θ_{ae} is the angle in electrical units, θ_a is the spatial angle. This same relationship applies to all angular measurements in a multi-pole machine; their values in electrical units will be equal to (poles/2) times their actual spatial values.

The coil voltage of a multi-pole machine passes through a complete cycle every time a pair of poles sweeps by, or (poles/2) times each revolution. The electrical frequency f_e of the voltage generated in a synchronous machine is therefore

$$f_e = \left(\frac{\text{poles}}{2}\right)\frac{n}{60}\ \text{Hz} \tag{4.2}$$

where n is the mechanical speed in revolutions per minute, and hence $n/60$ is the speed in revolutions per second. The electrical frequency of the generated voltage in radians per second is

$$\omega_e = \left(\frac{\text{poles}}{2}\right)\omega_m \tag{4.3}$$

where ω_m is the mechanical speed in radians per second.

The rotors shown in Figs. 4.4 and 4.6 have *salient*, or *projecting,* poles with *concentrated windings.* Figure 4.8 shows diagrammatically a *nonsalient-pole,* or *cylindrical,* rotor. The field winding on the rotor is a two-pole *distributed winding;* the coil sides are distributed in multiple slots around the rotor periphery and arranged to produce an approximately sinusoidal distribution of radial air-gap flux.

The relationship between electrical frequency and rotor speed of Eq. 4.2 can serve as a basis for understanding why some synchronous generators have salient-pole rotor structures while others have cylindrical rotors. Most power systems in the

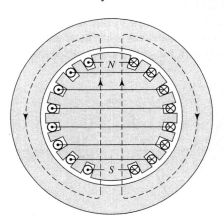

Figure 4.8 Elementary two-pole cylindrical-rotor field winding.

Figure 4.9 Rotor of a 100-MW turbine generator. A brushless excitation system, used to supply dc field current, is seen on the near end of the rotor. (*Photo courtesy of General Electric Company.*)

world operate at frequencies of either 50 or 60 Hz. A salient-pole construction is characteristic of hydroelectric generators because hydraulic turbines operate at relatively low speeds, and hence a relatively large number of poles is required to produce the desired frequency; a salient-pole construction is better adapted mechanically to this situation. Steam turbines and gas turbines operate best at relatively high speeds, and turbine-driven alternators or turbine generators are commonly two- or four-pole cylindrical-rotor machines. These cylindrical rotors are made from a single steel forging or from several forgings, as shown in Fig. 4.9.

Most of the world's power systems are three-phase systems and, as a result, with very few exceptions, synchronous generators are three-phase machines. For the production of a set of three voltages phase-displaced by 120 electrical degrees in time, a minimum of three coils phase-displaced 120 electrical degrees in space must be used. A simplified schematic view of a three-phase, two-pole machine with one coil per phase is shown in Fig. 4.10a. The three phases are designated by the letters a, b, and c. In an elementary four-pole machine, a minimum of two such sets of coils must be used, as illustrated in Fig. 4.10b; in an elementary multi-pole machine, the minimum number of coil sets is given by one half the number of poles.

The two coils in each phase of Fig. 4.10b are connected in series so that their voltages add, and the three phases may then be either Y- or Δ-connected. Figure 4.10c shows how the coils may be interconnected to form a Y connection. Note however, since the voltages in the coils of each phase are identical, a parallel connection is also possible, e.g., coil $(a, -a)$ in parallel with coil $(a', -a')$, and so on.

When a synchronous generator supplies electric power to a load, the armature current creates a magnetic flux wave in the air gap which rotates at synchronous speed, as shown in Section 4.5. This flux reacts with the flux created by the field current, and electromechanical torque results from the tendency of these two magnetic fields to align. In a generator this torque opposes rotation, and mechanical torque must be

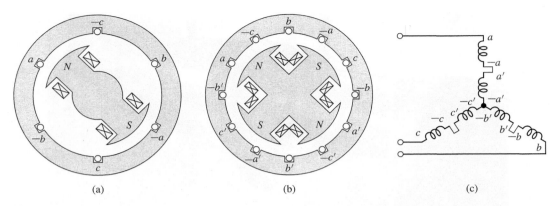

Figure 4.10 Schematic views of three-phase generators: (a) two-pole, (b) four-pole, and (c) *Y* connection of the windings.

applied from the prime mover to sustain rotation. This electromechanical torque is the mechanism through which the synchronous generator converts mechanical to electric energy.

The counterpart of the synchronous generator is the synchronous motor. Alternating current is supplied to the armature winding on the stator, and dc excitation is supplied to the field winding on the rotor. The magnetic field produced by the armature currents rotates at synchronous speed (equal to 2/poles times the electrical frequency of the armature currents). A steady electromechanical torque is produced when the rotor rotates in synchronism with the magnetic field produced by the armature currents. Hence the steady-state speed of a synchronous motor is determined by the number of poles and the frequency of the armature current and a synchronous motor operated from a constant-frequency ac source will operate at a constant steady-state speed.

In a motor the electromechanical torque is in the direction of rotation and balances the opposing torque required to drive the mechanical load. The flux produced by currents in the armature of a synchronous motor rotates ahead of that produced by the rotor field winding, thus pulling on the field winding (and hence on the rotor) and doing work. This is the opposite of the situation in a synchronous generator, where the field does work as its flux pulls on that of the armature. In both generators and motors, in addition to an electromechanical torque, a speed voltage (emf) is induced in the armature by the rotating field winding. As is discussed in Chapter 3, the production of both force or torque and a speed voltage are both essential components of electromechanical energy conversion.

Induction machines   A second type of ac machine is the *induction machine*. In an induction machine, the stator windings are essentially the same as those of a synchronous machine. However, the rotor windings are electrically short-circuited and frequently have no external connections; currents are induced by transformer action from the stator winding. A cutaway view of a squirrel-cage induction motor is shown in Fig. 4.11. Here the rotor "windings" are actually solid aluminum bars which are cast into the slots in the rotor and which are shorted together by cast aluminum

Figure 4.11 Cutaway view of a 460-V, 7.5-hp squirrel-cage induction motor.

rings at each end of the rotor. This type of rotor construction results in induction motors which are relatively inexpensive and highly reliable, factors contributing to their immense popularity and widespread application.

In contrast to a synchronous machine in which a field winding on the rotor is excited with dc current and the rotor rotates in synchronism with the flux wave produced by ac armature currents, the rotor windings of an induction machine are not excited by an external source. Rather, currents are induced in the shorted rotor windings as the rotor slips past the synchronously-rotating armature flux wave. Thus, induction machines are *asynchronous machines* and produce torque only when the rotor speed differs from synchronous speed.

Interestingly, although the rotor operates asynchronously, the flux wave produced by the induced rotor currents rotates in synchronism with the stator flux wave. This in fact is a requirement for, and consistent with, the ability of an induction machine to produce net torque. Induction motors operate at speeds less than the synchronous mechanical speed, in which case the armature flux in the induction motor leads that of the rotor and produces an electromechanical torque which pulls on the rotor just as is the case in a synchronous motor, A typical speed-torque characteristic for an induction motor is shown in Fig. 4.12.

Because rotor currents are by produced by induction, an induction machine may be regarded as a generalized transformer in which electric power is transformed between rotor and stator together with a change of frequency and a flow of mechanical power. Although induction machines are primarily used as motors, in recent years induction generators have been found to be well suited for some wind-power applications.

Figure 4.12 Typical induction-motor speed-torque characteristic.

4.2.2   DC machines

As has been discussed, the armature winding of a dc machine is on the rotor with current conducted to it by means of carbon brushes. The field winding is on the stator and is excited by direct current. A cutaway view of a dc motor is shown in Fig. 4.13.

Consider a very elementary two-pole dc generator as is shown in Fig. 4.14. The armature winding, consisting of a single coil of N turns, is indicated by the two coil sides a and $-a$ placed at diametrically opposite points on the rotor with the conductors parallel to the shaft. The rotor is normally turned at a constant speed by a source of mechanical power connected to the shaft. The air-gap flux distribution usually

Figure 4.13 Cutaway view of a 25-hp, 1750-rpm, 500-V dc motor. (*Photo courtesy of Baldor Electric/ABB.*)

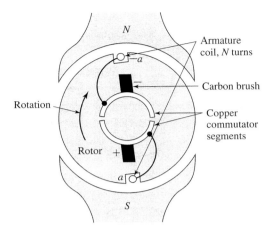

Figure 4.14 Elementary dc machine with commutator. The rotor, armature coil, and commutator rotate while the brushes remain stationary.

approximates a flat-topped wave, rather than the sine wave found in ac machines, and is shown in Fig. 4.15a. Rotation of the coil, shown schematically in Fig. 4.15a, generates a coil voltage which is a time function having the same waveform as the spatial flux-density distribution.

The function of a dc generator is the production of dc voltage and current. Thus the ac voltages and currents induced in the armature winding must be rectified. In a dc machine, rectification is produced mechanically by means of a *commutator* which is a cylinder formed of copper segments to which the armature coils are connected. These segments are otherwise insulated from each other by mica or some other highly insulating material and mounted on, but insulated from, the rotor shaft. Stationary carbon brushes held against the commutator surface connect the winding to the external armature terminals. The commutator and brushes can readily be seen in Fig. 4.13 and a simple two-segment commutator is shown in Fig. 4.14. The need for commutation is the reason why the armature windings of dc machines are found on the rotor.

For the elementary dc generator, the commutator takes the form shown in Fig. 4.14. To understand its function as a rectifier, note that the commutator at all times connects the coil side which is closest to the south pole to the positive brush and the coil side closest to the north pole is connected to the negative brush. Thus, each half rotation of the rotor, the brushes switch their polarity with respect to the coil polarity. As a result, although the coil voltage is an alternating voltage similar in form to the air-gap flux distribution shown in Fig. 4.15a, the commutator provides full-wave rectification, transforming the coil voltage to the voltage between brushes of Fig. 4.15b and making available a unidirectional voltage to the external circuit. The dc machine of Fig. 4.14 is, of course, simplified to the point of being unrealistic in the practical sense, and later it will be essential to examine the action of more realistic commutators.

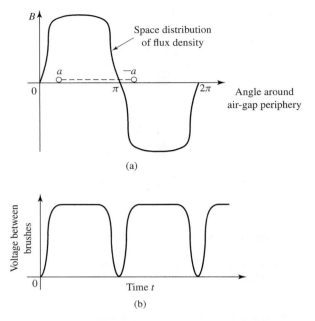

Figure 4.15 (a) Space distribution of air-gap flux density in an elementary dc machine. (b) Waveform of voltage between brushes.

The direct current in the field winding of a dc machine creates a magnetic flux distribution which is stationary with respect to the stator. Similarly, the effect of the commutator is such that when direct current flows through the brushes, the armature creates a magnetic flux distribution which is also fixed in space and whose axis, determined by the design of the machine and the position of the brushes, is typically perpendicular to the axis of the field flux.

Thus, just as in the ac machines discussed previously, it is the interaction of these two flux distributions that creates the torque of the dc machine. If the machine is acting as a generator, the electromechanical torque opposes rotation; if it is acting as a motor, the torque acts in the direction of rotation. Remarks similar to those already made concerning the roles played by the generated voltage and electromechanical torque in the energy conversion process in synchronous machines apply equally well to dc machines.

4.3   MMF OF DISTRIBUTED WINDINGS

Most armatures have distributed windings, i.e., windings which are spread over a number of slots around the air-gap periphery, as in Figs. 4.1 and 4.2. The individual coils are interconnected so that the result is a magnetic field having the same number of poles as the field winding.

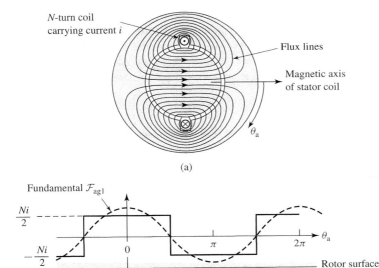

Figure 4.16 (a) Flux produced by a concentrated, full-pitch winding in a machine with a uniform air gap. (b) The air-gap mmf produced by current in this winding.

The study of the magnetic fields of distributed windings can be approached by examining the magnetic field produced by a winding consisting of a single N-turn coil which spans 180 electrical degrees, as shown in Fig. 4.16a. A coil which spans 180 electrical degrees is known as a *full-pitch coil*. The dot and cross indicate current flow toward and away from the reader, respectively. For simplicity, a concentric cylindrical rotor is shown. The dipole nature of the magnetic field produced by the current in the coil is shown by the flux lines in Fig. 4.16a. Since the permeability of the armature and field iron is much greater than that of air, it is sufficiently accurate for our present purposes to assume that all the reluctance of the magnetic circuit is in the air gap. From symmetry of the structure it is evident that the magnetic field intensity H_{ag} in the air gap at angle θ_a under one pole is the same in magnitude as that at angle $\theta_a + \pi$ under the opposite pole, but the fields are in the opposite direction.

Around any of the closed paths shown by the flux lines in Fig. 4.16a the mmf is Ni. Because we have assumed that the reluctance of the magnetic circuit is predominantly that of the air gap, the mmf drop in the iron can be neglected and all of the mmf drop will appear across the air gap. By symmetry we argued that the air-gap fields H_{ag} on opposite sides of the rotor are equal in magnitude but opposite in direction. It follows that the air-gap mmf should be similarly distributed; since each flux line crosses the air gap twice, the mmf drop across the air gap must be equal to half of the total or $Ni/2$.

Figure 4.16b shows the air gap and winding in developed form, i.e., laid out flat. The air-gap mmf distribution is shown by the step-like distribution of amplitude $Ni/2$. On the assumption of narrow slot openings, the mmf jumps abruptly by Ni in crossing from one side to the other of a coil. This mmf distribution is discussed again in Section 4.4, where the resultant magnetic fields are evaluated.

4.3.1 AC machines

Fourier analysis can be used to show that the air-gap mmf produced by a single coil such as the full-pitch coil of Fig. 4.16 consists of a fundamental space-harmonic component as well as a series of higher-order harmonic components. In the design of ac machines, serious efforts are made to distribute the coils making up the windings so as to minimize the higher-order harmonic components and to produce an air-gap mmf wave which consists predominantly of the space-fundamental sinusoidal component. It is thus appropriate here to assume that this has been done and to focus our attention on the fundamental component.

The rectangular air-gap mmf wave of the concentrated two-pole, full-pitch coil of Fig. 4.16b can be resolved into a Fourier series comprising a fundamental component and a series of odd harmonics. The fundamental component $\mathcal{F}_{\mathrm{ag1}}$ is

$$\mathcal{F}_{\mathrm{ag1}} = \frac{4}{\pi}\left(\frac{Ni}{2}\right)\cos\theta_{\mathrm{a}} \tag{4.4}$$

where θ_{a} is measured from the magnetic axis of the stator coil, as shown by the dashed sinusoid in Fig. 4.16b. It is a sinusoidal space wave of amplitude

$$(F_{\mathrm{ag1}})_{\mathrm{peak}} = \frac{4}{\pi}\left(\frac{Ni}{2}\right) \tag{4.5}$$

with its peak aligned with the magnetic axis of the coil.

Now consider a *distributed winding,* consisting of coils distributed in several slots. For example, Fig. 4.17a shows phase a of the armature winding of a somewhat simplified two-pole, three-phase ac machine. Phases b and c occupy the empty slots. The windings of the three phases are identical and are located with their magnetic axes 120 degrees apart. We direct our attention to the air-gap mmf of phase *a* alone, postponing the discussion of the effects of all three phases until Section 4.5. The winding is arranged in two layers, each full-pitch coil of N_{c} turns having one side in the top of a slot and the other coil side in the bottom of a slot a pole pitch away. In a practical machine, this two-layer arrangement simplifies the geometric problem of getting the end turns of the individual coils past each other when the winding is inserted in the stator.

Figure 4.17b shows one pole of this winding laid out flat. With the coils connected in series and hence carrying the same current, the mmf wave is a series of steps each of height $2N_{c}i_{a}$ (equal to the ampere-turns in the slot), where i_{a} is the winding current. Its space-fundamental component is shown by the sinusoid. It can be seen that the distributed winding produces an mmf wave which is a closer approximation to a sinusoidal mmf wave than that of the concentrated coil of Fig. 4.16.

(a)

(b)

Figure 4.17 The mmf of one phase of a distributed two-pole, three-phase winding with full-pitch coils.

The modified form of Eq. 4.4 for a distributed multi-pole winding having N_{ph} series turns per phase is

$$\mathcal{F}_{ag1} = \frac{4}{\pi} \left(\frac{k_w N_{ph}}{poles} \right) i_a \cos \left(\frac{poles}{2} \theta_a \right)$$

$$= \frac{4}{\pi} \left(\frac{k_w N_{ph}}{poles} \right) i_a \cos (\theta_{ae}) \qquad (4.6)$$

in which the factor $4/\pi$ arises from the Fourier-series analysis of the rectangular mmf wave of a concentrated full-pitch coil, as in Eq. 4.4, and the *winding factor* k_w takes into account the distribution of the winding. This factor is required because the mmfs produced by the individual coils of any one phase group have different magnetic axes and hence don't sum directly. When they are connected in series to form the phase winding, their phasor sum is then less than their numerical sum. (See Appendix B for details.) For most three-phase windings, k_w typically falls in the range of 0.85 to 0.95.

The factor $k_w N_{ph}$ is the *effective series turns per phase* for the fundamental mmf. The peak amplitude of the mmf wave of Eq. 4.6 is

$$(F_{ag1})_{peak} = \frac{4}{\pi} \left(\frac{k_w N_{ph}}{poles} \right) i_a \tag{4.7}$$

EXAMPLE 4.1

The two-pole phase-a armature winding of Fig. 4.17a can be considered to consist of eight N_c-turn, full-pitch coils connected in series, with each slot containing two coils. There are a total of 24 armature slots, and thus each slot is separated by $360°/24 = 15°$. Define the angle θ_a as being measured from the magnetic axis of phase a such that the four slots containing the coil sides labeled a are at $\theta_a = 67.5°, 82.5°, 97.5°$, and $112.5°$. The opposite sides of each coil are thus found in the slots found at $-112.5°, -97.5°, -82.5°$ and $-67.5°$, respectively. Assume this winding to be carrying current i_a.

(a) Write an expression for the space-fundamental mmf produced by the two coils whose sides are in the slots at $\theta_a = 112.5°$ and $-67.5°$. (b) Write an expression for the space-fundamental mmf produced by the two coils whose sides are in the slots at $\theta_a = 67.5°$ and $-112.5°$. (c) Write an expression for the space-fundamental mmf of the complete armature winding. (d) Determine the winding factor k_w for this distributed winding.

■ Solution

a. Noting that the magnetic axis of this pair of coils is at $\theta_a = (112.5° - 67.5°)/2 = 22.5°$ and that the total ampere-turns in each slot is equal to $2N_c i_a$, the mmf produced by this pair of coils can be found from analogy with Eq. 4.4 to be

$$(\mathcal{F}_{ag1})_{22.5°} = \frac{4}{\pi} \left(\frac{2N_c i_a}{2} \right) \cos (\theta_a - 22.5°)$$

b. This pair of coils produces the same space-fundamental mmf as the pair of part (a) with the exception that this mmf is centered at $\theta_a = -22.5°$. Thus

$$(\mathcal{F}_{ag1})_{-22.5°} = \frac{4}{\pi} \left(\frac{2N_c i_a}{2} \right) \cos (\theta_a + 22.5°)$$

c. By analogy with parts (a) and (b), the total space-fundamental mmf can be written as

$$(\mathcal{F}_{ag1})_{total} = (\mathcal{F}_{ag1})_{-22.5°} + (\mathcal{F}_{ag1})_{-7.5°} + (\mathcal{F}_{ag1})_{7.5°} + (\mathcal{F}_{ag1})_{22.5°}$$

$$= \frac{4}{\pi} \left(\frac{2N_c}{2} \right) i_a \left[\cos (\theta_a + 22.5°) + \cos (\theta_a + 7.5°) \right.$$

$$\left. + \cos(\theta_a - 7.5°) + \cos (\theta_a - 22.5°) \right]$$

$$= \frac{4}{\pi} \left(\frac{7.66 N_c}{2} \right) i_a \cos \theta_a$$

$$= 4.88 N_c i_a \cos \theta_a$$

d. Recognizing that, for this winding $N_{ph} = 8 N_c$, the total mmf of part (c) can be rewritten as

$$(\mathcal{F}_{ag1})_{total} = \frac{4}{\pi} \left(\frac{0.958 N_{ph}}{2} \right) i_a \cos \theta_a$$

Comparison with Eq. 4.6 shows that for this winding, the winding factor is $k_w = 0.958$.

Calculate the winding factor of the phase-a winding of Fig. 4.17 if the number of turns in the four coils in the two outer pairs of slots is reduced to six while the number of turns in the four coils in the inner slots remains at eight.

Look
✳ up in
Book or
online

Solution

$$k_w = 0.962$$

Equation 4.6 describes the space-fundamental component of the mmf wave produced by current in phase a of a distributed winding. If the phase-a current is sinusoidal in time, e.g., $i_a = I_{max} \cos \omega t$, the result will be an mmf wave which is stationary in space and varies sinusoidally both with respect to θ_a and in time. In Section 4.5 we will study the effect of currents in all three phases and will see that the application of three-phase currents will produce a rotating mmf wave.

In a directly analogous fashion, rotor windings are often distributed in slots to reduce the effects of space harmonics. Figure 4.18a shows the rotor of a typical two-pole round-rotor generator. Although the winding is symmetric with respect to the rotor axis, the number of turns per slot can be varied to control the various harmonics. In Fig. 4.18b it can be seen that there are fewer turns in the slots nearest the pole face (rotor axis). In addition, the designer can vary the spacing of the slots. As for distributed armature windings, the fundamental air-gap mmf wave of a multi-pole rotor winding can be expressed in the form of Eq. 4.6 in terms of the total number of series turns N_r, the winding current I_r, and a winding factor k_r as

$$\mathcal{F}_{ag1} = \frac{4}{\pi} \left(\frac{k_r N_r}{poles} \right) I_r \cos \left(\frac{poles}{2} \theta_r \right) \tag{4.8}$$

where θ_r is the spatial angle measured with respect to the rotor magnetic axis, as shown in Fig. 4.18b. Its peak amplitude is

$$(F_{ag1})_{peak} = \frac{4}{\pi} \left(\frac{k_r N_r}{poles} \right) I_r \tag{4.9}$$

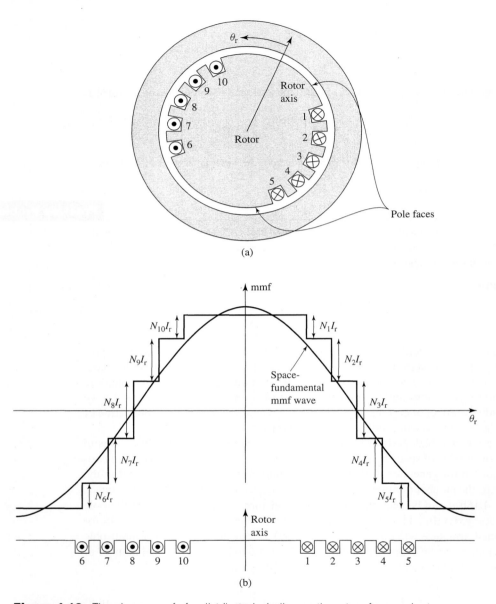

Figure 4.18 The air-gap mmf of a distributed winding on the rotor of a round-rotor generator.

4.3.2 DC Machines

Because of the restrictions imposed on the winding arrangement by the commutator, the mmf wave of a dc machine armature approximates a sawtooth waveform more nearly than the sine wave of ac machines. For example, Fig. 4.19 shows

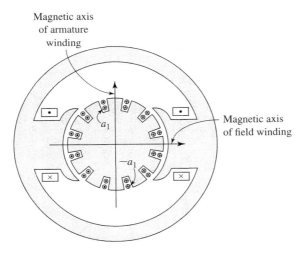

Figure 4.19 Cross section of a two-pole dc machine.

diagrammatically in cross section the armature of a two-pole dc machine. (In practice, in all but the smallest of dc machines, a larger number of coils and slots would probably be used.) The current directions are shown by dots and crosses. The armature winding coil connections are such that the armature winding produces a magnetic field whose axis is vertical and thus is perpendicular to the axis of the field winding. As the armature rotates, the coil connections to the external circuit are changed by the commutator such that the magnetic field of the armature remains vertical. Thus, the armature flux is always perpendicular to that produced by the field winding and a continuous unidirectional torque results. Commutator action is discussed in some detail in Section 7.2.

Figure 4.20a shows this winding laid out flat. The mmf wave is shown in Fig. 4.20b. On the assumption of narrow slots, it consists of a series of steps. The height of each step equals the number of ampere-turns $2N_c i_c$ in a slot, where N_c is the number of turns in each coil and i_c is the coil current, with a two-layer winding and full-pitch coils being assumed. The peak value of the mmf wave is along the magnetic axis of the armature, midway between the field poles. This winding is equivalent to a coil of $12N_c i_c$ A·turns distributed around the armature. On the assumption of symmetry at each pole, the peak value of the mmf wave at each armature pole is $6N_c i_c$ A·turns.

This mmf wave can be represented approximately by the sawtooth wave drawn in Fig. 4.20b and repeated in Fig. 4.20c. For a more realistic winding with a larger number of armature slots per pole, the triangular distribution becomes a close approximation. This mmf wave would be produced by a rectangular distribution of current density at the armature surface, as shown in Fig. 4.20c.

For our preliminary study, it is convenient to resolve the mmf waves of distributed windings into their Fourier series components. The fundamental component of the sawtooth mmf wave of Fig. 4.20c is shown by the sine wave. Its peak value is

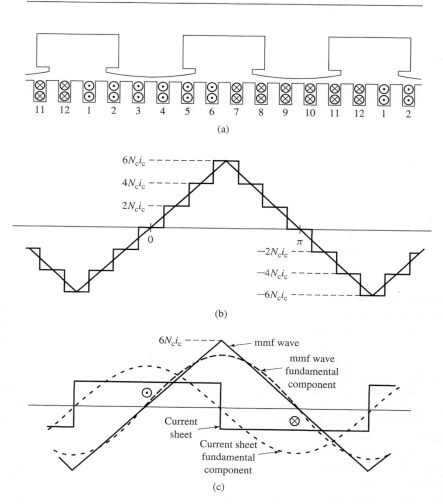

Figure 4.20 (a) Developed sketch of the dc machine of Fig. 4.19; (b) mmf wave; (c) equivalent sawtooth mmf wave, its fundamental component, and equivalent rectangular current sheet.

$8/\pi^2 = 0.81$ times the height of the sawtooth wave. This fundamental mmf wave is that which would be produced by the fundamental space-harmonic component of the rectangular current-density distribution of Fig. 4.20c.

Note that the air-gap mmf distribution depends only on the winding arrangement and symmetry of the magnetic structure at each pole. The air-gap flux density, however, depends not only on the mmf but also on the magnetic boundary conditions, primarily the length of the air gap, the effect of the slot openings, and the shape of the pole face. The designer takes these effects into account by means of detailed analyses, but these details need not concern us here.

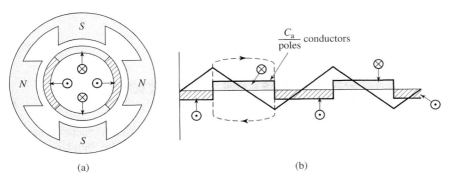

Figure 4.21 (a) Cross section of a four-pole dc machine; (b) development of current sheet and mmf wave.

DC machines often have a magnetic structure with more than two poles. For example, Fig. 4.21a shows schematically a four-pole dc machine. The field winding produces alternate north-south-north-south polarity, and the armature conductors are distributed in four belts of slots carrying currents alternately toward and away from the reader, as symbolized by the cross-hatched areas. This machine is shown in laid-out form in Fig. 4.21b. The corresponding sawtooth armature-mmf wave is also shown. On the assumption of symmetry of the winding and field poles, each successive pair of poles is like every other pair of poles. Magnetic conditions in the air gap can then be determined by examining any pair of adjacent poles (i.e. 360 electrical degrees).

The peak value of the sawtooth armature mmf wave can be written in terms of the total number of conductors in the armature slots as

$$(F_{ag})_{peak} = \left(\frac{C_a}{2m \times poles}\right) i_a \quad \text{A} \cdot \text{turns/pole} \qquad (4.10)$$

where

$\quad C_a$ = total number of conductors in armature winding

$\quad m$ = number of parallel paths through armature winding

$\quad i_a$ = armature current, A

This equation takes into account the fact that in some cases the armature may be wound with multiple current paths in parallel. It is for this reason that it is often more convenient to think of the armature in terms of the number of conductors (each conductor corresponding to a single current-carrying path within a slot). Thus i_a/m is the current in each conductor. This equation comes directly from the line integral around the dotted closed path in Fig. 4.21b which crosses the air gap twice and encloses $C_a/poles$ conductors, each carrying current i_a/m in the same direction. In more compact form,

$$(F_{ag})_{peak} = \left(\frac{N_a}{poles}\right) i_a \qquad (4.11)$$

where $N_a = C_a/(2m)$ is the number of series armature turns. From the Fourier series for the sawtooth mmf wave of Fig. 4.21b, the peak value of the corresponding space-fundamental mmf wave is given by

$$(F_{ag1})_{peak} = \frac{8}{\pi^2} \left(\frac{N_a}{poles} \right) i_a \tag{4.12}$$

4.4   MAGNETIC FIELDS IN ROTATING MACHINERY

We base our preliminary investigations of both ac and dc machines on the assumption of sinusoidal spatial distributions of mmf. This assumption will be found to give very satisfactory results for most problems involving ac machines because their windings are commonly distributed so as to minimize the effects of space harmonics. Because of the restrictions placed on the winding arrangement by the commutator, the mmf waves of dc machines inherently approach more nearly a sawtooth waveform. Nevertheless, an analysis based on a sinusoidal model brings out the essential features of dc machine performance. The results can readily be modified whenever necessary to account for any significant discrepancies.

It is often easiest to begin by examination of a two-pole machine, in which the electrical and mechanical angles and velocities are equal. The results can immediately be extrapolated to a multi-pole machine when it is recalled that electrical angles and angular velocities are related to mechanical angles and angular velocities by a factor of poles/2 (see, for example, Eq. 4.1).

The behavior of electric machinery is determined by the magnetic fields created by currents in the various windings of the machine. This section discusses how these magnetic fields and currents are related.

4.4.1   Machines with uniform air gaps

Figure 4.22a shows a single full-pitch, N-turn coil in a high-permeability magnetic structure ($\mu \to \infty$), with a concentric, cylindrical rotor. The air-gap mmf $\mathcal{F}_{ag}$ of this configuration is shown plotted versus angle θ_a in Fig. 4.22b. For such a structure, with a uniform air gap of length g at radius r_r (very much larger than g), it is quite accurate to assume that the magnetic field **H** in the air gap is predominantly radially directed and that it is constant in magnitude across the air gap.

The air-gap mmf distribution of Fig. 4.22b is equal to the line integral of H_{ag} across the air gap. For this case of constant radial H_{ag}, this integral is simply equal to the product of the air-gap radial magnetic field H_{ag} times the air-gap length g, and thus H_{ag} can be found simply by dividing the air-gap mmf by the air-gap length:

$$H_{ag} = \frac{\mathcal{F}_{ag}}{g} \tag{4.13}$$

Thus, in Fig. 4.22c, the radial field H_{ag} and the mmf can be seen to be identical in form, simply related by a factor of $1/g$.

The fundamental space-harmonic component of H_{ag} can be found directly from the fundamental component $\mathcal{F}_{ag1}$, given by Eq. 4.4.

$$H_{ag1} = \frac{\mathcal{F}_{ag1}}{g} = \frac{4}{\pi} \left(\frac{Ni}{2g} \right) \cos\theta_a \tag{4.14}$$

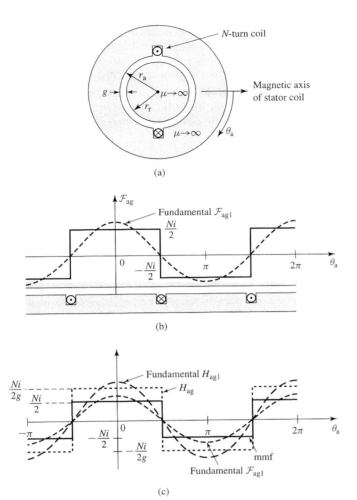

Figure 4.22 The air-gap mmf and radial component of H_{ag} for a concentrated full-pitch winding.

It is a sinusoidal space wave of amplitude

$$(H_{ag1})_{peak} = \frac{4}{\pi} \left(\frac{Ni}{2g} \right) \tag{4.15}$$

For a distributed winding such as that of Fig. 4.17 with winding factor k_w, the air-gap magnetic field intensity is easily found once the air-gap mmf is known. Thus, generalizing for the case of a multi-pole machine with N_{ph} series turns per pole, the fundamental component of H_{ag} can be found by dividing the fundamental component of the air-gap mmf (Eq. 4.6) by the air-gap length g.

$$H_{ag1} = \frac{4}{\pi} \left(\frac{k_w N_{ph}}{g \times poles} \right) i_a \cos(\theta_{ae}) \tag{4.16}$$

Note that the space-fundamental air-gap mmf $\mathcal{F}_{ag1}$ and air-gap magnetic field H_{ag1} produced by a distributed winding of winding factor k_w and N_{ph}/poles series turns per pole is equal to that produced by a concentrated, full-pitch winding of $(k_w N_{ph})$/poles turns per pole. In the analysis of machines with distributed windings, this result is useful since in considering space-fundamental quantities it permits the distributed solution to be obtained from the single N-turn-per-pole, full-pitch coil solution simply by replacing N by the effective number of turns per pole, $k_w N_{ph}$/poles, of the distributed winding.

EXAMPLE 4.2

A four-pole synchronous ac generator with a smooth air gap has a distributed rotor winding with 264 series turns, a winding factor of 0.935, and an air gap of length 0.7 mm. Assuming the mmf drop in the electrical steel to be negligible, find the rotor-winding current required to produce a peak, space-fundamental magnetic flux density of 1.6 T in the machine air gap.

■ **Solution**

The space-fundamental air-gap magnetic field can be found from the space-fundamental component of the air-gap mmf by dividing by the air-gap length g. Multiplying by the permeability of free space μ_0 then gives the space-fundamental air-gap magnetic flux density. Thus, from Eq. 4.9

$$(B_{ag1})_{peak} = \frac{\mu_0 (\mathcal{F}_{ag1})_{peak}}{g} = \frac{4\mu_0}{\pi g} \left(\frac{k_r N_r}{poles} \right) I_r$$

Solving for I_r gives

$$I_r = \left(\frac{\pi g \times poles}{4 \mu_0 k_r N_r} \right) (B_{ag1})_{peak}$$

$$= \left(\frac{\pi \times 0.0007 \times 4}{4 \times 4\pi \times 10^{-7} \times 0.935 \times 264} \right) 1.6$$

$$= 11.4 \text{ A}$$

Practice Problem 4.2

A 2-pole synchronous machine has an air-gap length of 2.2 cm and a field winding with a total of 830 series turns. When excited by a field current of 47 A, the peak, space-fundamental magnetic flux density in the machine air-gap is measured to be 1.35 T.

Based upon the measured flux density, calculate the field-winding winding factor k_r.

Solution

$$k_r = 0.952$$

4.4.2 Machines with Nonuniform Air Gaps

Figure 4.23a shows the structure of a typical dc machine, and Fig. 4.23b shows the structure of a typical salient-pole synchronous machine. Both machines consist of magnetic structures with extremely nonuniform air gaps. In such cases the air-gap magnetic-field distribution is more complex than that of uniform-air-gap machines.

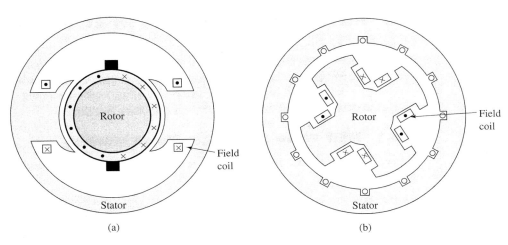

Figure 4.23 Structure of typical salient-pole machines: (a) dc machine and (b) salient-pole synchronous machine.

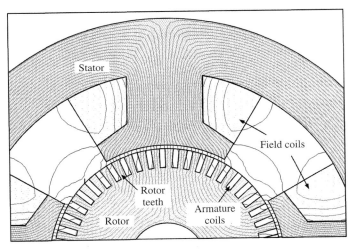

Figure 4.24 Finite-element solution showing the magnetic-field distribution in a salient-pole dc machine with the field coils excited (no current in armature coils).

Detailed analysis of the magnetic field distribution in such machines requires complete solutions of the field problem. For example, Fig. 4.24 shows the magnetic field distribution in a salient-pole dc generator as obtained by a finite-element program. However, experience has shown that through various simplifying assumptions, analytical techniques which yield reasonably accurate results can be developed. These techniques are illustrated in later chapters, where the effects of saliency on both dc and ac machines are discussed.

4.5 ROTATING MMF WAVES IN AC MACHINES

To understand the theory and operation of polyphase ac machines, it is necessary to study the nature of the mmf wave produced by a polyphase winding. Attention will be focused on a two-pole machine (or equivalently one pole pair of a multi-pole winding; $-\pi \leq \theta_{ae} \leq \pi$). We will begin with an analysis of a single-phase winding. This will help us to develop insight into the nature of a polyphase winding.

4.5.1 MMF Wave of a Single-Phase Winding

Figure 4.25a shows the space-fundamental mmf distribution of a single-phase winding. From Eq. 4.6,

$$\mathcal{F}_{ag1} = \frac{4}{\pi} \left(\frac{k_w N_{ph}}{\text{poles}} \right) i_a \cos (\theta_{ae}) \tag{4.17}$$

where θ_{ae} is given by Eq. 4.1. When this winding is excited by a current varying sinusoidally in time at electrical frequency ω_e

$$i_a = I_a \cos \omega_e t \tag{4.18}$$

the mmf distribution is given by

$$\mathcal{F}_{ag1} = F_{max} \cos (\theta_{ae}) \cos \omega_e t \tag{4.19}$$

Equation 4.19 has been written in a form to emphasize the fact that the result is an mmf distribution of maximum amplitude.

$$F_{max} = \frac{4}{\pi} \left(\frac{k_w N_{ph}}{\text{poles}} \right) I_a \tag{4.20}$$

This mmf distribution remains fixed in space with an amplitude that varies sinusoidally in time at frequency ω_e, as shown in Fig. 4.25a. Note that, to simplify the notation, Eq. 4.1 has been used to express the mmf distribution of Eq. 4.19 in terms of the electrical angle θ_{ae}.

Use of a common trigonometric identity[1] permits Eq. 4.19 to be rewritten in the form

$$\mathcal{F}_{ag1} = F_{max} \left[\frac{1}{2} \cos (\theta_{ae} - \omega_e t) + \frac{1}{2} \cos (\theta_{ae} + \omega_e t) \right] \tag{4.21}$$

which shows that the mmf of a single-phase winding can be resolved into two rotating mmf waves, each of amplitude equal to one-half the maximum amplitude of $\mathcal{F}_{ag1}$ with one, $\mathcal{F}_{ag1}^+$, rotating in the $+\theta_{ae}$ direction and the other, $\mathcal{F}_{ag1}^-$, rotating in the $-\theta_{ae}$ direction

$$\mathcal{F}_{ag1}^+ = \frac{1}{2} F_{max} \cos (\theta_{ae} - \omega_e t) \tag{4.22}$$

$$\mathcal{F}_{ag1}^- = \frac{1}{2} F_{max} \cos (\theta_{ae} + \omega_e t) \tag{4.23}$$

---

[1] $\cos \alpha \cos \beta = \frac{1}{2} \cos (\alpha - \beta) + \frac{1}{2} \cos (\alpha + \beta)$

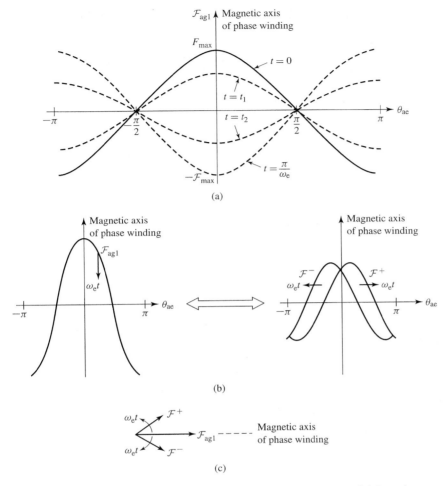

Figure 4.25 Single-phase-winding space-fundamental air-gap mmf: (a) mmf distribution of a single-phase winding at various times; (b) total mmf $\mathcal{F}_{ag1}$ decomposed into two traveling waves $\mathcal{F}^-$ and $\mathcal{F}^+$; (c) phasor decomposition of $\mathcal{F}_{ag1}$.

Both flux waves rotate in their respective directions with electrical angular velocity ω_e, corresponding to a mechanical angular velocity ω_m where

$$\omega_m = \left(\frac{2}{\text{poles}}\right)\omega_e = \left(\frac{\pi}{30}\right)n \tag{4.24}$$

where n is the rotational speed in r/min. This decomposition is shown graphically in Fig. 4.25b and in a phasor representation in Fig. 4.25c.

The fact that the air-gap mmf of a single-phase winding excited by a source of alternating current can be resolved into rotating traveling waves is an important conceptual step in understanding ac machinery. In single-phase ac machinery, the positive-traveling flux wave produces useful torque while the negative-traveling flux wave produces both negative and pulsating torque as well as losses. Although single-phase machines are designed so as to minimize the effects of the negative-traveling flux wave, they cannot be totally eliminated. On the other hand, as shown in Section 4.5.2, in polyphase ac machinery the windings are equally displaced in space phase, and the winding currents are similarly displaced in time phase, with the result that the negative-traveling flux waves of the various windings sum to zero while the positive-traveling flux waves reinforce, giving a single positive-traveling flux wave.

4.5.2 MMF Wave of a Polyphase Winding

In this section we study the mmf distributions of three-phase windings such as those found on the stator of three-phase induction and synchronous machines. The analyses presented can be readily extended to a polyphase winding with any number of phases. Once again attention is focused on a two-pole machine or one pair of poles of a multi-pole winding.

In a three-phase machine, the windings of the individual phases are displaced from each other by 120 electrical degrees in space around the air-gap circumference, as shown by coils $(a, -a)$, $(b, -b)$, and $(c, -c)$ in Fig. 4.26. The concentrated full-pitch coils shown here may be considered to represent distributed windings producing sinusoidal mmf waves centered on the magnetic axes of the respective phases. The space-fundamental sinusoidal mmf waves of the three phases are accordingly displaced 120 electrical degrees in space. Each phase is excited by an alternating current which varies in magnitude sinusoidally with time. Under balanced three-phase conditions, the instantaneous currents are

$$i_a = I_{max} \cos \omega_e t \tag{4.25}$$

$$i_b = I_{max} \cos (\omega_e t - 120°) \tag{4.26}$$

$$i_c = I_{max} \cos (\omega_e t + 120°) \tag{4.27}$$

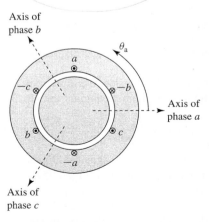

Figure 4.26 Simplified two-pole three-phase stator winding.

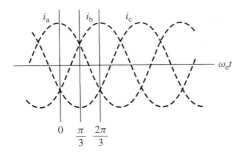

Figure 4.27 Instantaneous phase currents under balanced three-phase conditions.

where I_{max} is the maximum value of the current and the time origin is arbitrarily taken as the instant when the phase-a current is at its positive maximum. The phase sequence is assumed to be abc. The instantaneous currents are shown in Fig. 4.27. The dots and crosses in the coil sides (Fig. 4.26) indicate the reference directions for positive phase currents.

The mmf of phase a has been shown to be

$$\mathcal{F}_{a1} = \mathcal{F}_{a1}^{+} + \mathcal{F}_{a1}^{-} \tag{4.28}$$

where

$$\mathcal{F}_{a1}^{+} = \frac{1}{2} F_{max} \cos (\theta_{ae} - \omega_e t) \tag{4.29}$$

$$\mathcal{F}_{a1}^{-} = \frac{1}{2} F_{max} \cos (\theta_{ae} + \omega_e t) \tag{4.30}$$

and

$$F_{max} = \frac{4}{\pi} \left(\frac{k_w N_{ph}}{poles} \right) I_{max} \tag{4.31}$$

Note that to avoid excessive notational complexity, the subscript ag has been dropped; here the subscript "a1" indicates the space-fundamental component of the phase-a air-gap mmf.

Similarly, for phases b and c, whose axes are at $\theta_{ae} = 120°$ and $\theta_{ae} = -120°$ respectively, their air-gap mmfs can be shown to be

$$\mathcal{F}_{b1} = \mathcal{F}_{b1}^{+} + \mathcal{F}_{b1}^{-} \tag{4.32}$$

$$\mathcal{F}_{b1}^{+} = \frac{1}{2} F_{max} \cos (\theta_{ae} - \omega_e t) \tag{4.33}$$

$$\mathcal{F}_{b1}^{-} = \frac{1}{2} F_{max} \cos (\theta_{ae} + \omega_e t + 120°) \tag{4.34}$$

and

$$\mathcal{F}_{c1} = \mathcal{F}_{c1}^{+} + \mathcal{F}_{c1}^{-} \tag{4.35}$$

$$\mathcal{F}_{c1}^{+} = \frac{1}{2} F_{max} \cos (\theta_{ae} - \omega_e t) \tag{4.36}$$

$$\mathcal{F}_{c1}^{-} = \frac{1}{2} F_{max} \cos (\theta_{ae} + \omega_e t - 120°) \tag{4.37}$$

The total mmf is the sum of the contributions from each of the three phases

$$\mathcal{F}(\theta_{ae}, t) = \mathcal{F}_{a1} + \mathcal{F}_{b1} + \mathcal{F}_{c1} \tag{4.38}$$

This summation can be performed quite easily in terms of the positive- and negative-traveling waves. The negative-traveling waves sum to zero

$$
\begin{aligned}
\mathcal{F}^-(\theta_{ae}, t) &= \mathcal{F}_{a1}^- + \mathcal{F}_{b1}^- + \mathcal{F}_{c1}^- \\
&= \frac{1}{2} F_{max} \left[\cos(\theta_{ae} + \omega_e t) + \cos(\theta_{ae} + \omega_e t - 120°) \right. \\
&\quad \left. + \cos(\theta_{ae} + \omega_e t + 120°) \right] \\
&= 0
\end{aligned}
\tag{4.39}
$$

while the positive-traveling waves reinforce

$$
\begin{aligned}
\mathcal{F}^+(\theta_{ae}, t) &= \mathcal{F}_{a1}^+ + \mathcal{F}_{b1}^+ + \mathcal{F}_{c1}^+ \\
&= \frac{3}{2} F_{max} \cos(\theta_{ae} - \omega_e t)
\end{aligned}
\tag{4.40}
$$

Thus, the result of displacing the three windings by 120° in space phase and displacing the winding currents by 120° in time phase is a single positive-traveling mmf wave

$$\mathcal{F}(\theta_{ae}, t) = \frac{3}{2} F_{max} \cos(\theta_{ae} - \omega_e t) \tag{4.41}$$

The air-gap mmf wave described by Eq. 4.41 is a space-fundamental sinusoidal function of the electrical space angle θ_{ae} (and hence of the space angle $\theta_a = 2\,\theta_{ae}/poles$). It has a constant amplitude of $(3/2)\,F_{max}$, i.e., 1.5 times the peak amplitude of the air-gap mmf wave produced by the individual phases alone. It has a positive peak at angle $\theta_a = (2\,\omega_e\,t/poles)$. Thus, under balanced three-phase conditions, the three-phase winding produces an air-gap mmf wave which rotates at *synchronous angular velocity* ω_s

$$\omega_s = \left(\frac{2}{poles} \right) \omega_e \tag{4.42}$$

where

ω_e = angular frequency of the applied electrical excitation [rad/sec]

ω_s = synchronous spatial angular velocity of the air-gap mmf wave [rad/sec]

The corresponding *synchronous speed* n_s in r/min can be expressed in terms of the applied electrical frequency

$$f_e = \frac{\omega_e}{2\pi} \quad \text{Hz} \tag{4.43}$$

as

$$n_s = \left(\frac{120}{poles} \right) f_e \quad \text{r/min} \tag{4.44}$$

In general, a rotating field of constant amplitude will be produced by a q-phase winding ($q \geq 3$) excited by balanced q-phase currents of frequency f_e when the respective phase axes are located $2\pi/q$ electrical radians apart in space. The amplitude of this flux wave will be $q/2$ times the maximum contribution of any one phase, and the synchronous angular velocity will remain $\omega_s = (2\,\omega_e/\text{poles})$ radians per second. For a two phase machine, the phase axes are located $\pi/2$ electrical radians apart in space and the amplitude of the rotating flux wave will be equal to that of the individual phases.

In this section, we have seen that a polyphase winding excited by balanced polyphase currents produces a rotating mmf wave. Production of a rotating mmf wave and the corresponding rotating magnetic flux wave is key to the operation of polyphase rotating electrical machinery. It is the interaction of this magnetic flux wave with that of the rotor which produces torque. Constant torque is produced when rotor-produced magnetic flux wave rotates in synchronism with that of the stator.

4.5.3 Graphical Analysis of Polyphase MMF

For balanced three-phase currents as given by Eqs. 4.25 to 4.27, the production of a rotating mmf can also be shown graphically. Consider the state of affairs at $t = 0$ (Fig. 4.27), the moment when the phase-a current is at its maximum value I_{max}. The mmf of phase a then has its maximum value F_{max}, as shown by the vector $\mathbf{F}_a$ drawn along the magnetic axis of phase a in the two-pole machine shown schematically in Fig. 4.28a. At this moment, currents i_b and i_c are both $I_{max}/2$ in the negative direction, as shown by the dots and crosses in Fig. 4.28a indicating the actual instantaneous directions. The corresponding mmfs of phases b and c are shown by the vectors $\mathbf{F}_b$ and $\mathbf{F}_c$, both of magnitude $F_{max}/2$ drawn in the negative direction along the magnetic axes of phases b and c, respectively. The resultant, obtained by adding the individual contributions of the three phases, is a vector of magnitude $F = \frac{3}{2}F_{max}$ centered on the axis of phase a. It represents a sinusoidal space wave with its positive peak centered on the axis of phase a and having an amplitude $\frac{3}{2}$ times that of the phase-a contribution alone.

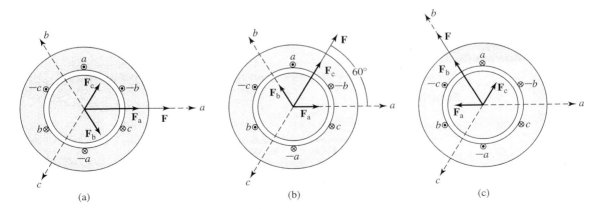

Figure 4.28 The production of a rotating magnetic field by means of three-phase currents.

At a later time $\omega_e t = \pi/3$ (Fig. 4.27), the currents in phases a and b are a positive half maximum, and that in phase c is a negative maximum. The individual mmf components and their resultant are now shown in Fig. 4.28b. The resultant has the same amplitude as at $t = 0$, but it has now rotated counter-clockwise 60 electrical degrees in space. Similarly, at $\omega_e t = 2\pi/3$ (when the phase-b current is a positive maximum and the phase-a and phase-c currents are a negative half maximum) the same resultant mmf distribution is again obtained, but it has rotated counter-clockwise 60 electrical degrees still farther and is now aligned with the magnetic axis of phase b (see Fig. 4.28c). As time passes, the resultant mmf wave retains its sinusoidal form and amplitude but rotates progressively around the air gap; the net result can be seen to be an mmf wave of constant amplitude rotating at a uniform angular velocity.

In one cycle the resultant mmf must be back in the position of Fig. 4.28a. The mmf wave therefore makes one revolution per electrical cycle in a two-pole machine. In a multi-pole machine the mmf wave travels one pole-pair per electrical cycle and hence one revolution in (poles/2) electrical cycles.

EXAMPLE 4.3

Consider a three-phase stator excited with balanced, 60-Hz currents. Find the synchronous angular velocity in rad/sec and speed in r/min for stators with two, four, and six poles.

■ **Solution**

For a frequency of $f_e = 60$ Hz, the electrical angular frequency is equal to

$$\omega_e = 2\pi f_e = 120\pi \text{ rad/sec}$$

Using Eqs. 4.42 and 4.44, the following table can be constructed:

Poles	n_s (r/min)	ω_s (rad/sec)
2	3600	120π
4	1800	60π
6	1200	40π

Practice Problem 4.3

Repeat Example 4.3 for a three-phase stator excited by balanced 50-Hz currents.

Solution

Poles	n_s (r/min)	ω_s (rad/sec)
2	3000	100π
4	1500	50π
6	1000	$100\pi/3$

4.6 GENERATED VOLTAGE

The general nature of the induced voltage has been discussed in Section 4.2. Quantitative expressions for the induced voltage will now be determined.

4.6.1 AC machines

An elementary ac machine is shown in cross section in Fig. 4.29. The coils on both the rotor and the stator have been shown as concentrated, multiple-turn, full-pitch coils. As we have seen, the performance of a machine with distributed windings can be determined from that of a machine with concentrated windings by multiplying the number of series turns in the winding by a winding factor. Under the assumption of a small air gap, the field winding on the rotor can be assumed to produce an essentially radial-directed space-fundamental sinusoidal air-gap flux of peak flux density B_{peak}.

As is derived in Example 4.2, if the air gap is uniform, B_{peak} can be found from

$$B_{peak} = \frac{4\mu_0}{\pi g} \left(\frac{k_f N_f}{poles} \right) I_f \tag{4.45}$$

where

$\qquad g$ = air-gap length

$\qquad N_f$ = total series turns in the field winding

$\qquad k_f$ = field-winding winding factor

$\qquad I_f$ = field current

When the rotor poles are in line with the magnetic axis of a stator phase winding, the flux linkage with that winding (of N_{ph} series turns per phase and winding factor

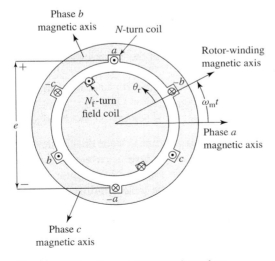

Phase b magnetic axis

N-turn coil

Rotor-winding magnetic axis

N_f-turn field coil

θ_r

$\omega_m t$

Phase a magnetic axis

Phase c magnetic axis

Figure 4.29 Cross-sectional view of an elementary three-phase ac machine.

k_w) is $k_w N_{ph} \Phi_p$, where Φ_p is the air-gap flux per pole. For the assumed sinusoidal air-gap flux-density of form

$$B = B_{peak} \cos\left(\frac{\text{poles}}{2}\theta_r\right) \tag{4.46}$$

Φ_p can be found as the integral of the flux density over the pole area

$$\Phi_p = l \int_{-\pi/\text{poles}}^{+\pi/\text{poles}} B_{peak} \cos\left(\frac{\text{poles}}{2}\theta_r\right) r\, d\theta_r$$

$$= \left(\frac{2}{\text{poles}}\right) 2\, l\, r\, B_{peak} \tag{4.47}$$

Here,

$$\theta_r = \text{angle measured from the rotor magnetic axis}$$
$$r = \text{radius to air gap}$$
$$l = \text{axial length of the stator/rotor iron}$$

Note that although Fig. 4.29 shows a two-pole machine, the analysis presented here is for the general case of a multi-pole machine.

As the rotor turns, the flux linkage of each stator phase varies cosinusoidally with the angle between the magnetic axes of that phase and that of the rotor field winding. With the rotor spinning at constant angular velocity ω_m, $\theta_r = \omega_m t$, and the flux linkage with the phase-a stator winding is thus

$$\lambda_a = k_w N_{ph} \Phi_p \cos\left(\left(\frac{\text{poles}}{2}\right)\omega_m t\right)$$

$$= k_w N_{ph} \Phi_p \cos \omega_e t \tag{4.48}$$

where time t is arbitrarily chosen as zero when the field winding magnetic axis coincides with that of phase a and ω_e is the electrical frequency in rad/sec given by Eq. 4.3.

By Faraday's law, the voltage induced in phase a is found from Eq. 4.48 as

$$e_a = \frac{d\lambda_a}{dt} = k_w N_{ph}\frac{d\Phi_p}{dt}\cos(\omega_e t) - \omega_e k_w N_{ph}\Phi_p \sin(\omega_e t) \tag{4.49}$$

The polarity of this induced voltage is such that if the stator coil were short-circuited, the induced voltage would cause a current to flow in the direction that would oppose any change in the flux linkage of the stator coil. Although Eq. 4.49 is derived on the assumption that only the field winding is producing air-gap flux, the equation applies equally well to the general situation where Φ_p is the net air-gap flux per pole produced by currents on both the rotor and the stator.

The first term on the right-hand side of Eq. 4.49 is a transformer voltage and is present only when the amplitude of the air-gap flux wave changes with time. The second term is the *speed voltage* generated by the relative motion of the air-gap flux wave and the stator coil. In the normal steady-state operation of most rotating machines, the amplitude of the air-gap flux wave is constant; under these conditions the first term is zero and the generated voltage is simply the speed voltage. The term *electromotive force* (abbreviated *emf*) is often used for the speed voltage. Thus, for constant air-gap flux,

$$e_a = -\omega_e k_w N_{ph} \Phi_p \sin(\omega_e t) \tag{4.50}$$

EXAMPLE 4.4

The so-called *cutting-of-flux* equation states that the voltage v induced in a wire of length l (in the frame of the wire) moving with respect to a constant magnetic field with flux density of magnitude B is given by

$$v = l v_{\perp} B$$

where $v_{\perp}$ is the component of the wire velocity perpendicular to the direction of the magnetic flux density.

Consider the two-pole elementary three-phase machine of Fig. 4.29. Assume the rotor-produced air-gap flux density to be of the form

$$B_{ag}(\theta_r) = B_{peak} \sin \theta_r$$

and the rotor to rotate at constant angular velocity ω_m. (Note that since this is a two-pole machine, $\omega_e = \omega_m$). Show that if one assumes that the armature-winding coil sides are in the air gap and not in the slots, the voltage induced in a full-pitch, N-turn concentrated armature phase coil can be calculated from the cutting-of-flux equation and that it is identical to that calculated using Eq. 4.50. Let the average air-gap radius be r and the air-gap length be g ($g \ll r$).

■ Solution

We begin by noting that the cutting-of-flux equation requires that the conductor be moving and the magnetic field be constant in time. Thus in order to apply it to calculating the stator magnetic field, we must translate our reference frame to the rotor.

In the rotor frame, the magnetic field is constant and the stator coil sides, when moved to the center of the air gap at radius r, appear to be moving with velocity $\omega_m r$ which is perpendicular to the radially-directed air-gap flux. If the rotor and phase-coil magnetic axes are assumed to be aligned at time $t = 0$, the location of a coil side as a function of time will be given by $\theta_r = -\omega_m t$. The voltage induced in one side of one turn can therefore be calculated as

$$e_1 = l v_{\perp} B_{ag}(\theta_r) = l \omega_m r B_{peak} \sin(-\omega_m t)$$

There are N turns per coil and two sides per turn. Thus the total coil voltage is given by

$$e = 2N e_1 = -2N l \omega_e r B_{peak} \sin \omega_e t$$

where ω_e has been substituted for ω_m.

From Eq. 4.50, the voltage induced in the full-pitched, 2-pole stator coil is given by

$$e = -\omega_e N \Phi_p \sin \omega_e t$$

Substituting $\Phi_p = 2B_{peak}lr$ from Eq. 4.47 gives

$$e = -\omega_e N(2B_{peak}lr)\sin\omega_e t$$

which is identical to the voltage determined using the cutting-of-flux equation.

In the normal steady-state operation of ac machines, we are usually interested in the rms values of voltages and currents rather than their instantaneous values. From Eq. 4.50 the maximum value of the induced voltage is

$$E_{max} = \omega_e k_w N_{ph}\Phi_p = 2\pi f_e k_w N_{ph}\Phi_p \tag{4.51}$$

where f_e is the electrical frequency of the generated voltage in Hz. Its rms value is

$$E_{rms} = \frac{2\pi f_e k_w N_{ph}\Phi_p}{\sqrt{2}} = \sqrt{2}\,\pi f_e k_w N_{ph}\Phi_p \tag{4.52}$$

Note that these equations are identical in form to the corresponding emf equations for a transformer. Relative motion of a coil and a constant-amplitude spatial flux-density wave in a rotating machine produces voltage in the same fashion as does a time-varying flux linking the stationary coils of a transformer. Rotation introduces the element of time variation and transforms a space distribution of flux density into a time variation of flux linkage and voltage.

The voltage induced in a single winding is a single-phase voltage. For the production of a set of balanced, three-phase voltages, it follows that three windings displaced 120 electrical degrees in space must be used, as shown in elementary form in Fig. 4.10. The machine of Fig. 4.10 is shown to be Y-connected and hence each winding voltage is a phase-neutral voltage. Thus, Eq. 4.52 gives the rms line-neutral voltage produced in this machine when N_{ph} is the total series turns per phase. For a Δ-connected machine, the voltage winding voltage calculated from Eq. 4.52 would be the machine line-line voltage.

EXAMPLE 4.5

A two-pole, three-phase, Y-connected, 60-Hz, round-rotor synchronous generator has a distributed field winding with N_f series turns and winding factor k_f. The armature winding has N_{ph} turns per phase and winding factor k_w. The air-gap length is g, and the mean air-gap radius is r. The armature-winding active length is l. The dimensions and winding data are

$$N_f = 68 \text{ series turns} \qquad k_f = 0.945$$
$$N_{ph} = 18 \text{ series turns/phase} \qquad k_w = 0.933$$
$$r = 0.53 \text{ m} \qquad g = 4.5 \text{ cm}$$
$$l = 3.8 \text{ m}$$

The rotor is driven by a steam turbine at a speed of 3600 r/min. For a field current of $I_f = 720$ A dc, compute (a) the peak fundamental mmf $(F_{ag1})_{peak}$ produced by the field winding, (b) the peak fundamental flux density $(B_{ag1})_{peak}$ in the air gap, (c) the fundamental flux per pole Φ_p, and (d) the rms value of the open-circuit voltage generated in the armature.

■ **Solution**

a. From Eq. 4.9

$$(F_{ag1})_{peak} = \frac{4}{\pi} \left(\frac{k_f N_f}{poles} \right) I_f = \frac{4}{\pi} \left(\frac{0.945 \times 68}{2} \right) 720$$

$$= \frac{4}{\pi} (32.1)720 = 2.94 \times 10^4 \text{ A} \cdot \text{turns/pole}$$

b. Using Eq. 4.13, we get

$$(B_{ag1})_{peak} = \frac{\mu_0 (F_{ag1})_{peak}}{g} = \frac{4\pi \times 10^{-7} \times 2.94 \times 10^4}{4.5 \times 10^{-2}} = 0.821 \text{ T}$$

Because of the effect of the slots containing the armature winding, most of the air-gap flux is confined to the stator teeth. The flux density in the teeth at a pole center is higher than the value calculated in part (b), probably by a factor of about 2. In a detailed design this flux density must be calculated to determine whether the teeth are excessively saturated.

c. From Eq. 4.47

$$\Phi_p = 2(B_{ag1})_{peak} lr = 2(0.821)(3.8)(0.53) = 3.31 \text{ Wb}$$

d. From Eq. 4.52 with $f_{me} = 60$ Hz

$$E_{rms,line-neutral} = \sqrt{2} \pi f_{me} k_w N_{ph} \Phi_p = \sqrt{2} \pi (60)(0.933)(18)(3.31)$$

$$= 14.8 \text{ kV rms}$$

The line-line voltage is thus

$$E_{rms,line-line} = \sqrt{3} (14.8 \text{ kV}) = 25.7 \text{ kV rms}$$

Practice Problem 4.4

The rotor of the machine of Example 4.5 is to be rewound. The new field winding will have a total of 76 series turns and a winding factor of 0.925. (a) Calculate the field current which will result in a peak air-gap flux density of 0.83 T. (b) Calculate the corresponding rms line-line open-circuit voltage which will result if this modified machine is operated at this value of field current and 3600 r/min.

Solution

a. $I_f = 664$ A
b. $E_{rms,line-line} = 26.0$ kV rms

4.6.2 DC Machines

In a dc machine, although the ultimate objective is the generation of dc voltage, ac voltages are produced in the armature-winding coils as these coils rotate through the dc flux distribution of the stationary field winding. The armature-winding alternating voltage must therefore be rectified. Mechanical rectification is provided by the commutator as has been discussed in Section 4.2.2.

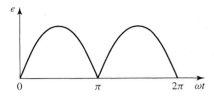

Figure 4.30 Sinusoidal approximation of the voltage between the brushes in the elementary dc machine of Fig. 4.14.

Consider the single N-turn armature coil of the elementary, two-pole dc machine of Fig. 4.14. The simple two-segment commutator provides full-wave rectification of the coil voltage. Although the spatial distribution of the air-gap flux in dc machines is typically far from sinusoidal, we can approximate the magnitude of the generated voltage by assuming a sinusoidal distribution. As we have seen, such a flux distribution will produce a sinusoidal ac voltage in the armature coil. The rectification action of the commutator will produce a dc voltage across the brushes as in Fig. 4.30. The average, or dc, value of this voltage can be found from taking the average of Eq. 4.50 (with $k_w = 1.0$)

$$E_a = \frac{1}{\pi} \int_0^\pi \omega_e N \Phi_p \sin (\omega_e t) \, d(\omega_e t) = \frac{2}{\pi} \omega_e N \Phi_p \qquad (4.53)$$

For dc machines it is usually more convenient to express the voltage E_a in terms of the mechanical speed ω_m (rad/sec) or n (r/min). Substitution of Eq. 4.24 in Eq. 4.53 for a multi-pole machine then yields

$$E_a = \left(\frac{\text{poles}}{\pi}\right) N \Phi_p \omega_m = \text{poles } N \Phi_p \left(\frac{n}{30}\right) \qquad (4.54)$$

The single-coil armature winding implied here is, of course, unrealistic in the practical sense, and it will be essential later to examine the action of commutators more carefully. Actually, Eq. 4.54 gives correct results for the more practical case of distributed armature windings as well, provided N is taken as the total number of turns in series between armature terminals. Usually the voltage is expressed in terms of the total number of active conductors C_a and the number m of parallel paths through the armature winding. Because it takes two coil sides to make a turn and $1/m$ of these are connected in series, the number of series turns is $N_a = C_a/(2m)$. Substitution in Eq. 4.54 then gives

$$E_a = \left(\frac{\text{poles}}{2\pi}\right) \left(\frac{C_a}{m}\right) \Phi_p \omega_m = \left(\frac{\text{poles}}{60}\right) \left(\frac{C_a}{m}\right) \Phi_p n \qquad (4.55)$$

4.7 TORQUE IN NON-SALIENT-POLE MACHINES

The behavior of any electromagnetic device as a component in an electromechanical system can be described in terms of its electrical-terminal equations and its displacement and electromechanical force or torque. The purpose of this section is to derive the terminal relationships and torque equations for an idealized elementary rotating machine, results which can be readily extended later to more complex machines. We derive these equations from two viewpoints and show that basically they stem from the same ideas.

The first viewpoint is essentially the same as that of Section 3.6. The machine will be regarded as a circuit element whose inductances depend on the angular position of the rotor. The flux linkages λ and magnetic field coenergy will be expressed in terms of the currents and inductances. The torque can then be found from the partial derivative of the coenergy with respect to the rotor position and the terminal voltages from the sum of the resistance drops Ri and the Faraday-law voltages $d\lambda/dt$. The result will be a set of nonlinear differential equations describing the dynamic performance of the machine.

The second viewpoint regards the machine as two groups of windings producing magnetic flux in the air gap, one group on the stator, and the other on the rotor. By making suitable assumptions regarding these fields (similar to those used to derive analytic expressions for the inductances), simple expressions can be derived for the flux linkages and the coenergy in the air gap in terms of the field quantities. The torque and generated voltage can then be found from these expressions. In this fashion, torque can be expressed explicitly as the tendency of two magnetic fields to align, in the same way that permanent magnets tend to align, and generated voltage can be expressed in terms of the relative motion between a field and a winding. These expressions lead to a simple physical picture of the normal steady-state behavior of rotating machines.

4.7.1 Coupled-Circuit Viewpoint

Consider the elementary smooth-air-gap machine of Fig. 4.31 with one winding on the stator and one on the rotor and with θ_m being the mechanical angle between the axes of the two windings. These windings are distributed over a number of slots so that their mmf waves can be approximated by space sinusoids. In Fig. 4.31a the coil sides $s, -s$ and $r, -r$ mark the positions of the centers of the conductor belts comprising the distributed windings. An alternative way of drawing these windings is shown in Fig. 4.31b, which also shows reference directions for voltages and currents. Here it is assumed that current in the arrow direction produces a magnetic field in the air gap in the arrow direction, so that a single arrow defines reference directions for both current and flux.

The stator and rotor are concentric cylinders and slot openings are neglected. Consequently, our elementary model does not include the effects of salient poles, which are investigated in later chapters. We also assume that the reluctances of the stator and rotor iron are negligible. Finally, although Fig. 4.31 shows a two-pole

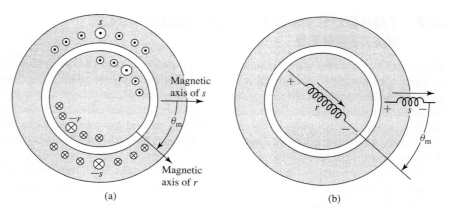

(a)   (b)

Figure 4.31 Elementary two-pole machine with smooth air gap: (a) winding distribution and (b) schematic representation.

machine, we will write the derivations that follow for the general case of a multi-pole machine, replacing θ_m by the electrical rotor angle

$$\theta_{me} = \left(\frac{\text{poles}}{2}\right)\theta_m \tag{4.56}$$

Based upon these assumptions, the stator and rotor self-inductances L_{ss} and L_{rr} can be seen to be constant, but the stator-to-rotor mutual inductance depends on the electrical angle θ_{me} between the magnetic axes of the stator and rotor windings. The mutual inductance is at its positive maximum when $\theta_{me} = 0$ or 2π, is zero when $\theta_{me} = \pm\pi/2$, and is at its negative maximum when $\theta_{me} = \pm\pi$. On the assumption of sinusoidal mmf waves and a uniform air gap, the space distribution of the air-gap flux wave is sinusoidal, and the mutual inductance will be of the form

$$\mathcal{L}_{sr}(\theta_{me}) = L_{sr} \cos(\theta_{me}) \tag{4.57}$$

where the script letter $\mathcal{L}$ denotes an inductance which is a function of the electrical angle θ_{me}; the italic capital letter L denotes a constant value. Thus L_{sr} is the magnitude of the mutual inductance; its value when the magnetic axes of the stator and rotor are aligned ($\theta_{me} = 0$). In terms of the inductances, the stator and rotor flux linkages λ_s and λ_r are

$$\lambda_s = L_{ss}i_s + \mathcal{L}_{sr}(\theta_{me})i_r = L_{ss}i_s + L_{sr}\cos(\theta_{me})i_r \tag{4.58}$$

$$\lambda_r = \mathcal{L}_{sr}(\theta_{me})i_s + L_{rr}i_r = L_{sr}\cos(\theta_{me})i_s + L_{rr}i_r \tag{4.59}$$

where the inductances can be calculated as discussed in Appendix B. In matrix notation

$$\begin{bmatrix} \lambda_s \\ \lambda_r \end{bmatrix} = \begin{bmatrix} L_{ss} & \mathcal{L}_{sr}(\theta_{me}) \\ \mathcal{L}_{sr}(\theta_{me}) & L_{rr} \end{bmatrix} \begin{bmatrix} i_s \\ i_r \end{bmatrix} \tag{4.60}$$

The terminal voltages v_s and v_r are

$$v_s = R_s i_s + \frac{d\lambda_s}{dt} \tag{4.61}$$

$$v_r = R_r i_r + \frac{d\lambda_r}{dt} \tag{4.62}$$

where R_s and R_r are the resistances of the stator and rotor windings respectively.

When the rotor is revolving, θ_{me} varies with time. Differentiation of Eqs. 4.58 and 4.59 and substitution of the results in Eqs. 4.61 and 4.62 then give

$$v_s = R_s i_s + L_{ss}\frac{di_s}{dt} + L_{sr}\cos(\theta_{me})\frac{di_r}{dt} - L_{sr}i_r\sin(\theta_{me})\frac{d\theta_{me}}{dt} \tag{4.63}$$

$$v_r = R_r i_r + L_{rr}\frac{di_r}{dt} + L_{sr}\cos(\theta_{me})\frac{di_r}{dt} - L_{sr}i_s\sin(\theta_{me})\frac{d\theta_{me}}{dt} \tag{4.64}$$

where

$$\frac{d\theta_{me}}{dt} = \left(\frac{poles}{2}\right)\omega_m = \omega_e \tag{4.65}$$

is the instantaneous speed in electrical radians per second. In a two-pole machine (such as that of Fig. 4.31), θ_{me} and ω_e are equal to the instantaneous shaft angle θ_m and the shaft speed ω_m respectively. In a multi-pole machine, they are related by Eqs. 4.56 and 4.3. The second and third terms on the right-hand sides of Eqs. 4.63 and 4.64 are $L(di/dt)$ induced voltages like those induced in stationary coupled circuits such as the windings of transformers. The fourth terms are caused by mechanical motion and are proportional to the instantaneous speed. These are the speed voltage terms which are associated with the interchange of power between the electric and mechanical systems.

The electromechanical torque can be found from the coenergy. From Eq. 3.70

$$W'_{fld} = \frac{1}{2}L_{ss}i_s^2 + \frac{1}{2}L_{rr}i_r^2 + L_{sr}i_s i_r \cos\theta_{me}$$

$$= \frac{1}{2}L_{ss}i_s^2 + \frac{1}{2}L_{rr}i_r^2 + L_{sr}i_s i_r \cos\left(\left(\frac{poles}{2}\right)\theta_m\right) \tag{4.66}$$

Note that the coenergy of Eq. 4.66 has been expressed specifically in terms of the shaft angle θ_m because the torque expression of Eq. 3.68 requires that the torque be obtained from the derivative of the coenergy with respect to the spatial angle θ_m and not with respect to the electrical angle θ_{me}. Thus, from Eq. 3.68

$$T = \left.\frac{\partial W'_{fld}(i_s, i_r, \theta_m)}{\partial \theta_m}\right|_{i_s, i_r} = -\left(\frac{poles}{2}\right)L_{sr}i_s i_r \sin\left(\frac{poles}{2}\theta_m\right)$$

$$= -\left(\frac{poles}{2}\right)L_{sr}i_s i_r \sin\theta_{me} \tag{4.67}$$

where T is the electromechanical torque acting to accelerate the rotor (i.e., a positive torque acts to increase θ_m). The negative sign in Eq. 4.67 means that the electromechanical torque acts in the direction to bring the magnetic fields of the stator and rotor into alignment.

Equations 4.63, 4.64, and 4.67 are a set of three equations relating the electrical variables v_s, i_s, v_r, i_r and the mechanical variables T and θ_m. These equations, together with the constraints imposed on the electrical variables by the networks connected to the terminals (sources or loads and external impedances) and the constraints imposed on the rotor (applied torques and inertial, frictional, and spring torques), determine the performance of the device and its characteristics as an energy-conversion device between the external electrical and mechanical systems. These are nonlinear differential equations and are difficult to solve except under special circumstances. We are not specifically concerned with their solution here; rather we are using them merely as steps in the development of the theory of rotating machines.

EXAMPLE 4.6

Consider the elementary two-pole, two-winding machine of Fig. 4.31. Its shaft is coupled to a mechanical device which can be made to absorb or deliver mechanical torque over a wide range of speeds. This machine can be connected and operated in several ways. For this example, let us consider the situation in which the rotor winding is excited with direct current I_r and the stator winding is connected to an ac source which can either absorb or deliver electric power. Let the stator current be

$$i_s = I_s \cos \omega_e t$$

where $t = 0$ is arbitrarily chosen as the moment when the stator current has its peak value.

a. Derive an expression for the magnetic torque developed by the machine as the speed is varied by controlling the mechanical device connected to its shaft.
b. Find the speed at which non-zero average torque will be produced if the stator frequency is 60 Hz.
c. With the assumed current-source excitations, what voltages are induced in the stator and rotor windings at synchronous speed ($\omega_m = \omega_e$)?

■ Solution

a. From Eq. 4.67 for a two-pole machine

$$T = -L_{sr} i_s i_r \sin \theta_m$$

For the conditions of this problem, with $\theta_m = \omega_m t + \delta$

$$T = -L_{sr} I_s I_r \cos \omega_e t \, \sin (\omega_m t + \delta)$$

where ω_m is the clockwise angular velocity impressed on the rotor by the mechanical drive and δ is the angular position of the rotor at $t = 0$. Using a trigonometric identity,[2] we have

$$T = -\frac{1}{2} L_{sr} I_s I_r \{\sin [(\omega_m + \omega_e)t + \delta] + \sin [(\omega_m - \omega_e)t + \delta]\}$$

---

[2] $\sin \alpha \cos \beta = \frac{1}{2}[\sin (\alpha + \beta) + \sin (\alpha - \beta)]$

The torque consists of two sinusoidally time-varying terms of frequencies $\omega_m + \omega_e$ and $\omega_m - \omega_e$. As shown in Section 4.5, ac current applied to the two-pole, single-phase stator winding in the machine of Fig. 4.31 creates two flux waves, one traveling in the positive θ_m direction with angular velocity ω_e and the second traveling in the negative θ_m direction also with angular velocity ω_e. It is the interaction of the rotor with these two flux waves which results in the two components of the torque expression.

b. Except when $\omega_m = \pm\omega_e$, the torque averaged over a sufficiently long time is zero. But if $\omega_m = \omega_e$, the rotor is traveling in synchronism with the positive-traveling stator flux wave, and the torque becomes

$$T = -\frac{1}{2}L_{sr}I_sI_r[\sin(2\omega_e t + \delta) + \sin\delta]$$

The first sine term is a double-frequency component whose average value is zero. The second term is the average torque

$$T_{avg} = -\frac{1}{2}L_{sr}I_sI_r \sin\delta$$

A nonzero average torque will also be produced when $\omega_m = -\omega_e$ which merely means rotation in the counter-clockwise direction; the rotor is now traveling in synchronism with the negative-traveling stator flux wave.

This machine is an idealized single-phase synchronous machine. With a stator frequency of 60 Hz, it will produce nonzero average torque for speeds of $\omega_m = \pm\omega_e = \pm2\pi 60$ rad/sec, corresponding to speeds of ±3600 r/min as can be seen from Eq. 4.44.

c. From the second and fourth terms of Eq. 4.63 (with $\theta_e = \theta_m = \omega_m t + \delta$), the voltage induced in the stator when $\omega_m = \omega_e$ is

$$e_s = -\omega_e L_{ss}I_s \sin\omega_e t - \omega_e L_{sr}I_r \sin(\omega_e t + \delta)$$

From the third and fourth terms of Eq. 4.64, the voltage induced in the rotor is

$$e_r = -\omega_e L_{sr}I_s[\sin\omega_e t \, \cos(\omega_e t + \delta) + \cos\omega_e t \, \sin(\omega_e t + \delta)]$$
$$= -\omega_e L_{sr}I_s \sin(2\omega_e t + \delta)$$

The backwards-rotating component of the stator flux induces a double-frequency voltage in the rotor, while the forward-rotating component, which is rotating in synchronism with the rotor, appears as a dc flux to the rotor, and hence induces no voltage in the rotor winding.

Now consider a uniform-air-gap machine with several stator and rotor windings. The same general principles that apply to the elementary model of Fig. 4.31 also apply to the multi-winding machine. Each winding has its own self inductance as well as mutual inductances with other windings. The self inductances and mutual inductances between pairs of windings on the same side of the air gap are constant on the assumption of a uniform gap and negligible magnetic saturation. However, the mutual inductances between pairs of stator and rotor windings vary as the cosine of the angle between their magnetic axes. Torque results from the tendency of the magnetic field of the rotor windings to line up with that of the stator windings. It can be expressed as the sum of terms like that of Eq. 4.67.

EXAMPLE 4.7

Consider a 4-pole, three-phase synchronous machine with a uniform air gap. Assume the armature-winding self and mutual inductances to be constant

$$L_{aa} = L_{bb} = L_{cc}$$

$$L_{ab} = L_{bc} = L_{ca}$$

Similarly, assume the field-winding self inductance L_f to be constant while the mutual inductances between the field winding and the three armature phase windings will vary with the angle θ_m between the magnetic axis of the field winding and that of phase a

$$\mathcal{L}_{af} = L_{af} \cos 2\theta_m$$

$$\mathcal{L}_{bf} = L_{af} \cos (2\theta_m - 120°)$$

$$\mathcal{L}_{cf} = L_{af} \cos (2\theta_m + 120°)$$

Show that when the field is excited with constant current I_f and the armature is excited by balanced-three-phase currents of the form

$$i_a = I_a \cos (\omega_e t + \delta)$$

$$i_b = I_a \cos (\omega_e t - 120° + \delta)$$

$$i_c = I_a \cos (\omega_e t + 120° + \delta)$$

the torque will be constant when the rotor travels at synchronous speed ω_s as given by Eq. 4.42.

■ Solution

The torque can be calculated from the coenergy as described in Section 3.6. This particular machine is a four-winding system and the coenergy will consist of four terms involving 1/2 the self-inductance multiplied by the square of the corresponding winding current as well as product-terms consisting of the mutual inductances between pairs of windings multiplied by the corresponding winding currents. Noting that only the terms involving the mutual inductances between the field winding and the three armature phase windings will contain terms that vary with θ_m, we can write the coenergy in the form

$$W'_{fld}(i_a, i_b, i_c, i_f, \theta_m) = \text{(constant terms)} + \mathcal{L}_{af} i_a i_f + \mathcal{L}_{bf} i_b i_f + \mathcal{L}_{cf} i_c i_f$$

$$= \text{(constant terms)} + L_{af} I_a I_f [\cos 2\theta_m \cos (\omega_e t + \delta)$$

$$+ \cos (2\theta_m - 120°) \cos (\omega_e t - 120° + \delta)$$

$$+ \cos (2\theta_m + 120°) \cos (\omega_e t + 120° + \delta)]$$

$$= \text{(constant terms)} + \frac{3}{2} L_{af} I_a I_f \cos (2\theta_m - \omega_e t - \delta)$$

The torque can now be found from the partial derivative of W'_{fld} with respect to θ_m

$$T = \left. \frac{\partial W'_{fld}}{\partial \theta_m} \right|_{i_a, i_b, i_c, i_f}$$

$$= -3 L_{af} I_a I_f \sin (2\theta_m - \omega_e t - \delta)$$

From this expression, we see that the torque will be constant when the rotor rotates at synchronous velocity ω_s such that

$$\theta_m = \omega_s t = \left(\frac{2}{\text{poles}}\right)\omega_e t = \left(\frac{\omega_e}{2}\right) t$$

in which case the torque will be equal to

$$T = 3L_{af}I_aI_f \sin\delta$$

Note that unlike the case of the single-phase machine of Example 4.6, the torque for this three-phase machine operating at synchronous velocity under balanced-three-phase conditions is constant. As we have seen, this is due to the fact that the stator mmf wave consists of a single rotating flux wave, as opposed to the single-phase case in which the stator phase current produces both a forward- and a backward-rotating flux wave. This backwards flux wave is not in synchronism with the rotor and hence is responsible for the double-frequency time-varying torque component seen in Example 4.6.

Practice Problem 4.5

For the four-pole machine of Example 4.7, find the synchronous speed at which a constant torque will be produced if the rotor currents are of the form

$$i_a = I_a \cos(\omega_e t + \delta)$$

$$i_b = I_a \cos(\omega_e t + 120° + \delta)$$

$$i_c = I_a \cos(\omega_e t - 120° + \delta)$$

Solution

$$\omega_s = -(\omega_e/2)$$

In Example 4.7 we found that, under balanced conditions, a four-pole synchronous machine will produce constant torque at a rotational angular velocity equal to half of the electrical excitation frequency. This result can be generalized to show that, under balanced operating conditions, a multiphase, multi-pole synchronous machine will produce constant torque at a rotor speed, at which the rotor rotates in synchronism with the rotating flux wave produced by the stator currents. Hence, this is known as the *synchronous speed* of the machine. From Eqs. 4.42 and 4.44, the synchronous speed is equal to $\omega_s = (2/\text{poles})\omega_e$ in rad/sec or $n_s = (120/\text{poles})f_e$ in r/min.

4.7.2 Magnetic Field Viewpoint

In the discussion of Section 4.7.1 the characteristics of a rotating machine as viewed from its electric and mechanical terminals have been expressed in terms of its winding inductances. This viewpoint gives little insight into the physical phenomena which occur within the machine. In this section, we will explore an alternative formulation in terms of the interacting magnetic fields.

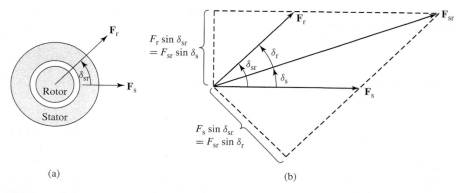

Figure 4.32 Simplified two-pole machine: (a) elementary model and (b) vector diagram of mmf waves. Torque is produced by the tendency of the rotor and stator magnetic fields to align. Note that these figures are drawn with δ_{sr} positive, i.e., with the rotor mmf wave $\mathbf{F_r}$ leading that of the stator $\mathbf{F_s}$.

As we have seen, currents in the rotor and stator windings each produce mmf distributions which in turn produce magnetic fields in the machine. The rotor and stator mmf waves are shown schematically in Fig. 4.32a for a two-pole machine with a smooth air gap. Torque is produced by the tendency of the corresponding rotor and stator magnetic fields to align their magnetic axes. A useful physical picture is that this situation is quite similar to that of two bar magnets pivoted at their centers on the same shaft; there will be a torque, proportional to the angular displacement of the bar magnets, which will act to align them. In the machine of Fig. 4.32a, the torque is proportional to the product of the amplitudes of the stator and rotor mmf waves and is also a function of the angle δ_{sr} measured from the axis of the stator mmf wave to that of the rotor. In fact, we will show that, for a smooth-air-gap machine, the torque is proportional to $\sin \delta_{sr}$.

In a typical machine, most of the flux produced by the stator and rotor windings crosses the air gap and links both windings; this is termed the *mutual flux,* directly analogous to the mutual or magnetizing flux in a transformer. However, some of the flux produced by the rotor and stator windings does not cross the air gap; this is analogous to the leakage flux in a transformer. These flux components are referred to as the *rotor leakage flux* and the *stator leakage flux.* Components of this leakage flux include slot and tooth-tip leakage, end-turn leakage, and space harmonics in the air-gap field.

Only the mutual flux is of direct concern in torque production. The leakage fluxes do affect machine performance however, by virtue of the voltages they induce in their respective windings. Their effect on the electrical characteristics is accounted for by means of leakage inductances, analogous to the use of inclusion of leakage inductances in the transformer models of Chapter 2.

When expressing torque in terms of the winding currents or their resultant mmfs, the resulting expressions do not include terms containing the leakage inductances.

Our analysis here, then, will be in terms of the resultant mutual flux. We shall derive an expression for the magnetic coenergy stored in the air gap in terms of the stator and rotor mmfs and the angle δ_{sr} between their magnetic axes. The torque can then be found from the partial derivative of the coenergy with respect to angle δ_{sr}.

For analytical simplicity, we will assume that the radial length g of the air gap (the radial clearance between the rotor and stator) is small compared with the radius of the rotor or stator. For a smooth-air-gap machine constructed from electrical steel with high magnetic permeability, it is possible to show that this will result in air-gap flux which is primarily radially directed and that there is relatively little difference between the flux density at the rotor surface, at the stator surface, or at any intermediate radial distance in the air gap. The air-gap field then can be represented as a radial field H_{ag} or B_{ag} whose intensity varies with the angle around the periphery. The line integral of H_{ag} across the gap then is simply $H_{ag}g$ and equals the *resultant air-gap mmf* $\mathcal{F}_{sr}$ produced by the stator and rotor windings; thus

$$H_{ag}g = \mathcal{F}_{sr} \tag{4.68}$$

where the script $\mathcal{F}$ denotes the mmf wave as a function of the angle around the periphery.

The mmf waves of the stator and rotor are spatial sine waves with δ_{sr} being the phase angle between their magnetic axes in electrical degrees. They can be represented by the space vectors $\mathbf{F}_s$ and $\mathbf{F}_r$ drawn along the magnetic axes of the stator- and rotor-mmf waves respectively, as in Fig. 4.32b. The resultant mmf acting to produce flux across the air gap is their vector sum and is represented by the space vector $\mathbf{F}_{sr}$. From the trigonometric formula for the diagonal of a parallelogram, its peak value is found from

$$F_{sr}^2 = F_s^2 + F_r^2 + 2F_s F_r \cos \delta_{sr} \tag{4.69}$$

in which the Fs are the peak values of the mmf waves. The resultant radial H_{ag} field is a sinusoidal space wave whose peak value $H_{ag,peak}$ is, from Eq. 4.68,

$$(H_{ag})_{peak} = \frac{F_{sr}}{g} \tag{4.70}$$

Now consider the magnetic field coenergy stored in the air gap. From Eq. 3.49, the coenergy density at a point where the magnetic field intensity is H is calculated as $(\mu_0/2)H^2$ in SI units. Thus, the coenergy density averaged over the volume of the air gap is $\mu_0/2$ times the average value of H_{ag}^2. The average value of the square of a sine wave is half its peak value. Hence,

$$\text{Average coenergy density} = \frac{\mu_0}{2}\left(\frac{(H_{ag})_{peak}^2}{2}\right) = \frac{\mu_0}{4}\left(\frac{F_{sr}}{g}\right)^2 \tag{4.71}$$

Based upon the small-gap approximation, the volume of the air gap is given by πDlg where l is the axial length of the air gap and D is its average diameter. The total coenergy can be found by multiplying the average coenergy density by the air-gap volume

$$W'_{\text{fld}} = \frac{\mu_0}{4} \left(\frac{F_{\text{sr}}}{g} \right)^2 \pi D l g = \frac{\mu_0 \pi D l}{4g} F_{\text{sr}}^2 \tag{4.72}$$

From Eq. 4.69 the coenergy stored in the air gap can now be expressed in terms of the peak amplitudes of the stator- and rotor-mmf waves and the space-phase angle between them; thus

$$W'_{\text{fld}} = \frac{\mu_0 \pi D l}{4g} \left(F_{\text{s}}^2 + F_{\text{r}}^2 + 2 F_{\text{s}} F_{\text{r}} \cos \delta_{\text{sr}} \right) \tag{4.73}$$

Recognizing that holding mmf constant is equivalent to holding current constant, an expression for the electromechanical torque T can now be obtained in terms of the interacting magnetic fields by taking the partial derivative of the field coenergy with respect to angle. For a two-pole machine

$$T = \frac{\partial W'_{\text{fld}}}{\partial \delta_{\text{sr}}} \bigg|_{F_{\text{s}}, F_{\text{r}}} = - \left(\frac{\mu_0 \pi D l}{2g} \right) F_{\text{s}} F_{\text{r}} \sin \delta_{\text{sr}} \tag{4.74}$$

The general expression for the torque for a multi-pole machine is

$$T = - \left(\frac{\text{poles}}{2} \right) \left(\frac{\mu_0 \pi D l}{2g} \right) F_{\text{s}} F_{\text{r}} \sin \delta_{\text{sr}} \tag{4.75}$$

In this equation, δ_{sr} is the electrical space-phase angle between the rotor and stator mmf waves and the torque T acts in the direction to accelerate the rotor. Thus when δ_{sr} is negative, the torque is positive (acting in a direction to accelerate the rotor) and the machine is operating as a motor. Similarly, a positive value of δ_{sr} corresponds to negative torque tending to de-accelerate the rotor as is the case when the machine is operating as a generator.

This important equation states that the torque is proportional to the peak values of the stator- and rotor-mmf waves F_{s} and F_{r} and to the sine of the electrical space-phase angle δ_{sr} between them. Equal and opposite torques are exerted on the stator and rotor. The minus sign means that the fields tend to align themselves.

One can now compare the results of Eq. 4.75 with that of Eq. 4.67. Recognizing that F_{s} is proportional to i_{s} and F_{r} is proportional to i_{r}, one sees that they are similar in form. In fact, they must be equal, as can be verified by substitution of the appropriate expressions for F_{s}, F_{r} (Section 4.3.1), and L_{sr} (Appendix B). Note that these results have been derived with the assumption that the iron reluctance is negligible. However, the two techniques are equally valid for finite iron permeability.

On referring to Fig. 4.32b, it can be seen that $F_{\text{r}} \sin \delta_{\text{sr}}$ is the component of the F_{r} wave in electrical space quadrature with the F_{s} wave. Similarly $F_{\text{s}} \sin \delta_{\text{sr}}$ is the component of the F_{s} wave in quadrature with the F_{r} wave. Thus, the torque is proportional to the product of one magnetic field and the component of the other in quadrature with it, much like the cross product of vector analysis. Also note that in Fig. 4.32b

$$F_{\text{s}} \sin \delta_{\text{sr}} = F_{\text{sr}} \sin \delta_{\text{r}} \tag{4.76}$$

and

$$F_r \sin \delta_{sr} = F_{sr} \sin \delta_s \tag{4.77}$$

where, as seen in Fig. 4.32, δ_r is the angle measured from the axis of the resultant mmf wave to the axis of the rotor mmf wave. Similarly, δ_s is the angle measured from the axis of the stator mmf wave to the axis of the resultant mmf wave.

The torque, acting to accelerate the rotor, can then be expressed in terms of the resultant mmf wave F_{sr} by substitution of either Eq. 4.76 or Eq. 4.77 in Eq. 4.75; thus

$$T = -\left(\frac{\text{poles}}{2}\right)\left(\frac{\mu_0 \pi Dl}{2g}\right) F_s F_{sr} \sin \delta_s \tag{4.78}$$

$$T = -\left(\frac{\text{poles}}{2}\right)\left(\frac{\mu_0 \pi Dl}{2g}\right) F_r F_{sr} \sin \delta_r \tag{4.79}$$

Comparison of Eqs. 4.75, 4.78, and 4.79 shows that the torque can be expressed in terms of the component magnetic fields due to *each* current acting alone, as in Eq. 4.75, or in terms of the *resultant* field and *either* of the components, as in Eqs. 4.78 and 4.79, *provided that we use the corresponding angle between the axes of the fields.* Ability to reason in any of these terms is a convenience in machine analysis.

In Eqs. 4.75, 4.78, and 4.79, the fields have been expressed in terms of the peak values of their mmf waves. When magnetic saturation is neglected, the fields can, of course, be expressed in terms of the peak values of their flux-density waves or in terms of total flux per pole. Thus the peak value B_{ag} of the field due to a sinusoidally distributed mmf wave in a uniform-air-gap machine is $\mu_0 F_{ag,peak}/g$, where $F_{ag,peak}$ is the peak value of the mmf wave. For example, the resultant mmf F_{sr} produces a resultant flux-density wave whose peak value is $B_{sr} = \mu_0 F_{sr}/g$. Thus, $F_{sr} = g B_{sr}/\mu_0$ and substitution in Eq. 4.79 gives

$$T = -\left(\frac{\text{poles}}{2}\right)\left(\frac{\pi Dl}{2}\right) B_{sr} F_r \sin \delta_r \tag{4.80}$$

One of the inherent limitations in the design of electromagnetic apparatus is the saturation flux density of magnetic materials. Because of saturation in the armature teeth the peak value B_{sr} of the resultant flux-density wave in the air gap is limited to about 1.5 to 2.0 T. The maximum permissible value of the winding current, and hence the corresponding mmf wave, is limited by the temperature rise of the winding and other design requirements. Because the resultant flux density and mmf appear explicitly in Eq. 4.80, this equation is in a convenient form for design purposes and can be used to estimate the maximum torque which can be obtained from a machine of a given size.

EXAMPLE 4.8

An 1800-r/min, four-pole, 60-Hz synchronous motor has an air-gap length of 1.2 mm. The average diameter of the air-gap is 27 cm, and its axial length is 32 cm. The rotor winding has 786 turns and a winding factor of 0.976. Assuming that thermal considerations limit the rotor current to 18 A, estimate the maximum torque and power output one can expect to obtain from this machine.

■ Solution

First, we can determine the maximum rotor mmf from Eq. 4.9

$$(F_r)_{max} = \frac{4}{\pi} \left(\frac{k_r N_r}{poles} \right) (I_r)_{max} = \frac{4}{\pi} \left(\frac{0.976 \times 786}{4} \right) 18 = 4395 \text{ A}$$

Assuming that the peak value of the resultant air-gap flux is limited to 1.5 T, we can estimate the maximum torque from Eq. 4.80 by setting δ_r equal to $-\pi/2$ (recognizing that negative values of δ_r, with the rotor mmf lagging the resultant mmf, correspond to positive, motoring torque)

$$T_{max} = \left(\frac{poles}{2} \right) \left(\frac{\pi Dl}{2} \right) B_{sr} (F_r)_{max}$$

$$= \left(\frac{4}{2} \right) \left(\frac{\pi \times 0.27 \times 0.32}{2} \right) 1.5 \times 4395 = 1789 \text{ N} \cdot \text{m}$$

For a synchronous speed of 1800 r/min, $\omega_m = n_s (\pi/30) = 1800 (\pi/30) = 60\pi$ rad/sec, and thus the corresponding power can be calculated as $P_{max} = \omega_m T_{max} = 337$ kW.

Practice Problem 4.6

Repeat Example 4.8 for a two-pole, 60-Hz synchronous motor with an air-gap length of 1.3 mm, an average air-gap diameter of 22 cm and an axial length of 41 cm. The rotor winding has a 900 turns and a winding factor of 0.965. The maximum rotor current is 22 A.

Solution

$T_{max} = 2585$ N · m and $P_{max} = 975$ kW

Alternative forms of the torque equation arise when it is recognized that the resultant flux per pole is

$$\Phi_p = (\text{average value of } B \text{ over a pole})(\text{pole area}) \tag{4.81}$$

and that the average value of a sinusoid over one-half wavelength is $2/\pi$ times its peak value. Thus

$$\Phi_p = \frac{2}{\pi} B_{peak} \left(\frac{\pi Dl}{poles} \right) = \left(\frac{2Dl}{poles} \right) B_{peak} \tag{4.82}$$

where B_{peak} is the peak value of the corresponding flux-density wave. For example, using the peak value of the resultant flux B_{sr} and substitution of Eq. 4.82 into Eq. 4.80 gives

$$T = -\frac{\pi}{2} \left(\frac{poles}{2} \right)^2 \Phi_{sr} F_r \sin \delta_r \tag{4.83}$$

where Φ_{sr} is the resultant flux per pole produced by the combined effect of the stator and rotor mmfs.

To recapitulate, we now have several forms in which the torque of a uniform-air-gap machine can be expressed in terms of its magnetic fields. *All are merely statements that the torque is proportional to the product of the magnitudes of the interacting fields and to the sine of the electrical space angle between their magnetic axes.* The negative sign indicates that the electromechanical torque acts in a direction to decrease the displacement angle between the fields. In our preliminary discussion of machine types, Eq. 4.83 will be the preferred form.

One further remark can be made concerning the torque equations and the thought process leading to them. There was no restriction in the derivation that the mmf wave or flux-density wave remain stationary in space. They may remain stationary, or they may be traveling waves, as discussed in Section 4.5. As we have seen, if the magnetic fields of the stator and rotor are constant in amplitude and travel around the air gap at the same speed, a steady torque will be produced by the tendency of the stator and rotor fields to align themselves in accordance with the torque equations.

4.8 LINEAR MACHINES

In general, each of the machine types discussed in this book can be produced in linear versions in addition to the rotary versions which are commonly found and which are discussed extensively in the following chapters. In fact, for clarity of discussion, many of the machine types discussed in this book are drawn in their developed (Cartesian coordinate) form, such as in Fig. 4.16b.

Linear motors can be found in some transportation systems, typically with the ac "stator" on the moving vehicle and with a conducting stationary "rotor" constituting the rails. In these systems, in addition to providing propulsion, the induced currents in the rail may be used to provide levitation, thus offering a mechanism for high-speed transportation without the difficulties associated with wheel-rail interactions on more conventional rail transport. Linear motors have also found application in the machine tool industry and in robotics where linear motion (required for positioning and in the operation of manipulators) is a common requirement. In addition, reciprocating linear machines are being constructed for driving reciprocating compressors and alternators.

The analysis of linear machines is quite similar to that of rotary machines. In general, linear dimensions and displacements replace angular ones, and forces replace torques. With these exceptions, the expressions for machine parameters are derived in an analogous fashion to those presented here for rotary machines, and the results are similar in form.

Consider the linear winding shown in Fig. 4.33. This winding, consisting of N turns per slot and carrying a current i, is directly analogous to the rotary winding shown in developed form in Fig. 4.22. In fact, the only difference is that the dependence on the angular position θ_a is replaced by a dependence on the linear position z.

The fundamental component of the mmf wave of Fig. 4.33 can be found directly from Eq. 4.14 simply by recognizing that this winding has a wavelength equal to β and that the fundamental component of this mmf wave varies as $\cos(2\pi z/\beta)$. Thus replacing the angle θ_a in Eq. 4.14 by $2\pi z/\beta$, we can find the fundamental component of the mmf wave directly as

$$H_{\text{ag1}} = \frac{4}{\pi}\left(\frac{Ni}{2g}\right)\cos\left(\frac{2\pi z}{\beta}\right) \tag{4.84}$$

Figure 4.33 The mmf and H field of a concentrated full-pitch linear winding.

If an actual machine has a distributed winding (similar to its rotary counterpart as shown in Fig. 4.17) consisting of a total of N_{ph} turns distributed over (poles/2) periods in z (i.e., over a length of $\beta \times$ poles/2), the fundamental component of H_{ag} can be found by analogy with Eq. 4.16

$$H_{ag1} = \frac{4}{\pi} \left(\frac{k_w N_{ph} i}{g \times \text{poles}} \right) \cos \left(\frac{2\pi z}{\beta} \right) \tag{4.85}$$

where k_w is the winding factor.

In a fashion analogous to the discussion of Section 4.5.2, a three-phase linear winding can be made from three windings such as those of Fig. 4.28, with each phase displaced in position by a distance $\beta/3$ and with each phase excited by balanced three-phase currents of angular frequency ω_e

$$i_a = I_{peak} \cos \omega_e t \tag{4.86}$$

$$i_b = I_{peak} \cos (\omega_e t - 120°) \tag{4.87}$$

$$i_c = I_{peak} \cos (\omega_e t + 120°) \tag{4.88}$$

Following the development of Eqs. 4.28 through 4.40, we can see that there will be a single positive-traveling mmf which can be written directly from Eq. 4.40 simply by replacing θ_a by $2\pi z/\beta$ as

$$\mathcal{F}^+(z, t) = \frac{3}{2} F_{max} \cos \left(\frac{2\pi z}{\beta} - \omega_e t \right) \qquad (4.89)$$

where F_{max} is given by

$$F_{max} = \frac{4}{\pi} \left(\frac{k_w N_{ph}}{poles} \right) I_{peak} \qquad (4.90)$$

From Eq. 4.89 we see that the result is an mmf which travels in the z direction with a linear velocity

$$v = \frac{\omega_e \beta}{2\pi} = f_e \beta \qquad (4.91)$$

where f_e is the exciting frequency in hertz.

From Eq. 4.89 and using Eq. 4.13, we can find the fundamental air-gap flux density

$$B_{ag1} = \left(\frac{\mu_0}{g} \right) \mathcal{F}^+(z, t) = \frac{3}{2} B_{max} \cos \left(\frac{2\pi z}{\beta} - \omega_e t \right) \qquad (4.92)$$

where

$$B_{max} = \frac{4 \mu_0}{\pi g} \left(\frac{k_w N_{ph}}{poles} \right) I_{peak} \qquad (4.93)$$

EXAMPLE 4.9

A three-phase linear ac motor has a winding with a wavelength of $\beta = 0.5$ m and an air gap of 1.0 cm in length. A total of 48 turns, with a winding factor $k_w = 0.92$, is distributed over a total winding length of $3\beta = 1.5$ m (poles = 6). Assume the windings to be excited with balanced three-phase currents of peak amplitude 700 A and frequency 25 Hz. Calculate (a) the amplitude of the fundamental component of the resultant mmf wave, (b) the amplitude of the corresponding air-gap flux density, and (c) the velocity of the traveling mmf wave.

■ **Solution**

a. From Eqs. 4.89 and 4.90, the amplitude of the fundamental component of the resultant mmf wave is

$$F_{peak} = \frac{3}{2} \frac{4}{\pi} \left(\frac{k_w N_{ph}}{poles} \right) I_{peak}$$

$$= \frac{3}{2} \frac{4}{\pi} \left(\frac{0.92 \times 48}{6} \right) 700$$

$$= 9840 \text{ A/m}$$

b. The amplitude of the corresponding flux-density wave is

$$B_{peak} = \left(\frac{\mu_0}{g} \right) F_{peak}$$

$$= \left(\frac{4 \pi \times 10^{-7}}{0.01} \right) 9840$$

$$= 1.24 \text{ T}$$

c. Finally, the velocity of the traveling wave can be determined from Eq. 4.91:

$$v = f_e \beta = 25 \times 0.5 = 12.5 \text{ m/s}$$

A three-phase linear synchronous motor has a wavelength of 0.93 m. It is observed to be traveling at speed of 83 km/hr. Calculate the frequency of the electrical excitation required under this operating condition.

Solution

$$f = 24.8 \text{ Hz}$$

Linear machines are not discussed specifically in this book. Rather, the reader is urged to recognize that the fundamentals of their performance and analysis correspond directly to those of their rotary counterparts. One major difference between these two machine types is that linear machines have *end effects,* corresponding to the magnetic fields which "leak" out of the air gap ahead of and behind the machine. These effects are beyond the scope of this book and have been treated in detail in the published literature.[3]

4.9   MAGNETIC SATURATION

The characteristics of electric machines depend heavily upon the use of magnetic materials. These materials are required to form the magnetic circuit and are used by the machine designer to obtain specific machine characteristics. As we have seen in Chapter 1, magnetic materials are less than ideal. As the magnetic flux they carry increases, they begin to saturate, with the result that their magnetic permeabilities begin to decrease, along with their effectiveness in contributing to the overall flux density in the machine.

Both electromechanical torque and generated voltage in all machines depend on the winding flux linkages. For specific mmfs in the windings, the fluxes depend on the reluctances of the iron portions of the magnetic circuits and on those of the air gaps. Saturation may therefore appreciably influence the characteristics of the machines.

Another aspect of saturation, more subtle and more difficult to evaluate without experimental and theoretical comparisons, concerns its influence on the basic premises from which the analytic approach to machinery is developed. Specifically, relations for the air-gap mmf are typically based on the assumption of negligible reluctance in the iron. When these relations are applied to practical machines with varying degrees of saturation in the iron, significant errors in the analytical results can be expected.

---

[3] See, for example, S. Yamamura, *Theory of Linear Induction Motors,* 2d ed., Halsted Press, 1978. Also, S. Nasar and I. Boldea, *Linear Electric Motors: Theory, Design and Practical Applications,* Prentice-Hall, 1987.

To improve these analytical relationships, in one approach the actual machine is replaced by an equivalent machine whose iron has negligible reluctance but whose air-gap length is increased by an amount sufficient to absorb the mmf drop in the iron of the actual machine.

Similarly, the effects of air-gap non-uniformities such as slots and ventilating ducts are also incorporated by increasing the effective air-gap length. Ultimately, these various approximate techniques must be verified and confirmed experimentally. In cases where such simple techniques are found to be inadequate, detailed analyses, such as those employing finite-element or other numerical techniques, can be used. Typically the use of these techniques represents a significant increase in modeling complexity.

Saturation characteristics of rotating machines are often presented in the form of an *open-circuit characteristic,* also called a *magnetization curve* or *saturation curve.* For a synchronous machine, the open-circuit saturation curve is obtained by operating the machine at constant speed and measuring the open-circuit armature voltage as a function of the field current. A typical open-circuit saturation curve for a synchronous machine takes the form shown in Fig. 4.34. This nature of this curve is determined both by the geometry of the machine under consideration as well as by the magnetization characteristics of the electrical steel used in the machine. The straight line tangent to the lower portion of the curve is the *air-gap line,* corresponding to low levels of flux density within the machine. Under these conditions the reluctance of the machine iron is typically negligible, and the mmf required to excite the machine is simply that required to overcome the reluctance of the air gap. If it were not for the effects of saturation, the air-gap line and open-circuit characteristic would coincide. Thus, the departure of the curve from the air-gap line as the field current is increased is an indication of the degree of saturation in the machine. In typical machines the ratio at rated voltage of the total mmf to that required by the air gap alone is between 1.1 and 1.25.

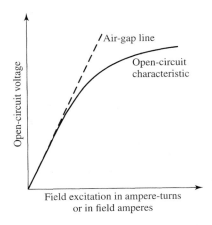

Figure 4.34 Typical open-circuit characteristic and air-gap line.

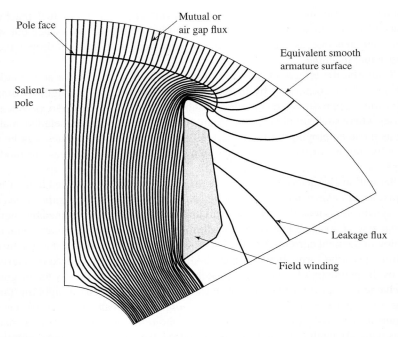

Figure 4.35 Finite-element solution for the flux distribution around a salient pole.

At the design stage, the open-circuit characteristic can be calculated using techniques such as finite-element analyses. A typical finite-element solution for the flux distribution around the pole of a salient-pole machine is shown in Fig. 4.35. The distribution of the air-gap flux found from this solution, together with the fundamental and third-harmonic components, is shown in Fig. 4.36.

In addition to saturation effects, Fig. 4.36 clearly illustrates the effect of a nonuniform air gap. As expected, the flux density over the pole face, where the air gap is small, is much higher than that away from the pole. This type of detailed analysis is of great use to a designer in obtaining specific machine characteristics.

As we have seen, the magnetization curve for an existing synchronous machine can be determined by operating the machine as an unloaded generator and measuring the values of terminal voltage corresponding to a series of values of field current. For an induction motor, the machine is operated at or close to synchronous speed (in which case very little current will be induced in the rotor windings), and the stator current is measured as a function of stator terminal voltage. The magnetization curve is produced by plotting the stator voltage as a function of stator current.

It should be emphasized that saturation in a fully loaded machine occurs as a result of the total mmf acting on the magnetic circuit. Since the flux distribution under load generally differs from that of no-load conditions, the details of the machine saturation characteristics may vary from the open-circuit curve of Fig. 4.34.

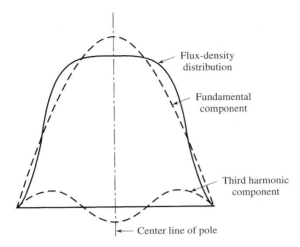

Figure 4.36 Flux-density wave corresponding to Fig. 4.38 with its fundamental and third-harmonic components.

4.10 LEAKAGE FLUX

In Section 2.4 we showed that in a two-winding transformer the flux created by each winding can be separated into two components. One component consists of flux which links both windings, and the other consists of flux which links only the winding creating the flux. The first component, called *mutual flux,* is responsible for coupling between the two coils. The second, known as *leakage flux,* contributes only to the self-inductance of each coil.

Note that the concept of mutual and leakage flux is meaningful only in the context of a multi-winding system. For systems of three or more windings, the bookkeeping must be done very carefully. Consider, for example, the three-winding system of Fig. 4.37. Shown schematically are the various components of flux created by a current in winding 1. Here φ_{123} is clearly mutual flux that links all three windings, and φ_{1l} is clearly leakage flux since it links only winding 1. However, φ_{12} is mutual flux with respect to winding 2 yet is leakage flux with respect to winding 3, while φ_{13} mutual flux with respect to winding 3 and leakage flux with respect to winding 2.

Electric machinery often contains systems of multiple windings, requiring careful bookkeeping to account for the flux contributions of the various windings. Although the details of such analysis are beyond the scope of this book, it is useful to discuss these effects in a qualitative fashion and to describe how they affect the basic machine inductances.

Air-Gap Space-Harmonic Fluxes   In this chapter we have seen that although single distributed coils create air-gap flux with a significant amount of space-harmonic content, it is possible to distribute these windings so that the space-fundamental component is emphasized while the harmonic effects are greatly reduced. As a result, we

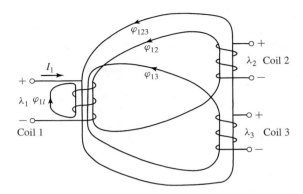

Figure 4.37 Three-coil system showing components of mutual and leakage flux produced by current in coil 1.

can neglect harmonic effects and consider only space-fundamental fluxes in calculating the self and mutual-inductance expressions of Eqs. B.24 and B.25.

Though often small, the space-harmonic components of air-gap flux do exist. In dc machines they are useful torque-producing fluxes and therefore can be counted as mutual flux between the rotor and stator windings. In ac machines, however, they may generate time-harmonic voltages or asynchronously rotating flux waves. These effects generally cannot be rigorously accounted for in most standard analyses. Nevertheless, it is consistent with the assumptions basic to these analyses to recognize that these fluxes form a part of the leakage flux of the individual windings which produce them.

Slot-Leakage Flux   Figure 4.38 shows the flux created by a single coil side in a slot. Notice that in addition to flux which crosses the air gap, contributing to the air-gap flux, there are flux components which cross the slot. In a slot with coils from a single phase, this flux links only the coil that is producing it; it also forms a component of

Figure 4.38 Flux created by a single coil side in a slot.

Figure 4.39 End view of the stator of a 16.5-kV 275-MVA 3600 r/min turbine generator. (*Photo courtesy of Siemens*)

the leakage inductance of the winding producing it. In other cases, coils of two phases share a single slot and some of the slot flux is mutual between the phases. However, since this flux does not cross the air gap, it remains leakage flux with respect to any windings on the rotor.

End-Turn Fluxes Figure 4.39 shows the stator end windings of an ac machine. The magnetic field distribution created by end turns is extremely complex. In general these fluxes do not contribute to useful rotor-to-stator mutual flux, and thus they, too, contribute to leakage inductance.

From this discussion we see that the self-inductance expression of Eq. B.24 must, in general, be modified by an additional term L_l, which represents the winding leakage inductance. This leakage inductance corresponds directly to the leakage inductance of a transformer winding as discussed in Chapter 1. Although the leakage inductance is usually difficult to calculate analytically and must be determined by approximate or empirical techniques, it plays an important role in machine performance.

4.11 SUMMARY

This chapter presents a brief and elementary description of three basic types of rotating machines: synchronous, induction, and dc machines. In all of them the basic principles are essentially the same. Voltages are generated by the relative motion of a magnetic field with respect to a winding, and torques are produced by the interaction of the magnetic fields of the stator and rotor windings. The characteristics of the various machine types are determined by the methods of connection and excitation of the windings, but the basic principles are essentially similar.

The basic analytical tools for studying rotating machines are expressions for the generated voltages and for the electromechanical torque. Taken together, they express the coupling between the electric and mechanical systems. To develop a reasonably quantitative theory without the confusion arising from too much detail, we have made several simplifying approximations. In the study of ac machines we have assumed sinusoidal time variations of voltages and currents and sinusoidal space distributions of air-gap flux density and mmf. On examination of the mmf produced by distributed ac windings we found that the space-fundamental component is the most important. On the other hand, in dc machines the armature-winding mmf is more nearly a sawtooth wave. For our preliminary study in this chapter, however, we have assumed sinusoidal mmf distributions for both ac and dc machines. We examine this assumption more thoroughly for dc machines in Chapter 7. Faraday's law results in Eq. 4.52 for the rms voltage generated in an ac machine winding or Eq. 4.55 for the average voltage generated between brushes in a dc machine.

On examination of the mmf wave of a three-phase winding, we found that balanced three-phase currents produce a constant-amplitude air-gap magnetic field rotating at synchronous speed, as shown in Fig. 4.28 and Eq. 4.41. The importance of this fact cannot be overstated, for it means that it is possible to operate such machines, either as motors or generators, under conditions of constant torque (and hence constant electrical power as is discussed in Appendix A), eliminating the double-frequency, time-varying torque inherently associated with single-phase machines. For example, imagine a multi-megawatt single-phase 60-Hz generator subjected to multi-megawatt instantaneous torque and power pulsation at 120 Hz! The discovery that poly-phase windings can produce rotating fields led to the invention of the simple, rugged, reliable, self-starting polyphase induction motor, which is analyzed in Chapter 6. (A single-phase induction motor will not start; it needs an auxiliary starting winding, as shown in Chapter 9.)

In single-phase machines, or in polyphase machines operating under unbalanced conditions, the backward-rotating component of the armature mmf wave induces currents and losses in the rotor structure. Thus, the operation of polyphase machines under balanced conditions not only eliminates the second-harmonic component of generated torque, it also eliminates a significant source of rotor loss and rotor heating. It was the invention of polyphase machines operating under balanced conditions that made possible the design and construction of large synchronous generators with ratings as large as 1000 MW.

Having assumed sinusoidally-distributed magnetic fields in the air gap, we then derived expressions for the magnetic torque. The simple physical picture for torque production is that of two magnets, one on the stator and one on the rotor, as shown schematically in Fig. 4.32a. The torque acts in the direction to align the magnets. To get a reasonably close quantitative analysis without being hindered by details, we assumed a smooth air gap and neglected the reluctance of the magnetic paths in the iron parts, with a mental note that this assumption may not be valid in all situations and a more detailed model may be required.

In Section 4.7 we derived expressions for the magnetic torque from two viewpoints, both based on the fundamental principles of Chapter 3. The first viewpoint regards the machine as a set of magnetically-coupled circuits with inductances which depend on the angular position of the rotor, as in Section 4.7.1. The second regards the machine from the viewpoint of the magnetic fields in the air gap, as in Section 4.7.2. It is shown that the torque can be expressed as the product of the stator field, the rotor field, and the sine of the angle between their magnetic axes, as in Eq. 4.75 or any of the forms derived from Eq. 4.75. The two viewpoints are complementary, and ability to reason in terms of both is helpful in reaching an understanding of how machines work.

This chapter has been concerned with basic principles underlying rotating-machine theory. By itself it is obviously incomplete. Many questions remain unanswered. How do we apply these principles to the determination of the characteristics of synchronous, induction, and dc machines? What are some of the practical problems that arise from the use of iron, copper, and insulation in physical machines? What are some of the economic and engineering considerations affecting rotating-machine applications? What are the physical factors limiting the conditions under which a machine can operate successfully? Appendix D discusses some of these problems. Taken together, Chapter 4 along with Appendix D serve as an introduction to the more detailed treatments of rotating machines in the following chapters.

4.12 CHAPTER 4 VARIABLES

β	Linear wavelength [m]
δ	Phase angle [rad]
λ	Flux linkages [Wb]
Φ_p	Air gap flux per pole [Wb]
θ_a	Stator spatial angle [rad]
θ_{ae}	Stator spatial angle in electrical units [rad]
θ_m	Rotor angular position [rad]
θ_{me}	Rotor angular position in electrical units [rad]
θ_r	Rotor spatial angle [rad]
$L, \mathcal{L}$	Inductance [H]
μ	Magnetic permeability [H/m]
μ_0	Permeability of free space $= 4\pi \times 10^{-7}$ [H/m]
ω_e	Electrical frequency [rad/sec]
ω_m	Mechanical angular velocity [rad/sec]
ω_s	Synchronous mechanical angular velocity [rad/sec]
B	Magnetic flux density [T]
C_a	Total number of turns in dc-machine armature winding
e, E, v	Voltage [V]
f_e	Electrical frequency [Hz]
$F, \mathcal{F}$	Magnetomotive force [A]

g	Air-gap length [m]
$H, \mathbf{H}$	Magnetic field intensity [A/m]
i, I	Current [A]
k_f, k_r, k_w	Winding factor
l, r, D	Linear dimensions [m]
m	Number of parallel paths in dc-machine armature winding
n	Angular velocity [r/min]
n_s	Synchronous angular velocity [r/min]
N	Number of turns
N_c	Number of turns per coil
N_f	Number of field-winding series turns
N_{ph}	Number of turns per phase
poles	Number of poles
q	Number of phases
t	Time [sec]
T	Torque [N·m]
v	Velocity [m/sec]
W'	Coenergy [J]
z	Linear position [m]

Subscripts:

a	Armature
a,b,c	Phase designations
ag	Air gap
c	Coil
f	Field
max	Maximum
r	Rotor
rms	Root mean square
s	Stator

4.13   PROBLEMS

4.1 The rotor of a six-pole synchronous generator is rotating at a mechanical speed of 1200 r/min.

    a. Express this mechanical speed in radians per second.

    b. What is the frequency of the generated voltage in hertz and in radians per second?

    c. What mechanical speed in revolutions per minute would be required to generate voltage at a frequency of 50 Hz?

4.2 The voltage generated in phase a of an unloaded three-phase synchronous generator is of the form $v_a(t) = \sqrt{2}\, V_a \cos(\omega t)$. (i) Write expressions for the voltage in the remaining two phases a and b. (ii) Write an expression for the line-line voltage $v_{ab}(t)$.

4.3 A wind turbine is connected to an 8-pole permanent-magnet generator through a gear with a speed-increase ratio of 1:10. The generator, whose output will be rectified, produces a voltage of 480 V rms, line-line at a speed of 900 r/min. Depending upon the speed of the wind, the wind-turbine will rotate at speeds in the range of 0.5 to 1.75 r/sec. Calculate the generator output frequency and voltage at wind-turbine speeds of (i) 0.5 r/sec and (ii) 1.75 r/sec.

4.4 A three-phase motor is used to drive a pump. When connected to a 50-Hz power system, it is observed (by the use of a stroboscope) that the motor speed decreases from 998 r/min when the pump is unloaded to 945 r/min as the pump is loaded.

    a.   Is this a synchronous or an induction motor?

    b.   How many poles does this motor have?

4.5 A three-phase, variable-frequency drive system is used to power a 4-pole synchronous motor. Calculate the speed of the motor in r/min if the drive frequency is 200 Hz.

4.6 The object of this problem is to illustrate how the armature windings of certain machines, i.e., dc machines, can be approximately represented by uniform current sheets, the degree of correspondence growing better as the winding is distributed in a greater number of slots around the armature periphery. For this purpose, consider an armature with eight slots uniformly distributed over 360 electrical degrees (corresponding to a span of one pole pair). The air gap is of uniform length, the slot openings are very small, and the reluctance of the iron is negligible.

    Lay out 360 electrical degrees of the armature with its slots in developed form in the manner of Fig. 4.20a and number the slots 1 to 8 from left to right. The winding consists of eight single-turn coils, each carrying a direct current of I_0. Coil sides placed in any of the slots 1 to 4 carry current directed into the paper; those placed in any of the slots 5 to 8 carry current out of the paper.

    a.   Consider that all eight coils are placed with one side in slot 1 and the other in slot 5. The remaining slots are empty. Draw the rectangular mmf wave produced by these slots.

    b.   Next consider that four coils have one side in slot 1 and the other in slot 5, while the remaining four coils have one side in slot 3 and the other in slot 7. Draw the component rectangular mmf waves produced by each group of coils, and superimpose the components to give the resultant mmf wave.

    c.   Now consider that two coils are placed in slots 1 and 5, two in slots 2 and 6, two in 3 and 7, and two in 4 and 8. Again superimpose the component rectangular waves to produce the resultant wave. Note that the task can be systematized and simplified by recognizing that the mmf wave is symmetric about its axis and takes a step at each slot which is directly proportional to the number of ampere-conductors in that slot.

    d. Let the armature now consist of 16 slots per 360 electrical degrees with one coil side per slot. Draw the resultant mmf wave.

4.7 A three-phase Y-connected ac machine is initially supplying a balanced three-phase load when one of the phase windings becomes open-circuited. Because there is no neutral connection on the winding, this requires that the currents in the remaining two windings become equal and opposite. Under this condition, calculate the relative magnitudes of the resultant positive- and negative-traveling mmf waves.

4.8 What is the effect on the rotating mmf and flux waves of a three-phase winding produced by balanced-three-phase currents if two of the phase connections are interchanges?

4.9 In a balanced two-phase machine, the two windings are displaced 90 electrical degrees in space, and the currents in the two windings are phase-displaced 90 electrical degrees in time. For such a machine, carry out the process leading to an equation for the rotating mmf wave corresponding to Eq. 4.41 (which is derived for a three-phase machine).

4.10 This problem investigates the advantages of short-pitching the stator coils of an ac machine. Figure 4.40a shows a single full-pitch coil in a two-pole machine. Figure 4.40b shows a fractional-pitch coil for which the coil sides are β radians apart, rather than π radians (180°) as is the case for the full-pitch coil.

    For an air-gap radial flux distribution of the form

$$B_{\mathrm{r}} = \sum_{n \text{ odd}} B_n \cos n\theta$$

where $n = 1$ corresponds to the fundamental space harmonic, $n = 3$ to the third space harmonic, and so on, the flux linkage of each coil is the integral of B_{r} over the surface spanned by that coil. Thus for the nth space harmonic, the ratio of the maximum fractional-pitch coil flux linkage to that of the

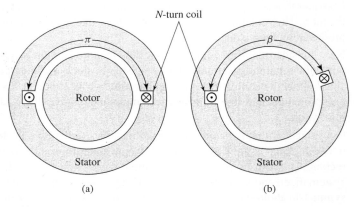

Figure 4.40   Problem 4.10: (a) full-pitch coil and (b) fractional-pitch coil.

full-pitch coil is

$$\frac{\int_{-\beta/2}^{\beta/2} B_n \cos n\theta \, d\theta}{\int_{-\pi/2}^{\pi/2} B_n \cos n\theta \, d\theta} = \frac{\int_{-\beta/2}^{\beta/2} \cos n\theta \, d\theta}{\int_{-\pi/2}^{\pi/2} \cos n\theta \, d\theta} = |\sin (n\beta/2)|$$

It is common, for example, to fractional-pitch the coils of an ac machine by 30 electrical degrees ($\beta = 5\pi/6 = 150°$). For $n = 1, 3, 5$ calculate the fractional reduction in flux linkage due to short pitching.

4.11 An eight-pole, 60-Hz synchronous machine has a rotor winding with a total of 608 series turns and a winding factor $k_r = 0.921$. The rotor length is 1.78 m, the rotor radius is 56 cm, and the air-gap length $= 2.85$ cm.

  a. What is the rated operating speed in r/min?

  b. Calculate the rotor-winding current required to achieve a peak fundamental air-gap flux density of 1.43 T.

  c. Calculate the corresponding fundamental flux per pole.

4.12 Assume that a phase winding of the synchronous machine of Problem 4.11 consists of one 5-turn, full-pitch coil per pole pair, with the coils connected in series to form the phase winding. If the machine is operating at rated speed and under the operating conditions of Problem 4.11, calculate the rms generated voltage per phase.

4.13 The synchronous machine of Problem 4.11 has a three-phase winding with 45 series turns per phase and a winding factor $k_w = 0.935$. For the flux condition and rated speed of Problem 4.11, calculate the rms-generated voltage per phase.

4.14 A four-pole, three-phase synchronous generator has a field winding with a total of 148 series turns and a winding factor $k_r = 0.939$. The rotor length is 72 cm, and its radius is 19 cm. The air-gap length 0.8 cm. The Δ-connected stator winding has 12 series turns per phase and a winding factor $k_w = 0.943$.

  a. The rated rms open-circuit line-line voltage of this motor is 575 V. Calculate the corresponding flux per pole and the peak of the fundamental component of the corresponding air-gap flux density.

  b. Calculate the field-current required to achieve rated open-circuit voltage.

  c. The stator winding is to be rewound so that the motor can be moved to an application for which it will be operated at 50-Hz at a terminal voltage 690 V. Assuming the stator-winding remains Δ connected, (i) calculate the minimal number of series turns per phase required to insure that the re-wound motor achieves rated open-circuit voltage at a field current which does not exceed that of part (b). (ii) Calculate the required field current.

4.15 Consider a two-pole machine with a smooth air gap. Assume that the rotor includes a single, 400-turn full-pitched field winding. The stator has an inside diameter of 15 cm and an axial length is 27 cm and the air gap length is 1.0 cm.

a. The field-winding is excited with a current of 4.6 A. Sketch a plot of the air-gap flux density as a function of angle (assume the field-coil sides to be located at ±90°). Calculate the peak fundamental amplitude of the air-gap flux wave.

Assume that each phase of the stator winding consists of a 30-turn full-pitched winding.

b. If the rotor is driven at a speed of 60 r/sec, plot the resultant voltage generated in the stator coil as a function of time. You may take zero time as the instant when the stator-winding flux linkage is at its maximum. Calculate the rms value of the fundamental component of this generated voltage.

4.16 A three-phase two-pole winding is excited by balanced three-phase 60-Hz currents as described by Eqs. 4.25 to 4.27. Although the winding distribution has been designed to minimize harmonics, there remains some third and fifth spatial harmonics. Thus the phase-a mmf can be written as

$$\mathcal{F}_a = i_a(A_1 \cos\theta_a + A_3 \cos 3\theta_a + A_5 \cos 5\theta_a)$$

Similar expressions can be written for phases b (replace θ_a by $\theta_a - 120°$) and c (replace θ_a by $\theta_a + 120°$). Calculate the total three-phase mmf. What is the angular velocity and rotational direction of each component of the mmf?

4.17 The nameplate of a dc generator indicates that it will produce an output voltage of 24 V dc when operated at a speed of 1800 r/min. By what factor must the number of armature turns be changed such that, for the same field-flux per pole, the generator will produce an output voltage of 48 V dc at a speed of 1400 r/min?

4.18 The armature of a four-pole dc generator has a total of 270 series turns. When operated at a speed of 1200 r/min, the open-circuit generated voltage is 240 V. Calculate Φ_p, the air-gap flux per pole.

4.19 The design of a four-pole, three-phase, 415-V, 50-Hz induction motor is to be based on a stator core of length 21 cm and inner diameter 17 cm. The stator winding distribution which has been selected has a winding factor $k_w = 0.936$.

The designer must pick the number of armature turns so that the flux density in the machine is large enough to make efficient use of the magnetic material without being so large as to result in excessive saturation. To achieve this objective, the machine is to be designed with a peak fundamental air-gap flux density close to 1.45 T. Calculate the required number of series turns per phase if the armature winding is to be (a) Y-connected and (b) Δ-connected.

4.20 For an air-gap length of 0.35 mm, calculate the self-inductance of an armature phase of the Y-connected induction motor of Problem 4.19 using the inductance formulas of Appendix B.

4.21 A two-pole, 60-Hz, three-phase, laboratory-size synchronous generator has a rotor radius of 5.71 cm, a rotor length of 18.0 cm, and an air-gap length of 0.25 mm. The rotor field winding consists of 264 turns with a winding factor of $k_r = 0.95$. The Y-connected armature winding consists of 45 turns per phase with a winding factor $k_w = 0.93$.

    a. Calculate the flux per pole and peak fundamental air-gap flux density which will result in an open-circuit, 60-Hz armature voltage of 120 V rms/phase (line-to-neutral).

    b. Calculate the dc field current required to achieve the operating condition of part (a).

    c. Calculate the peak value of the field-winding to armature-phase-winding mutual inductance.

4.22 A four-pole, 60-Hz, three-phase synchronous generator has a rotor radius of 55 cm, a rotor length of 3.23 m, and an air-gap length of 6.2 cm. The rotor field winding consists of 148 turns with a winding factor of $k_r = 0.962$. The Δ-connected armature winding consists of 24 series turns per phase with a winding factor $k_w = 0.935$.

    a. The generator is designed to achieve rated 60-Hz open-circuit voltage at a peak air-gap flux density of 1.30 T. Calculate the rated rms, line-line terminal voltage.

    b. Calculate the dc field current required to achieve the operating condition of part (a).

4.23 The generator of Problem 4.22 is to be re-wound to operate on a 50-Hz power system with a terminal voltage of 22 kV. The stator winding will be Y-connected.

    a. Calculate the number of turns per phase in the re-wound stator such that rated open-circuit terminal voltage will be achieved at field current as close as possible to that of the original generator.

    b. Calculate the dc field current required to achieve rated open-circuit voltage for the new generator.

4.24 Write a MATLAB script which calculates the required total series field turns and armature-winding series turns per phase for a three-phase, Y-connected synchronous motor given the following information:

    Rotor radius, R (meters)   Rotor length, l (meters)
    Air-gap length, g (meters)   Number of poles
    Electrical frequency, f_e (Hz)   Peak fundamental air-gap flux
                                       density, B_{peak} (T)
    Field-winding factor, k_f Armature-winding factor, k_w
    Rated rms open-circuit line-to-line terminal voltage, V_{rated} (V)
    Field-current at rated-open-circuit terminal voltage, I_f (A)

Exercise your program on a generator with the following parameters:

$$R = 8.4 \text{ cm} \quad l = 32 \text{ cm} \quad g = 0.65 \text{ mm}$$
$$\text{poles} = 4 \quad f_e = 50 \text{ Hz} \quad B_{peak} = 0.94 \text{ T}$$
$$k_f = 0.955 \quad k_w = 0.935 \quad V_{rated} = 415 \text{ V}$$
$$I_f = 8.0 \text{ A}$$

4.25 A four-pole, 60-Hz synchronous generator has a rotor length of 4.8 m, diameter of 1.13 m, and air-gap length of 5.9 cm. The field winding consists of a series connection of 244 turns with a winding factor of $k_r = 0.925$. The peak value of the fundamental air-gap flux density is limited to 1.15 T and the rotor winding current to 2800 A. Calculate the maximum torque (N·m) and power output (MW) which can be supplied by this machine.

4.26 Thermal considerations limit the field-current of the laboratory-size synchronous generator of Problem 4.21 to a maximum value of 2.6 A. If the peak fundamental air-gap flux density is limited to a maximum of 1.35 T, calculate the maximum torque (N·m) and power (kW) which can be produced by this generator.

4.27 Write a MATLAB script to solve for the maximum torque and power for a generator given the following information:

Rotor radius, R (meters)   Rotor length, l (meters)
Air-gap length, g (meters)   Number of poles
Electrical frequency, f_e Peak fundamental air-gap flux
             density, B_{peak} (T)
Field-winding factor, k_f Number of field-winding turns, N_f
Maximum field-current, $I_{f,max}$ (A)

Exercise your program on the laboratory generator of Problems 4.21 and 4.26.

4.28 Figure 4.41 shows in cross section a machine having a rotor winding f and two identical stator windings a and b whose axes are in quadrature. The self-inductance of each stator winding is L_{aa} and of the rotor is L_{ff}. The air gap is uniform. The mutual inductance between a stator winding depends on the angular position of the rotor and may be assumed to be of the form

$$M_{af} = M \cos\theta_0 \quad M_{bf} = M \sin\theta_0$$

where M is the maximum value of the mutual inductance. The resistance of each stator winding is R_a.

a. Derive a general expression for the torque T in terms of the angle θ_0, the inductance parameters, and the instantaneous currents i_a, i_b, and i_f. Does this expression apply at standstill? When the rotor is revolving?

b. Suppose the rotor is stationary and constant direct currents $i_a = I_0$, $i_b = I_0$, and $i_f = 2I_0$ are supplied to the windings in the directions indicated by the dots and crosses in Fig. 4.41. If the rotor is allowed to move, will it rotate continuously or will it tend to come to rest? If the latter, at what value of θ_0?

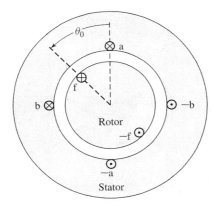

Figure 4.41 Elementary cylindrical-rotor, two-phase synchronous machine for Problem 4.28.

c. The rotor winding is now excited by a constant direct current I_f while the stator windings carry balanced two-phase currents

$$i_a = \sqrt{2}I_a \cos \omega t \qquad i_b = \sqrt{2}I_a \sin \omega t$$

The rotor is revolving at synchronous speed so that its instantaneous angular position is given by $\theta_0 = \omega t - \delta$, where δ is a phase angle describing the position of the rotor at $t = 0$. The machine is an elementary two-phase synchronous machine. Derive an expression for the torque under these conditions.

d. Under the conditions of part (c), derive an expression for the instantaneous terminal voltages of stator phases a and b.

4.29 Consider the two-phase synchronous machine of Problem 4.28. Derive an expression for the torque acting on the rotor if the rotor is rotating at constant angular velocity, such that $\theta_0 = \omega t + \delta$, and the phase currents become unbalanced such that

$$i_a = \sqrt{2}I_a \cos \omega t \qquad i_b = \sqrt{2}(I_a + I') \sin \omega t$$

What are the instantaneous and time-averaged torque under this condition?

4.30 Figure 4.42 shows in schematic cross section a salient-pole synchronous machine having two identical stator windings a and b on a laminated steel core. The salient-pole rotor is made of steel and carries a field winding f connected to slip rings.

Because of the nonuniform air gap, the self- and mutual inductances are functions of the angular position θ_0 of the rotor. Their variation with θ_0 can be approximated as:

$$L_{aa} = L_0 + L_2 \cos 2\theta_0 \qquad L_{bb} = L_0 - L_2 \cos 2\theta_0 \qquad M_{ab} = L_2 \sin 2\theta_0$$

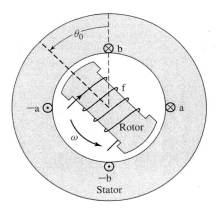

Figure 4.42 Schematic two-phase, salient-pole synchronous machine for Problem 4.30.

where L_0 and L_2 are positive constants. The mutual inductance between the rotor and the stator windings are functions of θ_0

$$M_{af} = M \cos \theta_0 \qquad M_{bf} = M \sin \theta_0$$

where M is also a positive constant. The self-inductance of the field winding, L_{ff}, is constant, independent of θ_0.

Consider the operating condition in which the field winding is excited by a direct current I_f and the stator windings are connected to a balanced two-phase voltage source of frequency ω. With the rotor revolving at synchronous speed, its angular position will be given by $\theta_0 = \omega t$. Under this operating condition, the stator currents will be of the form

$$i_a = \sqrt{2}I_a \cos (\omega t + \delta) \qquad i_b = \sqrt{2}I_a \sin (\omega t + \delta)$$

a. Derive an expression for the electromagnetic torque acting on the rotor.

b. Can the machine be operated as a motor and/or a generator? Explain.

c. Will the machine continue to supply torque if the field current I_f is reduced to zero? Support you answer with an expression for the torque and an explanation as to why such operation is or is not possible.

4.31 A three-phase linear ac motor has an armature winding of wavelength 35 cm. A three-phase balanced set of currents at a frequency of 120 Hz is applied to the armature.

a. Calculate the linear velocity of the armature mmf wave.

b. For the case of a synchronous rotor, calculate the linear velocity of the rotor.

c. For the case of an induction motor operating at a slip of 0.055, calculate the linear velocity of the rotor.

4.32 The linear-motor armature of Problem 4.31 has a total active length of 7 wavelengths, with a total of 322 turns per phase with a winding factor $k_w = 0.93$. For an air-gap length of 1.03 cm, calculate the rms magnitude of the balanced three-phase currents which must be supplied to the armature to achieve a peak space-fundamental air-gap flux density of 1.4 T.

4.33 A two-phase linear permanent-magnet synchronous motor has an air-gap of length 1.2 mm, a wavelength of 17 cm, and a pole width of 4.5 cm. The rotor is 6 wavelengths in length. The permanent magnets on the rotor are arranged to produce an air-gap magnetic flux distribution that is uniform over the width of a pole but which varies sinusoidally in space in the direction of rotor travel. The peak density of this air-gap flux is 0.87 T.

  a. Calculate the net flux per pole.

  b. Each armature phase consists of 12 turns per pole, with all the poles connected in series. Assuming that the armature winding extends many wavelengths past either end of the rotor, calculate the peak flux linkages of the armature winding.

  c. If the rotor is traveling at a speed of 6.3 m/sec, calculate the rms voltage induced in the armature winding.

5 CHAPTER

Synchronous Machines

As we have seen in Section 4.2.1, in a synchronous machine under steady-state conditions, the rotor, along with the magnetic field created by a dc field current or permanent magnet, rotates at the same speed as, or in synchronism with, the rotating magnetic field produced by the armature currents and a steady torque results. Thus, the steady-state speed of a synchronous machine is proportional to the frequency of the armature currents. An elementary picture of how a synchronous machine works is given in Section 4.2.1 with emphasis on torque production in terms of the interactions between the machine's magnetic fields.

Analytical methods of examining the steady-state performance of polyphase synchronous machines will be developed in this chapter. Initial consideration will be given to cylindrical-rotor machines; the effects of salient poles are taken up in Sections 5.6 and 5.7.

5.1 INTRODUCTION TO POLYPHASE SYNCHRONOUS MACHINES

As indicated in Section 4.2.1, a synchronous machine is one in which alternating current flows in the armature winding and dc rotor flux is produced by dc excitation to a field winding or by permanent magnets. The armature winding is almost invariably on the stator and is frequently a three-phase winding, as discussed in Chapter 4. The cylindrical-rotor construction shown in Figs. 4.10 and 4.11 is used for two- and four-pole turbine generators. The salient-pole construction shown in Fig. 4.9 is best adapted to multi-polar, slow-speed hydroelectric generators and to many synchronous motors.

The dc power required for excitation of a synchronous-machine field winding – approximately one to a few percent of the rating of the synchronous machine – is supplied by the *excitation system*. In the case of a permanent magnet synchronous machine, no power is required to excite the dc rotor flux and hence there is the potential for higher machine efficiency. There is a tradeoff however because with permanent-magnet excitation it is not possible to adjust the magnitude of the dc rotor flux in response to machine operating conditions.

In older machines, the field excitation current was typically supplied through *slip rings* from a dc machine, referred to as the *exciter*, which was often mounted on the same shaft as the synchronous machine. In more modern systems, the excitation is supplied from ac exciters and solid-state rectifiers (either simple diode bridges or phase-controlled rectifiers). In some cases, the rectification occurs in the stationary frame, and the rectified excitation current is fed to the rotor via slip rings. In other systems, referred to as *brushless excitation systems*, the alternator of the ac exciter is on the rotor, as is the rectification system, and the current is supplied directly to the field-winding without the need for slip rings. One such system is described in Appendix D.

As is discussed in Chapter 4, a single synchronous generator acts as a voltage source whose frequency is determined by the speed of its mechanical drive (or *prime mover*), as can be seen from Eq. 4.2. From Eqs. 4.44–4.47, 4.50 and 4.52, we see that the amplitude of the generated voltage is proportional to the rotor speed and the field current. As we will see, the generator terminal current and power factor are determined by the generator field excitation and the impedance of the generator and load.

Synchronous generators can be readily operated in parallel, and, in fact, the electricity supply systems of industrialized countries typically have scores or even hundreds of them operating in parallel, interconnected by thousands of miles of transmission lines, and supplying electric energy to loads scattered over areas of many thousands of square miles. These huge systems have grown in spite of the necessity for designing the system so that synchronism between generators is maintained following disturbances and the problems, both technical and administrative, which must be solved to coordinate the operation of such a complex system.

When a synchronous generator is connected to a large interconnected system containing many other synchronous generators, the voltage and frequency at its armature terminals are substantially fixed by the system. The magnetic flux corresponding to this applied voltage thus rotates at the synchronous speed (Eq. 4.44) as determined by the system electrical frequency f_e. As is discussed in Chapter 4, for the production of a steady, unidirectional electromechanical torque, the fields of the stator and rotor must rotate at the same speed, and therefore the rotor must turn at precisely the system-imposed synchronous speed. Because any individual generator is a small fraction of the total system generation, it cannot significantly affect the system voltage or frequency. It is thus often useful, when studying the behavior of an individual generator or group of generators, to represent the remainder of the system as a constant-frequency, constant-voltage source, commonly referred to as an *infinite bus*.

Many important features of synchronous-machine behavior can be understood from the analysis of a single machine connected to an infinite bus. The steady-state behavior of a synchronous machine can be visualized in terms of the torque equation. From Eq. 4.83, with changes in notation appropriate to synchronous-machine theory,

$$T = \frac{\pi}{2} \left(\frac{\text{poles}}{2} \right)^2 \Phi_R F_f \sin \delta_{RF} \tag{5.1}$$

where

$$\Phi_R = \text{resultant air-gap flux per pole}$$
$$F_f = \text{mmf of the dc field winding}$$
$$\delta_{RF} = \text{electrical phase angle between magnetic axes of } \Phi_R \text{ and } F_f$$

The minus sign of Eq. 4.83 has been omitted with the understanding that the electromechanical torque acts in the direction to bring the interacting fields into alignment. In normal steady-state operation, the electromechanical torque balances the mechanical torque applied to the shaft. In a generator, the prime-mover torque acts in the direction of rotation of the rotor, pushing the rotor mmf wave ahead of the resultant air-gap flux. The electromechanical torque then opposes rotation. The opposite situation exists in a synchronous motor, where the electromechanical torque is in the direction of rotation, in opposition to the retarding torque of the mechanical load on the shaft.

Variations in the electromechanical torque result in corresponding variations in the *torque angle*, δ_{RF}, as seen from Eq. 5.1. The relationship is shown in the form of a *torque-angle curve* in Fig. 5.1, where the field current (rotor mmf) and resultant air-gap flux are assumed constant. Positive values of torque represent generator action, corresponding to positive values of δ_{RF} for which the the rotor mmf wave leads the resultant air-gap flux.

As the prime-mover torque is increased, the magnitude of δ_{RF} must increase until the electromechanical torque balances the shaft torque. The readjustment process is actually a dynamic one, requiring a change in the mechanical speed of the rotor, typically accompanied by a damped mechanical oscillation of the rotor about its new steady-state torque angle. This oscillation is referred to as a *hunting transient*. In a practical machine undergoing such a transient, some changes in the amplitudes of the resultant flux-density and field-winding mmf wave may also occur because of various factors such as saturation effects, the effect of the machine leakage impedances, the response of the machine's excitation system, and so on. To emphasize the fundamental principles of synchronous-machine operation, such effects will be neglected in the present discussion.

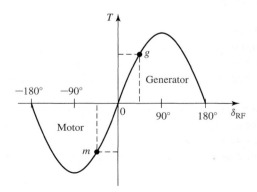

Figure 5.1 Torque-angle characteristic.

The adjustment of the rotor to its new angular position following a load change can be observed experimentally in the laboratory by viewing the machine rotor with stroboscopic light triggered from the applied armature voltage (thus having a flashing frequency which causes the rotor to appear stationary when it is turning at its normal synchronous speed). Alternatively, electronic sensors can be used to determine the shaft position relative to the synchronous reference frame associated with the stator voltage. The resultant signal can be displayed on an oscilloscope or recorded with a data-acquisition system.

As can be seen from Fig. 5.1, an increase in prime-mover torque will result in a corresponding increase in the torque angle. When δ_{RF} becomes 90°, the electromechanical torque reaches its maximum value, known as the *pull-out torque*. Any further increase in prime-mover torque cannot be balanced by a corresponding increase in synchronous electromechanical torque, with the result that synchronism will no longer be maintained and the rotor will speed up. This phenomenon is known as *loss of synchronism* or *pulling out of step*. Under these conditions, the generator is usually disconnected from the external electrical system by the automatic operation of circuit breakers, and the prime mover is quickly shut down to prevent dangerous overspeed. Note from Eq. 5.1 that the value of the pull-out torque can be increased by increasing either the field current or the resultant air-gap flux. However, this cannot be done without limit; the field current is limited by the ability to cool the field winding and the air-gap flux is limited by saturation of the machine iron. Also as seen from Fig. 5.1, a similar situation occurs in a synchronous motor for which an increase in the shaft load-torque beyond the pull-out torque will cause the rotor to lose synchronism and thus to slow down.

Since a synchronous motor develops torque only at synchronous speed, it cannot be started simply by the application of armature voltages of rated frequency. In some cases, a squirrel-cage structure is included in the rotor in which case the motor can be started as an induction motor and it will synchronize when it is close to synchronous speed. Alternatively, synchronous motors are often operated from variable-frequency/variable-voltage electronic drives which are controlled in such a fashion as to insure synchronous operation as the motor is brought up to its operating speed.

5.2 SYNCHRONOUS-MACHINE INDUCTANCES; EQUIVALENT CIRCUITS

In Section 5.1, synchronous-machine torque-angle characteristics are described in terms of the interacting air-gap flux and mmf waves. Our purpose now is to derive an equivalent circuit which represents the steady-state terminal volt-ampere characteristics.

A cross-sectional sketch of a three-phase cylindrical-rotor synchronous machine is shown schematically in Fig. 5.2. The figure shows a two-pole machine; alternatively, this can be considered as two poles of a multi-pole machine. The three-phase armature winding on the stator is of the same type used in the discussion of rotating magnetic fields in Section 4.5. Coils aa', bb', and cc' represent distributed windings producing

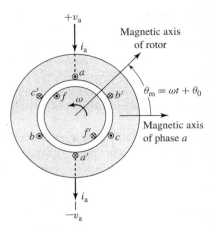

Figure 5.2 Schematic diagram of a two-pole, three-phase cylindrical-rotor synchronous machine.

sinusoidal mmf and flux-density waves in the air gap. The reference directions for the currents are shown by dots and crosses. The field winding ff' on the rotor also represents a distributed winding which produces a sinusoidal mmf and flux-density wave centered on its magnetic axis and rotating with the rotor.

When the flux linkages with armature phases a, b, c and field winding f are expressed in terms of the inductances and currents as follows,

$$\lambda_a = \mathcal{L}_{aa}i_a + \mathcal{L}_{ab}i_b + \mathcal{L}_{ac}i_c + \mathcal{L}_{af}i_f \tag{5.2}$$

$$\lambda_b = \mathcal{L}_{ba}i_a + \mathcal{L}_{bb}i_b + \mathcal{L}_{bc}i_c + \mathcal{L}_{bf}i_f \tag{5.3}$$

$$\lambda_c = \mathcal{L}_{ca}i_a + \mathcal{L}_{cb}i_b + \mathcal{L}_{cc}i_c + \mathcal{L}_{cf}i_f \tag{5.4}$$

$$\lambda_f = \mathcal{L}_{fa}i_a + \mathcal{L}_{fb}i_b + \mathcal{L}_{fc}i_c + \mathcal{L}_{ff}i_f \tag{5.5}$$

the induced voltages can be found from Faraday's law. Here, two like subscripts denote a self inductance and two unlike subscripts denote a mutual inductance between the two windings. The script $\mathcal{L}$ is used to indicate that in general, both the self and mutual inductances of a three-phase machine may vary with rotor angle, as is seen for example in Section C.2, where the effects of salient poles are analyzed.

Before we proceed, it is useful to investigate the nature of the various inductances. Based upon the cylindrical-rotor, sinusoidal-mmf assumptions, each of these inductances can be expressed in terms of constant coefficients.

5.2.1   Rotor Self-Inductance

With a cylindrical stator, the self-inductance of the field winding is independent of the rotor position θ_m when the harmonic effects of stator slot openings are neglected. Hence

$$\mathcal{L}_{ff} = L_{ff} = L_{ff0} + L_{fl} \tag{5.6}$$

where the italic L is used for an inductance which is independent of θ_m. The component L_{ff0} corresponds to that portion of $\mathcal{L}_{ff}$ due to the space-fundamental component of air-gap flux. This component can be computed from air-gap dimensions and winding data, as shown in Appendix B. The additional component L_{fl} accounts for field-winding leakage flux.

Under transient or unbalanced conditions, the flux linkages with the field winding, Eq. 5.5, vary with time, and the voltages induced in the rotor circuits have an important effect on machine performance. However, with the rotor rotating at synchronous speed and with balanced three-phase armature currents, the constant-amplitude magnetic flux produced by the armature currents rotates in synchronism with the rotor. Thus the field-winding flux linkage produced by this flux does not vary with time and hence does not induce voltage in the field winding. As a result, with constant dc voltage V_f applied to the field-winding terminals, the field direct current I_f can be determined by Ohm's law, $I_f = V_f/R_f$.

5.2.2 Stator-to-Rotor Mutual Inductances

The stator-to-rotor mutual inductances vary periodically with θ_{me}, the electrical angle between the magnetic axes of the field winding and the armature phase a as shown in Fig. 5.2 and as defined by Eq. 4.56. With the space-mmf and air-gap flux distribution assumed sinusoidal, the mutual inductance between the field winding f and phase a varies as $\cos \theta_{me}$; thus

$$\mathcal{L}_{af} = \mathcal{L}_{fa} = L_{af} \cos \theta_{me} \tag{5.7}$$

Similar expressions apply to phases b and c, with θ_{me} replaced by $\theta_{me} - 120°$ and $\theta_{me} + 120°$, respectively. Attention will be focused on phase a. The inductance L_{af} can be calculated as discussed in Appendix B.

With the rotor rotating at synchronous speed ω_s (Eq. 4.42), the rotor angle will vary as

$$\theta_m = \omega_s t + \delta_0 \tag{5.8}$$

where δ_0 is the angle of the rotor at time $t = 0$. From Eq. 4.56

$$\theta_{me} = \left(\frac{\text{poles}}{2}\right) \theta_m = \omega_e t + \delta_{e0} \tag{5.9}$$

Here, $\omega_e = (\text{poles}/2)\,\omega_s$ is the electrical frequency and δ_{e0} is the electrical angle of the rotor at time $t = 0$.

Thus, substituting into Eq. 5.7 gives

$$\mathcal{L}_{af} = \mathcal{L}_{fa} = L_{af} \cos(\omega_e t + \delta_{e0}) \tag{5.10}$$

5.2.3 Stator Inductances; Synchronous Inductance

With a cylindrical rotor, the air gap geometry is independent of θ_m if the effects of rotor slots are neglected. The stator self-inductances then are constant; thus

$$\mathcal{L}_{aa} = \mathcal{L}_{bb} = \mathcal{L}_{cc} = L_{aa} = L_{aa0} + L_{al} \tag{5.11}$$

where L_{aa0} is the component of self-inductance due to space-fundamental air-gap flux (Appendix B) and L_{al} is the additional component due to armature-winding leakage flux (see Section 4.10).

The armature phase-to-phase mutual inductances can be found on the assumption that the mutual inductance is due solely to space-fundamental air-gap flux.[1] From Eq. B.26 of Appendix B, we see that the air-gap mutual inductance of two identical windings displaced by α electrical degrees is equal to the air-gap component of their self inductance multiplied by $\cos \alpha$. Thus, because the armature phases are displaced by 120° electrical degrees and $\cos(\pm 120°) = -\frac{1}{2}$, the mutual inductances between the armature phases are equal and given by

$$\mathcal{L}_{ab} = \mathcal{L}_{ba} = \mathcal{L}_{ac} = \mathcal{L}_{ca} = \mathcal{L}_{bc} = \mathcal{L}_{cb} = -\frac{1}{2}L_{aa0} \tag{5.12}$$

Substituting Eqs. 5.11 and 5.12 for the self and mutual inductances into the expression for the phase-a flux linkages (Eq. 5.2) gives

$$\lambda_a = (L_{aa0} + L_{al})i_a - \frac{1}{2}L_{aa0}(i_b + i_c) + \mathcal{L}_{af}i_f \tag{5.13}$$

Under balanced three-phase armature currents (see Fig. 4.27 and Eqs. 4.25 to 4.27)

$$i_a + i_b + i_e = 0 \tag{5.14}$$

$$i_b + i_c = -i_a \tag{5.15}$$

Substitution of Eq. 5.15 into Eq. 5.13 gives

$$\lambda_a = (L_{aa0} + L_{al})i_a + \frac{1}{2}L_{aa0}i_a + \mathcal{L}_{af}i_f$$

$$= \left(\frac{3}{2}L_{aa0} + L_{al}\right)i_a + \mathcal{L}_{af}i_f \tag{5.16}$$

It is useful to define the *synchronous inductance* L_s as

$$L_s = \frac{3}{2}L_{aa0} + L_{al} \tag{5.17}$$

and thus

$$\lambda_a = L_s i_a + \mathcal{L}_{af}i_f \tag{5.18}$$

Note that the synchronous inductance L_s is the *effective inductance seen by phase a under steady-state, balanced three-phase machine operating conditions.* It is made up of three components. The first, L_{aa0}, is due to the space-fundamental air-gap component of the phase-a flux linkages due to phase-a currents alone. The second, L_{al}, known as the armature-winding *leakage inductance,* is due to the leakage component of phase-a flux linkages. The third component, $\frac{1}{2}L_{aa0}$, is due to the

---

[1] Since the armature windings in practical machines are generally wound with overlapping phase windings (i.e. portions of adjacent windings share the same slots), there is an additional component of the phase-to-phase mutual inductance which is due to slot leakage flux.

phase-a flux linkages due to the space-fundamental component of air-gap flux produced by currents in phases b and c. Under balanced three-phase conditions, the phase-b and -c currents are related to the current in phase a by Eq. 5.15. Thus the synchronous inductance is an *apparent inductance* in that it accounts for the flux linkages of phase a in terms of the current in phase a even though some of this flux linkage is due to currents in phases b and c. Hence, it should be remembered that, although L_s appears from Eq. 5.18 to be the self-inductance of phase a, that is not actually the case and that it is defined under the assumption of balanced 3-phase armature currents.

The significance of the synchronous inductance can be further appreciated with reference to the discussion of rotating magnetic fields in Section 4.5.2, where it was shown that under balanced three-phase conditions, the armature currents create a rotating magnetic flux wave in the air gap of magnitude equal to $\frac{3}{2}$ times the magnitude of that due to phase a alone, the additional component being due to the phase-b and -c currents. This corresponds directly to the $\frac{3}{2}L_{aa0}$ component of the synchronous inductance in Eq. 5.17; this component of the synchronous inductance accounts for the total space-fundamental air-gap component of phase-a flux linkages produced by the three armature currents under balanced three-phase conditions.

5.2.4 Equivalent Circuit

The phase-a terminal voltage is the sum of the armature-resistance voltage drop $R_a i_a$ and the induced voltage. The voltage e_{af} induced by the field winding flux (often referred to as the *generated voltage* or *internal voltage*) can be found from the time derivative of Eq. 5.18 with the armature current i_a set equal to zero. With dc excitation I_f in the field winding, substitution of Eq. 5.10 gives

$$e_{af} = \frac{d}{dt}(\mathcal{L}_{af}i_f) = -\omega_e L_{af} I_f \sin(\omega_e t + \delta_{e0}) \tag{5.19}$$

Using Eq. 5.18, the terminal voltage can then be expressed as

$$v_a = R_a i_a + \frac{d\lambda_a}{dt}$$

$$= R_a i_a + L_s \frac{di_a}{dt} + e_{af} \tag{5.20}$$

The generated voltage e_{af} of Eq. 5.19 is at frequency ω_e, equal to the electrical frequency of the generator terminal voltage. Its rms amplitude is given by

$$E_{af} = \frac{\omega_e L_{af} I_f}{\sqrt{2}} \tag{5.21}$$

Under this synchronous operating condition, all machine armature quantities (current and flux linkage) will also vary sinusoidally in time at this frequency. Thus, we can write the terminal-voltage equation, Eq. 5.20, in terms of rms complex amplitudes as

$$\hat{V}_a = R_a \hat{I}_a + j X_s \hat{I}_a + \hat{E}_{af} \tag{5.22}$$

where $X_s = \omega_e L_s$ is known as the *synchronous reactance*.

Figure 5.3 Synchronous-machine equivalent circuits:
(a) motor reference direction and (b) generator reference
direction.

The rms complex amplitude of the generated voltage $\hat{E}_{af}$ can be found by recognizing that

$$e_{af} = \text{Re}[\sqrt{2}\,\hat{E}_{af}\,e^{j\omega_e t}] \tag{5.23}$$

where the notation Re[ ] indicates the real part of a complex quantity. Thus from Eq. 5.19 we see that

$$\hat{E}_{af} = j\left(\frac{\omega_e L_{af} I_f}{\sqrt{2}}\right) e^{j\delta_{e0}} \tag{5.24}$$

An equivalent circuit in complex form is shown in Fig. 5.3a. The reader should note that Eq. 5.22 and Fig. 5.3a are written with the reference direction for $\hat{I}_a$ defined as positive into the machine terminals. This is known as the *motor reference direction* for the current.

Alternatively, the *generator reference direction* is defined with the reference direction for $\hat{I}_a$ chosen as positive out of the machine terminals, as shown in Fig. 5.3b. Under these choice of current reference direction, Eq. 5.22 becomes

$$\hat{V}_a = -R_a \hat{I}_a - j\,X_s \hat{I}_a + \hat{E}_{af} \tag{5.25}$$

Note that these two representations are equivalent; when analyzing a particular synchronous-machine operating condition the actual current will be the same. The sign of $\hat{I}_a$ will simply be determined by the choice of reference direction. Either choice is acceptable, independent of whether the synchronous machine under investigation is operating as a motor or a generator. However, since power tends to flow into a motor, it is perhaps intuitively more satisfying to choose a reference direction with current flowing into the machine for the analysis of motor operation. The opposite is true for generator operation, for which power tends to flow out of the machine. Most of the synchronous-machine analysis techniques presented here were first developed to analyze the performance of synchronous generators in electric power systems. As a result, the generator reference direction is more common and is generally used from this point on in the text.

Figure 5.4 Synchronous-machine equivalent circuit showing air-gap and leakage components of synchronous reactance and air-gap voltage.

Figure 5.4 shows an alternative form of the equivalent circuit in which the synchronous reactance is shown in terms of its components. From Eq. 5.17

$$X_s = \omega_e L_s = \omega_e L_{al} + \omega_e \left(\frac{3}{2} L_{aa0} \right)$$

$$= X_{al} + X_\varphi \tag{5.26}$$

where $X_{al} = \omega_e L_{al}$ is the armature *leakage reactance* and $X_\varphi = \omega_e \left(\frac{3}{2} L_{aa0} \right)$ is the reactance corresponding to the rotating space-fundamental air-gap flux produced by the three armature currents. The reactance X_φ is the effective *magnetizing reactance* of the armature winding under balanced three-phase conditions. The rms voltage $\hat{E}_R$ is the internal voltage generated by the resultant air-gap flux and is usually referred to as the *air-gap voltage* or the *voltage "behind" leakage reactance*.

It is important to recognize that the equivalent circuits of Figs. 5.3 and 5.4 are *single-phase, line-to-neutral equivalent circuits for a three-phase machine operating under balanced, three-phase conditions*. Thus, once the phase-a voltages and currents are found, either from the equivalent circuit or directly from the voltage equations (Eqs. 5.22 and 5.25), the currents and voltages for phases b and c can be found simply by phase-shifting those of phase a by $-120°$ and $120°$ respectively. Similarly, the total three-phase power of the machine can be found simply by multiplying that of phase a by three, unless the analysis is being performed in per unit (see Section 2.9), in which case the three-phase, per-unit power is equal to that found from solving for phase a alone and the factor of three is not needed.

EXAMPLE 5.1

A 60-Hz, three-phase synchronous motor is observed to have a terminal voltage of 460 V (line-line) and a terminal current of 120 A at a power factor of 0.95 lagging. The field-current under this operating condition is 47 A. The machine synchronous reactance is equal to 1.68 Ω (0.794 per unit on a 460-V, 100-kVA, three-phase base). Assume the armature resistance to be negligible.

Calculate (a) the generated voltage E_{af} in volts, (b) the magnitude of the field-to-armature mutual inductance L_{af}, and (c) the electrical power input to the motor in kW and in horsepower.

■ **Solution**

a. Using the motor reference direction for the current and neglecting the armature resistance, the generated voltage can be found from the equivalent circuit of Fig. 5.3a or Eq. 5.22 as

$$\hat{E}_{af} = \hat{V}_a - jX_s\hat{I}_a$$

We will choose the terminal voltage as our phase reference. Because this is a line-to-neutral equivalent, the terminal voltage V_a must be expressed as a line-to-neutral voltage

$$\hat{V}_a = \frac{460}{\sqrt{3}} = 265.6 \text{ V, line-to-neutral}$$

A lagging power factor of 0.95 corresponds to a power factor angle $\phi = -\cos^{-1}(0.95) = -18.2°$. Thus, the phase-a current is

$$\hat{I}_a = 120\,e^{-j18.2°} \text{ A}$$

Thus

$$\hat{E}_{af} = 265.6 - j1.68(120\,e^{-j18.2°})$$

$$= 278.8\,e^{-j43.4°} \text{ V, line-to-neutral}$$

and hence, the generated voltage E_{af} is equal to 278.8 V rms, line-to-neutral.

b. The field-to-armature mutual inductance can be found from Eq. 5.21. With $\omega_e = 120\pi$,

$$L_{af} = \frac{\sqrt{2}\,E_{af}}{\omega_e I_f} = \frac{\sqrt{2} \times 279}{120\pi \times 47} = 22.3 \text{ mH}$$

c. The three-phase power input to the motor P_{in} can be found as three times the power input to phase a. Hence,

$$P_{in} = 3V_a I_a \times (\text{power factor}) = 3 \times 265.6 \times 120 \times 0.95$$

$$= 90.8 \text{ kW} = 122 \text{ hp}$$

EXAMPLE 5.2

Assuming the input power and terminal voltage for the motor of Example 5.1 remain constant, calculate (a) the phase angle δ of the generated voltage and (b) the field current required to achieve unity power factor at the motor terminals.

■ **Solution**

a. For unity power factor at the motor terminals, the phase-a terminal current will be in phase with the phase-a line-to-neutral voltage $\hat{V}_a$. Thus

$$\hat{I}_a = \frac{P_{in}}{3V_a} = \frac{90.6 \text{ kW}}{3 \times 265.6 \text{ V}} = 114 \text{ A}$$

From Eq. 5.22,

$$\hat{E}_{af} = \hat{V}_a - jX_s\hat{I}_a$$

$$= 265.6 - j1.68 \times 114 = 328\,e^{-j35.8°} \text{ V, line-to-neutral}$$

Thus, $E_{af} = 328$ V line-to-neutral and $\delta = -35.8°$.

b. Having found L_{af} in Example 5.1, we can find the required field current from Eq. 5.21.

$$I_f = \frac{\sqrt{2}\,E_{af}}{\omega_e L_{af}} = \frac{\sqrt{2} \times 328}{377 \times 0.0223} = 55.2 \text{ A}$$

Practice Problem 5.1

The synchronous machine of Examples 5.1 and 5.2 is to be operated as a synchronous generator. For operation at 60 Hz with a terminal voltage of 460 V line-to-line, calculate the field current required to supply a load of 85 kW, 0.95 power-factor leading.

Solution

46.3 A

Practice Problem 5.2

Consider the synchronous motor of Example 5.1 operating at a terminal voltage of 460-V (line-line). Write a MATLAB script to plot the field current required to maintain unity-power-factor as the motor power is varied from 50 to 100 kW.

Solution

Figure 5.5 Plot of field current vs. motor power for Practice Problem 5.2.

It is helpful to have a rough idea of the order of magnitude of the impedance components of typical synchronous machines. For machines with ratings above a few hundred kVA, the armature-resistance voltage drop at rated current usually is less than 0.01 times rated voltage; i.e., the armature resistance usually is less than 0.01 per unit on the machine rating as a base. (The per-unit system is described in Section 2.9.) The armature leakage reactance usually is in the range of 0.1 to 0.2 per unit, and the synchronous reactance is typically in the range of 1.0 to 2.0 per unit.

In general, the per-unit armature resistance increases and the per-unit synchronous reactance decreases with decreasing size of the machine. In small machines, such as those in educational laboratories, the armature resistance may be in the vicinity of 0.05 per unit and the synchronous reactance in the vicinity of 0.5 per unit. In all but small machines, the armature resistance can usually be neglected in most analyses, except insofar as its effect on losses and heating is concerned.

5.3 OPEN- AND SHORT-CIRCUIT CHARACTERISTICS

The fundamental characteristics of a synchronous machine can be determined by a pair of tests, one made with the armature terminals open-circuited and the second with the armature terminals short-circuited. These tests are discussed here. Except for a few remarks on the degree of validity of certain assumptions, the discussions apply to both cylindrical-rotor and salient-pole machines.

5.3.1 Open-Circuit Saturation Characteristic and No-Load Rotational Losses

The *open-circuit characteristic* (also referred to as the *open-circuit saturation curve*) of a synchronous machine is a curve of open-circuit armature terminal voltage $V_{a,oc}$ (either in volts or in per unit) as a function of field current I_f when the machine is running at synchronous speed, as shown by curve labeled *occ* in Fig. 5.6. The open-circuit characteristic represents the relation between the space-fundamental component of the air-gap flux and the mmf acting on the magnetic circuit when the field winding constitutes the only mmf source. The effects of magnetic saturation can be clearly seen in Fig. 5.6; the characteristic bends downward with increasing field current as saturation of the magnetic material increases the reluctance of the flux paths in the machine and reduces the effectiveness of the field current in producing magnetic flux.

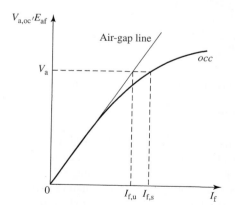

Figure 5.6 Open-circuit characteristic of a synchronous machine.

Note that with the machine armature winding open-circuited, the terminal voltage is equal to the generated voltage E_{af}. Thus the open-circuit characteristic is also a measurement of the relationship between the field current I_f and E_{af} and can therefore provide a direct measurement of the field-to-armature mutual inductance L_{af}. These two voltages will be used interchangeably in the discussion that follows.

As can be seen from Fig. 5.6, the open-circuit characteristic is initially linear as the field current is increased from zero. This portion of the curve (and its linear extension for higher values of field current) is known as the *air-gap line*. It represents the machine open-circuit voltage characteristic corresponding to unsaturated operating conditions, in which case the air-gap is the dominant reluctance in the flux path of the machine. Consider the field excitation required to achieve the open-circuit armature voltage V_a in Fig. 5.6. If there were no saturation, the machine open-circuit voltage characteristic would correspond to the air-gap line and this voltage would be produced by field current $I_{f,u}$. However, due to the effects of saturation, a field current of magnitude $I_{f,s}$ is required to produce the same voltage. The difference between $I_{f,s}$ and $I_{f,u}$ is a measure of the degree of saturation in the machine at that level of voltage.

EXAMPLE 5.3

An open-circuit test performed on a three-phase, 60-Hz synchronous generator shows that the rated open-circuit voltage of 13.8 kV is produced by a field current of 318 A. Extrapolation of the air-gap line from a complete set of measurements on the machine shows that the field-current corresponding to 13.8 kV on the air-gap line is 263 A. Calculate the saturated and unsaturated values of L_{af}.

■ **Solution**

From Eq. 5.21, L_{af} is found from

$$L_{af} = \frac{\sqrt{2}\,E_{af}}{\omega_e I_f}$$

Here, $E_{af} = 13.8\text{ kV}/\sqrt{3} = 7.97$ kV. Hence the saturated value of L_{af} is given by

$$(L_{af})_{sat} = \frac{\sqrt{2}\,(7.97 \times 10^3)}{120\,\pi\,\times 318} = 94\text{ mH}$$

and the unsaturated value is

$$(L_{af})_{unsat} = \frac{\sqrt{2}\,(7.97 \times 10^3)}{120\,\pi\,\times 263} = 114\text{ mH}$$

In this case, we see that saturation reduces the mutual inductance between the field and armature windings by approximately 18 percent.

Practice Problem 5.3

If the synchronous generator of Example 5.3 is operated at a speed corresponding to a generated voltage of 50 Hz, calculate (a) the open-circuit line-to-line terminal voltage corresponding to a field current of 318 A and (b) the field-current corresponding to that same voltage on the 50-Hz air-gap line.

Figure 5.7 Typical form of an open-circuit core-loss curve.

Solution

    a. 11.5 kV
    b. 263 A

When the machine is an existing one, the open-circuit characteristic is usually determined experimentally by driving the machine mechanically at synchronous speed with its armature terminals open-circuited and by measuring the terminal voltage as a function of field current. If the mechanical power required to drive the synchronous machine during the open-circuit test is measured, the *no-load rotational losses* can be obtained. These losses consist of friction and windage losses associated with rotation as well as the core loss corresponding to the flux in the machine at no load. The friction and windage losses at synchronous speed are constant, while the open-circuit core loss is a function of the flux, which in turn is proportional to the open-circuit voltage.

The mechanical power required to drive the machine at synchronous speed and unexcited is its friction and windage loss. When the field is excited, the mechanical power equals the sum of the friction, windage, and open-circuit core loss. The open-circuit core loss therefore can be found from the difference between these two values of mechanical power. A typical curve of open-circuit core loss as a function of open-circuit voltage takes the form of that found in Fig. 5.7. It is common to assume that the core loss under loaded conditions at a given terminal voltage is equal to the open-circuit core loss at the corresponding voltage.

5.3.2 Short-Circuit Characteristic and Load Loss

The *short-circuit characteristic* of a synchronous machine is a curve of short-circuit terminal current $I_{a,sc}$ (either in amperes or in per unit) as a function of field current. The short-circuit characteristic can be obtained by applying a three-phase short circuit through suitable current sensors to the armature terminals of a synchronous machine. With the machine driven at synchronous speed, the field current can be increased and

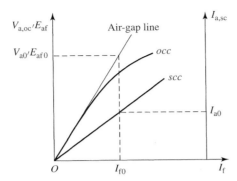

Figure 5.8 Open- and short-circuit characteristics of a synchronous machine.

a curve of armature current versus field current can be obtained.[2] An open-circuit characteristic *occ* and a short-circuit characteristic *scc* are shown in Fig. 5.8.

With the armature short-circuited, $V_a = 0$ and, from Eq. 5.25 (using the generator reference direction for current)

$$\hat{E}_{af} = \hat{I}_a(R_a + jX_s) \tag{5.27}$$

The corresponding phasor diagram is shown in Fig. 5.9. Because the resistance is much smaller than the synchronous reactance, the armature current lags the excitation voltage by very nearly 90°. Consequently the armature mmf wave is very nearly in line with the axis of the field poles and in opposition to the field mmf, as shown by phasors $\hat{A}$ and $\hat{F}$ representing the armature and field mmf waves, respectively.

The resultant mmf creates the resultant air-gap flux wave which generates the air-gap voltage $\hat{E}_R$ (see Fig. 5.4) equal to the voltage drop across the armature resistance R_a and leakage reactance X_{al}; as an equation,

$$\hat{E}_R = \hat{I}_a(R_a + jX_{al}) \tag{5.28}$$

In many synchronous machines the armature resistance is negligible, and the leakage reactance is between 0.10 and 0.20 per unit; a representative value is about 0.15 per unit. That is, at rated armature current the leakage reactance voltage drop is about 0.15 per unit (or 15 percent of the machine rated voltage). From Eq. 5.28, therefore, the air-gap voltage at rated armature current on short circuit is about 0.15 per unit; i.e., the resultant air-gap flux is only about 0.15 times its rated-voltage value. Consequently, the machine is operating in an unsaturated condition. The short-circuit armature current, therefore, is directly proportional to the field current over the range

---

[2] In reality, this test does not have to be conducted at synchronous speed. The short-circuit armature current will remain essentially constant with speed as long as the corresponding electrical frequency is sufficiently large that the synchronous reactance at that frequency is much larger than the armature resistance.

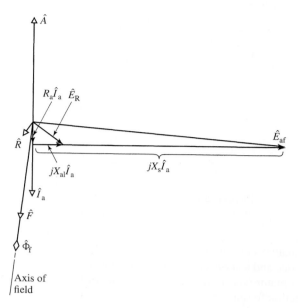

Figure 5.9 Phasor diagram for short-circuit conditions.

from zero to well above rated armature current; when plotted versus field current, it is thus a straight line as can be seen in Fig. 5.8.

The *unsaturated synchronous reactance* $X_{s,u}$ (corresponding to unsaturated operating conditions within the machine) can be found from the open- and short-circuit characteristics. At any convenient field excitation, such as I_{f0} in Fig. 5.8, the armature current on short circuit is I_{a0}, and the unsaturated generated voltage for the same field is equal to E_{af0}, as read from the air-gap line. Note that the voltage on the air-gap line should be used because the machine is assumed to be operating in an unsaturated condition.

If E_{af0} and I_{a0} are expressed in real units with E_{af0} being the rms line-to-neutral generated voltage, then from Eq. 5.27, with armature resistance R_a neglected, the unsaturated synchronous reactance $X_{s,u}$ in ohms per phase is calculated as

$$X_{s,u} = \frac{E_{af0}}{I_{a0}} \tag{5.29}$$

Because the air-gap line and the short-circuit characteristic are both linear, the value of synchronous reactance as calculated by Eq. 5.29 is independent of the specific value of field current I_{f0}. Note that the synchronous reactance in ohms per phase is calculated by using the phase or line-to-neutral voltage. Often the open-circuit saturation curve is given in terms of the line-to-line voltage, in which case the voltage must be converted to the line-to-neutral value by dividing by $\sqrt{3}$. If, on the other hand, $V_{a,oc}$ and $I_{a,sc}$ are expressed in per unit, the synchronous reactance as calculated by Eq. 5.29 will be in per unit.

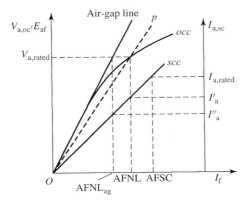

Figure 5.10 Open- and short-circuit characteristics showing equivalent magnetization line for saturated operating conditions.

For operation at or near rated terminal voltage, it is common to assume that the machine is equivalent to an unsaturated one with a linear magnetizing characteristic which starts at the origin and which passes through the rated-voltage point on the open-circuit characteristic, as shown by the dashed line Op in Fig. 5.10. Under this approximation, the machine can be represented by an equivalent circuit of the form of Fig. 5.3 with the generated voltage E_{af} linearly proportional to field current such that it is equal to rated voltage $V_{a,rated}$ (or one per unit) when I_f is equal to that value of field current, referred to as AFNL (**A**mperes **F**ield **N**o **L**oad), which produces rated open-circuit voltage $V_{a,rated}$ on the open-circuit characteristic as shown in Fig. 5.10.

Correspondingly, X_s is assumed equal to the rated-voltage *saturated synchronous reactance* given by

$$X_s = \frac{V_{a,rated}}{I_a'} \tag{5.30}$$

where I_a' is the armature current read from the short-circuit characteristic at the I_f = AFNL. As with the unsaturated synchronous reactance, if $V_{a,rated}$ and I_a' are expressed in per unit, the synchronous reactance will be in per unit. If $V_{a,rated}$ and I_a' are expressed in rms line-to-neutral volts and rms amperes per phase, respectively, the synchronous reactance will be in ohms per phase.

This method of handling the effects of saturation can be justified by recognizing that synchronous machines, for example synchronous generators with terminal-voltage regulation and connected to power systems, operate at a relatively constant terminal voltage. To a good approximation, ignoring the voltage drop across the armature-winding resistance and leakage reactance, this implies that the net air-gap flux in the machine, and hence the degree of saturation in the machine, remains relatively constant, independent of load. A fixed degree of saturation in-turn corresponds to a magnetic circuit with constant reluctances, which in turn implies a linear relationship between the field current I_f and the field-produced magnetic flux/terminal voltage V_a as shown in Fig. 5.10.

Although not commonly done, this same argument could be applied to determine the synchronous-machine equivalent-circuit parameters, E_{af} as a function of field current and X_s, for operation at terminal voltages other than rated value. For example, if the machine were operating at very low terminal voltages, the generated voltage would be calculated from the air-gap line and the corresponding unsaturated synchronous reactance would be given by

$$X_{s,u} = \frac{V_{a,rated}}{I_a''} \tag{5.31}$$

Comparing Figs 5.8 and 5.10, we see that Eqns. 5.30 and 5.31 are equivalent.

Note that, with the short-circuit terminal current expressed in per unit, the short-circuit current characteristic *scc* can be expressed as

$$I_{a,sc} = \frac{I_f}{\text{AFSC}} \quad \text{per unit} \tag{5.32}$$

where AFSC (**A**mperes **F**ield **S**hort **C**ircuit) is the value of field current which produces rated (1.0 per unit) short-circuit current. Thus, with $I_f = \text{AFNL}$, $E_{af} = V_{a,rated} = 1.0$ per unit and

$$I_a' = \frac{\text{AFNL}}{\text{AFSC}} \quad \text{per unit} \tag{5.33}$$

Thus, the per-unit saturated synchronous reactance can be calculated from Eq. 5.30 as

$$X_s = \frac{V_{a,rated}}{I_a'} = \frac{\text{AFSC}}{\text{AFNL}} \quad \text{per unit} \tag{5.34}$$

By a similar argument, the per-unit unsaturated synchronous reactance can be calculated as

$$X_{s,u} = \frac{V_{a,rated}}{I_a'} = \frac{\text{AFSC}}{\text{AFNL}_{ag}} \quad \text{per unit} \tag{5.35}$$

where AFNL_{ag} is the field current corresponding to rated open-circuit voltage on the air-gap line.

The *short-circuit ratio* (SCR) is defined as the ratio of AFNL to AFSC and thus it is equal to the inverse of the per-unit saturated synchronous reactance X_s

$$\text{SCR} = \frac{\text{AFNL}}{\text{AFSC}} \tag{5.36}$$

Note that as we have discussed, when the machine is operating at rated voltage, it is assumed that the generated voltage is linearly proportional to the field current with a slope such that the generated voltage is equal to the machine rated value (1.0 per unit) when the field current I_f is equal to AFNL, as represented by the dashed line Op in Fig. 5.10. Thus, for any given value of generated voltage, the field current can be found from the **per-unit value** of E_{af} as

$$I_f = E_{af} \times \text{AFNL} \quad \text{[A]} \tag{5.37}$$

EXAMPLE 5.4

The following data are taken from the open- and short-circuit characteristics of a 45-kVA, three-phase, Y-connected, 220-V (line-to-line), six-pole, 60-Hz synchronous machine. From the open-circuit characteristic:

Field current = 2.84 A   Line-to-line voltage = 220 V

and from the air-gap line:

Field current = 2.20 A   Line-to-line voltage = 202 V

From the short-circuit characteristic:

Field current, A	2.20	2.84
Armature current, A	118	152

Compute the unsaturated value of the synchronous reactance and its saturated value at rated voltage, both in ohms per phase and in per unit on the machine rating as a base.

■ Solution

To aid in visualizing the solution, the given voltages and currents are shown on the open- and short-circuit characteristics of Fig. 5.11. At a field current of 2.20 A the line-to-neutral voltage on the air-gap line is

$$V_{a,ag} = \frac{202}{\sqrt{3}} = 116.7 \text{ V}$$

and for the same field current the armature current on short circuit is 118 A.
Thus, from Eq. 5.29

$$X_{s,u} = \frac{116.7}{118} = 0.987 \text{ }\Omega/\text{phase}$$

Similarly, rated open-circuit terminal voltage of 220 V, corresponding to a line-to-neutral voltage of $220/\sqrt{3} = 127.0$ V is produced by a field current of 2.84 A. The corresponding

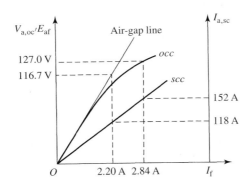

Figure 5.11 Plot of motor characteristics for Example 5.4.

short-circuit current is 152 A and thus from Eq. 5.30

$$X_s = \frac{127}{152} = 0.836 \ \Omega/\text{phase}$$

Noting that rated armature current is

$$I_{a,\text{rated}} = \frac{45{,}000}{\sqrt{3} \times 220} = 118 \text{ A}$$

we see from the given data that AFSC = 2.20 A and that AFNL = 2.84 A. Thus, from Eq. 5.34

$$X_s = \frac{\text{AFSC}}{\text{AFNL}} = \frac{2.20}{2.84} = 0.775 \text{ per unit}$$

Extrapolating the given air-gap line data to rated voltage, we can find

$$\text{AFNL}_{\text{ag}} = 220 \left(\frac{2.20}{220}\right) = 2.40 \text{ A}$$

and thus, from Eq. 5.35

$$X_{s,u} = \frac{\text{AFSC}}{\text{AFNL}_{\text{ag}}} = \frac{2.20}{2.40} = 0.917 \text{ per unit}$$

Note of course that the per-unit reactances can also be calculated by dividing their values in Ω/phase by the base impedance

$$Z_{\text{base}} = \frac{220^2}{45 \times 10^3} = 1.076 \quad \Omega$$

Equivalently, the reactances in Ω/phase can be calculated from their per-unit values by multiplying by Z_{base}.

Practice Problem 5.4

Calculate the saturated synchronous reactance (in Ω/phase and per unit) of an 85-kVA synchronous machine which achieves its rated open-circuit voltage of 460 V at a field current 8.7 A and which achieves rated short-circuit current at a field current of 11.2 A.

Solution

$$X_s = 3.21 \ \Omega/\text{phase} = 1.29 \text{ per unit}$$

Because the machine flux level is low under short-circuit conditions, the core loss under this condition is typically considered to be negligible. Thus the mechanical power required to drive the synchronous machine during a short-circuit test equals the sum of friction and windage loss (determined from the open-circuit test at zero field current) plus losses caused by the armature current. The losses caused by the armature current can then be found by subtracting friction and windage from the driving power. The losses caused by the short-circuit armature current are known collectively as the *short-circuit load loss*. A curve showing the typical form of short-circuit load loss plotted against armature current is shown in Fig. 5.12. Often this loss is assumed to vary parabolically with armature current.

Figure 5.12 Typical form of short-circuit load loss and stray load loss curves.

The short-circuit load loss consists of I^2R loss in the armature winding, local core losses caused by the armature leakage flux, and the small core loss component caused by the net resultant flux. For a q-phase machine, the short-circuit resistance dc loss $P_{\mathrm{arm,dc}}$, calculated as

$$P_{\mathrm{arm,dc}} = q I_{\mathrm{a,sc}}^2 R_{\mathrm{dc}} \qquad (5.38)$$

can be computed if the dc winding resistance R_{dc} is measured and corrected, when necessary, for the temperature of the windings during the short-circuit test. For copper conductors

$$\frac{R_{\mathrm{dc}}(T)}{R_{\mathrm{dc}}(t)} = \frac{234.5 + T}{234.5 + t} \qquad (5.39)$$

where R_T and R_t are the resistances at Celsius temperatures T and t, respectively. If this dc resistance loss is subtracted from the short-circuit load loss, the difference will be the loss due to skin effect and eddy currents in the armature conductors plus the local core losses caused by the armature leakage flux. This difference between the short-circuit load loss and the dc resistance loss is the additional loss caused by the alternating current in the armature. It is the *stray-load loss* described in Appendix D, commonly considered to have the same value under normal load conditions as on short circuit. It is a function of the armature current, as shown by the curve in Fig. 5.12.

As with any ac device, the *effective resistance of the armature*, $R_{\mathrm{a,eff}}$, can be computed as the power loss attributable to the armature current divided by the square of the current. On the assumption that the stray load loss is a function of only the armature current, the effective resistance of the armature can be determined from the short-circuit load loss:

$$R_{\mathrm{a,eff}} = \frac{\text{short-circuit load loss}}{(\text{short-circuit armature current})^2} \qquad (5.40)$$

If the short-circuit load loss and armature current are expressed in per unit, the effective resistance will be in per unit. If they are expressed in watts per phase and amperes per phase, respectively, the effective resistance will be in ohms per phase. Often, it is sufficiently accurate to find the value of $R_{\mathrm{a,eff}}$ at rated current and then to assume it to be constant.

EXAMPLE 5.5

For the 45-kVA, three-phase, Y-connected synchronous machine of Example 5.4, at rated armature current (118 A) the short-circuit load loss (total for three phases) is 1.80 kW at a temperature of 25°C. The dc resistance of the armature at this temperature is 0.0335 Ω/phase. Compute the effective armature resistance in per unit and in ohms per phase at 25°C.

■ **Solution**

The short-circuit load loss is $1.80/45 = 0.040$ per unit at $I_a = 1.00$ per unit. Therefore,

$$R_{a,eff} = \frac{0.040}{(1.00)^2} = 0.040 \text{ per unit}$$

On a per-phase basis the short-circuit load loss is $1800/3 = 600$ W/phase and consequently the effective resistance is

$$R_{a,eff} = \frac{600}{(118)^2} = 0.043 \text{ Ω/phase}$$

The ratio of ac-to-dc resistance is

$$\frac{R_{a,eff}}{R_{a,dc}} = \frac{0.043}{0.0335} = 1.28$$

Because this is a small machine, its per-unit resistance is relatively high. The effective armature resistance of machines with ratings above a few hundred kVA usually is less than 0.01 per unit.

Practice Problem 5.5

Consider a three-phase 13.8 kV 25-MVA synchronous generator whose three-phase short-circuit loss is 52.8 kW at rated armature current. Calculate (a) its rated armature current and (b) its effective armature resistance in Ω/phase and in per unit.

Solution

    a. 1046 A
    b. $R_{a,eff} = 0.0161$ Ω/phase $= 0.0021$ per unit

5.4 STEADY-STATE POWER-ANGLE CHARACTERISTICS

The maximum power a synchronous machine can deliver is determined by the maximum torque which can be applied without loss of synchronism with the external system to which it is connected.[3] The purpose of this section is to derive expressions

---

[3] In the context of this discussion, the term "maximum power" refers to the maximum power which can theoretically be delivered without loss of synchronism. In practice, this value may be significantly higher than the machine's rated power which is the practical operating power limit of the machine and which is determined by thermal limitations.

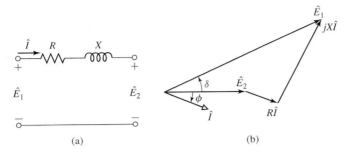

Figure 5.13 (a) Impedance interconnecting two voltages;
(b) phasor diagram.

for the steady-state power limits of synchronous machines in simple situations for which the external system can be represented as an impedance in series with a voltage source.

Since both the external system and the machine itself can be represented as an impedance in series with a voltage source, the study of power limits becomes merely a special case of the more general problem of the limitations on power flow through a series impedance. The impedance will include the synchronous impedance of the synchronous machine as well as an equivalent impedance of the external system (which may consist of transmission lines and transformer banks as well as additional synchronous machines).

Consider the simple circuit of Fig. 5.13a, consisting of two ac voltages, $\hat{E}_1$ and $\hat{E}_2$, connected by an impedance $Z = R + jX$ through which the current is $\hat{I}$. The phasor diagram is shown in Fig. 5.13b. Note that in this phasor diagram, the voltage $\hat{E}_2$ is chosen as the reference phasor and the reference direction for positive angles is counter-clockwise. Thus, in Fig. 5.13b, the phase angle δ of $\hat{E}_1$ is positive while the phase angle ϕ of the current can be seen to be negative.

The phasor current is

$$\hat{I} = \frac{\hat{E}_1 - \hat{E}_2}{Z} = \frac{E_1 e^{j\delta} - E_2}{R + jX} \qquad (5.41)$$

The power P_2 delivered through the impedance to voltage source $\hat{E}_2$ is

$$P_2 = \text{Re}[\hat{E}_2 \hat{I}^*] \qquad (5.42)$$

where the notation Re[ ] indicates the real part of a complex number and the superscript * indicates the complex conjugate.

If, as is frequently the case in the analysis of large power systems, the resistance R is negligible, then there is no power dissipated in the series impedance and the power P_1 supplied by the source $\hat{E}_1$ is equal to P_2. Under this assumption, Eq. 5.42 reduces to the simple form

$$P_1 = P_2 = \frac{E_1 E_2}{X} \sin \delta \qquad (5.43)$$

When the power-angle expression of Eq. 5.43 is compared with the expression of Eq. 5.1 for torque in terms of interacting flux and mmf waves, they are seen to be of the same form. This is no coincidence. Remember that torque and power are proportional when, as is the case here, speed is constant. What we are really saying is that Eq. 5.1, applied specifically to an idealized cylindrical-rotor synchronous machine and translated to circuit terms, becomes Eq. 5.43. A quick mental review of the background of each relation should show that they stem from the same fundamental considerations.

Equation 5.43 is a very important equation in the study of synchronous machines and indeed in the study of ac power systems in general. Eq. 5.43 is commonly referred to as the *power-angle characteristic*, and the angle δ is known as the *power angle*. Note that if δ is positive, $\hat{E}_1$ leads $\hat{E}_2$ and power flows from source $\hat{E}_1$ to $\hat{E}_2$. Similarly, when δ is negative, $\hat{E}_1$ lags $\hat{E}_2$ and power flows from source $\hat{E}_2$ to $\hat{E}_1$. From Eq. 5.43 the maximum power which can be transferred between sources 1 and 2 is

$$P_{1,\max} = P_{2,\max} = \pm\frac{E_1 E_2}{X} \tag{5.44}$$

which occurs when $\delta = \pm 90°$.

It should be emphasized that the derivation of Eqs. 5.41 to 5.43 is based on a single-phase, line-to-neutral ac circuit. When considering a three-phase system, if E_1 and E_2 are expressed in per unit or in terms of line-to-line voltages, Eq. 5.43 gives three-phase power directly. Alternatively, if E_1 and E_2 are the line-neutral voltages, the power must be multiplied by three to get the total three-phase power and Eq. 5.43 becomes

$$P_1 = P_2 = \frac{3E_1 E_2}{X} \sin\delta \tag{5.45}$$

Equations 5.43 and 5.45 are valid for any voltage sources $\hat{E}_1$ and $\hat{E}_2$ separated by a reactive impedance jX. Thus for a three-phase synchronous machine with generated voltage $\hat{E}_{af}$ and synchronous reactance X_s connected to a system whose Thevenin equivalent is a voltage source $\hat{V}_{eq}$ in series with a reactive impedance jX_{eq}, as shown in Fig. 5.14, the power-angle characteristic can be written

$$P = \frac{E_{af} V_{eq}}{X_s + X_{eq}} \sin\delta \tag{5.46}$$

if E_{af} and V_{eq} are expressed in terms of line-to-line voltages or in per unit (in which case P, X_s and X_{eq} must also be expressed in per unit) and

$$P = \frac{3E_{af} V_{eq}}{X_s + X_{eq}} \sin\delta \tag{5.47}$$

if E_{af} and V_{eq} are expressed in terms of line-to-neutral voltages. Here P is the power transferred from the synchronous machine to the system and δ is the phase angle of $\hat{E}_{af}$ with respect to $\hat{V}_{eq}$.

In a similar fashion, it is possible to write a power-angle characteristic in terms of X_s, E_{af}, the terminal voltage V_a, and the relative angle between them, or alternatively X_{eq}, V_a and V_{eq} and their relative angle. Although these various expressions are equally

Figure 5.14 Equivalent-circuit representation of a synchronous machine connected to an external system.

valid, they are not equally useful. For example, if the machine is operated with constant field current, both E_{af} and V_{eq} will remain constant as P is varied while the terminal voltage V_a will not. Thus, while Eqs. 5.46 and 5.47 give an easily solved relation between P and δ, a power-angle characteristic based upon V_a, V_{eq} and X_{eq} cannot be solved without an additional expression relating V_a to P.

Note that Eqs. 5.43, 5.45, 5.46 and 5.47 are derived based upon the choice of the generator reference direction for the current. If the motor reference direction is chosen, the sign of the current is reversed in Eq. 5.41 a minus sign must be included in these equations to account for the fact that with the choice of motor reference direction, P represents the power into the machine and positive input power will correspond to negative values of power angle δ.

From Eqs. 5.46 and 5.47 we see that the peak of the power-angle characteristic associated with synchronous-machine operation is proportional to the magnitude of the system voltage V_{eq} as well as to that of the generator internal voltage E_{af}. Thus, for constant system voltage, the maximum power which can be supplied by a synchronous generator or supplied to a synchronous motor can be increased by increasing the synchronous-machine field current and thus the internal voltage. Of course, this cannot be done without limit; neither the field current nor the machine fluxes can be raised past the point where losses become excessive and the machine cannot be adequately cooled.

In general, stability considerations dictate that a synchronous machine achieve steady-state operation for a power angle considerably less than 90°. Thus, the peak of the power-angle characteristic of a synchronous machine under normal operating conditions is considerably larger than the mechanical power supplied to it in the case of generator operation or the load power in the case of a synchronous motor.

EXAMPLE 5.6

A three-phase, 75-MVA, 13.8-KV synchronous generator with saturated synchronous reactance $X_s = 1.35$ per unit and unsaturated synchronous reactance $X_{s,u} = 1.56$ per unit is connected to an external system with equivalent reactance $X_{eq} = 0.23$ per unit and voltage $V_{eq} = 1.0$ per unit, both on the generator base. It achieves rated open-circuit voltage at a field current of 297 amperes.

a. Find the maximum power P_{max} (in MW and per unit) that can be supplied to the external system if the internal voltage of the generator is held equal to 1.0 per unit.

b. Using MATLAB, plot the per-unit terminal voltage of the generator as the generator output is varied from zero to P_{max} under the conditions of part (a).

■ Solution

a. From Eq. 5.46

$$P_{max} = \frac{E_{af} V_{eq}}{X_s + X_{eq}}$$

Note that although this is a three-phase generator, no factor of 3 is required because we are working in per unit.

Because the machine is operating with a terminal voltage near its rated value, we should express P_{max} in terms of the saturated synchronous reactance. Thus

$$P_{max} = \frac{1}{1.35 + 0.23} = 0.633 \text{ per unit} = 47.5 \text{ MW}$$

b. From the equivalent circuit of Fig 5.14, we see that the generator terminal current can be expressed as a function of the power angle δ is given by

$$\hat{I}_a = \frac{\hat{E}_{af} - \hat{V}_{eq}}{j(X_s + X_{eq})} = \frac{E_{af} e^{j\delta} - V_{eq}}{j(X_s + X_{eq})}$$

The generator terminal voltage is then given by

$$\hat{V}_a = \hat{V}_{eq} + jX_{eq}\hat{I}_a$$

and the generator power can be expressed as

$$P = \text{Re}[\hat{V}_a \hat{I}_a^*]$$

Thus the terminal voltage can be plotted as a function of the generator power by varying the power angle over the range 0 to 90°. Figure 5.15 is the desired MATLAB plot. The terminal voltage can be seen to vary from 1.0 to approximately 0.87 as the generator is loaded to its maximum value of 0.633 per unit.

Here is the MATLAB script:

```
clc
clear


% Solution for part (b)

%System parameters
Veq = 1.0;
Eaf = 1.0;
Xeq = .23;
Xs = 1.35;
```

Figure 5.15 MATLAB plot of terminal voltage vs. per-unit generator power for Example 5.6(b).

```
n = 1:101;
delta = (pi/2)*(n-1)/100;
Iahat = (Eaf *exp(j*delta) -  Veq)/(j*(Xs + Xeq));
Vahat = (Veq + j*Xeq*Iahat);
Vamag = abs(Vahat);
P = real(Vahat.*conj(Iahat));

%Now plot the results
plot(P,Vamag)
xlabel('Generator power [per unit]')
ylabel('Terminal voltage [per unit]')
```

Practice Problem 5.6

Consider the 75-MVA, 13.8 kV machine of Example 5.6. It is observed to be operating at terminal voltage of 13.7 kV and an output power of 53 MW at 0.87 pf lagging. Find (a) the phase current in kA, (b) the internal voltage in per unit and (c) the corresponding field current in amperes.

Solution

    a. $I_a = 2.57$ kA
    b. $E_{af} = 1.81$ per unit
    c. $I_f = 538$ amperes

As is demonstrated in Example 5.6, most large synchronous generators connected to a power system cannot be loaded to rated power with their internal voltage equal to rated voltage; the peak of the per-unit power-angle characteristic P_{max} is less than the generator rating. Thus, in order to properly load the generator, the field current must be increased, increasing the internal voltage, as the load is increased.

Although this can be done manually, it is typically done automatically through the action of an *automatic voltage regulator* (AVR). An automatic voltage regulator measures a system voltage (e.g., the generator terminal voltage) and controls the generator field current to maintain that voltage at a pre-specified value. As can be seen from Example 5.6, loading the machine with constant field current results in a reduction in terminal voltage. Thus, as will be demonstrated in Example 5.7, an AVR set to maintain terminal voltage will automatically respond to an increase in generator load by increasing the field current and hence the peak of the power angle characteristic, permitting the generator to be fully loaded.

EXAMPLE 5.7

Assume that the generator of Example 5.6 is equipped with an automatic voltage regulator set to maintain the generator terminal voltage at its rated value.

a. If the generator is loaded to its rated value, calculate the corresponding power angle, per-unit internal voltage, and field current.
b. Using MATLAB, plot the field current in amperes as a function of the generator per-unit power up to full load.

■ Solution

a. With the terminal voltage held constant at $V_a = 1.0$ per unit, the power can be expressed as

$$P = \frac{V_a V_{eq}}{X_{eq}} \sin \delta_t = \frac{1}{0.23} \sin \delta_t = 4.35 \sin \delta_t$$

where δ_t is the angle of the terminal voltage with respect to $\hat{V}_{eq}$. For $P = 1.0$ per unit, $\delta_t = 13.3°$ and hence $\hat{I}$ is equal to

$$\hat{I}_a = \frac{V_a e^{j\delta_t} - V_{eq}}{j X_{eq}} = 1.007 \, e^{j6.65°}$$

and

$$\hat{E}_{af} = \hat{V}_{eq} + j(X_{eq} + X_s)\hat{I}_a = 1.78 \, e^{j62.7°}$$

or $E_{af} = 1.78$ per unit, corresponding to a field current (from Eq. 5.37) of

$$I_f = 1.78 \times 297 = 529 \quad [\text{A}]$$

The corresponding power angle is 62.7°.

b. Figure 5.16 is the desired MATLAB plot. I_f can be seen to vary from 1.0 at $P = 0$ to 1.78 at $P = 1.0$.

Here is the MATLAB script:

```
clc
clear

%System parameters
```

Figure 5.16 MATLAB plot of field current vs. per-unit power for Example 5.7.

```
Veq = 1.0;
Xeq = .23;
Xs = 1.35;
AFNL = 297;

%Set terminal voltage to unity
Vterm = 1.0;

n = 1:101;
P = (n-1)/100;
deltat = asin(P*Xeq/(Vterm*Veq));
Ia = (Vterm *exp(j*deltat) -  Veq)/(j*Xeq);
Eaf = abs(Vterm + j*(Xs+Xeq)*Ia);
If = AFNL*Eaf;

%Now plot the results
plot(P,If)
xlabel('Power [per unit]')
ylabel('Field current  [A]')
```

EXAMPLE 5.8

A 2000-hp, 2300-V, three-phase, Y-connected, 30-pole, 60-Hz synchronous motor has a synchronous reactance of 1.95 Ω/phase and AFNL = 370 A. The motor is connected to a 60-Hz, 2300-V constant voltage source through a feeder of reactance 0.32 Ω/phase. For the purposes of this example, all losses may be neglected.

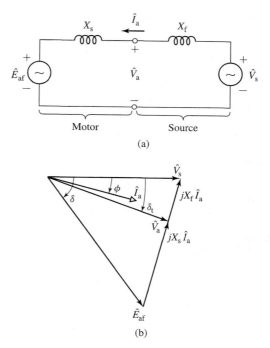

Figure 5.17 Equivalent circuit and phasor diagram for Example 5.8.

The motor has an automatic voltage regulator which is adjusted to maintain its terminal voltage at 2300 V. If the motor is operating at its rated power, calculate its terminal current, the reactive power supplied to the motor at its terminals, and the corresponding motor field current.

■ Solution

Although this machine is undoubtedly of the salient-pole type, we will solve the problem by simple cylindrical-rotor theory. The solution accordingly neglects reluctance torque and hence, as is discussed in Section 5.7, somewhat under-estimates the maximum power capability of the machine.

As shown in the equivalent circuit of Fig. 5.17(a), for the purpose of this example, we will use the motor reference direction for current. From Eq. 5.45 and the phasor diagram of Fig. 5.17(b), $V_a = V_s = 2300/\sqrt{3}$ V = 1328 V, line-to-neutral and with $P = 2000$ hp = 1492 kW,

$$\delta_t = -\sin^{-1}\left(\frac{PX_f}{3V_aV_s}\right)$$

$$= -\sin^{-1}\left(\frac{1492 \times 10^3 \times 0.32}{3 \times 1328^2}\right)$$

$$= -5.18°$$

where the minus sign is due to the fact that power flows from the source to the motor and hence $\hat{V}_a$ lags $\hat{V}_s$.

$$\hat{V}_a = V_a e^{j\delta_t} = 1328\ e^{-j5.18°}$$

Thus

$$\hat{I}_a = \frac{V_s - \hat{V}_a}{jX_f} = \frac{1328 - 1328e^{-j5.18°}}{j0.32} = 375\ e^{-j2.59°}\quad [\text{A}]$$

and the reactive power Q supplied to the motor is equal to

$$Q = \text{Im}[3\ \hat{V}_a \hat{I}_a^*] = -67.5\quad [\text{kVAR}]$$

where the notation Im[ ] indicates the imaginary part of a complex number and the superscript * indicates the complex conjugate. The fact that the reactive power into the motor is negative means that the motor is actually supply reactive power to the system under this operating condition.

From the single-phase, line-neutral equivalent circuit of Fig. 5.17(a) we see that

$$\hat{E}_{af} = \hat{V}_s - j(X_s + X_f)\hat{I}_a = 1328 + j(1.95 + 0.32) \times 375\ e^{-j2.59°}$$

$$= 1544\ e^{-j33.40°}\quad [\text{V}]$$

Note that line-to-neutral voltages must be used and thus $E_{af} = 1544$ V, line-to-neutral = 2674 V, line-to-line. Here we see that E_{af} is equal to 1.16 times the machine rated voltage (1.16 per unit) and thus we can calculate the field current from Eq. 5.37 as

$$I_f = 1.16 \times \text{AFNL} = 430\quad [\text{A}]$$

Practice Problem 5.7

Repeat Example 5.8 for source voltage of 2315 V.

Solution

$I_a = 375$ A

$Q = 23.5$ kVA

$I_f = 417$ A

5.5 STEADY-STATE OPERATING CHARACTERISTICS

The principal steady-state operating characteristics of a synchronous machine are described by the interrelations between terminal voltage, field current, armature current, power factor, and efficiency. A selection of performance characteristics of importance in practical application of synchronous machines are presented in this section.

Synchronous generators are usually rated in terms of a maximum apparent power (kVA or MVA) load at a specific voltage and power factor (often 80, 85, or 90 percent lagging) which they can carry continuously without overheating. Because they are typically operated with terminal voltage regulation, synchronous generators normally operate at a terminal voltage whose value is within ±5 percent of rated voltage. When the real-power loading and voltage are fixed, the allowable reactive-power loading is limited by either armature- or field-winding heating. The allowable operating region for a synchronous generator is frequently presented in the form of a *capability curve* which gives the maximum reactive-power loadings corresponding to various real power loadings with operation at rated terminal voltage.

A typical set of *capability curves* for a large, hydrogen-cooled turbine generator is shown in Fig. 5.18. Note that the three-curves seen in the figure correspond to differing pressure of the hydrogen cooling gas. Increasing the hydrogen pressure improves cooling and, as can be seen from Fig. 5.18, permits a larger overall loading of the machine.

Armature-winding heating is the limiting factor in the region from unity to rated power factor (0.85 lagging power factor in Fig. 5.18). For example, for a given real-power loading, increasing the reactive power past a point on the armature-heating limited portion of the capability curve will result in an armature current in excess of that which can be successfully cooled, resulting in armature-winding temperatures which will damage the armature-winding insulation and degrade its life. Similarly, for lower power factors, field-winding heating is the limiting factor.

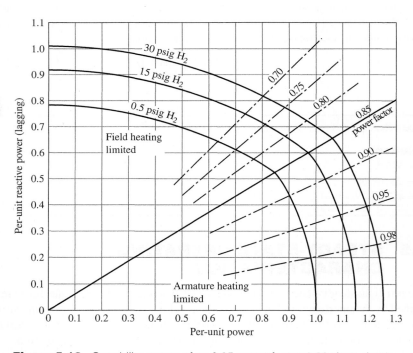

Figure 5.18   Capability curves of an 0.85 power factor, 0.80 short-circuit ratio, hydrogen-cooled turbine generator. Base MVA is rated MVA at 0.5 psig hydrogen.

Capability curves provide a valuable guide both to power system planners and to operators. As system planners consider modifications and additions to power systems, they can readily see whether the various existing or proposed generators can safely supply their required loadings. Similarly, power system operators can quickly see whether individual generators can safely respond to changes in system loadings which occur during the normal course of system operation.

The derivation of capability curves such as those in Fig. 5.18 can be seen as follows. Operation under conditions of constant terminal voltage and armature current (at the maximum value permitted by heating limitations) corresponds to a constant value of apparent output power determined by the product of terminal voltage and current. Since the per-unit apparent power S is given by

$$S = V_a I_a = \sqrt{P^2 + Q^2} \qquad (5.48)$$

where P represents the per-unit real power and Q represents the per-unit reactive power, we see that a constant apparent power corresponds to a circle centered on the origin on a plot of reactive power versus real power. Note also from Eq. 5.48, that, for constant terminal voltage, constant apparent power corresponds to constant armature-winding current and hence constant armature-winding heating. Such a circle, corresponding to the maximum acceptable level of armature heating, is shown in Fig. 5.19.

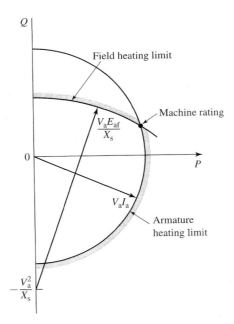

Figure 5.19 Construction used for the derivation of a synchronous generator capability curve.

Similarly, consider operation when terminal voltage is constant and field current (and hence generated voltage E_{af}) is limited to a maximum value, also determined by heating limitations. In per unit,

$$P - jQ = \hat{V}_a \hat{I}_a \tag{5.49}$$

From Eq. 5.25 (with $R_a = 0$)

$$\hat{E}_{af} = \hat{V}_a + jX_s \hat{I}_a \tag{5.50}$$

Equations 5.49 and 5.50 can be solved to yield

$$P^2 + \left(Q + \frac{V_a^2}{X_s} \right)^2 = \left(\frac{V_a E_{af}}{X_s} \right)^2 \tag{5.51}$$

This equation corresponds to a circle centered at $Q = -(V_a^2/X_s)$ as shown in Fig. 5.19 and determines the field-heating limitation on machine operation shown in Fig. 5.18. It is common to specify the rating (apparent power and power factor) of the machine as the point of intersection of the armature- and field-heating limitation curves as shown in Fig. 5.19.

As can be seen from the capability curves of Fig. 5.18, there are additional limitations imposed on operation of a generator when operating under-excited and absorbing reactive power ($Q < 0$). These limitations, not shown in Fig. 5.19, are associated with heating in the end regions of the stator core of a generator under under-excited operating conditions as well as stability limits imposed by the system to which a specific generator is connected.

EXAMPLE 5.9

Consider a synchronous generator rated at 13.8 kV, 150 MVA, 0.9 pf with a synchronous reactance of 1.18 pu and AFNL = 680 A. Recognizing that the rated power factor of the generator is determined by the intersection of the armature- and field-heating limitation curves, calculate the maximum field current which can be supplied to the generator without exceeding the field-heating limit.

■ **Solution**

Based upon the assumption that the rated power factor of this generator is determined by the intersection of the armature- and field-heating limitation curves as shown in Fig. 5.19, we see that at this operating point, $V_a = 1.0$ per unit and

$$I_a = 1.0 \, e^{j\phi}$$

where $\phi = -\cos^{-1}(0.9) = -25.84°$. Note that ϕ is negative because the reactive power $Q = \text{Im}[\hat{V}_a \hat{I}_a]^*$ is positive. From Eq. 5.50

$$\hat{E}_{af} = \hat{V}_a + jX_s \hat{I}_a = 1.0 + j1.18 \times 1.0 \, e^{-j25.84°} = 1.850 \, e^{j35.04°}$$

Thus we see that the field-heating limits the maximum value of generated voltage to 1.85 per and thus limits the field current to a maximum value of $1.85 \times \text{AFNL} = 1258$ A.

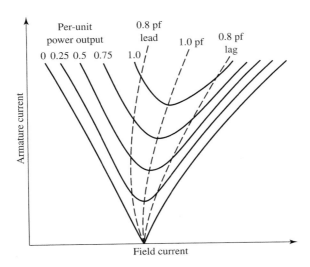

Figure 5.20 Typical form of synchronous-generator V curves.

For a given real-power loading and terminal voltage, the power factor at which a synchronous machine operates, and hence its armature current, can be controlled by adjusting its field excitation. A plot of armature current as a function of field current at constant real power and terminal voltage is known as a *V curve* because of its characteristic shape. A family of V curves for a synchronous generator corresponding to various real-power loadings takes the form of those shown in Fig. 5.20.

The dashed lines are loci of constant power factor; they are referred to as *compounding curves*, showing how the field current must be varied as the load is changed to maintain constant power factor. Points to the right of the unity-power-factor compounding curve correspond to over-excitation and lagging power factor; points to the left correspond to under-excitation and leading power factor. Synchronous-motor V curves and compounding curves are very similar to those of synchronous generators. In fact, if it were not for the small effects of armature resistance, motor and generator compounding curves would be identical except that the lagging- and leading-power-factor curves would be interchanged.

The nature of a V curve is best understood with the aid of a phasor diagram. Consider the phasor diagram of Fig. 5.21, representing Eq. 5.50 for a synchronous generator operating at constant terminal voltage V_a, constant real power P and three different values of field current. To simplify this discussion, we will assume that all quantities are expressed in per unit and thus the real power is given by

$$P = \text{Re}[\hat{V}_a \, \hat{I}_a^*] = V_a I_a \cos \phi \tag{5.52}$$

where ϕ is the angle of $\hat{I}_a$ with respect to $\hat{V}_a$. Because V_a and P are constant, we see from Eq. 5.52 that

$$I_a \cos \phi = \text{constant} \tag{5.53}$$

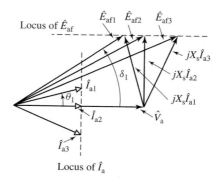

Figure 5.21 Phasor diagram for constant-power operation at constant terminal voltage.

and thus the projection of $\hat{I}_a$ onto $\hat{V}_a$ is constant. As a result, the tips of all the phasors $\hat{I}_a$ must lie along the vertical dotted line labeled "Locus of $\hat{I}a$" in Fig. 5.21. Similarly, because $\hat{E}_{af}$ is obtained by adding the phasor $jX_s\hat{I}_a$, which is perpendicular to the phasor $\hat{I}_a$, to $\hat{V}_a$, it can be shown that the tips of all the phasors $\hat{E}_{af}$ must lie along the horizontal dotted line labeled "Locus of $\hat{E}_{af}$" in Fig. 5.21.

Consider operation at current $\hat{I}_{a1}$ in Fig. 5.21, in which case the generator is operating at a leading power factor (ϕ_1 is positive) and hence its reactive power output, given by

$$Q = \mathrm{Im}[\hat{V}_a \, \hat{I}_a^*] = -V_a I_a \sin\phi \tag{5.54}$$

is negative, i.e. the generator is absorbing reactive power from the external system. Notice that under this operating condition, the corresponding generated voltage $\hat{E}_{af}$ has the smallest magnitude of the three operating points, corresponding to the smallest value of field current as can be seen from Eq. 5.37. When a synchronous generator is absorbing reactive power, it is said to be *under-excited*.

Next consider unity-power-factor operation, corresponding to the terminal current $\hat{I}_{a2}$ in the phasor diagram. We see that the magnitude of the corresponding generated voltage $\hat{E}_{af2}$ is larger than that of the first operating condition. Thus we see that if the generator is operating under-excited, an increase in field current will reduce the armature current and improve the power factor, reducing the reactive power absorbed by the generator. A minimum of armature current will occur when the generator is operating at unity power factor (zero reactive power).

As can be seen from the phasor diagram, a further increase in field current (and a corresponding increase in E_{af}) will result in an increase in armature current from its minimum value; for example, consider the operating point corresponding to terminal current $\hat{I}_{a3}$ and generated voltage $\hat{E}_{af3}$. Under these conditions the generator is operating at lagging power factor (ϕ_3 is negative) and hence the terminal reactive power is positive and the generator is supplying reactive power to the external system. When a synchronous generator is supplying reactive power, it is said to be *over-excited*.

EXAMPLE 5.10

Calculate the field current in amperes for the generator of Example 5.9 if it is operating at its rated terminal voltage and unity-power-factor with real-power loadings of 0.5, 0.75 and 1.0 per unit.

■ Solution

At unity power factor, the per-unit terminal current is

$$I_a = \frac{P}{V_a} = \frac{0.5}{1.0} = 0.5$$

As can be seen from the phasor diagram of Fig. 5.21, the phasor $j X_s \hat{I}_a$ is perpendicular to $\hat{V}_a$ and thus

$$E_{af} = \sqrt{V_a^2 + (X_s I_a)^2} = \sqrt{(1.0)^2 + (1.18 \times 0.5)^2} = 1.161$$

and from Eq. 5.37

$$I_f = E_{af} \times \text{AFNL} = 1.161 \times 680 = 789 \quad [\text{A}]$$

Similarly, for $P = 0.75$ per unit, $I_f = 908$ A and for $P = 1.0$ per unit, $I_f = 1,052$ A.

EXAMPLE 5.11

Using MATLAB, plot the per-unit terminal current vs. field current in amperes for the generator of Example 5.9 operating at rated terminal voltage and real power of 0.7 per unit as the generator power factor is varied from 0.8 leading to 0.8 lagging.

■ Solution

For the stated range of power factors, the power factor angle varies over the range $\phi_0 \geq \phi \geq -\phi_0$ where $\phi_0 = \cos^{-1}(0.8) = 36.87°$. From Eq. 5.52, we see that for a given value of ϕ, the per-unit terminal current can be found as

$$I_a = \frac{P}{V_a \, \cos \phi}$$

and thus

$$\hat{I}_a = \left(\frac{P}{V_a \, \cos \phi} \right) e^{j\phi}$$

The per-unit generated voltage can then be found from Eq. 5.50 and the field current from Eq. 5.37. The resultant plot is shown in Fig. 5.22.

Here is the MATLAB script:

```
clc
clear

% Generator parameters
Va = 1.0;
Xs = 1.18;
AFNL = 680;
P = 0.7;
```

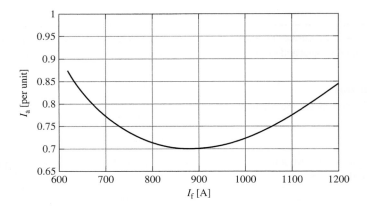

Figure 5.22 MATLAB plot of per-unit terminal current vs. field current for Example 5.11.

```
theta = acos(0.8)*(1:-.01:-1);
Ia = P./(Va*cos(theta));
Iahat = Ia.*exp(j*theta);
Eafhat = Va+j*Xs*Iahat;
Eaf = abs(Eafhat);
If = Eaf*AFNL;

plot(If,Ia,'LineWidth',2)
xlabel('I_f [A]','FontSize',20)
ylabel('I_a [per unit]','FontSize',20)
set(gca,'FontSize',20)
set(gca,'xlim',[600 1200])
grid on
```

As we have seen, synchronous generators can supply both real and reactive power. A special type of synchronous generator, designed to supply only reactive power, is referred to as a *synchronous condenser*. Synchronous condensers operate without prime movers[4] and their function is to supply or absorb reactive power to a power system, thereby controlling the system voltage at the point to which there are connected. To a simple approximation, they can be thought of as an adjustable ac voltage source controlled by their field current. Note that this type of operating corresponds to operating along the zero-real-power axis of the capability curves of Figs. 5.18 and 5.19.

---

[4] A relatively small motor sufficient to supply rotational losses can be used to bring them up to operating speed in order to parallel them to the power system.

EXAMPLE 5.12

Consider a synchronous condenser connected to a power system bus which can be represented by a Thevenin-equivalent voltage V_{eq} and series reactance X_{eq} as shown in Fig. 5.14. The synchronous condenser is rated at 75 MVA, 13.8 kV with a synchronous reactance of 0.95 per unit and AFNL = 830 A. If the equivalent system voltage is 13.75 kV and $X_{eq} = 0.02$ per unit on the generator base, calculate the generator field current required to raise the generator terminal voltage, and thus the local system voltage, to 13.8 kV and the reactive power supplied under that operating condition.

■ Solution

Under this operating condition, $V_{eq} = 13.75/13.80 = 0.9964$ per unit and the generator terminal voltage is $V_a = 1.0$ per unit. Because there is no real-power flow, we know that these voltages are in phase and thus the generator terminal current is

$$\hat{I}_a = \frac{(V_a - V_{eq})}{j X_{eq}} = \frac{(1.0 - 0.9964)}{j\,0.02} = -j\,0.181 \text{ per unit}$$

The per-unit generated voltage can then be found from Eq. 5.50 as

$$\hat{E}_{af} = V_a + j X_s \hat{I}_a = 1.172 \text{ perunit}$$

Thus from Eq. 5.37 the field current is equal to $I_f = 830 \times 1.172 = 973$ A.

Finally, the generator reactive power output is

$$Q = \text{Im}[\hat{V}_a \hat{I}_a^*] = 0.181 \text{ per unit} = 13.6 \text{ MVAR}$$

Practice Problem 5.8

Repeat Example 5.12 if the equivalent system voltage is 13.88 kV.

Solution

$I_f = 601$ A

$Q = -0.290$ per unit $= -21.7$ MVA

As in all electromechanical machines, the efficiency of a synchronous machine at any particular operating point is determined by losses; $I^2 R$ losses in the windings, core losses, stray-load losses, and mechanical losses. Because these losses change with operating condition and are somewhat difficult to measure accurately, various standard procedures have been developed to calculate the efficiency of synchronous machines.[5] The general principles for these calculations are described in Appendix D.

---

[5] See, for example, IEEE Std. 115-2009, "IEEE Guide: Test Procedures for Synchronous Machines," Institute of Electrical and Electronic Engineers, Inc., *www.ieee.org* and NEMA Standards Publication No. MG 1-2009, "Motors and Generators," National Electrical Manufacturers Association, *www.nema.org*

EXAMPLE 5.13

Data are given in Fig. 5.23 with respect to the losses of the 45-kVA, 220-V, 6-pole, 60-Hz, three-phase synchronous machine of Examples 5.4 and 5.5. Compute its efficiency when it is running as a synchronous motor at a terminal voltage of 220 V and with a power input to its armature of 45 kVA at 0.80 leading power factor. Assume the armature and field windings to be at a temperature of 75°C.

■ Solution

The I^2R losses must be computed on the basis of the dc resistances of the windings at 75°C. Correcting the winding resistances by means of Eq. 5.39 gives

a. Field-winding resistance R_f at 75°C $= 35.5\ \Omega$
b. Armature dc resistance R_a at 75°C $= 0.0399\ \Omega$/phase

Note that, because the stray-load loss is accounted for separately in Fig. 5.23, in this case we are calculating the armature loss using the dc resistance instead of the effective resistance of Eq. 5.40.

Friction and windage loss $= 0.91$ kW
Armature dc resistance at 25°C $= 0.0335\ \Omega$ per phase
Field-winding resistance at 25°C $= 29.8\ \Omega$

Figure 5.23 Losses in a three-phase, 45-kVA, Y-connected, 220-V, 60-Hz, six-pole synchronous machine (Example 5.13).

For the specified operating conditions, the motor is operating at its rated voltage and kVA and thus at rated armature current magnitude (1.0 per unit = 118 A). The per-unit armature current is thus

$$\hat{I}_a = 1.0e^{j\phi}$$

where $\phi = \cos^{-1}(0.8) = 36.9°$.

The per-unit generated voltage can be found as

$$\hat{E}_{af} = V_a - (R_a + jX_s)\hat{I}_a$$

Here $V_a = 1.0$ per unit and $X_s = 0.775$ as calculated in Example 5.4. R_a in per unit is calculated using the base impedance $Z_{base} = (220 \text{ V})^2/45 \text{ kVA} = 1.076 \ \Omega$ as

$$R_a = \frac{0.0399}{1.076} = 0.0371 \quad \text{per unit}$$

Thus

$$\hat{E}_{af} = 1.572e^{-j24.1°} \quad \text{per unit}$$

From Example 5.4, AFNL = 2.84 A and I_f can be found from Eq. 5.37 as $I_f = E_{af} \times$ AFNL = 4.47 A. The field I^2R loss is therefore

$$I_f^2 R_f = 4.47^2 \times 35.5 = 708 \text{ W}$$

The per-unit armature I^2R loss is

$$I_a^2 R_a = 3 \times 1.0^2 \times 0.0371 = 0.0371 \text{ per unit}$$

and thus $I_a^2 R_a = 0.0371 \times (45 \times 10^3) = 1670$ W.

From Fig. 5.23 at $I_a = 118$ A the stray-load loss = 0.36 kW. The stray-load loss is considered to account for the losses caused by the armature leakage flux. Core loss under load is primarily a function of the main core flux in the motor. As is discussed in Chapter 2, the voltage across the magnetizing branch in a transformer (corresponding to the transformer core flux) is calculated by subtracting the leakage impedance drop from the terminal voltage. In a directly analogous fashion, the main core flux in a synchronous machine (i.e., the air-gap flux) can be calculated as the voltage (often referred to as the *air-gap voltage*) behind the leakage impedance of the machine. Typically the armature resistance is small, and hence it is common to ignore the resistance and to calculate the voltage behind the leakage reactance. The core loss can then be estimated from the open-circuit core-loss curve at the voltage behind leakage reactance.

In this case, we do not know the machine leakage reactance. Thus, one approach would be simply to assume that the air-gap voltage is equal to the terminal voltage and to determine the core-loss under load from the core-loss curve at the value equal to the terminal voltage.[6] In this case, the motor terminal voltage is 220 V line-to-line and thus from Fig. 5.23, the open-circuit core loss is 1.20 kW.

---

[6] Although not rigorously correct, it has become common practice to ignore the leakage impedance drop when determining the under-load core loss.

To estimate the effect of ignoring the leakage reactance drop, let us assume that the leakage reactance of this motor is $X_{al} = 0.15$ per unit. Under this assumption, the per-unit air-gap voltage is equal to

$$\hat{V}_a - jX_{al}\hat{I}_a = 1.10e^{-j6.28°}$$

which corresponds to a line-to-line voltage magnitude of 242 V. From Fig. 5.23, the corresponding core-loss is 1.42 kW, 220 W higher than the value determined using the terminal voltage. We will use 1.42 kW for the purposes of this example.

Including the friction and windage loss of 0.91 kW, all losses have now been found:

$$\text{Total losses} = .708 + 1.67 + 0.36 + 1.42 + 0.91 = 5.07 \text{ kW}$$

The total motor input power is the input power to the armature plus the power dissipated in the field winding

$$\text{Input power} = 0.8 \times 45 + 0.708 = 36.7 \text{ kW}$$

and the output power is equal to the total input power minus the total losses

$$\text{Output power} = 36.7 - 5.07 = 31.6 \text{ kW}$$

Therefore

$$\text{Efficiency} = \frac{\text{Output power}}{\text{Input power}} = \frac{31.6}{36.7} = 0.862 = 86.2\%$$

Practice Problem 5.9

Repeat Example 5.13 for the case that the motor is operating at a power input of 45 kW, unity power factor.

Solution

$$\text{Efficiency} = 89.9\%$$

EXAMPLE 5.14

Experimental results are often presented either in tabular form or the form of plots, such as the loss data presented in Fig. 5.23. Frequently is is helpful to express this data in a functional form so that it can be easily incorporated into design and analysis programs. MATLAB includes a number of functions which can be used to accomplish this task. Based upon the following data points read from the curve of open-circuit core loss vs open-circuit voltage, use the MATLAB *spline* function to plot a curve of open-circuit core loss vs. open-circuit voltage.

Open-circuit voltage [V]	Open-circuit core loss [W]
0	0
50	200
80	600
110	1200
140	2000

Figure 5.24 MATLAB plot of open-circuit core loss vs. open-circuit voltage Example 5.14.

■ Solution

The plot of open-circuit core loss vs. open-circuit voltage is given in Fig. 5.24.
Here is the MATLAB script:

```
clc
clear

% Open-circuit voltage [V]
Voc(1) = 0;
Voc(2) = 50;
Voc(3) = 80;
Voc(4) = 110;
Voc(5) = 140;

%Core loss [W]
Pcore(1) = 0;
Pcore(2) = 200;
Pcore(3) = 600;
Pcore(4) = 1200;
Pcore(5) = 2000;

% Select a range of open-circuit voltages for plotting
VOC = 0:150;

% Use a the 'spline' function to calculate the
% corresponding core loss
```

```
PCORE = spline(Voc,Pcore,VOC);

% Plot the results

plot(VOC,PCORE/1000)
xlabel('Open-circuit voltage')
ylabel('Open-circuit core-loss [kW]')
```

5.6   EFFECTS OF SALIENT POLES; INTRODUCTION TO DIRECT- AND QUADRATURE-AXIS THEORY

The essential features of salient-pole machines are developed in this section based on physical reasoning. A mathematical treatment, based on an inductance formulation like that presented in Section 5.2, is given in Appendix C, where the dq0 transformation is developed.

5.6.1   Flux and MMF Waves

Because the air gap is uniform, the flux produced by an mmf wave in a uniform-air-gap machine is independent of the spatial alignment of the wave with respect to the field poles. However, in salient-pole machines, such as those shown schematically in Figs. 4.4 and 4.6, the preferred direction of magnetization is determined by the protruding field poles. The permeance along the polar axis, commonly referred to as the rotor *direct axis,* is appreciably greater than that along the interpolar axis, commonly referred to as the rotor *quadrature axis.*

The field winding produces flux which is aligned with the field pole and hence along the rotor direct axis. Thus, when phasor diagrams are drawn, the field-winding mmf and its corresponding flux $\hat{\Phi}_f$ are found along the rotor direct axis. The generated internal voltage is proportional to the time derivative of the field-winding flux, and thus its phasor $\hat{E}_{af}$ leads the flux $\hat{\Phi}_f$ by 90°. Following the convention that the quadrature axis leads the direct axis by 90°,[7] we see that **the generated-voltage phasor $\hat{E}_{af}$ lies along the quadrature axis.** Thus a key point in the analysis of synchronous-machine phasor diagrams is that, by locating the phasor $\hat{E}_{af}$, the location of both the quadrature axis and the direct axes is immediately determined. This forms the basis of the direct- and quadrature-axis formulation for the analysis of salient-pole machines in which all machine voltages and currents can be resolved into their *direct-* and *quadrature-axis components.*

----

[7] Alternatively, although less common, some authors choose to define the direct-axis as leading the quadrature-axis by 90°.

In a non-salient, cylindrical-rotor machine, a sinusoidally distributed mmf wave will produce a sinusoidal space-harmonic air-gap flux distribution. Such is not the case in a salient-pole machine in which the same sinusoidally distributed mmf wave will produce space-harmonic components of the air-gap flux in addition to the fundamental component. Fortunately, experience has shown that in many cases these space-harmonic flux components can be ignored and salient-pole machines are typically analyzed simply based upon the fundamental space-harmonic components of the air-gap flux and a recognition that the amplitudes of these flux components are determined both by the magnitude of their associated mmfs and the orientation of the mmfs with respect to the rotor direct axis. In the discussion which follows, a *direct-axis quantity* is one whose magnetic effect is aligned with the axes of the field poles; direct-axis mmfs produce flux along these axes. A *quadrature-axis quantity* is one whose magnetic effect is centered on the interpolar space.

Focusing our attention on the space-fundamental components of the air-gap flux and mmf, the effects of salient poles can be taken into account by resolving the armature current $\hat{I}_a$ into two components, one along the direct axis and the other along the quadrature axis as shown in the phasor diagram of Fig. 5.25. Thus

$$\hat{I}_a = \hat{I}_d + \hat{I}_q \tag{5.55}$$

Using generator notation for the armature current, with the armature current reference direction defined as being out of the armature terminals, positive armature current produces demagnetizing flux. Hence the positive direct-axis component $\hat{I}_d$ of the armature current shown in Fig. 5.25 produces a negative component of the space-fundamental armature flux $\hat{\Phi}_{ad}$ along the negative direct axis .

The quadrature-axis component of the armature current $\hat{I}_q$, in phase with the generated voltage, produces a component of the space-fundamental armature-reaction

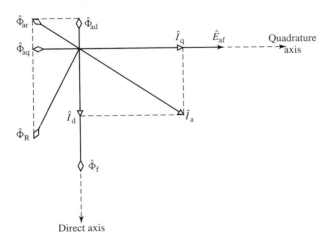

Figure 5.25 Phasor diagram of a salient-pole synchronous generator.

flux $\hat{\Phi}_{aq}$. The net space-fundamental armature-reaction flux $\hat{\Phi}_{ar}$ produced by the armature current is the phasor sum of the direct- and quadrature-axis components $\hat{\Phi}_{ad}$ and $\hat{\Phi}_{aq}$ as shown in the figure. The resultant flux $\hat{\Phi}_{R}$, which is the net air-gap component of the flux which links the armature-winding, is the sum of $\hat{\Phi}_{ar}$ and the field flux $\hat{\Phi}_{f}$.

5.6.2 Phasor Diagrams for Salient-Pole Machines

The inductive effects of the direct- and quadrature-axis armature flux waves can be accounted for by *direct-* and *quadrature-axis magnetizing reactances,* $X_{\varphi d}$ and $X_{\varphi q}$ respectively, similar to the magnetizing reactance X_{φ} of cylindrical-rotor theory. These reactances account for the inductive effects of the space-fundamental air-gap fluxes created by the armature currents along the direct and quadrature axes, $\hat{\Phi}_{ad}$ and $\hat{\Phi}_{aq}$ respectively. Because of the longer air gap between the poles and the correspondingly larger reluctance, the space-fundamental armature flux when the armature mmf is aligned with the quadrature axis is less than the space fundamental armature flux which would be created by the same armature current if the armature mmf wave were aligned with the direct axis. Hence, the quadrature-axis magnetizing reactance is less than that of the direct axis.

With each of the component currents $\hat{I}_{d}$ and $\hat{I}_{q}$ there is associated a component synchronous-reactance voltage drop, $j\hat{I}_{d}X_{d}$ and $j\hat{I}_{q}X_{q}$ respectively. The reactances X_{d} and X_{q} are, respectively, the *direct-* and *quadrature-axis synchronous reactances* and are equal to the sum of the direct- and quadrature-magnetizing reactances and the armature-winding leakage reactance. The direct- and quadrature-axis synchronous reactances are then given by

$$X_{d} = X_{\varphi d} + X_{al} \tag{5.56}$$

$$X_{q} = X_{\varphi q} + X_{al} \tag{5.57}$$

where X_{al} is the armature leakage reactance, assumed to be the same for direct- and quadrature-axis currents. Compare Eqs. 5.56 and 5.57 with Eq. 5.26 for the non salient-pole case. As we have discussed, the quadrature-axis synchronous reactance X_{q} is less than that of the direct axis X_{d} because of the greater reluctance of the longer air gap in the quadrature axis. Note that a small salient-pole effect is present even in cylindrical-rotor turbo-alternators because of the effect of the slots for the field winding on the rotor quadrature-axis.

As shown in the generator phasor diagram of Fig. 5.26, the generated voltage $\hat{E}_{af}$ equals the phasor sum of the terminal voltage $\hat{V}_{a}$ plus the armature-resistance drop $\hat{I}_{a}R_{a}$ and the component synchronous-reactance drops $j\hat{I}_{d}X_{d} + j\hat{I}_{q}X_{q}$.

$$\hat{E}_{af} = \hat{V}_{a} + R_{a}\hat{I}_{a} + jX_{d}\hat{I}_{d} + jX_{q}\hat{I}_{q} \tag{5.58}$$

From this phasor diagram we also see that, given the power-factor angle ϕ and the power angle δ, the magnitude of the component currents can be found as

$$I_{d} = I_{a}\sin(\delta - \phi) \tag{5.59}$$

$$I_{q} = I_{a}\cos(\delta - \phi) \tag{5.60}$$

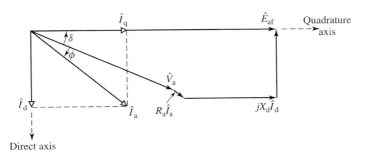

Figure 5.26 Phasor diagram for a synchronous generator showing the relationship between the voltages and the currents.

Note that it might appear from Fig. 5.26 that the appropriate angle is $\delta + \phi$. However, this is not correct because the phasor diagram of Fig. 5.26 is drawn for the case of a lagging power factor and hence the angle ϕ as drawn has a negative value.

Just as for the synchronous reactance X_s of a cylindrical-rotor machine, the reactances X_d and X_q are not constant with flux density but rather saturate as the machine flux density increases. It is common to find both unsaturated and saturated values specified for each of these parameters.[8] The saturated values apply to typical machine operating conditions for which the terminal voltage is near its rated value. For our purposes in this chapter and elsewhere in this book, we will not focus attention on this issue and, unless specifically stated, the reader may assume that the values of X_d and X_q given are the saturated values.

In drawing a phasor diagram such as that of Fig. 5.26, the armature current must be resolved into its direct- and quadrature-axis components. This resolution assumes that the phase angle $\delta - \phi$ of the armature current with respect to the generated voltage is known. Typically, however, although the power-factor angle ϕ at the machine terminals is known, the angle δ between the terminal voltage and the generated voltage is not known. It is thus necessary to locate the quadrature axis and to compute δ.

A portion of the phasor diagram of Fig. 5.26 is repeated in Fig. 5.27. Note that in this case, instead of adding the phasors $j\hat{I}_d X_d$ and $j\hat{I}_q X_q$ to the tip of the phasor $\hat{I}_a R_a$, the figure shows the addition of the phasors $j\hat{I}_d X_q$ and $j\hat{I}_q X_q$. Although the phasor $j\hat{I}_d X_q$ is somewhat shorter than the phasor $j\hat{I}_d X_d$ of Fig. 5.26, both are parallel to the quadrature axis and hence in each case, the addition of the phasor $j\hat{I}_q X_q$ results in a phasor which terminates on the quadrature axis.

The key point of the phasor diagram of Fig. 5.27 is that, from Eq. 5.55, $j(\hat{I}_d + \hat{I}_q)X_q = j\hat{I}_a X_q$ and thus **the quadrature axis can be located by adding the phasor $j\hat{I}_a X_q$ to the phasor $\hat{V}_a + \hat{I}_a R_a$.** Once the quadrature axis (and hence δ) is known, $\hat{I}_d$ and $\hat{I}_q$ can be determined and the generated voltage $\hat{E}_{af}$ can be found from Eq. 5.58.

---

[8] See, for example, IEEE Std. 115-2009, "IEEE Guide: Test Procedures for Synchronous Machines," Institute of Electrical and Electronic Engineers, Inc., *www.ieee.org*.

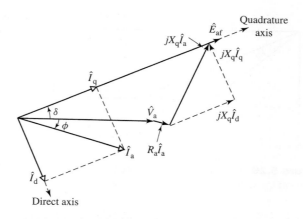

Figure 5.27 Phasor diagram illustrating the technique for locating the quadrature axis.

EXAMPLE 5.15

The reactances X_d and X_q of a salient-pole synchronous generator are 1.00 and 0.60 per unit respectively. The armature resistance may be considered to be negligible. Compute the per-unit generated voltage when the generator delivers its rated kVA at 0.80 lagging power factor and rated terminal voltage.

■ Solution

The phasor diagram is shown in Fig. 5.28. As is commonly done for such problems, the terminal voltage $\hat{V}_a$ will be used as the reference phasor, i.e., $\hat{V}_a = V_a\,e^{j0°} = V_a$. In this case, the machine is operating at rated terminal voltage and thus $V_a = 1.0$ per unit. In addition, because the machine is operating at its rated kVA, the magnitude of the armature current is $I_a = 1.0$ per unit.

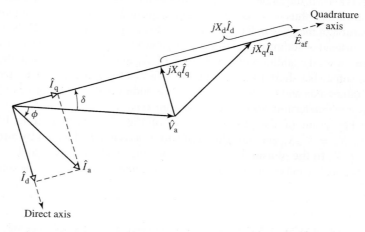

Figure 5.28 Generator phasor diagram for Example 5.15.

For a power factor of 0.8 lagging, the phase angle ϕ of the armature current is

$$\phi = -\cos^{-1}(0.8) = -36.9°$$

and thus

$$\hat{I}_a = I_a\, e^{j\phi} = 1.0\, e^{-j36.9°}$$

The quadrature axis is located by the phasor

$$\hat{E}' = \hat{V}_a + jX_q\hat{I}_a = 1.0 + j0.60 \times 1.0\, e^{-j36.9°} = 1.44\, e^{j19.4°}$$

Thus, $\delta = 19.4°$, and the phase angle between $\hat{E}_{af}$ and $\hat{I}_a$ is $\delta - \phi = 19.4° - (-36.9°) = 56.3°$.

The armature current can now be resolved into its direct- and quadrature-axis components. From Eqs. 5.59 and Eqs. 5.60

$$I_d = I_a \sin(\delta - \phi) = 1.00 \sin(56.3°) = 0.832$$

and

$$I_q = I_a \cos(\delta - \phi) = 1.00 \cos(56.3°) = 0.555$$

and thus, as phasors,

$$\hat{I}_d = 0.832\, e^{j(19.4° - 90°)} = 0.832\, e^{-j70.6°}$$

and

$$\hat{I}_q = 0.555\, e^{j19.4°}$$

We can now find $\hat{E}_{af}$ from Eq. 5.58

$$\hat{E}_{af} = \hat{V}_a + jX_d\hat{I}_d + jX_q\hat{I}_q$$

$$= 1.0 + j1.0 \times 0.832\, e^{-j70.6°} + j0.6 \times 0.555\, e^{j19.4°}$$

$$= 1.78\, e^{j19.4°}$$

and we see that $E_{af} = 1.78$ per unit. Note that, as expected, $\angle \hat{E}_{af} = 19.4° = \delta$, thus confirming that $\hat{E}_{af}$ lies along the quadrature axis.

Practice Problem 5.10

Repeat Example 5.15 for a power factors of (a) 0.95 leading and (b) 0.95 lagging.

Solution

a. $\hat{E}_{af} = 1.11\, e^{j35.1°}$ per unit
b. $\hat{E}_{af} = 1.59\, e^{j25.6°}$ per unit

EXAMPLE 5.16

In the simplified theory of Section 5.2, the synchronous machine is assumed to be representable by a single reactance, the synchronous reactance X_s of Eq. 5.26. The question naturally arises: How serious an approximation is involved if a salient-pole machine is treated in this simple fashion? Suppose that a salient-pole machine were treated by cylindrical-rotor theory as if it had a single synchronous reactance equal to its direct-axis value X_d? To investigate this question, we will repeat Example 5.15 under this assumption.

■ **Solution**

In this case, under the assumption that

$$X_q = X_d = X_s = 1.0 \text{ per unit}$$

the generated voltage can be found simply as

$$\hat{E}_{af} = V_a + jX_s \hat{I}_a = 1.0 + j1.0 \times 1.0 \, e^{-j36.9°}$$

$$= 1.79 \, e^{j26.6°} \quad \text{per unit}$$

Comparing this result with that of Example 5.15 (in which we found that $\hat{E}_{af} = 1.78e^{j19.4°}$), we see that the magnitude of the predicted generated voltage is relatively close to the correct value. As a result, we see that the calculation of the field current required for this operating condition will be relatively accurate under the simplifying assumption that the effects of saliency can be neglected.

However, the calculation of the power angle δ (19.4° versus a value of 26.6° if saliency is neglected) shows a considerably larger error. In general, such errors in the calculation of generator steady-state power angles may be of significance when studying the transient behavior of a system including a number of synchronous machines. Thus, although saliency can perhaps be ignored when doing "back-of-the-envelope" system calculations, it is rarely ignored in large-scale, computer-based system studies.

5.7 POWER-ANGLE CHARACTERISTICS OF SALIENT-POLE MACHINES

For the purposes of this section, we will consider a synchronous machine acting as a generator and will neglect the armature resistance R_a because it is usually small. With R_a neglected, Eq. 5.58 can be re-written in terms of the direct- and quadrature-axis voltage and current components as

$$\hat{E}_{af} = (\hat{V}_d + \hat{V}_q) + jX_d \hat{I}_d + jX_q \hat{I}_q \tag{5.61}$$

Recognizing that the phasors $\hat{E}_{af}$ and $jX_d I_d$ lies along the quadrature axis and $jX_q I_q$ lies along the negative direct axis, we can re-write Eq. 5.61 in terms of the magnitudes of its direct- and quadrature-axis components as

Direct axis:

$$0 = V_d - X_q I_q \tag{5.62}$$

Quadrature axis:

$$E_{af} = V_q + X_d I_d \tag{5.63}$$

These relationships are illustrated in the phasor diagram of Fig. 5.29. Note that Eqs. 5.61 through 5.63 are based upon the generator reference for current. For an

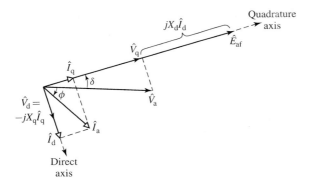

Figure 5.29 Phasor diagram illustrating the direct-
and quadrature-axis components of Eq. 5.61.

analysis based upon the motor reference direction, the sign of each term involving current must be reversed, i.e. replace $\hat{I}_d$ by $-\hat{I}_d$ and $\hat{I}_q$ by $-\hat{I}_q$.

The generator output power (per-phase or in per unit) can be calculated as

$$P = \mathrm{Re}[\hat{V}_a \hat{I}_a^*] \tag{5.64}$$

From the phasor diagram of Fig. 5.29, $\hat{V}_a$ and $\hat{I}_a$ can be written in terms of their axis-component magnitudes and the power-angle δ as

$$\hat{V}_a = \hat{V}_d + \hat{V}_q = -j V_d\, e^{j\delta} + V_q\, e^{j\delta} \tag{5.65}$$

$$\hat{I}_a = \hat{I}_d + \hat{I}_q = -j I_d\, e^{j\delta} + I_q\, e^{j\delta} \tag{5.66}$$

Substitution into Eq. 5.64 then gives

$$\begin{aligned} P &= \mathrm{Re}[(-j V_d\, e^{j\delta} + V_q\, e^{j\delta})(j I_d\, e^{-j\delta} + I_q\, e^{-j\delta})] \\ &= V_d I_d + V_q I_q \end{aligned} \tag{5.67}$$

From the phasor diagram of Fig. 5.29, we see that

$$V_d = V_a \sin\delta \tag{5.68}$$

$$V_q = V_a \cos\delta \tag{5.69}$$

and from Eqs. 5.62 and 5.63

$$I_d = \frac{E_{af} - V_q}{X_d} \tag{5.70}$$

$$I_q = \frac{V_d}{X_q} \tag{5.71}$$

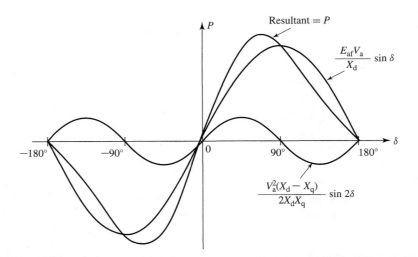

Figure 5.30   Power-angle characteristic of a salient-pole synchronous machine showing the fundamental component due to field excitation and the second-harmonic component due to reluctance torque.

Substitution of Eqs. 5.68 to 5.71 in Eq. 5.67 with appropriate trigonometric manipulation then gives the desired result

$$P = \frac{E_{af} V_a}{X_d} \sin \delta + \frac{V_a^2 (X_d - X_q)}{2 X_d X_q} \sin 2\delta \tag{5.72}$$

Equation 5.72 is directly analogous to Eq. 5.46 which applies to the case of a non-salient machine. It gives the power per phase when E_{af} and V_{eq} are expressed as line-neutral voltages and the reactances are in Ω/phase and the result must be multiplied by 3 to get the total three-phase power (analogous to Eq. 5.47). Alternatively, it gives the per-unit power if all the quantities are expressed in per unit and the total power when E_{af} and V_{eq} are expressed as line-line voltages.

The general form of this power-angle characteristic is shown in Fig. 5.30. The first term is the same as the expression obtained for a cylindrical-rotor machine (Eq. 5.46). The second term includes the effect of salient poles. It represents the fact that the air-gap flux wave creates torque, tending to align the field poles in the position of minimum reluctance. This term is the power corresponding to the *reluctance torque* and is of the same general nature as the reluctance torque discussed in Section 3.5. Note that the reluctance torque is independent of field excitation. Also note that, if $X_d = X_q$ as in a uniform-air-gap machine, there is no preferential direction of magnetization, the reluctance torque is zero, and Eq. 5.72 reduces to the power-angle equation for a cylindrical-rotor machine (Eq. 5.46).

Notice that the characteristic for negative values of δ is the same except for a reversal in the sign of P. That is, the generator and motor regions are identical if the effects of resistance (not included in the derivation of Eq. 5.72) are negligible. For

Figure 5.31 Single-line diagram of a salient-pole synchronous machine (SM) connected to an infinite bus through a series impedance.

generator action $\hat{E}_{af}$ leads $\hat{V}_a$ and δ and P are positive; for motor action $\hat{E}_{af}$ lags $\hat{V}_a$ and δ and P are negative. Steady-state operation is stable over the range where the slope of the power-angle characteristic is positive. Because of the reluctance torque, a salient-pole machine is "stiffer" than one with a cylindrical rotor; i.e., for equal voltages and equal values of X_d, a salient-pole machine develops a given torque at a smaller value of δ, and the maximum torque which can be developed is somewhat greater.

For a derivation based upon motor reference currents, the signs of I_d and I_q in Eqs. 5.62 and 5.63 are reversed and equation 5.72 becomes

$$P = -\left(\frac{E_{af}V_a}{X_d} \sin\delta + \frac{V_a^2(X_d - X_q)}{2X_dX_q} \sin 2\delta \right) \tag{5.73}$$

In this case, P is equal to the terminal power into the motor and, as expected, a negative value of δ corresponds to motoring operation gives a positive value of P.

Synchronous generators are commonly connected to an external system which can be represented by an infinite bus of voltage V_{eq} in series with an equivalent impedance of reactance X_{eq} as is shown in Fig. 5.31. The analysis leading to Eq. 5.72 can be directly applied to this configuration simply by replacing X_d with $X_d + X_{eq}$. X_q with $X_q + X_{eq}$ and V_a with V_{eq}.

EXAMPLE 5.17

The 2000-hp, 2300-V synchronous motor of Example 5.8 is assumed to have a synchronous reactance $X_s = 1.95\ \Omega/\text{phase}$. In actual fact, it is a salient-pole machine with reactances $X_d = 1.95\ \Omega/\text{phase}$ and $X_q = 1.40\ \Omega/\text{phase}$. Neglecting all losses, compute the maximum mechanical power in kilowatts which this motor can deliver if it is supplied with electric power directly from an infinite bus (Fig. 5.32a) at rated voltage and frequency and if its field excitation is held constant at that value which would result in unity-power-factor operation at rated load. The shaft load is assumed to be increased gradually so that transient swings are negligible and the steady-state power limit applies. Also, compute the value of δ corresponding to this maximum power operation.

■ **Solution**

To simplify our calculations, we will work this example in per unit. Based upon a rated voltage of 2300 V and rated power of 2000 hp = 1492 kW, the motor base impedance is

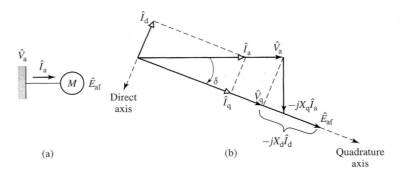

Figure 5.32 (a) Single-line diagram and (b) phasor diagram for motor of Example 5.17.

$2300^2/1492 \times 10^3 = 3.54$ Ω. Thus the per-unit reactances are $X_d = 1.95/3.55 = 0.550$ and $X_q = 1.40/3.54 = 0.395$.

Because we are considering motor operation, we will choose the motor reference for direction for current as shown in Fig. 5.32a. The analysis developed in this and previous sections based upon the generator reference direction for current can be readily applied to an analysis based upon the choice of motor reference direction simply by changing the sign of each term involving the current $\hat{I}_a$ or its direct- or quadrature-axis components.

As a result, as shown in the phasor diagram of Fig. 5.32b, drawn in this case for unity-power-factor operation, the quadrature-axis can be located by adding the phasor $-j X_q \hat{I}_a$ to the terminal voltage $\hat{V}_a$. Thus working in per unit with rated terminal voltage and kVA, $V_a = 1.0$ and $I_a = 1.0$ and for the phasor diagram of Fig. 5.32b we see that

$$\delta = -\tan^{-1}\left(\frac{I_a X_q}{V_a}\right) = -\tan^{-1}(0.394) = -21.6°$$

We can now find I_d and V_q

$$I_d = I_a \sin\delta = -0.367$$

$$V_q = V_a \cos\delta = 0.930$$

and from Eq. 5.63, modified as indicated for motor reference current

$$E_{af} = V_q - I_d X_d = 0.930 - (-0.367) \times 0.550 = 1.132$$

From Eq. 5.73 the power-angle characteristic for this motor is

$$P = -\left(\frac{E_{af} V_a}{X_d}\sin\delta + V_a^2 \frac{X_d - X_q}{2 X_d X_q}\sin(2\delta)\right)$$

$$= -2.058\sin\delta - 0.357\sin(2\delta)$$

The maximum motor input power occurs when $dP/d\delta = 0$

$$\frac{dP}{d\delta} = -2.058\cos\delta - 0.714\cos 2\delta$$

Setting this equal to zero and using the trigonometric identity

$$\cos 2\alpha = 2\cos^2 \alpha - 1$$

permit us to solve for the angle δ at which the maximum power occurs:

$$\delta = -73.2°$$

Therefore the maximum power output is

$$P_{max} = 2.17 \text{ per unit} = 3240\text{kW} = 4340 \text{ hp}$$

Practice Problem 5.11

A 325-MVA, 26-kV, 60-Hz, three-phase, salient-pole synchronous generator is observed to be operating at a power output of 250-MW and a lagging power factor of 0.89 at a terminal voltage of 26 kV. The generator synchronous reactances are $X_d = 1.95$ and $X_q = 1.18$, both in per unit. The generator achieves rated-open-circuit voltage at a field current AFNL = 342 A.

Calculate (a) the angle δ between the generator terminal voltage and the generated voltage, (b) the magnitude of the generated voltage E_{af} in per unit, and (c) the required field current in amperes.

Solution

    a. $31.8°$
    b. $E_{af} = 2.29$ per unit
    c. $I_f = 783$ A

EXAMPLE 5.18

Write a MATLAB script to plot the per-unit power-angle characteristics of the synchronous machine of Example 5.17 for $V_a = 1.0$ per unit and $E_{af} = 1.5$ per unit over the range $-90° \leq \delta \leq 90°$. Assume the generator reference direction such that positive power corresponds to electrical power out of the machine terminals. Also plot the power-angle characteristic neglecting the effects of saliency, i.e. assuming $X_q = X_d = 1.95 \ \Omega$/phase.

■ **Solution**
The power-angle characteristics are plotted in Fig. 5.33. Here is the MATLAB script:

```
clc
clear

%System parameters
Vbase = 2300;
Pbase = 2000*746;
Zbase = Vbase^2/Pbase;

%Calculate per-unit reactances
Xd = 1.95/Zbase;
Xq = 1.40/Zbase;
```

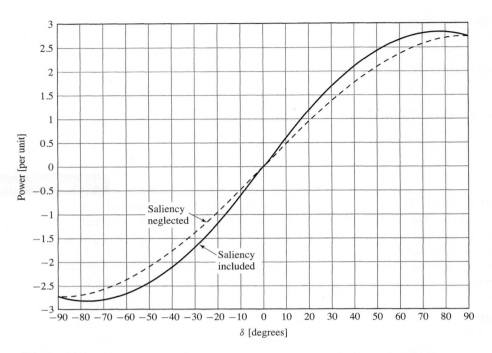

Figure 5.33 MATLAB plot of per-unit power vs. power angle for Example 5.18.

```
% Set Va and Eaf
Va = 1.0;
Eaf = 1.5;

% Range of delta in degrees
delta = -90:90;

% Power with saliency
Psalient = (Eaf*Va/Xd)*sind(delta) + (Va^2/2)*(1/Xq-1/Xd)*sind(2*delta);

% Power neglecting saliency
Pnonsalient = (Eaf*Va/Xd)*sind(delta);

%Plot the results
hold off
plot(delta,Psalient,'b','LineWidth',2)
hold on
plot(delta,Pnonsalient,'--r','LineWidth',2)
hold off
xlabel('\delta [degrees]')
ylabel('Power [per unit]')
```

5.8 PERMANENT-MAGNET AC MACHINES

Permanent-magnet ac machines are polyphase synchronous machines with permanent-magnet rotors. Thus they are similar to the synchronous machines discussed up to this point in this chapter with the exception that field windings are replaced by permanent magnets as a source of rotor excitation.

Figure 5.34 is a schematic diagram of a three-phase permanent-magnet ac machine. Comparison of this figure with Fig. 5.2 emphasizes the similarities between a permanent-magnet ac machine and a conventional wound-rotor synchronous machine. In fact, a permanent-magnet ac machine can be analyzed using the techniques of this chapter simply by assuming that the machine is excited by a field current of constant value, making sure to calculate the various machine inductances based on the effective permeability of the permanent-magnet rotor.

Small permanent-magnet motors are found in many applications, especially in the electronics industry, e.g., disk drives and fans, and in the automotive industry where they are used in fuel pumps, wipers, and power windows, doors and seats, etc. A growing application of larger permanent-magnet machines is in hybrid-electric vehicles and in even larger sizes in generators for large wind turbines. Although space- and time-harmonic fluxes produced by the stator may induce losses in the rotor structure of permanent-magnet machines, these rotors are relatively loss free because the magnets produce rotor flux without dissipation. As a result, with the increased emphasis on energy efficiency, permanent-magnet machines will be found in an increasing number of applications of continually increasing ratings.

The advantages of permanent magnets do not however come without a price. In addition to the actual cost of the permanent-magnetic materials themselves, there are technical challenges which must be taken into account, both at the design and application stage:

■ As discussed in Section 1.6, the characteristics of permanent-magnets are temperature dependent. The residual flux-density of rare-earth permanent

Figure 5.34 Schematic diagram of a three-phase permanent-magnet ac machine. The arrow indicates the direction of rotor magnetization.

magnets such as neodymium-iron-boron decreases as the magnet temperature increases. Since the machine will heat up under operating conditions, it is necessary to account for the corresponding reduction in generated voltage and torque-production.

■ Unlike a wound-rotor synchronous machine, the rotor excitation in a permanent-magnet machine is fixed. This poses challenges both with respect to control as well as for protection. For example:

Permanent-magnet motors are often designed such that the generated voltage is equal to rated terminal voltage at a speed (typically referred to as the motor's "base speed") significantly less than their maximum operating speed. Under these conditions, the drive supplying the motor must be capable of supplying the current required to limit the terminal voltage to its rated value.

In addition, problems can arise should the drive trip at high speed; although saturation will somewhat limit the motor terminal voltage, it may still be high enough to damage insulation. Similarly, problems can arise should a fault occurs, either externally to the motor or within the motor windings, since there is no way to to de-energize the rotor excitation. Unless there is a circuit-breaker or a fuse which can isolate the fault, fault current will continue to flow until the motor comes to a stop.

Because they are synchronous machines, permanent-magnet ac motors must be operated from variable-frequency motor drives. Figure 5.35 shows a cutaway view of a typical surface-permanent-magnet ac motor. This figure also shows a speed

Figure 5.35   Cutaway view of a surface-permanent-magnet ac motor. Also shown is the shaft speed and position sensor used to control the motor.

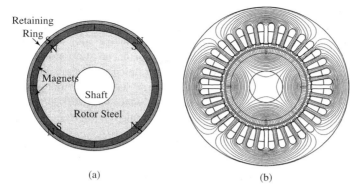

Retaining Ring

Magnets

Shaft

Rotor Steel

(a)

(b)

Figure 5.36 (a) Cross section of the rotor of a typical surface-permanent-magnet ac machine. (b) Open-circuit flux distribution.

and position sensor mounted on the rotor shaft. This sensor is used for control of the motor, as is discussed in Section 10.2.2. A number of techniques may be used for shaft-position sensing, including Hall-effect devices, light-emitting diodes and phototransistors in combination with a pulsed wheel, and inductance pickups.

The great majority of radial-air-gap permanent-magnet synchronous motors and generators tend to fall into two general classes; surface- and interior-permanent-magnet. Figure 5.36(a) shows a cross section of the rotor of a typical *surface-permanent-magnet* ac machine. These machines are characterized by a non-salient rotor of uniform cross section with magnets producing radial magnetic flux mounted on the surface of the rotor. As can be seen, Fig. 5.36(a) shows a four-pole rotor with radially-magnetized magnets of alternate polarity mounted on the rotor surface. Figure 5.36(b) shows a two-dimensional finite-element solution for the open-circuit flux distribution produced by this rotor in a typical stator.

In a surface-permanent-magnet machine, a non-magnetic retaining ring is frequently employed to support the magnets on the rotor against the centrifugal forces of rotation. The retaining ring increases the length of the magnetic gap between the rotor and the stator which in-turn reduces somewhat the torque-producing capability of the motor. The design of a retaining ring is thus a compromise; a thicker retaining ring increases the mechanical integrity of the rotor while a thinner ring increases the effectiveness of the magnetic circuit.

EXAMPLE 5.19

A four-pole, three-phase, surface-permanent-magnet motor has a synchronous inductance of 0.50 mH, an armature resistance of 11 mΩ, and a line-line generated voltage of 0.110 V/r/min (3.31 V/Hz). It is designed for nominal 1800 r/min operation but with over-speed capability to 2400 r/min at reduced power output. The motor can be operated up to a maximum terminal voltage of 208 V, line-line and a maximum terminal current of 185 A. For the purposes of this example, the armature resistance will be neglected.

The motor is supplied by a current-source drive which provides variable-frequency, balanced three-phase currents of adjustable magnitude and with a phase angle that can be varied with respect to the timing of a marker pulse obtained from a position sensor installed on the motor shaft. This phase adjustment can be used to align the flux wave produced by the stator currents arbitrarily with respect to the rotor direct axis. In order to insure that the flux density in the motor remains within acceptable limits, the drive has a V/Hz limit whose function is to insure that the motor terminal voltage does not exceed the rated V/Hz of the motor (in this case, the rated V/Hz is equal to 208 V/60 Hz = 3.47 V line-line per Hz).

a. With the drive supplying a terminal current of 185 A, calculate the maximum power and torque which the motor can supply at a speed of 1800 r/min. Calculate the d- and q-axis currents under this operating condition. Verify that under this operating condition, the motor terminal voltage will not exceed 208 V, line-line.

b. If the motor is operated at speed of 2400 r/min, calculate the maximum output power and torque which can be supplied by the motor assuming that the drive control limits the motor terminal voltage to its maximum value of 208 V line-line and its terminal current to 185 A. Also calculate the d- and q-axis components of the armature current under this operating condition.

■ **Solution**

a. At a speed of 1800 r/min, the electrical frequency is found from Eq. 4.2 to be 60 Hz. Using the notation E_{am} for the magnet-produced generated voltage, the corresponding generated voltage is thus

$$E_{am} = (3.31 \text{ V/Hz}) \times (60 \text{ Hz})$$

$$= 198.6 \text{ [V, line-line]} = 114.7 \text{ [V, line-neutral]}$$

and the synchronous reactance is

$$X_s = \omega_e L_s = (2\pi 60)(5.0 \times 10^{-4}) = 0.188 \ \Omega$$

Figure 5.37(a) is the line-neutral equivalent circuit from which we see that, because $\hat{E}_{am}$ is of fixed magnitude, for a fixed armature-current magnitude, the motor power will be maximum when $\hat{I}_a$ and $\hat{E}_{am}$ are in phase (and thus $\hat{I}_a$ lies along the quadrature axis). Note that this is a single-phase equivalent circuit and thus E_{am} is equal to its line-neutral

Figure 5.37 Example 5.19, part (a): (a) Line-neutral equivalent circuit. (b) Phasor diagram.

value of 114.7 V. Thus, the power output is equal to

$$P = 3E_{am}I_a = 3 \times 114.7 \times 185 = 63.6 \text{ kW}$$

and the torque is

$$T = \frac{P}{\omega_m} = 338 \text{ N·m}$$

where

$$\omega_m = \left(\frac{\pi}{30}\right) \times \text{rpm} = 60 \pi$$

Fig. 5.37(b) is the corresponding phasor diagram. Since the phasor $\hat{E}_{am}$ defines the location of the quadrature axis, under this operating condition the q-axis current is

$$I_q = I_a = 185 \text{ A}$$

and the d-axis current is $I_d = 0$. This result illustrates that, for given terminal-current magnitude, the torque in a non-salient permanent-magnet motor is maximized when the drive current is aligned with the rotor quadrature axis.

From the phasor diagram, we see that in this case the motor terminal voltage is

$$V_a = \sqrt{E_{am}^2 + (X_s I_a)^2} = 119.8 \text{ V, line-neutral} = 207.6 \text{ V, line-line}$$

and hence that the drive V/Hz limit will not be activated.

b. From Eq. 4.2, the electrical frequency corresponding to 2400 r/min operation is 80.0 Hz and thus the generated voltage is $E_{am} = 153$ V, line-neutral (265 V, line-line) and the synchronous reactance is $X_s = 0.251$ Ω. A terminal voltage of 208 V, line-line corresponds to a line-neutral voltage of $V_a = 120$ V. Figure 5.38(a) is the line-neutral equivalent circuit and Fig. 5.38(b) is the corresponding phasor diagram.

Because the magnitude of all of the legs of the phasor diagram of Fig. 5.38(b) are known, we can use the law of cosines to solve for the angle δ

$$\delta = -\cos^{-1}\left(\frac{V_a^2 + E_{am}^2 - (X_s I_a)^2}{2 V_a E_{am}}\right) = -14.0°$$

(a)   (b)

Figure 5.38 Example 5.19, part (b): (a) Line-neutral equivalent circuit. (b) Phasor diagram.

where the minus sign is included in recognition of the fact that δ is negative for motor operation. Thus

$$V_d = V_a \sin \delta = -29.0 \text{ V}$$

$$V_q = V_a \cos \delta = 117 \text{ V}$$

We can solve for $\hat{I}_a$ as

$$\hat{I}_a = \frac{V_a - \hat{E}_{am}}{jX_s} = \frac{V_a - E_{am}e^{j\delta}}{jX_s} = 185\, e^{j37.5°}$$

from which we see that $\phi = 37.5°$. Thus

$$I_d = I_a \sin(\phi - \delta) = -145 \text{ V}$$

$$I_q = I_a \cos(\phi - \delta) = 115 \text{ V}$$

From Eq. 5.67, multiplying by three to account for the fact that in this case we are calculating in real units with line-neutral voltages, the motor power output can be calculated as

$$P = 3(V_d I_d + V_q I_q) = 52.9 \text{ kW}$$

and the corresponding torque is

$$T = \frac{P}{\omega_m} = 211 \text{ N·m}$$

where $\omega_m = \text{rpm} \times (\pi/30) = 80\pi$.

At first thought, one might expect that the maximum output power of the motor would be simply determined by its rated current and voltage as $P = 3V_a I_a = 3 \times 120.1 \times 185 = 66.7$ kW. The difficulty in this case is that the magnet flux alone produces a generated voltage which is larger than the desired terminal voltage. As a result, the armature current must serve two functions; it must interact with the magnet flux to produce torque and it must provide an air-gap flux component which reduces the net-air gap flux to the value corresponding to a terminal voltage of 208 V, line-line. Specifically, the q-axis current (115 A) produces torque while the d-axis current (−145 A) reduces the net stator-winding flux as required to maintain the terminal voltage at 208 V. As will be discussed in Section 10.2.2, when a permanent-magnet motor is operated under vector or field-oriented control, this use of d-axis current to control terminal voltage is referred to as *field-weakening* or *flux-weakening*.

Practice Problem 5.12

Repeat part (b) of Example 5.19 assuming the motor is operating at 2200 r/min.

Solution

$P = 62.9$ kW $T = 273$ N·m

$I_d = -109$ A $I_q = 150$ A

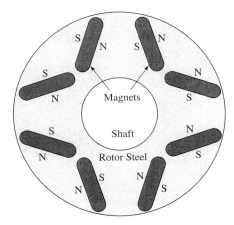

Figure 5.39 Cross section of the rotor of a typical interior-permanent-magnet ac machine.

Figure 5.39 shows a cross section of the rotor of a typical *interior-permanent-magnet* ac machine. In such machines, the magnets are placed in slots in the interior of the rotor. The rotor of Fig. 5.39 is a 4-pole rotor with pairs of magnets of alternating polarity. Figure 5.40(a) shows a two-dimensional finite-element solution for the open-circuit flux distribution produced by this rotor in a typical stator. Because of the presence of these slots, and the fact that the effective permeability of the magnets is close to that of free space, interior-permanent-magnet rotors exhibit saliency. As a result, they are similar to wound-rotor salient-pole synchronous machines and produce both reluctance and magnet torque.

There is, however, one significant difference between wound-rotor salient-pole synchronous machines and their interior-permanent-magnet machine counterparts. In wound-rotor salient-pole synchronous machines, the direct-axis inductance is larger than that of the quadrature axis. As can be seen from Fig. 5.40(a), direct-axis flux in the machine, in this case produced by the magnets alone, passes through the magnets. On the other hand, Fig. 5.40(b) shows that quadrature-axis flux passes around the magnets and remains in the rotor steel. The net result is that the rotor presents a larger reluctance to direct-axis flux than to quadrature-axis flux and hence, the quadrature-axis inductance is larger than that of the direct axis.

A careful examination of Fig. 5.40(a) also shows a concentration of magnet flux around the ends of each of the magnets. This flux concentration is critical to the performance of the rotor. From the rotor cross-section of Fig. 5.39, we see that there is magnetic material which surrounds each magnet. If the magnet material in these "flux bridges" were linear and of a reasonable permeability, they would simply shunt the majority of the magnet flux around the magnets and very little magnet flux, if any, would cross the airgap to interact with the stator.

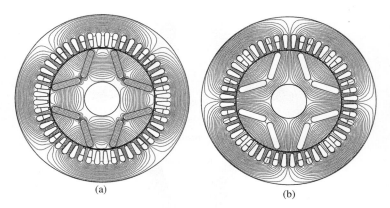

(a)   (b)

Figure 5.40 Flux distributions of the interior-permanent-magnet machine of Fig. 5.39. (a) Open-circuit flux distribution. (b) Quadrature-axis flux distribution.

In reality, the electrical steel is non-linear and saturation of the magnetic material in these flux bridges plays a key role in determining the performance of an interior-permanent-magnet machine. Because they are thin, they can carry only a small amount of flux before they saturate, in-turn forcing the majority of the magnet flux to cross the airgap. Notice however that the bridges also serve a second function of structural support; they hold the magnets and keep the rotor from flying apart. As with the retaining ring in a surface-permanent-magnet machine, the design of the bridges involves a compromise between structural integrity and magnetic performance; thin bridges are desirable to make most effective use of the flux produced by the rotor magnets while thick bridges are desirable to insure that the motor remains intact at its maximum operating speed.

The "V"-magnet arrangement of Fig. 5.39 is one of many which can be found in interior-permanent-magnet machines. For example, magnets may be oriented parallel or perpendicular radial lines, there may be multiple magnets in parallel slots, etc.[9] For each topology, saturating flux bridges or flux barriers (non-magnetic slots in the rotor steel) are required to guide the magnet flux across the air gap. Although the details of the various topologies vary, typically the rotor saliency will result in a quadrature-axis inductance which is larger than that of the direct axis.

Saturation also plays a role in determining the flux paths through the rotor when interior-permanent-magnet machines are loaded. As a result, although interior-permanent-magnet motors are frequently analyzed using the direct- and quadrature-axis theory of Sections 5.6 and 5.7, their direct- and quadrature-axis inductances may vary significantly with load.

---

[9] For an extensive discussion of permanent-magnet ac machines and their various topologies, see J.R. Hendershot & T.J.E. Miller, "Design of Brushless Permanent-Magnet Machines", Motor Design Books LLC, *http://www.motordesignbooks.com*.

EXAMPLE 5.20

In this example, we will consider a four-pole, three-phase, interior-permanent-magnet motor which is similar to that of Example 5.19 and is supplied by the same drive. Specifically, consider a motor with a direct-axis synchronous inductance of 0.50 mH and a quadrature-axis synchronous inductance of 2.30 mH, both of which will be considered to be constant and independent of the motor loading. As with the surface-permanent-magnet motor of Example 5.19, this motor has a line-line generated voltage of 3.31 V/Hz and it can be operated up to a maximum terminal voltage of 208 V, line-line and a maximum terminal current of 185 A.

Find the maximum output power and torque which the motor can achieve at a speed of 1800 r/min with the terminal voltage and current limited of their maximum values. Also find the corresponding direct- and quadrature-axis currents.

Solution

Because this is a salient pole machine, there will be both a magnet and reluctance torque and the power-angle capability of this machine can be expressed in terms of line-neutral voltages from Eq. 5.72 as

$$P = -3\left(\frac{E_{am} V_a}{X_d} \sin\delta + \frac{V_a^2(X_d - X_q)}{2X_d X_q} \sin 2\delta \right)$$

With the terminal voltage fixed at $V_a = 120.1$ V, line-neutral (208 V, line-line) and the generated voltage at 1800 r/min (60 Hz) equal to $E_{am} = 114.7$ V, line-neutral (198.6 V, line-line), one might be tempted to find the maximum power directly from the peak power of the power-angle characteristic. However, in this case, the terminal current cannot exceed the 185 A and hence the maximum power will be significantly less than that corresponding to the peak of the power-angle characteristic.

As a result, the desired solution is most easily found by a MATLAB search. Specifically, consider the phasor diagram of Fig. 5.41. Assuming I_a to be fixed at 185 A, for any given value of the angle γ one can write

$$I_d = I_a \sin\gamma$$

$$I_q = I_a \cos\gamma$$

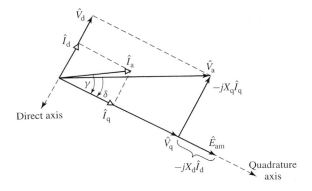

Figure 5.41 Phasor diagram for Example 5.20.

which then enables us to find the d- and q-axis components of the terminal voltage from Eqs. 5.62 and 5.63 (with the appropriate sign change for motor-reference current direction) as

$$V_d = -X_q I_q$$

$$V_q = E_{am} + X_d I_d$$

and thus we can find

$$V_a = \sqrt{V_d^2 + V_q^2}$$

By searching over γ for the value which corresponds to a terminal voltage of 208 V, line-line, the desired solution

$$P = 64.9 \text{ kW} \qquad T = 344 \text{ N·m}$$

$$I_d = -157 \text{ A} \qquad I_q = 98 \text{ A}$$

was obtained using the following MATLAB script:

```
clc
clear

% Machine parameters
VpHz = 3.31; % V [line-line]
Ld = 0.5e-3; % [H]
Lq = 2.3e-3; % [H]
Vrated = 208;
Irated = 185;

rpm = 1800;
fe = rpm/30;
omegae = 2*pi*fe;
omegam = omegae/2;

% Line-neutral Eam
Eam = fe*VpHz/sqrt(3);

% Synchronous reactances
Xd = omegae*Ld;
Xq = omegae*Lq;

%%%%%%%%%%%%%%%%%%%
% Set Ia = Irated and search over gamma
%%%%%%%%%%%%%%%%%%%

Ia = Irated;

N = 10000;
gamma = linspace(-pi/2,0,N);
```

```
% d- and q-axis currents
Iq = Ia*cos(gamma);
Id = Ia*sin(gamma);

% d- and q-axis voltages from Eqs.
% 5-60 and 5-61 (with a change to
% motor notation).

Vq = Eam+Xd.*Id;
Vd = -Xq.*Iq;

% Power
P = 3*(Vd.*Id+Vq.*Iq);

% Magnitude of Va
Va = sqrt(Vd.*Vd+Vq.*Vq);

% Find maximum power subject to not
% exceeding Vrated

PMAX = 0;
for n = 1:N
  if (sqrt(3)*Va(n) <= Vrated) && (P(n) > PMAX)
     PMAX = P(n);
     m = n;
  end
end

TMAX = PMAX/omegam;

ID = Id(m);
IQ = Iq(m);

fprintf('  P = %2.1f [kW]\n',PMAX/1000)
fprintf('  T = %2.1f [N-m]\n',TMAX)
fprintf('  Id = %3.1f [A], Iq = %3.1f [A]\n',ID,IQ)
```

Permanent-magnet ac motors are frequently referred to as *brushless motors* or *brushless dc motors*. This terminology comes about both because of the similarity, when combined with a variable-frequency, variable-voltage drive system, of their speed-torque characteristics to those of dc motors and because of the fact that one can view these motors as inside-out dc motors, with their field winding on the rotor and with their armature electronically commutated by the shaft-position sensor and by switches connected to the armature windings.

5.9   SUMMARY

Under steady-state operating conditions, the operation of a polyphase synchronous machine can be described in terms of the interaction of two magnetic fields as discussed in Section 4.7.2. Polyphase currents on the stator produce a rotating magnetic flux wave while dc currents (or a permanent magnet) on the rotor produce a flux wave which is stationary with respect to the rotor. Constant torque is produced only when the rotor rotates in synchronism with the stator flux wave. Under these conditions, there is a constant angular displacement between the rotor and stator flux waves and the result is a torque which is proportional to the sine of the displacement angle.

We have seen that a simple set of tests can be used to determine the significant parameters of a synchronous machine such as the synchronous reactance. Two such tests are an open-circuit test, in which the machine terminal voltage is measured as a function of field current, and a short-circuit test, in which the armature is short-circuited and the short-circuit armature current is measured as a function of field current. These test methods are a variation of a testing technique applicable not only to synchronous machines but also to any electrical system whose behavior can be approximated by a linear equivalent circuit to which Thevenin's theorem applies. From a Thevenin-theorem viewpoint, an open-circuit test gives the Thevenin-equivalent voltage, and a short-circuit test gives information regarding the Thevenin-equivalent impedance. From the more specific viewpoint of electromechanical machinery, an open-circuit test gives information regarding excitation requirements, core losses, and (for rotating machines) friction and windage losses; a short-circuit test gives information regarding the magnetic reactions of the load current, leakage impedances, and losses associated with the load current such as I^2R and stray load losses. The only real complication arises from the effects of magnetic nonlinearity, effects which can be taken into account approximately by considering the machine to be equivalent to an unsaturated one whose magnetization curve is the straight line Op of Fig. 5.10 and whose synchronous reactance is empirically adjusted for saturation as in Eq. 5.30.

In many cases, synchronous machines are operated in conjunction with an external system which can be represented as a constant-frequency, constant-voltage source known as an *infinite bus*. Under these conditions, the synchronous speed is determined by the frequency of the infinite bus, and the machine output power is proportional to the product of the bus voltage, the machine internal voltage (which is, in turn, proportional to the field excitation), and the sine of the phase angle between them (the power angle), and it is inversely proportional to the net reactance between them.

While the real power at the machine terminals is determined by the shaft power input to the machine (if it is acting as a generator) or the shaft load (if it is a motor), varying the field excitation varies the reactive power. For low values of field current, the machine will absorb reactive power from the system and the power angle will be large. Increasing the field current will reduce the reactive power absorbed by the machine as well as the power angle. At some value of field current, the machine power factor will be unity and any further increase in field current will cause the machine to supply reactive power to the system.

Once brought up to synchronous speed, synchronous motors can be operated quite efficiently when connected to a constant-frequency source. However, as we have seen, a synchronous motor develops torque only at synchronous speed and hence has no starting torque. To make a synchronous motor self-starting, a squirrel-cage winding, called an *amortisseur* or *damper winding*, can be inserted in the rotor pole faces. The rotor then comes up almost to synchronous speed by induction-motor action with the field winding unexcited. If the load and inertia are not too great, the motor will pull into synchronism when the field winding is energized from a dc source.

Increasingly frequently, synchronous motors are operated from polyphase variable-frequency drive systems. In this case they can be easily started and operated quite flexibly. Small permanent-magnet synchronous machines operated under such conditions are frequently referred to as *brushless motors* or *brushless-dc motors*, both because of the similarity of their speed-torque characteristics to those of dc motors and because of the fact that one can view these motors as inside-out dc motors, with the commutation of the stator windings produced electronically by the drive electronics.

5.10 CHAPTER 5 VARIABLES

δ	Electrical phase angle, torque angle [rad]
δ_{RF}	Electrical phase angle between magnetic axis of Φ_R and F_f [rad]
λ	Flux linkage [Wb]
ϕ	Phase angle [rad]
Φ	Flux [Wb]
Φ_R	Resultant air-gap flux per pole [Wb]
θ_m	Rotor position [Wb]
θ_{me}	Rotor position in electrical units [rad]
ω_e	Electrical frequency [rad/sec]
ω_m	Mechanical angular velocity [rad/sec]
ω_s	Synchronous angular velocity [rad/sec]
$\hat{A}$	Stator mmf phasor [A]
AFNL	Amperes Field No Load [A]
AFSC	Amperes Field Short Circuit [A]
e, v	Voltage [V]
E, V	Voltage [V, per unit]
$\hat{E}$	Voltage, complex amplitude [V, per unit]
e_{af}, E_{af}, E_{am}	Generated voltage [V]
$\hat{E}_{af}, \hat{E}_{am}$	Generated voltage, complex amplitude [V]
$\hat{E}_R$	Air-gap voltage, complex amplitude [V, per unit]
$\hat{F}$	Field mmf phasor [A]
F_f	mmf of the dc field winding [A]
poles	Number of poles
i, I	Current [A, per unit]
$\hat{I}$	Current, complex amplitude [A]

$L, \mathcal{L}$	Inductance [H]
L_{al}	Armature leakage inductance [H]
L_{fl}	Field-winding leakage inductance [H]
P	Power [W, per unit]
q	Number of phases
Q	Reactive power [VAR, per unit]
R	Resistance [Ω]
SCR	Short-circuit ratio
t	Time [sec], Temperature [C]
T	Torque [N·m], Temperature [C]
X	Reactance [Ω]
X_φ	Space-fundamental air-gap flux reactance [Ω]
X_{al}	Armature leakage reactance [Ω]
X_s	Synchronous reactance [Ω, per unit]
$X_{s,u}$	Unsaturated synchronous reactance [Ω, per unit]
Z	Impedance [Ω]

Subscripts:

a	Armature
a, b, c	Phase designations
ag	Air gap
arm	Armature
base	Base quantity
d	Direct axis
dc	Direct current
eff	Effective
eq	Equivalent
f	Field, feeder
in	Input
l	Leakage
m	Magnet
max	Maximum
oc	Open circuit
q	Quadrature axis
s	Synchronous, source
sat	Saturated
sc	Short circuit
t	Terminal
u	Unsaturated

5.11 PROBLEMS

5.1 The full-load torque angle of a synchronous motor at rated voltage and
frequency is 33 electrical degrees. Neglect the effects of armature resistance

and leakage reactance. If the field current is held constant, calculate the full-load torque angle following the following changes in operating condition?

   a. Frequency reduced 8 percent, load torque and applied voltage constant.

   b. Frequency reduced 8 percent, load power and applied voltage constant.

   c. Both frequency and applied voltage reduced 8 percent, load torque constant.

   d. Both frequency and applied voltage reduced 8 percent, load power constant.

5.2 The armature phase windings of a two-phase synchronous machine are displaced by 90 electrical degrees in space.

   a. What is the mutual inductance between these two windings?

   b. Repeat the derivation leading to Eq. 5.17 and show that the synchronous inductance is simply equal to the armature phase inductance; that is, $L_s = L_{aa0} + L_{al}$, where L_{aa0} is the component of the armature phase inductance due to space-fundamental air-gap flux and L_{al} is the armature leakage inductance.

5.3 Design calculations show the following parameters for a three-phase, cylindrical-rotor synchronous generator:

$$\text{Phase-a self-inductance } L_{aa} = 5.32 \text{ mH}$$

$$\text{Armature leakage inductance } L_{al} = 0.38 \text{ mH}$$

Calculate the air-gap component of the generator phase inductance L_{aa0}, the phase-phase mutual inductance L_{ab} and the synchronous inductances L_s.

5.4 Measurements show that a three-phase 50 MVA, 50 Hz synchronous generator has a synchronous inductance of 34.4 mH and a phase-phase mutual inductance of -10.1 mH. Calculate the fundamental component of the air-gap component of the phase inductance L_{aa0} and the leakage inductance L_{al}.

5.5 The open-circuit terminal voltage of a Y-connected, three-phase, 60-Hz synchronous generator is found to be 13.8 kV rms line-to-line when the field current is 515 A.

   a. Calculate the stator-to-rotor mutual inductance L_{af}.

   b. Calculate the rms line-line open-circuit terminal voltage for a field current of 345 A and with the generator speed reduced to produce a voltage of frequency 50 Hz.

5.6 The stator winding of the synchronous generator of Problem 5.5 is reconnected in Delta.

   a. With the generator operating at 60 Hz with a field current of 515 A, calculate the line-line and line-neutral open-circuit voltages.

   b. Calculate the stator-to-rotor mutual inductance L_{af}.

5.7 A 575-V, 50-kW, 60-Hz, three-phase synchronous motor has a synchronous reactance of $X_s = 4.65 \ \Omega$ and an armature-to-field mutual inductance, $L_{af} = 105$ mH. The motor is operating at rated speed and terminal voltage and at an output power of 40 kW. Ignoring losses in the motor, calculate the magnitude and phase angle of the line-to-neutral generated voltage $\hat{E}_{af}$ and the field current I_f if the motor is operating at (a) 0.9 power factor lagging, (b) unity power factor, and (c) 0.9 power factor leading.

5.8 Repeat Problem 5.7 assuming the synchronous motor is operating as a generator with an electrical output power of 40 kW.

5.9 The synchronous motor of Problem 5.7 is supplied from a 575-V source through a feeder with a reactive impedance of $X_f = 0.95\ \Omega$. The motor is operating at rated speed and source voltage and at an output power of 40 kW. Ignoring losses in the motor, calculate the magnitude and phase angle of the line-to-neutral generated voltage $\hat{E}_{af}$, the field current I_f and the line-to-line motor terminal voltage V_a if the motor is operating at (a) 0.9 power factor lagging, (b) unity power factor, and (c) 0.9 power factor leading as measured at the 575-V source.

5.10 Repeat Problem 5.9 assuming the synchronous motor is operating as a generator with an electrical output power of 40 kW.

5.11 A 50-Hz, two-pole, 825 kVA, 2300 V, three-phase synchronous machine has a synchronous reactance of 7.47 Ω and achieves rated open-circuit terminal voltage at a field current of 147 A.

    a.   Calculate the armature-to-field mutual inductance.

    b.   The machine is to be operated as a motor supplying a 700 kW load at its rated terminal voltage. Calculate the internal voltage E_{af} and the corresponding field current if the motor is operating at unity power factor.

    c.   For a constant load power of 700 kW, write a MATLAB script to plot the terminal current as a function of field current. For your plot, let the field current vary between a minimum value corresponding to a machine loading of 825 kVA, leading power factor, and a maximum value corresponding to a machine loading of 825 kVA, lagging power factor. What value of field current produces the minimum terminal current?

5.12 The manufacturer's data sheet for a 26-kV, 910-MVA, 60-Hz, three-phase synchronous generator indicates that it has a synchronous reactance $X_s = 1.95$ and a leakage reactance $X_{al} = 0.17$, both in per unit on the generator base. It achieves rated open-circuit voltage at a field current of 1775 A.
Calculate (a) the synchronous inductance in mH, (b) the armature leakage inductance in mH, (c) the armature phase inductance L_{aa} in mH, and (d) the armature-to-field mutual inductance, L_{af}.

5.13 A 350 MVA, 11 kV, 50 Hz, three-phase generator has a saturated synchronous of 1.18 per unit and an unsaturated synchronous reactance of 1.33 per unit. It achieves rated open-circuit at a field current of 427 A. Calculate (a) the saturated and unsaturated synchronous reactances in ohms/phase, (b) the field current required to achieve rated short-circuit current (AFSC).

5.14 The following readings are taken from the results of an open- and a short-circuit test on an 850-MVA, three-phase, Y-connected, 26-kV, two-pole, 60-Hz turbine generator driven at synchronous speed:

Field current, A	1690	3260
Armature current, short-circuit test, kA	9.82	18.9
Line voltage, open-circuit characteristic, kV	26.0	(31.8)
Line voltage, air-gap line, kV	(29.6)	(56.9)

The numbers in parentheses are extrapolations based upon the measured data. Find (a) the short-circuit ratio, (b) the unsaturated value of the synchronous reactance in ohms per phase and per unit, and (c) the saturated synchronous reactance in per unit and in ohms per phase.

5.15 Manufacturer supplied data for the open- and short-circuit characteristics for a 4.5-MW, 4160-V, three-phase, four-pole, 1800-r/min synchronous motor driven at rated speed are summarized in the following table.

Field current, A	203	218
Armature current, short-circuit test, A	625	672
Line voltage, open-circuit characteristic, V	3949	4160
Line voltage, air-gap line, V	4279	4601

Find:

a. the short-circuit ratio,

b. the unsaturated value of the synchronous reactance in ohms per phase and per unit,

c. the saturated synchronous reactance in ohms per phase and in per unit.

d. The armature leakage reactance is estimated to be 0.14 per unit on the motor rating as base. Calculate the air-gap component of the phase-a self inductance in Henries .

5.16 Write a MATLAB script which automates the calculations of Problems 5.14 and 5.15. The following minimum set of data is required:

- AFNL: The field current required to achieve rated open-circuit terminal voltage.
- The corresponding terminal voltage on the air-gap line.
- AFSC: The field current required to achieve rated short-circuit current on the short-circuit characteristic.

Your script should calculate (a) the short-circuit ratio, (b) the unsaturated value of the synchronous reactance in ohms per phase and per unit, and (c) the saturated synchronous reactance in per unit and in ohms per phase.

5.17 The following data are obtained from tests on a 175-MVA, 13.8-kV, three-phase, 60-Hz, 64-pole hydroelectric generator.
Open-circuit characteristic:

I_f, A	150	300	400	500	600	700	800	900	1000
Voltage, kV	2.7	5.5	7.1	8.7	10.1	11.3	12.5	13.7	14.5

Short-circuit test: $I_f = 925$ A, $I_a = 7320$ A

a. Find AFNL, AFNL_{ag} and AFSC. Hint: Use the MATLAB 'spline' function to find AFNL.

b. Find (i) the short-circuit ratio, (ii) the unsaturated value of the synchronous reactance in ohms per phase and per unit and (iii) the saturated synchronous reactance in per unit and in ohms per phase.

5.18 Using MATLAB, plot the field current required to achieve unity-power-factor operation for a motor operating at rated terminal voltage as the motor load varies from zero to full load. Exercise your program on the motor of Problem 5.15.

5.19 The motor of Problem 5.15 has a phase resistance of 42 mΩ and a field-winding resistance at $25°C = 0.218$ Ω, both at 25°C.

Loss data for the motor of Problem 5.15 are as follows:

 Open-circuit core loss at 4160 V $= 47$ kW

 Friction and windage loss $= 23$ kW

a. Compute the input power and efficiency when the motor is operating at rated output power, unity power factor, and rated terminal voltage. Assume the field-winding to be operating at a temperature of 125°C and the stator winding to be operating at 140°C.

b. Repeat the calculation of part (a) assuming the motor to be operating at a load of 3.5 MW and a leading power factor of 0.8.

5.20 A 125-MVA, 11-kV, three-phase, 50-Hz synchronous generator has a synchronous reactance of 1.33 per unit. The generator achieves rated open-circuit voltage at a field current of 325 A. The generator is operating on a system with an equivalent line-line voltage of 11 kV and an equivalent impedance of 0.17 per unit on the generator base. The generator is loaded to a real power of 110 MW.

a. (i) Calculate the generated voltage E_{af} in per unit and in kV (line-line) such that the system is operating at unity power factor at the external-system equivalent voltage. Calculate (ii) the corresponding field current, (iii) the corresponding generator terminal voltage in per unit and in kV (line-line) and (iv) the generator terminal power factor.

b. (i) Calculate the generated voltage E_{af} in per unit and in kV (line-line) such that the generator is operating its rated terminal voltage. Calculate (ii) the corresponding field current, and (iii) the generator terminal current in per unit and kA and (iv) the generator terminal power factor.

5.21 A 1000-kVA, 4160-V, three-phase, 60-Hz synchronous motor has a synchronous reactance of 19.4 Ω and achieves rated open-circuit voltage at a field current of 142 A. It is operated from a stiff power system which maintains the motor terminal voltage at its rated value.

a. The motor is initially operating at a load of 500 kW with the field current adjusted to achieve unity-power factor operation. Calculate the corresponding field current.

b. The load is suddenly increased to 800 kW. Calculate the resultant terminal power factor.

c. Calculate the field current required to return the motor to unity terminal power factor.

5.22 Consider the motor of Problem 5.15.

a. Compute the field current required when the motor is operating at rated voltage, 3.6 MW input power at 0.87 power factor leading. Account for saturation under load by the method described in the paragraph leading up to Eq. 5.30.

b. In addition to the data given in Problem 5.15 additional points on the open-circuit characteristic are given below:

Field current, A	200	225	250	275	300	325	350
Line-line voltage, V	3906	4247	4556	4846	5098	5325	5539

If the circuit breaker supplying the motor of part (a) is tripped, leaving the motor suddenly open-circuited, estimate the value of the motor terminal voltage following the trip (before the motor begins to slow down and before any protection circuitry reduces the field current). Hint: Use MATLAB and a spline fit to the open-circuit characteristic.

5.23 Consider the synchronous generator of Problem 5.12.

a. Find the minimum field current such that the generator, operating at its rated terminal voltage, can successfully supply per-unit output powers of 0.2, 0.4 and 0.6.

b. For each of the per-unit output powers of part (a), write a MATLAB script plot the per-unit armature current as a function of field current as the field current is varied from the minimum value to a maximum value of 5000 A.

5.24 Consider a synchronous generator operating at its rated terminal voltage whose synchronous reactance is 2.0 per unit, whose terminal current cannot exceed its rated value and whose maximum field current is limited to 1.75 times that required to achieve rated terminal voltage under open-circuit conditions.

a. What is the maximum per-unit real power which can be supplied by the machine such that the machine can continue to operate at its rated armature current? What is the corresponding per-unit reactive power and power factor?

b. What is the maximum per-unit reactive power that can be supplied by this machine?

5.25 A 45-MVA, 13.8 kV synchronous machine is operating as a synchronous condenser, as discussed in Appendix D (section D.4.1). It's short-circuit ratio is 1.68 and the field current at rated voltage, no load is 490 A. Assume the generator to be connected directly to an 13.8 kV source.

    a.   What is the saturated synchronous reactance of the generator in per unit and in ohms per phase?

The generator field current is adjusted to 260 A.

    b.   Draw a phasor diagram, indicating the terminal voltage, internal voltage, and armature current.

    c.   Calculate the armature current magnitude (per unit and amperes) and its relative phase angle with respect to the terminal voltage.

    d.   Under these conditions, does the synchronous condenser appear inductive or capacitive to the 11.5 kV system?

    e.   Repeat parts (b) through (d) for a field current of 740 A.

5.26   The synchronous condenser of Problem 5.25 is connected to a 13.8 kV system through a feeder whose series reactance is 0.09 per unit on the machine base. Using MATLAB, plot the line-line voltage (kV) at the synchronous-condenser terminals as the synchronous-condenser field current is varied between 260 A and 740 A.

5.27   A synchronous machine with a synchronous reactance of 1.13 per unit is operating as a generator at a real power loading of 0.75 per unit connected to a system with a series reactance of 0.06 per unit. An increase in its field current is observed to cause a decrease in armature current.

    a.   Before the increase, was the generator supplying or absorbing reactive power from the power system?

    b.   As a result of this increase in excitation, did the generator terminal voltage increase or decrease?

    c.   Repeat parts (a) and (b) if the synchronous machine is operating as a motor.

5.28   Various manufacturers have proposed building superconducting synchronous machines are designed with superconducting fields windings which can support large current densities and create large flux densities. Since in some configurations, the operating magnetic flux densities exceed the saturation flux densities of iron, these machines are typically designed without iron in the magnetic circuit; as a result, these machines exhibit no saturation effects and have low synchronous reactances.

Consider a two-pole, 60-Hz, 13.8-kV, 50-MVA superconducting generator which achieves rated open-circuit armature voltage at a field current of 1520 A. It achieves rated armature current into a three-phase terminal short circuit for a field current of 413 A.

    a.   Calculate the per-unit synchronous reactance.

Consider the situation in which this generator is connected to a 13.8 kV distribution feeder of negligible impedance and operating at an output power of 43 MW at 0.9 pf lagging. Calculate:

    b.   the field current in amperes, the reactive-power output in MVA, and the rotor angle for this operating condition.

    c.   the resultant rotor angle and reactive-power output in MVA if the field current is reduced to 1520 A while the shaft-power supplied by the prime mover to the generator remains constant.

5.29 A four-pole, 60-Hz, 26-kV, 550-MVA synchronous generator with a synchronous reactance of 1.67 per unit is operating on a power system which can be represented by a 26-kV infinite bus in series with a reactive impedance of $j0.43\ \Omega$. The generator is equipped with a voltage regulator that adjusts the field excitation such that the generator terminal voltage remains at 26.3 kV independent of the generator loading.

    a.   The generator output power is adjusted to 375 MW.

        i.   Using the infinite bus as a reference, draw a phasor diagram for this operating condition. Label the infinite bus voltage, the generator terminal voltage and the excitation voltage as well as the voltage drops across the system impedance and the synchronous reactance.

        ii.   Calculate the phase angle δ_t of the generator terminal voltage with respect to the infinite bus.

        iii.   Find the magnitude (in kA) of the generator terminal current.

        iv.   Find the generator terminal power factor.

        v.   Find the per-unit magnitude of the generator excitation voltage E_{af} and its phase angle δ with respect to the infinite bus.

    b.   Repeat part (a), (ii) - (v) for a generator output power of 500 MW.

5.30 The generator of Problem 5.29 achieves rated open-circuit armature voltage at a field current of 1170 A. Thermal limitations limit the maximum field current to 2350 A. The generator is operating on the system of Problem 5.29 with its voltage regulator set to maintain the terminal voltage at 1.01 per unit (26.3 kV).

    a.   The mechanical power supplied to the generator is increased until the generator terminal current or the field current reaches its maximum value, which ever comes first. Using MATLAB:

        i.   Find the maximum generator output power in MW.

        ii.   Plot the generator field current [A] as a function of the generator output power [MW].

        iii.   Plot the generator output reactive power [MVAR] as a function of the generator output power [MW].

    b.   Repeat part (a) if the voltage regulator is set to regulate the terminal voltage to 0.99 per unit (25.7 kV).

5.31 A 450 MVA, 26-kV generator is connected to a 345-kV power system through a 500-MVA, 26-kV:345-kV transformer which can be represented by a series reactance of 95 mΩ when referred to its low-voltage terminals. The generator has a saturated synchronous reactance of 1.73 per unit and a rated-open-circuit-voltage field current of 2140 A.

Under normal operating procedures, the generator is operated under automatic voltage regulation set to maintain its terminal voltage at 26 kV. In this problem you will investigate the possible consequences should the operators forget to switch over to the automatic voltage regulator and instead leave the field excitation constant at 2140 A.

    a.   (i) If the power system is represented simply by a 345-kV infinite (ignoring the effects of any equivalent impedance), can the generator be loaded to full load? If so, what is the power angle δ corresponding to full load? If not, what is the maximum load in MW that can be achieved? (ii) Find the value of field current which would be required to achieve rated load in MW at rated terminal voltage. Calculate the generator reactive power output under this operating condition.

    b.   Repeat part (a) with the power system now represented by a 345 kV infinite bus in series with a reactive impedance of 12.4 Ω.

    c.   Using MATLAB, plot the field-current as a function of generator load in MW for the system of part (b) assuming the generator is brought to full load with the automatic voltage regulator in operation maintaining the generator terminal voltage at its rated value.

5.32   Repeat Example 5.15 assuming the generator is operating at one-half of its rated kVA at a lagging power factor of 0.8 and rated terminal voltage.

5.33   Repeat the calculations of Problem 5.31 for a 450-MVA, 26-kV generator which has a direct-axis saturated inductance of 1.73 per unit and a quadrature-axis saturated inductance of 1.34 per unit but is otherwise identical to the generator of Problem 5.31.

5.34   Consider a salient-pole synchronous generator connected to an external system which can be represented by a 1.0 per-unit voltage source in series with a reactance of 0.12 per unit. The generator reactances are $X_d = 1.38$ per unit and $X_q = 0.92$ per unit. Assuming the generator is operated with a voltage regulator that maintains 1.0 per-unit terminal voltage, using MATLAB, plot the generated voltage E_{af} as a function of per-unit generator output power P over the range $0 \le P \le 1.0$.

5.35   Draw the steady-state, direct- and quadrature-axis phasor diagram for a salient-pole synchronous motor with reactances X_d and X_q and armature resistance R_a. From this phasor diagram, show that the torque angle δ between the generated voltage $\hat{E}_{af}$ (which lies along the quadrature axis) and the terminal voltage $\hat{V}_t$ is given by

$$\tan \delta = \frac{I_a X_q \cos \phi + I_a R_a \sin \phi}{V_t + I_a X_q \sin \phi - I_a R_a \cos \phi}$$

Here ϕ is the phase angle of the armature current $\hat{I}_a$ with respect to $\hat{V}_t$, considered to be negative when $\hat{I}_a$ lags $\hat{V}_t$.

5.36   Repeat Problem 5.35 for synchronous generator operation, in which case the equation for δ becomes

$$\tan \delta = \frac{I_a X_q \cos \phi + I_a R_a \sin \phi}{V_t - I_a X_q \sin \phi + I_a R_a \cos \phi}$$

5.37 What maximum percentage of its rated output power will a salient-pole motor deliver without loss of synchronism when operating at its rated terminal voltage with zero field excitation ($E_{af} = 0$) if $X_d = 1.15$ per unit and $X_q = 0.75$ per unit? Compute the per-unit armature current and reactive power for this operating condition.

5.38 The motor of prob 5.37 is operating at rated terminal voltage, rated power and at unity power factor.

   a. Calculate the per-unit field excitation (where 1.0 per unit excitation corresponds to a field current of AFNL). (b) Repeat the calculation of part (a) assuming the motor is non-salient, i.e. assume that $X_q = X_d = 1.15$ per unit.

5.39 Consider a salient-pole motor with $X_d = 0.93$ per unit and $X_q = 0.77$ per unit.

   a. The motor is operating at its rated terminal voltage and supplying rated shaft output power, unit power factor. Calculate its per-unit field excitation (where 1.0 per unit excitation corresponds to a field current of AFNL).

   b. The load on the motor suddenly drops to 0.5 per unit. Assuming that the field excitation does not change from that of part (a), calculate (i) the per-unit current and (ii) per-unit reactive power at the motor terminals. Hint: A MATLAB search may be simpler than attempting a direct analytical solution.

5.40 A salient-pole synchronous generator with saturated synchronous reactances $X_d = 1.72$ per unit and $X_q = 1.47$ per unit is connected to an infinite bus of through an external impedance $X_\infty = 0.09$ per unit on the generator base. The generator is operating at rated voltage and rated MVA at 0.95 power factor lagging, as measured at the generator terminals.

   a. Draw a phasor diagram, indicating the infinite-bus voltage, the armature current, the generator terminal voltage, the excitation voltage and the rotor angle (measured with respect to the infinite bus).

   b. Calculate the per-unit terminal, infinite bus and generated voltages, and the rotor angle in degrees as measured with respect to the infinite bus.

5.41 A salient-pole synchronous generator with saturated synchronous reactances $X_d = 0.87$ per unit and $X_q = 0.71$ per unit is connected to a rated-voltage infinite bus through an external impedance $X_\infty = 0.075$ per unit.

   a.   i. Assuming the generator to be supplying only reactive power. Find minimum and maximum per-unit field excitation (where 1.0 per unit is the field current required to achieve rated open-circuit voltage) such that the generator does not exceed its rated terminal current.

       ii. Using MATLAB, plot the armature current as a function of field excitation as the per-unit field excitation is varied between the limits determined in part (i).

   b. Now assuming the generator to be supplying 0.40 per unit rated real power, on the same axes add a plot of the per-unit armature current as a function of field excitation as the field current is varied in the range for which the armature current is less than 1.0 per unit.

c. Repeat part (b) for generator output powers of 0.6 and 0.8 per unit. The final result will be a plot of V-curves for this generator in this configuration.

5.42 A 150-MVA, 13.8-kV synchronous condenser is connected to a 138 kV power system through a 150-MVA 13.8 kV:138 kV transformer. The synchronous condenser generates rated open-circuit voltage at a field current of 2480 A and has a direct-axis synchronous inductance of 1.31 per unit and a quadrature-axis synchronous inductance of 0.98 per unit. The transformer can be represented by an 0.065 per-unit series reactance. For the purposes of this problem, you may represent the external system as a fixed 138 kV voltage source.

a. The synchronous condenser terminal voltage is observed to be 13.95 kV. Calculate its terminal current in kA, reactive power output in VVAR and field current in A.

b. The synchronous condenser is observed to be absorbing 85 MVAR of reactive power. Calculate its terminal voltage in kV, terminal current in kA and field current in A.

5.43 A three-phase, four-pole permanent-magnet ac motor is rated at 208 V line-line and an output 10 kW when operated at a speed of 2000 r/min. The motor is to be operated from a variable-speed drive at speeds up to 2500 r/min. The motor has a synchronous inductance of 5.6 mH and produces an open-circuit voltage of 185 V line-line at a speed of 2000 r/min.

For the purposes of this problem, you may consider the motor operating flux density to be proportional to the ratio of the motor terminal voltage divided by the operating electrical frequency and you may neglect any losses within the motor. The motor drive control algorithm insures that:

1. The motor operating flux density does not exceed the value corresponding to its rated voltage at 2000 r/min.

2. The motor terminal voltage does not exceed 208 V.

3. The motor terminal current does not exceed its rated value.

a. Calculate the motor electrical frequency at a speed of 2000 r/min.

b. Calculate the motor rated terminal current and power factor when the motor is operating at 2000 r/min and at its rated terminal voltage and output power.

c. Plot the maximum motor voltage as a function of speed over the range 0 to 2500 r/min.

d. Calculate the maximum motor output power when operated at a speed of 1500 r/min.

e. Calculate the maximum motor output power when operated at a speed of 2500 r/min.

Hint: Parts (d) and (e) may be most easily solved using MATLAB to search for the loading corresponding to rated terminal voltage.

5.44 A 7.5-kW, three-phase, permanent-magnet synchronous generator produces an open-circuit voltage of 208 V line-to-line, 60-Hz, when driven at a speed of 1800 r/min. When operating at rated speed and supplying a three-phase Y-connected resistive load, its terminal voltage is observed to be 189 V line-to-line for a power output of 6.8 kW.

a. Calculate the generator phase current under this operating condition.

b. Assuming the generator armature resistance to be negligible, calculate the generator 60-Hz synchronous reactance.

c. Calculate the generator terminal voltage which will result if the resistance is lowered such that the motor generator load is increased to 7.5 kW (again purely resistive) while the speed is maintained at 1800 r/min.

5.45 Small single-phase permanent-magnet ac generators are frequently used to generate the power for lights on bicycles. For this application, these generators are typically designed with a significant amount of leakage inductance in their armature winding. A simple model for these generators is an ac voltage source $e_a(t) = \omega K_a \cos \omega t$ in series with the armature leakage inductance L_a and the armature resistance R_a. Here ω is the electrical frequency of the generated voltage which is determined by the speed of the generator as it rubs against the bicycle wheel.

Assuming that the generator is running a light bulb which can be modeled as a resistance R_b, write an expression for the minimum frequency ω_{min} which must be achieved in order to insure that the light operates at constant brightness, independent of the speed of the bicycle.

5.46 An interior-permanent-magnet motor, rated at 25 kW, 460 V, 3600 r/min generates a 3600-r/min open-circuit voltage of 425 V line-line. Because of the magnets in the interior of the motor, oriented by definition along the rotor direct axis, the motor exhibits saliency and can be modeled by a direct-axis synchronous inductance of 2.20 Ω which is smaller than the quadrature-axis synchronous inductance of 3.98 Ω.

The motor is operating at a load of 18 kW at a terminal voltage of 460 V line-line. Calculate the motor terminal current and power factor. Hint: This may be most easily solved using to MATLAB search for the solution rather than by a closed-form solution .

6 CHAPTER

Polyphase Induction Machines

The objective of this chapter is to study the behavior of polyphase induction machines. Our analysis will begin with the development of single-phase equivalent circuits, the general form of which is suggested by the similarity of an induction machine to a transformer. These equivalent circuits can be used to study the electromechanical characteristics of an induction machine as well as the loading presented by the machine on its supply source, whether it is a fixed-frequency source such as a power system or a variable-frequency, variable-voltage motor drive.

6.1 INTRODUCTION TO POLYPHASE INDUCTION MACHINES

As indicated in Section 4.2.1, an *induction motor* is one in which alternating current is supplied to the stator directly and to the rotor by induction or transformer action from the stator. As in the synchronous machine, the stator winding is of the type discussed in Section 4.5. When excited from a balanced polyphase source, it will produce a magnetic field in the air gap rotating at synchronous speed as determined by the number of stator poles and the applied stator frequency f_e (Eq. 4.44).

The rotor of a polyphase induction machine may be one of two types. A *wound rotor* is built with a polyphase winding similar to, and wound with the same number of poles as, the stator. The terminals of the rotor winding are connected to insulated slip rings mounted on the shaft. Carbon brushes bearing on these rings make the rotor terminals available external to the motor. Wound-rotor induction machines are relatively uncommon, being found only in a limited number of specialized applications.

On the other hand, the polyphase induction motor shown in cutaway in Fig. 6.1 has a *squirrel-cage rotor* with a winding consisting of conducting bars embedded in slots in the rotor iron and short-circuited at each end by conducting end rings. The extreme simplicity and ruggedness of the squirrel-cage construction are outstanding advantages of this type of induction motor and make it by far the most commonly

Figure 6.1 Cutaway view of a three-phase squirrel-cage motor. The rotor cutaway shows the squirrel-cage laminations. (*Photo courtesy of Baldor Electric/ABB.*)

used type of motor in sizes ranging from fractional horsepower on up. Figure 6.2a shows the rotor of a small squirrel-cage motor while Fig. 6.2b shows the squirrel cage itself after the rotor laminations have been chemically etched away.

Let us assume that the rotor is turning at the steady speed of n r/min in the same direction as the rotating stator field. Let the synchronous speed of the stator field be n_s r/min as given by Eq. 4.44. The difference between synchronous speed and the

(a)

(b)

Figure 6.2 (a) The rotor of a small squirrel-cage motor. (b) The squirrel-cage structure after the rotor laminations have been chemically etched away.

rotor speed is commonly referred to as the *slip* of the rotor; in this case the rotor slip is $n_s - n$, as measured in r/min. Slip is most commonly defined as a fraction of synchronous speed as

$$s = \frac{n_s - n}{n_s} \tag{6.1}$$

It is this definition of slip which is used in the equations which characterize the performance of induction machines as developed in this chapter. Finally, slip is often expressed in percent, simply equal to 100 percent times the fractional slip of Eq. 6.1; e.g. a motor operating with a slip of $s = 0.025$ would be said to be operating at a slip of 2.5 percent.

The rotor speed in r/min can be expressed in terms of the slip s and the synchronous speed as

$$n = (1 - s)\, n_s \tag{6.2}$$

Similarly, the mechanical angular velocity ω_m can be expressed in terms of the synchronous angular velocity ω_s and the slip as

$$\omega_m = (1 - s)\, \omega_s \tag{6.3}$$

The relative motion of the stator flux and the rotor conductors induces voltages of frequency f_r

$$f_r = s f_e \tag{6.4}$$

referred to as the *slip frequency,* in the rotor. Thus, the electrical behavior of an induction machine is similar to that of a transformer but with the additional feature of frequency transformation produced by the relative motion of the stator and rotor windings. In fact, a wound-rotor induction machine can be used as a frequency changer.

The rotor terminals of an induction motor are short circuited; by construction in the case of a squirrel-cage motor and externally in the case of a wound-rotor motor. Slip-frequency voltages are induced in the rotor windings by the rotating air-gap flux. The rotor currents are then determined by the magnitudes of the induced voltages and the slip-frequency rotor impedance. At starting, the rotor is stationary ($n = 0$), the slip is unity ($s = 1$), and the rotor frequency equals the stator frequency f_e. The field produced by the rotor currents therefore revolves at the same speed as the stator field, and a starting torque results, tending to turn the rotor in the direction of rotation of the stator-inducing field. If this torque is sufficient to overcome the opposition to rotation created by the shaft load, the motor will come up to its operating speed. The operating speed can never equal the synchronous speed however, since the rotor conductors would then be stationary with respect to the stator field; no current would be induced in them, and hence no torque would be produced.

With the rotor revolving in the same direction of rotation as the stator field, the frequency of the rotor currents will be $s f_e$ and they will produce a rotating flux wave which will rotate at $s n_s$ r/min *with respect to the rotor* in the forward direction. But superimposed on this rotation is the mechanical rotation of the rotor at n r/min. Thus, with respect to the stator, the speed of the flux wave produced by the rotor currents is the sum of these two speeds and equals

$$sn_s + n = sn_s + n_s(1 - s) = n_s \qquad (6.5)$$

From Eq. 6.5 we see that the rotor currents produce an air-gap flux wave which rotates at synchronous speed and hence in synchronism with that produced by the stator currents. Because the stator and rotor fields each rotate synchronously, they are stationary with respect to each other and produce a steady torque, thus maintaining rotation of the rotor. Such torque, which exists for any mechanical rotor speed n other than synchronous speed, is called an *asynchronous torque*.

Figure 6.3 shows the form of a typical polyphase squirrel-cage induction motor torque-speed curve. The factors influencing the shape of this curve can be appreciated in terms of the torque equation, Eq. 4.83. Note that the resultant air-gap flux Φ_{sr} in this equation is approximately constant when the stator-applied voltage and frequency are constant. Also, recall that the rotor mmf F_r is proportional to the rotor current I_r. Equation 4.83 can then be expressed in the form

$$T = -K I_r \sin \delta_r \qquad (6.6)$$

where K is a constant and δ_r is the angle by which the rotor mmf wave leads the resultant air-gap mmf wave. The minus sign is included in Eq. 6.6 because the induced rotor current is in the direction to demagnetize the air-gap flux, whereas the rotor current is defined in Chapter 4 as being in the direction to magnetize the air-gap flux.

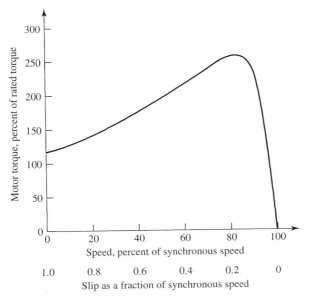

Figure 6.3 Typical induction-motor torque-speed curve for constant-voltage, constant-frequency operation.

Under normal running conditions the slip is small: 2 to 10 percent at full load in most squirrel-cage motors. The rotor frequency ($f_r = sf_e$) therefore is very low: correspondingly on the order of 1 to 6 Hz in 60-Hz motors. For these frequencies, the rotor impedance is largely resistive and hence independent of slip. The rotor-induced voltage, on the other hand, is proportional to slip and leads the resultant air-gap flux by 90°. Since the rotor windings are short-circuited, the rotor current must be equal to the negative of the voltage induced by the air-gap flux divided by the rotor impedance. Thus it is very nearly proportional to the slip, and proportional to and 180° out of phase with the rotor voltage. As a result, the rotor-mmf wave lags the resultant air-gap flux by approximately 90 electrical degrees, and therefore $\sin \delta_r \approx -1$.

Approximate proportionality of rotor current and hence torque with slip is therefore to be expected in the range where the slip is small. As slip increases, the rotor impedance increases because of the increasing contribution of the rotor leakage inductance and the increase of current and torque with slip becomes less than proportional. Also the rotor current lags farther behind the induced voltage, and the magnitude of $\sin \delta_r$ decreases, further decreasing the resultant torque. A more detailed analysis will show that the torque increases with increasing slip up to a maximum value and then decreases, as shown in Fig. 6.3. The maximum torque, or *breakdown torque,* which is typically a factor of two or more larger than the rated motor torque, limits the short-time overload capability of the motor.

We will see that the slip at which the peak torque occurs is proportional to the rotor resistance. For squirrel-cage motors this peak-torque slip is relatively small, much as is shown in Fig. 6.3. Thus, the squirrel-cage motor is substantially a constant-speed motor having a few percent drop in speed from no load to full load. In the case of a wound-rotor motor, the rotor resistance can be increased by inserting external resistance, hence increasing the slip at peak-torque, and thus decreasing the motor speed for a specified value of torque. Since wound-rotor induction machines are larger, more expensive, and require significantly more maintenance than squirrel-cage machines, this method of speed control is rarely used, and induction machines driven from constant-frequency sources tend to be limited to essentially constant-speed applications. In recent years, the use of solid-state, variable-voltage, variable-frequency drive systems makes it possible to readily control the speed of squirrel-cage induction machines and, as a result, they are now widely used in a wide-range of variable-speed applications.

6.2   CURRENTS AND FLUXES IN POLYPHASE INDUCTION MACHINES

For a coil-wound rotor, the flux-mmf situation can be seen with the aid of Fig. 6.4. This sketch shows the development of a simple two-pole, three-phase rotor winding in a two-pole field. It therefore conforms with the restriction that a wound rotor must have the same number of poles as the stator (although the number of phases need not be the same). The rotor flux-density wave is moving to the right at angular velocity ω_s and at slip angular velocity $s\omega_s$ with respect to the rotor winding, which in turn is

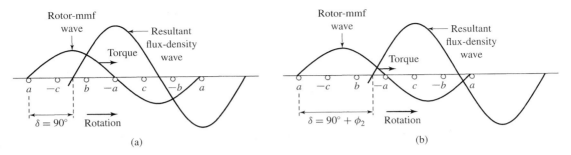

Figure 6.4 Developed rotor winding of an induction motor with its flux-density and mmf waves in their relative positions for (a) zero and (b) nonzero rotor leakage reactance.

rotating to the right at angular velocity $(1 - s)\omega_s$. It is shown in Fig. 6.4 in the position of maximum instantaneous voltage in phase a.

If the rotor leakage reactance, equal to $s\omega_s$ times the rotor leakage inductance, is very small compared with the rotor resistance (which is typically the case at the small slips corresponding to normal operation), the phase-a current will also be a maximum. As shown in Section 4.5, the rotor-mmf wave will then be centered on phase a; it is so shown in Fig. 6.4a. The displacement angle, or torque angle, δ_r, under these conditions is at its optimum value of $-90°$.

If the rotor leakage reactance is appreciable however, the phase-a current lags the induced voltage by the power-factor angle ϕ_2 of the rotor leakage impedance. The phase-a current will not be at maximum until a correspondingly later time. The rotor-mmf wave will then not be centered on phase a until the flux wave has traveled ϕ_2 degrees farther down the gap, as shown in Fig. 6.4b. The angle δ_r is now $-(90° + \phi_2)$. In general, therefore, the torque angle of an induction motor is

$$\delta_r = -(90° + \phi_2) \tag{6.7}$$

It departs from the optimum value of $-90°$ by the power-factor angle of the rotor leakage impedance at slip frequency. The electromechanical rotor torque is directed toward the right in Fig. 6.4, or in the direction of the rotating flux wave.

The comparable picture for a squirrel-cage rotor is given in Fig. 6.5. A 16-bar rotor placed in a two-pole field is shown in developed form. To simplify the drawing, only a relatively small number of rotor bars has been chosen and the number is an integral multiple of the number of poles, a choice normally avoided in practice in order to prevent harmful harmonic effects. In Fig. 6.5a the sinusoidal flux-density wave induces a voltage in each bar which has an instantaneous value indicated by the solid vertical lines.

At a somewhat later instant of time, the bar currents assume the instantaneous values indicated by the solid vertical lines in Fig. 6.5b, the time lag corresponding to the rotor power-factor angle ϕ_2. In this time interval, the flux-density wave has traveled in its direction of rotation with respect to the rotor through a space angle ϕ_2 and is then in the position shown in Fig. 6.5b. The corresponding rotor-mmf wave is shown by the step wave of Fig. 6.5c. The fundamental component is shown by

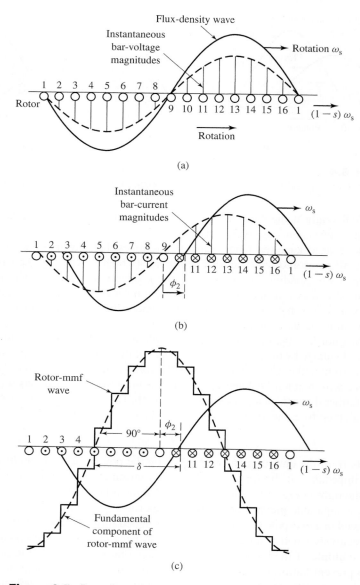

Figure 6.5 Reactions of a squirrel-cage rotor in a two-pole field.

the dashed sinusoid and the flux-density wave by the solid sinusoid. Study of these figures confirms the general principle that the number of rotor poles in a squirrel-cage rotor is determined by the inducing flux wave.

6.3 INDUCTION-MOTOR EQUIVALENT CIRCUIT

The foregoing considerations of flux and mmf waves can readily be translated to a steady-state equivalent circuit for a polyphase induction machine. In this derivation, only machines with symmetric polyphase windings excited by balanced polyphase voltages are considered. As in many other discussions of polyphase devices, it is helpful to think of three-phase machines as being Y-connected, so that currents are always line values and voltages always line-to-neutral values. In this case, we can derive the equivalent circuit for one phase, with the understanding that the voltages and currents in the remaining phases can be found simply by an appropriate phase shift of those of the phase under study ($\pm 120°$ in the case of a three-phase machine).

First, consider conditions in the stator. The synchronously-rotating air-gap flux wave generates balanced polyphase counter emfs in the phases of the stator. The stator terminal voltage differs from the counter emf by the voltage drop in the stator leakage impedance $Z_1 = R_1 + jX_1$. Thus

$$\hat{V}_1 = \hat{E}_2 + \hat{I}_1(R_1 + jX_1) \tag{6.8}$$

where

$\hat{V}_1$ = Stator line-to-neutral terminal voltage

$\hat{E}_2$ = Counter emf (line-to-neutral) generated by the resultant air-gap flux

$\hat{I}_1$ = Stator current

R_1 = Stator effective resistance

X_1 = Stator leakage reactance

The polarity of the voltages and currents are shown in the equivalent circuit of Fig. 6.6.

The resultant air-gap flux is created by the combined mmfs of the stator and rotor currents. Just as in the case of a transformer, the stator current can be resolved into two components: a load component and an exciting (magnetizing) component. The load component $\hat{I}_2$ produces an mmf that corresponds to the mmf of the rotor current. The exciting component $\hat{I}_\varphi$ is the additional stator current required to create the resultant air-gap flux and is a function of the emf $\hat{E}_2$. The exciting current can be resolved

Figure 6.6 Stator equivalent circuit for a polyphase induction motor.

into a core-loss component $\hat{I}_c$ in phase with $\hat{E}_2$ and a magnetizing component $\hat{I}_m$ lagging $\hat{E}_2$ by 90°. In the equivalent circuit, the exciting current can be accounted for by means of a shunt branch, formed by a *core-loss resistance* R_c and a *magnetizing reactance* X_m in parallel, connected across $\hat{E}_2$, as in Fig. 6.6. Both R_c and X_m are usually determined at rated stator frequency and for a value of E_2 close to the expected operating value; they are then assumed to remain constant for the small departures of E_2 associated with normal operation of the motor.

The equivalent circuit representing stator phenomena of Fig. 6.6 is exactly like that used to represent the primary of a transformer. To complete our model, the effects of the rotor must be incorporated. From the point of view of the stator equivalent circuit of Fig. 6.6, the rotor can be represented by an equivalent impedance Z_2

$$Z_2 = \frac{\hat{E}_2}{\hat{I}_2} \tag{6.9}$$

corresponding to the leakage impedance of an equivalent stationary secondary. To complete the equivalent circuit, we must determine Z_2 by representing the stator and rotor voltages and currents in terms of rotor quantities as referred to the stator.

As we saw in Section 2.3, from the point of view of the primary, the secondary winding of a transformer can be replaced by an equivalent secondary winding having the same number of turns as the primary winding. In a transformer where the turns ratio and the secondary parameters are known, this can be done by referring the secondary impedance to the primary by multiplying it by the square of the primary-to-secondary turns ratio. The resultant equivalent circuit is perfectly general from the point of view of primary quantities.

Similarly, in the case of a polyphase induction motor, if the rotor were to be replaced by an equivalent rotor with a polyphase winding with the same number of phases and turns as the stator but producing the same mmf and air-gap flux as the actual rotor, the performance as seen from the stator terminals would be unchanged. This concept, which we will adopt here, is especially useful in modeling squirrel-cage rotors for which the identity of the rotor "phase windings" is in no way obvious.

The rotor of an induction machine is short-circuited, and hence the impedance seen by induced voltage is simply the rotor short-circuit impedance. Consequently the relation between the slip-frequency leakage impedance Z_{2s} of the equivalent rotor and the slip-frequency leakage impedance Z_{rotor} of the actual rotor must be

$$Z_{2s} = \frac{\hat{E}_{2s}}{\hat{I}_{2s}} = N_{eff}^2 \left(\frac{\hat{E}_{rotor}}{\hat{I}_{rotor}} \right) = N_{eff}^2 Z_{rotor} \tag{6.10}$$

where N_{eff} is the effective turns ratio between the stator winding and that of the actual rotor winding. Here the subscript 2s refers to quantities associated with the referred rotor. Thus $\hat{E}_{2s}$ is the voltage induced in the equivalent rotor by the resultant air-gap flux, and $\hat{I}_{2s}$ is the corresponding induced current.

When one is concerned with the actual rotor currents and voltages, the turns ratio N_{eff} must be known in order to convert back from equivalent-rotor quantities to those of the actual rotor. However, for the purposes of studying induction-motor performance as seen from the stator terminals, there is no need for this conversion and a representation in terms of equivalent-rotor quantities is fully adequate. Thus an equivalent circuit based upon equivalent-rotor quantities can be used to represent both coil-wound and squirrel-cage rotors.

Having taken care of the effects of the stator-to-rotor turns ratio, we next must take into account the relative motion between the stator and the rotor with the objective of replacing the actual rotor and its slip-frequency voltages and currents with an equivalent stationary rotor with stator-frequency voltages and currents. Consider first the slip-frequency leakage impedance of the referred rotor.

$$Z_{2s} = \frac{\hat{E}_{2s}}{\hat{I}_{2s}} = R_2 + jsX_2 \qquad (6.11)$$

where

$R_2 =$ Referred rotor resistance

$sX_2 =$ Referred rotor leakage reactance at slip frequency

Note that here X_2 has been defined as the referred rotor leakage reactance at stator frequency f_e. Since the actual rotor frequency is $f_r = sf_e$, X_2 has been converted to the slip-frequency reactance simply by multiplying by the slip s. The slip-frequency equivalent circuit of one phase of the referred rotor is shown in Fig. 6.7. This is the equivalent circuit of the rotor as seen in the slip-frequency rotor reference frame.

We next observe that the resultant air-gap mmf wave is produced by the combined effects of the stator current $\hat{I}_1$ and the equivalent load current $\hat{I}_2$. Similarly, it can be expressed in terms of the stator current and the equivalent rotor current $\hat{I}_{2s}$. These two currents are equal in magnitude since $\hat{I}_{2s}$ is defined as the current in an equivalent rotor with the same number of turns per phase as the stator. Because the resultant air-gap mmf wave is determined by the phasor sum of the stator current and the rotor current of either the actual or equivalent rotor, $\hat{I}_2$ and $\hat{I}_{2s}$ must also be equal in phase (at their respective electrical frequencies) and hence we can write

$$\hat{I}_{2s} = \hat{I}_2 \qquad (6.12)$$

Finally, consider that the resultant flux wave induces both the slip-frequency emf induced in the referred rotor $\hat{E}_{2s}$ and the stator counter emf $\hat{E}_2$. If it were not for the effect of speed, these voltages would be equal in magnitude since the referred rotor

Figure 6.7 Rotor equivalent circuit for a polyphase induction motor at slip frequency.

winding has the same number of turns per phase as the stator winding. However, because the relative speed of the flux wave with respect to the rotor is s times its speed with respect to the stator, the relation between the magnitudes of these emfs is

$$E_{2s} = s E_2 \tag{6.13}$$

We can furthermore argue that since the phase angle between each of these voltages and the resultant flux wave is $90°$, then these two voltages must also be equal in a phasor sense at their respective electrical frequencies. Hence

$$\hat{E}_{2s} = s \hat{E}_2 \tag{6.14}$$

Division of Eq. 6.14 by Eq. 6.12 and use of Eq. 6.11 then gives

$$\frac{\hat{E}_{2s}}{\hat{I}_{2s}} = \frac{s \hat{E}_2}{\hat{I}_2} = Z_{2s} = R_2 + j s X_2 \tag{6.15}$$

Division by the slip s then gives

$$Z_2 = \frac{\hat{E}_2}{\hat{I}_2} = \frac{R_2}{s} + j X_2 \tag{6.16}$$

We have achieved our objective. Z_2 is the impedance of the equivalent stationary rotor which appears across the load terminals of the stator equivalent circuit of Fig. 6.6. The final result is shown in the single-phase equivalent circuit of Fig. 6.8. The combined effect of shaft load and rotor resistance appears as a reflected resistance R_2/s, a function of slip and therefore of the mechanical load. The current in the reflected rotor impedance equals the load component $\hat{I}_2$ of stator current; the voltage across this impedance equals the stator voltage $\hat{E}_2$. Note that when rotor currents and voltages are reflected into the stator, their frequency is also changed to stator frequency. All rotor electrical phenomena, when viewed from the stator, become stator-frequency phenomena, because the stator winding simply sees mmf and flux waves traveling at synchronous speed.

Figure 6.8   Single-phase equivalent circuit for a polyphase induction motor.

6.4 ANALYSIS OF THE EQUIVALENT CIRCUIT

The single-phase equivalent circuit of Fig. 6.8 can be used to determine a wide variety of steady-state performance characteristics of polyphase induction machines.
These include variations of current, speed, and losses as the load-torque requirements
change, as well as the starting torque, and the maximum torque. Note however that, in
practice, the equivalent-circuit parameters may be a function of operating conditions.
Specifically, temperature will affect the values of the resistances and the rotor parameters of a squirrel-cage motor may change with slip as discussed in Section 6.7.2.

The equivalent circuit shows that the total power P_{gap} transferred across the air
gap from the stator is

$$P_{gap} = q\ I_2^2 \left(\frac{R_2}{s} \right) \tag{6.17}$$

where q is the number of stator phases.

The total rotor I^2R loss, P_{rotor}, can be calculated from the I^2R loss in the equivalent rotor as

$$P_{rotor} = q\ I_{2s}^2\ R_2 \tag{6.18}$$

Since $I_{2s} = I_2$, we can write Eq. 6.18 as

$$P_{rotor} = q\ I_2^2\ R_2 \tag{6.19}$$

The electromechanical power P_{mech} developed by the motor can now be determined by subtracting the rotor power dissipation of Eq. 6.19 from the air-gap power
of Eq. 6.17.

$$P_{mech} = P_{gap} - P_{rotor} = q\ I_2^2 \left(\frac{R_2}{s} \right) - q\ I_2^2\ R_2 \tag{6.20}$$

or equivalently

$$P_{mech} = q\ I_2^2\ R_2 \left(\frac{1-s}{s} \right) \tag{6.21}$$

Comparing Eq. 6.17 with Eq. 6.21 gives

$$P_{mech} = (1-s) P_{gap} \tag{6.22}$$

and

$$P_{rotor} = s P_{gap} \tag{6.23}$$

We see then that, of the total power delivered across the air gap to the rotor, the fraction
$1 - s$ is converted to mechanical power and the fraction s is dissipated as I^2R loss in
the rotor conductors. Similarly, the power dissipated in the rotor can be expressed in
terms of the electromechanical power as

$$P_{rotor} = \left(\frac{s}{1-s} \right) P_{mech} \tag{6.24}$$

Figure 6.9 Alternative form of the polyphase induction motor equivalent circuit.

From Eqs. 6.23 and 6.24, it is evident that an induction motor operating at high slip is an inefficient device. The equivalent of Fig. 6.9 emphasizes the relationship between rotor loss and electromechanical power. The rotor power dissipation per stator phase corresponds to the power dissipated in the resistance R_2 while the electromechanical power per stator phase is equal to the power delivered to the resistance $R_2(1-s)/s$.

EXAMPLE 6.1

A three-phase, two-pole, 60-Hz induction motor is observed to be operating at a speed of 3502 r/min with an input power of 15.7 kW and a terminal current of 22.6 A. The stator-winding resistance is 0.20 Ω/phase. Calculate the I^2R power dissipated in rotor.

■ Solution

The power dissipated in the stator winding is given by

$$P_{\text{stator}} = 3I_1^2 R_1 = 3(22.6)^2 \times 0.2 = 306 \text{ W}$$

Hence the air-gap power is

$$P_{\text{gap}} = P_{\text{input}} - P_{\text{stator}} = 15.7 - 0.3 = 15.4 \text{ kW}$$

The synchronous speed of this machine can be found from Eq. 4.44

$$n_s = \left(\frac{120}{\text{poles}}\right) f_e = \left(\frac{120}{2}\right) 60 = 3600 \text{ r/min}$$

and hence from Eq. 6.1, the slip is $s = (3600 - 3502)/3600 = 0.0272$. Thus, from Eq. 6.23,

$$P_{\text{rotor}} = s P_{\text{gap}} = 0.0272 \times 15.4 \text{ kW} = 419 \text{ W}$$

Practice Problem 6.1

Calculate the rotor power dissipation for a three-phase, 460-V, 60-Hz, four-pole motor with an armature resistance of 0.056 Ω operating at a speed of 1738 r/min and with an input power of 47.4 kW and a terminal current of 76.2 A.

Solution

1.6 kW

The electromechanical torque T_{mech} corresponding to the power P_{mech} can be obtained by recalling that mechanical power equals torque times angular velocity. Thus,

$$P_{mech} = \omega_m \, T_{mech} = (1 - s) \, \omega_s \, T_{mech} \qquad (6.25)$$

For P_{mech} in watts and ω_s in rad/sec, T_{mech} will be in newton-meters.

Use of Eqs. 6.21 and 6.22 leads to

$$T_{mech} = \frac{P_{mech}}{\omega_m} = \frac{P_{gap}}{\omega_s} = \frac{q I_2^2 (R_2/s)}{\omega_s} \qquad (6.26)$$

With the synchronous mechanical angular velocity ω_s being given by

$$\omega_s = \left(\frac{2}{poles} \right) \omega_e \qquad (6.27)$$

where ω_e is the electrical frequency f_e expressed in rad/sec as

$$\omega_e = 2\pi f_e \qquad (6.28)$$

Eq. 6.26 can be written in terms of the electrical frequency ω_e as

$$T_{mech} = \left(\frac{poles}{2 \, \omega_e} \right) q I_2^2 (R_2/s) \qquad (6.29)$$

The mechanical torque T_{mech} and power P_{mech} are not the output values available at the shaft because friction, windage, and stray-load losses remain to be accounted for. It is obviously correct to subtract friction, windage, and other rotational losses from T_{mech} or P_{mech} and it is generally assumed that stray load effects can be subtracted in the same manner. The remainder is available as output power from the shaft for useful work. Thus

$$P_{shaft} = P_{mech} - P_{rot} \qquad (6.30)$$

and

$$T_{shaft} = \frac{P_{shaft}}{\omega_m} = T_{mech} - T_{rot} \qquad (6.31)$$

where P_{rot} and T_{rot} are the power and torque associated with the friction, windage, and remaining rotational losses.

Analysis of the transformer equivalent circuit is often simplified by either neglecting the magnetizing branch entirely or adopting the approximation of moving it out directly to the primary terminals. Such approximations are not used in the case of induction machines under normal running conditions because the presence of the air gap results in a relatively lower magnetizing impedance and correspondingly a relatively higher exciting current—30 to 50 percent of full-load current—and because the leakage reactances are also higher. Some simplification of the induction-machine equivalent circuit results if the core-loss resistance R_c is omitted and the associated core-loss effect is deducted from T_{mech} or P_{mech} at the same time that rotational losses and stray load effects are subtracted. The equivalent circuit then becomes that of Fig. 6.10a or b, and the error introduced is often relatively insignificant. Such

Figure 6.10 Equivalent circuits with the core-loss resistance R_c neglected corresponding to (a) Fig. 6.8 and (b) Fig. 6.9.

a procedure also has an advantage during motor testing, for then the no-load core loss need not be separated from friction and windage. These last circuits are used in subsequent discussions.

EXAMPLE 6.2

A three-phase Y-connected 460-V (line-to-line) 20-kW 60-Hz six-pole induction motor has the following parameter values in Ω/phase referred to the stator:

$$R_1 = 0.271 \quad R_2 = 0.188$$

$$X_1 = 1.12 \quad X_2 = 1.91 \quad X_m = 23.10$$

The total friction, windage, and core losses may be assumed to be constant at 320 W, independent of load.

For a slip of 1.6 percent, compute the speed, output torque and power, stator current, power factor, and efficiency when the motor is operated at rated voltage and frequency.

■ **Solution**

Let the impedance Z_{gap} (Fig. 6.10a) represent the per phase impedance presented to the stator by the magnetizing reactance and the rotor. Thus, from Fig. 6.10a

$$Z_{gap} = R_{gap} + jX_{gap} = \left(\frac{R_2}{s} + jX_2\right) \text{ in parallel with } jX_m$$

Substitution of numerical values gives, for $s = 0.016$,

$$R_{gap} + jX_{gap} = 8.48 + j6.74 \ \Omega$$

The stator input impedance can now be calculated as

$$Z_{in} = R_1 + jX_1 + Z_{gap} = 10.84 + j6.75 = 10.9 \angle 38.5° \ \Omega$$

The line-to-neutral terminal voltage is equal to

$$V_1 = \frac{460}{\sqrt{3}} = 266 \text{ V}$$

and hence the stator current can be calculated as

$$\hat{I}_1 = \frac{V_1}{Z_{\text{in}}} = \frac{266}{10.9 \angle 38.5°} = 24.5 \angle -38.5° \text{ A}$$

The stator current is thus 18.8 A and the power factor is equal to $\cos(-38.5°) = 0.783$ lagging.

The synchronous speed can be found from Eq. 4.44

$$n_s = \left(\frac{120}{\text{poles}}\right) f_e = \left(\frac{120}{6}\right) 60 = 1200 \text{ r/min}$$

or from Eq. 6.27

$$\omega_s = \frac{4\pi f_e}{\text{poles}} = \frac{4\pi \times 60}{6} = 40\pi \text{ rad/sec}$$

The rotor speed is

$$n = (1 - s)n_s = (1 - 0.016) \times 1200 = 1181 \text{ r/min}$$

or

$$\omega_m = (1 - s)\omega_s = (1 - 0.016) \times 40\pi = 123.7 \text{ rad/sec}$$

From Eq. 6.17,

$$P_{\text{gap}} = q I_2^2 \left(\frac{R_2}{s}\right)$$

Note however that because the only resistance included in Z_{gap} is R_2/s, the power dissipated in Z_{gap} is equal to the power dissipated in R_2/s and hence we can write

$$P_{\text{gap}} = q I_1^2 R_{\text{gap}} = 3(24.5)^2(8.21) = 14.80 \text{ kW}$$

We can now calculate P_{mech} from Eq. 6.21 and the shaft output power from Eq. 6.30. Thus

$$P_{\text{shaft}} = P_{\text{mech}} - P_{\text{rot}} = (1 - s)P_{\text{gap}} - P_{\text{rot}}$$

$$= (1 - 0.016) \times 14,800 - 320 = 14.24 \text{ kW}$$

and the shaft output torque can be found from Eq. 6.31 as

$$T_{\text{shaft}} = \frac{P_{\text{shaft}}}{\omega_m} = \frac{14,240}{123.7} = 115.2 \text{ N} \cdot \text{m}$$

The efficiency is calculated as the ratio of shaft output power to stator input power. The input power is given by

$$P_{\text{in}} = q\text{Re}[\hat{V}_1 \hat{I}_1^*] = 3 \text{ Re}[266 \times (24.5 \angle 38.5°)] = 15.29 \text{ kW}$$

Thus the efficiency η is equal to

$$\eta = \frac{P_{\text{shaft}}}{P_{\text{in}}} = \frac{14.24 \text{ kW}}{15.29 \text{ kW}} = 0.932 = 93.2\%$$

The complete performance characteristics of the motor can be determined by repeating these calculations for other assumed values of slip.

Find the speed, output power, and efficiency of the motor of Example 6.2 operating at rated voltage and frequency for a slip of 1.2 percent.

Solution

$$\text{Speed} = 1186 \text{ r/min}$$

$$P_{\text{shaft}} = 11.05 \text{ kW}$$

$$\text{Efficiency} = 93.4\%$$

6.5 TORQUE AND POWER BY USE OF THEVENIN'S THEOREM

When torque and power relations are to be emphasized, considerable simplification results from application of Thevenin's theorem to the induction-motor equivalent circuit. In its general form, Thevenin's theorem permits the replacement of any network of linear circuit elements and complex voltage sources, such as viewed from two terminals a and b (Fig. 6.11a), by a single complex voltage source $\hat{V}_{\text{eq}}$ in series with a single impedance Z_{eq} (Fig. 6.11b). The Thevenin-equivalent voltage $\hat{V}_{\text{eq}}$ is that appearing across terminals a and b of the original network when these terminals are open-circuited; the Thevenin-equivalent impedance Z_{eq} is that viewed from the same terminals when all voltage sources within the network are set equal to zero. For application to the induction-motor equivalent circuit, points a and b are taken as those so designated in Fig. 6.10a and b. The equivalent circuit then assumes the forms given in Fig. 6.12 where Thevenin's theorem has been used to transform the network to the left of points a and b into an equivalent voltage source $\hat{V}_{1,\text{eq}}$ in series with an equivalent impedance $Z_{1,\text{eq}} = R_{1,\text{eq}} + jX_{1,\text{eq}}$.

According to Thevenin's theorem, the equivalent source voltage $\hat{V}_{1,\text{eq}}$ is the voltage that would appear across terminals a and b of Fig. 6.10 with the rotor circuits

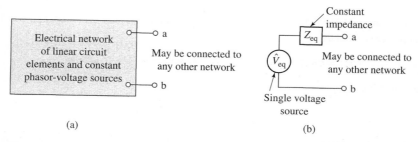

(a)   (b)

Figure 6.11 (a) General linear network and (b) its equivalent at terminals a-b by Thevenin's theorem.

Figure 6.12 Induction-motor equivalent circuits simplified by Thevenin's theorem.

removed. The result is a simple voltage divider and thus

$$\hat{V}_{1,eq} = \hat{V}_1 \left(\frac{jX_m}{R_1 + j(X_1 + X_m)} \right) \tag{6.32}$$

For most induction motors, negligible error results from neglecting the stator resistance in Eq. 6.32. The Thevenin-equivalent stator impedance $Z_{1,eq}$ is the impedance between terminals a and b of Fig. 6.10 viewed toward the source with the source voltage set equal to zero (or equivalently replaced by a short circuit) and therefore is

$$Z_{1,eq} = R_{1,eq} + jX_{1,eq} = (R_1 + jX_1) \text{ in parallel with } jX_m \tag{6.33}$$

or

$$Z_{1,eq} = \frac{jX_m(R_1 + jX_1)}{R_1 + j(X_1 + X_m)} \tag{6.34}$$

Note that the core-loss resistance R_c has been neglected in the derivation of Eqs. 6.32 through 6.34. Although this is a very commonly used approximation, its effect can be readily incorporated in the derivations presented here by replacing the magnetizing reactance jX_m by the magnetizing impedance Z_m, equal to the parallel combination of the core-loss resistance R_c and the magnetizing reactance jX_m.

From the Thevenin-equivalent circuit (Fig. 6.12)

$$\hat{I}_2 = \frac{\hat{V}_{1,eq}}{Z_{1,eq} + jX_2 + R_2/s} \tag{6.35}$$

and thus from the torque expression (Eq. 6.29)

$$\begin{aligned} T_{mech} &= \left(\frac{\text{poles}}{2\,\omega_e} \right) q|\hat{I}_2|^2(R_2/s) \\ &= \left(\frac{\text{poles}}{2\,\omega_e} \right) \left[\frac{qV_{1,eq}^2(R_2/s)}{(R_{1,eq} + (R_2/s))^2 + (X_{1,eq} + X_2)^2} \right] \end{aligned} \tag{6.36}$$

Eq. 6.36 expresses the electromechanical torque as a function of slip. The general shape of a typical *torque-speed* or *torque-slip curve* of an induction machine connected to a constant-voltage, constant-frequency source is shown in Figs. 6.13 and 6.14.

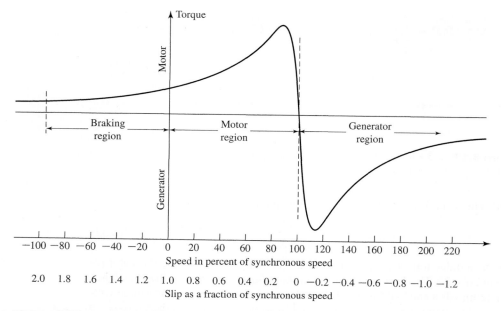

Figure 6.13 Induction-machine torque-slip curve showing braking, motor, and generator regions.

In normal motor operation, the rotor revolves in the direction of rotation of the magnetic field produced by the stator currents, the speed is between zero and synchronous speed, and the corresponding slip is between 1.0 and 0 (labeled "Motor region" in Fig. 6.13). Motor starting conditions are those of $s = 1.0$.

To obtain operation in the region of s greater than 1 (corresponding to a negative motor speed), the motor must be driven backward, against the direction of rotation of its magnetic field, by a source of mechanical power capable of counteracting the electromechanical torque T_{mech}. The chief practical usefulness of this region is in bringing motors to a quick stop by a method called *plugging*. By interchanging two stator leads in a three-phase motor, the phase sequence, and hence the direction of rotation of the magnetic field, is reversed suddenly and what was a small slip before the phase reversal becomes a slip close to 2.0 following the reversal. The motor speed thus becomes negative with respect to the synchronous stator flux wave and the resultant positive torque causes the motor slip to decrease. If the motor remains connected to the line, the motor will eventually accelerate towards a slip of 0. However, the motor can easily be stopped if it is disconnected from the line at zero speed ($s = 1$) before the motor can start in the other direction. Accordingly, the region from $s = 1.0$ to $s = 2.0$ is labeled "Braking region" in Fig. 6.13.

An induction machine will operate as a generator if its stator terminals are connected to a polyphase voltage source and its rotor is driven above synchronous speed (resulting in a negative slip) by a prime mover, as shown in Fig. 6.13. The source fixes the synchronous speed and supplies the reactive power input required to excite

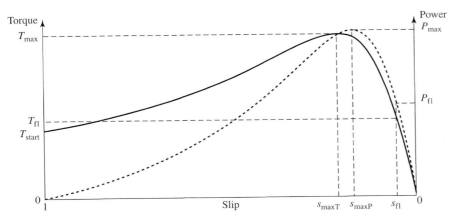

Figure 6.14 Typical motor-region torque (solid line) and power (dashed line) curves.

the air-gap magnetic field. One such application is that of an induction generator connected to a power system and driven by a wind turbine.

Figure 6.14 shows typical torque and power characteristics for an induction motor operating in the motor region ($0 \leq s \leq 1.0$). In the figure, the full-load operating conditions are indicated by slip s_{fl}, torque T_{fl}, and power P_{fl}. We see that the maximum torque (and power) capability is typically a few times that of its full-load value and that they occur at a significantly higher slip. The *maximum electromechanical torque,* or *breakdown torque, T_{max}* occurs at slip s_{maxT} while the maximum power P_{max} occurs at a somewhat smaller slip s_{maxP}.

An expression for T_{max} can be obtained readily from circuit considerations. As can be seen from Eq. 6.26, the electromechanical torque is a maximum when the power delivered to R_2/s in Fig. 6.12a is a maximum. It can be shown that this power will be greatest when the impedance of R_2/s equals the magnitude of the impedance $R_{1,eq} + j(X_{1,eq} + X_2)$ between it and the constant equivalent voltage $\hat{V}_{1,eq}$. Thus, maximum electromechanical torque will occur at a value of slip s_{maxT} for which

$$\frac{R_2}{s_{maxT}} = \sqrt{R_{1,eq}^2 + (X_{1,eq} + X_2)^2} \tag{6.37}$$

The slip s_{maxT} at maximum torque is therefore

$$s_{maxT} = \frac{R_2}{\sqrt{R_{1,eq}^2 + (X_{1,eq} + X_2)^2}} \tag{6.38}$$

and the corresponding torque is, from Eq. 6.36,

$$T_{max} = \left(\frac{poles}{2\,\omega_e}\right)\left[\frac{0.5q\,V_{1,eq}^2}{R_{1,eq} + \sqrt{R_{1,eq}^2 + (X_{1,eq} + X_2)^2}}\right] \tag{6.39}$$

EXAMPLE 6.3

For the motor of Example 6.2, determine (a) the load component I_2 of the stator current, the electromechanical torque T_{mech}, and the electromechanical power P_{mech} for a slip $s = 0.02$; (b) the maximum electromechanical torque and the corresponding speed; and (c) the electromechanical starting torque T_{start} and the corresponding stator load current $I_{2,start}$. Neglect rotational loss.

■ **Solution**

a. First reduce the circuit to its Thevenin-equivalent form. From Eq. 6.32

$$V_{1,eq} = |\hat{V}_{1,eq}| = 253.3 \text{ V}$$

and from Eq. 6.34,

$$R_{1,eq} + jX_{1,eq} = 0.246 + j1.071 \ \Omega$$

At $s = 0.02$, $R_2/s = 9.40$ and from Fig. 6.12a,

$$I_2 = \frac{V_{1,eq}}{\sqrt{(R_{1,eq} + R_2/s)^2 + (X_{1,eq} + X_2)^2}} = 25.1 \text{ A}$$

From Eq. 6.29

$$T_{mech} = \left(\frac{\text{poles}}{2 \, \omega_e}\right) q I_2^2 (R_2/s) = 141.2 \text{ N} \cdot \text{m}$$

and from Eq. 6.21

$$P_{mech} = q I_2^2 (R_2/s)(1 - s) = 17.4 \text{ kW}$$

b. At the maximum-torque point, from Eq. 6.38,

$$s_{maxT} = \frac{R_2}{\sqrt{R_{1,eq}^2 + (X_{1,eq} + X_2)^2}} = 0.063 = 6.3\%$$

and thus the speed at T_{max} is equal to $(1 - s_{maxT})n_s = (1 - 0.063) \times 1200 = 1125$ r/min.
From Eq. 6.39

$$T_{max} = \left(\frac{\text{poles}}{2 \, \omega_e}\right) \left[\frac{0.5 q V_{1,eq}^2}{R_{1,eq} + \sqrt{R_{1,eq}^2 + (X_{1,eq} + X_2)^2}}\right] = 237 \text{ N} \cdot \text{m}$$

c. At starting, $s = 1$. Therefore

$$I_{2,start} = \frac{V_{1,eq}}{\sqrt{(R_{1,eq} + R_2)^2 + (X_{1,eq} + X_2)^2}} = 84.1 \text{ A}$$

From Eq. 6.29

$$T_{start} = \left(\frac{\text{poles}}{2 \, \omega_e}\right) q I_2^2 R_2 = 31.7 \text{ N} \cdot \text{m}$$

Note that the starting torque calculated here is considerably smaller than the rated torque of the motor which is on the order of 160 N·m. As we shall see, an increase in starting torque can be obtained by means of an increase in rotor resistance. In squirrel-cage induction motors, this is accomplished through the use of double-cage or deep-bar rotors, as discussed in Section 6.7.2.

The rotor of the induction motor of Example 6.2 is replaced by a rotor with twice the rotor resistance but which is otherwise identical to the original rotor. Repeat the calculations of Example 6.3.

Solution

a. $I_2 = 13.1$ A, $T_{mech} = 77.5$ N·m, $P_{mech} = 9.5$ kW
b. $T_{max} = 237$ N·m at speed $= 1049$ r/min
c. At starting, $T_{start} = 62.1$ N·m, $I_{2,start} = 83.2$ A

For the induction motor of Example 6.2, find (a) the rotor resistance required to produce peak electromechanical torque at zero speed (i.e., $s_{maxT} = 1.0$) and (b) the corresponding torque T_{max}. (c) Using MATLAB,[1] plot the resultant torque-speed curve over the range $0 \leq s \leq 1.0$. You may ignore friction, windage, and core loss.

Solution

a. $R_2 = 2.99$ Ω
b. $T_{max} = 237$ N·m
c. The torque-speed curve is given in Fig. 6.15.

Figure 6.15 Plot of electromechanical torque vs. speed for Practice Problem 6.4.

Under the conditions of constant-frequency operation, a typical conventional induction motor with a squirrel-cage rotor is substantially a constant-speed motor

---

[1] MATLAB is a registered trademark of The MathWorks, Inc.

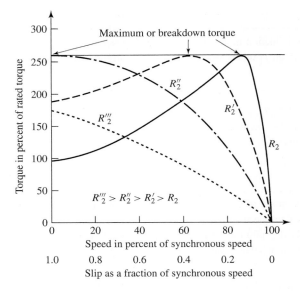

Figure 6.16 Induction-motor torque-slip curves showing effect of changing rotor-circuit resistance.

having about 10 percent or less drop in speed from no load to full load. In the case of a wound-rotor induction motor, speed variation can be obtained by inserting external resistance in the rotor circuit; the influence of increased rotor resistance on the torque-speed characteristic is shown by the dashed curves in Fig. 6.16. For such a motor, significant speed variations can be achieved as the rotor resistance is varied. Similarly, the zero-speed torque variations seen in Fig. 6.16 illustrate how the starting torque of a wound-rotor induction motor can be varied by varying the rotor resistance.

Notice from Eqs. 6.38 and 6.39 that the slip at maximum torque is directly proportional to rotor resistance R_2 but the value of the maximum torque is independent of R_2. When R_2 is increased by inserting external resistance in the rotor of a wound-rotor motor, the maximum electromechanical torque is unaffected but the speed at which it occurs can be directly controlled. This result can also be seen by observing that the electromechanical torque expression of Eq. 6.36 is a function of the ratio R_2/s. Thus, the torque is unchanged as long as the ratio R_2/s remains constant.

EXAMPLE 6.4

A three-phase, 460-V, 60-Hz, 40-kW, four-pole wound-rotor induction motor has the following parameters expressed in Ω/phase.

$$R_1 = 0.163 \quad X_1 = 0.793 \quad X_2 = 1.101 \quad X_m = 18.9$$

Using MATLAB, plot the electromechanical torque T_{mech} as a function of rotor speed in r/min for rotor resistances of $R_2 = 0.1, 0.2, 0.5, 1.0$ and $1.5\ \Omega$.

Figure 6.17 Electromechanical torque vs. speed for the wound-rotor induction motor of Example 6.4 for various values of the rotor resistance R_2.

■ **Solution**

The desired plot is shown in Fig. 6.17.

Here is the MATLAB script:

```
clc
clear

% Here are the motor parameters

V1 = 460/sqrt(3);
Nph = 3;
poles = 4;
fe = 60;

R1 = 0.163;
X1 = 0.793;
X2 = 1.101;
Xm = 18.87;

%Calculate the synchronous speed

omegas = 4*pi*fe/poles;
ns = 120*fe/poles;

%Calculate stator Thevenin equivalent
```

```
Z1eq = j*Xm*(R1+j*X1)/(R1 + j*(X1+Xm));
R1eq = real(Z1eq);
X1eq = imag(Z1eq);

V1eq = abs(V1*j*Xm/(R1 + j*(X1+Xm)));


%Here is the loop over rotor resistance

for m = 1:5

  if m == 1
    R2 = 0.1;
  elseif m==2
    R2 = 0.2;
  elseif m==3
    R2 = 0.5;
  elseif m==4
    R2 = 1.0;
  else
    R2 = 1.5;
  end

% Calculate the torque

  s = 0:.001:1;      %slip
  rpm = ns*(1-s);
  I2 = abs(V1eq./(Z1eq + j*X2 + R2./s));   %I2
  Tmech = Nph*I2.^2*R2./(s*omegas);   %Electromechanical torque

%Now plot

  plot(rpm,Tmech,'LineWidth',2)
  if m ==1
    hold on
  end

end   %End of resistance loop

hold off
xlabel('rpm','FontSize',20)
ylabel('T_{mech} [N\cdotm]','FontSize',20)
xlim([0 1800])
set(gca,'FontSize',20);
set(gca,'xtick',[0 500 1000 1500 1800])
```

```
set(gca,'ytick',[0 50 100 150 200 250 300])
grid on
```

Using MATLAB, re-consider Example 6.4 and plot the terminal current as a function of speed for the five values of R_2.

Solution

The plot of current vs. speed is given in Fig. 6.18.

Figure 6.18   Plot of current vs. speed for Practice Problem 6.5.

In applying the induction-motor equivalent circuit, the idealizations on which it is based should be kept in mind. This is particularly necessary when investigations are carried out over a wide speed range, such as is the case in investigations of motor starting. Saturation under the heavy inrush currents associated with starting conditions has a significant effect on the motor reactances. Moreover, the rotor currents are at slip frequency, which varies from stator frequency at zero speed to a low value at full-load speed. The current distribution in the rotor bars of squirrel-cage motors may vary significantly with frequency, giving rise to significant variations in rotor resistance. In fact, as discussed in Sections 6.7.2 and 6.7.3, motor designers can tailor the shape of the rotor bars in squirrel-cage motors to obtain various speed-torque characteristics. Errors from these causes can be kept to a minimum by using equivalent-circuit parameters corresponding as closely as possible to those of the proposed operating conditions.

6.6 PARAMETER DETERMINATION FROM NO-LOAD AND BLOCKED-ROTOR TESTS

The equivalent-circuit parameters needed for computing the performance of a polyphase induction motor under load can be obtained from the results of a no-load test, a blocked-rotor test, and measurements of the dc resistances of the stator windings. Stray-load losses, which must be taken into account when accurate values of efficiency are to be calculated, can also be measured by tests which do not require loading the motor. Stray-load-loss tests are not described here, however.[2]

6.6.1 No-Load Test

Like the open-circuit test on a transformer, the *no-load test* on an induction motor gives information with respect to exciting current and no-load losses. This test is ordinarily performed at rated frequency and with balanced polyphase voltages applied to the stator terminals. Readings are taken at rated voltage, after the motor has been running long enough for the bearings to be properly lubricated. We will assume that the no-load test is made with the motor operating at its rated electrical frequency f_{re} and that the following measurements are available from the no-load test:

$V_{1,nl}$ = The line-to-neutral terminal voltage [V]

$I_{1,nl}$ = The line current [A]

P_{nl} = The total polyphase electrical input power [W]

In polyphase machines it is most common to measure line-to-line voltage, and thus the line-to-neutral voltage must be then calculated (dividing by $\sqrt{3}$ in the case of a three-phase machine).

At no load, the rotor current is only the very small value needed to produce sufficient torque to overcome the friction and windage losses associated with rotation. The no-load rotor I^2R loss is, therefore, negligibly small. Unlike the continuous magnetic core in a transformer, the magnetizing path in an induction motor includes an air gap which significantly increases the required exciting current. Thus, in contrast to the case of a transformer, whose no-load primary I^2R loss is negligible, the no-load stator I^2R loss of an induction motor may be appreciable because of this larger exciting current.

Neglecting rotor I^2R losses and core loss, the *rotational loss*, P_{rot}, for normal running conditions can be found by subtracting the stator I^2R losses from the no-load input power

$$P_{rot} = P_{nl} - qI_{1,nl}^2 R_1 \qquad (6.40)$$

The total rotational loss at rated voltage and frequency under load usually is considered to be constant and equal to its no-load value. Note that the stator resistance R_1 varies

---

[2] For information concerning test methods, see IEEE Std. 112-2004, "Test Procedures for Polyphase Induction Motors and Generators," Institute of Electrical and Electronics Engineers, Inc., 345 East 47th Street, New York, New York, 10017.

with stator-winding temperature. Hence, when applying Eq. 6.40, care should be taken to use the value corresponding to the temperature of the no-load test.

Note that the derivations presented here ignore the core-loss and the associated core-loss resistance and assign all the no-load losses to friction and windage. Various tests can be performed to separate the friction and windage losses from the core losses. For example, if the motor is not energized, an external drive motor can be used to drive the rotor to the no-load speed and the rotational loss will be equal to the required drive-motor output power.

Alternatively, if the motor is operated at no load and rated speed and if it is then suddenly disconnected from the supply, the decay in motor speed will be determined by the rotational loss as

$$J \frac{d\omega_m}{dt} = -T_{rot} = -\frac{P_{rot}}{\omega_m} \tag{6.41}$$

Hence, if the rotor inertia J is known, the rotational loss at any speed ω_m can be determined from the resultant speed decay as

$$P_{rot}(\omega_m) = -\omega_m J \frac{d\omega_m}{dt} \tag{6.42}$$

Thus, the rotational losses at rated speed can be determined by evaluating Eq. 6.42 as the motor is first shut off when it is operating at rated speed.

If the no-load rotational losses are determined in this fashion, the core loss can be determined as

$$P_{core} = P_{nl} - P_{rot} - q I_{1,nl}^2 R_1 \tag{6.43}$$

Here P_{core} is the total *no-load core loss* corresponding to the voltage of the no-load test (typically rated voltage).

Under no-load conditions, the stator current is relatively low and, to a first approximation, one can neglect the corresponding voltage drop across the stator resistance and leakage reactance. Under this approximation, the voltage across the core-loss resistance will be equal to the no-load line-to-neutral voltage and the core-loss resistance can be determined as

$$R_c = \frac{q V_{1,nl}^2}{P_{core}} \tag{6.44}$$

Provided that the machine is operated close to rated speed and rated voltage, the refinement associated with separating out the core loss and specifically incorporating it in the form of a core-loss resistance in the equivalent circuit typically will not make a significant difference in the results of an analysis. Hence, it is common to ignore the core-loss resistance and to simply include the core loss with the rotational losses. For the purposes of analytical simplicity, this approach will be followed in the remainder of the text. However, if necessary, the reader should find it relatively straight forward to modify the remaining derivations to appropriately include the core-loss resistance.

Because the no-load slip, s_{nl}, is very small, the reflected rotor resistance R_2/s_{nl} is very large. The parallel combination of rotor and magnetizing branches then becomes

Figure 6.19 Approximate induction-motor equivalent circuit: No-load conditions.

jX_m in parallel with the rotor leakage reactance X_2 in series with a very large resistance and the impedance of this parallel combination therefore very nearly equals the magnetizing impedance jX_m. The corresponding equivalent circuit is shown in Fig. 6.19. Consequently the apparent reactance X_{nl} measured at the stator terminals at no load very nearly equals $X_1 + X_m$, which is the self-reactance X_{11} of the stator; i.e.,

$$X_{nl} \approx X_{11} = X_1 + X_m \tag{6.45}$$

The self-reactance of the stator can therefore be determined from the no-load measurements. The reactive power at no load Q_{nl} can be determined as

$$Q_{nl} = \sqrt{S_{nl}^2 - P_{nl}^2} \tag{6.46}$$

where

$$S_{nl} = q V_{1,nl} I_{1,nl} \tag{6.47}$$

is the total apparent power input at no load.

The no-load reactance X_{nl} can then be calculated from Q_{nl} and $I_{1,nl}$ as

$$X_{nl} = \frac{Q_{nl}}{q I_{1,nl}^2} \tag{6.48}$$

Noting that the no-load power factor is small (i.e., $Q_{nl} \gg P_{nl}$ and hence $R_1 \ll X_{11}$), the no-load reactance can often be approximated as

$$X_{nl} \approx \frac{V_{1,nl}}{I_{1,nl}} \tag{6.49}$$

6.6.2   Blocked-Rotor Test

Like the short-circuit test on a transformer, the *blocked-rotor test* on an induction motor gives information with respect to the leakage impedances. The rotor is blocked so that it cannot rotate (hence the slip is equal to unity), and balanced polyphase voltages are applied to the stator terminals. We will assume that the following measurements are

Figure 6.20 Induction-motor equivalent circuit: Blocked-rotor conditions.

available from the blocked-rotor test:

$V_{1,bl}$ = The line-to-neutral voltage [V]

$I_{1,bl}$ = The line current [V]

P_{bl} = The total polyphase electrical input power [W]

f_{bl} = The frequency of the blocked-rotor test [Hz]

In some cases, the blocked-rotor torque also is measured.

The equivalent circuit for blocked-rotor conditions (Fig. 6.20) is identical to that of a short-circuited transformer. An induction motor is more complicated than a transformer, however, because its leakage impedance may be affected by magnetic saturation of the leakage-flux paths associated with the stator slots and the rotor bars and by the frequency of the induced rotor currents (which affects the distribution of currents in the rotor bars as discussed in Section 6.7.2). The blocked-rotor impedance may also be affected by rotor position and the corresponding relative orientation of the rotor slots with the stator teeth, although this effect generally is small with squirrel-cage rotors.

Because leakage reactances are typically significantly affected by saturation, it is important to conduct blocked-rotor tests with current levels similar to those which are found in the machine at the operating condition for which the performance is later to be calculated. Similarly, for induction machines in which it is known that the distribution of rotor currents, and hence the rotor impedance, is affected by the rotor-current frequency, when possible the blocked-rotor test should be performed at a frequency which is approximately the same as that which occurs in the machine at the operating condition under consideration.

For example, if one is interested in the characteristics at slips near unity, as in starting, the blocked-rotor test should be taken at normal frequency and with currents near the values encountered in starting. If, however, one is interested in normal running characteristics, the blocked-rotor test should be taken at a reduced voltage which results in approximately rated current; the frequency should also be reduced, since the values of the effective rotor resistance and leakage inductance at the low rotor frequencies corresponding to small slips may differ appreciably from their values at normal frequency, particularly with double-cage or deep-bar rotors, as discussed in Section 6.7.2.

In practice, it is difficult to run tests at the low frequencies corresponding to running conditions with small slips. For example, the rotor-frequency in a 60-Hz machine running at a slip of 3 percent is 1.8 Hz. As a result, IEEE Standard 112 suggests a maximum blocked-rotor test frequency of 25 percent of rated frequency with the expectation that the rotor impedance at this frequency is not too different from that at small slips. The reactance at rated frequency can be obtained from this test value by multiplying the test reactance by the ratio of rated frequency to test frequency. The dependence of the rotor impedance on frequency is often negligible for many motors of less than 25-hp rating, and for these motors the rotor parameters determined by a blocked-rotor conducted at rated frequency are equally applicable to to starting and rated-load operating conditions.

Based upon blocked-rotor measurements, the blocked-rotor reactance can be found from the blocked-rotor reactive power

$$Q_{bl} = \sqrt{S_{bl}^2 - P_{bl}^2} \tag{6.50}$$

where

$$S_{bl} = q V_{1,bl} I_{1,bl} \tag{6.51}$$

is the total blocked-rotor apparent power. The blocked-rotor reactance, corrected to rated frequency, can then be calculated as

$$X_{bl} = \left(\frac{f_{re}}{f_{bl}} \right) \left(\frac{Q_{bl}}{q I_{1,bl}^2} \right) \tag{6.52}$$

where f_{bl} is the frequency of the blocked-rotor test.

The blocked-rotor resistance can be calculated from the blocked-rotor input power as

$$R_{bl} = \frac{P_{bl}}{q I_{1,bl}^2} \tag{6.53}$$

Once these parameters have been determined, the equivalent circuit parameters can be determined. Under blocked-rotor conditions, an expression for the stator input impedance can be obtained from examination of Fig. 6.20 as

$$Z_{bl} = R_1 + jX_1 + (R_2 + jX_2) \text{ in parallel with } jX_m$$

$$= R_1 + \frac{R_2 X_m^2}{R_2^2 + (X_m + X_2)^2}$$

$$+ j \left(X_1 + \frac{X_m (R_2^2 + X_2(X_m + X_2))}{R_2^2 + (X_m + X_2)^2} \right) \tag{6.54}$$

Here we have assumed that the reactances are at their rated-frequency values.

The corresponding blocked-rotor resistance is thus given by

$$R_{bl} = R_1 + \frac{R_2 X_m^2}{R_2^2 + (X_m + X_2)^2} \tag{6.55}$$

and the corresponding blocked-rotor reactance is

$$X_{bl} = X_1 + \frac{X_m\left(R_2^2 + X_2(X_m + X_2)\right)}{R_2^2 + (X_m + X_2)^2} \tag{6.56}$$

Our objective at this point is to solve Eqs. 6.55 and 6.56 for R_2 and X_2. As can be seen, these equations are sufficiently complex that there is no simple way to do this. However, it is typically appropriate to apply the approximation that $R_2 \ll X_m$, in which case Eqs. 6.55 and 6.56 can be reduced to

$$R_{bl} = R_1 + R_2 \left(\frac{X_m}{X_2 + X_m}\right)^2 \tag{6.57}$$

and

$$X_{bl} = X_1 + X_2 \left(\frac{X_m}{X_2 + X_m}\right) \tag{6.58}$$

From Eqs. 6.57 and 6.58, the rotor resistance R_2 and leakage reactance X_2 can be found as

$$R_2 = (R_{bl} - R_1) \left(\frac{X_2 + X_m}{X_m}\right)^2 \tag{6.59}$$

and

$$X_2 = (X_{bl} - X_1) \left(\frac{X_m}{X_m + X_1 - X_{bl}}\right) \tag{6.60}$$

In order to achieve maximum accuracy as with the no-load test, if possible the value of the stator resistance R_1 used in Eq. 6.59 should be corrected to the value corresponding to the temperature of the blocked-rotor test.

Substituting for X_m from Eq. 6.45 into Eq. 6.60 gives

$$X_2 = (X_{bl} - X_1) \left(\frac{X_{nl} - X_1}{X_{nl} - X_{bl}}\right) \tag{6.61}$$

Equation 6.61 expresses the rotor leakage reactance X_2 in terms of the measured quantities X_{nl} and X_{bl} and the unknown stator leakage reactance X_1. It is not possible to make an additional measurement from which X_1 and X_2 can be determined uniquely. Fortunately, the performance of the motor is affected relatively little by the way in which the total leakage reactance is distributed between the stator and rotor. Based upon a given motor class, IEEE Standard 112 recommends the empirical distribution shown in Table 6.1. The various motor classes are discussed in Section 6.7.3. If the motor class is unknown, it is common to assume that X_1 and X_2 are equal.

Once the fractional relationship between X_1 and X_2 has been determined, it can be substituted into Eq. 6.61 and X_2 (and hence X_1) can be found in terms of X_{nl} and X_{bl} by solving the resultant quadratic equation.

The magnetizing reactance X_m can then be determined from Eq. 6.45.

$$X_m = X_{nl} - X_1 \tag{6.62}$$

Finally, using the known stator resistance and the values of X_m and X_2 which are now known, the rotor resistance R_2 can now be determined from Eq. 6.59.

Table 6.1   Empirical distribution of leakage reactances in induction motors.

Motor class	Description	Fraction of $(X_1 + X_2)$	
		X_1	X_2
A	Normal starting torque, normal starting current	0.5	0.5
B	Normal starting torque, low starting current	0.4	0.6
C	High starting torque, low starting current	0.3	0.7
D	High starting torque, high slip	0.5	0.5
Wound rotor	Performance varies with rotor resistance	0.5	0.5

Source: IEEE Standard 112.

EXAMPLE 6.5

The following test data apply to a 135 kW (100-hp), three-phase, 460-V, 60-Hz, four-pole induction motor with a double-squirrel-cage rotor of design class B (normal-starting-torque, low-starting-current type):

Test 1: No-load test at 60 Hz

$$\text{Applied voltage } V = 459 \text{ V line-to-line}$$
$$\text{Average phase current } I_{1,nl} = 34.1 \text{ A}$$
$$\text{Power } P_{nl} = 1.25 \text{ kW}$$

Test 2: Blocked-rotor test at 15 Hz

$$\text{Applied voltage } V = 42.3 \text{ V line-to-line}$$
$$\text{Average phase current } I_{1,bl} = 169 \text{ A}$$
$$\text{Power } P_{bl} = 4.44 \text{ kW}$$

Test 3: Average dc resistance per stator phase (measured immediately after test 2)

$$R_1 = 30.3 \text{ m}\Omega$$

Test 4: Blocked-rotor test at 60 Hz

$$\text{Applied voltage } V = 455 \text{ V line-to-line}$$
$$\text{Average phase current } I_{1,bl} = 725 \text{ A}$$
$$\text{Power } P_{bl} = 147 \text{ kW}$$
$$\text{Measured starting torque } T_{start} = 603 \text{ N} \cdot \text{m}$$

a. Compute the no-load rotational loss and the equivalent-circuit parameters applying to normal running conditions. Assume the same temperature as in test 3. Neglect any effects of core loss, assuming that core loss can be lumped in with the rotational losses.
b. Compute the electromechanical starting torque from the input measurements of test 4. Assume the same temperature as in test 3.
c. To check the validity of the approximation leading to Eqs. 6.57 and 6.58, substitute the parameter values found in part (a) into Eqs. 6.55 and 6.56 and compare the results with the values of R_{bl} and X_{bl} calculated from the test results.

■ Solution

a. From Eq. 6.40, the rotational losses can be calculated as

$$P_{rot} = P_{nl} - q I_{1,nl}^2 R_1 = 1.14 \text{ kW}$$

The line-to-neutral no-load voltage is equal to $V_{1,nl} = 459/\sqrt{3} = 265$ V and thus, from Eqs. 6.46 and 6.47,

$$Q_{nl} = \sqrt{(q V_{1,nl} I_{1,nl})^2 - P_{nl}^2} = 27.1 \text{ kVA}$$

and thus from Eq. 6.48

$$X_{nl} = \frac{Q_{nl}}{q I_{1,nl}^2} = 7.76 \; \Omega$$

We can assume that the blocked-rotor test at a reduced frequency of 15 Hz and rated current reproduces approximately normal running conditions in the rotor. Thus, from test 2 and Eqs. 6.50 and 6.51 with $V_{1,bl} = 42.3/\sqrt{3} = 24.4$ V

$$Q_{bl} = \sqrt{(q V_{1,bl} I_{1,bl})^2 - P_{bl}^2} = 11.6 \text{ kVA}$$

and thus from Eq. 6.52

$$X_{bl} = \left(\frac{f_{re}}{f_{bl}}\right) \left(\frac{Q_{bl}}{q I_{1,bl}^2}\right) = \left(\frac{60}{15}\right) \left(\frac{11.6 \times 10^3}{3 \times 169^2}\right) = 0.540 \; \Omega$$

Since we are told that this is a Class B motor, we can refer to Table 6.1 and assume that $X_1 = 0.4(X_1 + X_2)$ or $X_1 = k X_2$, where $k = (2/3)$. Substituting into Eq. 6.61 results in a quadratic in X_2

$$k^2 X_2^2 + (X_{bl}(1-k) - X_{nl}(1+k))X_2 + X_{nl} X_{bl} = 0$$

or

Solving for X_2 gives two roots: 0.332 Ω and 28.4 Ω. Clearly, X_2 must be less than X_{nl} and hence it is easy to identify the proper solution as

$$X_2 = 0.332 \; \Omega$$

and thus

$$X_1 = 0.221 \; \Omega$$

From Eq. 6.62,

$$X_m = X_{nl} - X_1 = 7.54 \; \Omega$$

R_{bl} can be found from Eq. 6.53 as

$$R_{bl} = \frac{P_{bl}}{q I_{1,bl}^2} = 51.8 \text{ m}\Omega$$

and thus from Eq. 6.59

$$R_2 = (R_{bl} - R_1) \left(\frac{X_2 + X_m}{X_m}\right)^2 = 23.5 \text{ m}\Omega$$

The parameters of the equivalent circuit for small values of slip have now been calculated.

b. Although we could calculate the electromechanical starting torque from the equivalent-circuit parameters derived in part (a), we recognize that this is a double-squirrel-cage motor and hence these parameters (most specifically the rotor parameters) will differ significantly under starting conditions from their low-slip values calculated in part (a). Hence, we will calculate the electromechanical starting torque from the rated-frequency, blocked-rotor test measurements of test 4.

From the power input and stator I^2R losses, the air-gap power P_{gap} is

$$P_{gap} = P_{bl} - q I_{1,bl}^2 R_1 = 115 \text{ kW}$$

Since this is a four-pole machine, the synchronous speed can be found from Eq. 6.27 as $\omega_s = 60\pi$ rad/sec. Thus, from Eq. 6.26

$$T_{start} = \frac{P_{gap}}{\omega_s} = 611 \text{ N} \cdot \text{m}$$

The test value, $T_{start} = 603 \text{ N} \cdot \text{m}$ is a few percent less than the calculated value because the calculations do not account for the power absorbed in the stator core loss or in stray-load losses.

c. Substitution of the parameter values of part (a) into Eqs. 6.55 and 6.56 gives $R_{bl} = 51.8 \text{ m}\Omega$ and $X_{bl} = 0.540 \text{ }\Omega$. These values are identical to the corresponding values used to derive the parameters in part (a), hence confirming the validity of the approximation. Note that the validity of the assumption can also be verified by noting that it is based on the assumption that $R_2 \ll X_m$ which is certainly the case here.

Practice Problem 6.6

Repeat the equivalent-circuit parameter calculations of Example 6.5 part (a) under the assumption that the rotor and stator leakage reactances are equal (i.e., that $X_1 = X_2$).

Solution

$$R_1 = 30.3 \text{ m}\Omega \quad R_2 = 23.1 \text{ m}\Omega$$

$$X_1 = 0.275 \text{ }\Omega \quad X_m = 7.49 \text{ }\Omega \quad X_2 = 0.275 \text{ }\Omega$$

Calculation of the blocked-rotor reactance can be simplified if one assumes that $X_m \gg X_2$. Under this assumption, Eq. 6.58 reduces to

$$X_{bl} = X_1 + X_2 \tag{6.63}$$

X_1 and X_2 can then be found from Eq. 6.63 and an estimation of the fractional relationship between X_1 and X_2 (such as from Table 6.1).

Note that one might be tempted to approximate Eq. 6.59, the expression for R_2, in the same fashion. However, because the ratio $(X_2 + X_m)/X_m$ is squared, the approximation tends to result in unacceptably large errors and cannot be justified.

EXAMPLE 6.6

(*a*) Determine the parameters of the motor of Example 6.5 solving for the leakage reactances using Eq. 6.63. (*b*) Assuming the motor to be operating from a 460-V, 60-Hz source at a speed of 1765 r/min, use MATLAB to calculate the output power for the two sets of parameters.

■ Solution

a. As found in Example 6.5,

$$X_{nl} = 7.76 \ \Omega \quad X_{bl} = 0.540 \ \Omega$$

$$R_1 = 30.3 \ m\Omega \quad R_{bl} = 51.8 \ m\Omega$$

Thus, from Eq. 6.45,

$$X_1 + X_m = X_{nl} = 7.76 \ \Omega$$

and from Eq. 6.63

$$X_1 + X_2 = X_{bl} = 0.540 \ \Omega$$

From Table 6.1, $X_1 = 0.4(X_1 + X_2) = 0.216 \ \Omega$ and thus $X_2 = 0.324 \ \Omega$ and $X_m = 7.54 \ \Omega$.

Finally, from Eq. 6.59,

$$R_2 = (R_{bl} - R_1) \left(\frac{X_2 + X_m}{X_m} \right)^2 = 23.4 \ m\Omega$$

Comparison with Example 6.5 shows the following

Parameter	Example 6.5	Example 6.6
R_1	30.3 mΩ	30.3 mΩ
R_2	23.5 mΩ	23.4 mΩ
X_1	0.221 Ω	0.216 Ω
X_2	0.332 Ω	324 Ω
X_m	7.54 Ω	7.54 Ω

b. For the parameters of Example 6.5, $P_{shaft} = 128.2$ [kW] while for the parameters of part (a) of this example, $P_{shaft} = 129.7$ [kW]. Thus the approximation associated with Eq. 6.63 results in an error of approximately 1.2 percent from using the more exact expression of Eq. 6.58. This is a typical result and hence this approximation can be justified in many cases.

Here is the MATLAB script:

```
clc
clear

% Here are the two sets of parameters
% Set 1 corresponds to the solution from Example 6-5
% Set 2 corresponds to the solution from Example 6-6
```

```
R1(1) = 0.0303;          R1(2) = 0.0303;
R2(1) = 0.0235;          R2(2) = 0.0234;
X1(1) = 0.221;           X1(2) = 0.216;
X2(1) = 0.332;           X2(2) = 0.324;
Xm(1) = 7.54;            Xm(2) = 7.54;

nph = 3;
poles = 4;
Prot = 1140;

%Here is the operating condition

V1 = 460/sqrt(3);
fe = 60;
rpm = 1746;

%Calculate the synchronous speed
ns = 120*fe/poles;
omegas = 4*pi*fe/poles;

slip = (ns-rpm)/ns;
omegam = omegas*(1-slip);

%Loop over the two motors
for m = 1:2
  Zgap = j*Xm(m)*(j*X2(m)+R2(m)/slip)/(R2(m)/slip+j*(Xm(m)+X2(m)));
  Zin = R1(m) + j*X1(m) + Zgap;
  I1 = V1/Zin;
  I2 = I1*(j*Xm(m))/(R2(m)/slip+j*(Xm(m)+X2(m)));
  Tmech = nph*abs(I2)^2*R2(m)/(slip*omegas);   %Electromechanical torque
  Pmech = omegam*Tmech;   %Electromechanical power
  Pshaft = Pmech - Prot;

  if (m == 1)
    fprintf('\nExample 6-5 solution:')
  else
    fprintf('\nExample 6-6 solution:')
  end

  fprintf('\n    Pmech = %3.1f [kW], Pshaft = %3.1f [kW]\n', ...
    Pmech/1000,Pshaft/1000)
  fprintf('    I1 = %3.1f [A]\n',abs(I1));
end        % end of "for m = 1:2" loop
```

6.7 EFFECTS OF ROTOR RESISTANCE; WOUND AND DOUBLE-SQUIRREL-CAGE ROTORS

A basic limitation of induction motors with constant rotor resistance is that the rotor design has to be a compromise. High efficiency under normal running conditions requires a low rotor resistance, but a low rotor resistance results in a low starting torque and high starting current at a low starting power factor.

6.7.1 Wound-Rotor Motors

The use of a *wound rotor* is one effective way of avoiding the need for compromise. In a wound-rotor motor, the rotor is constructed with a polyphase winding similar to that of the stator. The terminals of the rotor windings are connected to slip rings. Stationary brushes in contact with the slip rings are used to connect the windings in series with external resistors which can be used to control the starting torque and current. As the motor comes up to speed, the resistor values can be varied and they can ultimately be short-circuited to achieve maximum efficiency at operating speeds.

The general nature of the effects on the torque-speed characteristics caused by varying rotor resistance has been shown in Fig. 6.16. By use of the appropriate value of rotor resistance, the maximum torque can be made to occur at standstill if high starting torque is needed. As the rotor speeds up, the external resistances can be decreased, making maximum torque available throughout the accelerating range. Since most of the rotor I^2R loss is dissipated in the external resistors, the rotor temperature rise during starting is lower than it would be if the resistance were incorporated in the rotor winding. For normal running, the rotor winding can be short-circuited directly at the brushes. The rotor winding itself is typically designed to have low resistance so that running efficiency is high and full-load slip is low. Besides their use when starting requirements are severe, wound-rotor induction motors can be used for adjustable-speed drives. Their chief disadvantage is greater cost and complexity than squirrel-cage motors.

The principal effects of varying rotor resistance on the starting and running characteristics of induction motors can be shown quantitatively by the following example.

EXAMPLE 6.7

A three-phase, 460-V, 60-Hz, four-pole, 500-hp wound-rotor induction motor, with its slip rings short-circuited, has the following properties:

Full-load slip = 1.5%

Rotor I^2R at full-load torque = 5.69 kW

Slip at maximum torque = 6%

Rotor current at maximum torque = 2.82 $I_{2,fl}$, where $I_{2,fl}$ is the full-load rotor current

Torque at 20% slip = 1.20 T_{fl}, where T_{fl} is the full-load torque

Rotor current at 20% slip = 3.95 $I_{2,fl}$

If the rotor-circuit resistance is increased to 5 R_{rotor} by connecting non-inductive resistances in series with each rotor slip ring, determine (a) the slip at which the motor will develop the same full-load torque, (b) total rotor-circuit $I^2 R$ loss at full-load torque, (c) horsepower output at full-load torque, (d) slip at maximum torque, (e) rotor current at maximum torque, (f) starting torque, and (g) rotor current at starting. Express the torques and rotor currents in per unit based on the full-load torque values.

■ Solution

The solution involves recognition of the fact that the effects of changes in the rotor resistance are seen from the stator in terms of changes in the referred resistance R_2/s. Examination of the equivalent circuit shows that, for specified applied voltage and frequency, everything concerning the stator performance is fixed by the value of R_2/s, the other impedance elements being constant. For example, if R_2 is doubled and s is simultaneously doubled, there will be no indication from the stator that anything has changed. The stator current and power factor, the power delivered to the air gap, and the torque will be unchanged as long as the ratio R_2/s remains constant.

Added physical significance can be given to the argument by examining the effects of simultaneously doubling R_2 and s from the viewpoint of the rotor. An observer on the rotor would see the resultant air-gap flux wave traveling past at twice the original slip speed, generating twice the original rotor voltage at twice the original slip frequency. The rotor reactance therefore is doubled, and since the original premise is that the rotor resistance also is doubled, the rotor impedance is doubled while the rotor power factor is unchanged. Since rotor voltage and impedance are both doubled, the effective value of the rotor current remains the same; only its frequency is changed. The air gap still has the same synchronously rotating flux and mmf waves with the same torque angle. An observer on the rotor would then agree with a counterpart on the stator that the torque is unchanged.

An observer on the rotor, however, would be aware of two changes not apparent in the stator: (1) the rotor $I^2 R$ loss will doubled, and (2) the rotor is turning more slowly and therefore developing less mechanical power with the same torque. In other words, more of the power absorbed from the stator goes into $I^2 R$ heat in the rotor, and less is available for mechanical power.

The preceding thought processes can be readily applied to the solution of this example.

a. If the rotor resistance is increased five times, the slip must increase five times for the same value of R_2/s and therefore for the same torque. But the original slip at full load is 0.015. The new slip at full-load torque therefore is $5 \times 0.015 = 0.075$.

b. The effective value of the rotor current is the same as its full-load value before addition of the series resistance, and therefore the rotor R_2/s loss is five times the full-load value of 5.69 kW, or

$$\text{Rotor } I^2 R = 5 \times 5.69 = 28.4 \text{ kW}$$

c. The increased slip has caused the per-unit speed at full-load torque to drop from $1 - s = 0.985$ down to $1 - s = 0.925$. Since the ratio R_2/s is unchanged, the torque is the same and hence the power output has dropped proportionally, or

$$P_{\text{mech}} = \left(\frac{0.925}{0.985} \right) 500 = 470 \text{ hp}$$

Because the air-gap power is unchanged, the decrease in electromechanical shaft power must be accompanied by a corresponding increase in rotor I^2R loss.

d. If rotor resistance is increased five times, the slip at maximum torque simply increases five times. But the original slip at maximum torque is 0.060. The new slip at maximum torque with the added rotor resistance therefore is

$$s_{maxT} = 5 \times 0.060 = 0.30$$

e. The effective value of the rotor current at maximum torque is independent of rotor resistance; only its frequency is changed when rotor resistance is varied. Therefore,

$$I_{2,maxT} = 2.82\, I_{2,fl}$$

f. With the rotor resistance increased five times, the starting torque will be the same as the original running torque at a slip of 0.20 and therefore equals the running torque without the series resistors, namely,

$$T_{start} = 1.20\, T_{fl}$$

g. The rotor current at starting with the added rotor resistances will be the same as the rotor current when running at a slip of 0.20 with the slip rings short-circuited, namely,

$$I_{2,start} = 3.95\, I_{2,fl}$$

Practice Problem 6.7

Consider the motor of Example 6.7. An external resistor is added to the rotor circuits such that the full-load torque is developed at a speed of 1719 r/min. Calculate (a) the added resistance in terms of the inherent rotor resistance R_{rotor}, (b) the rotor power dissipation at full load, and (c) the corresponding electromechanical power.

Solution

    a. Added resistance = $2\, R_{rotor}$
    b. Rotor $I^2R = 17.1$ kW
    c. $P_{mech} = 485$ hp

With the advent of variable-speed drives which can apply variable-frequency voltages and currents to the stator and hence can control the slip as a function of motor speed, it is possible to control the applied frequency, and hence the motor slip, to achieve maximum torque at any desired rotor speed, including under starting conditions. As a result, the use of wound-rotor motors has become less common because similar performance can now be obtained with squirrel-cage motors.

6.7.2 Deep-Bar and Double-Squirrel-Cage Rotors

A simple and ingenious way of obtaining a rotor resistance which automatically varies with speed makes use of the fact that, at standstill, the rotor frequency equals the stator frequency and, as the motor accelerates, the rotor frequency decreases to a very low

Figure 6.21 Deep rotor bar with slot-leakage flux shown in schematic form.

value at the speed associated with normal operating conditions. With suitable shapes and arrangements for rotor bars, squirrel-cage rotors can be designed so that their effective resistance at 60 Hz is several times their dc resistance. The various schemes all make use of the inductive effect of the slot-leakage flux on the current distribution in the rotor bars. This phenomenon is similar to the skin and proximity effect in any system of conductors carrying alternating current.

Consider first a squirrel-cage rotor having deep, narrow bars like that shown in cross section in Fig. 6.21. The general character of the slot-leakage flux produced by the current in the bar within this slot is shown in schematic form in the figure. If the rotor iron had infinite permeability, all the leakage-flux lines would close in paths below the slot, as shown. Now imagine the bar to consist of an infinite number of layers of differential depth; one at the bottom and one at the top are indicated crosshatched in Fig. 6.21. The leakage inductance of the bottom layer is greater than that of the top layer because the bottom layer is linked by more leakage flux. Because all the layers are electrically in parallel, under ac conditions the current in the low-reactance upper layers will be greater than that in the high-reactance lower layers. As a result, the current will be forced toward the top of the slot, and the phase of current in the upper layers will lead that of the current in the lower ones.

This nonuniform current distribution results in an increase in the effective bar resistance and a smaller decrease in the effective leakage inductance of the bar. Since the distortion in current distribution depends on an inductive effect, the effective resistance is a function of the frequency as well as the depth and shape of the bar and the permeability and resistivity of the bar material. Figure 6.22 shows a curve of the ratio of effective ac resistance to dc resistance as a function of frequency computed for a rectangular copper bar 2.5 cm deep. A squirrel-cage rotor with deep bars can be readily designed to have an effective resistance at stator frequency (corresponding to rotor standstill conditions) several times greater than its dc resistance. As the motor accelerates, the rotor frequency decreases and therefore the effective rotor resistance decreases, approaching its dc value at small slips.

An alternative way of attaining similar results is the double-cage arrangement shown in Fig. 6.23. In this case, the squirrel-cage winding consists of two layers of bars short-circuited by end rings. The upper bars are of smaller cross-sectional area than the lower bars and consequently have higher resistance. The general nature of the

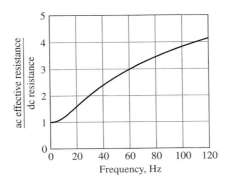

Figure 6.22 Skin effect in a copper rotor bar 2.5 cm deep.

slot-leakage field is shown in Fig. 6.23, from which it can be seen that the inductance of the lower bars is greater than that of the upper ones because of the flux crossing the slot between the two layers. The difference in inductance can be made quite large by properly proportioning the constriction in the slot between the two bars. At standstill, when rotor frequency equals stator frequency, there is relatively little current in the lower bars because of their high reactance; the effective resistance of the rotor at standstill is then approximately equal to that of the high-resistance upper layer. At the low rotor frequencies corresponding to small slips, however, reactance effects become negligible, and the rotor resistance then approaches that of the two layers in parallel.

Note that since the effective resistance and leakage inductance of double-cage and deep-bar rotors vary with frequency, the parameters R_2 and X_2, representing the referred effects of rotor resistance and leakage inductance as viewed from the stator, vary with rotor speed and are not constant. Strictly speaking, a more complicated form of equivalent circuit, with multiple parallel branches, is required in order to represent these cases.

Under steady-state conditions, the simple equivalent circuit derived in Section 6.3 can still be used to represent induction machines in these cases. However R_2 and X_2 must be varied with slip. All the basic relations still apply to the motor if the values

Figure 6.23 Double-squirrel-cage rotor bars with slot-leakage flux shown in schematic form.

of R_2 and X_2 are properly adjusted with changes in slip. For example, in computing the starting performance, R_2 and X_2 should be taken as their effective values at stator frequency, while in computing the running performance at small slips, R_2 should be taken as its effective value at a low frequency, and X_2 should be taken as the stator-frequency value of the reactance corresponding to a low-frequency effective value of the rotor leakage inductance. Over the normal running range of slips, the rotor resistance and leakage inductance usually can be considered constant at substantially their dc values.

6.7.3   Motor-Application Considerations

By use of double-cage and deep-bar rotors, squirrel-cage motors can be designed to have the good starting characteristics resulting from high rotor resistance and, at the same time, the good running characteristics resulting from low rotor resistance. The design is necessarily somewhat of a compromise, however, and such motors lack the flexibility of a wound-rotor machine with external rotor resistance. As a result, wound-rotor motors were commonly preferred when starting requirements were severe. However, as discussed in Section 6.7.2, when combined with power-electronics, squirrel-cage motors can achieve all the flexibility of wound-rotor motors, and hence wound-rotor motors are becoming increasingly less common even in cases where starting requirements are severe.

To meet the usual needs of industry, integral-horsepower, three-phase, squirrel-cage motors are available from manufacturers' stock in a range of standard ratings up to 200 hp at various standard frequencies, voltages, and speeds. (Larger motors are generally regarded as special-purpose rather than general-purpose motors.) Several standard designs are available to meet various starting and running requirements. Representative torque-speed characteristics of the four most common designs are shown in Fig. 6.24. These curves are fairly typical of 1800 r/min (synchronous-speed) motors in ratings from 7.5 to 200 hp although it should be understood that individual motors may differ appreciably from these average curves.

Briefly, the characteristic features of these designs are as follows.

Design Class A: Normal Starting Torque, Normal Starting Current, Low Slip
This design usually has a low-resistance, single-cage rotor. It emphasizes good running performance at the expense of starting. The full-load slip is low and the full-load efficiency is high. The maximum torque usually is well over 200 percent of full-load torque and occurs at a small slip (less than 20 percent). The starting torque at full voltage varies from about 200 percent of full-load torque in small motors to about 100 percent in large motors. The high starting current (500 to 800 percent of full-load current when started at rated voltage) is the principal disadvantage of this design.

In sizes below about 7.5 hp these starting currents usually are within the limits on inrush current which the distribution system supplying the motor can withstand, and across-the-line starting at full voltage then can be used. Otherwise, reduced-voltage starting must be used. Reduced-voltage starting results in a decrease in starting torque because the starting torque is proportional to the square of the voltage applied to the motor terminals. The reduced voltage for starting is usually obtained from an

Figure 6.24 Typical torque-speed curves for 1800-r/min general-purpose induction motors.

autotransformer, called a *starting compensator,* which may be manually operated or automatically operated by relays which cause full voltage to be applied after the motor is up to speed. A circuit diagram of one type of compensator is shown in Fig. 6.25. If a smoother start is necessary, series resistance or reactance in the stator may be used.

The class A motor is the basic standard design in sizes below about 7.5 and above about 200 hp. It is also used in intermediate ratings where design considerations may make it difficult to meet the starting-current limitations of the class-B design. Its field of application is about the same as that of the class-B design described next.

Design Class B: Normal Starting Torque, Low Starting Current, Low Slip This design has approximately the same starting torque as the class-A design but with 75 percent of the starting current. Full-voltage starting, therefore, may be used with larger sizes than with class A. The starting current is reduced by designing for relatively high leakage reactance, and the starting torque is maintained by use of a double-cage or deep-bar rotor. The full-load slip and efficiency are good, about the same as for the class A design. However, the use of high reactance slightly decreases the power factor and decidedly lowers the maximum torque (usually only slightly over 200 percent of full-load torque being obtainable).

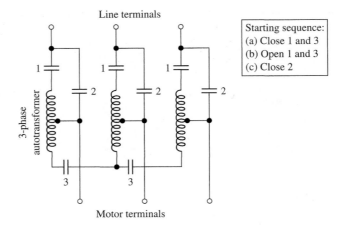

Figure 6.25 Connections of a one-step starting autotransformer.

This design is the most common in the 7.5 to 200-hp range of sizes. It is used for substantially constant-speed drives where starting-torque requirements are not severe, such as in driving fans, blowers, pumps, and machine tools.

Design Class C: High Starting Torque, Low Starting Current   This design uses a double-cage rotor with higher rotor resistance than the class-B design. The result is higher starting torque with low starting current but somewhat lower running efficiency and higher slip than the class-A and class-B designs. Typical applications are in driving compressors and conveyers.

Design Class D: High Starting Torque, High Slip   This design usually has a single-cage, high-resistance rotor (frequently brass bars). It produces very high starting torque at low starting current, high maximum torque at 50 to 100 percent slip, but runs at a high slip at full load (7 to 11 percent) and consequently has low running efficiency. Its principal uses are for driving intermittent loads involving high accelerating duty and for driving high-impact loads such as punch presses and shears. When driving high-impact loads, the motor is generally aided by a flywheel which helps supply the impact and reduces the pulsations in power drawn from the supply system. A motor whose speed falls appreciably with an increase in torque is required so that the flywheel can slow down and deliver some of its kinetic energy to the impact.

6.8 SUMMARY

In a polyphase induction motor, slip-frequency currents are induced in the rotor windings as the rotor slips past the synchronously-rotating stator flux wave. These rotor currents, in turn, produce a flux wave which rotates in synchronism with the stator flux wave; torque is produced by the interaction of these two flux waves. For increased load on the motor, the rotor speed decreases, resulting in larger slip, increased induced rotor currents, and greater torque.

Examination of the flux-mmf interactions in a polyphase induction motor shows that, electrically, the machine is a form of transformer. The synchronously-rotating air-gap flux wave in the induction machine is the counterpart of the mutual core flux in the transformer. The rotating field induces emfs of stator frequency in the stator windings and of slip frequency in the rotor windings (for all rotor speeds other than synchronous speed). Thus, the induction machine transforms voltages and at the same time changes frequency. When viewed from the stator, all rotor electrical and magnetic phenomena are transformed to stator frequency. The rotor mmf reacts on the stator windings in the same manner as the mmf of the secondary current in a transformer reacts on the primary. Pursuit of this line of reasoning leads to a single-phase equivalent circuit for polyphase induction machines which closely resemble that of a transformer.

For applications requiring substantially constant speed without excessively severe starting conditions, the squirrel-cage motor usually is unrivaled because of its ruggedness, simplicity, and relatively low cost. Its only disadvantage is its relatively low power factor (about 0.85 to 0.90 at full load for four-pole, 60-Hz motors and considerably lower at light loads and for lower-speed motors). The low power factor is a consequence of the fact that all the excitation must be supplied by lagging reactive power taken from the ac source.

One of the salient facts affecting induction-motor applications is that the slip at which maximum torque occurs can be controlled by varying the rotor resistance. A high rotor resistance gives high starting conditions but poor running performance. A low rotor resistance, however, may result in unsatisfactory starting conditions. As a result, the design of a squirrel-cage motor is, therefore, quite likely to be a compromise.

Marked improvement in the starting performance with relatively little sacrifice in running performance can be built into a squirrel-cage motor by using a deep-bar or double-cage rotor whose effective resistance increases with slip. A wound-rotor motor can be used for very severe starting conditions or when speed control by rotor resistance is required. Variable-frequency solid-state motor drives lend considerable flexibility to the application of induction motors in variable-speed applications. These issues are discussed in Chapter 10.

6.9 CHAPTER 6 VARIABLES

δ_r, ϕ	Phase angle [rad]
ω_m	Mechanical angular velocity [rad/sec]
ω_s	Synchronous angular velocity [rad/sec]
Φ_{sr}	Resultant air-gap flux [Wb]
$\hat{E}, \hat{V}$	Voltage, complex amplitude [V]
f_e	Electrical frequency [Hz]
f_r	Rotor electrical frequency [Hz]
F_r	Rotor mmf [A]
$\hat{I}$	Current, complex amplitude [A]
$\hat{I}_\varphi$	Exciting current, complex amplitude [A]
$\hat{I}_c$	Core-loss component of the exciting current, complex amplitude [A]

$\hat{I}_\mathrm{m}$	Magnetizing component of the exciting current, complex amplitude [A]
K	Constant
n	Angular velocity [r/min]
n_s	Synchronous angular velocity [r/min]
N	Number of turns
poles	Number of poles
q	Number of phases
R	Resistance [Ω]
s	Slip
T	Torque [N·m]
X	Reactance [Ω]
Z	Impedance [Ω]

Subscripts:

bl	Blocked
c	Core
eff	Effective
fl	Full load
gap	Gap
in	Input
m	Magnetizing
max	Maximum
maxT	Maximum torque
mech	Mechanical
nl	No load
re	Rated electric
rot	Rotational
s	Slip frequency
start	Starting

6.10   PROBLEMS

6.1   The nameplate on a 400-V, 35-kW, 50-Hz, four-pole induction motor indicates that its speed at rated load is 1458 r/min. Assume the motor to be operating at rated load.

   a.   What is the slip of the rotor?

   b.   What is the frequency of the rotor currents in Hz?

   c.   What is the angular velocity of the stator-produced air-gap flux wave with respect to the stator in rad/sec? With respect to the rotor?

   d.   What is the angular velocity of the rotor-produced air-gap flux wave with respect to the stator in rad/sec? With respect to the rotor?

6.2   A 60-Hz, two-pole, 208-V wound-rotor induction motor has a three-phase stator winding of 42 series turns/phase and a rotor winding of 38 series turns/phase. When operating at rated terminal voltage, the motor is observed to be operating at a speed of 3517 r/min. Calculations indicate that under this operating condition, the air-gap flux wave induces a voltage of 193 V, line-line in the stator winding. Calculate the corresponding voltage induced in the rotor winding.

6.3 Stray leakage fields will induce rotor-frequency voltages in a pickup coil mounted along the shaft of an induction motor. Measurement of the frequency of these induced voltages can be used to determine the rotor speed.

    a. What is the rotor speed in r/min of a 50-Hz, six-pole induction motor if the frequency of the induced voltage is 0.73 Hz?

    b. Calculate the frequency of the induced voltage produced by a four-pole, 60-Hz induction motor operating at a speed of 1763 r/min. What is the corresponding slip?

6.4 A three-phase induction motor runs at 1198 r/min at no load and 1119 r/min at full load when supplied from a 60-Hz, three-phase source.

    a. How many poles does this motor have?

    b. What is the slip in percent at full load?

    c. What is the corresponding frequency of the rotor currents?

    d. What is the speed in r/min of the rotor field with respect to the rotor? With respect to the stator?

6.5 Linear induction motors have been proposed for a variety of applications including high-speed ground transportation. A linear motor based on the induction-motor principle consists of a car riding on a track. The track is a developed squirrel-cage winding, and the car, which is 6.7 m long and 1.75 m wide, has a developed three-phase, 10-pole-pair armature winding. Power at 40 Hz is fed to the car from arms extending through slots to rails below ground level.

    a. What is the synchronous speed in km/hr?

    b. Will the car reach this speed? Explain your answer.

    c. What is the slip if the car is traveling 89 km/hr? What is the frequency of the track currents under this condition?

    d. If the control system controls the magnitude and frequency of the car currents to maintain constant slip, what is the frequency of the armature-winding currents when the car is traveling 75 km/hr? What is the frequency of the track currents under this condition?

6.6 The stator of a 208-V, 60-Hz induction motor is wound with 10-turn coils. The motor is to be re-wound for operation at 400-V, 50-Hz. Calculate the number of turns per coil for the re-wound motor so that it operates at the same flux-density as the original motor.

6.7 Describe the effect on the torque-speed characteristic of an induction motor produced by (a) halving the applied voltage and (b) halving both the applied voltage and the frequency. Sketch the resultant torque-speed curves relative

Figure 6.26 Interconnected induction and synchronous machines (Problem 6.8).

to that of rated-voltage and rated-frequency. Neglect the effects of stator resistance and leakage reactance.

6.8 A system such as that shown in Fig. 6.26 can be used to convert balanced 60-Hz voltages to other frequencies. The synchronous motor has six poles and drives the interconnected shaft in the clockwise direction. The induction machine has four poles and its stator windings are connected to the source in such a fashion as to produce a counter-clockwise rotating field (in the direction opposite to the rotation of the synchronous motor). The induction machine has a wound rotor whose terminals are brought out through slip rings.

  a. With the system supplied from a 50-Hz source, at what speed does the synchronous motor run?

  b. What is the frequency of the voltages produced at the slip rings of the induction motor?

  c. What will be the frequency of the voltages produced at the slip rings of the induction motor if two leads of the induction-motor stator are interchanged, reversing the direction of rotation of the resultant rotating field?

6.9 A three-phase, eight-pole, 60-Hz, 4160-V, 1000-kW squirrel-cage induction motor has the following equivalent-circuit parameters in ohms-per-phase referred to the stator:

$$R_1 = 0.187 \quad R_2 = 0.176 \quad X_1 = 1.66 \quad X_2 = 2.06 \quad X_m = 38.85$$

Determine the changes in these constants which will result from the following proposed design modifications. Consider each modification separately.

  a. Replace the stator winding with an otherwise identical winding with a wire size whose cross-sectional area is increased by 6 percent.

b. Decrease the inner diameter of the stator laminations such that the air gap is decreased by 15 percent.

c. Replace the aluminum rotor bars (conductivity 3.5×10^7 mhos/m) with copper bars (conductivity 5.8×10^7 mhos/m).

d. Reconnect the stator winding, originally connected in Y for 4160-V operation, in Δ for 2.4 kV operation.

6.10 The single-phase equivalent-circuit parameters for a three-phase induction motor in ohms-per-phase are

$$R_1 = 0.17 \quad R_2 = 0.24 \quad X_1 = 1.05 \quad X_2 = 0.87$$

$$X_m = 82.1 \quad R_c = 435$$

For a slip of 3.5 percent, and a terminal voltage of 460 V, line-line, calculate:

a. Calculate the motor phase current and input real and reactive power.

b. Calculate the mechanical output power and the power dissipated in the rotor. You may assume that the motor friction and windage losses are 270 W.

c. Calculate the motor core loss and the motor efficiency.

6.11 Write a MATLAB script which calculates the terminal current, power factor, shaft output power, and efficiency for an induction motor given its equivalent-circuit parameters and friction/windage loss. The input to your program will be the motor terminal voltage and operating slip. Exercise your program on the motor of Problem 6.10.

6.12 A three-phase, Y-connected, 460-V (line-line), 37-kW, 60-Hz, four-pole induction motor has the following equivalent-circuit parameters in ohms-per-phase referred to the stator:

$$R_1 = 0.070 \quad R_2 = 0.152 \quad X_1 = 0.743 \quad X_2 = 0.764 \quad X_m = 40.1$$

The total friction and windage losses may be assumed constant at 390 W, and the core loss may be assumed to be equal to 325 W. With the motor connected directly to a 460-V source, compute the speed, output shaft torque and power, input power, and power factor and efficiency for slips of 1, 2, and 3 percent. You may choose either to represent the core loss by a resistance connected directly across the motor terminals or by resistance R_c connected in parallel with the magnetizing reactance X_m.

6.13 A 460-V, three-phase, 4-pole induction motor is known to have the following single-phase equivalent-circuit parameters in ohms-per-phase Y

$$R_1 = 19.7 \times 10^{-3} \quad X_1 = 0.129 \quad X_2 = 0.187 \quad X_m = 13.9$$

The motor is observed to be operating at a terminal voltage of 450 V, line-line with an output power of 95 kW at a speed of 1780.7 r/min. Calculate the single-phase equivalent-circuit rotor resistance R_2 assuming that the motor core loss is 1200 W and the friction and windage loss is 700 W. Hint: Most easily solved using a MATLAB search.

6.14 A three-phase, 4-pole, 75 kW, 460-V induction motor has the following single-phase equivalent-circuit parameters in ohms-per-phase

$$R_1 = 24.5 \times 10^{-3} \quad R_2 = 55.2 \times 10^{-3}$$
$$X_1 = 0.267 \quad X_2 = 0.277 \quad X_m = 19.8$$

You may assume that the motor friction and windage loss of 1250 W remains constant over the normal range of operation and the core loss at 460 V is 780 W.

a. Calculate the motor slip, speed, terminal current, power factor and efficiency when operating at 460 V and supplying its rated output power. Hint: It may be easiest to search for the desired operating point using MATLAB.

b. Complete a table including the motor slip, speed, terminal current, power factor and efficiency when operating at 460 V for full load (part (a)), 75 percent, 50 percent, and 25 percent of rated load as well as no load.

6.15 The motor of Problem 6.14 is to be operated from a variable-voltage, variable-frequency, three-phase drive. The drive output voltage is 460 V line-line at 60 Hz and is proportional to frequency. Assume that the motor parameters (resistances and inductances) do not vary with applied voltage and frequency. You may also assume that, for this operation, the friction and windage loss varies with the cube of the motor speed (1250 W at 1800 r/min) and the core loss with the square of the applied frequency.

a. Calculate the motor slip, speed, terminal current, power factor, and efficiency when operating at 460 V and supplying its rated output power. Hint: It may be easiest to search for the desired operating point using MATLAB.

With the motor drive operating frequencies below 60 Hz, the maximum motor output power corresponds to that power which results in motor terminal current equal to that found in part (a).

b. Calculate the maximum load power which can be supplied by this system at a frequency of 50 Hz. Calculate the corresponding terminal voltage, slip, speed, power factor and efficiency.

6.16 Consider the induction motor of Problem 6.12 operating at its rated terminal voltage.

a. Find the motor speed in r/min corresponding to the rated shaft output power of 37 kW. (Hint: This can be easily done by writing a MATLAB script which searches over the motor slip.)

b. Similarly, find the speed in r/min at which the motor will operate with no external shaft load (assuming the motor load at that speed to consist only of the friction and windage losses).

c. Plot the motor efficiency versus output power as the motor output power varies from 5 kW to full load.

6.17 Write a MATLAB script to analyze the performance of a three-phase induction motor operating at its rated frequency and voltage. The inputs should be the rated motor voltage, power and frequency, the number of poles, the equivalent-circuit parameters, and the rotational loss. Given a specific speed, the program should calculate the motor output power, the input power and power factor, and the motor efficiency. Exercise your program on a 450-kW, 3.3 kV, three-phase, 50-Hz, four-pole induction motor operating at 1466 r/min whose rated speed rotational loss is 2.8 kW, whose core loss is 3.7 kW and whose equivalent-circuit parameters in ohms-per-phase are:

$$R_1 = 0.178 \quad R_2 = 0.28 \quad X_1 = 2.28 \quad X_2 = 2.69 \quad X_m = 215$$

6.18 A three-phase, 6-pole, 120 kW, 460-V aluminum-squirrel-cage induction motor has the following single-phase equivalent-circuit parameters in ohms-per-phase

$$R_1 = 15.3 \times 10^{-3} \quad R_2 = 34.5 \times 10^{-3}$$
$$X_1 = 0.183 \quad X_2 = 0.219 \quad X_m = 13.4$$

You may assume that the motor friction and windage loss of 1370 W remains constant over the normal range of operation and the core loss at 460 V is 1100 W.

a. Make a table including the motor slip, speed, terminal current, power factor, and efficiency when operating at 460 V and supplying rated power. Hint: It may be easiest to search for the desired operating points using MATLAB.

b. The manufacturer proposes replacing the rotor of this motor with an otherwise identical rotor except that the squirrel cage is cast from copper instead of aluminum. Assuming the electrical conductivity copper to be 1.5 times that of aluminum, repeat the calculation of part (a) for the motor operating with this new rotor. Expand your table of part (a) to include the performance of the copper-rotor motor and compare the results.

c. Compare the performance of this motor with the cast-aluminum and cast-copper rotors operating at rated voltage and 75 percent, 50 percent and 25 percent of rated load.

6.19 A 10-kW, 460-V, three-phase, Y-connected, 60-Hz, six-pole squirrel-cage induction motor develops rated torque at a slip of 3.2 percent when operated at rated voltage and frequency. For the purposes of this problem, rotational and core losses can be neglected. The following motor parameters, in ohms-per-phase, have been obtained:

$$R_1 = 1.26 \quad X_1 = X_2 = 1.56 \quad X_m = 60.6$$

Determine (i) the motor rated torque, (ii) the maximum torque and corresponding speed at rated voltage and frequency, and (iii) the starting torque and current at rated voltage and frequency.

6.20 A three-phase induction motor, operating at rated voltage and frequency, has a starting torque of 115 percent and a maximum torque of 230 percent, both with respect to its rated-load torque. Assuming constant rotor parameters with slip and neglecting the effects of stator resistance and rotational losses and assuming constant rotor resistance, determine:

a. the slip at maximum torque.

b. the slip at rated load.

c. the rotor current at starting (as a percentage of rotor current at rated load).

6.21 When operated at rated voltage and frequency, a three-phase squirrel-cage induction motor delivers full load at a slip of 7.6 percent and develops a maximum torque of 255 percent of full load at a slip of 62 percent. Neglect core and rotational losses and assume that the rotor resistance and inductance remain constant, independent of slip. Determine the torque at starting, with rated voltage and frequency, in per unit based upon its full-load value.

6.22 A three-phase, 6-pole, 125 kW, 575-V, 60-Hz aluminum-squirrel-cage induction motor has the following single-phase equivalent-circuit parameters in ohms-per-phase

$$R_1 = 19.5 \times 10^{-3} \quad R_2 = 30.6 \times 10^{-3}$$

$$X_1 = 0.249 \quad X_2 = 0.294 \quad X_m = 23.5$$

This motor is to be operated as a generator connected to a 575-V system which has a series-equivalent reactance of 0.19 Ω. Calculate the generator speed in r/min and the generator terminal voltage when the generator electrical output power is 110 kW.

6.23 A 1.5-MW, 2400-V, four-pole, 60-Hz induction machine has the following equivalent-circuit parameters in ohms-per-phase referred to the stator:

$$R_1 = 0.0384 \quad R_2 = 0.0845 \quad X_1 = 0.182 \quad X_2 = 0.0780 \quad X_m = 32.7$$

When operated as a motor, it achieves rated shaft output at a slip of 2.35 percent with an efficiency of 95.2 percent. The machine is to be used as a generator, driven by a wind turbine. It will be connected to a 60-Hz distribution system which can be represented by a 2400-V infinite bus.

a. From the given data calculate the total rotational and core losses at rated load.

b. With the wind turbine driving the induction machine at a slip of −2.35 percent, calculate (i) the electric power output in MW, (ii) the efficiency (electric power output per shaft input power) in percent, and (iii) the power factor measured at the machine terminals.

c. The actual distribution system to which the generator is connected has an effective impedance of $0.041 + j0.15$ Ω/phase. For a slip of −2.35 percent, calculate the electric power as measured (i) at the infinite bus and (ii) at the machine terminals.

6.24 Write a MATLAB script to plot the efficiency as a function of electric power output for the induction generator of Problem 6.23 as the speed varies from 1800 r/min to 1840 r/min. Assume the generator to be operating into the system with the feeder impedance of part (c) of Problem 6.23.

6.25 For a 75-kW, 460-V, three-phase, 60-Hz squirrel-cage motor operating at rated voltage and frequency, the rotor I^2R loss at maximum torque is 8.5 times that at full-load torque, and the slip at full-load torque is 0.026. Stator resistance and rotational losses may be neglected and the rotor resistance and inductance may be assumed to be constant. Expressing torque in per unit of the full-load torque, find (a) the slip at maximum torque, (b) the maximum torque, and (c) the starting torque.

6.26 A squirrel-cage induction motor runs at a full-load slip of 3.5 percent. The rotor current at starting is 4.8 times the rotor current at full load. The rotor resistance and inductance are independent of rotor frequency and rotational losses, stray-load losses, and stator resistance may be neglected. Expressing torque in per unit of the full-load torque, compute (a) the starting torque and (b) the maximum torque and the slip at which the maximum torque occurs.

6.27 A 460-V, three-phase, four-pole, 60-Hz squirrel-cage induction motor develops a maximum internal torque of 1160 N·m at a slip of 16 percent when operated at rated voltage and frequency. If the effect of stator resistance is neglected, determine the maximum internal torque that this motor would develop if it were operated at 380 V and 50 Hz. Under these conditions, at what speed in r/min would the maximum torque be developed?

6.28 A Δ-connected, 125-kW, 460-V, three-phase, four-pole, 50-Hz squirrel-cage induction motor has the following equivalent-circuit parameters in ohms-per-phase:

$$R_1 = 0.033 \quad R_2 = 0.045 \quad X_1 = 0.28 \quad X_2 = 0.31 \quad X_m = 7.7$$

a. Calculate the starting current and torque for this motor connected directly to a 460-V source.

b. To limit the starting current, it is proposed to connect the stator winding in Y for starting and then to switch to the Δ connection for normal operation. (i) What are the equivalent-circuit parameters in ohms-per-phase for the Y connection? (ii) With the motor Y-connected and running directly off of a 460-V source, calculate the starting current and torque.

6.29 A Δ-connected, 25-kW, 380-V, three-phase, six-pole, 50-Hz squirrel-cage induction motor has the following equivalent-circuit parameters in ohms-per-phase:

$$R_1 = 0.12 \quad R_2 = 0.15 \quad X_1 = 0.79 \quad X_2 = 0.76 \quad X_m = 26.2$$

The motor is connected to a fan which presents a load proportional to the cube of speed as

$$P_{fan} = 23 \left(\frac{\text{r/min}}{1000} \right)^3 \text{ kW}$$

The combined inertia of the motor and fan is equal to $1.8 \text{ kg} \cdot \text{m}^2$.
The motor is started by applying a terminal voltage of 230 V.

a. Calculate the steady-state operating speed of the fan.

b. Calculate the rms terminal current when the motor is first started.

c. Using MATLAB, plot (i) the motor speed and (ii) the rms motor current as a function of time. HINT: It is fairly easy to write a simple rectangular integration routine. Alternatively, you can implement your solution using MATLAB/Simulink.

6.30 A Δ-connected, 50-kW, 380-V, three-phase, 2-pole, 50-Hz squirrel-cage induction motor is known to have the following equivalent-circuit parameters in ohms-per-phase:

$$R_1 = 0.063 \quad R_2 = 0.095 \quad X_1 = 0.39 \quad X_2 = 0.32 \quad X_m = 14.8 \quad R_c = 113$$

At rated speed, the motor friction and windage loss is equal to 150 W.

a. For a no-load test conducted at rated voltage and frequency, calculate the no-load terminal current and input power.

b. For a blocked-rotor test conducted at a frequency of 12.5 Hz and at rated terminal current, calculate the blocked-rotor line-line voltage and input power.

c. Using the approximations of Section 6.6, calculate the motor equivalent-circuit parameters based upon the no-load and block-rotor "test" results determined in parts (a) and (b). Assume that R_1 is equal to the given value and that $X_1 = X_2$. Compare the resultant parameters with the given values.

6.31 The induction motor of Problem 6.30 is re-connected in Y to operate at a terminal voltage of 660 V. Repeat the calculations of Problem 6.30.

6.32 The following data apply to a 250-kW, 2300-V, three-phase, six pole, 60-Hz squirrel-cage induction motor:

■ Stator-resistance between phase terminals $= 0.52 \, \Omega$

■ No-load test at rated frequency and voltage:

Line current $= 2.1$ A   Three-phase power $= 2405$ W

The friction and windage loss at rated speed has been determined to 750 W.

■ Blocked-rotor test at 15 Hz:

Line voltage $= 182$ V   Line current $= 62.8$ A

Three-phase power $= 10.8$ kW

a. Calculate the no-load core loss.

b. Using reasonable engineering approximations, calculate the equivalent-circuit parameters in ohms. Assume that $X_1 = X_2$ and that the core-loss resistance R_c is connected directly at the motor terminals.

c. Compute the

  ■ stator current
  ■ input power
  ■ power factor
  ■ stator, core, and rotor power dissipation
  ■ output power
  ■ efficiency

when this motor is operating at rated voltage and frequency at a slip of 3.1 percent.

d. Repeat the calculation of part (c) assuming the core-loss-resistance R_c is connected in parallel with the magnetizing reactance X_m. Compare your results with those of part (c).

6.33 Two 150-kW, 460-V, three-phase, four-pole, 60-Hz squirrel-cage induction motors have identical stators and rotors of the same radius but differing rotor-bar dimensions. The dc resistance measured between any pair of stator terminals is 33.9 mΩ. Blocked-rotor tests at 60-Hz produce the following results:

Motor	Volts (line-to-line)	Amperes	Three-phase power [kW]
1	70.5	188.3	3.12
2	60.7	188.3	6.81

Determine the ratio of the internal starting torque developed by motor 2 to that of motor 1 (a) for the same current and (b) for the same voltage. Make reasonable assumptions.

6.34 Write a MATLAB script to calculate the Y-equivalent-circuit parameters of a three-phase induction motor from open-circuit and blocked-rotor tests. Input:

  ■ Rated frequency
  ■ Rotational loss at rated speed
  ■ No-load test at rated speed: Voltage, current, and power
  ■ Blocked-rotor test: Frequency, voltage, current, and power
  ■ Stator-resistance measured phase to phase
  ■ Assumed ratio X_1/X_2

Output:

  ■ Equivalent circuit parameters R_1, R_2, R_c, X_1, X_2, and X_m

If a value for rotational loss is not available, you may set it equal to zero.

a.   Base your MATLAB script on the approximations presented in Section 6.6. Exercise your program on a 2300-V, three-phase, 50-Hz, 150-kW induction motor whose test results are:

Stator-resistance between phase terminals $= 0.428\ \Omega$

No-load test at rated frequency and voltage:

Line current $= 12.8$ A   Three-phase power $= 2.31$ kW

Blocked-rotor test at 12.5 Hz:

Line-line voltage $= 142$ V   Line current $= 43.1$ A

Three-phase power $= 4.87$ kW

You may assume that $X_1 = 0.45(X_1 + X_2)$.

b.   Modify the parameters values found in part (a) such that when the complete equivalent-circuit of Fig. 6.8 is used to simulate the no-load and blocked-rotor tests, the simulated and test results match exactly. This can be easily done by adding a section of MATLAB code which searches over parameter values close to those found in part (a) for values which result in a complete equivalent circuit which matches the test results. Compare these "exact" parameter values with those found in part (a).

6.35 A 50-kW, 50-Hz, four-pole, 380-V three-phase, squirrel-cage induction motor develops full-load torque at 1447 r/min with the rotor short-circuited. It develops a maximum torque of 542 N·m. An external non-inductive resistance of 0.9 Ω is placed in series with each phase of the rotor, and the motor is observed to develop its rated torque at a speed of 1415 r/min. Calculate the rotor resistance per phase of the motor itself.

6.36 A 125-kW, 380-V, three-phase, six-pole, 50-Hz, wound-rotor induction motor develops a maximum internal torque of 225 percent at a slip of 17 percent when operated at rated voltage and frequency with its rotor short-circuited directly at the slip rings. Stator resistance and rotational losses may be neglected, and the rotor resistance and inductance may be assumed to be constant, independent of rotor frequency. Determine

a.   the slip at full load in percent.

b.   the rotor I^2R loss at full load in watts.

c.   the starting torque at rated voltage and frequency in per unit and in N · m.

If the rotor resistance is doubled (by inserting external series resistance at the slip rings) and the motor load is adjusted for such that the line current is equal to the value corresponding to rated load with no external resistance, determine

d.   the corresponding slip in percent and

e.   the torque in N · m.

6.37 A three-phase, Y-connected, 460-V (line-line), 25-kW, 60-Hz, four-pole wound rotor induction motor has the following equivalent-circuit parameters in ohms-per-phase referred to the stator:

$$R_1 = 0.10 \quad R_2 = 0.08 \quad R_c = 1270 \quad X_1 = 1.12 \quad X_2 = 1.22 \quad X_m = 253$$

   a. Neglecting any effects of rotational and core losses, use MATLAB to plot the internal torque versus speed curve for rated-voltage, rated-frequency operation.

   b. On the same plot, plot curves of internal torque versus speed for this motor assuming the rotor resistance increases by a factor of 5, 10 and 30.

   c. The motor is connected to a fan load whose torque requirement varies as the square of its speed and which requires 117 N·m at 1800 r/min. Plot the fan torque on the same plot.

   d. Calculate the fan speed in r/min and power in kW for each of four values of rotor resistance.

6.38 A 575-V, three-phase, four-pole, 60-Hz, 125-kW, wound-rotor induction motor develops an internal torque of 195 percent with a line current of 210 percent (torque and current expressed as a percentage of their full-load values) at a slip of 5.5 percent when running at rated voltage and frequency with its rotor terminals short-circuited. The rotor resistance is measured to be 95 mΩ between each slip ring and may be assumed to remain constant. A balanced set of Y-connected resistors is to be connected to the slip rings in order to limit the rated-voltage starting current to 210 percent of its rated value. What resistance must be chosen for each leg of the Y connection? What will be the starting torque under these conditions in percent of rated torque?

6.39 A 100-kW, three-phase, 60-Hz, 460-V, eight-pole wound-rotor induction motor develops its rated full-load output at a speed of 869 r/min when operated at rated voltage and frequency with its slip rings short-circuited. The maximum torque it can develop at rated voltage and frequency is 295 percent of full-load torque. The resistance of the rotor winding is 0.18 ohms-per-phase. Neglect any effects of rotational and stray-load loss and stator resistance.

   a. Compute the rotor I^2R loss at full load.

   b. Compute the speed at maximum torque in r/min.

   c. How much resistance must be inserted in series with the rotor windings to produce maximum starting torque?

With the rotor windings short-circuited, the motor is now run from a 50-Hz supply with the applied voltage adjusted so that the air-gap flux wave is essentially equal to that at rated 60-Hz operation.

   d. Compute the 50-Hz applied voltage.

   e. Compute the speed at which the motor will develop a torque equal to its rated 60-Hz value with its slip-rings shorted.

6.40 A 575-V, 175-kW, 60-Hz, 6-pole wound-rotor induction motor has the following parameters in ohms-per-phase

$$R_1 = 0.023 \quad R_2 = 0.081 \quad R_c = 287 \quad X_1 = 0.25 \quad X_2 = 0.29 \quad X_m = 57$$

The phase-phase resistance of the rotor as measured across the rotor slip rings is 0.23 Ω. For the purposes of this problem, you may assume that this motor is driving a constant-torque load of 950 N·m. Hint: This problem is most easily solved by using MATLAB to search for operating points that match the stated criterion.

a. Find the motor speed in r/min, load power, terminal current, efficiency and the rotor power dissipation if the motor is operated at rated voltage with the rotor slip rings shorted.

b. Calculate the external resistance in ohms-per-phase that must be added at the slip rings to set the motor speed to 1050 r/min. Again find the motor speed in r/min, load power, terminal current, efficiency and the rotor power dissipation. Also calculate the power dissipation in the external rotor resistors.

CHAPTER 7

DC Machines

D c machines are characterized by their versatility. By means of various combinations of shunt-, series-, and separately excited field windings they can be designed to display a wide variety of volt-ampere or speed-torque characteristics for both dynamic and steady-state operation. Because of the ease with which they can be controlled, systems of dc machines have been frequently used in applications requiring a wide range of motor speeds or precise control of motor output. In recent years, solid-state ac drive system technology has developed sufficiently that these systems are replacing dc machines in applications previously associated almost exclusively with dc machines. However, the versatility of dc machines in combination with the relative simplicity of their drive systems will insure their continued use in a wide variety of applications.

7.1 INTRODUCTION

The essential features of a dc machine are shown schematically in Fig. 7.1. The stator has salient poles and is excited by one or more field coils. The air-gap flux distribution created by the field windings is symmetric about the center line of the field poles. This axis is called the *field axis* or *direct axis*.

As discussed in Section 4.6.2, the ac voltage generated in each rotating armature coil is converted to dc in the external armature terminals by means of a rotating commutator and stationary brushes to which the armature leads are connected. The commutator-brush combination forms a mechanical rectifier, resulting in a dc armature voltage as well as an armature-mmf wave which is fixed in space. Commutator action is discussed in detail in Section 7.2.

The brushes are located so that commutation occurs when the coil sides are in the neutral zone, midway between the field poles. The axis of the armature-mmf wave then is 90 electrical degrees from the axis of the field poles, i.e., in the *quadrature axis*. In the schematic representation of Fig. 7.1a, the brushes are shown in the quadrature axis because this is the position of the coils to which they are connected. The armature-mmf wave then is along the brush axis, as shown. (The geometric position of the brushes

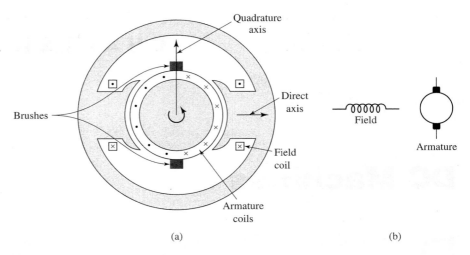

Figure 7.1   Schematic representations of a dc machine.

in an actual machine is approximately 90 electrical degrees from their position in the schematic diagram because of the shape of the end connections to the commutator. For example, see Fig. 7.7.) For simplicity, the circuit representation usually will be drawn as in Fig. 7.1b.

Although the magnetic torque and the speed voltage appearing at the brushes are somewhat dependent on the spatial waveform of the flux distribution, for convenience we continue to assume a sinusoidal flux-density wave in the air gap as was done in Chapter 4. The torque can then be found from the magnetic field viewpoint of Section 4.7.2.

By direct analogy to the derivation of of Eq. 4.83, the electromagnetic torque T_{mech} can be expressed in terms of the interaction of the direct-axis air-gap flux per pole Φ_d and the space-fundamental component F_{a1} of the armature-mmf wave. Specifically, Eq. 4.75 can be re-written in terms of the net direct-axis (stator) mmf (F_s replaced by F_d) and the fundamental net armature-winding (rotor) mmf (F_r replaced by F_{a1}).

$$T_{\mathrm{mech}} = -\left(\frac{\text{poles}}{2}\right)\left(\frac{\mu_0 \pi\, Dl}{2g}\right) F_d F_{a1} \sin \delta_{\mathrm{sr}} \tag{7.1}$$

By analogy to Eq. 4.82 and recognizing that $B_d = \mu_0 F_d / g$ we can solve for F_d in terms of the direct-axis flux as

$$F_d = \left(\frac{g \times \text{poles}}{2\mu_0 Dl}\right) \Phi_d \tag{7.2}$$

With the brushes in the quadrature axis, the angle between these fields is 90 electrical degrees, and its sine equals unity. Substitution of Eq. 7.2 into Eq. 7.1 with $\delta_{\mathrm{sr}} = 90°$ then gives

$$T_{\mathrm{mech}} = \frac{\pi}{2}\left(\frac{\text{poles}}{2}\right)^2 \Phi_d F_{a1} \tag{7.3}$$

in which the minus sign has been dropped because the positive direction of the torque can be determined from physical reasoning. The peak value of the sawtooth armature-mmf wave is given by Eq. 4.10, and its space fundamental F_{a1} is $8/\pi^2$ times its peak and thus

$$F_{a1} = \left(\frac{8}{\pi^2}\right)\left(\frac{C_a}{2m \cdot \text{poles}}\right)i_a \qquad (7.4)$$

Substitution of Eq. 7.4 into Eq. 7.3 then gives

$$T_{\text{mech}} = \left(\frac{\text{poles } C_a}{2\pi m}\right)\Phi_d i_a = K_a \Phi_d i_a \qquad (7.5)$$

where

i_a = Current in external armature circuit

C_a = Total number of conductors in armature winding

m = Number of parallel paths through winding

Here

$$K_a = \frac{\text{poles } C_a}{2\pi m} \qquad (7.6)$$

is a constant determined by the design of the winding.

The rectified voltage generated in the armature has already been found in Section 4.6.2 for an elementary single-coil armature, and its waveform is shown in Fig. 4.30. The effect of distributing the winding in several slots is shown in Fig. 7.2, in which each of the rectified sine waves is the voltage generated in one of the coils, with commutation taking place at the moment when the coil sides are in the neutral zone.

The generated voltage as observed from the brushes is the sum of the rectified voltages of all the coils in series between brushes and is shown by the rippling waveform labeled e_a in Fig. 7.2. With a dozen or so commutator segments per pole, the ripple becomes very small and the average generated voltage observed from the brushes equals the sum of the average values of the rectified coil voltages. From Eq. 4.55 the rectified voltage e_a between brushes, known also as the *speed voltage*, is

$$e_a = \left(\frac{\text{poles } C_a}{2\pi m}\right)\Phi_d \omega_m = K_a \Phi_d \omega_m \qquad (7.7)$$

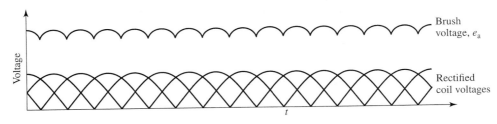

Figure 7.2 Rectified coil voltages and resultant voltage between brushes in a dc machine.

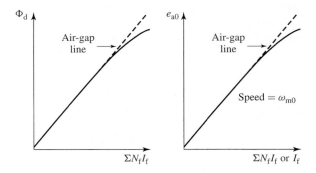

Figure 7.3 Typical form of magnetization curves of a dc machine.

where K_a is the winding constant defined in Eq. 7.6. The rectified voltage of a distributed winding has the same average value as that of a concentrated coil. The difference is that the ripple is greatly reduced.

From Eqs. 7.5 and 7.7, with all variables expressed in SI units,

$$e_a i_a = T_{mech} \, \omega_m = P_{mech} \tag{7.8}$$

Noting that the product of torque and mechanical speed is the mechanical power, this equation simply says that the instantaneous electric power associated with the speed voltage equals the instantaneous mechanical power associated with the magnetic torque, the direction of power flow being determined by whether the machine is acting as a motor or generator.

The direct-axis air-gap flux Φ_d is produced by the combined mmf $\sum N_f i_f$ of the field windings; the flux-mmf characteristic is referred to as the *magnetization curve* for the machine. The form of a typical magnetization curve is shown in Fig. 7.3a, in which it is assumed that the armature mmf has no effect on the direct-axis flux because the axis of the armature-mmf wave, as determined by the orientation of the brushes, is along the quadrature axis and hence perpendicular to the field axis. It will be necessary to re-examine this assumption later in this chapter, where the effects of saturation are investigated more thoroughly. Note that the magnetization curve of Fig. 7.3a does not pass through the origin. This behaviour will occur in cases where the field structure exhibits *residual magnetism,* i.e., where the magnetic material of the field does not fully demagnetize when the net field mmf is reduced to zero.

Because the armature emf is proportional to flux times speed, it is usually more convenient to express the magnetization curve in terms of the armature emf E_{a0} at a constant speed ω_{m0} as shown in Fig. 7.3b. The voltage E_a for a given flux at any other speed ω_m is proportional to the speed; i.e., from Eq. 7.7

$$\frac{e_a}{\omega_m} = K_a \Phi_d = \frac{e_{a0}}{\omega_{m0}} \tag{7.9}$$

Thus

$$e_a = \left(\frac{\omega_m}{\omega_{m0}} \right) e_{a0} \tag{7.10}$$

or, in terms of rotational speed in r/min

$$e_a = \left(\frac{n}{n_0}\right) e_{a0} \tag{7.11}$$

where n_0 is the rotational speed in r/min corresponding to the speed ω_{m0}.

In the case where only a single field winding is excited, the magnetization curve can be plotted most readily as a function of the field current i_f instead of the net field ampere-turns $\left(\sum N_f i_f\right)$ as is also shown in Figure 7.3b. This curve can easily be obtained by test methods; since the field current can be measured directly, no knowledge of any design details is required.

Over a fairly wide range of excitation the reluctance of the electrical steel in the machine is negligible compared with that of the air gap. In this region the flux is linearly proportional to the total mmf of the field windings, the constant of proportionality being the *direct-axis permeance* $\mathcal{P}_d$; thus

$$\Phi_d = \mathcal{P}_d \sum N_f i_f \tag{7.12}$$

The dashed straight line through the origin coinciding with the straight portion of the magnetization curves in Fig. 7.3 is called the *air-gap line*. This nomenclature refers to the fact that this linear magnetizing characteristic would be found if the reluctance of the magnetic material portion of the flux path remained negligible compared to that of the air gap, independent of the degree of magnetic saturation of the motor steel.

The outstanding advantages of dc machines arise from the wide variety of operating characteristics which can be obtained by selection of the method of excitation of the field windings. Various connection diagrams are shown in Fig. 7.4. The method of excitation profoundly influences both the steady-state characteristics and the dynamic behavior of the machine in control systems.

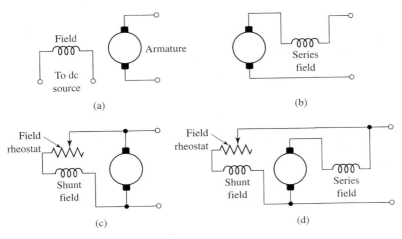

Figure 7.4 Field-circuit connections of dc machines: (a) separate excitation, (b) series, (c) shunt, (d) compound.

Consider first dc generators. The connection diagram of a *separately excited generator* is given in Fig. 7.4a. The required field current is a very small fraction of the rated armature current, on the order of 1 to 3 percent in the average generator. A small amount of power in the field circuit may control a relatively large amount of power in the armature circuit; i.e., the generator is a power amplifier. Separately excited generators are often used in feedback control systems when control of the armature voltage over a wide range is required.

The field windings of *self-excited generators* may be supplied in three different ways. The field may be connected in series with the armature (Fig. 7.4b), resulting in a *series generator*. The field may be connected in shunt with the armature (Fig. 7.4c), resulting in a *shunt generator,* or the field may be in two sections (Fig. 7.4d), one of which is connected in series and the other in shunt with the armature, resulting in a *compound generator*. With *self-excited generators,* residual magnetism must be present in the machine iron to get the self-excitation process started. The effects of residual magnetism can be clearly seen in Fig. 7.3, where the flux and voltage are seen to have nonzero values when the field current is zero.

Typical steady-state volt-ampere characteristics of dc generators are shown in Fig. 7.5, constant-speed operation being assumed. The relation between the steady-state generated emf E_a and the armature terminal voltage V_a is

$$V_a = E_a - I_a R_a \tag{7.13}$$

where I_a is the steady-state armature current output and R_a is the armature circuit resistance. In a generator, E_a is larger than V_a, and the electromagnetic torque T_{mech} is a counter torque opposing rotation.

The terminal voltage of a separately excited generator decreases slightly with an increase in the load current, principally because of the voltage drop in the armature

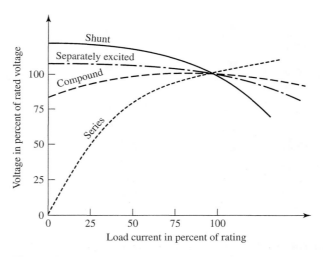

Figure 7.5 Volt-ampere characteristics of dc generators.

resistance. The field current of a series generator is the same as the load current, so that the air-gap flux and hence the voltage vary widely with load. As a consequence, series generators are not often used. The voltage of shunt generators drops off somewhat with load, but not in a manner that is objectionable for many purposes. Compound generators are normally connected so that the mmf of the series winding aids that of the shunt winding. The advantage is that through the action of the series winding the flux per pole can increase with load, resulting in a voltage output which is nearly constant or which even rises somewhat as load increases. The shunt winding usually contains many turns of relatively small wire. The series winding, wound on the outside, consists of a few turns of comparatively heavy conductor because it must carry the full armature current of the machine. The voltage of both shunt and compound generators can be controlled over reasonable limits by means of rheostats in the shunt field.

Any of the methods of excitation used for generators can also be used for motors. Typical steady-state dc-motor speed-torque characteristics are shown in Fig. 7.6, in which it is assumed that the motor terminals are supplied from a constant-voltage source. In a motor the relation between the emf E_a generated in the armature and the armature terminal voltage V_a is

$$V_a = E_a + I_a R_a \tag{7.14}$$

or

$$I_a = \frac{V_a - E_a}{R_a} \tag{7.15}$$

where I_a is now the armature-current input to the machine. The generated emf E_a is now smaller than the terminal voltage V_a, the armature current is in the opposite direction to that in a generator, and the electromagnetic torque is in the direction to sustain rotation of the armature.

Figure 7.6 Speed-torque characteristics of dc motors.

In *shunt-* and *separately excited motors,* the field flux is nearly constant. Consequently, increased torque must be accompanied by a very nearly proportional increase in armature current and hence by a small decrease in counter emf E_a to allow this increased current through the small armature resistance. Since counter emf is determined by flux and speed (Eq. 7.7), the speed must drop slightly. Like the squirrel-cage induction motor, the shunt motor is substantially a constant-speed motor having about 6 percent drop in speed from no load to full load. A typical speed-torque characteristic is shown by the solid curve in Fig. 7.6. Starting torque and maximum torque are limited by the armature current that can be successfully commutated.

An outstanding advantage of the shunt motor is ease of speed control. With a rheostat in the shunt-field circuit, the field current and flux per pole can be varied at will, and variation of flux causes the inverse variation of speed to maintain counter emf approximately equal to the impressed terminal voltage. A maximum speed range of about 4 or 6 to 1 can be obtained by this method, the limitation again being commutating conditions. By variation of the impressed armature voltage, very wide speed ranges can be obtained.

In the *series motor,* increase in load is accompanied by increases in the armature current and mmf and the stator field flux (provided the iron is not completely saturated). Because flux increases with load, speed must drop in order to maintain the balance between impressed voltage and counter emf; moreover, the increase in armature current caused by increased torque is smaller than in the shunt motor because of the increased flux. The series motor is therefore a varying-speed motor with a markedly drooping speed-torque characteristic of the type shown in Fig. 7.6. For applications requiring heavy torque overloads, this characteristic is particularly advantageous because the corresponding power overloads are held to more reasonable values by the associated speed drops. Very favorable starting characteristics also result from the increase in flux with increased armature current.

In the *compound motor,* the series field may be connected either *cumulatively,* so that its mmf adds to that of the shunt field, or *differentially,* so that it opposes. The differential connection is rarely used. As shown by the broken-dash curve in Fig. 7.6, a cumulatively compounded motor has speed-load characteristics intermediate between those of a shunt and a series motor, with the drop of speed with load depending on the relative number of ampere-turns in the shunt and series fields. It does not have the disadvantage of very high light-load speed associated with a series motor, but it retains to a considerable degree the advantages of series excitation.

The application advantages of dc machines lie in the variety of performance characteristics offered by the possibilities of shunt, series, and compound excitation. Some of these characteristics have been touched upon briefly in this section. Still greater possibilities exist if additional sets of brushes are added so that other voltages can be obtained from the commutator. Thus the versatility of dc-machine systems and their adaptability to control, both manual and automatic, are their outstanding features.

7.2 COMMUTATOR ACTION

The dc machine differs in several respects from the ideal model of Section 4.2.2. Although the basic concepts of Section 4.2.2 are still valid, a reexamination of the assumptions and a modification of the model are desirable. The crux of the matter is the effect of the commutator shown in Figs. 4.1 and 4.13.

Figure 7.7 shows diagrammatically the armature winding of Figs. 4.19 and 4.20a with the addition of the commutator, brushes, and connections of the coils to the commutator segments. The commutator is represented by the ring of segments in the center of the figure. The segments are insulated from each other and from the shaft. Two stationary brushes are shown by the black rectangles inside the commutator although in practical dc machines the brushes usually contact the outer surface, as shown in Fig. 4.13. The coil sides in the slots are shown in cross section by the small circles with dots and crosses in them, indicating currents toward and away from the reader, respectively, as in Fig. 4.19. The connections of the coils to the commutator segments are shown by the circular arcs. The end connections at the back of the armature are shown dashed for the two coils in slots 1 and 7, and the connections of these coils to adjacent commutator segments are shown by the heavy arcs. All coils are identical. The back end connections of the other coils have been omitted to avoid complicating the figure, but they can easily be traced by remembering that each coil has one side in the top of a slot and the other side in the bottom of the diametrically opposite slot.

In Fig. 7.7a the brushes are in contact with commutator segments 1 and 7. Current entering the right-hand brush divides equally between two parallel paths through the winding. The first path leads to the inner coil side in slot 1 and finally ends at the brush on segment 7. The second path leads to the outer coil side in slot 6 and also finally ends at the brush on segment 7. The current directions in Fig. 7.7a can readily be verified by tracing these two paths. They are the same as in Fig. 4.19. The effect is identical to that of a coil wrapped around the armature with its magnetic axis vertical, and a clockwise magnetic torque is exerted on the armature, tending to align its magnetic field with that of the field winding.

Now suppose the machine is acting as a generator driven in the counterclockwise direction by an applied mechanical torque. Figure 7.7b shows the situation after the armature has rotated through the angle subtended by half a commutator segment. The right-hand brush is now in contact with both segments 1 and 2, and the left-hand brush is in contact with both segments 7 and 8. The coils in slots 1 and 7 are now short-circuited by the brushes. The currents in the other coils are shown by the dots and crosses, and they produce a magnetic field whose axis again is vertical.

After further rotation, the brushes will be in contact with segments 2 and 8, and slots 1 and 7 will have rotated into the positions which were previously occupied by slots 12 and 6 in Fig. 7.7a. The current directions will be similar to those of Fig. 7.7a except that the currents in the coils in slots 1 and 7 will have reversed. The magnetic axis of the armature is still vertical.

During the time when the brushes are simultaneously in contact with two adjacent commutator segments, the coils connected to these segments are temporarily

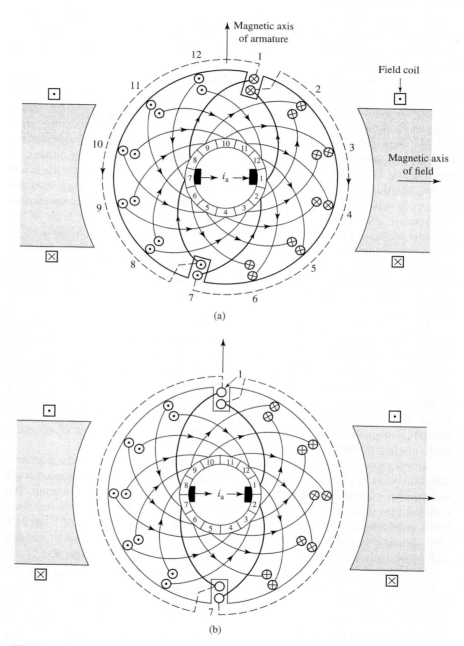

Magnetic axis
of armature

Field coil

Magnetic axis
of field

(a)

(b)

Figure 7.7 Dc machine armature winding with commutator and brushes.
(a), (b) Current directions for two positions of the armature.

Figure 7.8 Waveform of current in an armature coil with linear commutation.

removed from the main circuit comprising the armature winding, short-circuited by the brushes, and the currents in them are reversed. Ideally, the current in the coils being commutated should reverse linearly with time, a condition referred to as *linear commutation*. Serious departure from linear commutation will result in sparking at the brushes. Means for obtaining sparkless commutation are discussed in Section 7.9. With linear commutation the waveform of the current in any coil as a function of time is trapezoidal, as shown in Fig. 7.8.

The winding of Fig. 7.7 is simpler than that used in most dc machines. Ordinarily more slots and commutator segments would be used, and except in small machines, more than two poles are common. Nevertheless, the simple winding of Fig. 7.7 includes the essential features of more complicated windings.

7.3 ANALYTICAL FUNDAMENTALS: ELECTRIC-CIRCUIT ASPECTS

From Eqs. 7.3 and 7.7, the electromagnetic torque and generated voltage of a dc machine are, respectively,

$$T_{mech} = K_a \Phi_d I_a \tag{7.16}$$

and

$$E_a = K_a \Phi_d \omega_m \tag{7.17}$$

where

$$K_a = \frac{poles\ C_a}{2\pi m} \tag{7.18}$$

Here the capital-letter symbols E_a for generated voltage and I_a for armature current are used to emphasize that we are primarily concerned with steady-state considerations. The remaining symbols are as defined in Section 7.1. Equations 7.16 through 7.18 are basic equations for analysis of the machine. The quantity $E_a I_a$ is frequently referred to as the *electromagnetic power;* from Eqs. 7.16 and 7.17 it is related to electromagnetic torque by

$$T_{mech} = \frac{E_a I_a}{\omega_m} \tag{7.19}$$

The electromagnetic power differs from the mechanical power at the machine shaft by the rotational losses and differs from the electric power at the machine terminals by the shunt-field and armature $I^2 R$ losses. Once the electromagnetic

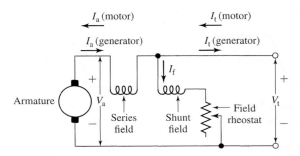

Figure 7.9   Motor or generator connection diagram with current directions. Long-shunt connection.

power $E_a I_a$ has been determined, numerical addition of the rotational losses for generators and subtraction for motors yields the mechanical power at the shaft.

The interrelations between voltage and current are immediately evident from the connection diagram of Fig. 7.9. Thus,

$$V_a = E_a \pm I_a R_a \tag{7.20}$$

$$V_t = E_a \pm I_a (R_a + R_s) \tag{7.21}$$

and the terminal current is

$$I_t = I_a \pm I_f \tag{7.22}$$

where the plus sign is used for a motor and the minus sign for a generator and R_a and R_s are the resistances of the armature and series field, respectively. Here, the voltage V_a refers to the terminal voltage of the armature winding and V_t refers to the terminal voltage of the dc machine, including the voltage drop across the series-connected field winding; they are equal if there is no series field winding.

Some of the terms in Eqs. 7.20 to 7.22 are omitted when the machine connections are simpler than those shown in Fig. 7.9. The resistance R_a is to be interpreted as that of the armature plus brushes unless specifically stated otherwise. Sometimes R_a is taken as the resistance of the armature winding alone and the brush-contact voltage drop is accounted for separately, usually assumed to be two volts.

EXAMPLE 7.1

A 25-kW 125-V separately excited dc machine is operated at a constant speed of 3000 r/min with a constant field current such that the open-circuit armature voltage is 125 V. The armature resistance is 0.02 Ω.

Compute the armature current, terminal power, and electromagnetic power and torque when the terminal voltage is (a) 128 V and (b) 124 V.

■ **Solution**

a. From Eq. 7.20, with $V_t = 128$ V and $E_a = 125$ V, the armature current is

$$I_a = \frac{V_t - E_a}{R_a} = \frac{128 - 125}{0.02} = 150 \text{ A}$$

in the motor direction, and the power input at the motor terminal is

$$V_t I_a = 128 \times 150 = 19.20 \text{ kW}$$

The electromagnetic power is given by

$$E_a I_a = 125 \times 150 = 18.75 \text{ kW}$$

In this case, the dc machine is operating as a motor and the electromagnetic power is hence smaller than the motor input power by the power dissipated in the armature resistance.

Finally, the electromagnetic torque is given by Eq. 7.19:

$$T_{mech} = \frac{E_a I_a}{\omega_m} = \frac{18.75 \times 10^3}{100\pi} = 59.7 \text{ N} \cdot \text{m}$$

b. In this case, E_a is larger than V_t and hence armature current will flow out of the machine, and thus the machine is operating as a generator. Hence

$$I_a = \frac{E_a - V_t}{R_a} = \frac{125 - 124}{0.02} = 50 \text{ A}$$

and the terminal power is

$$V_t I_a = 124 \times 50 = 6.20 \text{ kW}$$

The electromagnetic power is

$$E_a I_a = 125 \times 50 = 6.25 \text{ kW}$$

and the electromagnetic torque is

$$T_{mech} = \frac{6.25 \times 10^3}{100\pi} = 19.9 \text{ N} \cdot \text{m}$$

Practice Problem 7.1

The speed of the separately excited dc machine of Example 7.1 is observed to be 2950 r/min with the field current at the same value as in Example 7.1. For a terminal voltage of 125 V, calculate the terminal current and power and the electromagnetic power for the machine. Is it acting as a motor or a generator?

Solution

$$\text{Terminal current:} I_a = 104 \text{ A}$$
$$\text{Terminal power:} V_t I_a = 13.0 \text{kW}$$
$$\text{Electromechanical power:} E_a I_a = 12.8 \text{kW}$$

The machine is acting as a motor.

EXAMPLE 7.2

Consider again the separately excited dc machine of Example 7.1 with the field current maintained constant at the value that would produce a terminal voltage of 125 V at a speed of

3000 r/min. The machine is observed to be operating as a motor with a terminal voltage of 123 V and with a terminal power of 21.9 kW. Calculate the speed of the motor.

■ Solution

The terminal current can be found from the terminal voltage and power as

$$I_a = \frac{\text{Input power}}{V_t} = \frac{21.9 \times 10^3}{123} = 178 \text{ A}$$

Thus the generated voltage is

$$E_a = V_t - I_a R_a = 119.4 \text{ V}$$

From Eq. 7.11, the rotational speed can be found as

$$n = n_0 \left(\frac{E_a}{E_{a0}} \right) = 3000 \left(\frac{119.4}{125} \right) = 2866 \text{ r/min}$$

Practice Problem 7.2

Repeat Example 7.2 if the machine is observed to be operating as a generator with a terminal voltage of 124 V and a terminal power of 24 kW.

Solution

3069 r/min

For compound machines, another variation may occur. Figure 7.9 shows a *long-shunt connection* in that the shunt field is connected directly across the line terminals with the series field between it and the armature. An alternative possibility is the *short-shunt connection,* illustrated in Fig. 7.10, with the shunt field directly across the armature and the series field between it and the line terminals. The series-field current is then I_t instead of I_a, and the voltage equations are modified accordingly. There is so little practical difference between these two connections that the distinction can usually be ignored: unless otherwise stated, compound machines will be treated as though they were long-shunt connected.

Although the difference between terminal voltage V_t and armature generated voltage E_a is comparatively small for normal operation, it has a definite bearing

Figure 7.10 Short-shunt compound dc-machine connections.

on performance characteristics. This voltage difference divided by the armature resistance determines the value of armature current I_a and hence the strength of the armature flux. Complete determination of machine behavior requires a similar investigation of factors influencing the direct-axis flux or, more particularly, the net flux per pole Φ_d.

7.4 EFFECT OF ARMATURE MMF

Armature mmf has definite effects on both the space distribution of the air-gap flux and the magnitude of the net flux per pole. The effect on flux distribution is important because the limits of successful commutation are directly influenced; the effect on flux magnitude is important because both the generated voltage and the torque per unit armature current are influenced thereby. These effects and the problems arising from them are described in this section.

It was shown in Section 4.3.2 and Fig. 4.20 that the armature-mmf wave can be closely approximated by a sawtooth, corresponding to the wave produced by a finely distributed armature winding or current sheet. For a machine with brushes in the neutral position, the idealized mmf wave is shown by the dashed sawtooth in Fig. 7.11, in which a positive mmf ordinate denotes flux lines leaving the armature surface. Current directions in all windings other than the main field are indicated by black and cross-hatched bands. Because of the salient-pole field structure found in almost all dc machines, the associated space distribution of flux will not be triangular. The distribution of air-gap flux density with only the armature excited is given by the

Figure 7.11 Armature-mmf and flux-density distribution with brushes on neutral and only the armature excited.

Field iron

Armature
iron

Figure 7.12 Flux with only the armature excited and brushes on neutral.

solid curve of Fig. 7.11. As can readily be seen, it is appreciably decreased by the long air path in the interpolar space.

The axis of the armature mmf is fixed at 90 electrical degrees from the main-field axis by the brush position. The corresponding flux follows the paths shown in Fig. 7.12. The effect of the armature mmf is seen to be that of creating flux crossing the pole faces; thus its path in the pole shoes crosses the path of the main-field flux. For this reason, armature reaction of this type is called *cross-magnetizing armature reaction* and it causes a decrease in the resultant air-gap flux density under one half of the pole and an increase under the other half.

When the armature and field windings are both excited, the resultant air-gap flux-density distribution is of the form given by the solid curve of Fig. 7.13. Superimposed on this figure are the flux distributions with only the armature excited (long-dash curve) and only the field excited (short-dash curve). The effect of cross-magnetizing armature reaction in decreasing the flux under one pole tip and increasing it under the other can be seen by comparing the solid and short-dash curves. In general, the solid curve is not the algebraic sum of the two dashed curves because of the nonlinearity of the iron magnetic circuit. Because of saturation of the iron, the flux density is decreased by a greater amount under one pole tip than it is increased under the other. Accordingly, the resultant flux per pole is lower than would be produced by the field winding alone, a consequence known as the *demagnetizing effect of cross-magnetizing armature reaction*. Since it is caused by saturation, its magnitude is a nonlinear function of both the field current and the armature current. For normal machine operation at the flux densities used commercially, the effect is usually significant, especially at heavy loads, and must often be taken into account in analyses of performance.

The distortion of the flux distribution caused by cross-magnetizing armature reaction may have a detrimental influence on the commutation of the armature current, especially if the distortion becomes excessive. In fact, this distortion is usually an important factor limiting the short-time overload capability of a dc machine. Tendency toward distortion of the flux distribution is most pronounced in a machine, such as a shunt motor, where the field excitation remains substantially constant while the armature mmf may reach very significant proportions at heavy loads. The tendency is least pronounced in a series-excited machine, such as the series motor, for both the field and armature mmf increase with load.

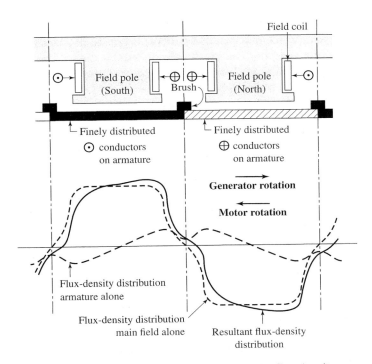

Figure 7.13 Armature, main-field, and resultant flux-density distributions with brushes on neutral.

The effect of cross-magnetizing armature reaction can be limited in the design and construction of the machine. The mmf of the main field should exert predominating control on the air-gap flux, so that the condition of weak field mmf and strong armature mmf should be avoided. The reluctance of the cross-flux path (essentially the armature teeth, pole shoes, and the air gap, especially at the pole tips) can be increased by increasing the degree of saturation in the teeth and pole faces, by avoiding too small an air gap, and by using a chamfered or eccentric pole face, which increases the air gap at the pole tips. These expedients affect the path of the main flux as well, but the influence on the cross flux is much greater. The best, but also the most expensive, curative measure is to compensate the armature mmf by means of a winding embedded in the pole faces, a measure discussed in Section 7.9.

If the brushes are not in the neutral position, the axis of the armature mmf wave is not 90° from the main-field axis. The armature mmf then produces not only cross magnetization but also a direct-axis demagnetizing or magnetizing effect, depending on the direction of brush shift. Shifting of the brushes from the neutral position is usually inadvertent due to incorrect positioning of the brushes or a poor brush fit. Before the invention of interpoles, however, shifting the brushes was a common method of securing satisfactory commutation, the direction of the shift being such that demagnetizing action was produced. It can be shown that brush shift in the direction of rotation in a generator or against rotation in a motor produces a direct-axis demagnetizing mmf which may result in unstable operation of a motor or excessive drop in voltage of a generator. Incorrectly placed brushes can be detected by a load test. If the brushes are on neutral, the terminal voltage of a generator or the speed of a motor should be the same for identical conditions of field excitation and armature current when the direction of rotation is reversed.

7.5 ANALYTICAL FUNDAMENTALS: MAGNETIC-CIRCUIT ASPECTS

The net flux per pole is that resulting from the combined mmfs of the field and armature windings. Although in a idealized, shunt- or separately excited dc machine the armature mmf produces magnetic flux only along the quadrature axis, in a practical device the armature current produces flux along the direct axis, either directly, as produced for example by a series field winding, or indirectly through saturation effects as discussed in Section 7.4. The interdependence of the generated armature voltage E_a and magnetic circuit conditions in the machine is accordingly a function of the sum of all the mmfs on the polar- or direct-axis flux path. First we consider the mmf intentionally placed on the stator main poles to create the working flux, i.e., the *main-field mmf*, and then we include armature-reaction effects.

7.5.1 Armature Reaction Neglected

With no load on the machine or with armature-reaction effects ignored, the resultant mmf is the algebraic sum of the mmfs acting on the main or direct axis. For the usual compound generator or motor having N_f shunt-field turns per pole and N_s series-field turns per pole,

$$\text{Direct-axis mmf} = N_f I_f + N_s I_s \qquad (7.23)$$

The series field current I_s is defined in Eq. 7.23 such it produces an mmf which adds to that of the shunt field winding. Note, however, that its polarity can be reversed in any given configuration and its operating current can hence be positive or negative. For a connection which produces positive series field current ($I_s > 0$), referred to as a *cummulative series-field connection*, its mmf indeed adds to that of the shunt field. For a connection which produces negative series field current ($I_s < 0$), referred to as a *differential series-field connection*, its mmf subtracts from that of the shunt field.

Additional terms will appear in Eq. 7.23 when there are additional field windings on the main poles and when, unlike the compensating windings of Section 7.9, they are wound concentric with the normal field windings to permit specialized control. When either the series or the shunt field is absent, the corresponding term in Eq. 7.23 is naturally omitted.

Equation 7.23 thus sums up in ampere-turns per pole the gross mmf of the direct-axis field windings acting on the main magnetic circuit. The magnetization curve for a dc machine is generally given in terms of current in only the principal field winding, which is almost invariably the shunt-field winding when one is present. The mmf units of such a magnetization curve and of Eq. 7.23 can be made the same by one of two rather obvious steps. The field current on the magnetization curve can be multiplied by the turns per pole in that winding, giving a curve in terms of ampere-turns per pole; or both sides of Eq. 7.23 can be divided by the turns in the shunt-field N_f, converting the units to an equivalent current in the shunt-field winding alone which produces the same mmf. Thus

$$I_{f,eq} = I_f + \left(\frac{N_s}{N_f} \right) I_s \tag{7.24}$$

in which case, Eq. 7.23 can be written as

$$\text{Direct-axis mmf} = N_f \left(I_f + \left(\frac{N_s}{N_f} \right) I_s \right) = N_f I_{f,eq} \tag{7.25}$$

This latter procedure is often the more convenient and the one more commonly adopted. As discussed in conjunction with Eq. 7.23, the connection of the series field winding will determine whether or not the series-field mmf adds to or subtracts from that of the main field winding.

An example of a *no-load magnetization characteristic* is given by the curve for $I_a = 0$ in Fig. 7.14, with values representative of those for a 100-kW, 250-V, 1200-r/min generator. Note that the mmf scale is given in both shunt-field current and ampere-turns per pole, the latter being derived from the former on the basis of a 1000 turns-per-pole shunt field. The characteristic can also be presented in normalized, or per-unit, form, as shown by the upper mmf and right-hand voltage scales. On these scales, 1.0 per-unit field current or mmf is that required to produce rated voltage at rated speed when the machine is unloaded; similarly, 1.0 per-unit voltage equals rated voltage.

Use of the magnetization curve with generated voltage, rather than flux, plotted on the vertical axis may be somewhat complicated by the fact that the speed of a dc machine need not remain constant and that speed enters into the relation between flux and generated voltage. Hence, generated voltage ordinates correspond to a unique machine speed. The generated voltage E_a at any speed ω_m is given by Eqs. 7.10 and 7.11, repeated here in terms of the steady-state values of generated voltage.

$$E_a = \left(\frac{\omega_m}{\omega_{m0}} \right) E_{a0} \tag{7.26}$$

or, in terms of rotational speed in r/min,

$$E_a = \left(\frac{n}{n_0} \right) E_{a0} \tag{7.27}$$

In these equations, ω_{m0} and n_0 are the magnetizing-curve speed in rad/sec and r/min respectively and E_{a0} is the corresponding generated voltage.

Mmf or shunt-field current, per unit

Figure 7.14 Magnetization curves for a 250-V 1200-r/min dc machine. Also shown are field-resistance lines for the discussion of self-excitation in Section 7.6.1.

EXAMPLE 7.3

A 100-kW, 250-V, 400-A, long-shunt compound generator has an armature resistance (including brushes) of 0.025 Ω, a series-field resistance of 0.005 Ω, and the magnetization curve of Fig. 7.14. There are 1000 shunt-field turns per pole and three series-field turns per pole. The series field is connected in such a fashion that positive armature current produces direct-axis mmf which adds to that of the shunt field (i.e. $I_s = I_a$).

Compute the terminal voltage at rated terminal current when the shunt-field current is 4.7 A and the speed is 1150 r/min. Neglect the effects of armature reaction.

■ **Solution**

As is shown in Fig. 7.9, for a long-shunt connection the armature and series field-currents are equal. Thus

$$I_s = I_a = I_t + I_f = 400 + 4.7 = 405 \text{ A}$$

From Eq. 7.24 the equivalent shunt-field winding current is

$$I_{f,eq} = I_f + \left(\frac{N_s}{N_f}\right) I_s$$

$$= 4.7 + \left(\frac{3}{1000}\right) 405 = 5.9 \quad \text{equivalent shunt-field amperes}$$

By examining the $I_a = 0$ curve of Fig. 7.14 at this equivalent shunt-field current, one reads a generated voltage of 274 V. Accordingly, the actual emf at a speed of 1150 r/min can be found from Eq. 7.27

$$E_a = \left(\frac{n}{n_0}\right) E_{a0} = \left(\frac{1150}{1200}\right) 274 = 263 \text{ V}$$

Then

$$V_t = E_a - I_a(R_a + R_s) = 263 - 405 \times (0.025 + 0.005) = 251 \text{ V}$$

Practice Problem 7.3

Repeat Example 7.3 for a terminal current of 375 A and a speed of 1190 r/min.

Solution

257 V

EXAMPLE 7.4

A 50-kW, 450-V, dc machine has the following characteristics:

Armature resistance: $R_a = 0.242 \ \Omega$
    Shunt field: $R_f = 167 \ \Omega$, 1250 turns/pole
    Series field: $R_s = 0.032 \ \Omega$, 1 turn/pole

The shunt-field resistance includes that of a rheostat, adjusted so that with the dc motor connected to a 450 V dc source, the motor operates at a speed of 1000 r/min at no load. For the purposes of this problem, assume armature-reaction to be negligible and that the motor terminal voltage is 450 V.

a. Consider first the motor in the shunt connection without the series field. Use MATLAB to plot the motor speed as a function of load.

b. Now consider the motor connected in the long-shunt connection of Fig. 7.9 with the series field connected such that the series-field mmf subtracts from that of the shunt field. Again use MATLAB to plot the motor speed over the load range of the motor.

■ **Solution**

a. From Eq. 7.8

$$P_{mech} = E_a I_a$$

Figure 7.15 Plot of r/min vs. motor load for Example 7.4(a).

Substituting Eq. 7.20 gives

$$P_{\text{mech}} = \frac{E_a(V_a - E_a)}{R_a}$$

which gives the following expression for E_a in terms of P_{mech}

$$E_a = \frac{V_a \pm \sqrt{V_a^2 - 4R_a P_{\text{mech}}}}{2}$$

Clearly the $+$ sign must be used since we know that $E_a = V_a$ when $P_{\text{mech}} = 0$. From the given motor characteristics, we see that $E_{a0} = 450$ V when $n_0 = 1000$ r/min. Thus from Eq. 7.11

$$n = \left(\frac{E_a}{E_{a0}}\right) n_0 = \frac{n_0\left(V_a + \sqrt{V_a^2 - 4R_a P_{\text{mech}}}\right)}{2E_{a0}}$$

This equation can be used to plot the rotor speed as a function of P_{mech} is varied from 0 to P_{rated}. The resultant plot is shown in Fig. 7.15.

b. Because the motor is connected in the long-shunt connection, the field current remains constant at a value of

$$I_{f0} = \frac{V_a}{R_f} = \frac{450}{167} = 2.70 \text{ A}$$

Furthermore, we know that when the machine is unloaded and operating at a speed $n_0 = 1000$ r/min, the corresponding direct-axis mmf produces a generated voltage of $E_{a0} = V_{\text{rated}} = 450$ V. We can thus write that at speed n_0

$$E_{a0} = \left(\frac{I_{f,\text{eq}}}{I_{f0}}\right) V_{\text{rated}}$$

where, recognizing that in this case $I_s = -I_a$, from Eq. 7.24

$$I_{f,\text{eq}} = I_{f0} - \left(\frac{N_s}{N_f}\right) I_a$$

Figure 7.16 Plot of r/min vs. motor load for Example 7.4(b).

Finally, from Eq. 7.11, we can write an expression for the generated voltage as a function of motor speed

$$E_a = \left(\frac{n}{n_0}\right) E_{a0} = \left(\frac{n}{n_0}\right)\left(1 - \left(\frac{N_s I_a}{N_f I_{f0}}\right)\right) V_{rated}$$

From Eq. 7.21, including the resistance of the series field, the armature current is given by

$$I_a = \frac{V_t - E_a}{(R_a + R_s)}$$

Appropriate manipulation of these equations gives an expression for the armature current I_a as a function of the motor speed

$$I_a = \frac{N_f I_{f0}(n_0 V_t - n V_{rated})}{n_0 N_f I_{f0}(R_a + R_s) - n N_s V_{rated}}$$

and the corresponding mechanical output power as a function of motor speed is then given by $P_{mech} = E_a I_a$. The desired plot is shown in Fig. 7.16 which was obtained by decrementing the motor speed from an initial value of 1100 r/min until the rated power of 50 kW was found.

Here is the MATLAB script for this example:

```
clc
clear

% Motor characteristics
Prated = 50e3; % Rated power
Vrated = 450; % Rated voltage
Ra = 0.242; % Armature resistance
Rf = 167; % Field resistance
Nf = 1250; % Field turns/pole
Rs = 0.032; % Series-field resistance
Ns = 1; % Series-field turns/pole
n0 = 1000; % No load speed
```

```
Ea0 = 450; % No load voltage

% Part (a)

Va = 450; % Terminal voltage

Pmech = linspace(0,Prated,100);
n = n0*(Va+sqrt(Va^2-4*Ra*Pmech))/(2*Ea0);

plot(Pmech/1000,n,'LineWidth',2)
xlabel('P_{mech} [kW]','FontSize',20)
ylabel('Speed [rpm]','FontSize',20)
set(gca,'FontSize',20)
set(gca,'xlim',[0 50])
set(gca,'xtick',[0 10 20 30 40 50])
grid on

disp('Hit any key for part (b)\n')
pause

% Part (b)
clear n Pmech

Vt = 450; % Terminal voltage
If0 = Vt/Rf;     % Shunt-field current

P = 0;
m=0;
while P < 50*1000
  m = m+1;
  n(m) = 1000-(m-1);
  Ia = Nf*If0*(n0*Vt-n(m)*Vrated)/(n0*Nf*If0*(Ra+Rs)-n(m)*Ns*Vrated);
  Ea = n(m)*Vrated*(If0-(Ns/Nf)*Ia)/(n0*If0);
  P = Ea*Ia;
  Pmech(m) = P;
end

plot(Pmech/1000,n,'LineWidth',2)
xlabel('P_{mech} [kW]','FontSize',20)
ylabel('Speed [rpm]','FontSize',20)
set(gca,'FontSize',20)
set(gca,'xlim',[0 50])
set(gca,'xtick',[0 10 20 30 40 50])
grid on
```

7.5.2 Effects of Armature Reaction Included

As described in Section 7.4, current in the armature winding gives rise to a demagnetizing effect caused by a cross-magnetizing armature reaction. Analytical inclusion of this effect is not straightforward because of the nonlinearities involved. One common approach has been to base analyses on the measured performance of the machine in question or for one of similar design and frame size. Data are taken with both the field and armature excited, and the tests are conducted so that the effects on generated emf of varying both the main-field excitation and the armature mmf can be noted. Numerical analysis, based upon techniques such as finite-element method, can also be used.

One form of summarizing and correlating the results is illustrated in Fig. 7.14. Curves are plotted not only for the no-load characteristic ($I_a = 0$) but also for a range of values of I_a. In the analysis of machine performance, the inclusion of armature reaction then becomes simply a matter of using the magnetization curve corresponding to the armature current involved. Note that the ordinates of all these curves give values of armature-generated voltage E_a, not terminal voltage under load. Note also that all the curves tend to merge with the air-gap line as the saturation of the iron decreases.

The load-saturation curves are displaced to the right of the no-load curve by an amount which is a function of I_a. The effect of armature reaction then is approximately the same as a demagnetizing mmf F_{ar} acting on the main-field axis. This additional term can then be included in Eq. 7.23, with the result that the net direct-axis mmf can be assumed to be

$$\text{Net mmf} = \text{gross mmf} - F_{ar} = N_f I_f + N_s I_s - F_{ar} \qquad (7.28)$$

The no-load magnetization curve can then be used as the relation between generated emf and net excitation under load with the armature reaction accounted for as a demagnetizing mmf. Over the normal operating range (about 240 to about 300 V for the machine of Fig. 7.14), the demagnetizing effect of armature reaction may be assumed to be approximately proportional to the armature current. The reader should be aware that the amount of armature reaction present in Fig. 7.14 is chosen so that some of its disadvantageous effects will appear in a pronounced form in subsequent numerical examples and problems illustrating generator and motor performance features. It is definitely more than one would expect to find in a normal, well-designed machine operating at normal currents.

EXAMPLE 7.5

Consider again the long-shunt compound dc generator of Example 7.3. As in Example 7.3, compute the terminal voltage at rated terminal current when the shunt-field current is 4.7 A and the speed is 1150 r/min. In this case however, include the effects of armature reaction.

■ **Solution**

As calculated in Example 7.3, $I_s = I_a = 405$ A and the gross mmf is equal to 5.9 equivalent shunt-field amperes. Given the resolution of the curves of Fig. 7.14, from the curve labeled $I_a = 400$, we can determine that the corresponding generated emf is 261 V (as compared to

274 V with armature reaction neglected). Thus from Eq. 7.27, the actual generated voltage at a speed of 1150 r/min is equal to

$$E_a = \left(\frac{n}{n_0}\right) E_{a0} = \left(\frac{1150}{1200}\right) 261 = 250 \text{ V}$$

Then

$$V_t = E_a - I_a(R_a + R_s) = 250 - 405(0.025 + 0.005) = 238 \text{ V}$$

EXAMPLE 7.6

To counter the effects of armature reaction, a fourth turn is added to the series-field winding of the dc generator of Examples 7.3 and 7.5, increasing its resistance to 0.007 Ω. Repeat the terminal-voltage calculation of Example 7.5.

■ **Solution**

As in Examples 7.3 and 7.5, $I_s = I_a = 405$ A. The main-field mmf can then be calculated as

$$\text{Gross mmf} = I_f + \left(\frac{N_s}{N_f}\right) I_s = 4.7 + \left(\frac{4}{1000}\right) 405$$

$$= 6.3 \quad \text{equivalent shunt-field amperes}$$

From the $I_a = 400$ curve of Fig. 7.14 with an equivalent shunt-field current of 6.3 A, one reads a generated voltage 269 V which corresponds to an emf at 1150 r/min of

$$E_a = \left(\frac{1150}{1200}\right) 269 = 258 \text{ V}$$

The terminal voltage can now be calculated as

$$V_t = E_a - I_a(R_a + R_s) = 258 - 405(0.025 + 0.007) = 245 \text{ V}$$

Practice Problem 7.4

Repeat Example 7.6 assuming that a fifth turn is added to the series field winding, bringing its total resistance to 0.009 Ω.

Solution

250 V

7.6 STEADY-STATE DC MACHINE PERFORMANCE

Although exactly the same principles apply to the analysis of a dc machine acting as a generator as to one acting as a motor, the general nature of the problems ordinarily encountered is somewhat different for the two methods of operation. For a generator, the speed is usually fixed by the prime mover, and problems often encountered are to determine the terminal voltage corresponding to a specified load and excitation or to find the excitation required for a specified load and terminal voltage. For a motor, however, problems frequently encountered are to determine the speed corresponding to a specific load and excitation or to find the excitation required for specified load and speed conditions; terminal voltage is often fixed at the value of the available source. The routine techniques of applying the common basic principles therefore differ to the extent that the problems differ.

7.6.1 Generator Analysis

Since the main-field current is independent of the generator voltage, separately excited generators are the simplest to analyze. For a given load, the equivalent main-field excitation is given by Eq. 7.24 and the associated armature-generated voltage E_a is determined by the appropriate magnetization curve. This voltage, together with Eq. 7.20 or 7.21, fixes the terminal voltage.

Shunt-excited generators will be found to self-excite under properly chosen operating conditions. Under these conditions, the generated voltage will build up spontaneously (typically initiated by the presence of a small amount of residual magnetism in the field structure) to a value ultimately limited by magnetic saturation. In self-excited generators, the shunt-field excitation depends on the terminal voltage and the series-field excitation depends on the armature current. Dependence of shunt-field current on terminal voltage can be incorporated graphically in an analysis by drawing the *field-resistance line,* the line 0a in Fig. 7.14, on the magnetization curve. The field-resistance line 0a is simply a graphical representation of Ohm's law applied to the shunt field. It is the locus of the terminal voltage versus shunt-field-current operating point. Thus, the line 0a is drawn for $R_f = 50\ \Omega$ and hence passes through the origin and the point (1.0 A, 50 V).

The tendency of a shunt-connected generator to self-excite can be seen by examining the buildup of voltage for an unloaded shunt generator. When the field circuit is closed, the small voltage from residual magnetism (the 6-V intercept of the magnetization curve, Fig. 7.14) causes a small field current. If the flux produced by the resulting ampere-turns adds to the residual flux, progressively greater voltages and field currents are obtained. If the field ampere-turns opposes the residual magnetism, the shunt-field terminals must be reversed to obtain buildup.

This process can be seen with the aid of Fig. 7.17. In Fig. 7.17, the generated voltage e_a is shown in series with the armature inductance L_a and resistance R_a. The shunt-field winding, shown connected across the armature terminals, is represented by its inductance L_f and resistance R_f. Recognizing that since there is no load current on the generator ($i_t = 0$), $i_a = i_f$ and thus the differential equation describing the buildup of the field current i_f is

$$(L_a + L_f)\frac{di_f}{dt} = e_a - (R_a + R_f)i_f \qquad (7.29)$$

From this equation it is clear that as long as the net voltage across the winding inductances $e_a - i_f(R_a + R_f)$ is positive, the field current and the corresponding generated voltage will increase. Buildup continues until the volt-ampere relations

Figure 7.17 Equivalent circuit for analysis of voltage buildup in a self-excited dc generator.

represented by the magnetization curve and the field-resistance line are simultaneously satisfied, which occurs at their intersection $e_a = (R_a + R_f)\, i_f$; in this case at $e_a = 250\,\text{V}$ for the line $0a$ in Fig. 7.14. From Eq. 7.29, it is clear that the field resistance line should also include the armature resistance. However, this resistance is in general much less than the field and is typically neglected.

Notice that if the field resistance is too high, as shown by line $0b$ for $R_f = 100\,\Omega$ in Fig. 7.14, the intersection is at very low voltage and buildup is not obtained. Notice also that if the field-resistance line is essentially tangent to the lower part of the magnetization curve, corresponding to a field resistance of 57 Ω in Fig. 7.14, the intersection may be anywhere from about 60 to 170 V, resulting in very unstable conditions. The corresponding resistance is the *critical field resistance,* above which buildup will not be obtained. The same buildup process and the same conclusions apply to compound generators; in a long-shunt compound generator, the series-field mmf created by the shunt-field current is entirely negligible.

For a shunt generator, the magnetization curve for the appropriate value of I_a is the locus of E_a versus I_f. The field-resistance line is the locus V_t versus I_f. Under steady-state operating conditions, at any value of I_f, the vertical distance between the line and the curve must be the $I_a R_a$ drop at the load corresponding to that condition. Determination of the terminal voltage for a specified armature current is then simply a matter of finding where the line and curve are separated vertically by the proper amount; the ordinate of the field-resistance line at that field current is then the terminal voltage. For a compound generator, however, the series-field mmf causes corresponding points on the line and curve to be displaced horizontally as well as vertically. The horizontal displacement equals the series-field mmf measured in equivalent shunt-field amperes, and the vertical displacement is still the $I_a R_a$ drop.

Great precision is evidently not obtained from the foregoing computational process. The uncertainties caused by magnetic hysteresis in dc machines make high precision unattainable in any event. In general, the magnetization curve on which the machine operates on any given occasion may range from the rising to the falling part of the rather fat hysteresis loop for the magnetic circuit of the machine, depending essentially on the magnetic history of the iron. The curve used for analysis is usually the mean magnetization curve, and thus the results obtained are substantially correct on the average. Significant departures from the average may be encountered in the performance of any dc machine at a particular time, however.

EXAMPLE 7.7

A 100-kW, 250-V, 400-A, 1200-r/min dc shunt generator has the magnetization curves (including armature-reaction effects) of Fig. 7.14. The armature-circuit resistance, including brushes, is 0.025 Ω. The generator is driven at a constant speed of 1200 r/min, and the excitation is adjusted (by varying the shunt-field rheostat) to give rated voltage at no load.

(a) Determine the terminal voltage at an armature current of 400 A. (b) A series field of four turns per pole having a resistance of 0.005 Ω is to be added. There are 1000 turns per pole in the shunt field. The generator is to be *flat-compounded* so that the full-load voltage is 250 V when the shunt-field rheostat is adjusted to give a no-load voltage of 250 V. Show how a resistance across the series field (referred to as a *series-field diverter*) can be adjusted to produce the desired performance.

■ **Solution**

a. The 50 Ω field-resistance line 0*a* (Fig. 7.14) passes through the 250-V, 5.0-A point of the no-load magnetization curve. At $I_a = 400$ A

$$I_a R_a = 400 \times 0.025 = 10 \text{ V}$$

Thus the operating point under this condition corresponds to a condition for which the terminal voltage V_t (and hence the shunt-field voltage) is 10 V less than the generated voltage E_a.

A vertical distance of 10 V exists between the magnetization curve for $I_a = 400$ A and the field-resistance line at a field current of 4.1 A, corresponding to $V_t = 205$ V. The associated line current is

$$I_t = I_a - I_f = 400 - 4 = 396 \text{ A}$$

Note that a vertical distance of 10 V also exists at a field current of 1.2 A, corresponding to $V_t = 60$ V. The voltage-load curve is accordingly double-valued in this region. It can be shown that this operating point is unstable and that the point for which $V_t = 205$ V is the normal operating point.

b. For the no-load voltage to be 250 V, the shunt-field resistance must be 50 Ω and the field-resistance line is 0*a* (Fig. 7.14). At full load, $I_f = 5.0$ A because $V_t = 250$ V. Then

$$I_a = 400 + 5.0 = 405 \text{ A}$$

and

$$E_a = V_t + I_a(R_a + R_p) = 250 + 405 \times (0.025 + R_p)$$

where R_p is the parallel combination of the series-field resistance $R_s = 0.005$ Ω and the diverter resistance R_d

$$R_p = \frac{R_s R_d}{(R_s + R_d)}$$

The series field and the diverter resistor are in parallel, and thus the shunt-field current can be calculated as

$$I_s = 405 \left(\frac{R_d}{R_s + R_d} \right) = 405 \left(\frac{R_p}{R_s} \right)$$

and the equivalent shunt-field amperes can be calculated from Eq. 7.24 as

$$I_{net} = I_f + \frac{4}{1000} I_s = 5.0 + \frac{4}{1000} I_s$$

$$= 5.0 + 1.62 \left(\frac{R_p}{R_s} \right)$$

This equation can be solved for R_p which can be, in turn, substituted (along with $R_s = 0.005\ \Omega$) in the equation for E_a to yield

$$E_a = 253.9 + 1.25 I_{net}$$

This can be plotted on Fig. 7.14 (E_a on the vertical axis and I_{net} on the horizontal axis). Its intersection with the magnetization characteristic for $I_a = 400$ A (strictly speaking, of course, a curve for $I_a = 405$ A should be used, but such a small distinction is obviously meaningless here) gives $I_{net} = 6.0$ A. Thus

$$R_p = \frac{R_s (I_{net} - 5.0)}{1.62} = 0.0031\ \Omega$$

and

$$R_d = 0.0082\ \Omega$$

Practice Problem 7.5

Repeat part (b) of Example 7.7, calculating the diverter resistance which would give a full-load voltage of 240-V if the excitation is adjusted for a no-load voltage of 250-V.

Solution

$$R_d = 1.9\ m\Omega$$

EXAMPLE 7.8

Although the dynamics of self-excitation are not a focus of this discussion, as we have seen in Section 3.9, the MATLAB/Simulink package can be used to investigate the nature of the voltage build-up in a self-excited dc machine. In this Example, we will use MATLAB/Simulink to plot the terminal voltage as a function of time for a somewhat idealized dc generator with the following characteristics:

$$R_a = 0.02\ \Omega \qquad L_a = 10\ mH$$
$$R_f = 100\ \Omega \qquad L_f = 220\ mH$$

Figure 7.18 Generated voltage versus field current for the idealized dc generator of Example 7.8. Also shown is the field-resistance line.

and whose generated voltage as a function of field current can be expressed as

$$E_a = \begin{cases} 120\,(I_f + 0.05) & I_f \leq 1.0\ \text{A} \\ 120\,(I_f + 0.05 - 0.1\,(I_f - 1.0)^3) & 1.0\ \text{A} < I_f \leq 2.7\ \text{A} \\ 120\,(2.259 + 0.133\,(I_f - 2.7) - 0.5\,(I_f - 2.7)^2) & \text{Otherwise} \end{cases} \quad (7.30)$$

This characteristic is shown in Fig. 7.18 along with the field-resistance line.

■ Solution

Equation 7.29 describes the desired voltage transient. It can be re-written in integral form as

$$i_f = \int_0^t \left(\frac{e_a - (R_a + R_f)i_f}{L_a + L_f} \right) dt$$

or in Laplace-transform form as implemented in MATLAB/Simulink

$$i_f = \frac{1}{s} \left(\frac{e_a - (R_a + R_f)i_f}{L_a + L_f} \right)$$

The MATLAB/Simulink representation of this equation is shown in Fig. 7.19. Note that in the Simulink model, the field current i_f is represented by the variable "ifld" to avoid a conflict with the MATLAB "if" function. The resultant plot of terminal voltage as a function of time is shown in Fig. 7.20.

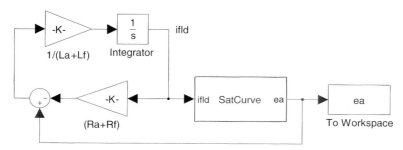

Figure 7.19 MATLAB/Simulink model for Example 7.8.

Figure 7.20   Plot of the terminal voltage versus time for the idealized dc generator of Example 7.8.

7.6.2   Motor Analysis

The terminal voltage of a motor is usually held substantially constant or controlled to a specific value. Hence, motor analysis most nearly resembles that for separately excited generators, although speed is now an important variable and often the one whose value is to be found. Analytical essentials include Eqs. 7.20 and 7.21 relating terminal voltage and generated voltage (counter emf); Eq. 7.24 for the main-field excitation; the magnetization curve for the appropriate armature current as the graphical relation between counter emf and excitation; Eq. 7.16 showing the dependence of electromagnetic torque on flux and armature current; and Eq. 7.17 relating counter emf to flux and speed. The last two relations are particularly significant in motor analysis. The former is pertinent because the interdependence of torque and the stator and rotor field strengths must often be examined. The latter is the usual medium for determining motor speed from other specified operating conditions.

Motor speed corresponding to a given armature current I_a can be found by first computing the actual generated voltage E_a from Eq. 7.20 or 7.21. Next the main-field excitation can be obtained from Eq. 7.24. Since the magnetization curve will be plotted for a constant speed ω_{m0}, which in general will be different from the actual motor speed ω_m, the generated voltage read from the magnetization curve at the foregoing main-field excitation will correspond to the correct flux conditions but to speed ω_{m0}. Substitution in Eq. 7.26 then yields the actual motor speed.

Note that knowledge of the armature current is postulated at the start of this process. When, as is frequently the case, the speed at a stated shaft power or torque output is to be found, an iterative procedure based on assumed values of I_a usually forms the basis for finding the solution.

EXAMPLE 7.9

A 100-hp, 250-V dc shunt motor has the magnetization curves (including armature-reaction effects) of Fig. 7.14. The armature circuit resistance, including brushes, is 0.025 Ω. No-load rotational losses are 2000 W and the stray-load losses equal 1.0% of the output. The field rheostat is adjusted for a no-load speed of 1100 r/min.

a. As an example of computing points on the speed-load characteristic, determine the speed in r/min and output in horsepower (1 hp = 746 W) corresponding to an armature current of 400 A.

b. Because the speed-load characteristic observed to in part (a) is considered undesirable, a *stabilizing winding* consisting of 1-1/2 cumulative series turns per pole is to be added. The resistance of this winding is assumed negligible. There are 1000 turns per pole in the shunt field. Compute the speed corresponding to an armature current of 400 A.

■ Solution

a. At no load, $E_a = 250$ V. The corresponding point on the 1200-r/min no-load saturation curve is

$$E_{a0} = 250 \left(\frac{1200}{1100} \right) = 273 \text{ V}$$

for which $I_f = 5.90$ A. The field current remains constant at this value.
  At $I_a = 400$ A, the actual counter emf is

$$E_a = 250 - 400 \times 0.025 = 240 \text{ V}$$

From Fig. 7.14 with $I_a = 400$ and $I_f = 5.90$, the value of E_a would be 261 V if the speed were 1200 r/min. The actual speed is then found from Eq. 7.27

$$n = 1200 \left(\frac{240}{261} \right) = 1100 \text{ r/min}$$

The electromagnetic power is

$$E_a I_a = 240 \times 400 = 96 \text{ kW}$$

Deduction of the rotational losses leaves 94 kW. With stray load losses accounted for, the power output P_0 is given by

$$94 \text{ kW} - 0.01 P_0 = P_0$$

or

$$P_0 = 93.1 \text{ kW} = 124.8 \text{ hp}$$

Note that the speed at this load is the same as at no load, indicating that armature-reaction effects have caused an essentially flat speed-load curve.

b. With $I_f = 5.90$ A and $I_s = I_a = 400$ A, the equivalent shunt-field current is

$$5.90 + \left(\frac{1.5}{1000} \right) 400 = 6.50 \text{ A}$$

From Fig. 7.14 the corresponding value of E_a at 1200 r/min would be 271 V. Accordingly, the speed is now

$$n = 1200 \left(\frac{240}{271} \right) = 1063 \text{ r/min}$$

The power output is the same as in part (a). The speed-load curve is now drooping, due to the effect of the stabilizing winding.

Repeat Example 7.9 for an armature current of $I_a = 200$ A.

Solution

 a. Speed $= 1097$ r/min and $P_0 = 46.5$ kW $= 62.4$ hp

 b. Speed $= 1085$ r/min

7.7 PERMANENT-MAGNET DC MACHINES

Permanent-magnet dc machines are widely found in a wide variety of low-power applications. The field winding is replaced by a permanent magnet, resulting in simpler construction. Permanent magnets offer a number of useful benefits in these applications. Chief among these is that they do not require external excitation and its associated power dissipation to create magnetic fields in the machine. The space required for the permanent magnets may be less than that required for the field winding, and thus permanent-magnet machines may be smaller, and in some cases cheaper, than their externally excited counterparts.

Alternatively, permanent-magnet dc machines are subject to limitations imposed by the permanent magnets themselves. These include the risk of demagnetization due to excessive currents in the motor windings or due to overheating of the magnet. In addition, permanent magnets are somewhat limited in the magnitude of air-gap flux density that they can produce. However, with the development of new magnetic materials such as samarium-cobalt and neodymium-iron-boron (Section 1.6), these characteristics are becoming less and less restrictive for permanent-magnet machine design.

Figure 7.21 shows a cutaway view of a typical integral-horsepower permanent-magnet dc motor. Unlike the salient-pole field structure characteristic of a dc machine with external field excitation, permanent-magnet motors typically have a smooth stator structure consisting of a cylindrical shell (or fraction thereof) of uniform-thickness permanent-magnet material magnetized in the radial direction. Such a structure is illustrated in Fig. 7.22, where the arrows indicate the direction of magnetization. The rotor of Fig. 7.22 has winding slots and has a commutator and brushes, as in all dc machines. Notice also that the outer shell in these motors serves a dual purpose: it is made up of a magnetic material and thus serves as a return path for magnetic flux as well as a support for the magnets.

Figure 7.23a defines the dimensions of a permanent-magnet dc motor similar to that of Fig. 7.22. Assume the following values:

$$\text{Rotor radius } R_r = 1.2 \text{ cm}$$
$$\text{Gap length } g = 0.05 \text{ cm}$$
$$\text{Magnet thickness } t_m = 0.35 \text{ cm}$$

Also assume that both the rotor and outer shell are made of infinitely permeable magnetic material ($\mu \to \infty$) and that the magnet is neodymium-iron-boron (see Fig. 1.19).

Figure 7.21 Cutaway view of a typical integral-horsepower permanent-magnet dc motor. (*Photo courtesy of Baldor Electric/ABB.*)

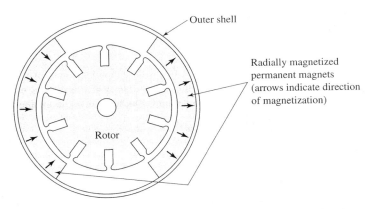

Outer shell

Radially magnetized permanent magnets (arrows indicate direction of magnetization)

Rotor

Figure 7.22 Cross section of a typical permanent-magnet motor. Arrows indicate the direction of magnetization in the permanent magnets.

Ignoring the effects of rotor slots, estimate the magnetic flux density B in the air gap of this motor.

■ Solution

Because the rotor and outer shell are assumed to be made of material with infinite magnetic permeability, the motor can be represented by a magnetic equivalent circuit consisting of an air gap of length $2g$ in series with a section of neodymium-iron-boron of length $2t_m$ (see Fig. 7.23b). Note that this equivalent circuit is approximate because the cross-sectional area of

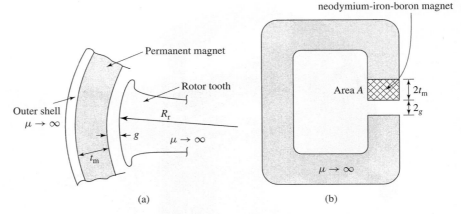

Figure 7.23   (a) Dimension definitions for the motor of Fig. 7.22, (b) approximate magnetic equivalent circuit.

the flux path in the motor increases with increasing radius, whereas it is assumed to be constant in the equivalent circuit.

The solution can be written down by direct analogy with Example 1.9. Replacing the air-gap length g with $2t_g$ and the magnet length l_m with $2t_m$, the equation for the load line can be written as

$$B_m = -\mu_0 \left(\frac{t_m}{g}\right) H_m = -7\mu_0 H_m$$

This relationship can be plotted on Fig. 1.19 to find the operating point from its intersection with the dc magnetization curve for neodymium-iron-boron. Alternatively, recognizing that, in SI units, the dc magnetization curve for neodymium-iron-boron is a straight line of the form

$$B_m = 1.06\mu_0 H_m + 1.25$$

we find that

$$B_m = B_g = 1.09 \text{ T}$$

Practice Problem 7.7

Estimate the magnetic flux density in the motor of Example 7.10 if the rotor radius is increased to $R_r = 1.3$ cm and the magnetic thickness is decreased to $t_m = 0.25$ cm.

Solution

$$B_m = B_g = 1.03 \text{ T}$$

Figure 7.24 shows an exploded view of an alternate form of permanent-magnet dc motor. In this motor, the armature windings are made into the form of a thin disk (with no iron in the armature). As in any dc motor, brushes are used to commutate

Figure 7.24 Exploded view of a disk-armature permanent-magnet servomotor. Magnets are Alnico. (*Photo courtesy of Kollmorgen Corporation.*)

the armature current, contacting the commutator portion of the armature which is at its inner radius. Currents in the disk armature flow radially, and the disk is placed between two sets of permanent magnets which create axial flux through the armature winding. The combination of axial magnetic flux and radial currents produces a torque which results in rotation, as in any dc motor. This motor configuration can be shown to produce large acceleration (due to low rotor inertia), no cogging torque (due to the fact that the rotor is nonmagnetic), and long brush life and high-speed capability (due

Figure 7.25 Equivalent circuit of a permanent-magnet dc motor.

to the fact that the armature inductance is low and thus there will be little arcing at the commutator segments).

The principal difference between permanent-magnet dc machines and those discussed previously in this chapter is that they have a fixed source of field flux which is supplied by a permanent magnet. As a result, the equivalent circuit for a permanent-magnet dc motor is identical to that of the externally-excited dc motor except that there are no field-winding connections. Figure 7.25 shows the equivalent circuit for a permanent-magnet dc motor.

From Eq. 7.17, the speed-voltage term for a dc motor can be written in the form $E_a = K_a \Phi_d \omega_m$ where Φ_d is the net flux along the field-winding axis and K_a is a geometric constant. In a permanent-magnet dc machine, Φ_d is constant and thus Eq. 7.17 can be reduced to

$$E_a = K_m \omega_m \tag{7.31}$$

where

$$K_m = K_a \Phi_d \tag{7.32}$$

is known as the *torque constant* of the motor and is a function of motor geometry and magnet properties.

Finally the torque of the machine can be easily found from Eq. 7.19 as

$$T_{mech} = \frac{E_a I_a}{\omega_m} = K_m I_a \tag{7.33}$$

In other words, the torque of a permanent-magnet motor is given by the product of the torque constant and the armature current.

EXAMPLE 7.11

A permanent-magnet dc motor is known to have an armature resistance of $1.03\ \Omega$. When operated at no load from a dc source of 50 V, it is observed to rotate at a speed of 2100 r/min and to draw a current of 1.25 A. Find (a) the torque constant K_m (b) the no-load rotational losses of the motor, and (c) the power output of the motor when it is operating at 1700 r/min from a 48-V source.

■ **Solution**

a. From the equivalent circuit of Fig. 7.25, the generated voltage E_a can be found as

$$E_a = V_t - I_a R_a$$
$$= 50 - 1.25 \times 1.03 = 48.7 \text{ V}$$

At a speed of 2100 r/min,

$$\omega_m = \left(\frac{2100 \text{ r}}{\text{min}}\right) \times \left(\frac{2\pi \text{ rad}}{\text{r}}\right) \times \left(\frac{1 \text{ min}}{60 \text{ sec}}\right)$$
$$= 220 \text{ rad/sec}$$

Therefore, from Eq. 7.31,

$$K_m = \frac{E_a}{\omega_m} = \frac{48.7}{220} = 0.22 \text{ V/(rad/sec)}$$

b. At no load, all the power supplied to the generated voltage E_a is used to supply rotational losses. Therefore

$$\text{Rotational losses} = E_a I_a = 48.7 \times 1.25 = 61 \text{ W}$$

c. At 1700 r/min,

$$\omega_m = 1700 \left(\frac{2\pi}{60}\right) = 178 \text{ rad/sec}$$

and

$$E_a = K_m \omega_m = 0.22 \times 178 = 39.2 \text{ V}$$

The input current can now be found as

$$I_a = \frac{V_t - E_a}{R_a} = \frac{48 - 39.2}{1.03} = 8.54 \text{ A}$$

The electromagnetic power can be calculated as

$$P_{\text{mech}} = E_a I_a = 39.2 \times 8.54 = 335 \text{ W}$$

Assuming the rotational losses to be constant at their no-load value (certainly an approximation), the output shaft power can be calculated:

$$P_{\text{shaft}} = P_{\text{mech}} - \text{rotational losses} = 274 \text{ W}$$

Practice Problem 7.8

The armature resistance of a small dc motor is measured to be 178 mΩ. With an applied voltage of 9 V, the motor is observed to rotate at a no-load speed of 14,600 r/min while drawing a current of 437 mA. Calculate (a) the rotational loss and (b) the motor torque constant K_m.

Solution

a. Rotational loss $= 3.90 \text{ W}$

b. $K_m = 5.84 \times 10^{-3} \text{ V/(rad/sec)}$

7.8 COMMUTATION AND INTERPOLES

One of the most important limiting factors on the satisfactory operation of a dc machine is the ability to transfer the necessary armature current through the brush contact at the commutator without sparking and without excessive local losses and heating of the brushes and commutator. Sparking causes destructive blackening, pitting, and wear of both the commutator and the brushes, conditions which rapidly become worse and burn away the copper and carbon. Sparking may be caused by faulty mechanical conditions, such as chattering of the brushes or a rough, unevenly worn commutator, or, as in any switching problem, by electrical conditions. The latter conditions are significantly influenced by the armature mmf and the resultant flux wave.

As indicated in Section 7.2, a coil undergoing commutation is in transition between two groups of armature coils: at the end of the commutation period, the coil current must be equal but opposite to that at the beginning. Figure 7.7b shows the armature in an intermediate position during which the coils in slots 1 and 7 are being commutated. The commutated coils are short-circuited by the brushes. During this period the brushes must continue to conduct the armature current I_a from the armature winding to the external circuit. The short-circuited coil constitutes an inductive circuit with time-varying resistances at the brush contact, with rotational voltages induced in the coil, and with both conductive and inductive coupling to the rest of the armature winding.

The attainment of good commutation is more an empirical art than a quantitative science. The principal obstacle to quantitative analysis lies in the electrical behavior of the carbon-copper (brush-commutator) contact film. Its resistance is nonlinear and is a function of current density, current direction, temperature, brush material, moisture, and atmospheric pressure. Its behavior in some respects is like that of an ionized gas or plasma. The most significant fact is that an unduly high current density in a portion of the brush surface (and hence an unduly high energy density in that part of the contact film) results in sparking and a breakdown of the film at that point. The boundary film also plays an important part in the lubrication of the rubbing surfaces. At high altitudes, definite steps must be taken to preserve it, or extremely rapid brush wear takes place.

The empirical basis of securing sparkless commutation, then, is to avoid excessive current densities at any point in the copper-carbon contact. This requirement, combined with the objective of utilizing all material to the fullest extent, leads designers to seek designs for which the current density is uniform over the brush surface during the entire commutation period. A linear change of current with time in the commutated coil, corresponding to linear commutation as shown in Fig. 7.8, brings about this condition and is accordingly the optimum.

The principal factor aiding linear commutation is the change in brush-contact resistance resulting from the linear decrease in area at the trailing brush edge and linear increase in area at the leading edge. Several electrical factors mitigate against linearity. Resistance in the commutated coil is one example. Usually, however, the voltage drop at the brush contacts is sufficiently large (of the order of 1.0 V) in comparison with the resistance drop in a single armature coil to permit the latter to be ignored. Coil inductance is a much more serious factor. Both the voltage of self-induction in the commutated coil and the voltage of mutual-induction from other coils (particularly those in the same slot) undergoing commutation at the same time oppose changes in current in the commutated coil. The sum of these two voltages is often referred to as the *reactance voltage*. Its result is that current values in the short-circuited coil lag behind in time the values dictated by linear commutation. This condition is known as *under commutation* or *delayed commutation*.

The effects of armature inductance thus tend to produce high losses and sparking at the trailing brush tip. For best commutation, inductance must be held to a minimum by using the fewest possible number of turns per armature coil and by using a multipolar design with a short armature. The effect of a given reactance voltage in delaying commutation is minimized when the resistive brush-contact voltage drop is significant compared with it. This fact is one of the main reasons for the use of carbon brushes with their appreciable contact drop. When good commutation is secured by virtue of resistance drops, the process is referred to as *resistance commutation*. It is typically used as the exclusive means only in fractional-horsepower machines.

Another important factor in the commutation process is the rotational voltage induced in the short-circuited coil. Depending on its sign, this voltage may hinder or aid commutation. In Fig. 7.13, for example, cross-magnetizing armature reaction creates a definite flux in the interpolar region. The direction of the corresponding rotational voltage in the commutated coil is the same as the current under the immediately preceding pole face. This voltage then encourages the continuance of current in the old direction and, like the resistance voltage, opposes its reversal. To aid commutation, the rotational voltage must oppose the reactance voltage. The general principle is to produce in the coil undergoing commutation a rotational voltage which approximately compensates for the reactance voltage, a principle called *voltage commutation*. Voltage commutation is used in almost all modern integral-horsepower commutating machines. The appropriate flux density is introduced in the commutating zone by means of small, narrow poles located between the main poles. These auxiliary poles are called *interpoles* or *commutating poles*. Figure 7.26 shows the stator of a 4-pole dc motor under construction in which the field poles and interpoles can be clearly seen.

The general appearance of interpoles and a schematic map of the flux produced when they alone are excited are shown in Fig. 7.27. The polarity of a commutating pole must be that of the main pole just ahead of it, i.e., in the direction of rotation for a generator, and just behind it for a motor. The interpole mmf must be sufficient to neutralize the cross-magnetizing armature mmf in the interpolar region and enough more to furnish the flux density required for the rotational voltage in the short-circuited armature coil to cancel the reactance voltage. Since both the armature mmf and the reactance voltage are proportional to the armature current, the commutating winding must be connected in series with the armature. To preserve the desired linearity, the commutating pole should operate at a relatively low flux level. By the use of commutating fields sparkless commutation can be obtained over a wide range in large dc machines.

Figure 7.26 The stator of a 4-pole dc motor under construction showing both the field poles and interpoles. (*Photo courtesy of Baldor Electric/ABB.*)

Figure 7.27 Interpoles and their associated component flux.

7.9 COMPENSATING WINDINGS

For machines subjected to heavy overloads, rapidly changing loads, or operation with a weak main field, there is the possibility of trouble other than simply sparking at the brushes. At the instant when an armature coil is located at the peak of a badly distorted flux wave (caused for example by the saturating effects associated with armature reaction), the coil voltage may be high enough to break down the air between the adjacent segments to which the coil is connected and result in flashover, or arcing, between segments. The breakdown voltage here is not high, because the air near the commutator is in a condition favorable to breakdown due to the presence of the plasma carrying the armature current between the brushes and the commutator. The maximum voltage between segments should be limited to a value on the order of 30 to 40 V, a fact which limits the average voltage between segments to lower values and thus determines the minimum number of segments which can be used in a proposed design.

Under transient conditions, high voltages between segments may result from the induced voltages associated with growth and decay of armature flux. Inspection of Fig. 7.12, for instance, may enable one to visualize very appreciable voltages of this nature being induced in a coil under the pole centers by the growth or decay of the armature flux shown in the sketch. Consideration of the sign of this induced voltage will show that it adds to the normal rotational emf when load is dropped from a generator or added to a motor. Flashing between segments may quickly spread around the entire commutator and, in addition to its possibly destructive effects on the commutator, constitutes a direct short circuit on the line. Even with interpoles present, therefore, armature reaction under the poles definitely limits the conditions under which a machine can operate.

These limitations can be considerably extended by compensating or neutralizing the armature mmf under the pole faces. Such compensation can be achieved by means of a *compensating* or *pole-face winding*, shown schematically in Fig. 7.28, embedded in slots in the pole face and having a polarity opposite of that of the adjoining armature winding. Since the axis of the compensating winding is the same as that of the armature, it will almost completely neutralize the armature reaction of the armature conductors under the pole faces when it is given the proper number of turns. It must be connected in series with the armature in order to carry a proportional current. The net effect of the main field, armature, commutating winding, and compensating winding on the air-gap flux is that, except for the commutation zone, the resultant flux-density distribution is substantially the same as that produced by the main field alone (Fig. 7.13). Furthermore, the addition of a compensating winding improves the speed of response of the machine because it reduces the armature-circuit time constant.

The main disadvantage of pole-face windings is their expense. They are used in machines designed for heavy overloads or rapidly changing loads (steel-mill motors are a good example of machines subjected to severe duty cycles) or in motors intended to operate over wide speed ranges by shunt-field control. By way of a schematic

Figure 7.28 Schematic section of a dc machine showing a compensating winding.

Figure 7.29 Schematic connection diagram of a dc machine.

summary, Fig. 7.29 shows the circuit diagram of a compound machine with a compensating winding. The relative position of the coils in this diagram indicates that the commutating and compensating fields act along the armature axis, and the shunt and series fields act along the axis of the main poles. Rather complete control of air-gap flux around the entire armature periphery is thus achieved.

7.10 SERIES UNIVERSAL MOTORS

Figure 7.30 shows a dc machine connection with a series-connected field winding. For this connection the direct-axis flux Φ_d is proportional to the armature current. Hence from Eq. 7.17, the generated voltage E_a is proportional to the product of the armature current and the motor speed, and from Eq. 7.19 we see that the torque will be proportional to the square of the armature current.

The dashed line in Fig. 7.31 shows a typical speed-torque characteristic for such a series-connected motor under dc operating conditions. Note that because the torque is proportional to the square of the armature current, the torque depends only upon the magnitude of the armature voltage and not its polarity; reversing the polarity of the applied voltage will not change the magnitude or direction of the applied torque.

If the rotor and stator structures of a series connected motor are properly laminated to reduce ac eddy-current losses, the resultant motor is referred to as a *series universal motor*. The series universal motor has the convenient ability to run on either alternating or direct current and with similar characteristics. Such a single-phase series motor

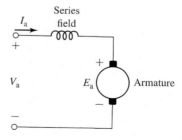

Figure 7.30 Series-connected universal machine.

Figure 7.31 Typical torque-speed characteristics of a series universal motor.

therefore is commonly called a *universal motor*. The torque angle is fixed by the brush position and is normally at its optimum value of 90°. If alternating current is supplied to a series universal motor, the torque will always be in the same direction, although it will pulsate in magnitude at twice line frequency. Average torque will be produced, and the performance of the motor will be generally similar to that with direct current.

Small universal motors are used where light weight is important, as in vacuum cleaners, kitchen appliances, and portable tools, and usually operate at high speeds (1500 to 15,000 r/min). Typical characteristics are shown in Fig. 7.31. The ac and dc characteristics differ somewhat for two reasons: (1) With alternating current, reactance-voltage drops in the field and armature absorb part of the applied voltage; therefore for a specified current and torque the rotational counter emf generated in the armature is less than with direct current, and the speed tends to be lower. (2) With alternating current, the magnetic circuit may be appreciably saturated at the peaks of the current wave. Thus the rms value of the flux may be appreciably less with alternating current than with the same rms value of direct current. The torque therefore tends to be less with alternating than with direct current. The universal motor provides the highest horsepower per dollar in the fractional-horsepower range, at the expense of noise, relatively short life, and high speed.

To obtain control of the speed and torque of a series universal motor, the applied ac voltage may be varied by the use of a electronic switching element called a Triac. The firing angle of the Triac can be manually adjusted, as in a trigger-controlled electric drill, or it can be controlled by a speed control circuit, as in some portable tools and appliances. The combination of a series motor and a solid-state device provides an economical, controllable motor package.

7.11 SUMMARY

This chapter has discussed the significant operating characteristics of dc machines. In general, the outstanding advantage of dc machines lies in their flexibility and versatility. Before the widespread availability of ac motor drives, dc machines were essentially the only choice available for many applications which required a high degree of control. Their principal disadvantages stem from the complexity associated with the armature winding and the commutator/brush system. Not only does this additional complexity increase the cost over competing ac machines, it also increases the need for maintenance and reduces the potential reliability of these machines. Yet the advantages of dc motors remain, and they continue to retain a competitive position in both large sizes for industrial applications and in smaller sizes for a wide variety of applications.

Dc generators are a simple solution to the problem of converting mechanical energy to electric energy in dc form, although ac generators feeding rectifier systems are certainly an option which must be considered. Among dc generators themselves, separately excited and cumulatively compounded, self-excited machines are the most common. Separately excited generators have the advantage of permitting a wide range of output voltages, whereas self-excited machines may produce unstable voltages at lower output voltages where the field-resistance line becomes essentially tangent to the magnetization curve. Cumulatively compounded generators may produce a substantially flat voltage characteristic or one which rises with load, whereas shunt- or separately excited generators may produce a drooping voltage characteristic unless external regulating means (such as a series field winding) are added.

Among dc motors, the outstanding characteristics of each type are as follows. The series motor operates with a decidedly drooping speed as load is added, the no-load speed usually being prohibitively high; the torque is proportional to almost the square of the current at low flux levels and to some power between 1 and 2 as saturation increases. The shunt motor at constant field current operates at a slightly drooping but almost constant speed as load is added, the torque being almost proportional to armature current; equally important, however, is the fact that its speed can be controlled over wide ranges by shunt-field control, armature-voltage control, or a combination of both. Depending on the relative strengths of the shunt and series field, the cumulatively compounded motor is intermediate between the other two and may be given essentially the advantages of one or the other.

In a wide variety of low-power applications in systems which are run from a dc source (automotive applications, portable electronics, etc.), dc machines are the most cost-effective choice. These dc machines are constructed in a wide-range of configurations, and many of them are based upon permanent-magnet excitation. In spite of the wide variety of dc machines which can be found in these various applications, their performance can readily be determined using the models and techniques presented in this chapter.

7.12   CHAPTER 7 VARIABLES

δ, ϕ	Phase angle [rad]
Φ_d	Direct-axis flux [Wb]
μ	Magnetic permeability [H/m]

μ_0	Permeability of free space = $4\pi \times 10^{-7}$ [H/m]
θ_a	Spatial angle [rad]
ω_m	Mechanical angular velocity [rad/sec]
C_a	Total number of turns in dc-machine armature winding
D, l	Linear dimensions [m]
e, E	Voltage [V]
F_{a1}	Net fundamental armature-winding (rotor) mmf [A]
F_{ar}	Armature-reaction mmf [A]
F_d	Net direct-axis (stator) mmf [A]
g	Gap length [m]
i, I	Current [A]
k_w	Winding factor
K_a	Winding constant
K_m	Torque constant [N·m/A]
L	Inductance [H]
m	Number of parallel paths through the armature winding
n	Angular velocity [r/min]
N	Number of turns
N_c	Number of turns per coil
N_{ph}	Series turns per phase
P	Power [W]
$\mathcal{P}$	Permeance [H]
poles	Number of poles
R	Resistance [Ω]
R_r	Rotor radius [m]
t_m	Magnet thickness [m]
T	Torque [N·m]

Subscripts:

a	Armature
ag	Air gap
c	Coil
d	Direct axis, diverter
eq	Equivalent
f	Field
L	Line
m	Magnet
mech	Mechanical
p	Parallel
r	Rotor
s	Stator, series field, Laplace operator
t	Terminal

7.13 PROBLEMS

7.1 Consider a separately excited dc motor. Describe the speed variation of the motor operating unloaded under the following conditions:

a. The armature terminal voltage is varied while the field current is held constant.

b. The field current is varied while the armature terminal voltage is held constant.

c. The field winding is connected in shunt directly to the armature terminals and the armature terminal voltage is then varied.

7.2 A dc shunt motor operating unloaded at an armature terminal voltage of 125 V is observed to be operating at a speed of 1420 r/min. When the motor is operated unloaded at the same armature terminal voltage but with an additional resistance of 8 Ω in series with the shunt field, the motor speed is observed to be 1560 r/min.

a. Calculate the resistance of the shunt field.

b. Calculate the motor speed which will result if the series resistance is increased from 8 Ω to 20 Ω.

c. With the field resistance at its original value, calculate the motor speed if it is operated unloaded at a terminal voltage of 90 V.

7.3 A shunt-connected, 75-kW, 250-V dc motor has an armature resistance of 45 mΩ and a field resistance of 185 Ω. When operated at 250 V, its no-load speed is 1850 r/min.

a. The motor is operating under load at a terminal voltage of 250 V and a terminal current of 290 A. Calculate (i) the motor speed in r/min, (ii) the load power in kW, and (iii) the load torque in N·m.

b. Assuming the load torque remains constant as a function of speed at the value calculated in part (a), calculate (i) the motor speed and (ii) the terminal current if the terminal voltage is reduced to 200 V.

c. Repeat part (b) if the load torque of part (a) varies with the square of the speed.

7.4 For each of the following changes in operating condition for a separately excited dc motor, describe how the armature current and speed will vary under the following circumstances. You may assume the armature resistance is negligible.

a. Halving the armature terminal voltage while the field flux and load torque remain constant.

b. Halving the armature terminal voltage while the field flux and load power remain constant.

c. Doubling the field flux while the armature terminal voltage and load torque remain constant.

d. Halving both the field flux and armature terminal voltage while the load power remains constant.

e. Halving the armature terminal voltage while the field flux remains constant and the load torque varies as the square of the speed.

Only brief quantitative statements describing the general nature of the effect are required, e.g., "speed-doubled."

7.5 The constant-speed magnetization curve for a 35-kW, 250-V dc machine at a speed of 1500 r/min is shown in Fig. 7.32. This machine is separately excited and has an armature resistance of 95 mΩ. This machine is to be operated as a dc generator while driven from a synchronous motor at constant speed.

a. What is the rated armature current of this machine?

b. With the generator speed held at 1500 r/min and if the armature current is limited to its rated value, calculate the maximum power output of the generator and the corresponding armature voltage for constant field currents of (i) 1.0 A, (ii) 2.0 A and (iii) 2.5 A.

c. Repeat part (b) if the speed of the synchronous generator is reduced to 1250 r/min.

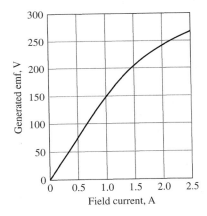

Figure 7.32 1500 r/min magnetization curve for the dc generator of Problem 7.5.

7.6 The dc generator of Problem 7.5 is to be operated at a constant speed of 1500 r/min into a load resistance of 2.0 Ω.

a. Using the "spline()" function of MATLAB and the points of the magnetization curve of Fig. 7.32 at 0, 0.5, 1.0, 1.5, 2.0, and 2.5 A, create a MATLAB plot of the magnetization curve of Fig. 7.32.

b. Using the "spline()" function as in part (a), use MATLAB to plot (i) the terminal voltage and (ii) the power delivered to the load as the generator field current is varied from 0 to 2.5 A.

7.7 The dc machine of Problem 7.5 is to be operated as a motor supplied by a constant armature terminal voltage of 250 V. If saturation effects are ignored, the magnetization curve of Fig. 7.32 becomes a straight line with a constant slope of 150 volts per ampere of field current. For the purposes of this problem, you may assume that saturation effects can be neglected.

    a. Assuming that the field current is held constant at 1.67 A, plot the motor speed as a function of motor shaft power as the shaft power varies from 0 to 35kW.

    b. Now assuming that the field current can be adjusted in order to maintain the motor speed constant at 1500 r/min, calculate the required field current as a function of motor shaft power as the shaft power varies from 0 to 35kW.

7.8 Repeat Problem 7.7 including the saturation effects represented by the saturation curve of Fig. 7.32. For part (a), set the field current equal to the value required to produce an open-circuit armature terminal voltage of 250 V at 1500 r/min. (Hint: This problem is most easily solved using MATLAB and its "spline()" function as in Problem 7.6.)

7.9 The 1750-r/min no-load magnetization curve of a separately-excited 550-V, 100-kW dc machine is given by

E_a, V	509	531	547	560	571	581	589	596	603	609	615
I_f, A	2.5	2.7	2.9	3.1	3.3	3.5	3.7	3.9	4.1	4.3	4.5

The field winding has 1175 turns/pole and a resistance of 163 Ω. The armature resistance is 57 mΩ.

The machine is operated as a shunt-connected generator at speed of 1700 r/min.

    a. Calculate the no-load terminal voltage.

    b. When loaded to a terminal current of 180 A, the generator terminal voltage is observed to be 527 V. Calculate the armature reaction in A-turns/pole.

    c. Calculate the generator terminal voltage if the speed is increased to 1750 r/min and the terminal current is maintained at 180 A.

Hint: This problem can be solved either graphically or by use of the MATLAB "spline()" function to represent the magnetization curve.

7.10 The dc machine of Problem 7.9 is operated as a separately excited motor at a terminal voltage of 550 V.

    a. Repeat part (b) of Problem 7.9 to calculate the armature reaction at a terminal current of 180 A.

    b. The motor is operating at a field current of 2.6 A. Plot the motor speed as a function of the armature current as the armature current varies over the range 0 to 180 A. You may assume that the armature reaction is linear proportional to the terminal current.

7.11 A 35-kW, 250-V shunt motor has an armature resistance of 0.13 Ω and a field resistance of 117 Ω. At no load and rated voltage, the speed is 1975 r/min and the armature current is 7.4 A. At full load and rated voltage, the armature current is 152 A and, because of armature reaction, the flux is 8 percent less than its no-load value. What is the full-load speed?

7.12 A 20-kW, 250-V, 1150 r/min shunt generator is driven by a prime mover whose speed is 1195 r/min when the generator delivers no load. The speed falls to 1145 r/min when the generator delivers 20 kW and may be assumed to decrease in proportion to the generator output. The generator is to be changed into a short-shunt compound generator by equipping it with a series field winding which will cause its voltage to rise from 230 V at no load to 250 V for a load of 80A. It is estimated that the series field winding will have a resistance of 0.049 Ω. The armature resistance (including brushes) is 0.152 Ω. The shunt field winding has 650 turns per pole.

To determine the effect of armature reaction, the machine is run as a separately excited generator and the following load data are obtained:

$$\text{Armature terminal voltage} = 250 \text{ V}$$
$$\text{Armature current} = 80.0 \text{ A}$$
$$\text{Field current} = 1.62 \text{ A}$$
$$\text{Speed} = 1145 \text{ r/min}$$

The magnetization curve at 1195 r/min is as follows:

E_a, V	230	240	250	260	270	280
I_f, A	1.05	1.13	1.25	1.44	1.65	1.91

Determine

a. the armature reaction in equivalent demagnetizing ampere-turns per pole for $I_a = 80$ A and

b. the necessary number of series-field turns per pole.

HINT: This problem can be solved either graphically or by use of the MATLAB "spline()" function to represent the magnetization curve.

7.13 When operated from a 300-V dc supply, a dc series motor operates at 1225 r/min with a line current of 70 A. Its armature-circuit resistance is 0.13 Ω and its series-field resistance is 0.09 Ω. Due to saturation effects, the flux produced by an armature current of 25 A is 54 percent of that at an armature current of 70 A. Find the motor speed when the armature voltage is 300 V and the armature current is 25 A.

7.14 Consider the long-shunt, 250-V, 100-kW dc machine of Example 7.3. Assuming the machine is operated as a motor at a constant supply voltage of 250-V with a constant shunt-field current of 4.8 A, use MATLAB to plot the motor speed as a function of load. Use the MATLAB "spline()" function to represent the magnetization curve of Fig. 7.14. Neglect armature-reaction effects. Include two plots, one for the case where the series-field ampere-turns add to those of the shunt field and the second for the case where the series-field ampere-turns oppose those of the shunt field.

7.15 A 250-V, 75-kW separately-excited dc motor is used as an adjustable-speed drive over the range from 0 to 2400 r/min. It has an armature resistance of 42 mΩ. When operated at a speed of 2400 r/min, the motor achieves its rated terminal voltage at a field current of 4.5 A. Speeds from 0 to 1450 r/min are obtained by adjusting the armature terminal voltage (up to 250 V at 1450 r/min) with the field current kept constant. Speeds from 1450 r/min to 2400 r/min are obtained by decreasing the field current with the armature terminal voltage remaining at 250 V. For the purposes of this problem, you may neglect armature-reaction effects.

    a.   Calculate the field current, terminal current and torque corresponding to operation at an armature terminal of 250 V and a load of 250 hp.

    b.   With the load torque equal to that found in part (a), calculate the field and armature currents corresponding to operation at an armature terminal voltage of 250 V and a speed of 1450 r/min.

    c.   For the motor operating at a constant torque equal to that found in part (a) and operating with the given speed-control algorithm plot (i) the armature current, (ii) the armature voltage, and (iii) the field current, each versus speed over the entire range.

7.16 A separately excited 550-V, 200-kW dc motor is used to drive loads over the speed range of 1500 to 3800 r/min. The motor has an armature resistance of 45 mΩ and a field winding of 1200 turns/pole. At a speed of 3500 r/min, the motor achieves rated open-circuit armature voltage at a field current of 0.9 A. You may assume that the open-circuit voltage varies linearly with field current and may neglect the effects of armature reaction.

Consider a load which requires 180 kW at a speed of 3800 r/min, 125 kW at a speed of 1500 r/min and whose torque varies linearly this speed range.

    a.   If the motor is operated at a constant armature terminal voltage of 550 V, calculate the field current required to operate the load at speeds of 1500, 2500, 3000, and 3800 r/min and calculate the corresponding armature current and armature power dissipation at each speed.

    b.   If the motor is initially operating at a speed of 3800 and an armature terminal voltage of 550 V, calculate the armature terminal voltage required to operate the load at speeds of 1500, 2500, 3000, and 3800 r/min and the corresponding armature current and armature power dissipation if the field current is held constant and the motor speed is varied by means of armature-voltage control.

7.17 For the dc-motor of Problem 7.16, at an armature current of 350 A, the demagnetizing effect of armature reaction has been determined to be 180 A-turns/pole. Repeat the calculations of Problem 7.16 including armature-reaction effects. You may assume that the effect of armature-reaction is linearly proportional to the armature current.

7.18 Consider a separately excited dc motor, whose armature terminals are connected to a constant-voltage source, driving a load requiring constant electromagnetic torque. Show that if $E_a > 0.5V_t$ (the normal situation), increasing the resultant air-gap flux decreases the speed, whereas if $E_a < 0.5V_t$ (as might be brought about by inserting a relatively high resistance in series with the armature), increasing the resultant air-gap flux increases the speed.

7.19 A four-pole, 25 kW, 250 V separately excited dc motor is mechanically coupled to a three-phase, four-pole, 25-kVA, 460-V, cylindrical-pole synchronous generator. The dc motor is connected to a constant 250-V dc supply, and the ac generator is connected to a 460-V, fixed-voltage, fixed-frequency, three-phase supply. The synchronous reactance of the synchronous generator is 0.78 per unit. The armature resistance of the dc motor is 22 mA. All unspecified losses are to be neglected.

  a. If the two machines act as a motor-generator set receiving power from the dc source and delivering power to the ac supply, what is the generated voltage E_{af} of the ac machine in volts/phase (line-to-neutral) when it delivers 30 kW at unity power factor? What is the internal voltage of the dc motor?

  b. Leaving the field current of the ac machine at the value corresponding to the condition of part (a), what adjustment can be made to reduce the power transfer between the two machines to zero? Under this condition of zero power transfer, what is the armature current of the dc machine? What is the armature current of the ac machine?

  c. Leaving the field current of the ac machine as in parts (a) and (b), what adjustment can be made to cause the transfer of 30 kW from the ac source to the dc source? Under these conditions what are the armature current and internal voltage of the dc machine? What will be the magnitude and phase of the current of the ac machine?

7.20 A 150-kW, 600-V, 600 r/min dc series-wound railway motor has a combined field and armature resistance (including brushes) of 0.125 Ω. The full-load current at rated voltage and speed is 250 A. The magnetization curve at 400 r/min is as follows:

Generated emf, V	360	380	400	420	440	460	480
Series-field current, A	220	238	256	276	305	346	404

Determine the internal starting torque when the starting current is limited to 470 A. Assume the armature reaction to be equivalent to a demagnetizing mmf which varies as the square of the current. (Hint: This problem can be solved either graphically or by use of the MATLAB "spline()" function to represent the magnetization curve.)

7.21   A axial-flow fan has the following speed-load characteristic

Speed, r/min	770	880	990	1100	1210	1320
Power, kW	5.8	7.8	10.4	13.4	17.3	22.2

The fan is driven by a 25 kW, 230-V, four-pole dc shunt motor. The motor has an armature winding with two parallel paths and $C_a = 784$ active conductors. The armature-circuit resistance is 0.195 Ω. The armature flux per pole is $\Phi_d = 5.9 \times 10^{-3}$ Wb and armature reaction effects can be neglected. No-load rotational losses (to be considered constant) are estimated to be 1125 W.

a.   Determine the motor terminal voltage and current and the fan power when the the fan is operating at a speed of 1285 r/min.

b.   Determine the motor terminal current and fan speed and power if the terminal voltage is decreased to 180 V. (HINT: This problem can be easily solved using MATLAB with the fan characteristic represented by the MATLAB "spline()" function.)

7.22   A shunt-connected dc motor operating from a 230-V line draws a full-load armature current of 53.7 A and runs at a speed of 1250 r/min at both no load and full load. The following data is available on this motor:

■   Armature-circuit resistance (including brushes) = 0.15 Ω
■   Shunt-field turns per pole = 1650 turns

The magnetizing curve taken with the machine operating as a motor at no load and 1250 r/min is

E_a, V	180	200	220	240	250
I_f, A	0.98	1.15	1.46	1.93	2.27

a.   Determine the shunt-field current of this motor at no load and 1250 r/min when connected to a 230-V line. Assume negligible armature reaction at no load.

b.   Determine the effective armature reaction at full load in ampere-turns per pole.

c.   How many series-field turns should be added to make this machine into a long-shunt cumulatively compounded motor whose speed will be 1150 r/min when the armature current is 53.7 A and the applied voltage is 230 V? Assume that the series field has a resistance of 0.037 Ω.

d.   If a series-field winding having 21 turns per pole and a resistance of 0.037 Ω is installed, determine the speed when the armature current is 53.7 A and the applied voltage is 230 V.

(HINT: This problem can be solved either graphically or by use of the MATLAB "spline()" function to represent the magnetization curve.)

7.23 A 12.5-kW, 230-V shunt motor has 2400 shunt-field turns per pole, an armature resistance (including brushes) of 0.18 Ω, and a commutating-field resistance of 0.035 Ω. The shunt-field resistance (exclusive of rheostat) is 375 Ω. When the motor is operated at no load with rated terminal voltage and varying shunt-field resistance, the following data are obtained:

Speed, r/min	1665	1704	1743	1782	1821	1860
I_f, A	0.555	0.517	0.492	0.468	0.447	432

The no-load armature current is negligible. When the motor is operating at full load and rated terminal voltage with a field current of 0.468 A, the armature current is 58.2 A and the speed is 1770 r/min.

a. Calculate the full-load armature reaction in equivalent demagnetizing ampere-turns per pole.

b. Calculate the electromagnetic and load torques and the rotational loss at the given operating condition.

c. What starting torque will the motor produce with a field current of 0.555 A if the starting armature current is limited to 85 A? Assume that the armature reaction under these conditions is equal to 175 ampere-turns per pole.

d. Design a series field winding to give a speed of 1575 r/min when the motor is loaded to an armature current of 58.2 A and when the shunt field current is adjusted to give a no-load speed of 1800 r/min. Assume the series field will have a resistance of 0.045 Ω.

(HINT: This problem can be solved either graphically or by use of the MATLAB "spline()" function to represent the magnetization curve.)

7.24 When operated at rated voltage, a 230-V shunt motor runs at 1500 r/min at full load and at no load. The full-load armature current is 125 A. The shunt field winding has 1700 turns per pole. The resistance of the armature circuit (including brushes and interpoles) is 0.12 Ω. The magnetization curve at 1500 r/min is

E_a, V	200	210	220	230	240	250
I_f, A	0.40	0.44	0.49	0.55	0.61	0.71

a. Compute the demagnetizing effect of the armature reaction at full load.

b. A long-shunt cumulative series field winding having three turns per pole and a resistance of 0.038 Ω is added to the machine. Compute the speed at full-load current and rated voltage. The shunt field current will remain equal to that of part (a).

c. With the series-field winding of part (b) installed, compute the internal starting torque in N·m if the starting armature current is limited to 190 A.

Assume that the corresponding demagnetizing effect of armature reaction is 270 ampere-turns per pole.

(HINT: This problem can be solved either graphically or by use of the MATLAB "spline()" function to represent the magnetization curve.)

7.25 A 350-V dc shunt motor has an armature-circuit resistance of 0.21 Ω. When operating from a 350-V supply and driving a constant-torque load, the motor is observed to be drawing an armature current of 84 A. An external resistance of 1.2 Ω is now inserted in series with the armature while the shunt field current is unchanged. Neglecting the effects of rotational losses and armature reaction, calculate

a.   the resultant armature current and

b.   the fractional speed change of the motor.

7.26 A 75-kW, 460-V shunt motor has an armature resistance of 0.082 Ω and a field-circuit resistance of 237 Ω. The motor delivers rated output power at rated voltage when its armature current is 171 A. When the motor is operating at rated voltage, the speed is observed to be 1240 r/min when the machine is loaded such that the armature current is 103.5 A.

a.   Calculate the rated-load speed of this motor.

In order to protect both the motor and the dc supply under starting conditions, an external resistance will be connected in series with the armature winding (with the field winding remaining directly across the 460-V supply). The resistance will then be automatically adjusted in steps so that the armature current does not exceed 180 percent of rated current. The step size will be determined such that, until all the external resistance is switched out, the armature current will not be permitted to drop below rated value. In other words, the machine is to start with 180 percent of rated armature current and as soon as the current falls to rated value, sufficient series resistance is to be cut out to restore the current to 180 percent. This process will be repeated until all of the series resistance has been eliminated.

b.   Find the maximum value of the series resistance.

c.   How much resistance should be cut out at each step in the starting operation and at what speed should each step change occur?

7.27 The manufacturer's data sheet for a permanent-magnet dc motor indicates that it has a torque constant $K_m = 0.28$ V/(rad/sec) and an armature resistance of 1.75 Ω. For a constant applied armature voltage of 100 V dc, calculate

a.   the no-load speed of the motor in r/min and

b.   its stall (zero-speed) current and torque (in N·m).

c.   Plot the motor torque as a function of speed.

d.   The motor is used to power a small pump which requires a torque of 9 N·m at a speed of 2000 r/min and which varies as the square of speed. Find the operating speed when the pump is driven by the dc motor at a terminal voltage of 85 V.

e.   Armature-voltage control applied to the dc motor is to be used to control the speed of the pump of part (d). Plot the required dc-motor terminal voltage as a function of speed.

7.28 Measurements on a small permanent-magnet dc motor indicate that it has an armature resistance of 8.9 Ω. With an applied armature voltage of 9 V, the motor is observed to achieve a no-load speed of 13,340 r/min while drawing an armature current of 45.0 mA.

a.   Calculate the motor torque constant K_m in V/(rad/sec).

b.   Calculate the no-load rotational losses in mW.

Assume the motor to be operating from an applied armature voltage of 9 V.

c.   Find the stall current and torque of the motor.

d.   At what speeds will the motor achieve an output power of 2 W? Estimate the motor efficiency under these operating conditions. Assume that the rotational loss varies as the cube of the speed.

7.29 Write a MATLAB script to calculate the parameters of a permanent-magnet dc motor. The inputs will be the armature resistance and the no-load armature voltage, speed, and armature current. The output should be the no-load rotational loss and the torque constant K_m. Exercise your script on a motor with an armature resistance of 6 Ω, no-load voltage of 7.5 V, no-load armature current of 22 mA and no-load speed of 8500 r/min.

7.30 The dc motor of Problem 7.28 will be used to drive a load which requires a power of 1.2 W at a speed of 8750 r/min. The combined inertia of the motor and load is 3.2×10^{-6} kg·m². Using MATLAB or MATLAB/Simulink, plot the motor speed and armature current as a function of time assuming the system is initially at rest and 9 V is suddenly applied to the motor terminals at time $t = 0$.

7.31 The 75-kW dc motor and current-limiting resistance system of Problem 7.26 are to be used to drive a constant-torque load of 500 N·m. The combined inertia of the motor and load is 6.5 kg·m². Using MATLAB or MATLAB/Simulink, assuming the motor to be initially at rest when 460 V dc is applied to the system, plot the motor speed and the motor current, both as a function of time.

8 CHAPTER

Variable-Reluctance Machines and Stepping Motors

$\mathbf{V}$ ariable reluctance machines[1] (often abbreviated as *VRMs*) are perhaps the simplest of electrical machines. They consist of a stator with excitation windings and a magnetic rotor with saliency. Rotor conductors are not required because torque is produced by the tendency of the rotor to align with the stator-produced flux wave in such a fashion as to maximize the stator flux linkages that result from a given applied stator current. The stator-winding inductances of these machines are functions of the rotor angular position and hence the torque produced by these machines can be evaluated using the techniques of Chapter 3.

Although the concept of the VRM has been around for a long time, only in the past few decades have these machines begun to see widespread use in engineering applications. This is due in large part to the fact that, although they are simple in construction, they are somewhat complicated to control. For example, the position of the rotor must be known in order to properly energize the phase windings to produce torque. It is the widespread availability and low cost of digital computation in combination with power electronics that has made the VRM competitive with other motor technologies in a wide range of applications.

By sequentially exciting the phases of a VRM, the rotor will rotate in a step-wise fashion through a specific angle per step. *Stepper motors* are designed to take advantage of this characteristic. Such motors often combine the use of a variable-reluctance geometry with permanent magnets to produce increased torque and precision position accuracy.

---

[1] Variable-reluctance machines are often referred to as *switched-reluctance machines* (*SRMs*) to indicate the combination of a VRM and the switching inverter required to drive it. This term is popular in the technical literature.

8.1 BASICS OF VRM ANALYSIS

Common variable-reluctance machines can be categorized into two types: singly salient and doubly salient. In both cases, their most noticeable features are that there are no windings or permanent magnets on their rotors and that their only source of excitation consists of stator windings. This can be a significant feature because it means that all the resistive winding losses in the VRM occur on the stator. Because the stator can typically be cooled much more effectively and easily than the rotor, the result is often a smaller motor for a given rating and frame size.

As is discussed in Chapter 3, to produce torque, VRMs must be designed such that the stator-winding inductances vary with the position of the rotor. Figure 8.1a shows a cross-sectional view of a *singly salient VRM*, which can be seen to consist of a nonsalient stator and a two-pole salient rotor, both constructed of high-permeability magnetic material. In the figure, a two-phase stator winding is shown although any number of phases are possible.

Figure 8.2a shows the form of the variation of the stator inductances as a function of rotor angle θ_m for a singly salient VRM of the form of Fig. 8.1a. Notice that the inductance of each stator phase winding varies with rotor position such that the inductance is maximum when the rotor axis is aligned with the magnetic axis of that phase and minimum when the two axes are perpendicular. The figure also shows that the mutual inductance between the phase windings is zero when the rotor is aligned with the magnetic axis of either phase but otherwise varies periodically with rotor position.

Figure 8.1b shows the cross-sectional view of a two-phase *doubly salient VRM* in which both the rotor and stator have salient poles. In this machine, the stator has four poles, each with a winding. However, the windings on opposite poles are of the same phase; they may be connected either in series or in parallel. Thus this machine is quite similar to that of Fig. 8.1a in that there is a two-phase stator winding and a two-pole salient rotor. Similarly, the phase inductance of this configuration varies from a maximum value when the rotor axis is aligned with the axis of that phase to a minimum when they are perpendicular.

Unlike the singly-salient machine of Fig. 8.1a, under the assumption of negligible iron reluctance the mutual inductances between the phases of the doubly-salient VRM of Fig. 8.1b will be zero, with the exception of a small, essentially-constant component associated with leakage flux. In addition, the saliency of the stator enhances the difference between the maximum and minimum inductances, which in turn enhances the torque-producing characteristics of the doubly salient machine. Figure 8.2b shows the form of the variation of the phase inductances for the doubly salient VRM of Fig. 8.1b.

The relationship between flux linkage and current for the singly salient VRM is of the form

$$\begin{bmatrix} \lambda_1 \\ \lambda_2 \end{bmatrix} = \begin{bmatrix} L_{11}(\theta_m) & L_{12}(\theta_m) \\ L_{12}(\theta_m) & L_{22}(\theta_m) \end{bmatrix} \begin{bmatrix} i_1 \\ i_2 \end{bmatrix} \tag{8.1}$$

Here $L_{11}(\theta_m)$ and $L_{22}(\theta_m)$ are the self-inductances of phases 1 and 2, respectively, and $L_{12}(\theta_m)$ is the mutual inductances. Note that, by symmetry

$$L_{22}(\theta_m) = L_{11}(\theta_m - 90°) \tag{8.2}$$

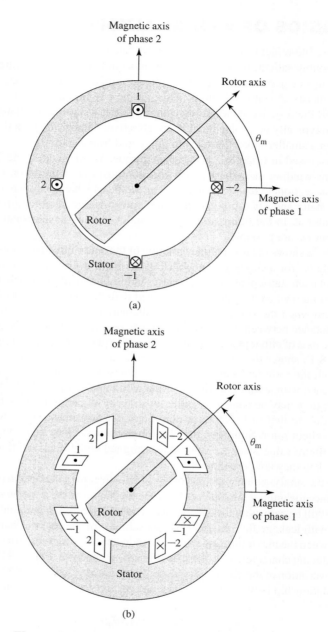

Figure 8.1   Basic two-phase VRMs: (a) singly salient and (b) doubly salient.

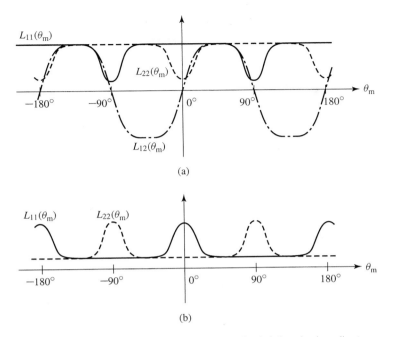

Figure 8.2 Plots of inductance versus θ_m for (a) the singly salient VRM of Fig. 8.1a and (b) the doubly salient VRM of Fig. 8.1b.

Note also that all of these inductances are periodic with a period of 180° because rotation of the rotor through 180° from any given angular position results in no change in the magnetic circuit of the machine.

From Eq. 3.68 the electromagnetic torque of this system can be determined from the coenergy as

$$T_{mech} = \frac{\partial W'_{fld}(i_1, i_2, \theta_m)}{\partial \theta_m} \qquad (8.3)$$

where the partial derivative is taken while holding currents i_1 and i_2 constant. Here, the coenergy can be found from Eq. 3.70

$$W'_{fld} = \frac{1}{2}L_{11}(\theta_m)i_1^2 + L_{12}(\theta_m)i_1 i_2 + \frac{1}{2}L_{22}(\theta_m)i_2^2 \qquad (8.4)$$

Thus, combining Eqs. 8.3 and 8.4 gives the torque as

$$T_{mech} = \frac{1}{2}i_1^2 \frac{dL_{11}(\theta_m)}{d\theta_m} + i_1 i_2 \frac{dL_{12}(\theta_m)}{d\theta_m} + \frac{1}{2}i_2^2 \frac{dL_{22}(\theta_m)}{d\theta_m} \qquad (8.5)$$

For the double salient VRM of Fig. 8.1b, the mutual-inductance term $dL_{12}(\theta_m)/d\theta_m$ is zero and the torque expression of Eq. 8.5 simplifies to

$$T_{mech} = \frac{1}{2}i_1^2 \frac{dL_{11}(\theta_m)}{d\theta_m} + \frac{1}{2}i_2^2 \frac{dL_{22}(\theta_m)}{d\theta_m} \qquad (8.6)$$

Substitution of Eq. 8.2 then gives

$$T_{mech} = \frac{1}{2}i_1^2 \frac{dL_{11}(\theta_m)}{d\theta_m} + \frac{1}{2}i_2^2 \frac{dL_{11}(\theta_m - 90°)}{d\theta_m} \tag{8.7}$$

Equations 8.6 and 8.7 illustrate an important characteristic of VRMs in which mutual-inductance effects are negligible. In such machines the torque expression consists of a sum of terms, each of which is proportional to the square of an individual phase current. As a result, the torque depends only on the magnitude of the phase currents and not on their polarity. Thus the electronics which supply the phase currents to these machines can be unidirectional; i.e., bidirectional currents are not required.

Since the phase currents in these machines are typically switched on and off by solid-state switches such as transistors or thyristors and since each switch need only handle currents in a single direction, this means that the motor drive requires only half the number of switches (as well as half the corresponding control electronics) that would be required in a corresponding bidirectional drive. The result is a drive system which is less complex and may be less expensive.

The assumption of negligible mutual inductance is valid for the doubly salient VRM of Fig. 8.1b both due to symmetry of the machine geometry and due to the assumption of negligible iron reluctance. In practice, even in situations where symmetry might suggest that the mutual inductances are zero or can be ignored because they are independent of rotor position (e.g., the phases are coupled through leakage fluxes), significant nonlinear and mutual-inductance effects can arise due to saturation of the machine iron. In such cases, although the techniques of Chapter 3, and indeed torque expressions of the form of Eq. 8.3, remain valid, analytical expressions are often difficult to obtain (see Section 8.4).

At the design and analysis stage, the winding flux-current relationships and the motor torque can be determined by using numerical-analysis packages which can account for the nonlinearity of the machine magnetic material. Once a machine has been constructed, measurements can be made, both to validate the various assumptions and approximations which were made at the design stage as well as to accurately characterize actual machine performance.

From this point on, we shall use the symbol p_s to indicate the number of stator poles and p_r to indicate the number of rotor poles, and the corresponding machine will be called a p_s/p_r machine. Example 8.1 examines a 4/2 VRM.

EXAMPLE 8.1

A 2-phase, 4/2 VRM is shown in Fig. 8.3. Its dimensions are

$$R = 3.8 \text{ cm} \qquad \alpha = \beta = 60° = \pi/3 \text{ rad}$$
$$g = 2.54 \times 10^{-2} \text{ cm} \qquad D = 13.0 \text{ cm}$$

and the poles of each phase winding are connected in series such that there are a total of $N = 100$ turns (50 turns per pole) in each phase winding. Assume the rotor and stator to be of infinite magnetic permeability.

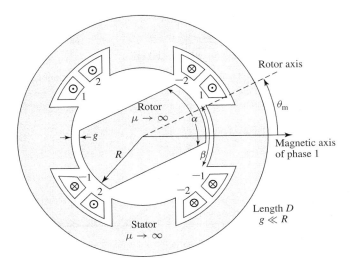

Figure 8.3 4/2 VRM for Example 8.1.

a. Neglecting leakage and fringing fluxes, plot the phase-1 inductance $L(\theta_m)$ as a function of θ_m.
b. Plot the torque, assuming (*i*) $i_1 = I_1$ and $i_2 = 0$ and (*ii*) $i_1 = 0$ and $i_2 = I_2$.
c. Calculate the net torque (in N · m) acting on the rotor when both windings are excited such that $i_1 = i_2 = 5$ A and at angles (*i*) $\theta_m = 0°$, (*ii*) $\theta_m = 45°$, (*iii*) $\theta_m = 75°$.

■ Solution

a. Using the magnetic circuit techniques of Chapter 1, we see that the maximum inductance L_{max} for phase 1 occurs when the rotor axis is aligned with the phase-1 magnetic axis. From Eq. 1.30, we see that L_{max} is equal to

$$L_{max} = \frac{N^2 \mu_0 \alpha R D}{2g}$$

where $\alpha R D$ is the cross-sectional area of the air gap and $2g$ is the total gap length in the magnetic circuit. For the values given,

$$
\begin{aligned}
L_{max} &= \frac{N^2 \mu_0 \alpha R D}{2g} \\
&= \frac{(100)^2 (4\pi \times 10^{-7})(\pi/3)(3.8 \times 10^{-2})(0.13)}{2 \times (2.54 \times 10^{-4})} \\
&= 0.128 \text{ H}
\end{aligned}
$$

Neglecting fringing, the inductance $L(\theta_m)$ will vary linearly with the air-gap cross-sectional area as shown in Fig. 8.4a. Note that this idealization predicts that the inductance is zero when there is no overlap when in fact there will be some small value of inductance, as shown in Fig. 8.2.

b. From Eq. 8.7, the torque consists of two terms

$$T_{\text{mech}} = \frac{1}{2}i_1^2 \frac{dL_{11}(\theta_m)}{d\theta_m} + \frac{1}{2}i_2^2 \frac{dL_{11}(\theta_m - 90°)}{d\theta_m}$$

and $dL_{11}/d\theta_m$ can be seen to be the stepped waveform of Fig. 8.4b whose maximum values are given by $\pm L_{\text{max}}/\alpha$ (with α expressed in radians!). Thus the torque is as shown in Fig. 8.4c.

Figure 8.4 (a) $L_{11}(\theta_m)$ versus θ_m, (b) $dL_{11}(\theta_m)/d\theta_m$ versus θ_m, and (c) torque versus θ_m.

c. The peak torque due to each of the windings is given by

$$T_{max} = \left(\frac{L_{max}}{2\alpha}\right) i^2 = \left(\frac{0.128}{2(\pi/3)}\right) 5^2 = 1.53 \text{ N} \cdot \text{m}$$

(i) From the plot in Fig. 8.4c, at $\theta_m = 0°$, the torque contribution from phase 2 is clearly zero. Although the phase-1 contribution appears to be indeterminate, in an actual machine the torque change from T_{max_1} to $-T_{max_1}$ at $\theta_m = 0°$ would have a finite slope and the torque would be zero at $\theta = 0°$. Thus the net torque from phases 1 and 2 at this position is zero.

Notice that the torque at $\theta_m = 0$ is zero independent of the current levels in phases 1 and 2. This is a problem with the 4/2 configuration of Fig. 8.3 since the rotor can get "stuck" at this position (as well as at $\theta_m = \pm 90°$, 180°) and should that happen, there is no way that electrical torque can be produced to move it.

(ii) At $\theta_m = 45°$ both phases are providing torque. That of phase 1 is negative while that of phase 2 is positive. Because the phase currents are equal, the torques are thus equal and opposite and the net torque is zero. However, unlike the case of $\theta_m = 0°$, the torque at this point can be made either positive or negative simply by appropriate selection of the phase currents.

(iii) At $\theta_m = 75°$ phase 1 produces no torque while phase 2 produces a positive torque of magnitude T_{max_2}. Thus the net torque at this position is positive and of magnitude 1.53 N · m. Notice that there is no combination of phase currents that will produce a negative torque at this position since the phase-1 torque is always zero while that of phase 2 can only be positive (or zero).

Practice Problem 8.1

Repeat the calculation of Example 8.1, part (c), for the case in which $\alpha = \beta = 70°$.

Solution

  i. $T = 0 \text{ N} \cdot \text{m}$
  ii. $T = 0 \text{ N} \cdot \text{m}$
  iii. $T = 1.59 \text{ N} \cdot \text{m}$

Example 8.1 illustrates a number of important considerations for the design of VRMs. Clearly these machines must be designed to avoid the occurrence of rotor positions for which none of the phases can produce torque. This is of concern in the design of 4/2 machines which will always have such positions if they are constructed with uniform, symmetric air gaps.

It is also clear that to operate VRMs with specified torque characteristics, the phase currents must be applied in a fashion consistent with the rotor position. For example, positive torque production from each phase winding in Example 8.1 can be seen from Fig. 8.4c to occur only for specific values of θ_m. Thus operation of VRMs must include some sort of rotor-position sensing as well as a controller which determines both the sequence and the waveform of the phase currents to achieve the desired operation. This is typically implemented by using electronic switching devices (transistors, thyristors, gate-turn-off devices, etc.) under the supervision of a microprocessor-based controller.

Although a 4/2 VRM such as in Example 8.1 can be made to work, as a practical matter it is not particularly useful because of undesirable characteristics such as its zero-torque positions and the fact that there are angular locations at which it is not possible to achieve a positive torque. For example, because of these limitations, this machine cannot be made to generate a constant torque independent of rotor angle; certainly no combination of phase currents can result in torque at the zero-torque positions or positive torque in the range of angular locations where only negative torque can be produced. As discussed in Section 8.2, these difficulties can be eliminated by 4/2 designs with asymmetric geometries, and so practical 4/2 machines can be constructed.

As has been seen in this section, the analysis of VRMs is conceptually straight-forward. In the case of linear machine iron (no magnetic saturation), determining the torque is simply a matter of calculating the stator-phase inductances (self and mutual) as a function of rotor position, expressing the coenergy in terms of these inductances, and then calculating the derivative of the coenergy with respect to angular position (holding the phase currents constant when taking the derivative). Similarly, as discussed in Section 3.8, the electric terminal voltage for each of the phases can be found from the sum of the time derivative of the phase flux linkage and the iR drop across the phase resistance.

In the case of nonlinear machine iron (where saturation effects are important) as is discussed in Section 8.4, the coenergy can be found by appropriate integration of the phase flux linkages, and the torque can again be found from the derivative of the coenergy with respect to the angular position of the rotor. In either case, there are no rotor windings and typically no other rotor currents in a well-designed variable-reluctance motor; hence, unlike other ac machine types (synchronous and induction), there are no electrical dynamics associated with the machine rotor. This greatly simplifies their analysis.

Although VRMs are simple in concept and construction, their operation is some-what complicated and requires sophisticated control and motor-drive electronics to achieve useful operating characteristics. These issues and others are discussed in Sections 8.2 to 8.5.

8.2 PRACTICAL VRM CONFIGURATIONS

Practical VRM drive systems (the motor and its inverter) are designed to meet operating criteria such as

- Low cost.
- Constant torque independent of rotor angular position.
- A desired operating speed range.
- High efficiency.
- A large torque-to-mass ratio.

As in any engineering situation, the final design for a specific application will involve a compromise between the variety of options available to the designer. Because VRMs require some sort of electronics and control to operate, often the designer is concerned with optimizing a characteristic of the complete drive system, and this will impose additional constraints on the motor design.

VRMs can be built in a wide variety of configurations. In Fig. 8.1, two forms of a 4/2 machine are shown: a singly salient machine in Fig. 8.1a and a doubly salient machine in Fig. 8.1b. Although both types of design can be made to work, a doubly salient design is often the superior choice because it can generally produce a larger torque for a given frame size.

This can be seen qualitatively (under the assumption of a high-permeability, non-saturating magnetic structure) by reference to Eq. 8.7, which shows that the torque is a function of $dL_{11}(\theta_m)/d\theta_m$, the derivative of the phase inductance with respect to angular position of the rotor. Clearly, all else being equal, the machine with the largest derivative will produce the largest torque.

This derivative can be thought of as being determined by the ratio of the maximum to minimum phase inductances L_{max}/L_{min}. In other words, we can write,

$$
\begin{aligned}
\frac{dL_{11}(\theta_m)}{d\theta_m} &\cong \frac{L_{max} - L_{min}}{\Delta\theta_m} \\
&= \frac{L_{max}}{\Delta\theta_m}\left(1 - \frac{L_{min}}{L_{max}}\right)
\end{aligned}
\tag{8.8}
$$

where $\Delta\theta_m$ is the angular displacement of the rotor between the positions of maximum and minimum phase inductance. From Eq. 8.8, we see that, for a given L_{max} and $\Delta\theta_m$, the largest value of L_{max}/L_{min} will give the largest torque. Because of its geometry, a doubly salient structure will typically have a lower minimum inductance and thus a larger value of L_{max}/L_{min}; hence it will produce a larger torque for the same rotor structure.

For this reason doubly salient machines are the predominant type of VRM, and hence for the remainder of this chapter we consider only doubly salient VRMs. In general, doubly salient machines can be constructed with two or more poles on each of the stator and rotor. It should be pointed out that once the basic structure of a VRM is determined, L_{max} is fairly well determined by such quantities as the number of turns, air-gap length, and basic pole dimensions. The challenge to the VRM designer is to achieve a small value of L_{min}. This is a difficult task because L_{min} is dominated by leakage fluxes and other quantities which are difficult to calculate and analyze.

As shown in Example 8.1, the geometry of a symmetric 4/2 VRM with a uniform air gap gives rise to rotor positions for which no torque can be developed for any combination of excitation of the phase windings. These torque zeros can be seen to occur at rotor positions where all the stator phases are simultaneously at a position of either maximum or minimum inductance. Since the torque depends on the derivative of inductance with respect to angular position, this simultaneous alignment of maximum and minimum inductance points necessarily results in zero net torque.

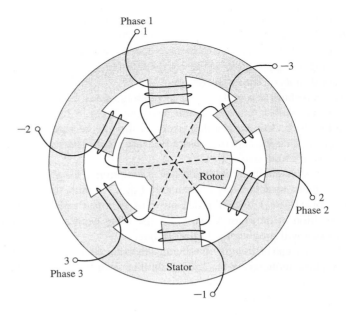

Figure 8.5 Cross-sectional view of a 6/4 three-phase VRM.

Figure 8.5 shows a 6/4 VRM from which we see that a fundamental feature of the 6/4 machine is that no such simultaneous alignment of phase inductances is possible. As a result, this machine does not have any zero-torque positions. This is a significant point because it eliminates the possibility that the rotor might get stuck in one of these positions at standstill, requiring that it be mechanically moved to a new position before it can be started. In addition to the fact that there are not positions of simultaneous alignment for the 6/4 VRM, it can be seen that there also are no rotor positions at which only a torque of a single sign (either positive or negative) can be produced. Hence by proper control of the phase currents, it should be possible to achieve constant-torque, independent of rotor position.

In the case of a symmetric VRM with p_s stator poles and p_r rotor poles, a simple test can be used to determine if zero-torque positions exist. If the ratio p_s/p_r (or alternatively p_r/p_s if p_r is larger than p_s) is an integer, there will be zero-torque positions. For example, for a 6/4 machine the ratio is 1.5, and there will be no zero-torque positions. However, the ratio is 2.0 for a 6/3 machine, and there will be zero-torque positions.

In some instances, design constraints may dictate that a machine with an integral pole ratio is desirable. In these cases, it is possible to eliminate the zero-torque positions by constructing a machine with an asymmetric rotor. For example, the rotor radius can be made to vary with angle as shown in grossly exaggerated fashion in Fig. 8.6a. This design, which also requires that the width of the rotor pole be wider than that of the stator, will not produce zero torque at positions of alignment because $dL(\theta_m)/d\theta_m$ is not zero at these points, as can be seen with reference to Fig. 8.6b.

(a)

(b)

Figure 8.6 A 4/2 VRM with nonuniform air gap: (a) exaggerated schematic view and (b) plots of $L(\theta_m)$ and $dL(\theta_m)/d\theta_m$ versus θ_m.

An alternative procedure for constructing an integral-pole-ratio VRM without zero-torque positions is to construct a stack of two or more VRMs in series, aligned such that each of the VRMs is displaced in angle from the others and with all the rotors sharing a common shaft. In this fashion, the zero-torque positions of the individual VRMs will not align, thus eliminating zero torque positions from the complete machine. For example, a series stack of two two-phase, 4/2 VRMs such as that of Example 8.1 (Fig. 8.3) with a 45° angular displacement between the individual VRMs will result in a four-phase VRM without zero-torque positions.

Generally VRMs are wound with a single coil on each pole. Although it is possible to control each of these windings separately as individual phases, it is common practice to combine them into groups of poles which are excited simultaneously. For example, the 4/2 VRM of Fig. 8.3 is shown connected as a two-phase machine. As shown in Fig. 8.5, a 6/4 VRM is commonly connected as a three-phase machine with opposite poles connected to the same phase and in such a fashion that the windings drive flux in the same direction through the rotor.

In some cases, VRMs are wound with a parallel set of windings on each phase. This configuration, known as a *bifilar winding,* in some cases can result in a simple inverter configuration and thus a simple, inexpensive motor drive.

In general, when a given phase is excited, the torque is such that the rotor is pulled to the nearest position of maximum flux linkage. As excitation is removed from that phase and the next phase is excited, the rotor "follows" as it is then pulled to a new maximum flux-linkage position. Thus, the rotor speed is determined by the frequency of the phase currents. However, unlike the case of a synchronous machine, the relationship between the rotor speed and the frequency and sequence of the phase-winding excitation can be quite complex, depending on the number of rotor poles and the number of stator poles and phases. This is illustrated in Example 8.2.

EXAMPLE 8.2

Consider a four-phase, 8/6 VRM. If the stator phases are excited sequentially, with a total time of T_0 sec required to excite the four phases (i.e., each phase is excited for a time of $T_0/4$ sec), find the angular velocity of the stator flux wave and the corresponding angular velocity of the rotor. Neglect any system dynamics and assume that the rotor will instantaneously track the stator excitation.

■ Solution

Figure 8.7 shows in schematic form an 8/6 VRM. The details of the pole shapes are not of importance for this example and thus the rotor and stator poles are shown simply as arrows indicating their locations. The figure shows the rotor aligned with the stator phase-1 poles. This position corresponds to that which would occur if there were no load on the rotor and the stator phase-1 windings were excited, since it corresponds to a position of maximum phase-1 flux linkage.

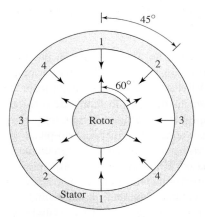

Figure 8.7 Schematic view of a four-phase 8/6 VRM. Pole locations are indicated by arrows.

Consider next that the excitation on phase 1 is removed and phase 2 is excited. At this point, the stator flux wave has rotated 45° in the clockwise direction. Similarly, as the excitation on phase 2 is removed and phase 3 is excited, the stator flux wave will move an additional 45° clockwise. Thus the angular velocity ω_s of the stator flux wave can be calculated quite simply as $\pi/4$ rad (45°) divided by $T_0/4$ sec, or $\omega_s = \pi/T_0$ rad/sec.

Note, however, that this is not the angular velocity of the rotor itself. As the phase-1 excitation is removed and phase 2 is excited, the rotor will move in such a fashion as to maximize the phase-2 flux linkages. In this case, Fig. 8.7 shows that the rotor will move 15° counterclockwise since the nearest rotor poles to phase 2 are actually 15° ahead of the phase-2 poles. Thus the angular velocity of the rotor can be calculated as $-\pi/12$ rad (15°, with the minus sign indicating counterclockwise rotation) divided by $T_0/4$ sec, or $\omega_m = -\pi/(3T_0)$ rad/sec.

In this case, the rotor travels at one-third the angular velocity of the stator excitation and in the opposite direction!

Practice Problem 8.2

Repeat the calculation of Example 8.2 for the case of a four-phase, 8/10 VRM.

Solution

$$\omega_m = \pi/(5T_0) \text{ rad/sec}$$

Example 8.2 illustrates the complex relationship that can exist between the excitation frequency of a VRM and the "synchronous" rotor frequency. This relationship is directly analogous to that between two mechanical gears for which the choice of different gear shapes and configurations gives rise to a wide range of speed ratios. It is difficult to derive a single rule which will describe this relationship for the immense variety of VRM configurations which can be envisioned. It is, however, a fairly simple matter to follow a procedure similar to that shown in Example 8.2 to investigate any particular configuration of interest.

Further variations on VRM configurations are possible if the main stator and rotor poles are subdivided by the addition of individual teeth (which can be thought of as a set of small poles excited simultaneously by a single winding). The basic concept is illustrated in Fig. 8.8, which shows a schematic view of three poles of a three-phase VRM with a total of six main stator poles. Such a machine, with the stator and rotor poles subdivided into teeth, is known as a *castleated* VRM, the name resulting from the fact that the stator teeth appear much like the towers of a medieval castle.

In Fig. 8.8 each stator pole has been divided into four subpoles by the addition of four teeth of width $6\frac{3}{7}^\circ$ (indicated by the angle β in the figure), with a slot of the same width between each tooth. The same tooth/slot spacing is chosen for the rotor, resulting in a total of 28 teeth on the rotor. Notice that this number of rotor teeth and the corresponding value of β were chosen so that when the rotor teeth are aligned with those of the phase-1 stator pole, they are not aligned with those of phases 2 and 3. In this fashion, successive excitation of the stator phases will result in a rotation of the rotor.

Castleation further complicates the relationship between the rotor speed and the frequency and sequence of the stator-winding excitation. For example, from Fig. 8.8 it can be seen that for this configuration, when the excitation of phase 1 is removed

Figure 8.8 Schematic view of a three-phase castleated VRM with six stator poles and four teeth per pole and 28 rotor poles.

and phase 2 is excited (corresponding to a rotation of the stator flux wave by 60° in the clockwise direction), the rotor will rotate by an angle of $(2\beta/3) = 4\frac{2}{7}°$ in the counterclockwise direction.

From the preceding analysis, we see that the technique of castleation can be used to create VRMs capable of operating at low speeds (and hence producing high torque for a given stator power input) and with very precise rotor position accuracy. For example, the machine of Fig. 8.8 can be rotated precisely by angular increments of $(2\beta/3)$. The use of more teeth can further increase the position resolution of these machines. Such machines can be found in applications where low speed, high torque, and precise angular resolution are required. This castleated configuration is one example of a class of VRMs commonly referred to as *stepping motors* because of their capability to produce small steps in angular resolution.

8.3 CURRENT WAVEFORMS FOR TORQUE PRODUCTION

As is seen in Section 8.1, the torque produced by a VRM in which saturation and mutual-inductance effects can be neglected is determined by the summation of terms consisting of the derivatives of the phase inductances with respect to the rotor angular position, each multiplied by the square of the corresponding phase current. For example, we see from Eqs. 8.6 and 8.7 that the torque of the two-phase, 4/2 VRM of Fig. 8.1b is given by

$$T_{\text{mech}} = \frac{1}{2}i_1^2\frac{dL_{11}(\theta_m)}{d\theta_m} + \frac{1}{2}i_2^2\frac{dL_{22}(\theta_m)}{d\theta_m}$$

$$= \frac{1}{2}i_1^2\frac{dL_{11}(\theta_m)}{d\theta_m} + \frac{1}{2}i_2^2\frac{dL_{11}(\theta_m - 90°)}{d\theta_m} \tag{8.9}$$

For each phase of a VRM, the phase inductance is periodic in rotor angular position, and thus the area under the curve of $dL/d\theta_m$ calculated over a complete period of $L(\theta_m)$ is zero, i.e.,

$$\int_0^{2\pi/p_r} \frac{dL(\theta_m)}{d\theta_m}\, d\theta_m = L(2\pi/p_r) - L(0) = 0 \tag{8.10}$$

where p_r is the number of rotor poles.

The average torque produced by a VRM can be found by integrating the torque equation (Eq. 8.9) over a complete period of rotation. Clearly, if the stator currents are held constant, Eq. 8.10 shows that the average torque will be zero. Thus, to produce a time-averaged torque, the stator currents must vary with rotor position. The desired average output torque for a VRM depends on the nature of the application. For example, motor operation requires a negative time-averaged shaft torque. Similarly, braking or generator action requires negative time-averaged torque.

Positive torque is produced when a phase is excited at angular positions with positive $dL/d\theta_m$ for that phase, and negative torque is produced by excitation at positions at which $dL/d\theta_m$ is negative. Consider a three-phase, 6/4 VRM (similar to that shown in Fig. 8.5) with 40° rotor and stator poles. The inductance versus rotor position for this machine will be similar to the idealized representation shown in Fig. 8.9.

Operation of this machine as a motor requires a net positive torque. Alternatively, it can be operated as a generator under conditions of net negative torque. Noting that positive torque is generated when excitation is applied at rotor positions at which

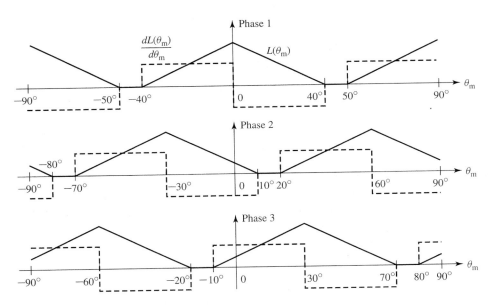

Figure 8.9 Idealized inductance and $dL/d\theta_m$ curves for a three-phase 6/4 VRM with 40° rotor and stator poles.

$dL/d\theta_m$ is positive, we see that a control system as required applies excitation to the individual phase-winding based upon the position of the rotor. It is, in fact, the need for this sort of control that makes VRM drive systems more complex than might perhaps be thought, considering only the simplicity of the VRM itself.

One of the reasons that VRMs have found application in a wide variety of situations is because the widespread availability and low cost of microprocessors and power electronics have brought the cost of the sensing and control required to successfully operate VRM drive systems down to a level where these systems can be competitive with competing technologies. Although the control of VRM drives is more complex than that required for dc, induction, and permanent-magnet ac motor systems, in many applications the overall VRM drive system turns out to be less expensive and more flexible than the competition.

Assuming that the appropriate rotor-position sensor and control system is available, the question still remains as to how to excite the armature phases. From Fig. 8.9, one possible excitation scheme would be to apply a constant current to each phase at those angular positions at which $dL/d\theta_m$ is positive and zero current otherwise.

If this is done, the resultant torque waveform will be that of Fig. 8.10. Note that because the torque waveforms of the individual phases overlap, the resultant torque will not be constant but rather will have a pulsating component on top of its average value. In general, torque profiles with significant pulsating components are typically considered problematic both because they may produce damaging stresses in the VRM and because they may result in the generation of excessive vibration and noise.

Consideration of Fig. 8.9 shows that there are alternative excitation strategies which can reduce the torque pulsations of Fig. 8.10. Perhaps the simplest strategy is to excite each phase for only 30° of angular position instead of the 40° which resulted in Fig. 8.9. Thus, each phase would simply be turned off as the next phase is turned on, and there would be no torque overlap between phases.

Although this strategy would be an ideal solution to the problem, as a practical matter it is not possible to implement. The difficulty is that because each phase winding has a self-inductance, it is not possible to instantaneously switch on or off

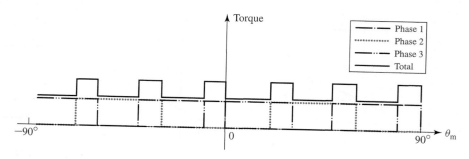

Figure 8.10   Individual phase torques and total torque for the motor of Fig. 8.9. Each phase is excited with a constant current I_0 only at positions where $dL/d\theta_m > 0$.

the phase currents. Specifically, for a VRM with independent (uncoupled) phases,[2] the voltage-current relationship of the jth phase is given by

$$v_j = R_j i_j + \frac{d\lambda_j}{dt} \tag{8.11}$$

where

$$\lambda_j = L_{jj}(\theta_m) i_j \tag{8.12}$$

Thus,

$$v_j = R_j i_j + \frac{d}{dt}[L_{jj}(\theta_m) i_j] \tag{8.13}$$

Equation 8.13 can be rewritten as

$$v_j = \left\{ R_j + \frac{d}{dt}[L_{jj}(\theta_m)] \right\} i_j + L_{jj}(\theta_m) \frac{di_j}{dt} \tag{8.14}$$

or

$$v_j = \left[R_j + \frac{dL_{jj}(\theta_m)}{d(\theta_m)} \frac{d\theta_m}{dt} \right] i_j + L_{jj}(\theta_m) \frac{di_j}{dt} \tag{8.15}$$

Although Eqs. 8.13 through 8.15 are mathematically complex and often require numerical solution, they clearly indicate that some time is required to build up currents in the phase windings following application of voltage to that phase. A similar analysis can be done for conditions associated with removal of the phase currents. The delay time associated with current build up can limit the maximum achievable torque while the current decay time can result in negative torque if current is still flowing when $dL(\theta_m)/d\theta_m$ reverses sign. These effects are illustrated in Example 8.3 which also shows that in cases where winding resistance can be neglected, an approximate solution to these equations can be found.

EXAMPLE 8.3

Consider the idealized 4/2 VRM of Example 8.1. Assume that it has a winding resistance of $R = 0.2 \ \Omega$/phase and a leakage inductance of $L_l = 5$ mH in each phase. For a constant rotor speed of 400 r/min, calculate (a) the phase-1 current as a function of time during the interval $-60° \leq \theta_m \leq 0°$, assuming that a constant voltage of $V_0 = 100$ V is applied to phase 1 just as $dL_{11}(\theta_m)/d\theta_m$ becomes positive (i.e., at $\theta_m = -60° = -\pi/3$ rad), and (b) the decay of phase-1 current if a negative voltage of -200 V is applied at $\theta_m = 0°$ and maintained until the current reaches zero. (c) Using MATLAB[†], plot these currents as well as the corresponding torque. Also calculate the integral under the torque-versus-time plot and compare it to the integral under the torque-versus-time curve for the time period during which the torque is positive.

---

[2] The reader is reminded that in some cases the assumption of independent phases is not justified, and then a more complex analysis of the VRM is required (see the discussion following the derivation of Eq. 8.5).

[†] MATLAB is a registered trademark of The MathWorks, Inc.

■ Solution

a. From Eq. 8.15, the differential equation governing the current buildup in phase 1 is given by

$$v_1 = \left[R + \frac{dL_{11}(\theta_{\mathrm{m}})}{d\theta_{\mathrm{m}}} \frac{d\theta_{\mathrm{m}}}{dt} \right] i_1 + L_{11}(\theta_{\mathrm{m}}) \frac{di_1}{dt}$$

At 400 r/min,

$$\omega_{\mathrm{m}} = \frac{d\theta_{\mathrm{m}}}{dt} = 400 \text{ r/min} \times \frac{\pi}{30} \left[\frac{\text{rad/sec}}{\text{r/min}} \right] = \frac{40\,\pi}{3} \text{ rad/sec}$$

From Fig. 8.4 (for $-60° \le \theta_{\mathrm{m}} \le 0°$)

$$L_{11}(\theta_{\mathrm{m}}) = L_l + \frac{L_{\max}}{\pi/3} \left(\theta_{\mathrm{m}} + \frac{\pi}{3} \right)$$

Thus

$$\frac{dL_{11}(\theta_{\mathrm{m}})}{d\theta_{\mathrm{m}}} = \frac{3L_{\max}}{\pi}$$

and

$$\frac{dL_{11}(\theta_{\mathrm{m}})}{d\theta_{\mathrm{m}}} \frac{d\theta_{\mathrm{m}}}{dt} = \left(\frac{3\,L_{\max}}{\pi} \right) \omega_{\mathrm{m}} = 5.12 \ \Omega$$

which is much greater than the resistance $R = 0.2 \ \Omega$

    This will enable us to obtain an approximate solution for the current by neglecting the Ri term in Eq. 8.13. We must then solve

$$\frac{d(L_{11}i_1)}{dt} = v_1$$

for which the solution is

$$i_1(t) = \frac{\int_0^t v_1 dt}{L_{11}(t)} = \frac{V_1 t}{L_{11}(t)}$$

where $V_1 = 100$ V. Substituting

$$\theta_{\mathrm{m}} = -\frac{\pi}{3} + \omega_{\mathrm{m}} t$$

into the expression for $L_{11}(\theta_{\mathrm{m}})$ gives

$$L_{11}(t) = L_l + \left(\frac{3L_{\max}}{\pi} \right) \omega_{\mathrm{m}}\, t$$

and thus

$$i_1(t) = \frac{100\,t}{0.005 + 5.12\,t}$$

which is valid until $\theta_{\mathrm{m}} = 0°$ at $t = t_1 = 25$ msec, at which point $i_1(t_1) = 18.8$ A.

b. During the period of current decay, the solution proceeds as in part (a). From Fig. 8.4, for $0° \le \theta_{\mathrm{m}} \le 60°$, $dL_{11}(\theta_{\mathrm{m}})/dt = -5.12 \ \Omega$ and again the Ri term can again be ignored in Eq. 8.15. As a result, during this period, the phase-1 current can again be solved by integration

$$i_1(t) = i_1(t_1) + \frac{\int_{t_1}^{t} v_1 dt}{L_{11}(t)} = \frac{V_2 (t - t_1)}{L_{11}(t)}$$

where $V_2 = -200$ V and

$$L_{11}(t) = L_l + \left(\frac{3 L_{max}}{\pi}\right) \omega_m (2t_1 - t)$$

From this equation, we see that the current reaches zero at $t = 33.45$ msec.

c. The torque can be found from Eq. 8.9 by setting $i_2 = 0$. Thus

$$T_{mech} = \frac{1}{2} i_1^2 \frac{dL_{11}}{d\theta_m}$$

Using MATLAB and the results of parts (a) and (b), the current waveform is plotted in Fig. 8.11a and the torque in Fig. 8.11b. The integral under the torque curve is 0.228 N · m · sec while that under the positive portion of the torque curve corresponding to positive torque is 0.030 N · m · sec. Thus we see that the negative torque produces a 16 percent reduction in average torque from that which would otherwise be available if the current could be reduced instantaneously to zero.

Notice first from the results of part (b) and from Fig. 8.11a that, in spite of applying a negative voltage of twice the magnitude of the voltage used to build up the current, current continues to flow in the winding for 8.4 ms after reversal of the applied voltage. From Fig. 8.11b, we see that the result is a significant period of negative torque production. In practice, this may, for example, dictate a control scheme which reverses the phase current in advance of the time that the sign of $dL(\theta_m)/d\theta_m$ reverses, achieving a larger average torque by trading off some reduction in average positive torque against a larger decrease in average negative torque.

This example also illustrates another important aspect of VRM operation. For a system of resistance of 0.2 Ω and constant inductance, one would expect a steady-state current of $100/0.2 = 500$ A. Yet in this system the steady-state current is less than 20 A. The reason for this is evident from Eqs. 8.14 and 8.15 where we see that $dL_{11}(\theta_m)/dt = 5.12 \Omega$ appears as an apparent resistance in series with the winding resistance which is much larger than the winding resistance itself. The corresponding voltage drop (the speed voltage) is of sufficient magnitude to limit the steady-state current to a value of $100/5.12 = 19.5$ A.

Here is the MATLAB script:

```
clc
clear

% Inductances
Ll = 0.005; % Leakage inductance
Lmax = 0.128; % Maximum value of variable inductance

% Operating parameters
rpm = 400;
omegam = rpm*pi/30;
```

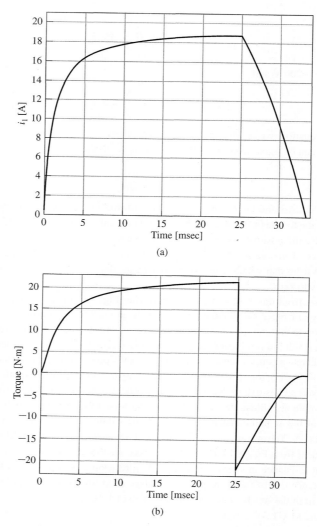

Figure 8.11 Example 8.3: (a) phase-1 current and
(b) corresponding torque profile.

```
% Voltages
V1 = 100; % Positive voltage
V2 = -200; % Negative voltage

% Step through time
delt = 1e-5;
sw = 1;
n = 0;
```

```
% Initialize torque integrals
int1 = 0;
int2 = 0;

while sw > 0;
    n = n+1;
    t(n) = 2*delt*(n-1);
    thetam = -pi/3+omegam*t(n);

    if thetam <= 0
        i1(n) = V1*t(n)/(L1+(3*Lmax*omegam/pi)*t(n));
        dL11dtheta = 3*Lmax/pi;
        Torque(n) = 0.5*dL11dtheta*i1(n)^2;
        int1 = int1 + Torque(n)*delt;
    else
        m = find(i1 == max(i1));
        L11 = L1+(3*Lmax*omegam/pi)*(2*t(m)-t(n));
        i1(n) = max(i1)+V2*(t(n)-t(m))./L11;
        if i1(n) < 0
            sw = -1;
        end
        dL11dtheta = -3*Lmax/pi;
        Torque(n) = 0.5*dL11dtheta*i1(n)^2;
        int2 = int2 + Torque(n)*delt;
    end
end

% Plot the current
plot(t*1000,i1,'LineWidth',2)
set(gca,'ylim',[0 21]);
set(gca,'xlim',[0 34]);
set(gca,'FontSize',20)
set(gca,'xtick',[0 5 10 15 20 25 30])
xlabel('Time [msec]','FontSize',20)
ylabel('i_1 [A]','FontSize',20)
grid on

pause

% Plot the Torque

plot(t*1000,Torque,'LineWidth',2)
ylim([-23 23]);
xlim([0 34]);
set(gca,'FontSize',20)
```

```
xlabel('Time [msec]','FontSize',20)
ylabel('Torque [N\cdotm]','FontSize',20)
set(gca,'xtick',[0 5 10 15 20 25 30])
set(gca,'ytick',[-20 -15 -10 -5 0 5 10 15 20])
grid on

fprintf('int1 = %g N-m-s\n',int1)
fprintf('int2 = %g N-m-s\n',int2)
```

Practice Problem 8.3

Reconsider Example 8.3 under the condition that a voltage of -250 V is applied to turn off the phase current. Use MATLAB to calculate the integral under the torque-versus-time plot and compare it to the integral under the torque-versus-time curve for the time period during which the torque is positive.

Solution

The current returns to zero at $t = 32.2$ msec. The integral under the negative portion of the torque curve is 0.030 N · m · s while that under the positive portion of the torque curve remains equal to 0.228 N · m · s. In this case, the negative torque produces a 13 percent reduction in torque from that which would otherwise be available if the current could be reduced instantaneously to zero.

Example 8.3 illustrates important aspects of VRM performance which do not appear in an idealized analysis such as that of Example 8.1 but which play an extremely important role in practical applications. It is clear that it is not possible to readily apply phase currents of arbitrary wave shapes. Winding inductances (and their time derivatives) significantly affect the current waveforms that can be achieved for a given applied voltage.

In general, the problem becomes more severe as the rotor speed is increased. Consideration of Example 8.3 shows, for a given applied voltage, (1) that as the speed is increased, the current will take a larger fraction of the available time during which $dL(\theta_m)/d\theta_m$ is positive to achieve a given level and (2) that the steady-state current which can be achieved is progressively lowered. One common method for maximizing the available torque is to apply the phase voltage somewhat in advance of the time when $dL(\theta_m)/d\theta_m$ begins to increase. This gives the current time to build up to a significant level before torque production begins.

Yet a more significant difficulty (also illustrated in Example 8.3) is that just as the currents require a significant amount of time to increase at the beginning of a turn-on cycle, they also require time to decrease at the end. As a result, if the phase excitation is removed at or near the end of the positive $dL(\theta_m)/d\theta_m$ period, it is highly likely that there will be phase current remaining as $dL(\theta_m)/d\theta_m$ becomes negative, so there will be a period of negative torque production, reducing the effective torque-producing capability of the VRM.

One way to avoid such negative torque production would be to turn off the phase excitation sufficiently early in the cycle that the current will have decayed essentially to zero by the time that $dL(\theta_m)/d\theta_m$ becomes negative. However, there is clearly a point of diminishing returns, because turning off the phase current while $dL(\theta_m)/d\theta_m$ is positive also reduces positive torque production. As a result, it is often necessary to accept a certain amount of negative torque (to get the required positive torque) and to compensate for it by the production of additional positive torque from another phase.

Another possibility is illustrated in Fig. 8.12. Figure 8.12a shows the cross-sectional view of a 4/2 VRM similar to that of Fig. 8.3 with the exception that the rotor pole angle has been increased from 60° to 75°, with the result that the rotor pole overhangs that of the stator by 15°. As can be seen from Fig. 8.12b, this results in a region of constant inductance separating the positive and negative $dL(\theta_m)/d\theta_m$ regions, which in turn provides additional time for the phase current to be turned off before the region of negative torque production is reached.

Figure 8.12 A 4/2 VRM with 15° rotor overhang: (a) cross-sectional view and (b) plots of $L_{11}(\theta_m)$ and $dL_{11}(\theta_m)/d\theta_m$ versus θ_m.

Although Fig. 8.12 shows an example with 15° of rotor overhang, in any particular design the amount of overhang would be determined as part of the overall design process and would depend on such issues as the amount of time required for the phase current to decay and the operating speed of the VRM. Also included in this design process must be recognition that the use of wider rotor poles will result in a larger value of L_{min}, which itself tends to reduce torque production (see the discussion of Eq. 8.8) and to increase the time for current buildup.

Under conditions of constant-speed operation, it is often desirable to achieve constant torque independent of rotor position. Such operation will minimize pulsating torques which may cause excessive noise and vibration and perhaps ultimately lead to component failure due to material fatigue. This means that as the torque production of one phase begins to decrease, that of another phase must increase to compensate. As can be seen from torque waveforms such as those found in Fig. 8.11, this represents a complex control problem for the phase excitation, and totally ripple-free torque will be difficult to achieve in many cases.

EXAMPLE 8.4

The analytic solutions of Example 8.3 are possible because the inductance variations of the idealized 4/2 VRM are of a simple form and because the winding resistance is sufficiently small that it can be ignored without significant loss of accuracy. In general, both the inclusion of resistive effects and the fact that inductance variations in practical machines are more complex that the idealized variation of the example make Eq. 8.13 difficult or impossible to solve analytically.

As a result, the analysis of VRMs require numerical analysis. Although we will not examine such analyses in any detail in this chapter, a simple example will be shown here using the MATLAB/Simulink.[3] Specifically, we will re-examine the steady-state performance of the 4/2 VRM of Example 8.3, including the effects of winding resistance and with both windings controlled with the same algorithm described in Ex. 8.3. (a) Using Simulink, we will plot the phase-1 current and the torque. (b) Again using Simulink, we will examine the effects of modifying the phase-voltage algorithm to advance the switching angle for the voltages by 5 degrees, i.e., to apply +100 V to each phase, 5 degrees before the derivative of the phase voltage turns positive and −200 V, 5 degrees before the derivative turns negative.

■ Solution

a. Figure 8.13 shows the Simulink block diagram. The various blocks are:

- ■ Block "L": This block calculates the phase inductances as a function of the rotor angle θ_m (see Fig. 8.4(a)).
- ■ Block "dLdtheta": This block calculates the derivatives of the phase inductances as a function of the rotor angle θ_m (see Fig. 8.4(b)).

---

[3] "MATLAB" and "Simulink" are registered trademarks of The MathWorks, Inc., 3 Apple Hill Drive, Natick, MA 01760, http://www.mathworks.com. Both Matlab and Simulink are avalailable in a Student Edition.

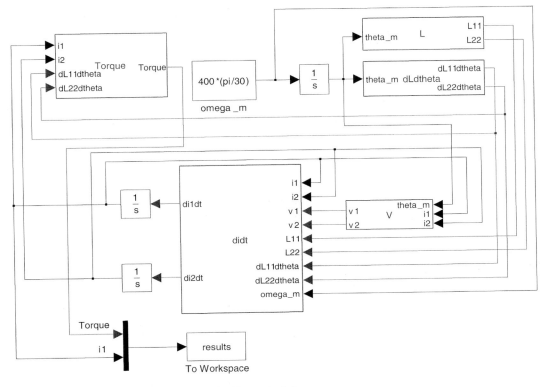

Figure 8.13 Simulink block diagram for Example 8.4

■ Block "V": This block calculates the voltages applied to each phase as a function of the angle θ_m and the phase currents; it turns off the applied -250 V voltage when the phase currents reach zero or first turn negative (since, because the simulation is solved numerically, it is unlikely that they will be identically zero at any point as they decay).

■ Block "didt": This block calculates the derivatives of the phase currents from Eq. 8.15

$$\frac{di_j}{dt} = \frac{1}{L_{jj}}\left(v_j - \left[R_j + \frac{dL_{jj}(\theta_m)}{dt}\omega_m\right]i_j\right)$$

where

$$\omega_m = \frac{d\theta_m}{dt}$$

Note that at a constant speed of 400 r/min,

$$\omega_m = \frac{400\,\pi}{30}$$

Because of the numerical implementation, it is possible that a slightly negative value of phase current will appear at the input of this block and thus there is additional

Figure 8.14 (a) Phase-1 current and (b) the torque profile for one revolution for part (a) of Example 8.4.

code in this block to re-set the currents to zero should a negative value of current appear at the input.

■ Block "Torque": This block calculates the electromechanical torque of Eq. 8.9.

Figure 8.14(a) shows a plot of the phase-1 current during one revolution of the rotor. The maximum value of the current is 18.4 A as compared to 18.8 A calculated in Example 8.3. The total torque produced by phases 1 and 2 is plotted in Fig. 8.14(b). It has a average value of 10.1 N·m.

b. By advancing the switching angle by 5 degrees, the current in each phase winding is seen to rise rapidly because the $dL_{jj}/d\theta_m$ term in Eq. 8.15 is initially zero and the current build up is thus limited only by the phase-winding leakage inductance and resistance. This can be seen from the phase-1 current waveform plotted in Fig. 8.15a, where the peak current is equal to 47.6 A as opposed to 18.4 A in part (a). As a result, there is significant phase current flowing when, 5 degrees after the application of voltage, $dL/d\theta_m$ becomes positive and the motor immediately begins to develop torque, as can be seen from torque waveform plotted in Fig. 8.15(b).

Although turning off the phase current "early," i.e., while $dL/d\theta_m$ is positive, reduces the positive torque, it results in less negative torque once $dL/d\theta_m$ becomes

(a)

(b)

Figure 8.15 (a) Phase-1 current and (b) the torque profile for one revolution with the voltage-switching angle advanced by 5 degrees for part (b) of Example 8.4.

negative. The net result is greater average torque; in this case the average torque is 19.2 N·m as compared to 10.1 N·m found in part (a) without the advancing the switching angles

8.4 NONLINEAR ANALYSIS

Like most electric machines, VRMs employ magnetic materials both to direct and shape the magnetic fields in the machine and to increase the magnetic flux density that can be achieved from a given amplitude of current. To obtain the maximum benefit from the magnetic material, practical VRMs are operated with the magnetic flux density high enough so that the magnetic material is in saturation under normal operating conditions.

As with the synchronous, induction, and dc machines discussed in Chapters 5–7, the actual operating flux density is determined by trading off such quantities as cost, efficiency, and torque-to-mass ratio. However, because the VRM and its drive

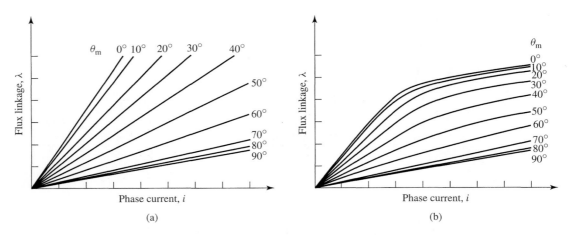

Figure 8.16 Plots of λ versus *i* for a VRM with (a) linear and (b) nonlinear magnetics.

electronics are quite closely interrelated, VRM design typically involves additional trade-offs that in turn affect the choice of operating flux density.

Figure 8.2 shows typical inductance-versus-angle curves for the VRMs of Fig. 8.1. Such curves are characteristic of all VRMs. It must be recognized that the use of the concept of inductance is strictly valid only under the condition that the magnetic circuit in the machine is linear so that the flux density (and hence the winding flux linkage) is proportional to the winding current. This linear analysis is based on the assumption that the magnetic material in the motor has constant magnetic permeability and was used for all the analyses earlier in this chapter.

An alternate representation of the flux-linkage versus current characteristic of a VRM is shown in Fig. 8.16. This representation consists of a series of plots of the flux linkage versus current at various rotor angles. In this figure, the curves correspond to a machine with a two-pole rotor such as in Fig. 8.1, and hence a plot of curves from 0° to 90° is sufficient to completely characterize the machine.

Figure 8.16a shows set of λ-i characteristics such as which would be measured in a machine with linear magnetics, i.e., constant magnetic permeability and no magnetic saturation. For each rotor angle, the curve is a straight line whose slope corresponds to the inductance $L(\theta_m)$ at that angular position. In fact, a plot of $L(\theta_m)$ versus θ_m such as in Fig. 8.2 is an equivalent representation to that of Fig. 8.16a.

In practice, VRMs do operate with their magnetic material in saturation and their λ-i characteristics take on the form of Fig. 8.16b. Notice that for low current levels, the curves are linear, corresponding to the assumption of linear magnetics of Fig. 8.16a. However, for higher current levels, saturation begins to occur and the curves bend over steeply, with the result that there is significantly less flux linkage for a given current level. Finally, note that saturation effects are maximum at $\theta_m = 0°$ (for which the rotor and stator poles are aligned) and minimal for higher angles as the rotor approaches the nonaligned position.

Saturation has two important, somewhat contradictory effects on VRM performance. On the one hand, saturation limits flux densities for a given current level and

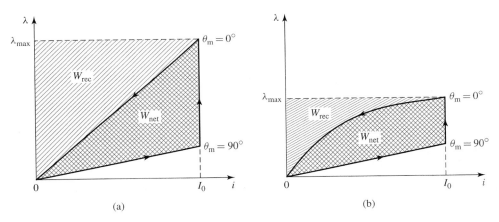

Figure 8.17 (a) Flux-linkage-current trajectory for the (a) linear and (b) nonlinear machines of Fig. 8.16.

thus tends to limit the amount of torque available from the VRM. On the other hand, it can be shown that saturation tends to lower the required inverter volt-ampere rating for a given VRM output power and thus tends to make the inverter smaller and less costly. A well-designed VRM system will be based on a trade-off between the two effects.[4]

These effects of saturation can be investigated by considering the two machines of Figs. 8.16a and b operating at the same rotational speed and under the same operating condition. For the sake of simplicity, we assume a somewhat idealized condition in which the phase-1 current is instantaneously switched on to a value I_0 at $\theta_m = -90°$ (the unaligned position for phase 1) and is instantaneously switched off at $\theta_m = 0°$ (the aligned position). This operation is similar to that discussed in Example 8.1 in that we will neglect the complicating effects of the current buildup and decay transients which are illustrated in Examples 8.3 and 8.4.

Because of rotor symmetry, the flux linkages for negative rotor angles are identical to those for positive angles. Thus, the flux linkage-current trajectories for one current cycle can be determined from Figs. 8.16a and b and are shown for the two machines in Figs. 8.17a and b.

As each trajectory is traversed, the power input to the winding is given by its volt-ampere product

$$p_{in} = iv = i\frac{d\lambda}{dt} \tag{8.16}$$

The net electric energy input to the machine (the energy that is converted to mechanical work) in a cycle can be determined by integrating Eq. 8.16 around the

[4] For a discussion of saturation effects in VRM drive systems, see T. J. E. Miller, "Converter Volt-Ampere Requirements of the Switched Reluctance Motor," *IEEE Trans. Ind. Appl.*, IA-21:1136–1144 (1985).

trajectory

$$\text{Net work} = \int p_{\text{in}} \, dt = \oint i \, d\lambda \qquad (8.17)$$

This can be seen graphically as the area enclosed by the trajectory, labeled W_{net} in Figs. 8.17a and b. Note that the saturated machine converts less useful work per cycle than the unsaturated machine. As a result, to get a machine of the same power output, the saturated machine will have to be larger than a corresponding (hypothetical) unsaturated machine. This analysis demonstrates the effects of saturation in lowering torque and power output.

The peak energy input to the winding from the inverter can also be calculated. It is equal to the integral of the input power from the start of the trajectory to the point $(I_0, \lambda_{\text{max}})$:

$$\text{Peak energy} = \int_0^{\lambda_{\text{max}}} i \, d\lambda \qquad (8.18)$$

This is the total area under the λ-i curve, shown in Fig. 8.17a and b as the sum of the areas labeled W_{rec} and W_{net}.

Since we have seen that the energy represented by the area W_{net} corresponds to useful output energy, it is clear that the energy represented by the area W_{rec} corresponds to additional energy input that is required to make the VRM operate (i.e., it goes into creating the magnetic fields in the VRM). This energy produces no useful work; rather it corresponds to reactive power which is recycled back in and out of the inverter during the course of a cycle.

The inverter volt-ampere rating is determined by the average power per phase processed by the inverter as the motor operates, equal to the peak energy input to the VRM divided by the time T between cycles. Similarly, the average output power per phase of the VRM is given by the net energy input per cycle divided by T. Thus the ratio of the inverter volt-ampere rating to power output is

$$\frac{\text{Inverter volt-ampere rating}}{\text{Net output area}} = \frac{\text{area}(W_{\text{rec}} + W_{\text{net}})}{\text{area}(W_{\text{net}})} \qquad (8.19)$$

In general, the inverter volt-ampere rating determines its cost and size. Thus, for a given power output from a VRM, a smaller ratio of inverter volt-ampere rating to output power means that the inverter will be both smaller and cheaper. Comparison of Figs. 8.17a and b shows that this ratio is smaller in the machine which saturates; the effect of saturation is to lower the amount of energy which must be recycled each cycle and hence the volt-ampere rating of the inverter required to supply the VRM.

EXAMPLE 8.5

Consider a symmetrical two-phase 4/2 VRM whose λ-i characteristic can be represented by the following λ-i expression (for phase 1) as a function of θ_{m} over the range $0 \leq \theta_{\text{m}} \leq 90°$

$$\lambda_1 = \left(0.005 + 0.09 \left(\frac{90° - \theta_{\text{m}}}{90°} \right) \left(\frac{8.0}{8.0 + i_1} \right) \right) i_1$$

Phase 2 of this motor is identical to that of phase 1, and there is no significant mutual inductance between the phases. Assume that the winding resistance is negligible.

a. Using MATLAB, plot a family of λ_1-i_1 curves for this motor as θ_m varies from 0 to 90° in 10° increments and as i_1 is varied from 0 to 30 A.

b. Again using MATLAB, use Eq. 8.19 and Fig. 8.17 to calculate the ratio of the inverter volt-ampere rating to the VRM net power output for the following idealized operating cycle:

   i. The current is instantaneously raised to 25 A when $\theta_m = -90°$.

   ii. The current is then held constant as the rotor rotates to $\theta_m = 0°$.

   iii. At $\theta_m = 0°$, the current is reduced to zero.

c. Assuming the VRM to be operating as a motor using the cycle described in part (b) and rotating at a constant speed of 2500 r/min, calculate the net electromechanical power supplied to the rotor.

■ Solution

a. The λ_1-i_1 curves are shown in Fig. 8.18a.

b. Figure 8.18b shows the areas W_{net} and W_{rec}. Note that, as pointed out in the text, the λ-i curves are symmetrical around $\theta_m = 0°$ and thus the curves for negative values of θ_m are identical to those for the corresponding positive values. The area W_{net} is bounded by the λ_1-i_1 curves corresponding to $\theta_m = 0°$ and $\theta_m = 90°$ and the line $i_1 = 25$ A. The area W_{rec} is bounded by the line $\lambda_1 = \lambda_{max}$ and the λ_1-i_1 curve corresponding to $\theta_m = 0°$, where $\lambda_{max} = \lambda_1(25 \text{ A}, 0°)$.

Using MATLAB to integrate the areas, the desired ratio can be calculated from Eq. 8.19 as

$$\frac{\text{Inverter volt-ampere rating}}{\text{Net output power}} = \frac{\text{area}(W_{rec} + W_{net})}{\text{area}(W_{net})} = 1.55$$

c. Energy equal to area(W_{net}) is supplied by each phase to the rotor twice during each revolution of the rotor. If area(W_{net}) is measured in joules, the power in watts supplied per phase is thus equal to

$$P_{phase} = 2\left(\frac{\text{area}(W_{net})}{T}\right) \text{ W}$$

where T is the time for one revolution (in seconds).

From MATLAB, area(W_{net}) = 9.91 joules and for 2500 r/min, $T = 60/2500 = 0.024$ sec,

$$P_{phase} = 2\left(\frac{9.91}{0.024}\right) = 825 \text{ W}$$

and thus

$$P_{mech} = 2P_{phase} = 1650 \text{ W}$$

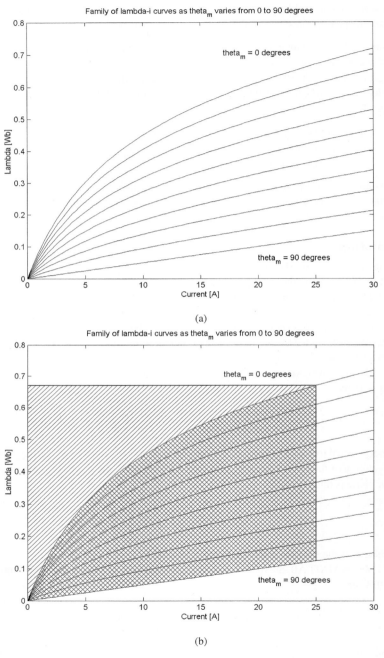

Figure 8.18 (a) λ_1-i_1 curves for Example 8.5. (b) Areas used in the calculation of part (b).

Here is the MATLAB script:

```
clc
clear

%(a) First plot the lambda-i characteristics

for m = 1:10
theta(m) = 10*(m-1);
   for n=1:101
i(n) = 30*(n-1)/100;
Lambda(n) = i(n)*(0.005 + 0.09*((90-theta(m))/90)*(8/(i(n)+8)));
   end

   plot(i,Lambda)
   if m==1
hold
   end
end

hold
xlabel('Current [A]')
ylabel('Lambda [Wb]')
title('Family of lambda-i curves as theta_m varies from 0 to 90 degrees')
text(17,.7,'theta_m = 0 degrees')
text(20,.06,'theta_m = 90 degrees')

%(b) Now integrate to find the areas.

%Peak lambda at 0 degrees, 25 Amps
lambdamax = 25*(0.005+0.09*(8/(25+8)));

AreaWnet = 0;
AreaWrec = 0;

% 100 integration step
deli = 25/100;

for n=1:101
   i(n) = 25*(n-1)/100;
   AreaWnet = AreaWnet + deli*i(n)*(0.09)*(8/(i(n)+8));
   AreaWrec = AreaWrec + deli*(lambdamax - i(n)*(0.005+0.09*(8/(i(n)+8))));
end
```

```
Ratio = (AreaWrec + AreaWnet)/AreaWnet;

fprintf('\nPart(b) Ratio = %g',Ratio)

%(c) Calculate the power

rpm = 2500;
rps = 2500/60;
T = 1/rps;
Pphase = 2*AreaWnet/T;
Ptot = 2*Pphase;

fprintf('\n\nPart(c) AreaWnet = %g [Joules]',AreaWnet)
fprintf('\n          Pphase = %g [W] and Ptot = %g [W]\n',Pphase,Ptot)
```

Practice Problem 8.4

Consider a two-phase VRM which is identical to that of Example 8.5 with the exception of an additional 5 mH of leakage inductance in each phase.

a. Calculate the ratio of the inverter volt-ampere rating to the VRM net power output for the following idealized operating cycle:

  i. The current is instantaneously raised to 25 A when $\theta_m = -90°$.
  ii. The current is then held constant as the rotor rotates to $\theta_m = 10°$.
  iii. At $\theta_m = 10°$, the current is reduced to zero.

b. Assuming the VRM to be operating as a motor using the cycle described in part (a) and rotating at a constant speed of 2500 r/min, calculate the net electromechanical power supplied to the rotor.

Solution

a.

$$\frac{\text{Inverter volt-ampere rating}}{\text{Net output power}} = 1.75$$

b. $P_{mech} = 1467$ W

Saturation effects clearly play a significant role in the performance of most VRMs and must be taken into account. In addition, the idealized operating cycle illustrated in Example 8.5 cannot, of course, be achieved in practice since some rotor motion is likely to take place over the time scale over which current changes occur. As a result, it is often necessary to resort to numerical-analysis packages such as finite-element programs as part of the design process for practical VRM systems. Many of these programs incorporate the ability to model the nonlinear effects of magnetic saturation as well as mechanical (e.g., rotor motion) and electrical (e.g., current buildup) dynamic effects.

As we have seen, the design of a VRM drive system typically requires that a trade-off be made. On the one hand, saturation tends to increase the size of the VRM for a given power output. On the other hand, on comparing two VRM systems with the same power output, the system with the higher level of saturation will typically require an inverter with a lower volt-ampere rating. Thus the ultimate design will be determined by a trade-off between the size, cost, and efficiency of the VRM and of the inverter.

8.5 STEPPING MOTORS

As we have seen, when the phases of a VRM are energized sequentially in an appropriate step-wise fashion, the VRM will rotate a specific angle for each step. Motors designed specifically to take advantage of this characteristic are referred to as *stepping motors* or *stepper motors*. Frequently stepping motors are designed to produce a large number of steps per revolution, for example 50, 100, or 200 steps per revolution (corresponding to a rotation of 7.2°, 3.6° and 1.8° per step).

An important characteristic of the stepping motor is its compatibility with digital-electronic systems. These systems are common in a wide variety of applications and continue to become more powerful and less expensive. For example, the stepping motor is often used in digital control systems where the motor receives open-loop commands in the form of a train of pulses to turn a shaft or move an object a specific distance. Typical applications include paper-feed and print-head-positioning motors in printers and plotters, drive and head-positioning motors in disk drives and CD players, and worktable and tool positioning in numerically controlled machine tools. In many applications, position information can be obtained simply by keeping count of the pulses sent to the motor, in which case position sensors and feedback control are not required.

The angular resolution of a VRM is determined by the number of rotor and stator teeth and can be greatly enhanced by techniques such as *castleation,* as is discussed in Section 8.2. Stepping motors come in a wide variety of designs and configurations. In addition to variable-reluctance configurations, these include permanent-magnet and hybrid configurations. The use of permanent magnets in combination with a variable-reluctance geometry can significantly enhance the torque and positional accuracy of a stepper motor.

The VRM configurations discussed in Sections 8.1 through 8.3 consist of a single rotor and stator with multiple phases. A stepping motor of this configuration is called a *single-stack, variable-reluctance stepping motor.* An alternate form of variable-reluctance stepping motor is known as a *multistack variable-reluctance stepping motor.* In this configuration, the motor can be considered to be made up of a set of axially displaced, single-phase VRMs mounted on a single shaft.

Figure 8.19 shows a multistack variable-reluctance stepping motor. This type of motor consists of a series of stacks, each axially displaced, of identical geometry and each excited by a single phase winding, as shown in Fig. 8.20. The motor of Fig. 8.19 has three stacks and three phases, although motors with additional phases and stacks are common. For an n_s-stack motor, the rotor or stator (but not both) on each stack is

Figure 8.19   Cutaway view of a three-phase, three-stack variable-reluctance stepping motor. (*Photo Courtesy of Warner Electric, an Altra Industrial Motion Company.*)

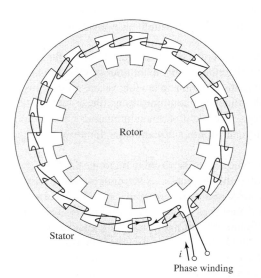

Figure 8.20   Diagram of one stack and phase of a multiphase, multistack variable-reluctance stepping motor, such as that in Fig. 8.19. For an n_s-stack motor, the rotor or stator (but not both) on each stack is displaced by $1/n_s$ times the pole pitch.

displaced by $1/n_s$ times the pole-pitch angle. In Fig. 8.19, the rotor poles are aligned, but the stators are offset in angular displacement by one-third of the pole pitch. By successively exciting the individual phases, the rotor can be turned in increments of this displacement angle.

A schematic diagram of a two-phase stepping motor with a permanent-magnet, two-pole rotor is shown in Fig. 8.21. Note that this machine is in fact a two-phase synchronous machine, similar for example to the three-phase permanent-magnet ac machine of Fig. 5.34. The distinction between such a stepping motor and a synchronous motor arises not from the construction of the motor but rather from how the motor is operated. The synchronous motor is typically intended to drive a load at a specified speed, and the stepping motor is typically intended to control the position of a load.

The rotor of the stepping motor of Fig. 8.21 assumes the angles $\theta_m = 0, 45°$, $90°, \ldots$ as the windings are excited in the sequence:

1. Positive current in phase 1 alone.
2. Equal-magnitude positive currents in phase 1 and phase 2.
3. Positive current in phase 2 alone.
4. Equal-magnitude negative current in phase 1 and positive current in phase 2.
5. Negative current in phase 1 alone.
6. And so on.

Note that if a ferromagnetic rotor were substituted for the permanent-magnet rotor, the rotor would move in a similar fashion.

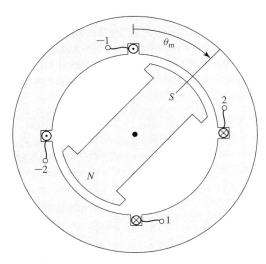

Figure 8.21 Schematic diagram of a
two-phase permanent-magnet stepping motor.

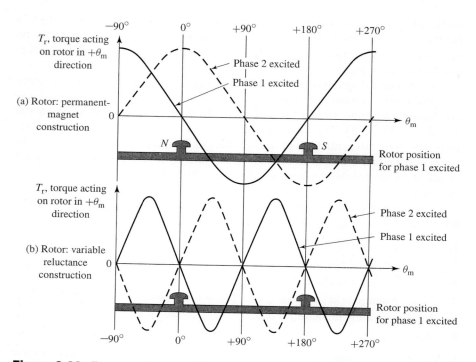

Figure 8.22   Torque-angle curves for the stepping motor of Fig. 8.21: (a) permanent-magnet rotor and (b) variable-reluctance rotor.

The stepping motor of Fig. 8.21 can also be used for 90° steps by exciting the coils singly. In the latter case, only a permanent-magnet rotor can be used. This can be seen from the torque-angle curves for the two types of rotors shown in Fig. 8.22. Whereas the permanent-magnet rotor produces peak torque when the excitation is shifted 90°, the ferromagnetic rotor produces zero torque and may move in either direction.

The rotor position in the permanent-magnet stepping motor of Fig. 8.21 is defined by the winding currents with no ambiguity and depends on the direction of the phase currents. Reversing the phase currents will cause the rotor to reverse its orientation. This is in contrast to VRM configurations with a ferromagnetic rotor, in which two rotor positions are equally stable for any particular set of phase currents, and hence the rotor position cannot be determined uniquely. Permanent-magnet stepping motors are also unlike their VRM counterparts in that torque tending to align the rotor with the stator poles will be generated even when there is no excitation applied to the phase windings. Thus the rotor will have preferred unexcited rest positions, a fact which can be used to advantage in some applications.

EXAMPLE 8.6

Using the techniques of Chapter 3 and neglecting saturation effects, the torque of a two-phase, permanent-magnet stepping motor of the form of Fig. 8.21 can be expressed as

$$T_{mech} = T_0 \, (i_1 \cos \theta_m + i_2 \sin \theta_m)$$

where T_0 is a positive constant that depends upon the motor geometry and the properties of the permanent magnet.

Calculate the rest (zero-torque) positions which will result if the motor is driven by a drive such that each phase current can be set equal to three values $-I_0$, 0, and I_0. Using such a drive, what is the motor step size?

■ Solution

In general, the zero-torque positions of the motor can be found by setting the torque expression to zero and solving for the resultant rotor position. Thus setting

$$T_{\text{mech}} = T_0 \, (i_1 \sin \theta_{\text{m}} - i_2 \cos \theta_{\text{m}}) = 0$$

gives

$$i_1 \sin \theta_{\text{m}} - i_2 \cos \theta_{\text{m}} = 0$$

or

$$\theta_{\text{m}} = \tan^{-1} \left(\frac{i_2}{i_1} \right)$$

Note that not all of these zero-torque positions correspond to stable equilibrium positions. For example, operation with $i_1 = I_0$ and $i_2 = 0$ gives two zero-torque positions: $\theta_{\text{m}} = 0°$ and $\theta_{\text{m}} = 180°$. Yet only the position $\theta_{\text{m}} = 0°$ is stable. This is directly analogous to the case of a hanging pendulum which sees zero torque both when it is hanging downward ($\theta = 0°$) and when it is sitting inverted ($\theta = 180°$). Yet, it is clear that the slightest perturbation of the position of the inverted pendulum will cause it to rotate downwards and that it will eventually come to rest in the stable hanging position.

Stable rest positions of the rotor are determined by the requirement that a restoring torque is produced as the rotor moves from that position. Thus, a negative torque should result if the rotor moves in the $+\theta_{\text{m}}$ direction, and a positive torque should result for motion in the $-\theta_{\text{m}}$ direction. Mathematically, this can be expressed as an additional constraint on the torque at the rest position

$$\left. \frac{\partial T_{\text{mech}}}{\partial \theta_{\text{m}}} \right|_{i_1, i_2} < 0$$

where the partial derivative is evaluated at the zero-torque position and is taken with the phase currents held constant. Thus, in this case, the rest position must satisfy the additional constraint that

$$\left. \frac{\partial T_{\text{mech}}}{\partial \theta_{\text{m}}} \right|_{i_1, i_2} = -T_0 \, (i_1 \cos \theta_{\text{m}} + i_2 \sin \theta_{\text{m}}) < 0$$

From this equation, we see for example that with $i_1 = I_0$ and $i_2 = 0$, at $\theta_{\text{m}} = 0°$, $\partial T_{\text{mech}}/\partial \theta_{\text{m}} < 0$ and thus $\theta_{\text{m}} = 0°$ is a stable rest position. Similarly, at $\theta_{\text{m}} = 180°$, $\partial T_{\text{mech}}/\partial \theta_{\text{m}} > 0$ and thus $\theta_{\text{m}} = 180°$ is not a stable rest position.

Using these relationships, Table 8.1 lists the stable rest positions of the rotor for the various combinations of phase currents.

From this table we see that this drive results in a step size of $45°$.

Table 8.1   Rotor rest positions for Example 8.6.

i_1	i_2	θ_m
0	0	—
0	$-I_0$	270°
0	I_0	90°
$-I_0$	0	180°
$-I_0$	$-I_0$	225°
$-I_0$	I_0	135°
I_0	0	0°
I_0	$-I_0$	315°
I_0	I_0	45°

Practice Problem 8.5

In order to achieve a step size of 22.5°, the motor drive of Example 8.6 is modified so that each phase can be driven by currents of magnitude 0, $\pm k I_0$, and $\pm I_0$. Find the required value of the constant k.

Solution

$$k = \tan^{-1}(22.5°) = 0.4142$$

In Example 8.6 we see that stable equilibrium positions of an unloaded stepping motor satisfy the conditions that there is zero torque, i.e.,

$$T_{\text{mech}} = 0 \tag{8.20}$$

and that there is positive restoring torque, i.e.,

$$\left.\frac{\partial T_{\text{mech}}}{\partial \theta_m}\right|_{i_1,i_2} < 0 \tag{8.21}$$

In practice, there will of course be a finite load torque tending to perturb the stepping motor from these idealized positions. For open-loop control systems (i.e., control systems in which there is no mechanism for position feedback), a high degree of position control can be achieved by designing the stepping motor to produce large restoring torque (i.e., a large magnitude of $\partial T_{\text{mech}}/\partial \theta_m$). In such a stepping motor, load torques will result in only a small movement of the rotor from the idealized positions which satisfy Eqs. 8.20 and 8.21.

Example 8.6 also shows how carefully controlled combinations of phase currents can enhance the resolution of a stepper motor. This technique, referred to as *microstepping,* can be used to achieve increased step resolution of a wide variety of stepper motors. As the following example shows, microstepping can be used to produce extremely fine position resolution. The increased resolution comes, however, at the expense of an increase in complexity of the stepping-motor drive electronics and control algorithms, which must accurately control the distribution of current to multiple phases simultaneously.

EXAMPLE 8.7

Consider again the two-phase, permanent-magnet stepping motor of Example 8.6. Calculate the rotor position which will result if the phase currents are controlled to be sinusoidal functions of a reference angle θ_{ref} in the form

$$i_1 = I_0 \cos \theta_{\text{ref}}$$

$$i_2 = I_0 \sin \theta_{\text{ref}}$$

■ Solution

Substitution of the current expressions into the torque expression of Example 8.6 gives

$$T_{\text{mech}} = T_0 \, (i_1 \cos \theta_{\text{m}} + i_2 \sin \theta_{\text{m}}) = T_0 I_0 \, (\cos \theta_{\text{ref}} \cos \theta_{\text{m}} + \sin \theta_{\text{ref}} \sin \theta_{\text{m}})$$

Use of the trigonometric identity $\cos(\alpha - \beta) = \cos\alpha \cos\beta + \sin\alpha \sin\beta$ gives

$$T_{\text{mech}} = T_0 I_0 \, \cos(\theta_{\text{ref}} - \theta_{\text{m}})$$

From this expression and using the analysis of Example 8.6, we see that the rotor equilibrium position will be equal to the reference angle, i.e., $\theta_{\text{m}} = \theta_{\text{ref}}$. In a practical implementation, a digital controller is likely to be used to increment θ_{ref} in finite steps, which will result in finite steps in the position of the stepping-motor.

The *hybrid stepping motor* combines characteristics of the variable-reluctance and permanent-magnet stepping motors. A photo of a hybrid stepping motor is shown in Fig. 8.23, and a schematic view of a hybrid stepping motor is shown in Fig. 8.24. The hybrid-stepping-motor rotor configuration appears much like that of a multistack variable-reluctance stepping motor. In the rotor of Fig. 8.24a, two identical rotor stacks are displaced axially along the rotor and displaced in angle by one-half the rotor pole pitch, while the stator pole structure is continuous along the length of the rotor. Unlike the multistack variable-reluctance stepping motor, in the hybrid stepping motor, the

Figure 8.23 Disassembled 1.8°/step hybrid stepping motor.

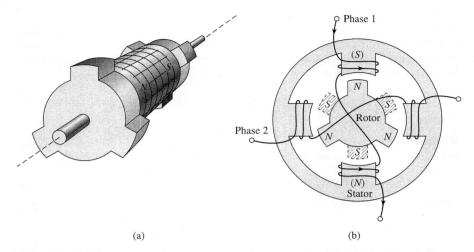

Phase 1

(S)

N

S

S

Rotor

Phase 2

N

N

(N)
Stator

(a)   (b)

Figure 8.24   Schematic view of a hybrid stepping motor. (a) Two-stack rotor showing the axially directed permanent magnet and the pole pieces displaced by one-half the pole pitch. (b) End view from the rotor north poles and showing the rotor south poles at the far end (shown crosshatched). Phase 1 of the stator is energized to align the rotor as shown.

rotor stacks are separated by an axially directed permanent magnet. As a result, in Fig. 8.24a one end of the rotor can be considered to have a north magnetic pole and the other end a south magnetic pole. Figure 8.24b shows a schematic end view of a hybrid stepping motor. The stator has four poles with the phase-1 winding wound on the vertical poles and the phase-2 winding wound on the horizontal poles. The rotor is shown with its north-pole end at the near end of the motor and the south-pole end (shown crosshatched) at the far end.

In Fig. 8.24b, phase 1 is shown excited such that the top stator pole is a south pole while the bottom pole is a north pole. This stator excitation interacts with the permanent-magnet flux of the rotor to align the rotor with a pole on its north-pole end vertically upward and a pole on its south-pole end vertically downward, as shown in the figure. Note that if the stator excitation is removed, there will still be a permanent-magnet torque tending to maintain the rotor in the position shown.

To turn the rotor, excitation is removed from phase 1, and phase 2 is excited. If phase 2 is excited such that the right-hand stator pole is a south pole and the left-hand one is a north pole, the rotor will rotate 30° counterclockwise. Similarly, if the opposite excitation is applied to the phase-2 winding, a 30° rotation in the clockwise direction will occur. Thus, by alternately applying phase-1 and phase-2 excitation of the appropriate polarity, the rotor can be made to rotate in either direction by a specified angular increment.

Practical hybrid stepping motors are generally built with more rotor poles than are indicated in the schematic motor of Fig. 8.24, in order to give much better angular resolution. Correspondingly, the stator poles are often castleated (see Fig. 8.8) to further increase the angular resolution. In addition, they may be built with more than two stacks per rotor.

The hybrid stepping motor design offers advantages over the permanent-magnet design discussed earlier. It can achieve small step sizes easily and with a simple magnet structure while a purely permanent-magnet motor would require a multipole permanent magnet. In comparison with the variable-reluctance stepping motor, the hybrid design may require less excitation to achieve a given torque because some of the excitation is supplied by the permanent magnet. In addition, the hybrid stepping motor will tend to maintain its position when the stator excitation is removed, as does the permanent-magnet design.

The actual choice of a stepping-motor design for a particular application is determined based on the desired operating characteristics, availability, size, and cost. In addition to the three classifications of stepping motors discussed in this chapter, a number of other different and often quite clever designs have been developed. Although these encompass a wide range of configurations and construction techniques, the operating principles remain the same.

8.6 SUMMARY

Variable-reluctance machines are perhaps the simplest of electrical machines. They consist of a stator with excitation windings and a magnetic rotor with saliency. Torque is produced by the tendency of the salient-pole rotor to align with excited magnetic poles on the stator.

VRMs are synchronous machines in that they produce net torque only when the rotor motion is in some sense synchronous with the applied stator mmf. This synchronous relationship may be complex, with the rotor speed being some specific fraction of the applied electrical frequency as determined not only by the number of stator and rotor poles but also by the number of stator and rotor teeth on these poles. In fact, in some cases, the rotor will be found to rotate in the direction opposite to the rotation direction of the applied stator mmf.

Successful operation of a VRM depends on exciting the stator phase windings in a specific fashion correlated to the instantaneous position of the rotor. Thus, rotor position must be measured, and a controller must be employed to determine the appropriate excitation waveforms and to control the output of the inverter. Typically chopping is required to obtain these waveforms. The net result is that although the VRM is itself a simple device, somewhat complex electronics are typically required to make a complete drive system.

The significance of VRMs in engineering applications stems from their low cost, reliability, and controllability. Because their torque depends only on the square of the applied stator currents and not on their direction, these machines can be operated from unidirectional drive systems, reducing the cost of the power electronics. However, it is only relatively recently, with the advent of low-cost, flexible power electronic circuitry and microprocessor-based control systems, that VRMs have begun to see widespread application in systems ranging from traction drives to high-torque, precision position control systems for robotics applications.

Practical experience with VRMs has shown that they have the potential for high reliability. This is due in part to the simplicity of their construction and to the fact that there are no windings on their rotors. In addition, VRM drives can be operated successfully (at a somewhat reduced rating) following the failure of one or more phases, either in the machine or in the inverter. VRMs typically have a large number of stator phases (four or more), and significant output can be achieved even if some of these phases are out of service. Because there is no rotor excitation, there will be no voltage generated in a phase winding which fails open-circuited or current generated in a phase winding which fails short-circuited, and thus the machine can continue to be operated without risk of further damage or additional losses and heating.

Because VRMs can be readily manufactured with a large number of rotor and stator teeth (resulting in large inductance changes for small changes in rotor angle), they can be constructed to produce very large torque per unit volume. There is, however, a trade-off between torque and velocity, and such machines will have a low rotational velocity (consistent with the fact that only so much power can be produced by a given machine frame size). On the opposite extreme, the simple configuration of a VRM rotor and the fact that it contains no windings suggest that it is possible to build extremely rugged VRM rotors. These rotors can withstand high speeds, and motors which operate in excess of 200,000 r/min have been built.

Finally, we have seen that saturation plays a large role in VRM performance. As recent advances in power electronic and microelectronic circuitry have brought VRM drive systems into the realm of practicality, so have advances in computer-based analytical techniques for magnetic-field analysis. Use of these techniques now makes it practical to perform optimized designs of VRM drive systems which are competitive with alternative technologies in many applications.

Stepping motors are closely related to VRMs in that excitation of each successive phase of the stator results in a specific angular rotation of the rotor. Stepping motors come in a wide variety of designs and configurations. These include variable-reluctance, permanent-magnet, and hybrid configurations. The rotor position of a variable-reluctance stepper motor is not uniquely determined by the phase currents since the phase inductances are not unique functions of the rotor angle. The addition of a permanent magnet changes this situation and the rotor position of a permanent-magnet stepper motor is a unique function of the phase currents.

Stepping motors are the electromechanical companions to digital electronics. By proper application of phase currents to the stator windings, these motors can be made to rotate in well-defined steps ranging down to a fraction of a degree per pulse. They are thus essential components of digitally controlled electromechanical systems where a high degree of precision is required. They are found in a wide range of applications including numerically controlled machine tools, in printers and plotters, and in disk drives.

8.7 CHAPTER 8 VARIABLES

α, β	Spatial angles [rad]
λ	Flux linkage [Wb]
μ_0	Permeability of free space $= 4\pi \times 10^{-7}$ [H/m]
θ_m	Rotor position [rad]
ω_m	Mechanical angular velocity [rad/sec]
D	Diameter [m]
g	Gap length [m]
i	Current [A]
L	Inductance [H]
N	Number of turns
p	Power [W]
R	Radius [m], resistance [Ω]
t	Time [sec]
T	Torque [N·m], time [sec]
v	Voltage [V]
W_{net}	Energy corresponding to output power [J]
W_{rec}	Recycled energy corresponding to reactive power power [J]
W'_{fld}	Coenergy [J]

Subscripts:

in	Input
max	Maximum
mech	Mechanical
ref	Reference

8.8 PROBLEMS

8.1 Repeat Example 8.1 for a machine identical to that considered in the example except that the stator pole-face angle is $\beta = 50°$ and the air-gap length is 2×10^{-2} cm.

8.2 In the paragraph preceding Eq. 8.1, the text states that "under the assumption of negligible iron reluctance the mutual inductances between the phases of the doubly salient VRM of Fig. 8.1b will be zero, with the exception of a small, essentially constant component associated with leakage flux." Neglect any leakage flux effects and use magnetic circuit techniques to show that this statement is true.

8.3 Use magnetic-circuit techniques to show that the phase-to-phase mutual inductance in the 6/4 VRM of Fig. 8.5 is zero under the assumption of infinite rotor- and stator-iron permeability. Neglect any contributions of leakage flux.

8.4 A 6/4 VRM of the form of Fig. 8.5 has the following properties:

> Stator pole angle $\beta = 30°$
> Rotor pole angle $\alpha = 30°$
> Air-gap length $g = 0.45$ mm
> Rotor outer radius $R = 6.3$ cm
> Active length $D = 8$ cm

This machine is connected as a three-phase motor with opposite poles connected in series to form each phase winding. There are 45 turns per pole (90 turns per phase). The rotor and stator iron can be considered to be of infinite permeability and hence mutual-inductance effects can be neglected.

a. Defining the zero of rotor angle θ_m at the position when the phase-1 inductance is maximum, plot and label the inductance of phase 1 as a function of rotor angle.

b. On the plot of part (a), plot the inductances of phases 2 and 3.

c. Find the phase-1 current I_0 which results in a magnetic flux density of 1.1 T in the air gap under the phase-1 pole face when the rotor is in a position of maximum phase-1 inductance.

d. Assuming that the phase-1 current is held constant at the value found in part (c) and that there is no current in phases 2 and 3, plot the torque as a function of rotor position.

The motor is to be driven from a three-phase current-source inverter which can be switched on or off to supply either zero current or a constant current of magnitude I_0 independently to each of the three phases.

e. Under the idealized assumption that the currents can be instantaneously switched, determine the sequence of phase currents (as a function of rotor position) that will result in constant positive motor torque, independent of rotor position.

f. If the frequency of the stator excitation is such that a time $T_0 = 40$ msec is required to sequence through all three phases under the excitation conditions of part (e), find the rotor angular velocity and its direction of rotation.

8.5 Repeat Problem 8.4 for a 6/4 VRM with rotor and stator pole angles of 35°. Use the same assumptions as in Problem 8.4.

8.6 In Section 8.2, when discussing Fig. 8.5, the text states: "In addition to the fact that there are not positions of simultaneous alignment for the 6/4 VRM, it can be seen that there also are no rotor positions at which only a torque of a single sign (either positive or negative) can be produced." Show that this statement is true.

8.7 Consider a three-phase 6/8 VRM. The stator phases are excited sequentially, requiring a total time of 10 msec. Find the angular velocity of the rotor in r/min.

8.8 The phase windings of the castleated machine of Fig. 8.8 are to be excited by turning the phases on and off individually (i.e., only one phase can be on at any given time).

    a. Describe the sequence of phase excitations required to move the rotor to the right (clockwise) by an angle of approximately $21.4°$.

    b. The stator phases are to be excited as a regular sequence of pulses. Calculate the phase order and the time between pulses required to produce a steady-state rotor rotation of 95 r/min in the counterclockwise direction.

8.9 Replace the 28-tooth rotor of Problem 8.8 with a rotor with 26 teeth.

    a. Phase 1 is excited, and the rotor is allowed to come to rest. If the excitation on phase 1 is removed and excitation is applied to phase 2, calculate the resultant direction and magnitude (in degrees) of rotor rotation.

    b. The stator phases are to be excited as a regular sequence of pulses. Calculate the phase order and the time between pulses required to produce a steady-state rotor rotation of 50 r/min in the counterclockwise direction.

8.10 Repeat Problem 8.8 for a castleated VRM of the form of Fig. 8.8 which has 5 teeth per stator pole, 40 rotor poles and $\beta = 4.5°$.

8.11 Repeat Example 8.3 for a rotor speed of 380 r/min.

8.12 Repeat Example 8.3 under the condition that the rotor speed is 450 r/min and that a negative voltage of -250 V is used to turn off the phase current.

8.13 Use MATLAB/Sumulink to reproduce the simulation of Example 8.4. Use your simulation to calculate the average torque for the switching-angle advanced by $2.5°$ and $7.5°$.

8.14 The three-phase 6/4 VRM of Problem 8.4 has a winding resistance of $0.17\ \Omega$/phase and a leakage inductance of 4.2 mH in each phase. Assume that the rotor is rotating at a constant angular velocity of 1675 r/min.

    a. Plot the phase-1 inductance as a function of the rotor angle θ_m.

    b. A voltage of 105 V is applied to phase 1 as the rotor reaches the position $\theta_m = -30°$ and is maintained constant until $\theta_m = 0°$. Calculate and plot the phase-1 current as a function of time during this period.

    c. When the rotor reaches $\theta = 0°$, the applied voltage is reversed so that a voltage of -105 V is applied to the winding. This voltage is maintained until the winding current reaches zero, at which point the winding is open-circuited. Calculate and plot the current decay during the time until the current decays to zero.

    d. Calculate and plot the torque during the time periods investigated in parts (b) and (c).

8.15 Assume that the VRM of Examples 8.1 and 8.3 is modified by replacing its rotor with a rotor with $75°$ pole-face angles as shown in Fig. 8.12a. All other dimensions and parameters of the VRM are unchanged.

a.   Calculate and plot $L(\theta_m)$ for this machine.

b.   Repeat Example 8.3 except that the constant voltage 100 V is first applied at $\theta_m = -67.5°$ when $dL(\theta_m)/d\theta_m$ becomes positive and the constant voltage of -100 V is then applied at $\theta_m = -7.5°$ (i.e., when $dL(\theta_m)/d\theta_m$ becomes zero) and is maintained until the winding current reaches zero.

c.   Plot the corresponding torque.

8.16   Repeat Example 8.5 for a symmetrical two-phase 4/2 VRM whose λ-i characteristic can be represented by the following expression (for phase 1) as a function of θ_m over the range $0 \le \theta_m \le 90°$:

$$\lambda_1 = \left(0.01 + 0.18 \left(\frac{90° - \theta_m}{90°}\right)\left(\frac{8.0}{9.0 + i_1}\right)^{1.25}\right) i_1$$

8.17   Consider a two-phase stepper motor with a permanent-magnet rotor such as shown in Fig. 8.21 and whose torque-angle curve is as shown in Fig. 8.22a. This machine is to be excited by a four-bit digital sequence corresponding to the following winding excitation:

bit			bit		
1	**2**	i_1	**3**	**4**	i_2
0	0	0	0	0	0
0	1	$-I_0$	0	1	$-I_0$
1	0	I_0	1	0	I_0
1	1	0	1	1	0

a.   Make a table of 4-bit patterns which will produce rotor angular positions of $0, 45°, \ldots, 315°$.

b.   By sequencing through the bit pattern found in part (a) the motor can be made to rotate. What time interval (in milliseconds) between bit-pattern changes will result in a rotor speed of 1400 r/min?

8.18   Consider a two-phase, permanent-magnet stepping motor with a torque-current relationship of the form

$$T_{\text{mech}} = T_0(i_1 \cos \theta_m + i_2 \sin \theta_m)$$

as in Example 8.6 with $T_0 = 3$ N $\cdot$ m. The motor is driven by a two-phase current source controlled based upon the rotor position such that

$$i_1 = I_0 \cos (\theta_m + \phi) \qquad i_2 = I_0 \sin (\theta_m + \phi)$$

The motor is driving a load whose power varies as the speed to the 2.5 power and which draws 3.5 kW at a speed of 1400 r/min. The combined inertia of the motor and load is 0.85 kg $\cdot$ m^2.

Assuming the motor is initially at rest when the drive is turned on with $I_0 = 8$ A, write a MATLAB/Simulink simulation of this system and plot the motor speed as a function of time for $\gamma = 0$ and $\gamma = \pi/4$.

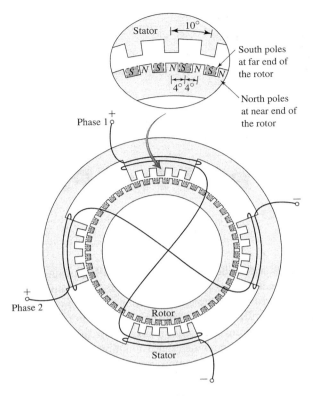

Figure 8.25 Castleated hybrid stepping motor for Problem 8.19.

8.19 Figure 8.25 shows a two-phase hybrid stepping motor with castleated poles
on the stator. The rotor is shown in the position it occupies when current is
flowing into the positive lead of phase 1.

   a. If phase 1 is turned off and phase 2 is excited with current flowing into its
positive lead, calculate the corresponding angular rotation of the rotor. Is
it in the clockwise or counterclockwise direction?

   b. Describe an excitation sequence for the phase windings which will result
in a steady rotation of the rotor in the clockwise direction.

   c. Determine the frequency of the phase currents required to achieve a rotor
speed of 10 r/min.

8.20 Consider a multistack, multiphase variable-reluctance stepping motor, such
as that shown schematically in Fig. 8.20, with 16 poles on each of the rotor
and stator stacks and three stacks with one phase winding per stack. The
motor is built such that the stator poles of each stack are aligned.

   a. Calculate the angular displacement between the rotor stacks.

   b. Determine the frequency of phase currents required to achieve a rotor
speed of 750 r/min.

9
CHAPTER

Single- and Two-Phase Motors

This chapter discusses single-phase motors. While focusing on induction motors, synchronous-reluctance, hysteresis, and shaded-pole induction motors are also discussed. Note that another common single-phase motor, the series universal motor, is discussed in Section 7.10. Most induction motors of fractional-kilowatt (fractional horsepower) rating are single-phase motors. In residential and commercial applications, they are found in a wide range of equipment including refrigerators, air conditioners and heat pumps, fans, pumps, washers, and dryers.

In this chapter, we will describe these motors qualitatively in terms of rotating-field theory and will begin with a rigorous analysis of a single-phase motor operating off a single winding. However, most single-phase induction motors are actually two-phase motors with unsymmetrical windings; the two windings are typically quite different, with different numbers of turns and/or winding distributions. Thus this chapter also discusses two-phase motors and includes a development of a quantitative theory for the analysis of single-phase induction motors when operating off both their main and auxiliary windings.

9.1 SINGLE-PHASE INDUCTION MOTORS: QUALITATIVE EXAMINATION

Structurally, the most common types of single-phase induction motors resemble polyphase squirrel-cage motors except for the arrangement of the stator windings. An induction motor with a squirrel-cage rotor and a single-phase stator winding is represented schematically in Fig. 9.1. Instead of being a concentrated coil, the actual stator winding is distributed in slots to produce an approximately sinusoidal space distribution of mmf. As we saw in Section 4.5.1, a single-phase winding produces equal forward- and backward-rotating mmf waves. By symmetry, it is clear that such a motor inherently will produce no starting torque since at standstill, it will produce equal torque in both directions. However, we will show that if it is started by auxiliary

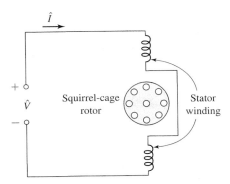

Figure 9.1 Schematic view of a single-phase induction motor.

means, the result will be a net torque in the direction in which it is started, and hence the motor will continue to run.

Before we consider auxiliary starting methods, we will discuss the basic properties of the schematic motor of Fig. 9.1. If the stator current is a cosinusoidal function of time, the resultant air-gap mmf is given by Eq. 4.19

$$\mathcal{F}_{\text{ag1}} = F_{\text{max}} \cos{(\theta_{\text{ae}})} \cos{\omega_e t} \tag{9.1}$$

which, as shown in Section 4.5.1, can be written as the sum of positive- and negative-traveling mmf waves of equal magnitude. The positive-traveling wave is given by

$$\mathcal{F}_{\text{ag1}}^{+} = \frac{1}{2} F_{\text{max}} \cos{(\theta_{\text{ae}} - \omega_e t)} \tag{9.2}$$

and the negative-traveling wave is given by

$$\mathcal{F}_{\text{ag1}}^{-} = \frac{1}{2} F_{\text{max}} \cos{(\theta_{\text{ae}} + \omega_e t)} \tag{9.3}$$

Each of these component mmf waves produces induction-motor action, but the corresponding torques are in opposite directions. With the rotor at rest, the forward and backward air-gap flux waves created by the combined mmfs of the stator and rotor currents are equal, the component torques are equal, and no starting torque is produced. If the forward and backward air-gap flux waves were to remain equal when the rotor revolves, each of the component fields would produce a torque-speed characteristic similar to that of a polyphase motor with negligible stator leakage impedance, as illustrated by the dashed curves f and b in Fig. 9.2a. The resultant torque-speed characteristic, which is the algebraic sum of the two component curves, shows that if the motor were started by auxiliary means, it would produce torque in whatever direction it was started.

The assumption that the air-gap flux waves remain equal when the rotor is in motion is a rather drastic simplification of the actual state of affairs. First, the effects of stator leakage impedance are ignored. Second, the effects of induced rotor currents are not properly accounted for. Both these effects will ultimately be included in the

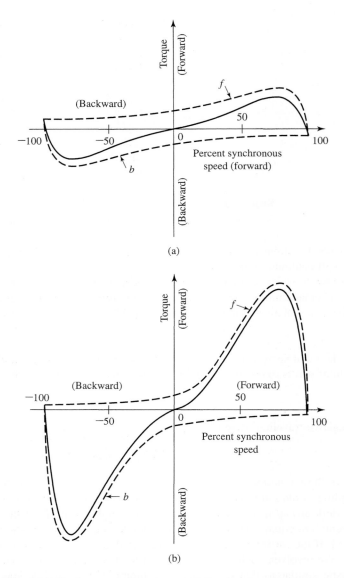

Figure 9.2 Torque-speed characteristic of a single-phase induction motor (a) on the basis of constant forward and backward flux waves, (b) taking into account changes in the flux waves.

detailed quantitative theory of Section 9.3. The following qualitative explanation shows that the performance of a single-phase induction motor is considerably better than would be predicted on the basis of equal forward and backward flux waves.

When the rotor is in motion, the component rotor currents induced by the corresponding backward field are greater than at standstill, and their power factor is lower. Their mmf, which opposes that of the stator current, results in a reduction of the backward flux wave. Conversely, the magnetic effect of the component currents induced by the forward field is less than at standstill because the rotor currents are less and their power factor is higher. As speed increases, therefore, the forward flux wave increases while the backward flux wave decreases. The sum of these flux waves must remain roughly constant since it must induce the stator counter emf, which is approximately constant if the stator leakage-impedance voltage drop is small.

Hence, with the rotor in motion, the torque of the forward field is greater and that of the backward field less than in Fig. 9.2a, the true situation being about that shown in Fig. 9.2b. In the normal running region at a few percent slip, the forward field is several times greater than the backward field, and the flux wave does not differ greatly from the constant-amplitude revolving field in the air gap of a balanced polyphase motor. In the normal running region, therefore, the torque-speed characteristic of a single-phase motor is not too greatly inferior to that of a polyphase motor having the same rotor and operating with the same maximum air-gap flux density.

In addition to the torques shown in Fig. 9.2, double-stator-frequency torque pulsations are produced by the interactions of the oppositely rotating flux and mmf waves which rotate past each other at twice synchronous speed. These interactions produce no average torque, but they tend to make the motor noisier and less efficient than a polyphase motor. Such torque pulsations are unavoidable in a single-phase motor because of the pulsations in instantaneous power input inherent in a single-phase circuit. The effects of the pulsating torque can be minimized by using an elastic mounting for the motor. The torque referred to on the torque-speed curves of a single-phase motor is the time average of the instantaneous torque.

9.2 STARTING AND RUNNING PERFORMANCE OF SINGLE-PHASE INDUCTION AND SYNCHRONOUS MOTORS

Single-phase induction motors are classified in accordance with their starting methods and are usually referred to by names descriptive of these methods. Selection of the appropriate motor is based on the starting- and running-torque requirements of the load, the duty cycle of the load, and the limitations on starting and running current from the supply line for the motor. The cost of single-phase motors increases with their rating and with their performance characteristics such as starting-torque-to-current ratio. Typically, in order to minimize cost, an application engineer will select the motor with the lowest rating and performance that can meet the specifications of the application. Where a large number of motors are to be used for a specific purpose, a special motor may be designed in order to ensure the least cost. In the fractional-kilowatt motor business, small differences in cost are important.

Starting methods and the resulting torque-speed characteristics are considered qualitatively in this section. A quantitative theory for analyzing these motors is developed in Section 9.4.2.

9.2.1   Split-Phase Motors

Split-phase motors have two stator windings, a *main winding* (also referred to as the *run winding*) which we will refer to with the subscript "main" and an *auxiliary winding* (also referred to as the *start winding*) which we will refer to with the subscript "aux." As in a two-phase motor, the axes of these windings are displaced 90 electrical degrees in space, and they are connected as shown in Fig. 9.3a. The auxiliary winding has a higher resistance-to-reactance ratio than the main winding, with the result that the two currents will be out of phase, as indicated in the phasor diagram of Fig. 9.3b, which is representative of conditions at starting. Since the auxiliary-winding current $\hat{I}_{\text{aux}}$ leads the main-winding current $\hat{I}_{\text{main}}$, the stator field first reaches a maximum along the axis of the auxiliary winding and then somewhat later in time reaches a maximum along the axis of the main winding.

The winding currents are equivalent to unbalanced two-phase currents, and the motor is equivalent to an unbalanced two-phase motor. The result is a rotating stator field which causes the motor to start. After the motor starts, the auxiliary winding is disconnected, usually by means of a centrifugal switch that operates at about 75 percent of synchronous speed. The simple way to obtain the high resistance-to-reactance ratio for the auxiliary winding is to wind it with smaller wire than the main winding, a permissible procedure because, although the losses in this winding are large, it operates only during starting. Its reactance can be reduced somewhat by placing it in the tops of the slots. A typical torque-speed characteristic for such a motor is shown in Fig. 9.3c.

Split-phase motors have moderate starting torque with low starting current. Typical applications include fans, blowers, centrifugal pumps, and office equipment. Typical ratings are 50 to 500 watts; in this range they are the lowest-cost motors available.

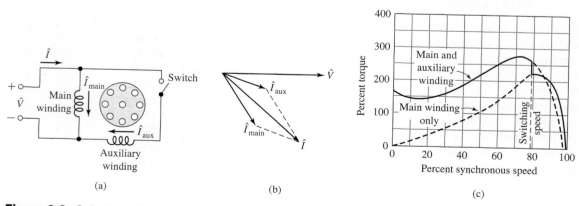

Figure 9.3 Split-phase motor: (a) connections, (b) phasor diagram at starting, and (c) typical torque-speed characteristic.

9.2.2 Capacitor-Type Motors

Capacitors can be used to improve motor starting performance, running performance, or both, depending on the size and connection of the capacitor. The *capacitor-start motor* is also a split-phase motor, but the time-phase displacement between the two currents is obtained by means of a capacitor in series with the auxiliary winding, as shown in Fig. 9.4a. Again the auxiliary winding is disconnected after the motor has started, and consequently the auxiliary winding and capacitor can be designed at minimum cost for intermittent service.

By using a *starting capacitor* of appropriate value, the auxiliary-winding current $\hat{I}_{aux}$ at standstill can be made to lead the main-winding current $\hat{I}_{main}$ by 90 electrical degrees, as it would in a balanced two-phase motor (see Fig. 9.4b). In practice, the best compromise between starting torque, starting current, and cost typically results with a phase angle somewhat less than 90°. A typical torque-speed characteristic is shown in Fig. 9.4c, high starting torque being an outstanding feature. These motors are used for compressors, pumps, refrigeration and air-conditioning equipment, and other hard-to-start loads.

In the *permanent-split-capacitor motor,* the capacitor and auxiliary winding are not cut out after starting; the construction can be simplified by omission of the switch, and the power factor, efficiency, and torque pulsations improved. For example, the capacitor and auxiliary winding could be designed for perfect two-phase operation (i.e., no backward flux wave) at any one desired load. The losses due to the backward field at this operating point would then be eliminated, with resulting improvement in efficiency. The double-stator-frequency torque pulsations would also be eliminated, with the capacitor serving as an energy storage reservoir for smoothing out the pulsations in power input from the single-phase line, resulting in quieter operation. Starting torque must be sacrificed because the choice of capacitance is necessarily a compromise between the best starting and running values. The resulting torque-speed characteristic and a schematic diagram are given in Fig. 9.5.

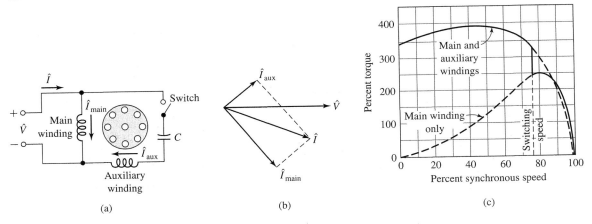

Figure 9.4 Capacitor-start motor: (a) connections, (b) phasor diagram at starting, and (c) typical torque-speed characteristic.

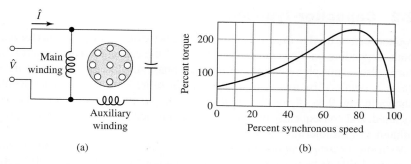

(a)   (b)

Figure 9.5 Permanent-split-capacitor motor and typical torque-speed characteristic.

If two capacitors are used, one for starting and one for running, theoretically optimum starting and running performance can both be obtained. One way of accomplishing this result is shown in Fig. 9.6a. The small value of capacitance required for optimum running conditions is permanently connected in series with the auxiliary winding, and the much larger value required for starting is obtained by a capacitor connected in parallel with the running capacitor via a switch which opens as the motor comes up to speed. Such a motor is known as a *capacitor-start, capacitor-run motor*.

The capacitor for a capacitor-start motor has a typical value of 300 μF for a 500-W motor. Since it must carry current for just the starting time, the capacitor is a special compact ac electrolytic type made for motor-starting duty. The capacitor for the same motor permanently connected has a typical rating of 40 μF, and since it operates continuously, the capacitor is an ac paper, foil, and oil type. The cost of the various motor types is related to performance: the capacitor-start motor has the lowest cost, the permanent-split-capacitor motor next, and the capacitor-start, capacitor-run motor the highest cost.

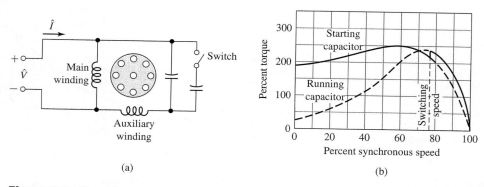

(a)   (b)

Figure 9.6 Capacitor-start, capacitor-run motor and typical torque-speed characteristic.

EXAMPLE 9.1

A 2.5-kW 120-V 60-Hz capacitor-start motor has the following impedances for the main and auxiliary windings (at starting):

$$Z_{main} = 4.5 + j3.7 \; \Omega \qquad \text{main winding}$$

$$Z_{aux} = 9.5 + j3.5 \; \Omega \qquad \text{auxiliary winding}$$

Find the value of starting capacitance that will place the main and auxiliary winding currents in quadrature at starting.

■ Solution

The currents $\hat{I}_{main}$ and $\hat{I}_{aux}$ are shown in Fig. 9.4a and b. The impedance angle of the main winding is

$$\phi_{main} = \tan^{-1} \left(\frac{3.7}{4.5} \right) = 39.6°$$

To produce currents in time quadrature with the main winding, the impedance angle of the auxiliary winding circuit (including the starting capacitor) must be

$$\phi = 39.6° - 90.0° = -50.4°$$

The combined impedance of the auxiliary winding and starting capacitor is equal to

$$Z_{total} = Z_{aux} + jX_c = 9.5 + j(3.5 + X_c) \; \Omega$$

where $X_c = -\frac{1}{\omega C}$ is the reactance of the capacitor and $\omega = 2\pi \times 60$ rad/sec. Thus

$$\tan^{-1} \left(\frac{3.5 + X_c}{9.5} \right) = -50.4°$$

$$\frac{3.5 + X_c}{9.5} = \tan(-50.4°) = -1.21$$

and hence

$$X_c = -1.21 \times 9.5 - 3.5 = -15.0 \; \Omega$$

The capacitance C is then

$$C = \frac{-1}{\omega X_c} = \frac{-1}{2\pi \times 60 \times (-15.0)} = 177 \; \mu F$$

Consider the motor of Example 9.1. Find the phase angle between the main- and auxiliary-winding currents if the 177-μF capacitor is replaced by a 200-μF capacitor.

Solution

85.2°

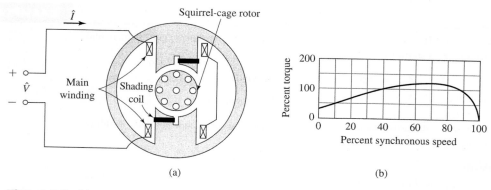

Figure 9.7   Shaded-pole induction motor and typical torque-speed characteristic.

9.2.3 Shaded-Pole Induction Motors

As illustrated schematically in Fig. 9.7a, the *shaded-pole induction motor* usually has salient poles with one portion of each pole surrounded by a short-circuited turn of copper called a *shading coil*. Induced currents in the shading coil cause the flux in the shaded portion of the pole to lag the flux in the other portion. The result is similar to a rotating field moving in the direction from the unshaded to the shaded portion of the pole; currents are induced in the squirrel-cage rotor and a low starting torque is produced. A typical torque-speed characteristic is shown in Fig. 9.7b. Their efficiency is low, but shaded-pole motors are the least expensive type of subfractional-kilowatt motor. They are found in ratings up to about 50 watts.

9.2.4 Self-Starting Synchronous-Reluctance Motors

Any one of the induction-motor types described above can be made into a *self-starting synchronous-reluctance motor*. Anything which makes the reluctance of the air gap a function of the angular position of the rotor with respect to the stator coil axis will produce reluctance torque when the rotor is revolving at synchronous speed. For example, suppose some of the teeth are removed from a squirrel-cage rotor, leaving the bars and end rings intact, as in an ordinary squirrel-cage induction motor. Figure 9.8a shows a lamination for such a rotor designed for use with a four-pole stator. The stator may be polyphase or any one of the single-phase types described above.

The motor will start as an induction motor and at light loads will speed up to a small value of slip. The reluctance torque arises from the tendency of the rotor to try to align itself in the minimum-reluctance position with respect to the synchronously revolving forward air-gap flux wave, in accordance with the principles discussed in Chapter 3. At a small slip, this torque alternates slowly in direction; the rotor is accelerated during a positive half cycle of the torque variation and decelerated during the succeeding negative half cycle. If the moment of inertia of the rotor and its mechanical load are sufficiently small, the rotor will be accelerated from slip speed up to synchronous speed during an accelerating half cycle of the reluctance torque.

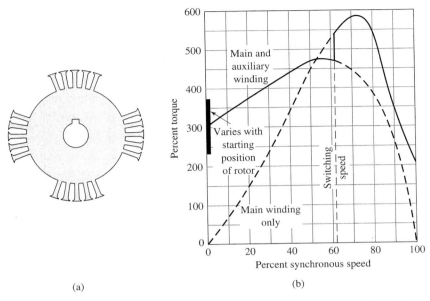

(a)   (b)

Figure 9.8 Rotor punching for four-pole synchronous-reluctance motor and typical torque-speed characteristic.

The rotor will then pull into synchronism and continue to run at synchronous speed. The presence of any backward-revolving stator flux wave will produce torque ripple and additional losses, but synchronous operation will be maintained provided the load torque is not excessive.

A typical torque-speed characteristic for a split-phase-start synchronous-reluctance motor is shown in Fig. 9.8b. Notice the high values of induction-motor torque. The reason for this is that in order to obtain satisfactory synchronous-motor characteristics, it has been found necessary to build synchronous-reluctance motors in frames which would be suitable for induction motors of two or three times their synchronous-motor rating. Also notice that the principal effect of the salient-pole rotor on the induction-motor characteristic is at standstill, where considerable "cogging" is evident; i.e., the torque varies considerably with rotor position.

9.2.5 Hysteresis Motors

The phenomenon of hysteresis can be used to produce mechanical torque. In its simplest form, the rotor of a *hysteresis motor* is a smooth cylinder of magnetically hard steel, without windings or teeth. It is placed inside a slotted stator carrying distributed windings designed to produce as nearly as possible a sinusoidal space distribution of flux, since undulations in the flux wave greatly increase the losses. In single-phase motors, the stator windings usually are of the permanent-split-capacitor type, as in Fig. 9.5. The capacitor is chosen so as to result in approximately balanced

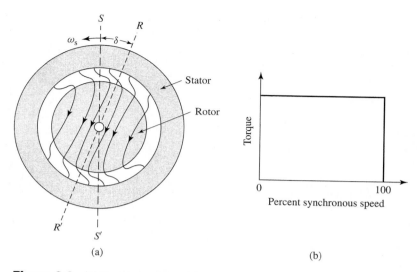

Figure 9.9 (a) General nature of the magnetic field in the air gap and rotor of a hysteresis motor; (b) idealized torque-speed characteristic.

two-phase conditions within the motor windings. The stator then produces a primarily space-fundamental air-gap field revolving at synchronous speed.

The instantaneous magnetic flux distribution in the air gap and rotor are indicated schematically in Fig. 9.9a for a two-pole stator. The axis SS' of the stator-mmf wave revolves at synchronous speed. Because of hysteresis, the magnetization of the rotor lags behind the inducing mmf wave, and therefore the axis RR' of the rotor flux wave lags behind the axis of the stator-mmf wave by the hysteretic lag angle δ (Fig. 9.9a). If the rotor is stationary, starting torque is produced proportional to the product of the fundamental components of the stator mmf and rotor flux and the sine of the torque angle δ. The rotor then accelerates if the torque of the load is less than the developed torque of the motor.

As long as the rotor is turning at less than synchronous speed, each region of the rotor is subjected to a repetitive hysteresis cycle at slip frequency. While the rotor accelerates, the lag angle δ remains constant if the flux is constant, since the angle δ depends merely on the hysteresis loop of the rotor material and is independent of the rate at which the loop is traversed. The motor therefore develops constant torque right up to synchronous speed, as shown in the idealized torque-speed characteristic of Fig. 9.9b. This feature is one of the advantages of the hysteresis motor. In contrast with a reluctance motor, which must "snap" its load into synchronism from an induction-motor torque-speed characteristic, a hysteresis motor can synchronize any load which it can accelerate, no matter how great the inertia. After reaching synchronism, the motor continues to run at synchronous speed and adjusts its torque angle so as to develop the torque required by the load.

The hysteresis motor is inherently quiet and produces smooth rotation of its load. Furthermore, the rotor takes on the same number of poles as the stator field. The motor lends itself to multi-speed synchronous operation when the stator is wound with several sets of windings and utilizes pole-changing connections. The hysteresis motor can accelerate and synchronize high-inertia loads because its torque is uniform from standstill to synchronous speed.

9.3 REVOLVING-FIELD THEORY OF SINGLE-PHASE INDUCTION MOTORS

As discussed in Section 9.1, the stator-mmf wave of a single-phase induction motor can be shown to be equivalent to two constant-amplitude mmf waves revolving at synchronous speed in opposite directions. Each of these component stator-mmf waves induces its own component rotor currents and produces induction-motor action just as in a balanced polyphase motor. This double-revolving-field concept not only is useful for qualitative visualization but also can be developed into a quantitative theory applicable to a wide variety of induction-motor types. We will not discuss the full quantitative theory here.[1] However, we will consider the simpler, but important case of a single-phase induction motor running on only its main winding.

Consider conditions with the rotor stationary and only the main stator winding excited. The motor then is equivalent to a transformer with its secondary short-circuited. The equivalent circuit is shown in Fig. 9.10a, where $R_{1,\mathrm{main}}$ and $X_{1,\mathrm{main}}$ are, respectively, the resistance and leakage reactance of the main winding, $X_{\mathrm{m,main}}$ is the magnetizing reactance, and $R_{2,\mathrm{main}}$ and $X_{2,\mathrm{main}}$ are the standstill values of the rotor resistance and leakage reactance referred to the main stator winding by use of the appropriate turns ratio. Core loss, which is omitted here, will be accounted for later as if it were a rotational loss. The applied voltage is $\hat{V}$, and the main-winding current is $\hat{I}_{\mathrm{main}}$. The voltage $\hat{E}_{\mathrm{main}}$ is the counter emf generated in the main winding by the stationary pulsating air-gap flux wave produced by the combined action of the stator and rotor currents.

In accordance with the double-revolving-field concept of Section 9.1, the stator mmf can be resolved into half-amplitude forward and backward rotating fields. At standstill the amplitudes of the forward and backward resultant air-gap flux waves both equal to half the amplitude of the pulsating field. In Fig. 9.10b the portion of the equivalent circuit representing the effects of the air-gap flux is split into two equal portions, representing the effects of the forward and backward fields, respectively.

Next consider conditions after the motor has been brought up to speed by some auxiliary means and is running on only its main winding in the direction of the forward field at a per-unit slip s. The rotor currents induced by the forward field are of slip frequency sf_{e}, where f_{e} is the stator applied electrical frequency. Just as in any polyphase motor with a symmetric polyphase or squirrel-cage rotor, these rotor currents produce an mmf wave traveling forward at slip speed with respect to the rotor and therefore at synchronous speed with respect to the stator. The resultant of

---

[1] For an extensive treatment of single-phase motors, see, for example, C. B. Veinott, *Fractional- and Subfractional-Horsepower Electric Motors,* McGraw-Hill, New York, 1970.

(a)

(b)   (c)

Figure 9.10 Equivalent circuits for a single-phase induction motor: (a) rotor blocked; (b) rotor blocked, showing effects of forward and backward fields; (c) running conditions.

the forward waves of stator and rotor mmf creates a resultant forward wave of air-gap flux, which generates a counter emf $\hat{E}_{\text{main,f}}$ in the main winding of the stator. The reflected effect of the rotor as viewed from the stator is like that in a polyphase motor and can be represented by an impedance $0.5R_{2,\text{main}}/s + j0.5X_{2,\text{main}}$ in parallel with $j0.5X_{\text{m,main}}$ as in the portion of the equivalent circuit of Fig. 9.10c labeled "f." The factors of 0.5 come from the resolution of the pulsating stator mmf into forward and backward components.

Now consider conditions with respect to the backward field. While the rotor is operating at a slip s with respect to the forward field, its slip with respect to the backward field is $2 - s$. The backward field then induces rotor currents whose frequency is $(2 - s) f_{\text{e}}$. For small slips, these rotor currents are of almost twice stator frequency.

At a small slip, the rotor currents will consist of a high-frequency component from the backward field superposed on a low-frequency component from the forward field. As viewed from the stator, the rotor-mmf wave of the backward-field-induced rotor current travels at synchronous speed but in the backward direction. The equivalent-circuit representing these internal reactions from the viewpoint of the stator is like that of a polyphase motor whose slip is $2 - s$ and is shown in the portion of the equivalent circuit (Fig. 9.10c) labeled "b." As with the forward field, the factors of 0.5 come from the resolution of the pulsating stator mmf into forward and backward components. The voltage $\hat{E}_{\text{main,b}}$ across the parallel combination representing the backward field is the counter emf generated in the main winding of the stator by the resultant backward field.

By use of the equivalent circuit of Fig. 9.10c, the stator current, power input, and power factor can be computed for any assumed value of slip when the applied voltage and the motor impedances are known. To simplify the notation, let

$$Z_f \equiv R_f + jX_f \equiv \left(\frac{R_{2,\text{main}}}{s} + jX_{2,\text{main}} \right) \text{ in parallel with } jX_{m,\text{main}} \qquad (9.4)$$

and

$$Z_b \equiv R_b + jX_b \equiv \left(\frac{R_{2,\text{main}}}{2-s} + jX_{2,\text{main}} \right) \text{ in parallel with } jX_{m,\text{main}} \qquad (9.5)$$

The impedances representing the reactions of the forward and backward fields from the viewpoint of the single-phase main stator winding are $0.5Z_f$ and $0.5Z_b$, respectively, in Fig. 9.10c.

Examination of the equivalent circuit (Fig. 9.10c) confirms the conclusion, reached by qualitative reasoning in Section 9.1 (Fig. 9.2b), that the forward air-gap flux wave increases and the backward wave decreases when the rotor is set in motion. When the motor is running at a small slip, the reflected effect of the rotor resistance in the forward field, $0.5R_{2,\text{main}}/s$, is much larger than its standstill value, while the corresponding effect in the backward field, $0.5R_{2,\text{main}}/(2-s)$, is smaller. The forward-field impedance therefore is larger than its standstill value, while that of the backward field is smaller. The forward-field counter emf $\hat{E}_{\text{main,f}}$ therefore is larger than its standstill value, while the backward-field counter emf $\hat{E}_{\text{main,b}}$ is smaller; i.e., the forward air-gap flux wave increases, while the backward flux wave decreases.

Mechanical power and torque can be computed by application of the torque and power relations developed for polyphase motors in Chapter 6. The torques produced by the forward and backward fields can each be treated in this manner. The interactions of the oppositely rotating flux and mmf waves cause torque pulsations at twice stator frequency but produce no average torque.

As in Eq. 6.26, the electromagnetic torque $T_{\text{main,f}}$ of the forward field in newton-meters equals $1/\omega_s$ times the power $P_{\text{gap,f}}$ in watts delivered by the stator winding to the forward field, where ω_s is the synchronous angular velocity in mechanical radians per second; thus

$$T_{\text{main,f}} = \frac{1}{\omega_s} P_{\text{gap,f}} \qquad (9.6)$$

When the magnetizing impedance is treated as purely inductive, $P_{\text{gap,f}}$ is the power absorbed by the impedance $0.5Z_f$; that is,

$$P_{\text{gap,f}} = I^2(0.5R_f) \qquad (9.7)$$

where R_f is the resistive component of the forward-field impedance defined in Eq. 9.4.

Similarly, the internal torque $T_{\text{main,b}}$ of the backward field is

$$T_{\text{main,b}} = \frac{1}{\omega_s} P_{\text{gap,b}} \qquad (9.8)$$

where $P_{gap,b}$ is the power delivered by the stator winding to the backward field, or

$$P_{gap,b} = I^2(0.5R_b) \tag{9.9}$$

where R_b is the resistive component of the backward-field impedance Z_b defined in Eq. 9.5.

The torque of the backward field is in the opposite direction to that of the forward field, and therefore the net internal torque T_{mech} is

$$T_{mech} = T_{main,f} - T_{main,b} = \frac{1}{\omega_s}(P_{gap,f} - P_{gap,b}) \tag{9.10}$$

Since the rotor currents produced by the two component air-gap fields are of different frequencies, the total rotor I^2R loss is the numerical sum of the losses caused by each field. In general, as shown by comparison of Eqs. 6.17 and 6.19, the rotor I^2R loss caused by a rotating field equals the slip of the field times the power absorbed from the stator. Thus

$$\text{Forward-field rotor } I^2R = s\,P_{gap,f} \tag{9.11}$$

$$\text{Backward-field rotor } I^2R = (2-s)\,P_{gap,b} \tag{9.12}$$

$$\text{Total rotor } I^2R = s\,P_{gap,f} + (2-s)\,P_{gap,b} \tag{9.13}$$

Since power is torque times angular velocity and the angular velocity of the rotor is $(1-s)\omega_s$, using Eq. 9.10, the internal power P_{mech} converted to mechanical form, in watts, is

$$P_{mech} = (1-s)\omega_s T_{mech} = (1-s)(P_{gap,f} - P_{gap,b}) \tag{9.14}$$

As in the polyphase motor, the internal torque T_{mech} and internal power P_{mech} are not the output values because rotational losses remain to be accounted for. It is obviously correct to subtract friction and windage losses from T_{mech} or P_{mech} and it is usually assumed that core losses can be treated in the same manner. For the small changes in speed encountered in normal operation, the rotational losses are often assumed to be constant.[2]

EXAMPLE 9.2

A $\frac{1}{4}$-hp, 110-V, 60-Hz, four-pole, capacitor-start motor has the following equivalent circuit parameter values (in Ω) and losses:

$$R_{1,main} = 2.02 \qquad X_{1,main} = 2.79 \qquad R_{2,main} = 4.12$$

$$X_{2,main} = 2.12 \qquad X_{m,main} = 66.8$$

$$\text{Core loss} = 24 \text{ W} \qquad \text{Friction and windage loss} = 13 \text{ W}$$

---

[2] For a treatment of the experimental determination of motor constants and losses, see Veinott, op. cit., Chapter 18.

For a slip of 0.05, determine the stator current, power factor, power output, speed, torque, and efficiency when this motor is running as a single-phase motor at rated voltage and frequency with its starting winding open.

■ Solution

The first step is to determine the values of the forward- and backward-field impedances at the assigned value of slip. The following relations, derived from Eq. 9.4, simplify the computations of the forward-field impedance Z_f:

$$R_f = \left(\frac{X_{m,main}^2}{X_{22}}\right)\frac{1}{s\,Q_{2,main} + 1/(s\,Q_{2,main})} \qquad X_f = \frac{X_{2,main}X_{m,main}}{X_{22}} + \frac{R_f}{s\,Q_{2,main}}$$

where

$$X_{22} = X_{2,main} + X_{m,main} \qquad \text{and} \qquad Q_{2,main} = \frac{X_{22}}{R_{2,main}}$$

Substitution of numerical values gives, for $s = 0.05$,

$$Z_f = R_f + jX_f = 31.9 + j40.3 \ \Omega$$

Corresponding relations for the backward-field impedance Z_b are obtained by substituting $2 - s$ for s in these equations. When $(2 - s)Q_{2,main}$ is greater than 10, as is usually the case, less than 1 percent error results from use of the following approximate forms:

$$R_b = \frac{R_{2,main}}{2 - s}\left(\frac{X_{m,main}}{X_{22}}\right)^2 \qquad X_b = \frac{X_{2,main}X_{m,main}}{X_{22}} + \frac{R_b}{(2 - s)Q_{2,main}}$$

Substitution of numerical values gives, for $s = 0.05$,

$$Z_b = R_b + jX_b = 1.98 + j2.12 \ \Omega$$

Addition of the series elements in the equivalent circuit of Fig. 9.10c gives

$$R_{1,main} + jX_{1,main} = 2.02 + j2.79$$

$$0.5(R_f + jX_f) = 15.95 + j20.15$$

$$\underline{0.5(R_b + jX_b) = 0.99 + j1.06}$$

$$\text{Total Input } Z = 18.96 + j24.00 = 30.6 \ \angle 51.7°$$

$$\text{Stator current } I = \frac{V}{Z} = \frac{110}{30.6} = 3.59 \text{ A}$$

$$\text{Power factor} = \cos(51.7°) = 0.620$$

$$\text{Power input} = P_{in} = VI \times \text{power factor} = 110 \times 3.59 \times 0.620 = 244 \text{ W}$$

The power absorbed by the forward field (Eq. 9.7) is

$$P_{gap,f} = I^2(0.5R_f) = 3.59^2 \times 15.95 = 206 \text{ W}$$

The power absorbed by the backward field (Eq. 9.9) is

$$P_{gap,b} = I^2(0.5R_b) = 3.59^2 \times 0.99 = 12.8 \text{ W}$$

The internal mechanical power (Eq. 9.14) is

$$P_{mech} = (1 - s)(P_{gap,f} - P_{gap,b}) = 0.95(206 - 13) = 184 \text{ W}$$

Assuming that the core loss can be combined with the friction and windage loss, the rotational loss becomes $24 + 13 = 37$ W and the shaft output power is the difference. Thus

$$P_{\text{shaft}} = 184 - 37 = 147 \text{ W} = 0.197 \text{ hp}$$

From Eq. 4.42, the synchronous speed in rad/sec is given by

$$\omega_s = \left(\frac{2}{\text{poles}} \right) \omega_e = \left(\frac{2}{4} \right) 120\pi = 188.5 \text{ rad/sec}$$

or in terms of r/min from Eq. 4.44

$$n_s = \left(\frac{120}{\text{poles}} \right) f_e = \left(\frac{120}{4} \right) 60 = 1800 \text{ r/min}$$

$$\text{Rotor speed} = (1 - s)(\text{synchronous speed})$$

$$= 0.95 \times 1800 = 1710 \text{ r/min}$$

and

$$\omega_m = 0.95 \times 188.5 = 179 \text{ rad/sec}$$

The torque can be found from Eq. 9.14.

$$T_{\text{shaft}} = \frac{P_{\text{shaft}}}{\omega_m} = \frac{147}{179} = 0.821 \text{ N} \cdot \text{m}$$

and the efficiency is

$$\eta = \frac{P_{\text{shaft}}}{P_{\text{in}}} = \frac{147}{244} = 0.602 = 60.2\%$$

As a check on the power bookkeeping, compute the losses:

$$I^2 R_{1,\text{main}} = (3.59)^2 (2.02) = 26.0$$

$$\text{Forward-field rotor } I^2 R \text{ (Eq. 9.11)} = 0.05 \times 206 = 10.3$$

$$\text{Backward-field rotor } I^2 R \text{ (Eq. 9.12)} = 1.95 \times 12.8 = 25.0$$

$$\text{Rotational losses} = \underline{37.0}$$

$$98.3 \text{ W}$$

From $P_{\text{in}} - P_{\text{shaft}}$, the total losses $= 97$ W which checks within accuracy of computations.

Practice Problem 9.2

Assume the motor of Example 9.2 to be operating at a slip of 0.065 and at rated voltage and frequency. Determine (a) the stator current and power factor and (b) the power output.

Solution

    a. 4.0 A, power factor $= 0.70$ lagging
    b. 190 W

Examination of the order of magnitude of the numerical values in Example 9.2 suggests approximations which usually can be made. These approximations pertain particularly to the backward-field impedance. Note that the impedance $0.5(R_b + jX_b)$ is only about 5 percent of the total motor impedance for a slip near full load. Consequently, an approximation as large as 20 percent of this impedance would cause only about 1 percent error in the motor current. Although, strictly speaking, the backward-field impedance is a function of slip, very little error usually results from computing its value at any convenient slip in the normal running region, e.g., 5 percent, and then assuming R_b and X_b to be constants.

Corresponding to a slightly greater approximation, the shunting effect of $jX_{m,main}$ on the backward-field impedance can often be neglected, whence

$$Z_b \approx \frac{R_{2,main}}{2-s} + jX_{2,main} \tag{9.15}$$

This equation gives values of the backward-field resistance that are a few percent high, as can be seen by comparison with the exact expression given in Example 9.2. Neglecting s in Eq. 9.15 would tend to give values of the backward-field resistance that would be too low, and therefore such an approximation would tend to counteract the error in Eq. 9.15. Consequently, for small slips

$$Z_b \approx \frac{R_{2,main}}{2} + jX_{2,main} \tag{9.16}$$

In a polyphase motor (Section 6.5), the maximum internal torque and the slip at which it occurs can easily be expressed in terms of the motor parameters; the maximum internal torque is independent of rotor resistance. No such simple expressions exist for a single-phase motor. The single-phase problem is much more involved because of the presence of the backward field, the effect of which is twofold: (1) it absorbs some of the applied voltage, thus reducing the voltage available for the forward field and decreasing the forward torque developed; and (2) the backward field produces negative torque, reducing the effective developed torque. Both of these effects depend on rotor resistance as well as leakage reactance. Consequently, unlike the polyphase motor, the maximum internal torque of a single-phase motor is influenced by rotor resistance; increasing the rotor resistance decreases the maximum torque and increases the slip at which maximum torque occurs.

Principally because of the effects of the backward field, a single-phase induction motor is somewhat inferior to a polyphase motor using the same rotor and the same stator core. The single-phase motor has a lower maximum torque which occurs at a lower slip. For the same torque, the single-phase motor has a higher slip and greater losses, largely because of the backward-field rotor I^2R loss. The volt-ampere input to the single-phase motor is greater, principally because of the power and reactive volt-amperes consumed by the backward field. The stator I^2R loss also is somewhat higher in the single-phase motor, because one phase, rather than several, must carry all the current. Because of the greater losses, the efficiency is lower, and the temperature rise for the same torque is higher. A larger frame size must be used for a single-phase motor than for a polyphase motor of the same power and speed rating. Because of the larger frame size, the maximum torque can be made comparable with that of a physically smaller but equally rated polyphase motor. In spite of the larger frame size and the necessity for auxiliary starting arrangements, general-purpose single-phase motors in the standard fractional-kilowatt ratings cost approximately the same as correspondingly rated polyphase motors because of the much greater volume of production of the former.

9.4   TWO-PHASE INDUCTION MOTORS

As we have seen, most single-phase induction motors are actually constructed in the form of two-phase motors, with two stator windings in space quadrature. The main and auxiliary windings are typically quite different, with a different number of turns, wire size, and turns distribution. This difference, in combination with the capacitor that is typically used in series with the auxiliary winding, guarantees that the mmfs produced by the two winding currents will be quite unbalanced; at best they may be balanced at one specific operating point. We will thus discuss various analytical techniques for two-phase motors, both to expand our understanding and insight into machine performance and also to develop techniques for the analysis of single- and two-phase motors.

Under balanced operating conditions, a symmetrical two-phase motor can be analyzed using techniques developed in Chapter 6 for three-phase motors, modified only slightly to take into account the fact that there are two phases rather than three. In this section, we will first discuss one technique that can be used to analyze a symmetrical two-phase motor operating under unbalanced operating conditions. We will then formally derive an analytical model for an unsymmetrical two-phase motor that can be applied to the general case single-phase motors operating off both their main and auxiliary windings.

9.4.1   Unbalanced Operation of Symmetrical Two-Phase Machines; The Symmetrical-Component Concept

When operating from the main winding alone, the single-phase motor is the extreme case of a motor operating under unbalanced stator-current conditions. In some cases, unbalanced voltages or currents are produced in the supply network to a motor, e.g., when a line fuse is blown. In other cases, unbalanced voltages are produced by the starting impedances of single-phase motors, as described in Section 9.2. The purpose of this section is to develop the symmetrical-component theory of two-phase induction motors from the double-revolving-field concept and to show how the theory can be applied to a variety of problems involving induction motors having two stator windings in space quadrature.

First consider in review what happens when balanced two-phase voltages are applied to the stator terminals of a two-phase machine having a uniform air gap, a symmetrical polyphase or cage rotor, and two identical stator windings α and β in space quadrature. The stator currents are equal in magnitude and in time quadrature.

Figure 9.11 Single-phase equivalent circuits for a two-phase motor under unbalanced conditions: (a) forward field and (b) backward field.

When the current in winding α is at its instantaneous maximum, the current in winding β is zero and the stator-mmf wave is centered on the axis of winding α. Similarly, the stator-mmf wave is centered on the axis of winding β at the instant when the current in winding β is at its instantaneous maximum. The stator-mmf wave therefore travels 90 electrical degrees in space in a time interval corresponding to a 90° phase change of the applied voltage, with the direction of its travel depending on the phase sequence of the currents. A more complete analysis in the manner of Section 4.5 shows that the traveling wave has constant amplitude and constant angular velocity. This fact is, of course, the basis for the theory of the balanced operation of induction machines.

The behavior of the motor for balanced two-phase applied voltages of either phase sequence can be readily determined. Thus, if the rotor is turning at a slip s in the direction from winding α toward winding β, the terminal impedance per phase is given by the equivalent circuit of Fig. 9.11a when the applied voltage $\hat{V}_\beta$ lags the applied voltage $\hat{V}_\alpha$ by 90°. Throughout the rest of this treatment, this phase sequence is called *positive sequence* and is designated by the subscript "f" since positive-sequence currents result in a forward field. With the rotor running at the same speed and in the same direction, the terminal impedance per phase is given by the equivalent circuit of Fig. 9.11b when $\hat{V}_\beta$ leads $\hat{V}_\alpha$ by 90°. This phase sequence is called *negative sequence* and is designated by subscript "b", since negative-sequence currents produce a backward field.

Suppose now that *two* balanced two-phase voltage sources of *opposite phase sequence* are connected in series and applied simultaneously to the motor, as indicated in Fig. 9.12a, where phasor voltages $\hat{V}_f$ and $j\hat{V}_f$ applied, respectively, to windings α and β form a balanced system of positive sequence, and phasor voltages $\hat{V}_b$ and $-j\hat{V}_b$ form another balanced system but of negative sequence.

The resultant voltage V_α applied to winding α is, as a phasor,

$$\hat{V}_\alpha = \hat{V}_f + \hat{V}_b \tag{9.17}$$

and that applied to winding β is

$$\hat{V}_\beta = j\hat{V}_f - j\hat{V}_b \tag{9.18}$$

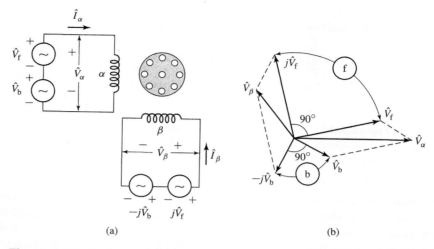

Figure 9.12 Synthesis of an unbalanced two-phase system from the sum of two balanced systems of opposite phase sequence.

Fig. 9.12b shows a generalized phasor diagram in which the forward, or positive-sequence, system is given by the phasors $\hat{V}_f$ and $j\hat{V}_f$ and the backward, or negative-sequence, system is given by the phasors $\hat{V}_b$ and $-j\hat{V}_b$. The resultant voltages, given by the phasors $\hat{V}_\alpha$ and $\hat{V}_\beta$ are not, in general, either equal in magnitude or in time quadrature. From this discussion we see that an unbalanced two-phase system of applied voltages V_α and V_β can be synthesized by combining two balanced voltage sets of opposite phase sequence.

The symmetrical-component systems are, however, much easier to work with than their unbalanced resultant system. Thus, it is easy to compute the component currents produced by each symmetrical-component system of applied voltages because the induction motor operates as a balanced two-phase motor for each component system. By superposition, the actual current in a winding then is the sum of its components. Thus, if $\hat{I}_f$ and $\hat{I}_b$ are, respectively, the positive- and negative-sequence component phasor currents in winding α, then the corresponding positive- and negative-sequence component phasor currents in winding β are, respectively, $j\hat{I}_f$ and $-j\hat{I}_b$, and the actual winding currents $\hat{I}_\alpha$ and $\hat{I}_\beta$ are

$$\hat{I}_\alpha = \hat{I}_f + \hat{I}_b \tag{9.19}$$

$$\hat{I}_\beta = j\hat{I}_f - j\hat{I}_b \tag{9.20}$$

The inverse operation of finding the symmetrical components of specified voltages or currents must be performed often. Solution of Eqs. 9.17 and 9.18 for the phasor components $\hat{V}_f$ and $\hat{V}_b$ in terms of known phasor voltages $\hat{V}_\alpha$ and $\hat{V}_\beta$ gives

$$\hat{V}_f = \frac{1}{2}(\hat{V}_\alpha - j\hat{V}_\beta) \tag{9.21}$$

$$\hat{V}_b = \frac{1}{2}(\hat{V}_\alpha + j\hat{V}_\beta) \tag{9.22}$$

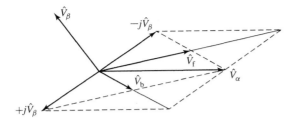

Figure 9.13 Resolution of unbalanced two-phase voltages into symmetrical components.

These operations are illustrated in the phasor diagram of Fig. 9.13. Obviously, similar relations give the phasor symmetrical components $\hat{I}_f$ and $\hat{I}_b$ of the current in winding α in terms of specified phasor currents $\hat{I}_m$ and $\hat{I}_a$ in the two phases; thus

$$\hat{I}_f = \frac{1}{2}(\hat{I}_\alpha - j\hat{I}_\beta) \tag{9.23}$$

$$\hat{I}_b = \frac{1}{2}(\hat{I}_\alpha + j\hat{I}_\beta) \tag{9.24}$$

EXAMPLE 9.3

The equivalent-circuit parameters of a 5-hp 220-V 60-Hz four-pole two-phase squirrel-cage induction motor in ohms per phase are

$$R_1 = 0.534 \qquad X_1 = 2.45 \qquad X_m = 70.1 \qquad R_2 = 0.956 \qquad X_2 = 2.96$$

This motor is operated from an unbalanced two-phase 60-Hz source whose phase voltages are, respectively, 230 and 210 V, the smaller voltage leading the larger by 80°. For a slip of 0.05, find (a) the positive- and negative-sequence components of the applied voltages, (b) the positive- and negative-sequence components of the stator-phase currents, (c) the effective values of the phase currents, and (d) the internal mechanical power.

■ **Solution**

We will solve this example using MATLAB.[3]

a. Let $\hat{V}_\alpha$ and $\hat{V}_\beta$ denote the voltages applied to the two phases, respectively. Then

$$\hat{V}_\alpha = 230\angle 0° = 230 + j0 \text{ V}$$

$$\hat{V}_\beta = 210\angle 80° = 36.4 + j207 \text{ V}$$

From Eqs. 9.21 and 9.22 the forward and backward components of voltages are, respectively,

$$\hat{V}_f = 218.4 - j18.2 = 219.2\angle -4.8° \text{ V}$$

$$\hat{V}_b = 11.6 + j18.2 = 21.6\angle 57.5° \text{ V}$$

---

[3] MATLAB is a registered trademark of The MathWorks, Inc.

b. Because of the ease with which MATLAB handles complex numbers, there is no need to use approximations such as are derived in Example 9.2. Rather, the forward- and backward-field input impedances of the motor can be calculated from the equivalent circuits of Figs. 9.11a and b. Dividing the forward-field voltage by the forward-field input impedance gives

$$\hat{I}_f = \frac{\hat{V}_f}{R_1 + jX_1 + Z_f} = 9.3 - j6.3 = 11.2\angle -34.2° \text{ A}$$

Similarly, dividing the backward-field voltage by the backward-field input impedance gives

$$\hat{I}_b = \frac{\hat{V}_b}{R_1 + jX_1 + Z_b} = 3.7 - j1.5 = 4.0\angle -21.9° \text{ A}$$

c. The winding currents can be calculated from Eqs. 9.19 and 9.20

$$\hat{I}_\alpha = \hat{I}_f + \hat{I}_b = 13.0 - j7.8 = 15.2\angle -31.0° \text{ A} \tag{9.25}$$

$$\hat{I}_\beta = j\hat{I}_f - j\hat{I}_b = 4.8 + j5.6 = 7.4\angle 49.1° \text{ A} \tag{9.26}$$

Note that the winding currents are much more unbalanced than the applied voltages. Even though the motor is not overloaded insofar as shaft load is concerned, the losses are appreciably increased by the current unbalance, and the stator winding with the greatest current may overheat.

d. The power delivered across the air gap by the forward field is equal to the forward-field equivalent-circuit input power minus the corresponding stator loss

$$P_{\text{gap,f}} = 2\left(\text{Re}[\hat{V}_f \hat{I}_f^*] - I_f^2 R_1\right) = 4149 \text{ W}$$

where the factor of 2 accounts for the fact that this is a two-phase motor. Similarly, the power delivered to the backward field is

$$P_{\text{gap,b}} = 2\left(\text{Re}[\hat{V}_b \hat{I}_b^*] - I_b^2 R_1\right) = 14.5 \text{ W}$$

Here, the symbol Re[ ] indicates the real part of a complex number, and the superscript * indicates the complex conjugate.

Finally, from Eq. 9.14, the internal mechanical power developed is equal to $(1 - s)$ times the total air-gap power or

$$P_{\text{mech}} = (1 - s)(P_{\text{gap,f}} - P_{\text{gap,b}}) = 3927 \text{ W}$$

If the core losses, friction and windage, and stray load losses are known, the shaft output can be found by subtracting them from the internal power. The friction and windage losses depend solely on the speed and are the same as they would be for balanced operation at the same speed. The core and stray load losses, however, are somewhat greater than they would be for balanced operation with the same positive-sequence voltage and current. The increase is caused principally by the $(2 - s)$-frequency core and stray losses in the rotor caused by the backward field.

Here is the MATLAB script:

```
clc
clear

% Useful constants
f = 60; %60 Hz system
omega = 2*pi*f;
s = 0.05; % slip

% Parameters

R1 = 0.534;
X1 = 2.45;
Xm = 70.1;
R2 = 0.956;
X2 = 2.96;

% Winding voltages

Valpha = 230;
Vbeta = 210 * exp(j*80*pi/180);

%(a)  Calculate Vf and Vb from Equations and 9-21 and 9-22

Vf = 0.5*(Valpha - j*Vbeta);
Vb = 0.5*(Valpha + j*Vbeta);

magVf = abs(Vf);
angleVf = angle(Vf)*180/pi;

magVb = abs(Vb);
angleVb = angle(Vb)*180/pi;

fprintf('\n(a)')
fprintf('\n  Vf = %.1f + j %.1f  = %.1f at angle %.1f degrees V', ...
real(Vf),imag(Vf),magVf,angleVf);
fprintf('\n  Vb = %.1f + j %.1f  = %.1f at angle %.1f degrees V\n', ...
real(Vb),imag(Vb),magVb,angleVb);

%(b) First calculate the forward-field input impedance of the motor from
% the equivalent circuit of Fig. 9-12(a).

Zf = R1 + j*X1 + j*Xm*(R2/s+j*X2)/(R2/s+j*(X2+Xm));
```

```
%Now calculate the forward-field current.

If = Vf/Zf;

magIf = abs(If);
angleIf = angle(If)*180/pi;

% Next calculate the backward-field input impedance of the motor from
% Fig. 9-12(b).

Zb = R1 + j*X1 + j*Xm*(R2/(2-s)+j*X2)/(R2/(2-s)+j*(X2+Xm));

%Now calculate the backward-field current.

Ib = Vb/Zb;

magIb = abs(Ib);
angleIb = angle(Ib)*180/pi;

fprintf('\n(b)')
fprintf('\n  If = %.1f + j %.1f  = %.1f at angle %.1f degrees A', ...
real(If),imag(If),magIf,angleIf);
fprintf('\n  Ib = %.1f + j %.1f  = %.1f at angle %.1f degrees A\n', ...
real(Ib),imag(Ib),magIb,angleIb);

%(c) Calculate the winding currents from Eqs. 9-19 and 9-20

Ialpha = If + Ib;

Ibeta = j*(If - Ib);

magIalpha = abs(Ialpha);
angleIalpha = angle(Ialpha)*180/pi;

magIbeta = abs(Ibeta);
angleIbeta = angle(Ibeta)*180/pi;

fprintf('\n(c)')
fprintf('\n  Ialpha = %.1f + j %.1f  = %.1f at angle %.1f degrees A', ...
real(Ialpha),imag(Ialpha),magIalpha,angleIalpha);
fprintf('\n  Ibeta = %.1f + j %.1f  = %.1f at angle %.1f degrees A\n', ...
real(Ibeta),imag(Ibeta),magIbeta,angleIbeta);

%(d) Power delivered to the forward field is equal to the
% forward-field input power less the stator-winding I^2R loss
```

```
Pgf = 2*(real(Vf*conj(If)) - R1*magIf^2);

% Power delivered to the backward field is equal to the
% backward-field input power less the stator-winding I^2R loss

Pgb = 2*(real(Vb*conj(Ib)) - R1*magIb^2);

% The electromagnetic power is equal to (1-s) times the
% net air-gap power

Pmech = (1-s)*(Pgf - Pgb);

fprintf('\n(d)')
fprintf('\n  Power to forward field = %.1f W',Pgf)
fprintf('\n  Power to backward field = %.1f W',Pgb)
fprintf('\n  Pmech = %.1f W\n',Pmech)
fprintf('\n')
```

For the motor of Example 9.3, use MATLAB to produce a plot of the internal mechanical power as a function of slip as the slip varies from $s = 0.04$ to $s = 0.05$ for the unbalanced voltages assumed in the example. On the same axes (using dashed lines), plot the internal mechanical power for balanced two-phase voltages of 220-V magnitude and 90° phase shift.

Solution

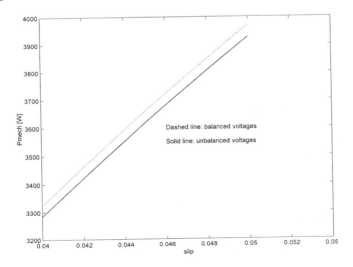

Figure 9.14 MATLAB plot for Practice Problem 9.3.

9.4.2   The General Case: Unsymmetrical Two-Phase Induction Machines

As we have discussed, a single-phase induction motor with a main and auxiliary winding is an example of an unsymmetrical two-phase induction motor. In this section we will develop a model for such two-phase motors, using notation appropriate to the single-phase motor. We will assume, as is commonly the case, that the magnetic axes of the windings are in space quadrature but that they are unsymmetrical in that they may have a different number of turns, a different winding distribution, and so on.

Our analytical approach is to represent the rotor by an equivalent two-phase winding as shown in schematic form in Fig. 9.15 and to start with flux-linkage/current relationships for the rotor and stator of the form

$$
\begin{bmatrix} \lambda_{main} \\ \lambda_{aux} \\ \lambda_{r1} \\ \lambda_{r2} \end{bmatrix} =
\begin{bmatrix}
L_{main} & 0 & \mathcal{L}_{main,r1}(\theta_{me}) & \mathcal{L}_{main,r2}(\theta_{me}) \\
0 & L_{aux} & \mathcal{L}_{aux,r1}(\theta_{me}) & \mathcal{L}_{aux,r2}(\theta_{me}) \\
\mathcal{L}_{main,r1}(\theta_{me}) & \mathcal{L}_{aux,r1}(\theta_{me}) & L_r & 0 \\
\mathcal{L}_{main,r2}(\theta_{me}) & \mathcal{L}_{aux,r2}(\theta_{me}) & 0 & L_r
\end{bmatrix}
\begin{bmatrix} i_{main} \\ i_{aux} \\ i_{r1} \\ i_{r2} \end{bmatrix}
$$

$$(9.27)$$

where θ_{me} is the rotor angle measured in electrical radians.

L_{main} = Self-inductance of the main winding

L_{aux} = Self-inductance of the auxiliary winding

L_r = Self-inductance of the equivalent rotor windings

$\mathcal{L}_{main,r1}(\theta_{me})$ = Mutual inductance between the main winding and equivalent rotor winding 1

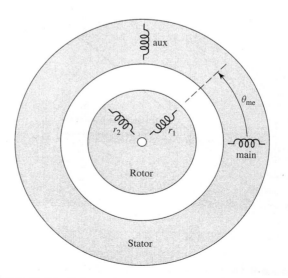

Figure 9.15   Schematic representation of a two-phase induction motor with an equivalent two-phase rotor.

$\mathcal{L}_{\mathrm{main,r2}}(\theta_{\mathrm{me}})$ = Mutual inductance between the main winding and equivalent rotor winding 2

$\mathcal{L}_{\mathrm{aux,r1}}(\theta_{\mathrm{me}})$ = Mutual inductance between the auxiliary winding and rotor winding 1

$\mathcal{L}_{\mathrm{aux,r2}}(\theta_{\mathrm{me}})$ = Mutual inductance between the auxiliary winding and rotor winding 2

Assuming a sinusoidal distribution of air-gap flux, the mutual inductances between the main winding and the rotor will be of the form

$$\mathcal{L}_{\mathrm{main,r1}}(\theta_{\mathrm{me}}) = L_{\mathrm{main,r}} \cos \theta_{\mathrm{me}} \tag{9.28}$$

and

$$\mathcal{L}_{\mathrm{main,r2}}(\theta_{\mathrm{me}}) = -L_{\mathrm{main,r}} \sin \theta_{\mathrm{me}} \tag{9.29}$$

where $L_{\mathrm{main,r}}$ is the amplitude of the mutual inductance.

The mutual inductances between the auxiliary winding will be of the same form with the exception that the auxiliary winding is displaced by 90 electrical degrees in space from the main winding. Hence we can write

$$\mathcal{L}_{\mathrm{aux,r1}}(\theta_{\mathrm{me}}) = L_{\mathrm{aux,r}} \sin \theta_{\mathrm{me}} \tag{9.30}$$

and

$$\mathcal{L}_{\mathrm{aux,r2}}(\theta_{\mathrm{me}}) = L_{\mathrm{aux,r}} \cos \theta_{\mathrm{me}} \tag{9.31}$$

Note that the auxiliary winding will typically have a different number of turns (and perhaps a different winding distribution) from that of the main winding. Thus, for modeling purposes, it is often convenient to write

$$L_{\mathrm{aux,r}} = a \, L_{\mathrm{main,r}} \tag{9.32}$$

where

$$a = \text{Turns ratio} = \frac{\text{Effective turns of auxiliary winding}}{\text{Effective turns of main winding}} \tag{9.33}$$

Similarly, if we write the self-inductance of the magnetizing branch as the sum of a leakage inductance $L_{\mathrm{main,l}}$ and a magnetizing inductance L_{m}

$$L_{\mathrm{main}} = L_{\mathrm{main,l}} + L_{\mathrm{m}} \tag{9.34}$$

then the self-inductance of the auxiliary winding can be written in the form

$$L_{\mathrm{aux}} = L_{\mathrm{aux,l}} + a^2 \, L_{\mathrm{m}} \tag{9.35}$$

The voltage equations for this machine can be written in terms of the winding currents and flux linkages as

$$v_{\mathrm{main}} = i_{\mathrm{main}} R_{\mathrm{main}} + \frac{d\lambda_{\mathrm{main}}}{dt} \tag{9.36}$$

$$v_{\mathrm{aux}} = i_{\mathrm{aux}} R_{\mathrm{aux}} + \frac{d\lambda_{\mathrm{aux}}}{dt} \tag{9.37}$$

$$v_{\mathrm{r1}} = 0 = i_{\mathrm{r1}} R_{\mathrm{r}} + \frac{d\lambda_{\mathrm{r1}}}{dt} \tag{9.38}$$

$$v_{\mathrm{r2}} = 0 = i_{\mathrm{r2}} R_{\mathrm{r}} + \frac{d\lambda_{\mathrm{r2}}}{dt} \tag{9.39}$$

where R_{main}, R_{aux} and R_r are the resistances of the main, auxiliary, and rotor windings, respectively. Note that the rotor-winding voltages are set equal to zero because the rotor windings of an induction motor are internally shorted.

When modeling a split-phase induction motor (Section 9.2.1) the main and auxiliary windings are simply connected in parallel, and thus v_{main} and v_{aux} are both set equal to the single-phase supply voltage when the motor is started. Following the time that the auxiliary winding is disconnected, the auxiliary-winding current is zero, and the motor is represented by a reduced-order model which includes only the main winding and the two equivalent rotor windings.

When modeling the various capacitor motors of Section 9.2.2, the circuit equations must take into account the fact that, while the main winding is connected directly to the single-phase supply, a capacitor is connected between the supply and the auxiliary-winding terminals. Depending upon the type of motor being modeled, the auxiliary winding may or may not be switched out as the motor comes up to speed.

Finally, the techniques of Section 3.5 can be used to show that the electromagnetic torque of this motor can be written as

$$
\begin{aligned}
T_{\text{mech}} &= i_{\text{main}} i_{\text{r}1} \left(\frac{d\mathcal{L}_{\text{main,r1}}(\theta_{\text{me}})}{d\theta_m} \right) + i_{\text{main}} i_{\text{r}2} \left(\frac{d\mathcal{L}_{\text{main,r2}}(\theta_{\text{me}})}{d\theta_m} \right) \\
&\quad + i_{\text{aux}} i_{\text{r}1} \left(\frac{d\mathcal{L}_{\text{aux,r1}}(\theta_{\text{me}})}{d\theta_m} \right) + i_{\text{aux}} i_{\text{r}2} \left(\frac{d\mathcal{L}_{\text{aux,r2}}(\theta_{\text{me}})}{d\theta_m} \right) \\
&= \left(\frac{\text{poles}}{2} \right) [-L_{\text{main,r}} \left(i_{\text{main}} i_{\text{r}1} \sin\theta_{\text{me}} + i_{\text{main}} i_{\text{r}2} \cos\theta_{\text{me}} \right) \\
&\quad + L_{\text{aux,r}} \left(i_{\text{aux}} i_{\text{r}1} \cos\theta_{\text{me}} - i_{\text{aux}} i_{\text{r}2} \sin\theta_{\text{me}} \right)]
\end{aligned}
\tag{9.40}
$$

where $\theta_m = (2/\text{poles})\theta_{\text{me}}$ is the rotor angle in radians.

Analogous to the development of the equivalent circuits derived in Chapter 6 for polyphase induction machines and earlier in this chapter for single-phase machines, the equations derived in this section can be further developed by assuming steady-state operation, with constant mechanical speed ω_{me}, corresponding to a slip s, and constant electrical supply frequency ω_e. Consistent with this assumption, the rotor currents will be at frequencies $\omega_r = \omega_e - \omega_{\text{me}} = s\,\omega_e$ (produced by the stator positive-sequence field) and $\omega_r = \omega_e + \omega_{\text{me}} = (2-s)\omega_e$ (produced by the stator negative-sequence field). After considerable algebraic manipulation, which includes using Eqs. 9.38 and 9.39 to eliminate the rotor currents, the main- and auxiliary-winding flux-linkage/current relationships of Eq. 9.27 can be written as phasor equations

$$
\hat{\lambda}_{\text{main}} = \left[L_{\text{main}} - jL_{\text{main,r}}^2 (\hat{K}^+ + \hat{K}^-) \right] \hat{I}_{\text{main}} + L_{\text{main,r}} L_{\text{aux,r}} (\hat{K}^+ - \hat{K}^-) \hat{I}_{\text{aux}}
\tag{9.41}
$$

and

$$
\hat{\lambda}_{\text{aux}} = -L_{\text{main,r}} L_{\text{aux,r}} (\hat{K}^+ - \hat{K}^-) \hat{I}_{\text{main}} + \left[L_{\text{aux}} - jL_{\text{aux,r}}^2 (\hat{K}^+ + \hat{K}^-) \right] \hat{I}_{\text{aux}}
\tag{9.42}
$$

where

$$\hat{K}^+ = \frac{s\omega_e}{2(R_r + js\omega_e L_r)} \tag{9.43}$$

and

$$\hat{K}^- = \frac{(2-s)\omega_e}{2(R_r + j(2-s)\omega_e L_r)} \tag{9.44}$$

Similarly, the voltage equations, Eqs. 9.36 and 9.37 become

$$\hat{V}_{main} = \hat{I}_{main} R_{main} + j\omega_e \hat{\lambda}_{main} \tag{9.45}$$

$$\hat{V}_{aux} = \hat{I}_{aux} R_{aux} + j\omega_e \hat{\lambda}_{aux} \tag{9.46}$$

The rotor currents will each consist of positive- and negative-sequence components. The complex amplitudes of the positive sequence components (at frequency $s\omega_e$) are given by

$$\hat{I}_{r1}^+ = \frac{-js\omega_e[L_{main,r}\hat{I}_{main} + jL_{aux,r}\hat{I}_{aux}]}{2(R_r + js\omega_e L_r)} \tag{9.47}$$

and

$$\hat{I}_{r2}^+ = -j\hat{I}_{r1}^+ \tag{9.48}$$

while the complex amplitudes of the negative sequence components (at frequency $(2-s)\omega_e$) are given by

$$\hat{I}_{r1}^- = \frac{-j(2-s)\omega_e[L_{main,r}\hat{I}_{main} - jL_{aux,r}\hat{I}_{aux}]}{2(R_r + j(2-s)\omega_e L_r)} \tag{9.49}$$

and

$$\hat{I}_{r2}^- = j\hat{I}_{r1}^- \tag{9.50}$$

Finally, again after careful algebraic manipulation, the time-averaged electromagnetic torque can be shown to be given by

$$<T_{mech}> = \left(\frac{poles}{2}\right) Re\left[(L_{main,r}^2 \hat{I}_{main}\hat{I}_{main}^* + L_{aux,r}^2 \hat{I}_{aux}\hat{I}_{aux}^*)(\hat{K}^+ - \hat{K}^-)^*\right.$$
$$\left. + jL_{main,r}L_{aux,r}(\hat{I}_{main}^*\hat{I}_{aux} - \hat{I}_{main}\hat{I}_{aux}^*)(\hat{K}^+ + \hat{K}^-)^*\right] \tag{9.51}$$

where the symbol Re[ ] again indicates the real part of a complex number and the superscript * indicates the complex conjugate. Note that Eq. 9.51 is derived based upon the assumption that the various currents are expressed as rms quantities.

EXAMPLE 9.4

Consider the case of a symmetrical two-phase motor such as is discussed in Section 9.4.1. In this case, Eqs. 9.27 through 9.39 simplify with equal self and mutual inductances and resistances for the two windings. Using the notation of Section 9.4.1, "α" and "β" replacing "main" and "aux," the flux-linkage/current relationships of Eq. 9.41 and 9.42 become

$$\hat{\lambda}_\alpha = \left[L_\alpha - jL_{\alpha,r}^2(\hat{K}^+ + \hat{K}^-)\right]\hat{I}_\alpha + L_{\alpha,r}^2(\hat{K}^+ - \hat{K}^-)\hat{I}_\beta$$

$$\hat{\lambda}_\beta = -L_{\alpha,r}^2(\hat{K}^+ - \hat{K}^-)\hat{I}_\alpha + \left[L_\alpha - jL_{\alpha,r}^2(\hat{K}^+ + \hat{K}^-)\right]\hat{I}_\beta$$

and the voltage equations (Eqs. 9.45 and 9.46) become

$$\hat{V}_\alpha = \hat{I}_\alpha R_\alpha + j\omega_e\hat{\lambda}_\alpha$$

$$\hat{V}_\beta = \hat{I}_\beta R_\alpha + j\omega_e\hat{\lambda}_\beta$$

Show that when operated from a positive sequence set of voltages such that $\hat{V}_\beta = -jV_\alpha$ the single-phase equivalent circuit for this motor is that of the forward-field (positive-sequence) equivalent circuit of Fig. 9.11a.

■ Solution

Substitution of the positive-sequence voltages in the above equations and solution for the impedance $Z_\alpha = \hat{V}_\alpha/\hat{I}_\alpha$ gives

$$Z_\alpha = R_\alpha + j\omega_e L_\alpha + \frac{(\omega_e L_{\alpha,r})^2}{(R_r/s + j\omega_e L_r)}$$

$$= R_\alpha + jX_\alpha + \frac{X_{\alpha,r}^2}{(R_r/s + jX_r)}$$

This equation can be rewritten as

$$Z_\alpha = R_\alpha + j(X_\alpha - X_{\alpha,r}) + \frac{jX_{\alpha,r}[j(X_r - X_{\alpha,r}) + R_r/s]}{(R_r/s + jX_r)}$$

Setting $R_\alpha \Rightarrow R_1$, $(X_\alpha - X_{\alpha,r}) \Rightarrow X_1$, $X_{\alpha,r} \Rightarrow X_m$, $(X_r - X_{\alpha,r}) \Rightarrow X_2$, and $R_r \Rightarrow R_2$, we see that this equation does indeed correspond to the input impedance of an equivalent circuit of the form of Fig. 9.11a.

Practice Problem 9.4

Analogous to the calculation of Example 9.4, show that when operated from a negative sequence set of voltages such that $\hat{V}_\beta = jV_\alpha$ the single-phase equivalent circuit is that of the backward-field (negative-sequence) equivalent circuit of Fig. 9.11b.

Solution

Under negative-sequence conditions, the impedance Z_α is equal to

$$Z_\alpha = R_\alpha + j\omega_e L_\alpha' + \frac{(\omega_e L_{\alpha,r})^2}{(R_r/(2-s) + j\omega_e L_r)}$$

$$= R_\alpha + jX_\alpha + \frac{X_{\alpha,r}^2}{(R_r/(2-s) + jX_r)}$$

As in Example 9.4, this can be shown to correspond to an equivalent circuit of the form of Fig. 9.11b.

EXAMPLE 9.5

A two-pole, single-phase induction motor has the following parameters:

$$L_{main} = 80.6 \text{ mH} \qquad R_{main} = 0.58 \ \Omega$$
$$L_{aux} = 196 \text{ mH} \qquad R_{aux} = 3.37 \ \Omega$$
$$L_r = 4.7 \ \mu\text{H} \qquad R_r = 37.6 \ \mu\Omega$$
$$L_{main,r} = 0.588 \text{ mH} \qquad L_{aux,r} = 0.909 \text{ mH}$$

It is operated from a single-phase, 230-V rms, 60-Hz source as a permanent-split-capacitor motor with a 35 μF capacitor connected in series with the auxiliary winding. In order to achieve the required phase shift of the auxiliary-winding current, the windings must be connected with the polarities shown in Fig. 9.16. The motor has a rotational losses of 40 W and 105 W of core loss.

Consider motor operation at 3500 r/min.

a. Find the main-winding, auxiliary-winding and source currents and the magnitude of the capacitor voltage.
b. Find the time-averaged electromagnetic torque and shaft output power.
c. Calculate the motor input power and its electrical efficiency. Note that since core loss isn't explicitly accounted for in the model derived in this section, you may simply consider it as an additional component of the input power.
d. Plot the motor time-averaged electromagnetic torque as a function of speed from standstill to synchronous speed.

■ Solution

MATLAB, with its ease of handling complex numbers, is ideal for the solution of this problem.

a. The main winding of this motor is directly connected to the single-phase source. Thus we directly set $\hat{V}_{main} = \hat{V}_s$. However, the auxiliary winding is connected to the single-phase source through a capacitor and its polarity is reversed. Thus we must write

$$\hat{V}_{aux} + \hat{V}_C = -\hat{V}_s$$

where the capacitor voltage is given by

$$\hat{V}_C = j\hat{I}_{aux}X_C$$

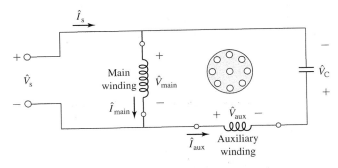

Figure 9.16 Permanent-split-capacitor induction-motor connections for Example 9.5.

Here the capacitor impedance X_C is equal to

$$X_C = -\frac{1}{(\omega_e C)} = -\frac{1}{(120\pi \times 35 \times 10^{-6})} = -75.8 \ \Omega$$

Setting $\hat{V}_s = V_0 = 230$ V and substituting these expressions into Eqs. 9.45 and 9.46 and using Eqs. 9.41 and 9.42 then gives the following matrix equation for the main- and auxiliary-winding currents.

$$\begin{bmatrix} (R_{main} + j\omega_e \hat{A}_1) & j\omega_e \hat{A}_2 \\ -j\omega_e \hat{A}_2 & (R_{aux} + jX_c + j\omega_e \hat{A}_3) \end{bmatrix} \begin{bmatrix} \hat{I}_{main} \\ \hat{I}_{aux} \end{bmatrix} = \begin{bmatrix} V_0 \\ -V_0 \end{bmatrix}$$

where

$$\hat{A}_1 = L_{main} - jL_{main,r}^2 (\hat{K}^+ + \hat{K}^-)$$

$$\hat{A}_2 = L_{main,r} L_{aux,r} (\hat{K}^+ - \hat{K}^-)$$

and

$$\hat{A}_3 = L_{aux} - jL_{aux,r}^2 (\hat{K}^+ + \hat{K}^-)$$

The parameters $\hat{K}^+$ and $\hat{K}^-$ can be found from Eqs. 9.43 and 9.44 once the slip is found using Eq. 6.1

$$s = \frac{n_s - n}{n_s} == \frac{3600 - 3500}{3600} = 0.278$$

This matrix equation can be readily solved using MATLAB with the result

$$\hat{I}_{main} = 15.9 \angle -37.6° \text{ A}$$

$$\hat{I}_{aux} = 5.20 \angle -150.7° \text{ A}$$

and

$$\hat{I}_s = 18.5 \angle -22.7° \text{ A}$$

The magnitude of the capacitor voltage is

$$|\hat{V}_C| = |\hat{I}_{aux} X_C| = 374 \text{ V}$$

b. Using MATLAB the time-averaged electromagnetic torque can be found from Eq. 9.51 to be

$$<T_{mech}> = 9.74 \text{ N} \cdot \text{m}$$

The shaft power can then be found by subtracting the rotational losses P_{rot} from the air-gap power

$$P_{shaft} = \omega_m <T_{mech}> - P_{rot}$$

$$= \left(\frac{2}{poles} \right)(1 - s)\omega_e (<T_{mech}>) - P_{rot}$$

$$= 3532 \text{ W}$$

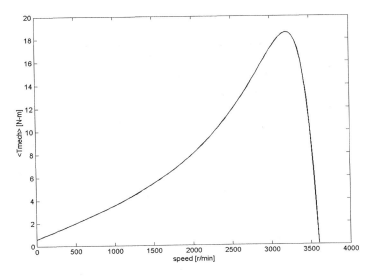

Figure 9.17 Time-averaged electromagnetic torque versus speed for the single-phase induction motor of Example 9.5.

c. The power input to the main winding can be found as

$$P_{main} = Re\left[V_0 \hat{I}_{main}^*\right] = 2893 \text{ W}$$

and that into the auxiliary winding, including the capacitor (which dissipates no power)

$$P_{aux} = Re\left[-V_0 \hat{I}_{aux}^*\right] = 1043 \text{ W}$$

The total input power, including the core loss power P_{core} is found as

$$P_{in} = P_{main} + P_{aux} + P_{core} = 4041 \text{ W}$$

Finally, the efficiency can be determined

$$\eta = \frac{P_{shaft}}{P_{in}} == 0.874 = 87.4\%$$

d. The plot of $<T_{mech}>$ versus speed generated by MATLAB is found in Fig. 9.17.

Here is the MATLAB script:

```
clc
clear

% Source parameters
V0 = 230;
omegae = 120*pi;

% Motor parameters
poles = 2;
```

```
Lmain = .0806;
Rmain = 0.58;
Laux = 0.196;
Raux = 3.37;
Lr = 4.7e-6;
Rr = 37.6e-6;
Lmainr = 5.88e-4;
Lauxr = 9.09e-4;
C = 35e-6;
Xc = -1/(omegae*C);
Prot = 40;
Pcore = 105;

% Run through program twice.  If calcswitch = 1, then
% calculate at speed of 3500 r/min only.  The second time
% program will produce the plot for part (d).

for calcswitch = 1:2

if calcswitch == 1
  mmax = 1;
else
   mmax = 101;
end

for m = 1:mmax

if calcswitch == 1
   speed(m) = 3500;
else
   speed(m) = 3599*(m-1)/100;
end

% Calculate the slip
ns = (2/poles)*3600;
s = (ns-speed(m))/ns;

% part (a)
% Calculate the various complex constants
Kplus = s*omegae/(2*(Rr + j*s*omegae*Lr));
Kminus = (2-s)*omegae/(2*(Rr + j*(2-s)*omegae*Lr));
A1 = Lmain - j*Lmainr^2*(Kplus+Kminus);
A2 = Lmainr*Lauxr*(Kplus-Kminus);
A3 = Laux - j*Lauxr^2*(Kplus+Kminus);
```

```
% Set up the matrix
M(1,1) = Rmain + j*omegae*A1;
M(1,2) = j*omegae*A2;
M(2,1) = -j*omegae*A2;
M(2,2) = Raux + j*Xc+ j*omegae*A3;

% Here is the voltage vector
V = [V0 ; -V0];

% Now find the current matrix

I = M\V;

Imain = I(1);
Iaux = I(2);
Is = Imain-Iaux;

magImain = abs(Imain);
angleImain = angle(Imain)*180/pi;
magIaux = abs(Iaux);
angleIaux = angle(Iaux)*180/pi;
magIs = abs(Is);
angleIs = angle(Is)*180/pi;

%Capacitor voltage
Vcap = Iaux*Xc;
magVcap = abs(Vcap);

% part (b)
Tmech1 = conj(Kplus-Kminus);
Tmech1 = Tmech1*(Lmainr^2*Imain*conj(Imain)+Lauxr^2*Iaux*conj(Iaux));
Tmech2 = j*Lmainr*Lauxr*conj(Kplus+Kminus);
Tmech2 = Tmech2*(conj(Imain)*Iaux-Imain*conj(Iaux));
Tmech(m) = (poles/2)*real(Tmech1+Tmech2);
Pshaft = (2/poles)*(1-s)*omegae*Tmech(m)-Prot;


%part (c)
Pmain = real(V0*conj(Imain));
Paux = real(-V0*conj(Iaux));
Pin = Pmain+Paux+Pcore;
eta = Pshaft/Pin;
```

```
if calcswitch == 1
    fprintf('part (a):')
    fprintf('\n    Imain = %g A at angle %g degrees',magImain,angleImain)
    fprintf('\n    Iaux = %g A at angle %g degrees',magIaux,angleIaux)
    fprintf('\n    Is = %g A at angle %g degrees',magIs,angleIs)
    fprintf('\n    Vcap = %g V\n',magVcap)
    fprintf('\npart (b):')
    fprintf('\n    Tmech = %g N-m',Tmech)
    fprintf('\n    Pshaft = %g W\n',Pshaft)
    fprintf('\npart (c):')
    fprintf('\n    Pmain = %g W',Pmain)
    fprintf('\n    Paux = %g W',Paux)
    fprintf('\n    Pin = %g W',Pin)
    fprintf('\n    eta = %g percent\n\n',100*eta)
else
    plot(speed,Tmech)
    xlabel('speed [r/min]')
    ylabel('<Tmech> [N-m]')

end

end %end of for m loop
end %end of for calcswitch loop
```

<hr>

Practice Problem 9.5

---

a. Calculate the efficiency of the single-phase induction motor of Example 9.5 operating at a speed of 3475 r/min.
b. Search over the range of capacitor values from 25 μF to 45 μF to find the capacitor value which will give the maximum efficiency at this speed and the corresponding efficiency.

Solution

a. 86.4%
b. 41.8 μF, 86.6%

9.5 SUMMARY

One theme of this chapter is a continuation of the induction-machine theory of Chapter 6 and its application to the single-phase induction motor. This theory is expanded by a step-by-step reasoning process from the simple revolving-field theory of the symmetrical polyphase induction motor. The basic concept is the resolution of the stator-mmf wave into two constant-amplitude traveling waves revolving around the air gap at synchronous speed in opposite directions. If the slip for the forward field is s, then that for the backward field is $(2 - s)$. Each of these component fields produces induction-motor action, just as in a symmetrical polyphase motor. From the view-point of the stator, the reflected effects of the rotor can be visualized and expressed quantitatively in terms of simple equivalent circuits. The ease with which the internal reactions can be accounted for in this manner is the essential reason for the usefulness of the double-revolving-field theory.

For a single-phase winding, the forward- and backward-component mmf waves are equal, and their amplitude is half the maximum value of the peak of the stationary pulsating mmf produced by the winding. The resolution of the stator mmf into its forward and backward components then leads to the physical concept of the single-phase motor described in Section 9.1 and finally to the quantitative theory developed in Section 9.3 and to the equivalent circuits of Fig. 9.10.

In most cases, single-phase induction motors are actually two-phase motors with unsymmetrical windings operated off a single phase source. Thus to complete our understanding of single-phase induction motors, it is necessary to examine the per-formance of two-phase motors. Hence, the next step is the application of the double-revolving-field picture to a symmetrical two-phase motor with unbalanced applied voltages, as in Section 9.4.1. This investigation leads to the symmetrical-component concept, whereby an unbalanced two-phase system of currents or voltages can be re-solved into the sum of two balanced two-phase component systems of opposite phase sequence. Resolution of the currents into symmetrical-component systems is equiv-alent to resolving the stator-mmf wave into its forward and backward components, and therefore the internal reactions of the rotor for each symmetrical-component system are the same as those which we have already investigated. A very sim-ilar reasoning process, not considered here, leads to the well-known three-phase symmetrical-component method for treating problems involving unbalanced opera-tion of three-phase rotating machines. The ease with which the rotating machine can be analyzed in terms of revolving-field theory is the chief reason for the usefulness of the symmetrical-component method.

Finally, the chapter ends in Section 9.4.2 with the development of an analytical theory for the general case of a two-phase induction motor with unsymmetrical wind-ings. This theory permits us to analyze the operation of single-phase motors running off both their main and auxiliary windings.

9.6 CHAPTER 9 VARIABLES

δ, ϕ	Phase angle [rad]
θ_{ae}	Stator spatial angle in electrical units [rad]
θ_m	Rotor position [rad]
θ_{me}	Rotor position in electrical units [rad]
λ	Flux linkage [Wb]
$\hat{\lambda}$	Flux linkage, complex amplitude [Wb]
ω_e	Electrical frequency [rad/sec]
ω_m	Rotor angular velocity [rad/sec]
ω_{me}	Rotor angular velocity in electrical units [rad/sec]
ω_r	Rotor electrical frequency [rad/sec]

ω_s	Synchronous angular velocity [rad/sec]
a	Turns ratio
C	Capacitance [F]
$\hat{E}, \hat{V}$	Voltage, complex amplitude [A]
f_e	Electrical frequency [Hz]
$F, \mathcal{F}$	Magnetomotive force [A]
i, I	Current [A]
$\hat{I}$	Current, complex amplitude [A]
$k_{2,\text{main}}, \hat{K}^+, \hat{K}^-, \hat{A}_1, \hat{A}_2, \hat{A}_3$	Useful parameters
$L, \mathcal{L}$	Inductance [H]
n	Angular velocity [r/min]
n_s	Synchronous angular velocity [r/min]
P	Power [W]
R	Resistance [Ω]
s	Slip
t	Time [sec]
T	Torque [N · m]
v, V	Voltage [V]
X	Reactance [Ω]
X_c	Capacitive reactance [Ω]
Z	Impedance [Ω]

Subscripts:

α, β	Phase designations
aux	Auxiliary winding
b	Backward field
C	Capacitor
f	Forward field
gap	Air gap
m	Magnetizing
main	Main winding
max	Maximum
r	Rotor
rot	Rotation
s	Supply

9.7   PROBLEMS

9.1 A 750-W, 120-V, 60-Hz capacitor-start motor has the following parameters for the main and auxiliary windings (at starting):

$$Z_{\text{main}} = 6.43 + j9.67 \ \Omega \qquad \text{main winding}$$
$$Z_{\text{aux}} = 10.6 + j12.2 \ \Omega \qquad \text{auxiliary winding}$$

a. Find the magnitude and the phase angles of the currents in the two windings when rated voltage is applied to the motor under starting conditions.

    b.   Find the value of starting capacitance that will place the main- and auxiliary-winding currents in time quadrature at starting.

    c.   Repeat part (a) when the capacitance of part (b) is inserted in series with the auxiliary winding. Find the magnitude and phase (with respect to the applied voltage) of auxiliary-winding voltage.

9.2 Repeat Problem 9.1 if the motor is operated from a 120-V, 50-Hz source.

9.3 Given the applied electrical frequency and the corresponding impedances Z_{main} and Z_{aux} of the main and auxiliary windings at starting, write a MATLAB script to calculate the value of the capacitance, which, when connected in series with the starting winding, will produce a starting winding current which will lag that of the main winding by 90°. Exercise your program on the 60-Hz motor of Problem 9.1.

9.4 A 120-V, 60-Hz, two-pole, permanent-split-capacitor, single-phase induction motor has a rated output power of 500 W. When operated at its rated voltage and load with an auxiliary-winding capacitance of 41.3 μF, the main-winding current is observed to be 4.89 A at a phase angle (with respect to the applied voltage) of $-55.8°$ and the auxiliary-winding current is observed to be 3.32 A at a phase angle of 34.2°.

    a.   Calculate the motor power input, power factor, and efficiency.

    b.   Calculate the impedances Z_{main} and Z_{aux} of the main and auxiliary windings.

    c.   The main and auxiliary windings differ only in their number of turns. The main winding has 180 turns/pole. Calculate the turns/pole of the auxiliary winding.

    d.   Show that under this operating condition, the combined mmfs of the main and auxiliary windings produce only a single rotating flux wave.

9.5 Repeat Example 9.2 for slip of 0.035;

9.6 A 600-W, 115-V, 60-Hz, six-pole, capacitor-start motor has the following equivalent-circuit parameter values (in Ω) and losses:

$$R_{1,main} = 1.07 \quad R_{2,main} = 1.47$$

$$X_{1,main} = 1.83 \quad X_{m,main} = 34.3 \quad X_{2,main} = 1.12$$

$$\text{Core loss} = 57 \text{ W} \quad \text{Friction and windage loss} = 17.7 \text{ W}$$

For a slip of 0.065, determine the stator current, power factor, power output, speed, torque, and efficiency when this motor is running as a single-phase motor at rated voltage and frequency with its starting winding open.

9.7 A 750-W, four-pole, 120-V, 60-Hz single-phase induction motor has the following parameters (resistances and reactances in Ω/phase):

$$R_{1,main} = 0.55 \quad R_{2,main} = 1.70$$

$$X_{1,main} = 0.83 \quad X_{m,main} = 41.5 \quad X_{2,main} = 0.72$$

$$\text{Core loss} = 57 \text{ W} \quad \text{Friction and windage loss} = 17.7 \text{ W}$$

Find the speed, stator current, torque, power output, and efficiency when the motor is operating at rated voltage and a slip of 7.2 percent.

9.8 Write a MATLAB script to produce plots of the speed and efficiency of the single-phase motor of Problem 9.7 as a function of output power over the range $0 \leq P_{\text{out}} \leq 750$ W.

9.9 To modify the 750-W, 120-V single-phase induction motor of Problem 9.7 to operate on a 240-V system, the main winding is to be re-wound with an otherwise identical winding with twice the number of turns using wire of one-half the cross sectional area.

    a. Calculate the main-winding parameters of the re-wound motor.

    b. With the re-wound motor operating from the 240-V source from its main winding alone, find the slip for which the motor output is 700 W. Calculate the corresponding main-winding current and motor efficiency.

9.10 At standstill the currents in the main and auxiliary windings of a four-pole, capacitor-start induction motor are $I_{\text{main}} = 18.9$ A and $I_{\text{aux}} = 12.1$ A rms respectively. The auxiliary-winding current leads the main-winding current by $58°$. The effective turns per pole (i.e., the number of turns corrected for the effects of winding distribution) are $N_{\text{main}} = 47$ and $N_{\text{aux}} = 73$. The windings are in space quadrature.

    a. Determine the amplitudes of the forward and backward stator-mmf waves.

    b. Suppose it were possible to adjust the magnitude and phase of the auxiliary-winding current. What magnitude and phase would produce a purely forward mmf wave?

9.11 Derive an expression in terms of $Q_{2,\text{main}}$ for the nonzero speed of a single-phase induction motor at which the internal torque is zero. (See Example 9.2.)

9.12 The equivalent-circuit parameters of an 7.5-kW 230-V 60-Hz four-pole two-phase squirrel-cage induction motor in ohms per phase are

$$R_1 = 0.266 \qquad X_1 = 1.27 \qquad X_{\text{m}} = 34.1 \qquad R_2 = 0.465 \qquad X_2 = 1.39$$

This motor is operated from an unbalanced two-phase 60-Hz source whose phase voltages are, respectively, 232 and 198 V, the smaller voltage leading the larger by $75°$. For a slip of 0.047, find

    a. the positive and negative-sequence components of the applied voltages and the resultant motor currents,

    b. the phase currents in each of the windings, and

    c. the internal mechanical power.

9.13 Consider the two-phase squirrel-cage induction motor of Problem 9.12 operating at a constant speed of 1725 rpm with the voltage of the first winding held constant at 230 V.

    a. Assume that the voltage of the second winding varies from 200 V to 240 V with a constant phase angle of $90°$ leading that of the first winding. Plot the internal mechanical power as a function of the voltage of the second winding.

b. Assume that the voltage of the second winding is held constant at 230 V while its phase angle varies from 70° to 110° leading that of the first winding. Plot the internal mechanical power as a function of the phase angle of the second winding.

9.14 Consider the two-phase motor of Example 9.3.

   a. Find the starting torque for the conditions specified in the example.

   b. Compare the result of part (a) with the starting torque which the motor would produce if 220-V balanced two-phase voltages were applied to the motor.

   c. Show that if the stator voltages $\hat{V}_\alpha$ and $\hat{V}_{\text{beta}}$ of a two-phase induction motor are in time quadrature but unequal in magnitude, the starting torque is the same as that developed when balanced two-phase voltages of magnitude $\sqrt{V_\alpha V_\beta}$ are applied.

9.15 The induction motor of Problem 9.12 is supplied from an unbalanced two-phase source by a feeder having an impedance $Z = 0.32 + j1.5\ \Omega/\text{phase}$. The source voltages can be expressed as

$$\hat{V}_\alpha = 237\angle 0° \quad \hat{V}_\beta = 211\angle 73°$$

For a slip of 5.2 percent, show that the induction-motor terminal voltages correspond more nearly to a balanced two-phase set than do those of the source.

9.16 The equivalent-circuit parameters in ohms per phase referred to the stator for a two-phase 1.5 kW, 220-V, four-pole, 60-Hz squirrel-cage induction motor are given below. The no-load rotational loss is 106 W.

$$R_1 = 0.49 \quad R_2 = 2.6 \quad X_1 = X_2 = 3.7 \quad X_{\text{m}} = 66$$

   a. The voltage applied to phase α is $220\angle 0°$ V and that applied to phase β is $204\angle 80°$ V. Find the net air-gap torque at a slip $s = 0.042$.

   b. What is the starting torque with the applied voltages of part (a)?

   c. The applied voltages are readjusted so that $\hat{V}_\alpha = 220\angle 0°$ V and $\hat{V}_\beta = 220\angle 90°$ V. Find the slip at which the full load output power is achieved.

   d. While the motor is running as in part (c), phase β is open-circuited. What is the power output of the machine at a slip $s = 0.042$?

   e. What voltage appears across the open phase-β terminals under the conditions of part (d)?

9.17 A 120-V, 60-Hz, capacitor-run, two-pole, single-phase induction motor has the following parameters:

$$L_{\text{main}} = 41.1\ \text{mH} \qquad R_{\text{main}} = 0.331\ \Omega$$
$$L_{\text{aux}} = 89\ \text{mH} \qquad R_{\text{aux}} = 1.55\ \Omega$$
$$L_{\text{r}} = 2.04\ \mu\text{H} \qquad R_{\text{r}} = 15.0\ \mu\Omega$$
$$L_{\text{main,r}} = 0.30\ \text{mH} \qquad L_{\text{aux,r}} = 0.461\ \text{mH}$$

You may assume that the motor has 48 W of core loss and 23 W of rotational losses. The motor windings are connected with the polarity shown in Fig. 9.16 with a 46 μF run capacitor.

a.   Calculate the motor starting torque.

With the motor operating at a speed of 3475 r/min, calculate

b.   the main and auxiliary-winding currents,

c.   the total line current and the motor power factor,

d.   the output power, and

e.   the electrical input power, and the efficiency.

Note that this problem is most easily solved using MATLAB.

9.18 A 230-V, 50-Hz, capacitor-run, four-pole, single-phase induction motor has the following parameters:

$$L_{main} = 135 \text{ mH} \qquad R_{main} = 1.22 \text{ } \Omega$$
$$L_{aux} = 363 \text{ mH} \qquad R_{aux} = 5.17 \text{ } \Omega$$
$$L_r = 6.77 \text{ } \mu\text{H} \qquad R_r = 259 \text{ } \mu\Omega$$
$$L_{main,r} = 1.16 \text{ mH} \qquad L_{aux,r} = 1.43 \text{ mH}$$

You may assume that the motor has 62 W of core loss and 27 W of rotational losses. The motor windings are connected with the polarity shown in Fig. 9.16 with an 18 μF run capacitor.

a.   With the motor operating at 230 rpm, find the speed at which the motor produces an output power of 1.5 kW.

b.   Find the motor current and efficiency at the operating condition of part (a).

9.19 The single-phase induction machine of Problem 9.18 is to be operated at 230-V on a 60-Hz system. Calculate the capacitance required to maximize the motor efficiency at a speed of 1710 rpm. You may assume that the core loss remains equal to 62 W and the rotational loss increases to 39 W. For operation at 230 V and 1710 rpm with this capacitance, calculate the motor power output, efficiency, and terminal current.

9.20 Consider the single-phase motor of Problem 9.17. Write a MATLAB script to search over the range of capacitor values from 50 μF to 100 μF to find the value which will maximize the motor efficiency at a motor speed of 3475 r/min. What is the corresponding maximum efficiency?

9.21 In order to raise the starting torque, the single-phase induction motor of Problem 9.17 is to be converted to a capacitor-start, capacitor-run motor. Write a MATLAB script to find the minimum value of starting capacitance required to raise the starting torque to 0.55 N $\cdot$ m.

9.22 Consider the single-phase induction motor of Example 9.5 operating over the speed range 3350 r/min to 3580 r/min.

a.   Use MATLAB to plot the output power over the given speed range.

b.   Plot the efficiency of the motor over this speed range.

c.   On the same plot as that of part (b), plot the motor efficiency if the run capacitor is increased to 30 μF.

CHAPTER 10

Speed and Torque Control

Electric motors are employed in many applications which require control of speed and torque. For much of the twentieth century ac machines tended to be employed primarily as single-speed devices. Typically they were operated from fixed-frequency sources (in most cases this was the 50- or 60-Hz power grid) while the control of speed requires a variable-frequency source. Thus, applications requiring variable speed and controlled torque were serviced by dc machines, which can provide highly flexible speed control, although at some cost since they are more complex, more expensive, and require more maintenance than their ac counterparts.

The availability of solid-state power switches and micro-processors for control changed this picture immensely. It is now possible to build power-electronic systems capable of supplying the variable-voltage/current, variable-frequency waveforms required to achieve variable-speed performance as well as torque control from ac machines. As a result, ac machines have now replaced dc machines in many traditional applications, and a wide range of new applications have been developed.

The objective of this chapter is to discuss various techniques for the control of electric machines. Since an in-depth discussion of this topic is both too extensive for a single chapter and beyond the scope of this book, the presentation here will necessarily be introductory in nature. We will present basic techniques for speed and torque control and will illustrate typical configurations of drive electronics that are used to implement the control algorithms. It should be recognized that system dynamics can play a critical role in some applications, with concerns ranging from speed of response to overall system stability. Although the techniques presented here form the basis for dynamic analyses, the discussion of this chapter is focused on steady-state operation.

In the discussion of torque control for synchronous and induction machines, the techniques of *field-oriented* or *vector control* are introduced and the analogy is made with torque control in dc motors. This material is somewhat more sophisticated mathematically than the speed-control discussion and requires application of the dq0 transformations developed in Appendix C. The chapter is written such that this material can be omitted at the discretion of the instructor without detracting from the discussion of speed control.

10.1   CONTROL OF DC MOTORS

Before the widespread application of power-electronic drives to control ac machines, dc motors were by far the machines of choice in applications requiring flexibility of control. Although in recent years ac drives have become quite common, the ease of control of dc machines insures their continued use in various applications.

10.1.1   Speed Control

The three most common speed-control methods for dc motors are adjustment of the flux, usually by means of field-current control, adjustment of the resistance associated with the armature circuit, and adjustment of the armature terminal voltage.

Field-Current Control   In part because it involves control at a relatively low power level (the power into the field winding is typically a small fraction of the power into the armature of a dc machine), *field-current control* is frequently used to control the speed of a dc motor with separately excited or shunt field windings. The connection diagram for a separately excited dc machine is found in Fig. 7.4a and the corresponding equivalent circuit is shown in Fig. 10.1. The method is, of course, also applicable to compound motors. The shunt field current can be adjusted by means of a variable resistance in series with the shunt field. Alternatively, for a separately excited field winding the field current can be supplied by power-electronic circuits which can be used to rapidly change the field current in response to a wide variety of control signals.

   To examine the effect of field-current control, let us begin with the case of a dc motor driving a load of constant torque T_{load}. From Eqs. 7.12 and 7.17, the generated voltage of a dc motor can be written as

$$E_a = K_f i_f \omega_m \tag{10.1}$$

where i_f is the field current, ω_m is the angular velocity in rad/sec, and $K_f = K_a \mathcal{P}_d N_f$ is a geometric constant which depends upon the dimensions of the motor, and the properties of the magnetic material used to construct the motor, as well as the number of turns in the field winding. Note that strictly speaking, K_f is not constant since it is

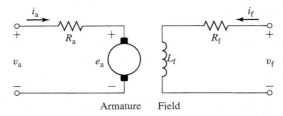

Figure 10.1   Equivalent circuit for a separately excited dc motor.

proportional to the direct-axis permeance, which typically varies as the flux-level in the motor increases to the point that the effects of magnetic saturation become significant.

The electromagnetic torque is given by Eq. 7.19 as

$$T_{\text{mech}} = \frac{E_a I_a}{\omega_m} = K_f i_f I_a \tag{10.2}$$

and the armature current can be seen from the equivalent circuit of Fig. 10.1 to be given by

$$I_a = \frac{(V_a - E_a)}{R_a} \tag{10.3}$$

Setting the motor torque T_{mech} equal to the load torque T_{load}, Eqs. 10.1 through 10.3 can be solved for ω_m

$$\omega_m = \frac{(V_a - I_a R_a)}{K_f i_f} = \frac{\left(V_a - \frac{T_{\text{load}} R_a}{K_f i_f}\right)}{K_f i_f} \tag{10.4}$$

From Eq. 10.4, recognizing that the armature resistance voltage drop $I_a R_a$ is generally quite small in comparison to the armature voltage V_a, we see that for a given armature voltage and load torque, the motor speed will increase with decreasing field current and decrease as the field current is increased. The lowest speed obtainable is that corresponding to maximum field current (the field current is limited by heating considerations); the highest speed is limited mechanically by the mechanical integrity of the rotor and electrically by the effects of armature reaction under weak-field conditions giving rise to poor commutation.

Armature current is typically limited by motor cooling capability. In many dc motors, cooling is aided by a shaft-driven fan whose cooling capacity is a function of motor speed. To examine in an approximate fashion the limitations on the allowable continuous motor output as the speed is changed, we will neglect the influence of changing ventilation and assume that the armature current I_a cannot exceed its rated value, in order to insure that the motor will not overheat. In addition, in our approximate argument we will neglect the effect of rotational losses (which of course also change with motor speed). Because the voltage drop across the armature resistance is relatively small, the speed voltage E_a will remain essentially constant at a value slightly below the applied armature voltage; any change in field current will be compensated for by a change in motor speed.

Thus under constant-terminal-voltage operation with varying field current, the maximum $E_a I_a$, and hence the allowable motor output power, remain substantially constant as the speed is varied. A dc motor controlled in this fashion is referred to as a *constant-power drive*. Torque, however, varies directly with field flux and therefore has its highest allowable value at the highest field current and hence lowest speed. Field-current control is thus best suited to drives requiring increased torque at low speeds. When a motor so controlled is used with a load requiring constant torque over the speed range, the power-rating and size of the machine are determined by the product of the torque and the highest speed. Such a drive is inherently over sized at the lower speeds, which is the principal economic factor limiting the practical speed range of large motors.

EXAMPLE 10.1

A 25-kW, 3600 r/min, 240-V dc motor has an armature resistance of 47 mΩ and a separately excited field winding with a resistance of 187 Ω and an inductance of 4.2 H. With an armature terminal voltage of 240 V, the no-load speed is found to be 3600 r/min with a field current of 0.34 A.

Assuming the armature terminal voltage to remain constant at 240 V and the motor to be driving a load which varies with speed as

$$P_{load} = 10.4 \left(\frac{n}{3600} \right)^3 \text{ kW}$$

where n is the motor speed in r/min, calculate the required field-voltage range such that the speed can be varied between 1800 and 3600 r/min. The effect of rotational losses can be ignored.

■ Solution

The load torque is equal to the load power divided by the motor speed ω_m expressed in rad/sec. First expressing the power in terms of $\omega_m = n\pi/30$

$$P_{load} = 22.4 \left(\frac{\omega_m}{120\pi} \right)^3 \text{ kW}$$

The load torque is then given by

$$T_{load} = \frac{P_{load}}{\omega_m} = 4.18 \times 10^{-4} \, \omega_m^2 \text{ N} \cdot \text{m}$$

Thus, at 1800 r/min, $\omega_m = 60\pi$ and $T_{load} = 14.9$ N · m. At 3600 r/min, $\omega_m = 120\pi$ and $T_{load} = 59.4$ N · m.

Before solving for i_f, we must find the value of K_f, which can be found from the no-load data. Specifically, we see that with a terminal voltage of 240 V and a field current of 0.34 A, the no-load motor speed is 3600 r/min ($\omega_m = 120\pi$). Since under no-load conditions $E_a \approx V_a$, we can find K_f from Eq. 10.1 as

$$K_f = \frac{E_a}{i_f \, \omega_m} = \frac{240}{0.34 \times 120\pi} = 1.87 \text{ V/(A} \cdot \text{rad/sec)}$$

To find the required field current for a given motor speed ω_m, we can solve Eq. 10.4 for I_f

$$i_f = \frac{V_a}{2K_f\omega_m} \left(1 \pm \sqrt{1 - \frac{4\omega_m T_{load} R_a}{V_a^2}} \right)$$

Recognizing that R_a is small and hence that $i_f \approx V_a/(K_f\omega_m)$ we see that the positive sign should be used and thus

$$i_f = \frac{V_a}{2K_f\omega_m} \left(1 + \sqrt{1 - \frac{4\omega_m T_{load} R_a}{V_a^2}} \right)$$

Once the field current has been found, the field voltage can be found as

$$V_f = R_f i_f$$

This leads to the following table:

r/min	T_{load} [N · m]	I_f [A]	V_f [V]
1800	14.9	0.679	127
3600	59.4	0.334	62.5

Thus, the controller must supply voltages in range from 62 to 127 V.

Armature-Circuit Resistance Control   Armature-circuit resistance control provides a means of obtaining reduced speed by the insertion of external series resistance in the armature circuit. It can be used with series, shunt, and compound motors; for the last two types, the series resistor must be connected between the shunt field and the armature, not between the line and the motor. It is a common method of speed control for series motors and is generally analogous in action to wound-rotor-induction-motor control by the addition of external series rotor resistance.

Depending upon the value of the series armature resistance, the speed may vary significantly with load, since the speed depends on the voltage drop in this resistance and hence on the armature current demanded by the load. For example, a 1200-r/min shunt motor whose speed under load is reduced to 750 r/min by series armature resistance will return to almost 1200-r/min operation if the load is removed because the no-load current produces a voltage drop across the series resistance which is insignificant. The disadvantage of poor speed regulation may not be important in a series motor, which is used only where varying-speed service is required or can be tolerated.

A significant disadvantage of this method of speed control is that the power loss in the external resistor is large, especially when the speed is greatly reduced. In fact, for a constant-torque load, the power input to the motor plus resistor remains constant, while the power output to the load decreases in proportion to the speed. Operating costs are therefore comparatively high for lengthy operation at reduced speeds. Because of its low initial cost however, the series-resistance method (or the variation of it discussed in the next paragraph) can be attractive economically for applications which require only short-time or intermittent speed reduction. Unlike field-current control, armature-resistance control results in a *constant-torque drive* because both the field-flux and, to a first approximation, the allowable armature current remain constant as speed changes.

A variation of this control scheme is given by the *shunted-armature method*, which may be applied to a series motor, as in Fig. 10.2a, or a shunt motor, as in Fig. 10.2b. In effect, resistors R_1 and R_2 act as a voltage divider applying a reduced voltage to the armature. Greater flexibility is possible because two resistors can now be adjusted to provide the desired performance. For series motors, the no-load speed can be adjusted to a finite, reasonable value, and the scheme is therefore applicable to the production of slow speeds at light loads. For shunt motors, the speed regulation in the low-speed range is appreciably improved because the no-load speed is definitely lower than the value with no controlling resistors.

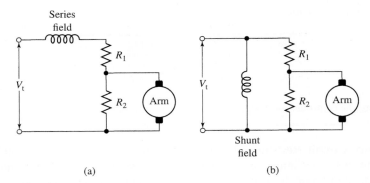

Figure 10.2 Shunted-armature method of speed control applied to (a) a series motor and (b) a shunt motor.

Armature-Terminal Voltage Control   Armature-terminal voltage control can be readily implemented using power-electronic inverter systems. Many inverter configurations exist. For example, Fig. 10.3 shows the topology of a full H-bridge inverter. With switches S1 and S3 closed, the armature voltage is equal to V_{dc} while with switches S2 and S4 closed, the armature voltage is equal to $-V_{dc}$. Clearly, using such an H-bridge configuration in combination with an appropriate choice of control signals to the switches, rapidly switching between V_{dc} and $-V_{dc}$, allows this system to achieve any desired average armature voltage in the range $-V_{dc} \leq V_a \leq V_{dc}$. This type of control is referred to *pulse-width modulation* (PWM).

Armature-voltage control takes advantage of the fact that, because the voltage drop across the armature resistance is relatively small, a change in the armature terminal voltage of a shunt motor is accompanied in the steady state by a substantially equal change in the speed voltage. With constant shunt field current and hence constant field flux, this change in speed voltage must be accompanied by a proportional change in motor speed. Thus, motor speed can be controlled directly by means of the armature terminal voltage.

Figure 10.3 Armature-terminal voltage control implemented with a full H-bridge inverter.

EXAMPLE 10.2

A 500-V, 75-kW (100-hp), 2500 r/min, separately excited dc motor has the following parameters:

Field resistance:	$R_f = 109\ \Omega$
Rated field voltage:	$V_{f0} = 300$ V
Armature resistance:	$R_a = 0.084\ \Omega$
Geometric constant:	$K_f = 0.694$ V/(A · rad/sec)

Assuming the field voltage to be held constant at 300 V and the motor to be operating at rated torque, calculate the variation in motor speed as a function of terminal voltage as the armature voltage is varied from 250 V to 500 V.

■ **Solution**

With constant field voltage, the field current is equal to

$$I_f = \frac{V_f}{R_f} = \frac{300}{109} = 2.75\ \text{A}$$

The rated speed of this motor is $\omega_{m,rated} = 2500 \times (\pi/30) = 262$ rad/sec and thus rated torque is equal to

$$T_{rated} = \frac{P_{rated}}{\omega_{m,rated}} = \frac{75 \times 10^3}{262} = 286\ \text{N} \cdot \text{m}$$

From Eq. 10.2, we see that for rated-torque operation with constant field current, the armature current will be constant

$$I_a = \frac{T_{m,rated}}{K_f I_f} = \frac{286}{0.694 \times 2.75} = 150\ \text{A}$$

Finally, we can find the motor speed from Eq. 10.4 as

$$\omega_m = \frac{(V_a - I_a R_a)}{K_f I_f} = 0.524 \times (V_a - 78.5)\ \text{rad/sec}$$

and we see that the motor speed will vary linearly with terminal voltage. Specifically, at $V_a = 250$ V, $\omega_m = 124.3z$ rad/sec (1187 r/min) and at $V_a = 500$ V, $\omega_m = 255.2$ rad/sec (2437 r/min).

Calculate the change in armature voltage required to maintain the motor of Example 10.2 at a speed of 2000 r/min as the load is changed from zero to full-load torque.

Solution

$$12.5\ \text{V}$$

EXAMPLE 10.3

The motor of Example 10.2 is initially operating at a speed of 2150 r/min at a power of 45 kW. The field winding is supplied from a constant-voltage dc source of 300 V.

a. Calculate (i) the load torque, (ii) the terminal current, and (iii) the terminal voltage.

b. The motor and load have a combined inertia of $J = 17.5$ kg·m². Assuming the load torque to remain constant with speed, calculate the motor speed as a function of time if the terminal voltage is suddenly decreased by 100 V.

■ **Solution**

a. (i) At 2150 r/min, $\omega_m = 2150 \times (\pi/30) = 225$ rad/sec.

$$T_{\text{load}} = \frac{P_{\text{load}}}{\omega_m} = \frac{45 \times 10^3}{225} = 200 \text{ N} \cdot \text{m}$$

(ii) From Example 10.2, $I_f = 2.75$ A and thus the from Eq. 10.1, the speed voltage is

$$E_a = K_f I_f \omega_m = 0.694 \times 2.75 \times 225 = 430 \text{ V}$$

and hence from Eq. 10.2

$$I_a = \frac{T_{\text{load}} \, \omega_m}{E_a} = \frac{200 \times 225}{430} = 105 \text{ A}$$

(iii) Under this operating condition, the terminal voltage is equal to

$$V_a = E_a + R_a I_a = 430 + 0.084 \times 105 = 440 \text{ V}$$

b. The motor speed is governed by the differential equation

$$J \frac{d\omega_m}{dt} = T_{\text{mech}} - T_{\text{load}}$$

where

$$T_{\text{mech}} = K_f I_f I_a = K_f I_f \left(\frac{V_a - E_a}{R_a} \right) = K_f I_f \left(\frac{V_a - K_f I_f \omega_m}{R_a} \right)$$

Combining these equations gives a differential equation for ω_m

$$J \frac{d\omega_m}{dt} + \left(\frac{(K_f I_f)^2}{R_a} \right) \omega_m = \left(\frac{K_f I_f}{R_a} \right) V_a - T_{\text{load}}$$

Substituting $T_{\text{load}} = 200$ N · m and $V_a = 340$ V gives

$$\frac{d\omega_m}{dt} + 2.47 \, \omega_m = 430$$

whose solution is

$$\omega_m = \omega_{m,\infty} + (\omega_{m0} - \omega_{m,\infty})e^{-t/\tau}$$

where $\omega_{m0} = 225$ rad/sec (2150 r/min), $\omega_{m,\infty} = 181$ rad/sec (1730 r/min), and $\tau = 405$ msec. The motor speed is plotted as a function of time in Fig. 10.4.

Frequently the control of motor voltage is combined with field-current control in order to achieve the widest possible speed range. With such dual control, base speed can be defined as the speed at which the motor achieves rated voltage at its nominal/rated armature flux. Below base speed, the maximum terminal voltage is typically limited to the rated voltage scaled by the fraction of base speed at a given operating point. For operation above base speed, the terminal voltage is typically limited to its rated value, accomplished in part by a reduction in field current.

Figure 10.4 Plot of speed versus time for Example 10.3(b) resulting from a step in armature voltage from 440 V to 340 V.

Because both the maximum armature voltage and current are restricted to constant values, the range above base speed is limited to a constant maximum power. In contrast, the range below base speed is limited to a constant maximum torque because, as in armature-resistance control, the flux and the allowable armature current remain approximately constant. The overall output limitations are therefore as shown in Fig. 10.5a for approximate allowable torque and in Fig. 10.5b for approximate allowable power. The constant-torque characteristic is well suited to many applications in the machine-tool industry, where many loads consist largely of overcoming the friction of moving parts and hence have essentially constant torque requirements.

The speed regulation and the limitations on the speed range above base speed are those already presented with reference to field-current control; the maximum speed thus does not ordinarily exceed four times base speed and preferably not twice base

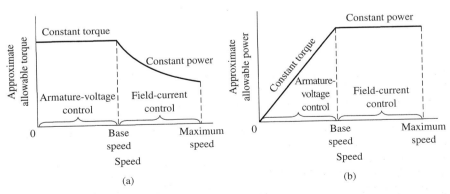

Figure 10.5 (a) Torque and (b) power limitations of combined armature-voltage and field-current methods of speed control.

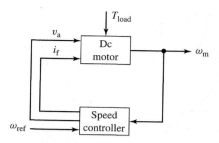

Figure 10.6 Block diagram for a speed-control system for a separately excited or shunt-connected dc motor.

speed. For conventional machines, the lower limit for reliable and stable operation is about one-tenth of base speed, corresponding to a total maximum-to-minimum range not exceeding 40:1.

With armature reaction ignored, the decrease in speed from no-load to full-load torque is caused entirely by the full-load armature-resistance voltage drop. This full-load armature-resistance voltage drop is constant over the voltage-control range, since full-load torque and hence full-load current are usually regarded as constant in that range. When measured in r/min, therefore, the speed decrease from no-load to full-load torque is a constant, independent of the no-load speed. The torque-speed curves accordingly are closely approximated by a series of parallel straight lines for the various motor-field adjustments. Note that a speed decrease of, say, 40 r/min from a no-load speed of 1200 r/min is often of little importance; a decrease of 40 r/min from a no-load speed of 120 r/min, however, may at times be of critical importance and require corrective steps in the layout of the system.

Figure 10.6 shows a block diagram of a feedback-control system that can be used to regulate the speed of a separately excited or shunt-connected dc motor. The inputs to the dc-motor block include the armature voltage and the field current as well as the load torque T_{load}. The resultant motor speed ω_m is fed back to a controller block which represents both the control logic and power electronics and which controls the armature voltage and field current applied to the dc motor, based upon a reference speed signal ω_{ref}. Depending upon the design of the controller, with such a scheme it is possible to control the steady-state motor speed to a high degree of accuracy independent of the variations in the load torque.

EXAMPLE 10.4

Figure 10.7 shows the block diagram for a simple speed control system to be applied to the dc motor of Example 10.2. In this controller, the field voltage (not shown) is held constant at its rated value of 300 V. Thus, the control is applied only to the armature voltage and takes the form

$$V_a = V_{a0} + G\,(\omega_{ref} - \omega_m)$$

where V_{a0} is the armature voltage when $\omega_m = \omega_{ref}$ and G is a multiplicative constant.

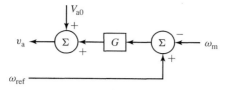

Figure 10.7 Simple dc-motor speed controller for Example 10.4.

With the reference speed set to 2000 r/min ($\omega_{\text{ref}} = 2000 \times \pi/30$), calculate V_{a0} and G so that the motor speed is 2000 r/min at no load and drops only by 25 r/min when the torque is increased to its rated full-load value.

■ **Solution**

As was found in Example 10.2, the field current under this condition will be 2.75 A. At no load, 2000 r/min,

$$V_a \approx E_a = K_f I_f \omega_m = 0.694 \times 2.75 \times 2000 \left(\frac{\pi}{30}\right) = 400 \text{ V}$$

and thus $V_{a0} = 400$ V.

The full-load torque was found in Example 10.3 to be $T_{\text{rated}} = 286$ N·m and thus the armature current required to achieve rated full-load torque can be found from Eq. 10.2

$$I_a = \frac{T_{\text{rated}}}{K_f I_f} = \frac{286}{0.694 \times 2.75} = 150 \text{ A}$$

At a speed of 1975 r/min, E_a will be given by

$$E_a = K_f I_f \omega_m = 0.694 \times 2.75 \times 1975 \left(\frac{\pi}{30}\right) = 395 \text{ V}$$

and thus

$$V_a = E_a + I_a R_a = 395 + 150 \times 0.084 = 408 \text{ V}$$

Solving for G gives

$$G = \frac{V_a - V_{a0}}{\omega_{\text{ref}} - \omega_m} = \frac{408 - 400}{(2000 - 1975)\left(\frac{\pi}{30}\right)} = 3.06 \text{ V·sec/rad}$$

Practice Problem 10.2

Consider again the motor and controller of Example 10.4. If the load is reduced to half of the rated full-load torque, calculate (a) the speed of the motor and (b) the corresponding load power.

Solution

  a. 1988 r/min
  b. 29.6 kW

EXAMPLE 10.5

The dc-motor of Example 10.2 is to be used in an industrial process which requires that the motor speed be maintained in the range of 2200 r/min (at no load) and 2185 r/min (at a full load torque of 200 N·m). The dc-motor field current will be held constant at its rated value and the motor speed will be controlled by varying the armature terminal voltage.

a. The motor is initially operated unloaded and the armature voltage is adjusted to set the speed to 2200 r/min ($\omega_m = 2200 \times (\pi/30) = 230.4$ rad/sec). Calculate the required armature voltage.

b. With the voltage held constant at the value V_{a0} found in part (a), calculate the steady-state terminal current and motor speed if the motor is loaded to the full-load torque of 200 N·m.

c. In order to meet the speed-range specification, a speed controller of the form shown in Fig. 10.7 will be used. Calculate the value of the gain G such that the motor speed is 2185 r/min when it is loaded to a torque of 200 N·m and with $\omega_{ref} = 230.4$ rad/sec.

d. Assuming the combined inertia of the motor and load is $J = 22.4$ kg·m^2 and that a constant-torque load of 200 N·m is applied suddenly at time t = 0.1 sec, use MATLAB/Simulink to plot the motor speed, armature current, and terminal voltage as a function of time with the motor operating both with and without the speed controller.

■ **Solution**

a. At no load, $I_a \approx 0$ and thus $V_a \approx E_a$. Rated field current for this motor is $I_f = 300$ V/109 $\Omega = 2.75$ A and at 2200 r/min, $\omega_m = 230.4$ rad/sec. Thus from Eq. 10.1

$$V_{a0} \approx E_a = K_f I_f \omega_m = 440 \text{ V}$$

b. From Eq. 10.2

$$I_a = \frac{T_{load}}{K_f I_f} = 105 \text{ A}$$

and from Eq. 10.4

$$\omega_m = \frac{(V_a - I_a R_a)}{K_f I_f} = 225.8 \text{ rad/sec}$$

corresponding to a speed of 2156 r/min.

c. At a speed of 2185 r/min, $\omega_m = 2185 \times (30/\pi) = 228.8$ rad/sec and thus

$$E_a = K_f I_f \omega_m = 437 \text{ V}$$

The armature current required to produce a steady-state load torque of 200 N·m is equal to 105 A independent of motor speed and thus we can find the required terminal voltage as

$$V_a = E_a + I_a R_a = 437 + 105 \times 0.084 = 445.8 \text{ V}$$

Solving for G from the block diagram of Fig. 10.7 gives

$$G = \frac{V_a - V_{a0}}{\omega_{ref} - \omega_m} = \frac{445.8 - 400.1}{230.4 - 228.8} = 3.7 \text{ V/(rad/sec)}$$

d. MATLAB/Simulink requires that dynamic equations be formulated in terms of integral equations. The motor speed is determined by the differential equation

$$J \frac{d\omega_m}{dt} = T_{mech} - T_{load}$$

or in integral form

$$\omega_m = \omega_{m0} + \frac{1}{J} \int_0^t (T_{mech} - T_{load}) dt$$

where $\omega_0 = 230.4$ rad/sec is the initial motor speed (2200 r/min) and from Eq. 10.2

$$T_{mech} = \frac{E_a I_a}{\omega_m}$$

where from Eq. 10.3

$$I_a = \frac{V_a - E_a}{R_a}$$

and from Eq. 10.1

$$E_a = K_f I_f \omega_m$$

With the controller

$$V_a = V_{a0} + G(\omega_m - \omega_{ref})$$

where ω_{ref} is set equal to ω_{m0} so that the controller attempts to maintain the motor speed at 2200 r/min. Without the controller, $V_a = V_{a0}$.

Figure 10.8 is the resultant Simulink model. The block labeled "Initialization" calls a MATLAB script which pre-loads the model parameters and initial conditions for the simulation. The speed controller block includes a switch which can be used prior to simulation to turn the speed controller on and off. The load switch operates automatically at 0.1 seconds to apply the 200 N · m load.

Figure 10.8 Simulink model for Example 10.5.

Plots of motor speed, armature current and terminal voltage are found in Fig. 10.9. Notice that not only does the controller result in the desired speed regulation but it also produces a faster response time.

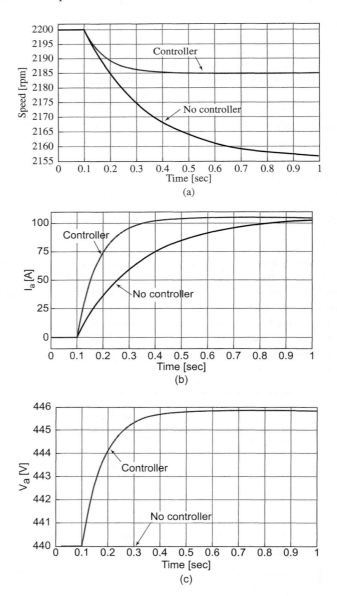

Figure 10.9 Example 10.5: Plot of (a) motor speed, (b) I_a, and (c) terminal voltage V_a versus time for Example 10.5.

In the case of permanent-magnet dc motors, the field flux is, of course, fixed by the permanent magnet (with the possible exception of any effects of temperature changes on the magnet properties as the motor heats up). From Eqs. 10.1 and 10.2, we see that the speed voltage can be written in the form

$$E_a = K_m \omega_m \qquad (10.5)$$

and that the electromagnetic torque can be written as

$$T_{mech} = K_m I_a \qquad (10.6)$$

Comparison of Eqs. 10.5 and 10.6 with Eqs. 10.1 and 10.2 show that the analysis of a permanent-magnet dc motor is identical to that of a shunt or separately excited dc motor with the exception that the torque-constant K_m must be substituted for the term $K_f I_f$.

EXAMPLE 10.6

The permanent-magnet dc motor of Example 7.11 has an armature resistance of 1.03 Ω and a torque constant $K_m = 0.22$ V/(rad/sec). Assume the motor to be driving a constant-power load of 800 W (including rotational losses), and calculate the motor speed as the armature voltage is varied from 40 to 50 V.

■ **Solution**

The motor power output (including rotational losses) is given by the product $E_a I_a$ and thus we can write

$$P_{load} = E_a I_a = K_m \omega_m I_a$$

Solving for ω_m gives

$$\omega_m = \frac{P_{load}}{K_m I_a}$$

The armature current can be written as

$$I_a = \frac{(V_a - E_a)}{R_a} = \frac{(V_a - K_m \omega_m)}{R_a}$$

These two equations can be combined to give an equation for ω_m of the form

$$\omega_m^2 - \left(\frac{V_a}{K_m}\right)\omega_m + \frac{P_{load} R_a}{K_m^2} = 0$$

from which we can find

$$\omega_m = \frac{V_a}{2K_m}\left[1 \pm \sqrt{1 - \frac{4P_{load} R_a}{V_a^2}}\right]$$

Recognizing that, if the voltage drop across the armature resistance is small, $V_a \approx E_a = K_m \omega_m$, we pick the positive sign and thus

$$\omega_m = \frac{V_a}{2K_m}\left[1 + \sqrt{1 - \frac{4P_{load} R_a}{V_a^2}}\right]$$

Substituting values, we find that for $V_a = 40$ V, $\omega_m = 169.2$ rad/sec (1616 r/min) and for $V_a = 50$ V, $\omega_m = 217.5$ rad/sec (2077 r/min).

Calculate the speed variation (in r/min) of the permanent-magnet dc motor of Example 10.6 if the armature voltage is held constant at 50 V and the load power varies from 100 W to 500 W.

Solution

2077 r/min to 1540 r/min

10.1.2   Torque Control

As we have seen, the electromagnetic torque of a dc motor is proportional to the armature current I_a and is given by

$$T_{mech} = K_f I_f I_a \tag{10.7}$$

in the case of a separately excited or shunt motor and

$$T_{mech} = K_m I_a \tag{10.8}$$

in the case of a permanent-magnet motor.

From these equations we see that torque can be controlled directly by controlling the armature current. Current control can be readily implemented with power-electronics. Fig. 10.10 shows in schematic terms three possible configurations for switching a dc-current (typically supplied from a so-called dc-link inductor) to create a variable dc which can be applied directly to the armature terminals of a dc motor.

In Fig. 10.10a, a phase-controlled rectifier, in combination with a dc-link filter inductor, can be used to create a variable dc-link current which can be applied directly to the armature terminals of a dc motor. In Fig. 10.10b, a constant dc-link current is produced by a diode rectifier. The armature terminal voltage is then varied by a pulse-width modulation scheme in which switch S is alternately opened and closed. When switch S is opened, the current I_{dc} flows into the dc-motor armature while when switch S is closed, the armature is shorted and I_a decays. Thus, the duty cycle of switch S will control the average current into the armature. Finally, Fig 10.10c shows an H-bridge configuration. Appropriate control of the four switches S1 through S4

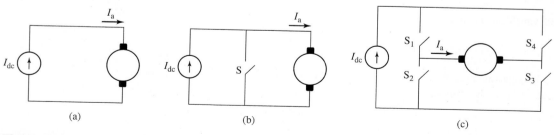

Figure 10.10   Three typical configurations for armature-current control. (a) Variable dc-link current (produced by a phase-controlled rectifier) applied directly to the dc-motor armature terminals. (b) Constant dc-link current with single-polarity pulse-width modulation. (c) Constant dc-link current with a full H-bridge.

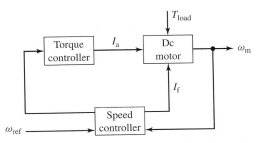

Figure 10.11 Block diagram of a dc-motor speed-control system using direct-control of motor torque.

allows this PWM system to achieve any desired armature average current in the range $-I_{dc} \leq I_a \leq I_{dc}$.

Note that in each of the PWM configurations of Fig. 10.10b and c, rapid changes in instantaneous current through the dc machine armature can give rise to large voltage spikes, which can damage the machine insulation as well as give rise to flashover and voltage breakdown of the commutator. In order to eliminate these effects, a practical system must include some sort of filter across the armature terminals (such as a large capacitor) to limit the voltage rise and to provide a low-impedance path for the high-frequency components of the drive current.

Figure 10.11 shows a typical controller in which torque control is surrounded by a speed-feedback loop. This looks similar to the speed control of Fig. 10.6. However, instead of controlling the armature voltage, in this case the output of the speed controller is a torque reference signal T_{ref} which in turn serves as the input to the torque controller. In addition to providing potentially faster control response because of the direct control of torque, another advantage of such a system is that it automatically limits the dc-motor armature current to acceptable levels under all operating conditions, as is shown in Example 10.7.

EXAMPLE 10.7

Consider the 100-hp dc motor of Example 10.2 to be driving a load whose torque varies linearly with speed such that it equals rated full-load torque (286 N · m) at a speed of 2500 r/min. We will assume the combined moment of inertia of the motor and load to equal to 15 kg·m². The field voltage is to be held constant at 300 V.

a. Calculate the armature voltage and current required to achieve speeds of 2000 and 2500 r/min and the corresponding speed voltages.

b. Assume that the motor is operated from an armature-voltage controller and that the armature voltage is suddenly switched from its 2000 r/min to its 2500 r/min value. Calculate the resultant motor speed and armature current as a function of time.

c. Assume that the motor is operated from an armature-current controller and that the armature current is suddenly switched from its 2000 r/min to its 2500 r/min value. Calculate the resultant motor speed as a function of time.

■ Solution

a. Neglecting any rotational losses, the armature current can be found from Eq. 10.2 by setting $T_{mech} = T_{load}$

$$I_a = \frac{T_{load}}{K_f I_f}$$

$$T_{load} = \left(\frac{\omega_m}{\omega_f}\right) T_{fl}$$

where n is the motor speed in rad/sec, $\omega_f = 2500 \times (\pi/30) = 261.8$ rad/sec (2500 r/min), and $T_{fl} = 286$ N · m gives

$$I_a = \frac{\omega_m T_{fl}}{\omega_f K_f I_f}$$

Solving for $V_a = E_a + I_a R_a$ then allows us to complete the following table:

[r/min]	ω_m [rad/sec]	E_a [V]	V_a [V]	I_a [A]	T_{load} [N · m]
2000	209.4	400	410	120	229
2500	261.8	500	513	150	286

b. The dynamic equation governing the speed of the motor is

$$J\frac{d\omega_m}{dt} = T_{mech} - T_{load}$$

Under armature-voltage control,

$$T_{mech} = K_f I_f I_a = K_f I_f \left(\frac{V_a - E_a}{R_a}\right)$$

$$= K_f I_f \left(\frac{V_a - K_f I_f \omega_m}{R_a}\right)$$

and thus the governing differential equation is

$$J\frac{d\omega_m}{dt} = K_f I_f \left(\frac{V_a - K_f I_f \omega_m}{R_a}\right) - \left(\frac{T_{fl}}{\omega_f}\right)\omega_m$$

or

$$\frac{d\omega_m}{dt} + \frac{1}{J}\left(\frac{T_{fl}}{\omega_f} + \frac{(K_f I_f)^2}{R_a}\right)\omega_m - \frac{K_f I_f V_a}{J R_a}$$

$$= \frac{d\omega_m}{dt} + 2.97\,\omega_m - 1.52 V_a = 0$$

From this differential equation, we see that with the motor initially at $\omega_m = \omega_i = 209$ rad/sec, if the armature voltage V_a is suddenly switched from $V_i = 410$ V to $V_f = 513$ V, the speed will rise exponentially to $\omega_m = \omega_f = 261.8$ rad/sec as

$$\omega_m = \omega_f + (\omega_i - \omega_f)e^{-t/\tau}$$

$$= 261.8 - 52.4 e^{-t/\tau} \text{ rad/sec}$$

where $\tau = 1/2.97 = 340$ msec. Expressed in terms of r/min

$$n = 2500 - 500e^{-t/\tau} \text{ r/min}$$

At the instant the voltage is first switched to to 513 V, the speed voltage will be equal to its 2000 r/min value of $E_i = 400$ V. Thus the initial value armature current will be

$$I_{a,i} = \frac{(V_f - E_i)}{R_a} = \frac{513 - 400}{0.084} = 1345 \text{ A}$$

The armature current will decrease exponentially with the same 340 msec time constant from this initial value to its final value of 150 A. Thus,

$$I_a = 150 + 1195e^{-t/\tau} \text{ A}$$

Notice that it is unlikely that the supply to the dc motor can supply this large initial current (roughly nine times the rated full-load armature current) and, in addition, the high current and corresponding high torque could potentially cause damage to the dc motor commutator, brushes, and armature winding. Hence, as a practical matter, a practical controller would undoubtedly limit the rate of change of the armature voltage to avoid such sudden steps in voltage, with the result that the speed change would not occur as rapidly as calculated here.

c. The dynamic equation governing the speed of the motor remains the same as that in part (b) as does the equation for the load torque. However, in this case, because the motor is being operated from a current controller, the electromagnetic torque will remain constant at $T_{mech} = T_{fl} = 286$ N · m after the current is switched from its initial value of 120 A to its final value of 150 A.

Thus

$$J \frac{d\omega_m}{dt} = T_{mech} - T_{load} = T_f - \left(\frac{T_{fl}}{\omega_f}\right)\omega_m$$

or

$$\frac{d\omega_m}{dt} + \left(\frac{T_{fl}}{J\omega_f}\right)\omega_m - \frac{T_{fl}}{J}$$

$$= \frac{d\omega_m}{dt} + 7.28 \times 10^{-2}\,\omega_m - 19.1 = 0$$

In this case, the speed will rise exponentially to $\omega_m = \omega_f = 261.8$ rad/sec as

$$\omega_m = \omega_f + (\omega_i - \omega_f)e^{-t/\tau}$$

$$= 261.8 - 52.4\,e^{-t/\tau} \text{ rad/sec}$$

where now the time constant $\tau = 1/0.0728 = 13.7$ sec.

Clearly, the change in motor speed under the current controller is much slower. However, at no point during this transient do either the motor current or the motor torque exceed their rated value. In addition, should faster response be desired, the armature current (and hence motor torque) could be set temporarily to a fixed value higher than the rated value (e.g., two or three times rated as compared to the factor of 9 found in part (b)), thus limiting the potential for damage to the motor.

Consider the dc motor/load combination of Example 10.7 operating under current (torque) control to be operating in the steady-state at a speed of 2000 r/min at an armature current of 119 A. If the armature current is suddenly switched to 250 A, calculate the time required for the motor to reach a speed of 2500 r/min.

Solution

3.6 sec

10.2 CONTROL OF SYNCHRONOUS MOTORS

10.2.1 Speed Control

As discussed in Chapters 4 and 5, synchronous motors are essentially constant-speed machines, with their speed being determined by the frequency of the armature currents as described by Eqs. 4.42 and 4.44. Specifically, Eq. 4.42 shows that the synchronous angular velocity is proportional to the electrical frequency of the applied armature voltage and inversely proportional to the number of poles in the machine

$$\omega_s = \left(\frac{2}{\text{poles}} \right) \omega_e \tag{10.9}$$

where

ω_s = synchronous spatial angular velocity of the air-gap mmf wave [rad/sec]
$\omega_e = 2\pi f_e$ = angular frequency of the applied electrical excitation [rad/sec]
f_e = applied electrical frequency [Hz]

Clearly, the simplest means of synchronous motor control is speed control via control of the frequency of the applied armature voltage, driving the motor by a polyphase voltage-source inverter such as the three-phase inverter shown in Fig. 10.12. The rectifier section produces dc-voltage V_{dc} on the "dc-link" capacitor and controlling the switches in the Inverter section can be used to produce pulse-width-modulated (PWM) ac voltage waveforms of variable amplitude. The dc-link voltage V_{dc} can itself be varied, for example, through the use of a phase control in the rectifier section.

The frequency of the inverter output waveforms can of course be varied by controlling the switching frequency of the inverter switches. For ac-machine applications, coupled with this frequency control must be control of the amplitude of the applied voltage, as we will now see.

From Faraday's Law, we know that the air-gap component of the armature voltage in an ac machine is proportional to the peak flux density in the machine and the electrical frequency. Thus, if we neglect the voltage drop across the armature resistance and leakage reactance, we can write

$$V_a = \left(\frac{f_e}{f_{\text{rated}}} \right) \left(\frac{B_{\text{peak}}}{B_{\text{rated}}} \right) V_{\text{rated}} \tag{10.10}$$

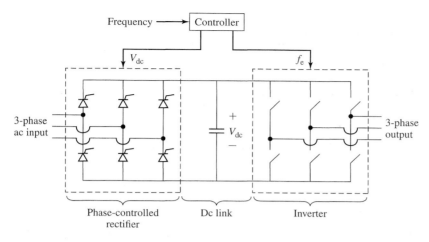

Figure 10.12 Three-phase voltage-source inverter.

where V_a is the amplitude of the armature voltage, f_e is the operating frequency, and B_{peak} is the peak air-gap flux density. V_{rated}, f_{rated}, and B_{rated} are the corresponding rated-operating-point values.

Consider a situation in which the frequency of the armature voltage is varied while its amplitude is maintained at its rated value ($V_a = V_{rated}$). Under these conditions, from Eq. 10.10 we see that

$$B_{peak} = \left(\frac{f_{rated}}{f_e}\right) B_{rated} \tag{10.11}$$

Equation 10.11 clearly demonstrates the problem with constant-voltage, variable-frequency operation. Specifically, for a given armature voltage, the machine flux density is inversely proportional to frequency and thus as the frequency is reduced, the flux density will increase. Thus for a typical machine which operates in saturation at rated voltage and frequency, any reduction in frequency will further increase the flux density in the machine. In fact, a significant drop in frequency will increase the flux density to the point of potential machine damage due both to increased core loss and to the increased machine currents required to support the higher flux density.

As a result, for frequencies less than or equal to rated frequency, it is typical to operate a machine at constant flux density. From Eq. 10.10, with $B_{peak} = B_{rated}$

$$V_a = \left(\frac{f_e}{f_{rated}}\right) V_{rated} \tag{10.12}$$

which can be rewritten as

$$\frac{V_a}{f_e} = \frac{V_{rated}}{f_{rated}} \tag{10.13}$$

From Eq. 10.13, we see that constant-flux operation can be achieved by maintaining a constant ratio of armature voltage to frequency. This is referred to as *constant-volts-per-hertz* (constant V/Hz) operation. It is typically maintained from rated frequency down to the low frequency at which the armature resistance voltage drop becomes a significant component of the applied voltage.

The machine terminal current is typically limited by thermal constraints. Thus, provided the machine cooling is not affected by rotor speed, the maximum permissible terminal current will remain constant at its rated value I_{rated}, independent of the applied frequency. As a result, for frequencies below rated frequency, with V_a proportional to f_e, the maximum machine power will be proportional to $f_e V_{rated} I_{rated}$. The maximum torque under these conditions can be found by dividing the power by the rotor speed ω_s, which is also proportional to f_e as can be seen from Eq. 10.9. Thus, we see that the maximum torque is proportional to $V_{rated} I_{rated}$, and hence it is constant at its rated-operating-point value.

Similarly, we see from Eq. 10.10 that if the machine is operated at frequencies in excess of rated frequency with the voltage at its rated value, the air-gap flux density will drop below its rated value. Thus, in order to maintain the flux density at its rated value, it would be necessary to increase the terminal voltage for frequencies in excess of rated frequency. However, in order to avoid insulation damage, it is common to maintain the machine terminal voltage at its rated value for frequencies in excess of rated frequency. Under this condition, with both terminal current and voltage limited to their rated values, the maximum power will be constant and equal to $V_{rated} I_{rated}$, the rated power. The corresponding maximum torque will then vary inversely with machine speed as $V_{rated} I_{rated}/\omega_s$. The maximum operating speed for this operating regime will be determined either by the maximum frequency which can be supplied by the drive electronics or by the maximum speed at which the rotor can be operated without risk of damage due to mechanical concerns such as excessive centrifugal force or to the presence of a resonance in the shaft system.

Figure 10.13 shows a plot of maximum power and maximum torque versus speed for a synchronous motor under variable-frequency operation. The operating regime below rated frequency and speed is referred to as the *constant-torque regime* and that above rated speed is referred to as the *constant-power regime*.

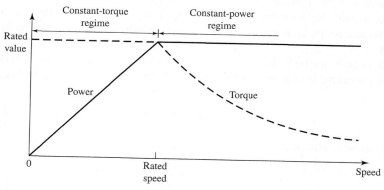

Figure 10.13   Variable-speed operating regimes for a synchronous motor.

EXAMPLE 10.8

The 45-kVA, 220-V, 60-Hz, six-pole, three-phase synchronous machine of Example 5.4 is to be operated as a motor and driven from a variable-frequency, three-phase voltage-source inverter which provides 220 V at 60 Hz and which maintains constant V/Hz as the frequency is reduced. The machine has a saturated synchronous reactance of 0.836 per unit and achieves rated open-circuit voltage at a field current of 2.84 A. For the purposes of this example, assume that the motor losses are negligible.

a. With the motor operating at 60 Hz, 220 V and at rated power, unity power factor, calculate (i) the motor speed in r/min and (ii) the motor field current.
b. If the inverter frequency is reduced to 50 Hz and the motor load adjusted to rated torque, calculate the (i) the resulting motor speed and (ii) and the motor field current required to again achieve unity-power-factor operation.

■ **Solution**

a. (i) The motor will operate at its synchronous speed which can be found from Eq. 4.44

$$n_s = \left(\frac{120}{\text{poles}}\right) f_e = \left(\frac{120}{6}\right) 60 = 1200 \text{ r/min}$$

(ii) As seen in Chapter 5, the field current can be determined from the generated voltage. For motor operation,

$$\hat{E}_{af} = \hat{V}_a - jX_s\hat{I}_a = 1.0 - j0.836 \times 1.0 = 1.30 \angle -39.9° \text{ per unit}$$

where V_a has been chosen as the reference phasor. Thus the field current is

$$I_f = 1.30 \times 2.84 = 3.70 \text{ A}$$

Note that we have chosen to solve for E_{af} in per unit. A solution in real units would of course have produced the same result.

b. (i) When the frequency is reduced from 60 Hz to 50 Hz, the motor speed will drop from 1200 r/min to 1000 r/min.

(ii) Let us again consider the equation for the generated voltage

$$\hat{E}_{af} = \hat{V}_a - jX_s\hat{I}_a$$

where here we will assume that the equation is written in real units with the voltages equal to their line-neutral values.

As the inverter frequency is reduced from 60 Hz, the inverter voltage will drop proportionally since the inverter maintains constant V/Hz. Thus we can write

$$V_a = \left(\frac{\omega_m}{\omega_{m0}}\right) V_{a0}$$

where the subscript 0 is used to indicate a 60-Hz value as found in part (a). Reactance is also proportional to frequency and thus

$$X_s = \left(\frac{\omega_m}{\omega_{m0}}\right) X_{s0}$$

The generated voltage is proportional to both the motor speed (and hence the frequency) and the field current, and thus we can write

$$E_{af} = \left(\frac{\omega_m}{\omega_{m0}}\right) \left(\frac{I_f}{I_{f0}}\right) E_{af0}$$

Finally, if we recognize that, to operate at rated torque and unity power factor under this reduced frequency condition, the motor armature current will have to be equal to the value found in part (a), i.e., $I_a = I_{a0}$, we can write the generated voltage equation as

$$\left(\frac{\omega_m}{\omega_{m0}}\right) \left(\frac{I_f}{I_{f0}}\right) \hat{E}_{af0} = \left(\frac{\omega_m}{\omega_{m0}}\right) \hat{V}_{a0} - j \left(\frac{\omega_m}{\omega_{m0}}\right) X_{s0} \hat{I}_{a0}$$

or

$$\left(\frac{I_f}{I_{f0}}\right) \hat{E}_{af0} = \hat{V}_{a0} - j X_{s0} \hat{I}_{a0}$$

Since the subscripted quantities correspond to the solution of part (a), they must satisfy

$$\hat{E}_{af0} = \hat{V}_{a0} - j X_{s0} \hat{I}_{a0}$$

and thus we see that we must have $I_f = I_{f0}$. In other words, the field current for this operating condition is equal to that found in part (a), or $I_f = 3.70$ A.

Practice Problem 10.5

Consider 50-Hz operation of the synchronous motor of Example 10.8, part (b). If the load torque is reduced to 75 percent of rated torque, calculate the field current required to achieve unity power factor.

Solution

3.35 A

Although during steady-state operation the speed of a synchronous motor is determined by the frequency of the drive, speed control by means of frequency control is of limited use in practice. This is due in most part to the fact that it is difficult for the rotor of a synchronous machine to track arbitrary changes in the frequency of the applied armature voltage. In addition, starting is a major problem, and, as a result, the rotors of synchronous motors are often equipped with a squirrel-cage winding known as an *amortisseur* or *damper winding* similar to the squirrel-cage winding in an induction motor, as shown in Fig. 5.3. Following the application of a polyphase voltage to the armature, the rotor will come up almost to synchronous speed by induction-motor action with the field winding unexcited. If the load and inertia are not too great, the motor will pull into synchronism when the field winding is subsequently energized.

Problems with changing speed result from the fact that, in order to develop torque, the rotor of a synchronous motor must remain in synchronism with the stator flux. Control of synchronous motors can be greatly enhanced by control algorithms in which the stator flux and its relationship to the rotor flux are controlled directly. Such control, which amounts to direct control of torque, is discussed in Section 10.2.2.

10.2.2 Torque Control

Direct torque control in an ac machine, which can be implemented in a number of different ways, is commonly referred to as *field-oriented control* or *vector control*. To facilitate our discussion of field-oriented control, it is helpful to return to the discussion of Section 5.6.1. Under this viewpoint, which is formalized in Appendix C, stator quantities (flux, current, voltage, etc.) are resolved into components which rotate in synchronism with the rotor. *Direct-axis* quantities represent those components which are aligned with the field-winding axis, and *quadrature-axis* components are aligned perpendicular to the field-winding axis.

Section C.2 of Appendix C derives the basic machine relations in dq0 variables for a synchronous machine consisting of a field winding and a three-phase stator winding. The transformed flux-current relationships are found to be

$$\lambda_d = L_d i_d + L_{af} i_f \tag{10.14}$$

$$\lambda_q = L_q i_q \tag{10.15}$$

$$\lambda_f = \frac{3}{2} L_{af} i_d + L_{ff} i_f \tag{10.16}$$

where the subscripts d, q, and f refer to armature direct-, quadrature-axis, and field-winding quantities respectively. Note that throughout this chapter we will assume balanced operating conditions, in which case zero-sequence quantities will be zero and hence will be ignored.

The corresponding transformed voltage equations are

$$v_d = R_a i_d + \frac{d\lambda_d}{dt} - \omega_{me} \lambda_q \tag{10.17}$$

$$v_q = R_a i_q + \frac{d\lambda_q}{dt} + \omega_{me} \lambda_d \tag{10.18}$$

$$v_f = R_f i_f + \frac{d\lambda_f}{dt} \tag{10.19}$$

where $\omega_{me} = (poles/2)\omega_m$ is the electrical angular velocity of the rotor.

Finally, the electromagnetic torque acting on the rotor of a synchronous motor is shown to be (Eq. C.31)

$$T_{mech} = \frac{3}{2} \left(\frac{poles}{2} \right) (\lambda_d i_q - \lambda_q i_d) \tag{10.20}$$

Under steady-state, balanced-three-phase operating conditions, $\omega_{me} = \omega_e$ where ω_e is the electrical frequency of the armature voltage and current in rad/sec. Because the armature-produced mmf and flux waves rotate in synchronism with the rotor and hence with respect to the dq reference frame, under these conditions an observer in the dq reference frame will see constant fluxes, and hence one can set $d/dt = 0$.[1]

---

[1] This can easily be derived formally by substituting expressions for the balanced-three-phase armature currents and voltages into the transformation equations.

Letting the subscripts F, D, and Q indicate the corresponding constant, steady-state values of field-, direct- and quadrature-axis quantities respectively, the flux-current relationships of Eqs. 10.14 through 10.16 then become

$$\lambda_D = L_d i_D + L_{af} i_F \tag{10.21}$$

$$\lambda_Q = L_q i_Q \tag{10.22}$$

$$\lambda_F = \frac{3}{2} L_{af} i_D + L_{ff} i_F \tag{10.23}$$

Armature resistance is typically quite small, and, if we neglect it, the steady-state voltage equations (Eqs. 10.17 through 10.19) then become

$$v_D = -\omega_e \lambda_Q \tag{10.24}$$

$$v_Q = \omega_e \lambda_D \tag{10.25}$$

$$v_F = R_f i_F \tag{10.26}$$

Finally, we can write Eq. 10.20 as

$$T_{mech} = \frac{3}{2} \left(\frac{poles}{2} \right) (\lambda_D i_Q - \lambda_Q i_D) \tag{10.27}$$

From this point on, we will focus our attention on machines in which the effects of saliency can be neglected. In this case, the direct- and quadrature-axis synchronous inductances are equal and we can write

$$L_d = L_q = L_s \tag{10.28}$$

where L_s is the synchronous inductance. Substitution into Eqs. 10.21 and 10.22 and then into Eq. 10.27 gives

$$T_{mech} = \frac{3}{2} \left(\frac{poles}{2} \right) [(L_s i_D + L_{af} i_F) i_Q - L_s i_Q i_D]$$

$$= \frac{3}{2} \left(\frac{poles}{2} \right) L_{af} i_F i_Q \tag{10.29}$$

Equation 10.29 shows that torque is produced by the interaction of the field flux (proportional to the field current) and the quadrature-axis component of the armature current, in other words, the component of armature current that is orthogonal to the field flux. We also see that, for a non-salient machine, the direct-axis component of armature current, which is aligned with the field flux, produces no torque.

This result is fully consistent with the generalized torque expressions which are derived in Chapter 4. Consider for example Eq. 4.75 which expresses the torque in terms of the product of the stator and rotor mmfs (F_s and F_r respectively) and the sine of the angle between them.

$$T = -\left(\frac{poles}{2} \right) \left(\frac{\mu_0 \pi D l}{2g} \right) F_s F_r \sin \delta_{sr} \tag{10.30}$$

where δ_{sr} is the electrical space angle between the stator and rotor mmfs. This shows clearly that no torque will be produced by the direct-axis component of the armature mmf which, by definition, is that component of the stator mmf which is aligned with that of the field winding on the rotor.

Equation 10.29 shows the torque in a nonsalient synchronous motor is proportional to the product of the field current and the quadrature-axis component of the armature current. This is directly analogous to torque production in a dc machine for which Eqs. 7.13 and 7.16 can be combined to show that the torque is proportional to the product of the field current and the armature current.

The analogy between a non-salient synchronous machine and dc machine can be further reinforced. Consider Eq. 5.21, which expresses the rms value of the line-neutral generated voltage of a synchronous generator as

$$E_{af} = \frac{\omega_e L_{af} i_F}{\sqrt{2}} \tag{10.31}$$

Substitution into Eq. 10.29 gives

$$T_{mech} = \frac{3}{2}\left(\frac{poles}{\sqrt{2}}\right)\frac{E_{af}i_Q}{\omega_e} \tag{10.32}$$

This is directly analogous to Eq. 7.19 ($T_{mech} = E_a I_a/\omega_m$) for a dc machine in which the torque is proportional to the product of the generated voltage and the armature current.

The brushes and commutator of a dc machine force the commutated armature current and armature flux along the quadrature axis such that $I_d = 0$. It is the interaction of the quadrature-axis flux with the direct-axis field flux that produces the torque.[2] A field-oriented controller which senses the position of the rotor and controls the quadrature-axis component of armature current produces the same effect in a synchronous machine.

Although the direct-axis component of the armature current does not play a role in torque production, it does play a role in determining the resultant stator flux and hence the machine terminal voltage, as can be readily shown. Specifically, from the transformation equations of Appendix C,

$$v_a = v_D \cos(\omega_e t) - v_Q \sin(\omega_e t) \tag{10.33}$$

and thus the rms amplitude of the line-neutral armature voltage is equal to[3]

$$V_a = \sqrt{\frac{v_D^2 + v_Q^2}{2}} = \omega_e \sqrt{\frac{\lambda_D^2 + \lambda_Q^2}{2}}$$

$$= \omega_e \sqrt{\frac{(L_s i_D + L_{af} i_F)^2 + (L_s i_Q)^2}{2}} \tag{10.34}$$

---

[2] In a practical dc motor, the brushes may be adjusted away from this ideal condition somewhat to improve commutation. In this case, some direct-axis current will result, producing a small direct-axis component of armature flux.

[3] Strictly speaking, armature resistance should be included in the voltage expression, in which case the rms amplitude of the armature voltage would be given by the expression

$$V_a = \sqrt{\frac{v_D^2 + v_Q^2}{2}} = \sqrt{\frac{(R_a i_D - \omega_e \lambda_Q)^2 + (R_a i_Q + \omega_e \lambda_D)^2}{2}}$$

Dividing the rms line-neutral voltage V_a by the electrical frequency ω_e, we get an expression for the rms armature line-neutral flux linkage

$$(\lambda_a)_{rms} = \frac{V_a}{\omega_e} = \sqrt{\frac{\lambda_D^2 + \lambda_Q^2}{2}} = \sqrt{\frac{(L_s i_D + L_{af} i_F)^2 + (L_s i_Q)^2}{2}} \quad (10.35)$$

Similarly, the transformation equations of Appendix C can be used to show that the rms amplitude of the armature current is equal to

$$I_a = \sqrt{\frac{i_D^2 + i_Q^2}{2}} \quad (10.36)$$

From Eq. 10.29 we see that torque is controlled by the product $i_F i_Q$ of the field current and the quadrature-axis component of the armature current. Thus, simply specifying a desired torque is not sufficient to uniquely determine either i_F or i_Q. In fact, under the field-oriented-control viewpoint presented here, there are actually three indpendent variables, i_F, i_Q and i_D, and, in general, three constraints will be required to uniquely determine them. In addition to specifying the desired torque, a typical controller will implement additional constraints on the terminal flux-linkage and current using the basic relationships found in Eqs. 10.35 and 10.36.

Figure 10.14a shows a typical field-oriented torque-control system in block-diagram form. The control system calculates reference values (set points) for the various motor currents, indicated by the subscript "ref". We will assume ideal controller performance such that under steady-state conditions the currents supplied to the motor are equal to their reference values, i.e., $i_D = (i_d)_{ref}$, $i_Q = (i_q)_{ref}$, and $i_F = (i_f)_{ref}$, and we will use these values interchangeably as appropriate.

The torque-controller block, which calculates the quadrature-axis current reference value $(i_q)_{ref}$, has two reference inputs, torque (T_{ref}) and field current $((i_f)_{ref})$. $(i_f)_{ref}$ is calculated by an auxiliary controller which also determines the reference value $(i_d)_{ref}$ of the direct-axis current.

The torque controller calculates $(i_q)_{ref}$ from Eq. 10.29 based upon T_{ref} and $(i_f)_{ref}$

$$(i_q)_{ref} = \frac{2}{3} \left(\frac{2}{poles} \right) \frac{T_{ref}}{L_{af}(i_f)_{ref}} \quad (10.37)$$

Note that a position sensor is required to determine the angular position of the rotor in order to implement the dq0 to abc transformation which determines the reference values for the motor phase currents which are supplied by the 3-phase current-source inverter.

In many applications, the ultimate control objective is not to control motor torque but to control speed or position. Figure 10.14b shows how the torque-control system of Fig. 10.14b can be used as a component of a speed-control system, with speed feedback forming an outer control loop around the inner torque-control loop.

EXAMPLE 10.9

Consider again the 45-kVA, 220-V, six-pole synchronous motor of Example 10.8 operating at 60 Hz with a field current of 3.70 A. If the motor is loaded to rated torque and operating at

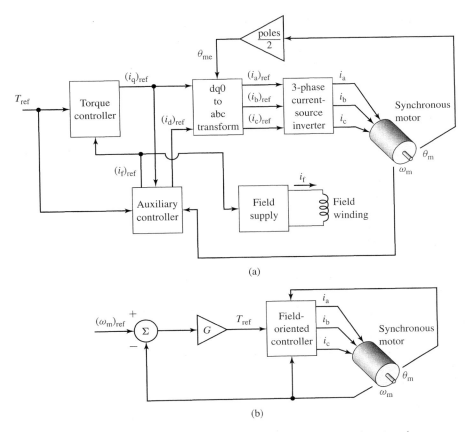

Figure 10.14 (a) Block diagram of a field-oriented torque-control system for a synchronous motor. (b) Block diagram of a synchronous-motor speed-control loop built around a field-oriented torque control system.

rated speed in the steady-state under a field-oriented control system such that $i_D = 0$, calculate (a) the per-unit armature current and (b) the motor terminal voltage in per unit.

■ Solution

a. We must first calculate L_{af}. From Example 10.8, we see that the motor produces rated 60-Hz open-circuit voltage (220-V rms, line-line) at a field current of 2.84 A. From Eq. 10.31

$$L_{af} = \frac{\sqrt{2}\, E_{af}}{\omega_e i_F}$$

where E_{af} is the rms, line-neutral generated voltage. Thus

$$L_{af} = \frac{\sqrt{2} \times (220/\sqrt{3})}{120\pi \times 2.84} = 0.168\ \text{H}$$

Rated torque for this six-pole motor is equal to

$$T_{\text{rated}} = \frac{P_{\text{rated}}}{(\omega_{\text{m}})_{\text{rated}}} = \frac{P_{\text{rated}}}{(\omega_{\text{e}})_{\text{rated}} \times (2/\text{poles})}$$

$$= \frac{45 \times 10^3}{120\pi \times (2/6)} = 358 \text{ N} \cdot \text{m}$$

Thus, setting $T_{\text{ref}} = T_{\text{rated}} = 358 \text{ N} \cdot \text{m}$ and $i_F = 3.70$ A, we can find i_Q from Eq. 10.37 as

$$i_Q = \frac{2}{3}\left(\frac{2}{\text{poles}}\right)\frac{T_{\text{ref}}}{L_{\text{af}} \, i_F} = \frac{2}{3}\left(\frac{2}{6}\right)\frac{358}{0.168 \times 3.70} = 128 \text{ A}$$

With $i_D = 0$, from Eq. 10.36 the rms armature current is equal to

$$I_a = \frac{i_Q}{\sqrt{2}} = 90.5 \text{ A}$$

The base current of this motor is

$$I_{\text{base}} = \frac{P_{\text{base}}}{\sqrt{3} \, V_{\text{base}}} = \frac{45 \times 10^3}{\sqrt{3} \times 220} = 118 \text{ A}$$

and thus $I_a = 90.5/118 = 0.77$ per unit.

b. With $i_D = 0$, from Eq. 10.21

$$\lambda_D = L_{\text{af}} i_F = 0.168 \times 3.70 = 0.622 \text{ Wb}$$

The base-inductance impedance of this machine is

$$Z_{\text{base}} = \frac{V_{\text{base}}^2}{P_{\text{base}}} = \frac{220^2}{45 \times 10^3} = 1.08 \; \Omega$$

and the corresponding base inductance is

$$L_{\text{base}} = \frac{Z_{\text{base}}}{(\omega_{\text{e}})_{\text{base}}} = \frac{1.08}{120 \, \pi} = 2.87 \text{ mH}$$

and thus the synchronous inductance is $L_s = 0.836 \times 2.87 \text{ mH} = 2.40 \text{ mH}$.

From Eq. 10.22 (with $L_q = L_s$ since this is a non-salient motor)

$$\lambda_Q = L_s i_Q = (2.40 \times 10^{-3}) \times 128 = 0.307 \text{ Wb}$$

Finally, from Eq. 10.34, the line-neutral voltage under this operating condition is

$$V_a = \omega_{\text{e}} \sqrt{\frac{\lambda_D^2 + \lambda_Q^2}{2}} = (120 \, \pi) \sqrt{\frac{0.620^2 + 0.307^2}{2}} = 184 \text{ V}$$

corresponding to a line-line terminal voltage of 320 V, considerably in excess of the 220 V rated voltage. In practice, in addition to the fact that this operation is likely to damage the motor insulation, it is unlikely to be achieved because the motor would be highly saturated and hence the synchronous inductance and field-armature mutual inductance will be lower than assumed here.

In the next example, we will see how a different choice of i_F, i_D, and i_Q can produce the same torque at a reduced terminal voltage.

EXAMPLE 10.10

In this example, we will re-visit Example 10.9 with the objective of examining a field-oriented controller which sets the motor torque equal to its rated value T_{rated} and which checks if the rms line-neutral armature flux linkage $(\lambda_a)_{\text{rms}}$ is greater than the rated value and if so, supplies direct-axis current to reduce $(\lambda_a)_{\text{rms}}$ to its rated value.

Write a MATLAB script that applies this algorithm and searches over field currents up to 5.0 A for an operating point which requires the minimum value of armature current. Note that because the motor is operating at rated speed and frequency and because the armature flux linkage is constrained to the rated value at maximum, the motor terminal voltage will not exceed the rated value of 220 V line-line as opposed to the 320 V result with the controller of Example 10.9.

■ Solution

From Eq. 10.35, the rated value of the rms line-neutral flux linkage (corresponding to rated terminal voltage) is equal to

$$(\lambda_a)_{\text{rated}} = \frac{V_{\text{rated}}}{\omega_e} = \frac{220/\sqrt{3}}{120\,\pi} = 337 \text{ mWb}$$

The MATLAB script will implement the following algorithm:

■ From Eq. 10.35 we see that there is a maximum value of i_Q such that i_D can be adjusted (by varying i_F) to set $(\lambda_a)_{\text{rms}}$ equal to $(\lambda_a)_{\text{rated}}$

$$(i_Q)_{\text{max}} = \frac{\sqrt{2}\,(\lambda_a)_{\text{rated}}}{L_s}$$

■ Based upon the requirement to achieve rated torque T_{rated}, the corresponding minimum value of field current can be found from Eq. 10.29 as

$$(i_F)_{\text{min}} = \frac{2}{3}\left(\frac{2}{\text{poles}}\right)\frac{T_{\text{rated}}}{L_{\text{af}}(i_Q)_{\text{max}}}$$

■ For each value of field current i_F, calculate i_Q from Eq. 10.37 as

$$i_Q = \frac{2}{3}\left(\frac{2}{\text{poles}}\right)\frac{T_{\text{rated}}}{L_{\text{af}}\,i_F}$$

■ Setting $i_D = 0$, calculate the rms line-neutral armature flux linkage from Eq. 10.35

$$(\lambda_a)_{\text{rms}} = \sqrt{\frac{(L_{\text{af}}i_F)^2 + (L_s i_Q)^2}{2}}$$

■ Check if $(\lambda_a)_{\text{rms}}$ is greater than the rated value $(\lambda_a)_{\text{rated}}$. If yes, then using Eq. 10.35, calculate the direct-axis current required to set the rms line-neutral flux linkage equal to the rated value.

$$i_D = \frac{\sqrt{2\,(\lambda_a)_{\text{rated}}^2 - (L_s\,i_Q)^2} - L_{\text{af}}i_F}{L_s}$$

■ The rms line-neutral armature flux linkage can be calculated from Eq. 10.35 as

$$(\lambda_a)_{\text{rms}} = \sqrt{\frac{(L_s i_D + L_{\text{af}}i_F)^2 + (L_s i_Q)^2}{2}}$$

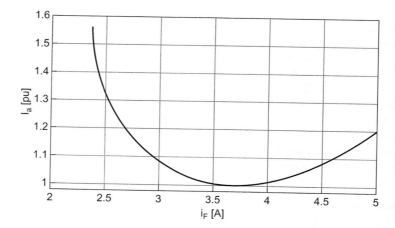

Figure 10.15   Plot of per-unit armature current versus field current for Example 10.10.

and the rms line-neutral terminal voltage can be calculated as

$$V_a = \omega_e (\lambda_a)_{rms}$$

■ Finally, the rms armature current can be calculated from Eq. 10.36 as

$$I_a = \sqrt{\frac{i_D^2 + i_Q^2}{2}}$$

and its per-unit value as I_a / I_{rated}.

Figure 10.15 is a plot of the resultant armature current versus field current. The minimum armature current of 1.00 per unit (118 A) occurs at a field current of 3.70 A. The direct- and quadrature-axis currents under this condition are $i_D = -107$ A and $i_Q = 128$ A and the corresponding terminal voltage is 220 V, line-line.

Here is the MATLAB script:

```
clc
clear

%%%%%%%%%%%%%
% Motor parameters
%%%%%%%%%%%%%%

Prated = 45e3;
Vrated = 220;
Irated = Prated/(sqrt(3)*Vrated);
poles = 6;
Lspu = 0.836;
AFNL = 2.84;
frated = 60;
```

```
omegaerated = 2*pi*frated;
omegamrated = omegaerated*(2/poles);

% Base impedance and inductance
Zbase = Vrated^2/Prated;
Lbase = Zbase/omegaerated;

% Synchronous inductance
Ls = Lspu*Lbase;

% Rated line-neutral voltage
Varated = Vrated/sqrt(3);

% Calculate Laf
Laf = sqrt(2)*Varated/(omegaerated*AFNL);

% Rated rms line-neutral flux linkage
Lambdaarated = Varated/omegaerated;

% Maximum value of iQ so that flux linkage
% can be limited to rated value
iQmax = sqrt(2)*Lambdaarated/Ls;

% Rated torque
Trated = Prated/omegamrated;

% Define range of iF starting with minimum value
% of field current to insure rated torque.
iFmin = (2/3)*(2/poles)*Trated/(Laf*iQmax);
iFmax = 5.0;

% Search over the field current to find that value
% which results in minimum armature current
deliF = 0.001;
n = 0;
iF = iFmin;

while iF <= iFmax
  n = n+1;
  ifld(n) = iF;
  iQ(n) = (2/3)*(2/poles)*Trated./(Laf*iF);
  iD(n) = 0;
  Lambdaarms = sqrt(((Laf*iF)^2+(Ls*iQ(n))^2)/2);
% iD required if Lambdaarms > Lambdaarated
  if Lambdaarms > Lambdaarated
```

```
        iD(n) = (sqrt(2*Lambdaarated^2-(Ls*iQ(n))^2) - Laf*iF)/Ls;
    end
    Ia(n) = sqrt((iD(n)*iD(n) + iQ(n)*iQ(n))/2);
    Iapu(n) = Ia(n)/Irated;
    iF = iF + deliF;
end

% Find index to minimum Ia
m = find(Ia == min(Ia));

Ia_min = Ia(m);
Iapu_min = Iapu(m);
iF_min = ifld(m);
iD_min = iD(m);
iQ_min = iQ(m);
lambdaa_min = sqrt(((Laf*iF_min+Ls*iD_min)^2+(Ls*iQ_min)^2)/2);
Va_min = omegaerated*lambdaa_min;

fprintf('At iF = %1.2f:\n',iF_min)
fprintf('   Va = %3.1f [V, l-1]\n',sqrt(3)*Va_min)
fprintf('   Ia = %2.1f [A] = %1.2f [pu]\n',Ia_min,Iapu_min)
fprintf('   iQ = %2.1f [A], iD = %2.1f [pu]\n\n',iQ_min,iD_min)

% Plot the results
hold off
plot(ifld,Iapu,'LineWidth',2)
set(gca,'FontSize',20)
xlabel('i_F [A]','FontSize',20)
ylabel('I_a [pu]','FontSize',20)
set(gca,'ylim',[0.98,1.6])
set(gca,'ytick',[1.0 1.1 1.2 1.3 1.4 1.5 1.6])
set(gca,'xlim',[2 5])
set(gca,'xtick',[2.0 2.5 3.0 3.5 4.0 4.5 5.0])
grid on
```

As we have discussed, a practical field-oriented control must determine values for all three currents i_F, i_D, and i_Q. In Example 10.9 two of these values were chosen relatively arbitrarily ($i_F = 2.84$ and $i_D = 0$) and the result was a control that achieved the desired torque but with a terminal voltage 30 percent in excess of the motor-rated voltage. In a practical system, additional constraints are required to achieve an acceptable control algorithm. One such algorithm would be to require that the motor operate at rated flux and at minimum armature current, subject to the constraint that the terminal voltage not exceed its rated value, as is illustrated in Example 10.10, with negative direct-axis current added as needed to reduce the armature flux linkages.

The discussion of this section has focused upon synchronous machines with field windings and the corresponding capability to control the field excitation. The basic concept, of course, also applies to synchronous machines with permanent magnets on the rotor. However, in the case of permanent-magnet synchronous machines, the effective field excitation is fixed and, as a result, there is one less degree of freedom for the field-oriented control algorithm.

For a permanent-magnet synchronous machine, since the effective equivalent field current is fixed by the permanent magnet, the quadrature-axis current is determined directly by the desired torque. Consider a three-phase permanent-magnet motor which produces rated rms, line-neutral open-circuit $(E_{af})_{rated}$ at electrical frequency ω_e. From Eq. 10.31 we see that the equivalent $L_{af}i_F$ product for this motor, which we will refer to by the symbol Λ_{PM}, is

$$\Lambda_{PM} = \frac{\sqrt{2}(E_{af})_{rated}}{\omega_e} \qquad (10.38)$$

Thus, the direct-axis flux-current relationship for this motor, corresponding to Eq. 10.21, becomes

$$\lambda_D = L_d i_D + \Lambda_{PM} \qquad (10.39)$$

and the torque expression of Eq. 10.29 becomes

$$T_{mech} = \frac{3}{2}\left(\frac{\text{poles}}{2}\right)\Lambda_{PM}i_Q \qquad (10.40)$$

From Eq. 10.40 we see that, for a permanent-magnet synchronous machine under field-oriented control, the quadrature-axis current is uniquely determined by the desired torque and Eq. 10.37 becomes

$$(i_Q)_{ref} = \frac{2}{3}\left(\frac{2}{\text{poles}}\right)\frac{T_{ref}}{\Lambda_{PM}} \qquad (10.41)$$

Once $(i_Q)_{ref}$ has been specified, the only remaining control choice remains to determine the desired value for the direct-axis current, $(i_D)_{ref}$. One possibility is simply to set $(i_D)_{ref} = 0$. This will clearly result in the lowest possible armature current for a given torque. However, as we have seen in Example 10.9, in some cases, this will result in a terminal voltage in excess of the rated voltage of the machine. As a result, under these conditions it is common to supply direct-axis current so as to reduce the direct-axis flux linkage of Eq. 10.39, which will in turn reduce the terminal voltage. This technique is commonly referred to as *flux weakening* and comes at the expense of increased armature current.[4] Figure 10.16 shows the block diagram for a field-oriented-control system for use with a permanent-magnet motor.

---

[4] See T. M. Jahns, "Flux-Weakening Regime Operation of an Interior Permanent Magnet Synchronous Motor Drive," *IEEE Transactions on Industry Applications,* Vol. 23, pp. 681–689.

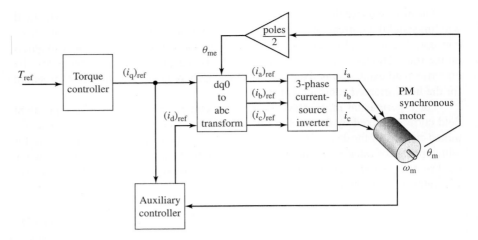

Figure 10.16   Block diagram of a field-oriented torque-control system for a permanent-magnet synchronous motor.

EXAMPLE 10.11

A 25-kW, 4000-r/min, 220-V, two-pole, three-phase permanent-magnet synchronous motor produces rated open-circuit voltage at a rotational speed of 3200 r/min and has a synchronous inductance of 1.75 mH. Assume the motor is to be operated under field-oriented control at 2800 r/min and 65 percent of rated torque.

a. Calculate the required quadrature-axis current.
b. If the motor is operated with quadrature-axis current only ($i_D = 0$), calculate the resultant per-unit armature flux linkage.
c. If the field-oriented controller is set to maintain the armature flux-linkage at its rated value (1.0 per unit), calculate the corresponding value of i_D and the corresponding rms and per-unit values of the armature current.

■ Solution

a. The rated speed of this machine is

$$(\omega_m)_{rated} = 4000 \left(\frac{\pi}{30}\right) = 419 \text{ rad/sec}$$

and the rated torque is

$$T_{rated} = \frac{P_{rated}}{(\omega_m)_{rated}} = \frac{25 \times 10^3}{419} = 59.7 \text{ N} \cdot \text{m}$$

This motor achieves its rated-open-circuit voltage of $220/\sqrt{3} = 127$ V rms at a speed of $n = 3200$ r/min. The corresponding electrical frequency is

$$\omega_e = \left(\frac{\text{poles}}{2}\right) \left(\frac{\pi}{30}\right) n = \left(\frac{\pi}{30}\right) 3200 = 335 \text{ rad/sec}$$

From Eq. 10.38,

$$\Lambda_{PM} = \frac{\sqrt{2}(E_{af})_{rated}}{\omega_e} = \frac{\sqrt{2} \times 127}{335} = 0.536 \text{ Wb}$$

Thus, setting $T_{ref} = 0.65 \times T_{rated} = 38.8 \text{ N} \cdot \text{m}$, from Eq. 10.41 we find that

$$(i_Q)_{ref} = \frac{2}{3}\left(\frac{2}{\text{poles}}\right)\frac{T_{ref}}{\Lambda_{PM}} = \frac{2}{3}\left(\frac{38.8}{0.536}\right) = 48.3 \text{ A}$$

c. With $(i_D)_{ref} = 0$,

$$\lambda_D = \Lambda_{PM} = 0.536 \text{ Wb}$$

and

$$\lambda_Q = L_s i_Q = 1.75 \times 10^{-3} \times 48.3 = 0.0845 \text{ Wb}$$

Thus, from Eq. 10.35, the rms line-neutral armature flux is equal to

$$\lambda_a = \sqrt{\frac{\lambda_D^2 + \lambda_Q^2}{2}} = \sqrt{\frac{0.536^2 + 0.0845^2}{2}} = 0.384 \text{ Wb}$$

The base rms line-neutral armature flux can be determined from the base line-neutral voltage ($(V_a)_{base} = 127$ V) and the base frequency ($(\omega_e)_{base} = 419$ rad/sec (66.7 Hz)) as

$$(\lambda_a)_{base} = \frac{(V_a)_{base}}{(\omega_e)_{base}} = 0.303 \text{ Wb}$$

Thus, the per-unit armature flux is equal to $0.384/0.303 = 1.27$ per unit. From this calculation we see that the motor is significantly saturated at this operating condition. In fact, the calculation is probably not accurate because such a degree of saturation will most likely give rise to a reduction in the synchronous inductance as well as the magnetic coupling between the rotor and the stator.

c. In order to maintain rated armature flux linkage, the control will have to produce a direct-axis component of armature current to reduce the direct-axis flux linkage such that the total armature flux linkage is equal to the rated value $(\lambda_a)_{base}$. Specifically, we must have

$$\lambda_D = \sqrt{2(\lambda_a)_{base}^2 - \lambda_Q^2} = \sqrt{2 \times 0.303^2 - 0.0844^2} = 0.420 \text{ Wb}$$

We can now find i_D from Eq. 10.39 (setting $L_d = L_s$)

$$i_D = \frac{\lambda_D - \Lambda_{PM}}{L_s} = \frac{0.420 - 0.536}{1.75 \times 10^{-3}} = -66.3 \text{ A}$$

The corresponding rms armature current is

$$I_a = \sqrt{\frac{i_D^2 + i_Q^2}{2}} = \sqrt{\frac{66.3^2 + 48.3^2}{2}} = 58.0 \text{ A}$$

The base rms armature current for this machine is equal to

$$I_{base} = \frac{P_{base}}{\sqrt{3}V_{base}} = \frac{25 \times 10^3}{\sqrt{3}\,220} = 65.6 \text{ A}$$

and hence the per-unit armature current is equal to $58.0/65.6 = 0.88$ per unit.

Comparing the results of parts (b) and (c) we see how flux weakening by the introduction of direct-axis current can be used to control the terminal voltage of a permanent-magnet synchronous motor under field-oriented control.

Practice Problem 10.6

Consider again the motor of Example 10.11. Repeat the calculations of parts (b) and (c) of Example 10.11 for the case in which the motor is operating at 80 percent of rated torque at a speed of 2500 r/min.

Solution

For part (b) $\lambda_a = 1.27$ per unit.
For part (c), $I_a = 0.98$ per unit.

EXAMPLE 10.12

In this example, we will examine the field-oriented control of a 2-pole, three-phase permanent-magnet motor designed for constant maximum torque for speeds below base speed and constant maximum power for speeds above base speed. When operated at rated flux, the motor achieves its rated terminal voltage of 460 V at a base speed of 3000 r/min and has a maximum safe operating current of 80 A. The motor is designed so that it can be operated in excess of base speed at a maximum terminal voltage of 460 V up to a speed of 7000 r/min. The motor is non-salient, has a synchronous inductance of 4.85 mH and achieves rated open-circuit voltage at a speed of 4900 r/min.

The motor is supplied by an electronic drive which includes a field-oriented controller with a speed feedback loop as shown in block-diagram form in Fig. 10.17. For this application, the controller gain has been set to $G = 31.4$ N · m/(rad/sec). The drive control algorithm implements the following features:

■ The drive output current is limited to the motor maximum safe operating current $I_{a,\max} = 80$ A.

■ The drive will supply only quadrature-axis current up to the point that direct-axis current is required to insure that the motor flux density does not exceed its rated value and that

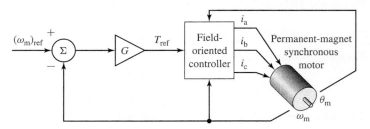

Figure 10.17 Block diagram of the synchronous-motor speed-control loop for the permanent-magnet synchronous motor of Example 10.12.

the terminal voltage does not exceed 460 V. If the required combination of quadrature-axis current and direct-axis current exceeds the maximum safe operating current, the drive will reduce the quadrature-axis current, hence reducing the motor torque, until no motor operating constraints (flux linkages, terminal voltage and current) are exceeded.

To investigate the performance of the controller, we will assume that the motor is driving a load which draws a constant power of 30 kW over the speed range of 2800 – 7000 r/min. For the purposes of this example, we will neglect the effects of losses and armature resistance.

a. The motor is observed to be operating at a speed of 2800 r/min. (i) Calculate the motor torque and the corresponding reference speed $(\omega_m)_{ref}$. (ii) Calculate the direct- and quadrature-axis currents. (iii) Calculate the armature current and the motor terminal voltage.
b. The reference speed is set to 7000 r/min. (i) Calculate the corresponding motor speed and torque. (ii) Calculate the direct- and quadrature-axis currents and the armature current in amperes.
c. The motor and load have a combined inertia of $J = 0.10$ kg·m². With the motor initially operating at 2800 r/min, the reference speed is suddenly switched to 7000 r/min. Use MATLAB/Simulink to plot the motor speed, torque, terminal voltage, and currents (q-axis, d-axis and armature rms) as a function of time.

■ **Solution**

Some preliminary calculations:

■ From Eq. 10.35, the rms rated line-neutral armature flux linkage is calculated from the rated line-neutral voltage and the base speed $((\omega_e)_{base} = (\omega_m)_{base} = 3000 \times (\pi/30) = 314.2$ r/min)

$$(\lambda_a)_{rated} = \frac{460/\sqrt{3}}{314.2} = 845 \text{ mWb}$$

■ The motor achieves rated open-circuit voltage at a speed of 4900 r/min $(\omega_e = 4900 \times (\pi/30) = 513.1$ rad/sec) and from Eq. 10.38,

$$\Lambda_{PM} = \frac{\sqrt{2} \, (E_{af})_{rated}}{\omega_e} = \frac{\sqrt{2} \, (460/\sqrt{3})}{513.1} = 732 \text{ mWb}$$

a. (i) At 2800 r/min with $\omega_m = 2800 \times (\pi/30) = 293.2$ rad/sec, the corresponding torque is

$$T_{load} = \frac{P_{load}}{\omega_m} = 102.3 \text{ N·m}$$

From the block diagram of Fig. 10.17 setting $T_{ref} = T_{load}$, the reference speed can be calculated as

$$(\omega_m)_{ref} = \omega_m + \frac{T_{load}}{G} = 293.2 + \frac{102.3}{31.4} = 296.5 \text{ rad/sec}$$

corresponding to a speed of 2831 r/min.

(ii) The value of quadrature-axis current required to produce the desired torque is calculated from Eq. 10.41

$$i_Q = \frac{2}{3}\left(\frac{2}{\text{poles}}\right)\frac{T_{\text{load}}}{\Lambda_{\text{PM}}} = 93.2 \text{ A}$$

This is is a non-salient motor with $L_d = L_q = L_s = 4.85$ mH. Hence, from Eq. 10.22

$$\lambda_Q = L_s i_Q = 452 \text{ mWb}$$

From Eq. 10.39, with $i_D = 0$,

$$\lambda_D = \Lambda_{\text{PM}} = 732 \text{ mWb}$$

and thus from Eq. 10.35

$$(\lambda_a)_{\text{rms}} = \sqrt{\frac{\lambda_D^2 + \lambda_Q^2}{2}} = 608 \text{ mWb}$$

which is less than $(\lambda_a)_{\text{rated}}$. Because the motor is operating below base speed, this guarantees that the terminal voltage will be less than 460 V. Thus flux weakening will not be required and the controller will set $i_D = 0$.

(iii) From Eq. 10.36 the armature current is

$$I_a = \frac{i_Q}{\sqrt{2}} = 65.9 \text{ A}$$

which is within the safe operating limit of the motor.

Finally, from Eq. 10.35, with $\omega_e = \omega_m = 293.2$ rad/sec, the rms line-neutral voltage is

$$V_a = \omega_e(\lambda_a)_{\text{rms}} = 293.2 \times 0.608 = 178.4 \text{ V}$$

corresponding to a line-line voltage of 308.9 V which is, as expected, considerably less than the rated terminal voltage.

b. (i) In this case, the reference speed is given as $n_{\text{ref}} = 7000$ r/min and hence the motor speed n must be found by equating the reference torque

$$T_{\text{ref}} = G(\omega_{\text{ref}} - \omega_m) = G(n_{\text{ref}} - n) \times (\pi/30)$$

with the load torque

$$T_{\text{load}} = \frac{P_{\text{load}}}{\omega_m} = \frac{P_{\text{load}}}{n \times (\pi/30)}$$

This results in a quadratic equation for n

$$n^2 - n_{\text{ref}}\, n + \left(\frac{P_{\text{load}}}{G}\right)\left(\frac{30}{\pi}\right)^2 = 0$$

which has two solutions, 12 r/min and the clearly correct value of 6988 r/min ($\omega_m = 731.7$ rad/sec). The load torque is thus

$$T_{\text{load}} = \frac{P_{\text{load}}}{\omega_m} = 41.0 \text{ N} \cdot \text{m}$$

(ii) The quadrature-axis current can again be calculated from Eq. 10.41

$$i_Q = \frac{2}{3}\left(\frac{2}{\text{poles}}\right)\frac{T_{\text{load}}}{\Lambda_{\text{PM}}} = 37.3 \text{ A}$$

Because the motor is operating above base speed, if necessary the controller will limit both the rms line-neutral flux armature linkage to its rated value and the motor line-line terminal voltage to its rated value of 460 V. To check whether controller action must be included, we will start by assuming that flux weakening with direct-axis current is not required. With $i_D = 0$, from Eq. 10.35, the rms line-neutral armature flux linkage would be

$$(\lambda_a)_{\text{rms}} = \sqrt{\frac{\lambda_{\text{PM}}^2 + (L_s i_Q)^2}{2}} = 0.533 \text{ Wb}$$

which again is less than $(\lambda_a)_{\text{rated}}$. However, because the motor is operating above base speed, it is necessary to check the corresponding terminal voltage. From Eq. 10.35 with $\omega_e = \omega_m = 731.7$ rad/sec, the rms line-neutral voltage is

$$V_a = \omega_e(\lambda_a)_{\text{rms}} = 390.0 \text{ V}$$

corresponding to a line-line voltage of 675.8 V which is in excess of the rated terminal voltage.

Thus, under this operating condition, flux weakening is required and the controller will supply negative direct-axis current sufficient to limit the line-line terminal voltage to 460 V (265.6 V line-neutral). The required rms line-neutral armature flux linkage is

$$(\lambda_a)_{\text{rms}} = \frac{V_a}{\omega_e} = \frac{265.6}{731.7} = 363 \text{ mWb}$$

and thus

$$\lambda_D = \sqrt{2(\lambda_a)_{\text{rms}}^2 - \lambda_Q^2} = \sqrt{2(\lambda_a)_{\text{rms}}^2 - (L_s i_Q)^2} = 480 \text{ mWb}$$

We can find i_D from Eq. 10.39

$$i_D = \frac{\lambda_D - \lambda_{\text{PM}}}{L_s} = -51.9 \text{ A}$$

Note that, as expected, i_D is negative as required to produce flux weakening by reducing the direct-axis flux.

From Eq. 10.36 the armature current is

$$I_a = \frac{i_Q}{\sqrt{2}} = 45.2 \text{ A}$$

which is again well within the safe operating range of the motor.

c. We will assume that the drive can supply phase currents to the motor that exactly match the required d- and q-axis currents and hence produce exactly the required torque. As a result, we will write the simulation directly in terms of the d- and q-axis quantities without the need to transform to phase variables.

The basic equations required for this simulation are those describing the speed controller of Fig. 10.17

$$T_{\text{ref}} = G(\omega_{\text{ref}} - \omega_m) = G(n_{\text{ref}} - n) \times (\pi/30)$$

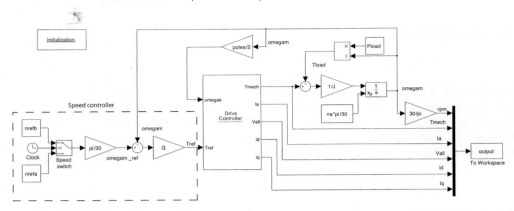

Figure 10.18 Simulink model for Example 10.12.

and the first-order differential equation describing the motor speed

$$J\frac{d\omega_m}{dt} = T_{mech} - T_{load}$$

where

$$T_{load} = \frac{P_{load}}{\omega_m}$$

In integral form as required by Simulink, the motor speed given by

$$\omega_m = \omega_{m0} + \frac{1}{J}\int_0^t (T_{mech} - T_{load})dt$$

where ω_{m0} is the motor speed at the start of the sumulation; in this case $\omega_{m0} = 2800 \times (\pi/30) = 293.2$ rad/sec.

Figure 10.18 is the block diagram of the Simulink model. The block labeled "Initialization" calls a MATLAB script which pre-loads the model parameters and initial conditions for the simulation. The element labeled "Speed switch" initiates the speed change by switching the reference speed from $n_{ref,a} = 2831$ r/min to $n_{ref,b} = 7000$ r/min.

The drive control algorithm is implemented in the subsystem labeled "Drive Controller" by the following MATLAB function:

```
function [Tmech,Ia,Vall,id,iq] = Control(Iamax,Tref, ...
    LambdaPM,L_s,Vrated,lambdaarated,omegae,poles)


Tmechmax = LambdaPM*(Iamax*sqrt(2))*(3/2)*(poles/2);

% Set Tmech = Tref to start
Tmech = Tref;
if Tmech > Tmechmax
   Tmech = Tmechmax;
end

% First pass at iq and id
iq = (2/3)*(2/poles)*Tmech/LambdaPM;
```

```
id = 0;

% Loop to find Tmech if necessary
sw = 0;
while (sw == 0)
   % Check if corresponding Ia is greater than Iamax. If so
   % reduce iq
   if iq > sqrt(2)*Iamax;
      iq = 0.999*sqrt(2)*Iamax;
   end

   % Find largest acceptable negative id
   id1 = -LambdaPM/L_s;
   id2 = -sqrt(2*Iamax^2-iq^2);
   idmin = max(id1,id2);

   % Find the corresponding minimum value of lambdaarms
   lambdaarmsmin = sqrt(((LambdaPM+L_s*idmin)^2 + (L_s*iq)^2 )/2);
   Vamin = omegae*lambdaarmsmin;

   % Check if these minimum values acceptable
   if (lambdaarmsmin <= lambdaarated) && ...
           (Vamin <= Vrated/sqrt(3))
      % Acceptable. First find out if id is needed by assuming
      % iq only and checking lambdaarms and Va
      sw = 1; %Set switch to exit Tmech loop
      lambdaarms = sqrt((LambdaPM^2+(L_s*iq)^2)/2);
      Va = omegae*lambdaarms;
      if (lambdaarms <= lambdaarated) && (Va <= Vrated/sqrt(3))
         id = 0; % No id needed
         sw = 1;
      else
         % id needed. Find the value that meets both constraints
         id1 = (sqrt(2*lambdaarated^2-(L_s*iq)^2) - LambdaPM)/L_s;
         id2 = (sqrt(2*(Vrated/(sqrt(3)*omegae))^2-(L_s*iq)^2) ...
             - LambdaPM)/L_s;
         % Required id is the minimum (largest negative) value
         id = min(id1,id2);
      end
   else
      % Minimum values not acceptable. Reduce Tmech and loop
      % until an acceptable Tmech is found
      Tmech = 0.999*Tmech;
      % Corresponding iq
      iq = (2/3)*(2/poles)*Tmech/LambdaPM;
```

```
      end
end % end of 'while sw == 0

% Calculate Ia and Va
Ia = sqrt((id^2+iq^2)/2); % RMS armature current
lambdaarms = sqrt(((LambdaPM+L_s*id)^2+(L_s*iq)^2)/2);
Va = omegae*lambdaarms;
Vall = sqrt(3)*Va; % Line-line voltage
```

The motor speed is plotted in Fig. 10.19a. Notice that the speed switch is controlled to apply the change in reference speed at 0.1 sec after the start of the simulation. The motor then takes slightly more than 0.9 sec to reach its final speed of 6988 r/min.

Immediately following the change in reference speed, the reference torque signal from the speed-controller jumps to a large value

$$T_{\text{ref}} = (n_{\text{ref},b} - n_{\text{ref},a})\,(\pi/30)\,G = 13.7 \text{ kN} \cdot \text{m}$$

Because the rms drive current is limited to 80 A, corresponding to a maximum possible value of quadrature-axis current of $i_{q,\max} = 80\sqrt{2}) = 113$ A, the maximum

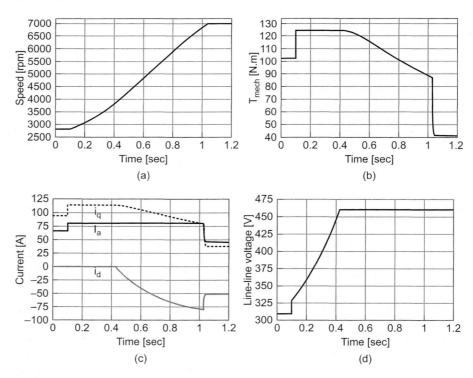

Figure 10.19 Simulation results for Example 10.12: (a) speed, (b) torque, (c) currents, and (d) line-line voltage.

motor torque will be limited by the drive to

$$T_{\text{mech,max}} = \frac{3}{2} \left(\frac{\text{poles}}{2} \right) \Lambda_{\text{PM}} \, i_{\text{q,max}} = 124.2 \text{ N} \cdot \text{m}$$

as can be seen in Fig. 10.19b where the motor torque immediately steps to this value as the reference speed is switched to 7000 r/min. From Fig. 10.19c we see that the rms armature current I_a and quadrature axis current also immediately step to their respective maximum values of 80 A and 113 A respectively.

As can be seen in Fig. 10.19d, the corresponding terminal voltage steps to 328 V which is less than the motor rated voltage of 460 V. As a result, flux weakening is not required and direct-axis current is set equal to zero. As the motor speed increases, we see that the q-axis current remains constant at its maximum value while the terminal voltage increases. As can be seen from the figure, the terminal voltages reaches 460 V when the motor speed is approximately 4000 at around 0.42 seconds. At this point, flux weakening is required to limit the terminal voltage and the drive must supply negative d-axis current, as can be seen in Fig. 10.19c. This in turn requires that the drive reduce the q-axis component of armature current in order to limit the rms armature current to 80 A and there is a corresponding reduction in motor torque, both of which can be seen in Fig. 10.19. Finally, we see that as the motor speed approaches the reference value of 7000 r/min, the reference torque drops rapidly and the motor speed, torque, and currents settle to the steady-state values as calculated in part (b).

10.3 CONTROL OF INDUCTION MOTORS

10.3.1 Speed Control

Induction motors supplied from a constant-frequency source admirably fulfill the requirements of substantially constant-speed drives. Many motor applications, however, require several speeds or even a continuously adjustable range of speeds. From the earliest days of ac power systems, engineers have been interested in the development of adjustable-speed ac motors.

The synchronous speed of an induction motor can be changed by (a) changing the number of poles or (b) varying the line frequency. The operating slip can be changed by (c) varying the line voltage, (d) varying the rotor resistance, or (e) applying voltages of the appropriate frequency to the rotor circuits. The salient features of speed-control methods based on these five possibilities are discussed in the following five sections.

Pole-Changing Motors In pole-changing motors, the stator winding is designed so that, by simple changes in coil connections, the number of poles can be changed in the ratio 2 to 1. Either of two synchronous speeds can then be selected. The rotor is almost always of the squirrel-cage type, which reacts by producing a rotor field having the same number of poles as the inducing stator field. With two independent sets of stator windings, each arranged for pole changing, as many as four synchronous speeds can be obtained in a squirrel-cage motor, for example, 600, 900, 1200, and 1800 r/min for 60-Hz operation.

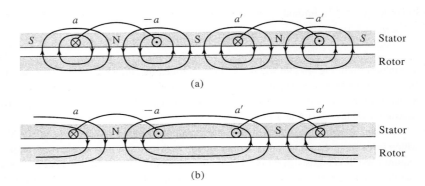

Figure 10.20   Principles of the pole-changing winding.

The basic principles of the pole-changing winding are shown in Fig. 10.20, in which aa and $a'a'$ are two coils comprising part of the phase-a stator winding. An actual winding would, of course, consist of several coils in each group. The windings for the other stator phases (not shown in the figure) would be similarly arranged. In Fig. 10.20a the coils are connected to produce a four-pole field; in Fig. 10.20b the current in the $a'a'$ coil has been reversed by means of a controller, the result being a two-pole field.

Figure 10.21 shows the four possible arrangements of these two coils: they can be connected in series or in parallel, and with their currents either in the same direction (four-pole operation) or in the opposite direction (two-pole operation). Additionally, the machine phases can be connected either in Y or Δ, resulting in eight possible combinations.

Note that for a given phase voltage, the different connections will result in differing levels of air-gap flux density. For example, a change from a Δ to a Y connection

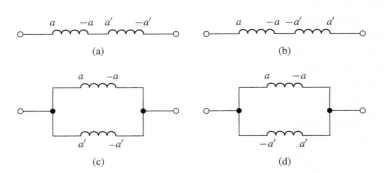

Figure 10.21   Four possible arrangements of phase-a stator coils in a pole-changing induction motor: (a) series-connected, four-pole; (b) series-connected, two-pole; (c) parallel-connected, four-pole; (d) parallel-connected, two-pole.

will reduce the coil voltage (and hence the air-gap flux density) for a given coil arrangement by $\sqrt{3}$. Similarly, changing from a connection with two coils in series to two in parallel will double the voltage across each coil and therefore double the magnitude of the air-gap flux density. These changes in flux density can, of course, be compensated for by changes in the applied winding voltage. In any case, they must be considered, along with corresponding changes in motor torque, when the configuration to be used in a specific application is considered.

Armature-Frequency Control   The synchronous speed of an induction motor can be controlled by varying the frequency of the applied armature voltage. This method of speed control is identical to that discussed in Section 10.2.1 for synchronous machines. In fact, the same inverter configurations used for synchronous machines, such as the three-phase voltage-source inverter of Fig. 10.12, can be used to drive induction motors. As is the case with any ac motor, to maintain approximately constant flux density, the armature voltage should also be varied directly with the frequency (constant-volts-per-hertz).

The torque-speed curve of an induction motor for a given frequency can be calculated by using the methods of Chapter 6 within the accuracy of the motor parameters at that frequency. Consider the torque expression of Eq. 6.36 which is repeated here

$$T_{\text{mech}} = \frac{1}{\omega_s} \left[\frac{n_{\text{ph}} V_{1,\text{eq}}^2 (R_2/s)}{(R_{1,\text{eq}} + (R_2/s))^2 + (X_{1,\text{eq}} + X_2)^2} \right] \tag{10.42}$$

where $\omega_s = (2/\text{poles})\omega_e$ and ω_e is the electrical excitation frequency of the motor in rad/sec,

$$\hat{V}_{1,\text{eq}} = \hat{V}_1 \left(\frac{j X_m}{R_1 + j(X_1 + X_m)} \right) \tag{10.43}$$

and

$$R_{1,\text{eq}} + j X_{1,\text{eq}} = \frac{j X_m (R_1 + j X_1)}{R_1 + j(X_1 + X_m)} \tag{10.44}$$

To investigate the effect of changing frequency, we will assume that R_1 is negligible. In this case,

$$\hat{V}_{1,\text{eq}} = \hat{V}_1 \left(\frac{X_m}{X_1 + X_m} \right) \tag{10.45}$$

$$R_{1,\text{eq}} = 0 \tag{10.46}$$

and

$$X_{1,\text{eq}} = \frac{X_m X_1}{X_1 + X_m} \tag{10.47}$$

Let the subscript 0 represent the rated-frequency values of each of the induction-motor parameters. As the electrical-excitation frequency is varied, we can write

$$(X_{1,eq} + X_2) = \left(\frac{\omega_e}{\omega_{e0}}\right)(X_{1,eq} + X_2)_0 \tag{10.48}$$

Under constant-volts-per-hertz control, we can also write the equivalent source voltage as

$$\hat{V}_1 = \left(\frac{\omega_e}{\omega_{e0}}\right)(\hat{V}_1)_0 \tag{10.49}$$

and hence, since $\hat{V}_{1,eq}$ is equal to $\hat{V}_1$ multiplied by a reactance ratio which stays constant with changing frequency,

$$\hat{V}_{1,eq} = \left(\frac{\omega_e}{\omega_{e0}}\right)(\hat{V}_{1,eq})_0 \tag{10.50}$$

Finally, we can write the motor slip as

$$s = \frac{\omega_s - \omega_m}{\omega_s} = \frac{\text{poles}}{2}\left(\frac{\Delta\omega_m}{\omega_e}\right) \tag{10.51}$$

where $\Delta\omega_m = \omega_s - \omega_m$ is the difference between the synchronous and mechanical angular velocities of the motor.

Substitution of Eqs. 10.48 through 10.51 into Eq. 10.42 gives

$$T_{mech} = \frac{n_{ph}[(V_{1,eq})_0]^2(R_2/\Delta\omega_m)}{\left[\left(\frac{2\omega_{e0}}{\text{poles}}\right)(R_2/\Delta\omega_m)\right]^2 + [(X_{1,eq} + X_2)_0]^2} \tag{10.52}$$

Equation 10.52 shows the general trend in which we see that the frequency dependence of the torque-speed characteristic of an induction motor appears only in the term $R_2/\Delta\omega_m$. Thus, under the assumption that R_1 is negligible, as the electrical supply frequency to an induction motor is changed, the shape of the speed-torque curve as a function of $\Delta\omega_m$ (the difference between the synchronous speed and the motor speed) will remain unchanged. As a result, the torque-speed characteristic will simply shift along the speed axis as $\omega_e(f_e)$ is varied.

A set of such curves is shown in Fig. 10.22a. Note that as the electrical frequency (and hence the synchronous speed) is decreased, a given value of $\Delta\omega_m$ corresponds to a larger slip. Thus, for example, if the peak torque of a four-pole motor driven at 60 Hz occurs at 1638 r/min, corresponding to a slip of 9 percent, when driven at 30 Hz, the peak torque will occur at 738 r/min, corresponding to a slip of 18 percent.

In practice, the effects of R_1 may not be fully negligible, especially for large values of slip. If this is the case, the shape of the speed-torque curves will vary somewhat with the applied electrical frequency. Figure 10.22b shows a typical family of curves for this case.

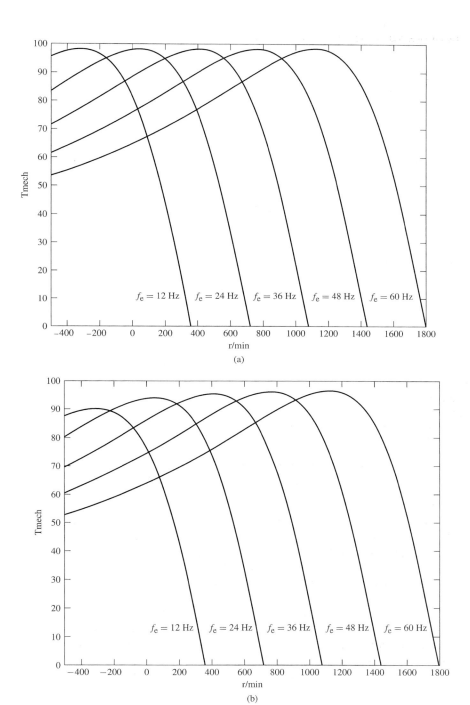

Figure 10.22 A family of typical induction-motor speed-torque curves for a four-pole motor for various values of the electrical supply frequency. (a) R_1 sufficiently small so that its effects are negligible. (b) R_1 not negligible.

EXAMPLE 10.13

A three-phase, 575-V, 60-Hz, 100-kW, four-pole induction motor has the following parameters in Ω/phase:

$$X_1 = 0.239 \quad X_2 = 0.344 \quad X_m = 35.4091.4$$

$$R_1 = 0.102 \quad R_2 = 0.125$$

This motor is to be operated from a variable-frequency, constant-volts-per-hertz motor drive whose terminal voltage is 575 V at 60 Hz.

The motor is driving a load whose power can be assumed to vary as

$$P_{\text{load}} = 92.0 \left(\frac{n}{1800} \right)^3 \text{ kW}$$

where n is the load speed in r/min. Motor rotational losses can be assumed to be negligible.

Write a MATLAB script to find the line-line terminal voltage, the motor slip and speed in r/min, the motor load in kW, and the terminal current and power factor for (a) a source frequency of 60 Hz and (b) a source frequency of 40 Hz.

■ **Solution**

As the electrical frequency f_e is varied, the motor reactances will vary

$$X = X_0 \left(\frac{f_e}{60} \right)$$

where X_0 is the reactance value at 60 Hz. Similarly, the line-neutral armature voltage must be varied as

$$V_1 = \frac{220}{\sqrt{3}} \left(\frac{f_e}{60} \right) = 127 \left(\frac{f_e}{60} \right) \text{ V}$$

From Eq. 4.42, the synchronous angular velocity of the motor is equal to

$$\omega_s = \left(\frac{4\pi}{\text{poles}} \right) f_e = \pi f_e \text{ rad/sec}$$

and, at any given motor speed ω_m, the corresponding slip is given by

$$s = \frac{\omega_s - \omega_m}{\omega_s}$$

Using Eqs. 10.42 through 10.44, the motor speed can be found by searching over ω_m for that speed at which $P_{\text{load}} = \omega_m T_{\text{mech}}$. The terminal current and power factor can be calculated from the motor input impedance as shown in Chapter 6. If this is done, the result is:

a. For $f_e = 60$ Hz:

   Terminal voltage = 575 V line-line
   Speed = 1736 r/min
   Slip = 3.56 %
   P_{load} = 82.5 kW
   Terminal current = 91.4 A
   Power factor = 90.6%

b. For $f_e = 40$ Hz:

  Terminal voltage $= 383$ V line-line
  Speed $= 1172$ r/min
  Slip $= 2.34$ %
  $P_{\text{load}} = 25.4$ kW
  Terminal current $= 41.7$ A
  Power factor $= 91.8\%$

  Here is the MATLAB script:

```
clc
clear

%Here are the 60-Hz motor parameters

V10 = 575/sqrt(3);
Nph = 3;
poles = 4;
fe0 = 60;
R1 = 0.102;
R2 = 0.125;
X10 = 0.239;
X20 = 0.344;
Xm0 = 35.40;

% Loop over two frequency values
fe1 = 60;
fe2 = 40;

for m = 1:2,
  if m == 1
    fe = fe1;
  else
    fe = fe2;
  end

% Calculate the reactances and the voltage
  X1 = X10*(fe/fe0);
  X2 = X20*(fe/fe0);
  Xm = Xm0*(fe/fe0);
  V1 = V10*(fe/fe0);

%Calculate the synchronous speed
```

```
omegas = 4*pi*fe/poles;
ns = 120*fe/poles;

%Calculate stator Thevenin equivalent
V1eq = abs(V1*j*Xm/(R1 + j*(X1+Xm)));
Z1eq = j*Xm*(R1+j*X1)/(R1 + j*(X1+Xm));

%Search over the slip until the Pload = Pmech
slip = 0.;
error = 1;
while error >= 0
  slip = slip + 0.00001;
  rpm = ns*(1-slip);
  omegam = omegas*(1-slip);
  I2hat = V1eq/(Z1eq+j*X2+R2/slip);
  I2 = abs(I2hat);
  Pmech = 3*I2^2*R2*(1-slip)/slip;
  Pload = 92e3*(rpm/1800)^3;
  error = Pload - Pmech;
end %End of while loop

% Find I1
Z2 = R2/slip + j*X2;
Zm = j*Xm;
Z1 = R1+j*X1;
Zin = Z1+Zm*Z2/(Zm+Z2);
I1hat = V1/Zin;
I1 = abs(I1hat);

% Calculate the power factor
pf = Pmech/(3*V1*I1);

fprintf('\nFor fe = %g [Hz]:',fe)
fprintf('\n  Terminal voltage = %g [V l-l]',V1*sqrt(3))
fprintf('\n  rpm = %g',rpm)
fprintf('\n  slip = %g [percent] ',100*slip)
fprintf('\n  Pload = %g [kW]',Pload/1000)
fprintf('\n  I1 = %g [A]',I1)
fprintf('\n  pf = %1.2f [percent]',100*pf)
fprintf('\n\n')

end % End of for m = 1:2 loop
```

Repeat Example 10.13 for a source frequency of 50 Hz.

Solution

Terminal voltage $= 479$ V line-line
Speed $= 1456$ r/min
Slip $= 2.94\,\%$
$P_{\text{load}} = 48.7$ kW
Terminal current $= 63.9$ A
Power factor $= 91.8\%$

Line-Voltage Control   The internal torque developed by an induction motor is proportional to the square of the voltage applied to its primary terminals, as shown by the two torque-speed characteristics in Fig. 10.23. If the load has the torque-speed characteristic shown by the dashed line, the speed will be reduced from n_1 to n_2. This method of speed control is commonly used with small squirrel-cage motors driving fans, where cost is an issue and the inefficiency of high-slip operation can be tolerated. It is characterized by a rather limited range of speed control.

Rotor-Resistance Control   The possibility of speed control of a wound-rotor motor by changing its rotor-circuit resistance has already been pointed out in Section 6.7.1. The torque-speed characteristics for three different values of rotor resistance are shown in Fig. 10.24. If the load has the torque-speed characteristic shown by the dashed line, the speeds corresponding to each of the values of rotor resistance are n_1, n_2, and n_3. This method of speed control has characteristics similar to those of dc shunt-motor speed control by means of resistance in series with the armature.

   The principal disadvantages of both line-voltage and rotor-resistance control are low efficiency at reduced speeds and poor speed regulation with respect to change in load. In addition, the cost and maintenance requirements of wound-rotor induction motors are sufficiently high that squirrel-cage motors combined with solid-state drives have become the preferred option in most applications.

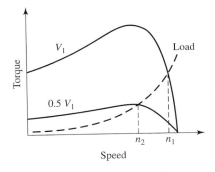

Figure 10.23 Speed control by means of line voltage.

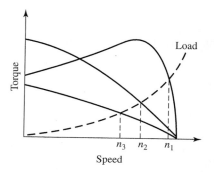

Figure 10.24 Speed control by means of rotor resistance.

10.3.2 Torque Control

In Section 10.2.2 we developed the concept of field-oriented control for synchronous machines. Under this viewpoint, the armature flux and current are resolved into two components which rotate synchronously with the rotor and with the air-gap flux wave. The components of armature current and flux which are aligned with the field-winding are referred to as *direct-axis components* while those which are perpendicular to this axis are referred to as *quadrature-axis components*.

It turns out that the same viewpoint which we applied to synchronous machines can be applied to induction machines. As is discussed in Section 6.1, in the steady-state the mmf and flux waves produced by both the rotor and stator windings of an induction motor rotate at synchronous speed and in synchronism with each other. Thus, the torque-producing mechanism in an induction machine is equivalent to that of a synchronous machine. The difference between the two is that, in an induction machine, the rotor currents are not directly supplied but rather are induced as the induction-motor rotor slips with respect to the rotating flux wave produced by the stator currents. Thus, unlike as in the case of a synchronous machine, although the rotor and stator flux waves rotate synchronously in an induction motor, they do not rotate synchronously with the rotor.

To examine the application of field-oriented control to induction machines, we begin with the dq0 transformation of Section C.3 of Appendix C. This transformation transforms both the stator and rotor quantities into a synchronously rotating reference frame. Under balanced-three-phase, steady-state conditions, zero-sequence quantities will be zero and the remaining direct- and quadrature-axis quantities will be constant. Hence the flux-linkage current relationships of Eqs. C.52 through C.58 become

$$\lambda_D = L_S i_D + L_m i_{DR} \tag{10.53}$$

$$\lambda_Q = L_S i_Q + L_m i_{QR} \tag{10.54}$$

$$\lambda_{DR} = L_m i_D + L_R i_{DR} \tag{10.55}$$

$$\lambda_{QR} = L_m i_Q + L_R i_{QR} \tag{10.56}$$

In these equations, the subscripts D, Q, DR, and QR represent the constant values of the direct- and quadrature-axis components of the stator and rotor quantities respectively. It is a straightforward matter to show that the inductance parameters can be determined from the equivalent-circuit parameters as

$$L_\mathrm{m} = \frac{X_{\mathrm{m}0}}{\omega_{\mathrm{e}0}} \tag{10.57}$$

$$L_\mathrm{S} = L_\mathrm{m} + \frac{X_{10}}{\omega_{\mathrm{e}0}} \tag{10.58}$$

$$L_\mathrm{R} = L_\mathrm{m} + \frac{X_{20}}{\omega_{\mathrm{e}0}} \tag{10.59}$$

where the subscript 0 indicates the rated-frequency value.

Under steady-state conditions, the transformed voltage equations Eqs. C.63 through C.64 and C.66 through C.67 become

$$v_\mathrm{D} = R_\mathrm{a} i_\mathrm{D} - \omega_\mathrm{e} \lambda_\mathrm{Q} \tag{10.60}$$

$$v_\mathrm{Q} = R_\mathrm{a} i_\mathrm{Q} + \omega_\mathrm{e} \lambda_\mathrm{D} \tag{10.61}$$

$$0 = R_\mathrm{aR} i_\mathrm{DR} - (\omega_\mathrm{e} - \omega_\mathrm{me}) \lambda_\mathrm{QR} \tag{10.62}$$

$$0 = R_\mathrm{aR} i_\mathrm{QR} + (\omega_\mathrm{e} - \omega_\mathrm{me}) \lambda_\mathrm{DR} \tag{10.63}$$

where ω_me is the rotor electrical angular velocity.

One can show that the resistances are related to those of the equivalent circuit as

$$R_\mathrm{a} = R_1 \tag{10.64}$$

and

$$R_\mathrm{aR} = R_2 \tag{10.65}$$

For the purposes of developing a field-oriented control scheme, we will begin with the torque expression of Eq. C.70

$$T_\mathrm{mech} = \frac{3}{2} \left(\frac{\mathrm{poles}}{2} \right) \left(\frac{L_\mathrm{m}}{L_\mathrm{R}} \right) (\lambda_\mathrm{DR} i_\mathrm{Q} - \lambda_\mathrm{QR} i_\mathrm{D}) \tag{10.66}$$

For the derivation of the dq0 transformation in Section C.3, the reference frame is chosen to be the synchronous frame of the stator and rotor flux waves, thus rotating with the angular velocity $\omega_\mathrm{s} = (2/\mathrm{poles})\,\omega_\mathrm{e}$. It is not necessary for the purposes of the derivation to specify the absolute angular location of the reference frame. It is convenient at this point to choose the direct axis of the reference frame aligned with the rotor flux.

If this is done, there will be no rotor flux aligned with the reference-frame quadrature axis. Hence

$$\lambda_\mathrm{QR} = 0 \tag{10.67}$$

and the torque expression of Eq. 10.66 becomes

$$T_{\text{mech}} = \frac{3}{2} \left(\frac{\text{poles}}{2} \right) \left(\frac{L_{\text{m}}}{L_{\text{R}}} \right) \lambda_{\text{DR}} i_{\text{Q}} \tag{10.68}$$

From Eq. 10.62 we see that

$$i_{\text{DR}} = 0 \tag{10.69}$$

and thus

$$\lambda_{\text{DR}} = L_{\text{m}} i_{\text{D}} \tag{10.70}$$

and

$$\lambda_{\text{D}} = L_{\text{S}} i_{\text{D}} \tag{10.71}$$

From Eqs. 10.70 and 10.71 we see that by aligning the synchronously rotating reference frame with the axis of the rotor flux and thus setting $\lambda_{\text{QR}} = 0$, the direct-axis rotor flux (which is, indeed, the total rotor flux) as well as the direct-axis flux are determined by the direct-axis component of the armature current. Notice the direct analogy with a dc motor. In a dc motor, the field- and direct-axis armature fluxes are determined by the field current and in this field-oriented control scheme, the rotor and direct-axis armature fluxes are determined by the direct-axis armature current. In other words, in this field-oriented control scheme, the direct-axis component of armature current serves the same function as the field current in a dc machine.

The torque equation, Eq. 10.68, completes the analogy with the dc motor. We see that once the rotor direct-axis flux λ_{DR} is set by the direct-axis armature current, the torque is then determined by the quadrature-axis armature current just as the torque is determined by the armature current in a dc motor.

In a practical implementation of the technique which we have derived, the direct- and quadrature-axis currents i_{D} and i_{Q} must be transformed into the three motor phase currents $i_{\text{a}}(t)$, $i_{\text{b}}(t)$, and $i_{\text{c}}(t)$. This can be done using the inverse dq0 transformation of Eq. C.48 which requires knowledge of θ_{s}, the electrical angle between the axis of phase a, and the direct-axis of the synchronously rotating reference frame.

Since it is not possible to measure the axis of the rotor flux directly, it is necessary to calculate θ_{s}, where $\theta_{\text{s}} = \omega_{\text{e}} t + \theta_0$ as given by Eq. C.46. Solving Eq. 10.63 for ω_{e} gives

$$\omega_{\text{e}} = \omega_{\text{me}} - R_{\text{aR}} \left(\frac{i_{\text{QR}}}{\lambda_{\text{DR}}} \right) \tag{10.72}$$

From Eq. 10.56 with $\lambda_{\text{QR}} = 0$ we see that

$$i_{\text{QR}} = -\left(\frac{L_{\text{m}}}{L_{\text{R}}} \right) i_{\text{Q}} \tag{10.73}$$

Eq. 10.73 in combination with Eq. 10.70 then gives

$$\omega_{\text{e}} = \omega_{\text{me}} + \frac{R_{\text{aR}}}{L_{\text{R}}} \left(\frac{i_{\text{Q}}}{i_{\text{D}}} \right) = \omega_{\text{me}} + \frac{1}{\tau_{\text{R}}} \left(\frac{i_{\text{Q}}}{i_{\text{D}}} \right) \tag{10.74}$$

where $\tau_{\text{R}} = L_{\text{R}}/R_{\text{aR}}$ is the rotor time constant.

We can now integrate Eq. 10.74 to find

$$\bar{\theta}_s = \left[\omega_{me} + \frac{1}{\tau_R} \left(\frac{i_Q}{i_D} \right) \right] t + \theta_0 \qquad (10.75)$$

where $\bar{\theta}_s$ indicates the calculated value of θ_s (often referred to as the *estimated value* of θ_s). In the more general dynamic sense

$$\bar{\theta}_s = \int_0^t \left[\omega_{me} + \frac{1}{\tau_R} \left(\frac{i_Q}{i_D} \right) \right] dt' + \theta_0 \qquad (10.76)$$

Note that both Eqs. 10.75 and 10.76 require knowledge of θ_0, the value of $\bar{\theta}_s$ at $t = 0$. Although we will not prove it here, it turns out that in a practical implementation, the effects of an error in this initial angle decay to zero with time, and hence it can be set to zero without any loss of generality.

Figure 10.25a shows a block diagram of a field-oriented torque-control system for an induction machine. The block labeled "Estimator" represents an algorithm which implements the integration of Eq. 10.76, which calculates the estimate of θ_s required by the transformation from dq0 to abc variables.

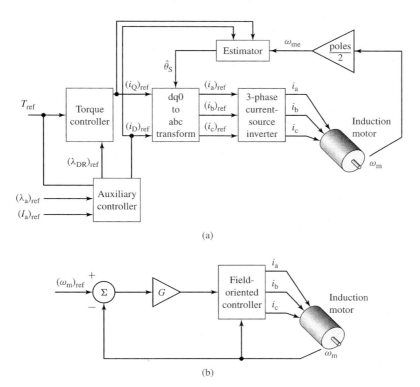

(a)

(b)

Figure 10.25 (a) Block diagram of a field-oriented torque-control system for an induction motor. (b) Block diagram of an induction-motor speed-control loop built around a field-oriented torque control system.

Note that a speed sensor is required to provide the rotor speed measurement required by the estimator. Also notice that the estimator requires knowledge of the rotor time constant $\tau_R = L_R/R_{aR}$. In general, this will not be known exactly, both due to uncertainty in the machine parameters as well as the fact that the rotor resistance R_{aR} will undoubtedly change with temperature as the motor is operated. It can be shown that errors in τ_R result in an offset in the estimate of θ_s, which in turn will result in an error in the estimate for the position of the rotor flux with the result that the applied armature currents will not be exactly aligned with the direct- and quadrature-axes. The torque controller will still work basically as expected, although there will be corresponding errors in the torque and rotor flux.

As with the synchronous motor, the rms armature flux-linkages can be found from Eq. 10.35 as

$$(\lambda_a)_{rms} = \sqrt{\frac{\lambda_D^2 + \lambda_Q^2}{2}} \tag{10.77}$$

Combining Eqs. 10.54 and 10.73 gives

$$\lambda_Q = L_S i_Q + L_m i_{QR} = \left(L_S - \frac{L_m^2}{L_R} \right) i_Q \tag{10.78}$$

Substituting Eqs. 10.71 and 10.78 into Eq. 10.77 gives

$$(\lambda_a)_{rms} = \sqrt{\frac{L_S^2 i_D^2 + \left(L_S - \frac{L_m^2}{L_R} \right)^2 i_Q^2}{2}} \tag{10.79}$$

Finally, as discussed in the footnote to Eq. 10.34, the rms line-neutral armature voltage can be found as

$$V_a = \sqrt{\frac{v_D^2 + v_Q^2}{2}} = \sqrt{\frac{(R_a i_D - \omega_e \lambda_Q)^2 + (R_a i_Q + \omega_e \lambda_D)^2}{2}}$$

$$= \sqrt{\frac{\left(R_a i_D - \omega_e \left(L_S - \frac{L_m^2}{L_R} \right) i_Q \right)^2 + (R_a i_Q + \omega_e L_S i_D)^2}{2}} \tag{10.80}$$

These equations show that the armature flux linkages and terminal voltage are determined by both the direct- and quadrature-axis components of the armature current. Thus, the block labeled "Torque Controller" in Fig. 10.25a must calculate reference values for the direct- and quadrature-axis currents $(i_D)_{ref}$ and $(i_Q)_{ref}$ which both achieve the desired torque and meet the constraints on armature flux linkages (to avoid saturation in the motor), armature current $(I_a)_{rms} = \sqrt{(i_D^2 + i_Q^2)/2}$ (to avoid excessive armature heating), and armature voltage (to avoid potential insulation damage).

Note that, as we discussed with regard to synchronous machines in Section 10.2.2, the torque-control system of Fig. 10.25a is typically embedded within a larger control loop. One such example is the speed-control loop of Fig. 10.25b.

EXAMPLE 10.14

The three-phase, 575-V, 60-Hz, 100-kW, four-pole induction motor of Example 10.13 is to be driven by a field-oriented speed-control system (similar to that of Fig. 10.25b). The controller is programmed to achieve the desired reference torque subject to insuring that motor voltage and rms armature flux linkages not exceed the machine rated values and that the motor terminal current not exceed 100 A rms in order to avoid overheating the motor. If the desired electromagnetic torque cannot be achieved without exceeding one or more constraints, the controller will reduce the motor torque sufficiently to insure that all constraints are satisfied.

Find the direct- and quadrature-axis currents, the rms amplitude of the armature current, the electrical frequency, and the rms terminal voltage if the electromagnetic power is 82.5 kW and the motor is operating at a speed of 1736 r/min.

■ Solution

This example is most easily solved by writing a MATLAB script to implement the controller algorithm. We must first determine the parameters for this machine. From Eqs. 10.57 through Eq. 10.65

$$L_m = \frac{X_{m0}}{\omega_{e0}} = \frac{35.4}{120\pi} = 93.90 \text{ mH}$$

$$L_S = L_m + \frac{X_{10}}{\omega_{e0}} = 91.90 + \frac{0.239}{120\pi} = 93.54 \text{ mH}$$

$$L_R = L_m + \frac{X_{20}}{\omega_{e0}} = 93.90 + \frac{0.344}{120\pi} = 94.81 \text{ mH}$$

$$R_a = R_1 = 0.102 \text{ } \Omega$$

$$R_{aR} = R_2 = 0.125 \text{ } \Omega$$

The rated rms line-neutral terminal voltage for this machine is $(V_a)_{rated} = 575/\sqrt{3} = 332.0$ V and thus the rated rms armature flux linkage for this machine is

$$(\lambda_a)_{rms,rated} = \frac{(V_a)_{rated}}{\omega_{e0}} = \frac{332.0}{120\,\pi} = 0.881 \text{ Wb}$$

Because we know that this is an achievable operating point (see Example 10.13), we do not need to include that portion of the algorithm which reduces the motor torque in the event the operating point cannot be achieved without exceeding the motor operating constraints.

For the specified operating condition

$$\omega_m = n\left(\frac{\pi}{30}\right) = 1736\left(\frac{\pi}{30}\right) = 181.8 \text{ rad/sec}$$

and the mechanical torque is

$$T_{mech} = \frac{P_{mech}}{\omega_m} = \frac{82.5 \times 10^3}{181.8} = 453.8 \text{ N} \cdot \text{m}$$

We will implement the relevant portion of the control algorithm as follows:

- ■ Step 1: As an initial estimate, set $\lambda_{DR} = \sqrt{2} \times (\lambda_a)_{rms,rated}$
- ■ Step 2: Calculate i_Q from Eq. 10.68

$$i_Q = \frac{2}{3}\left(\frac{2}{poles}\right)\left(\frac{L_R}{L_m}\right)\left(\frac{T_{mech}}{\lambda_{DR}}\right)$$

- Step 3: Calculate i_D from Eq. 10.70

$$i_D = \frac{\lambda_{DR}}{L_m}$$

and the rms armature current from Eq. 10.36

$$I_a = \sqrt{\frac{i_D^2 + i_Q^2}{2}}$$

- Step 4: From Eqs. 10.71 and 10.78 calculate

$$\lambda_D = L_S i_D$$

$$\lambda_Q = \left(L_S - \frac{L_m^2}{L_R} \right)$$

and the corresponding rms armature flux linkage from Eq. 10.77

$$(\lambda_a)_{rms} = \sqrt{\frac{\lambda_D^2 + \lambda_Q^2}{2}}$$

- Step 5: Calculate the rms line-neutral terminal voltage from Eq. 10.80

$$V_a = \sqrt{\frac{(R_a i_D - \omega_e \lambda_Q)^2 + (R_a i_Q + \omega_e \lambda_D)^2}{2}}$$

- Step 6: Check to see if all the constraints are satisfied. Specifically, the acceptable solution must have

$$I_a \leq 100 \text{ A}$$

$$(\lambda_a)_{rms} \leq (\lambda_a)_{rms,rated}$$

and

$$V_a \leq (V_a)_{rated}$$

If all the constraints are satisfied, the operating condition has been found. If not, reduce λ_{DR} and return to Step 2.

This algorithm is implemented by the following MATLAB script

```
clc
clear

%Here are the 60-Hz motor parameters
Varated = 575/sqrt(3);
poles = 4;
R1 = 0.102;
R2 = 0.125;
X10 = 0.239;
X20 = 0.344;
Xm0 = 35.40;

fe0 = 60;
```

```
omegae0 = 2*pi*fe0;
Lm = Xm0/omegae0;
LS = Lm+X10/omegae0;
LR = Lm+X20/omegae0;
Ra = R1;
RaR = R2;

% Maximum armature current
Iamax = 100;

% Rated rms armature flux linkages
lambdaarmsrated = Varated/omegae0;
lambdaarmsrated_peak = sqrt(2)*lambdaarmsrated;

% Specified operating condition
rpm = 1736;
omegam = rpm*pi/30;
omegame = omegam*(poles/2);
Pmech = 82.5e3;
Tmech = Pmech/omegam;

% Starting value of lambdaDR
lambdaDR = lambdaarmsrated_peak;

% Loop to find controller output
sw = 0;
while sw == 0;

   iQ = (2/3)*(2/poles)*(LR/Lm)*(Tmech/lambdaDR);
   iD = lambdaDR/Lm;
   Ia = sqrt((iD^2+iQ^2)/2);
   omegae = omegame+ (RaR/LR)*(iQ/iD);
   fe = omegae/(2*pi);
   lambdaD = LS*iD;
   lambdaQ = (LS-Lm^2/LR)*iQ;
   lambdaarms = sqrt((lambdaD^2+lambdaQ^2)/2);
   Va = sqrt(((Ra*iD-omegae*lambdaQ)^2 +(Ra*iQ+omegae*lambdaD)^2)/2);

   if (lambdaarms > lambdaarmsrated) || (Va > Varated) || (Ia > Iamax)
     lambdaDR = 0.999*lambdaDR;
   else
     sw = 1;
   end
 end % End of loop
```

```
fprintf('iQ = %3.1f, iD = %3.1f [A]\n',iQ,iD)
fprintf('Ia = %3.1f [A]\n',Ia)
fprintf('omegame = %3.1f [rad/sec], omegae = %3.1f [rad/sec]\n',omegame,omegae)
fprintf('fe = %3.1f [Hz]\n',fe)
fprintf('Va = %3.1f [V,l-n], Va = %3.1f [V,l-l]\n',Va,Va*sqrt(3))
```

Running the MATLAB script produces the following results:

$$i_D = 12.6 \text{ A} \quad i_Q = 128.7 \text{ A} \quad I_a = 91.4 \text{ A}$$

$$f_e = 60.0 \text{ Hz} \quad V_a = 574.9 \text{ A}$$

Note that the field-oriented control algorithm for this operating condition results in essentially the same motor voltage, current, and applied electrical frequency as the volts-per-hertz control of Example 10.13 part (a). This is not surprising; the motor responds to its terminal voltages and currents and not to the algorithm that produces them and in this case both algorithms apply essentially the same voltages and currents to this motor.

Practice Problem 10.8

Consider again the induction motor and field-oriented control system of Example 10.14. Assume that the speed is readjusted to 1172 r/min and that the electromagnetic power is 25.4 kW, corresponding to the operating condition of Example 10.13 part (b). Find the direct- and quadrature-axis currents, the rms amplitude of the armature current, the electrical frequency, and the rms terminal voltage.

Solution

$$i_D = 13.1 \text{ A} \quad i_Q = 56.5 \text{ A} \quad I_a = 41.0 \text{ A}$$

$$f_e = 40.0 \text{ Hz} \quad V_a = 389.7 \text{ A}$$

Notice that, in this case, the volts-per-hertz algorithm of Example 10.13 and the field-oriented algorithm of Example 10.14 give slightly different values of terminal voltage and current for operation at the same power and speed. The reason for this is because the volts-per-hertz algorithm approximates constant armature flux density based upon the terminal voltage (which includes the voltage drop across the armature resistance) while the field-oriented algorithm computes the armature flux density directly.

The ability to independently control the rotor flux and the torque has important control implications. Consider, for example, the dynamic response of the direct-axis rotor flux to a change in direct-axis current. Equation 10.62, with $\lambda_{qR} = 0$, becomes

$$0 = R_{aR}i_{dR} + \frac{d\lambda_{dR}}{dt} \tag{10.81}$$

Substituting for i_{dR} in terms of λ_{dR} from Eq. 10.55

$$i_{dR} = \frac{\lambda_{dR} - L_m i_d}{L_R} \tag{10.82}$$

gives a differential equation for the rotor flux linkages λ_{DR}

$$\frac{d\lambda_{dR}}{dt} + \left(\frac{R_{aR}}{L_R}\right)\lambda_{dR} = \left(\frac{L_m}{L_R}\right)i_d \qquad (10.83)$$

From Eq. 10.83 we see that the response of the rotor flux to a step change in direct-axis current i_d is relatively slow; λ_{dR} will change exponentially with the rotor time constant of $\tau_R = L_R/R_{aR}$. Since the torque is proportional to the product $\lambda_{dR}i_q$ we see that fast torque response will be obtained from changes in i_q. Thus, for example, to implement a step change in torque, a practical control algorithm might start with a step change in $(i_Q)_{ref}$ to achieve the desired torque change, followed by an adjustment in $(i_D)_{ref}$ (and hence λ_{dR}) to readjust the armature current or terminal voltage as desired. This adjustment in $(i_D)_{ref}$ would be coupled with a compensating adjustment in $(i_Q)_{ref}$ to maintain the torque at its desired value.

As discussed in Example 10.14, under any steady-state operating condition both a volts-per-hertz controller and a field-oriented controller can achieve the same operating point. It is the capability of a field-oriented controller to rapidly control torque and respond to changes in operating conditions that distinguishes it from a volts-per-hertz controller in many applications.

10.4 CONTROL OF VARIABLE-RELUCTANCE MOTORS

Unlike dc and ac (synchronous or induction) machines, variable-reluctance motors (VRMs) cannot be simply "plugged in" to a dc or ac source and then be expected to run. As is discussed in Chapter 8, the phases must be excited with (typically unipolar) currents, and the timing of these currents must be carefully correlated with the position of the rotor poles in order to produce useful, time-averaged torque. The result is that, although the VRM itself is perhaps the simplest of rotating machines, a practical VRM drive system is relatively complex.

VRM drive systems are competitive only because this complexity can be realized easily and inexpensively through the use of power and microelectronic circuitry. These drive systems require a fairly sophisticated level of controllability for even the simplest modes of VRM operation. Once the capability to implement this control is available, fairly sophisticated control features can be added (typically in the form of additional software) at little additional cost, further increasing the competitive position of VRM drives.

In addition to the VRM itself, the basic VRM drive system consists of the following components: a rotor-position sensor, a controller, and an inverter. The function of the rotor-position sensor is to provide an indication of shaft position which can be used to control the timing and waveform of the phase excitation. This is directly analogous to the timing signal used to control the firing of the cylinders in an automobile engine.

The controller is typically implemented in software in microelectronic (microprocessor) circuitry. Its function is to determine the sequence and waveforms of the phase excitation required to achieve the desired motor speed-torque characteristics. In addition to set points of desired speed and/or torque and shaft position (from the shaft-position sensor), sophisticated controllers often employ additional inputs including shaft-speed and phase-current magnitude. Along with the basic control function of determining the desired torque for a given speed, the more sophisticated controllers attempt to provide excitations which are in some sense optimized (for maximum efficiency, stable transient behavior, etc.).

The control circuitry consists typically of low-level electronics which cannot be used to directly supply the currents required to excite the motor phases. Rather its output consists of signals which control an inverter which in-turn supplies the phase currents. Control of the VRM is achieved by the application of an appropriate set of currents to the VRM phase windings.

Figures 10.26a to c show three common configurations found in inverter systems for driving VRMs. These configurations are referred to as H-bridge inverters. The switches labeled by "S" represent power-electronic components such as transistors or TRIACS (switchable diodes). The elements labeled "D" are diodes, circuit elements which carry current only in a single direction (in the direction of the arrow formed by the diode symbol). Diodes can be modeled as a short-circuit for currents flowing in the arrow direction and as an open circuit when currents attempt to reverse.

Each inverter in Fig. 10.26 is shown in a two-phase configuration. As can be seen, extension of each configuration to drive additional phases can be readily accomplished. The configuration of Fig. 10.26a is perhaps the simplest. Closing switches

Figure 10.26 Inverter configurations. (a) Two-phase inverter which uses two switches per phase. (b) Two-phase inverter which uses a split supply and one switch per phase. (c) Two-phase inverter with bifilar phase windings and one switch per phase.

S_{1a} and S_{1b} connects the phase-1 winding across the supply ($v_1 = V_0$) and causes the winding current to increase. Opening just one of the switches forces a short across the winding and the current will decay through the associated connected diode, while opening both switches connects the winding across the supply with negative polarity through the diodes D_{1a} and D_{1b} ($v_1 = -V_0$) and the winding current will decay more rapidly. Note that this configuration is capable of regeneration (returning energy to the supply), but not of supplying negative current to the phase winding. However, since the torque in a VRM is proportional to the square of the phase current, there is no need for negative winding current.

The average winding current can be controlled through the process of pulse-width modulation, under which a series of switch configurations alternately charge and discharge a phase winding. Using this technique, an inverter such as that of Fig. 10.26a can readily be made to supply the range of waveforms required to drive a VRM.

The inverter configuration of Fig. 10.26a is perhaps the simplest of H-bridge configurations which provide regeneration capability. Its main disadvantage is that it requires two switches per phase. In many applications, the cost of the switches (and their associated drive circuitry) dominates the cost of the inverter, and the result is that this configuration is less attractive in terms of cost when compared to other configurations which require one switch per phase.

Figure 10.26b shows one such configuration. This configuration requires a split supply (i.e., two supplies of voltage V_0) but only a single switch and diode per phase. Closing switch S_1 connects the phase-1 winding to the upper dc source. Opening the switch causes the phase current to transfer to diode D_1, connecting the winding to the bottom dc source. Phase 1 is thus supplied by the upper dc source and regenerates through the bottom source. Note that to maintain symmetry and to balance the energy supplied from each source equally, phase 2 is connected oppositely so that it is supplied from the bottom source and regenerates into the top source.

The major disadvantages of the configuration of Fig. 10.26b are that it requires a split supply and that when the switch is opened, the switch must withstand a voltage of $2V_0$. This can be readily seen by recognizing that when diode D_1 is forward-biased and carrying current it looks like a short circuit and thus the switch S_1 is connected across the two supplies. Such switches are likely to be more expensive than the switches required by the configuration of Fig. 10.26a. Both of these issues will tend to offset some of the economic advantage which can be gained by the elimination of one switch and one diode as compared with the inverter circuit of Fig. 10.26a.

A third inverter configuration is shown in Fig. 10.26c. This configuration requires only a single dc source and uses only a single switch and diode per phase. This configuration achieves regeneration through the use of *bifilar* phase windings. In a bifilar winding, each phase is wound with two separate windings which are closely coupled magnetically (this can be achieved by winding the two windings at the same time) and can be thought of as the primary and secondary windings of a transformer.

When switch S_1 is closed, the primary winding of phase 1 is energized, exciting phase 1. Opening the switch induces a voltage in the secondary winding (note the polarity indicated by the dots in Fig. 10.26c) in such a direction as to forward-bias diode D_1. The result is that current is transferred from the primary to the secondary winding with a polarity such that the current in the phase decays to zero and energy is returned to the source.

Although this configuration requires only a single dc source, it requires a switch which must withstand a voltage in excess of $2V_0$ (the degree of excess being determined by the voltage developed across the primary leakage reactance as current is switched from the primary to the secondary windings) and requires the more complex bifilar winding in the machine. In addition, the switches in this configuration must include snubbing circuitry (typically consisting of a resistor-capacitor combination) to protect them from transient overvoltages. These overvoltages result from the fact that although the two windings of the bifilar winding are wound such that they are as closely coupled as possible, perfect coupling cannot be achieved. As a result, there will be energy stored in the leakage fields of the primary winding which must be dissipated when the switch is opened.

As is discussed in Chapter 8, VRM operation requires control of the current applied to each phase. For example, one control strategy for constant torque production is to apply constant current to each phase during the time that $dL/d\theta_m$ for that phase is constant. This results in constant torque proportional to the square of the phase-current magnitude. The magnitude of the torque can be controlled by changing the magnitude of the phase current.

The control required to drive the phase windings of a VRM is made more complex because the phase-winding inductances change both with rotor position and with current levels due to saturation effects in the magnetic material. As a result, it is not possible in general to implement an open-loop PWM scheme based on a pre-calculated algorithm. Rather, pulse-width-modulation is typically accomplished through the use of current feedback. The instantaneous phase current can be measured and a switching scheme can be devised such that a switch can be turned off when the current has been found to reach a desired maximum value and turned on when the current decays to a desired minimum value. In this manner the average phase current is controlled to a pre-determined function of the rotor position and desired torque.

This section has provided a brief introduction to the topic of drive systems for variable-reluctance machines. In most cases, many additional issues must be considered before a practical drive system can be implemented. For example, accurate rotor-position sensing is required for proper control of the phase excitation, and the control loop must be properly compensated to ensure its stability. In addition, the finite rise and fall times of current buildup in the motor phase windings will ultimately limit the maximum achievable rotor torque and speed.

The performance of a complete VRM drive system is intricately tied to the performance of all its components, including the VRM, its controller, and its inverter. In this sense, the VRM is quite different from the induction, synchronous, and dc machines discussed earlier in this chapter. As a result, it is useful to design the complete drive system as an integrated package and not to design the individual components (VRM, inverter, controller, etc.) separately. The inverter configurations of Fig. 10.26 are representative of a number of possible inverter configurations which can be used in VRM drive systems. The choice of an inverter for a specific application must be made based on engineering and economic considerations as part of an integrated VRM drive system design.

10.5 SUMMARY

This chapter introduces various techniques for the control of electric machines. The broad topic of electric machine control requires a much more extensive discussion than is possible here so our objectives have been somewhat limited. Most noticeably, the discussion of this chapter focuses almost exclusively on steady-state behavior, and the issues of transient and dynamic behavior are not considered.

The starting point is a discussion of dc motors, for which it is convenient to subdivide the control techniques into two categories: speed and torque control. The algorithm for speed control in a dc motor is relatively straightforward. With the exception of a correction for voltage drop across the armature resistance, the steady-state speed is determined by the condition that the generated voltage must be equal to the applied armature voltage. Since the generated voltage is proportional to the field flux and motor speed, we see that the steady-state motor speed is proportional to the armature voltage and inversely proportional to the field flux.

An alternative viewpoint is that of torque control. Because the commutator/brush system maintains a constant angular relationship between the field and armature flux, the torque in a dc motor is simply proportional to the product of the armature current and the field flux. As a result, dc motor torque can be controlled directly by controlling the armature current as well as the field flux.

Because synchronous motors develop torque only at synchronous speed, the speed of a synchronous motor is simply determined by the electrical frequency of the applied armature excitation. Thus, steady-state speed control is simply a matter of armature frequency control. Torque control is also possible. By transforming the stator quantities into a reference frame rotating synchronously with the rotor (using the dq0 transformation of Appendix C), we found that torque is proportional to the field flux and the component of armature current in space quadrature with the field flux. This is directly analogous to the torque production in a dc motor. Control schemes which adopt this viewpoint are referred to as *vector* or *field-oriented* control.

Induction machines operate asynchronously; rotor currents are induced by the relative motion of the rotor with respect to the synchronously rotating stator-produced flux wave. When supplied by a constant-frequency source applied to the armature winding, the motor will operate at a speed somewhat lower than synchronous speed, with the motor speed decreasing as the load torque is increased. As a result, precise speed regulation is not a simple matter, although in most cases the speed will not vary from synchronous speed by an excessive amount.

Analogous to the situation in a synchronous motor, in spite of the fact that the rotor of an induction motor rotates at less than synchronous speed, the interaction between the rotor and stator flux waves is indeed synchronous. As a result, a transformation into a synchronously rotating reference frame results in rotor and stator flux waves which are constant. The torque can then be expressed in terms of the product of the rotor flux linkages and the component of armature current in quadrature with the rotor flux linkages (referred to as the *quadrature-axis component* of the armature current) in a fashion directly analogous to the field-oriented viewpoint of a synchronous motor. Furthermore, it can be shown that the rotor flux linkages are proportional to the direct-axis component of the armature current, and thus the direct-axis component of armature current behaves much like the field current in a synchronous motor. This field-oriented viewpoint of induction machine control, in combination with the power-electronic and control systems required to implement it, has led to the widespread applicability of induction machines to a wide range of variable-speed applications.

Finally, this chapter ends with a brief discussion of the control of variable-reluctance machines. To produce useful torque, these machines typically require relatively complex, nonsinusoidal current waveforms whose shape must be controlled as a function of rotor position. Typically, these waveforms are produced by pulse-width modulation combined with current feedback using an H-bridge inverter of the type discussed in Section 10.4. The details of these waveforms depend heavily upon the geometry and magnetic properties of the VRM and can vary significantly from motor to motor.

10.6 CHAPTER 10 VARIABLES

λ	Flux linkage [Wb]
Λ_{PM}	Permanent magnet direct-axis flux linkages [Wb]
ω_e	Electrical frequency [rad/sec]
ω_m	Rotor angular velocity [rad/sec]
ω_{me}	Rotor angular velocity in electrical units [rad/sec]
ω_s	Synchronous angular velocity [rad/sec]
τ	Time constant [sec]
θ_s	Rotor flux-axis angle [rad]
$\bar{\theta}_s$	Estimated value of θ_s [rad]
B	Flux density [T]
D, l	Linear dimensions [m]
e, E	Voltage
E_{af}	Generated voltage [per unit]
$\hat{E}_{af}$	Generated voltage, complex amplitude [per unit]
f	Frequency [Hz]
f_e	Electrical frequency [Hz]
F	Magnetomotive force [A]
G	Gain [Volt/(rad/sec)], [N·m/(rad/sec)]
i	Current [A]
I	Current [A, per unit]
$\hat{I}$	Current, complex amplitude [per unit]
J	Moment of inertia [kg·m^2]
K_f	Geometric constant [Ω/(rad/sec)]
K_m	Torque constant [V/(rad/sec)]

L	Inductance [H]
L_s	Synchronous inductance
n	Angular velocity [r/min]
n_s	Synchronous angular velocity [r/min]
P	Power [W]
poles	Number of poles
R	Resistance [Ω]
s	Slip
t	Time [sec]
τ	Time constant [sec]
T	Torque [N $\cdot$ m]
v	Voltage [V]
V	Voltage [V, per unit]
$\hat{V}$	Voltage, complex amplitude [V, per unit]
X_m	Magnetizing reactance [Ω, per unit]
X_s	Synchronous reactance [Ω, per unit]

Subscripts:

a	Armature
base	Base quantity
d, D, DR	Direct-axis component
dc	Direct current
eq	Equivalent
f, F	Field, final
fl	Full load
i	Initial
max	Maximum
mech	Mechanical
min	Minimum
q, Q, QR	Quadrature-axis component
R	Rotor
S	Stator
ref	Reference
rms	Root mean square

10.7 REFERENCES

Many excellent books are available which provide a much more thorough discussion of electric-machinery control than is possible in the introductory discussion presented here. This bibliography lists a few of the many textbooks available for readers who wish to study this topic in more depth.

Boldea, I., *Reluctance Synchronous Machines and Drives*. New York: Clarendon Press·Oxford, 1996.

Holmes, G., and Lipo, T., *Pulse Width Modulation for Power Converters: Principles and Practice*, IEEE Press, John Wiley & Sons, 2003.

Kenjo, T., *Stepping Motors and Their Microprocessor Controls.* New York: Clarendon Press·Oxford, 1984.

Leonhard, W., *Control of Electric Drives.*, 2nd ed. Berlin: Springer, 1996.

Miller, T. J. E., *Brushless Permanent-Magnet and Reluctance Motor Drives.* New York: Clarendon Press·Oxford, 1989.

Miller, T. J. E., *Switched Reluctance Motors and Their Controls.* New York: Magna Press Publishing and Clarendon Press·Oxford, 1993.

Mohan, N., *Advanced Electric Drives: Analysis, Control and Modeling Using Simulink.* Minneapolis: MNPERE (http://www.MNPERE.com), 2001.

Mohan, N., *Electric Drives: An Integrative Approach.* Minneapolis: MNPERE (http://www.MNPERE.com), 2001.

Murphy, J. M. D., and F. G. Turnbull, *Power Electronic Control of AC Motors.* New York: Pergamon Press, 1988.

Novotny, D. W., and T. A. Lipo, *Vector Control and Dynamics of AC Drives.* New York: Clarendon Press·Oxford, 1996.

Subrahmanyam, V., *Electric Drives: Concepts and Applications.* New York: McGraw-Hill, 1996.

Trzynadlowski, A. M., *Control of Induction Motors.* San Diego, California: Academic Press, 2001.

Vas, P., *Sensorless Vector and Direct Torque Control.* Oxford: Oxford University Press, 1998.

Wu, B., *High-Power Converters and AC Drives,* IEEE Press, John Wiley & Sons, 2006.

10.8   PROBLEMS

10.1 When operating at rated voltage, a 2.5-kW, 120-V, 1725 r/min separately excited dc motor achieves a no-load speed of 1708 r/min at a field current of 0.85 A. The motor has an armature resistance of 163 mA and a shunt-field resistance of 114 Ω. For the purposes of this problem you may assume the rotational losses to be negligible.

This motor is to be used to control the speed of a load whose torque is constant at 13.7 N · m over the speed range of 1400–1750 r/min. The motor will be operated at a constant armature voltage of 120 V. The field winding will be supplied from the 120-V dc armature supply via a pulse-width modulation system and the average field voltage and current, and hence the motor speed, will be varied by adjusting the duty cycle of the pulse-width modulation; a duty cycle variation between 0 and 1.0 will result in a linear variation of the average field voltage over the range of 0 to 120 V.

a.   Calculate the field current required to achieve operation at 13.7 N · m torque and 1750 r/min. Calculate the corresponding PWM duty cycle *D*.

b.   Calculate the field current required to achieve operation at 13.7 N · m torque and 1400 r/min. Calculate the corresponding PWM duty cycle.

c.   Plot the required PWM duty cycle as a function of speed over the desired speed range of 1400 to 1750 r/min.

10.2 Repeat Problem 10.1 for a load whose torque is 13.7 N·m at 1500 r/min and which varies as the speed to the 1.8 power.

10.3 The dc motor of problem 10.1 has a field-winding inductance $L_f = 3.4$ H and a moment of inertia $J = 0.105$ kg·m^2. The motor is operating at rated terminal voltage and an initial speed of 1500 r/min driving a constant-torque load of 13.7 N · mu.

   a. Calculate the initial field current I_f and PWM duty cycle D.

   At time $t = 0$, the PWM duty cycle is suddenly switched from the value found in part (a) to $D = 0.75$.

   b. Calculate the final values of the field current and motor speed after the transient has died out.

   c. Solve for the field-current as a function of time.

   d. Using MATLAB/Simulink, plot the motor speed and armature current as a function of time.

10.4 The dc motor and load of Example 10.1 have a combined inertia of $J = 2.1$ kg·m^2. The motor is initially operating with an armature voltage of 240 V and field voltage of 62.5 V at a speed of 3600 rpm when the field voltage is suddenly switched to 110 V.

   a. Calculate the resultant steady-state motor speed and armature current.

   b. Using MATLAB/Simulink, plot the motor speed and armature current as a function of time.

10.5 A shunt-connected 240-V, 20-kW, 3400 r/min dc motor has the following parameters

Field resistance:	R_f	$= 197\ \Omega$
Armature resistance	R_a	$= 0.134\ \Omega$
Geometric constant	K_f	$= 0.531$ V/(A · rad/sec)

When operating at rated voltage, no-load, the motor current is 1.93 A.

   a. Calculate the no-load speed and rotational loss.

   b. Assuming the rotational loss to be constant, use MATLAB to plot the motor output power as a function of speed. Limit your plot to a maximum power output of 20 kW.

   c. Armature-voltage control is to be used to maintain constant motor speed as the motor is loaded. For this operating condition, the shunt field voltage will be held constant at 240-V. Plot the armature voltage as a function of power output required to maintain the motor at a constant speed of 3325 r/min.

   d. Consider the situation for armature-voltage control is applied to this motor while the field winding remains connected in shunt across the armature terminals. Repeat part (c) for this operating condition. Is such operation feasible? Why is the motor behavior significantly different from that in part (c)?

10.6 The data sheet for a small permanent-magnet dc motor provides the following parameters:

$$
\begin{aligned}
\text{Rated voltage:} \qquad & V_{\text{rated}} = 6 \text{ V} \\
\text{No-load speed:} \qquad & n_{\text{nl}} = 15025 \text{ r/min} \\
\text{No-load current:} \qquad & I_{\text{nl}} = 0.2 \text{ A} \\
\text{Stall current:} \qquad & I_{\text{stall}} = 1.9 \text{ A}
\end{aligned}
$$

a. Calculate the armature resistance R_a and the torque constant K_m.

b. Calculate the no-load rotational loss.

c. Driving a propellor on a small model airplane, the motor is observed to be operating at a speed of 12000 r/min at a terminal voltage of 6.0 V. Assuming the rotational loss varies as the cube of speed, calculate the power supplied to the propeller. Calculate the motor efficiency at this operating condition.

10.7 A small permanent-magnet dc motor is characterized by the following parameters:

$$
\begin{aligned}
\text{Rated voltage:} \qquad & V_{\text{rated}} = 3 \text{ V} \\
\text{Rated output power:} \qquad & P_{\text{rated}} = 0.32 \text{ W} \\
\text{No-load speed:} \qquad & n_{\text{nl}} = 13100 \text{ r/min} \\
\text{Torque constant:} \qquad & K_m = 0.214 \text{ mV/(r/min)} \\
\text{Stall torque:} \qquad & T_{\text{stall}} = 0.106 \text{ oz·in}
\end{aligned}
$$

a. Calculate the motor armature resistance.

b. Calculate the no-load rotational loss.

c. Assume the motor to be connected to a load such that the total shaft power (actual load plus rotational loss) is equal 300 mW at a speed of 13000 r/min. Assuming the total load to vary as the cube of the motor speed, write a MATLAB script to plot the motor speed as a function of terminal voltage for $1.0 \text{ V} \le V_a \le 3.0 \text{ V}$.

10.8 The data sheet for a 350-W permanent-magnet dc motor provides the following parameters:

$$
\begin{aligned}
\text{Rated voltage:} \qquad & V_{\text{rated}} = 24 \text{ V} \\
\text{Armature resistance:} \qquad & R_a = 97 \text{ m}\Omega \\
\text{No-load speed:} \qquad & n_{\text{nl}} = 3580 \text{ r/min} \\
\text{No-load current:} \qquad & I_{a,\text{nl}} = 0.47 \text{ A}
\end{aligned}
$$

a. Calculate the motor torque-constant K_m in V/(rad/sec).

b. Calculate the no-load rotational loss.

c. The motor is supplied is supplied from a 30-V dc supply through a PWM inverter. Table 10.1 gives the measured motor current as a function of the PWM duty cycle D. Complete the table by calculating the motor speed and the load power for each value of D. Assume that the rotational losses vary as the cube of the motor speed.

Table 10.1 Motor-performance data for Problem 10.8

D	I_a [A]	r/min	P_{load} [W]
0.80	14.70		
0.75	12.79		
0.70	11.55		
0.65	10.34		
0.60	9.20		
0.55	8.07		
0.50	7.02		

10.9 The motor of Problem 10.8 has a moment of inertia of $J = 1.33 \times 10^{-3}$ kg·m². For the purposes of this problem, assume that the motor is unloaded and neglect any effects of rotational loss.

a. Calculate the time to achieve a speed of 3500 r/min if the motor is supplied by a constant armature current of 15 A and

If the motor is supplied by a constant terminal voltage of 24 V,

b. calculate the time to achieve a speed of 3500 r/min and

c. plot the motor speed and armature current as a function of time.

10.10 A 1200-W, 240-V, 3600-r/min permanent-magnet dc motor is to be operated from a current-source inverter so as to provide direct control of the motor torque. The motor torque constant is $K_m = 0.645$ V/(rad/sec) its armature resistance is 2.33 Ω. The motor rotational loss at a speed of 3600 r/min is 109 W. Assume that the rotational loss can be represented as a constant loss torque as the motor speed varies.

a. Calculate the rated armature current of this motor. What is the corresponding mechanical torque in N · m?

b. The current source supplying a current of 4.4 A to the motor armature and the motor speed is measured to be 3120 r/min. Calculate the load torque and power.

c. Assume the load torque of part (b) to vary linearly with speed and the motor and load to have a combined inertia of 9.2×10^{-3} kg·m². Plot the motor speed as a function of time if the armature current of part (b) is suddenly increased to 5.0 A.

10.11 The dc motor of Problem 10.10 is to be controlled by a speed controller of the form shown in Fig. 10.7. With the reference speed set to 3600 r/min $\omega_m = 120\pi$, find

a. the reference voltage V_{a0} such that the no-load motor speed is 3600 rpm and

b. the gain G such that the motor speed is 3550 r/min when the motor load is equal to 1.2 kW and the corresponding armature voltage.

10.12 The dc motor of Problems 10.10 and 10.11 is operating with the controller of Problem 10.11 with a reference speed of 3600 r/min. The motor is connected to an ac generator whose rotational loss is 95 W at 3600 rpm and can be considered to be proportional to speed. The combined inertia of the motor and generator is 0.02 kg·m². The generator is initially unloaded and operating at 3600 r/min when it is loaded to a torque of 3.0 N·m. Assuming the generator load torque remains constant with speed, use MATLAB/Simulink to plot the motor speed, terminal voltage and armature current as a function of time.

10.13 A 500-V, 50-kW, 2200 r/min, separately excited dc motor has the following parameters:

Field resistance:	$R_f = 127\ \Omega$
Rated field voltage:	$V_{f0} = 300$ V
Armature resistance:	$R_a = 0.132\ \Omega$
Geometric constant:	$K_f = 0.886$ V/(A · rad/sec)

This motor is applied in an application for which the load torque varies between no load and 220 N · m. The combined inertia of the motor and load is 6.5 N · m. The application requires that the motor speed remains in the range of 2125 r/min and 2150 r/min over this load range. Repeat the calculations and MATLAB/Simulink simulation of Example 10.5 for this motor and speed and load range.

10.14 A 75 kW, 480 V, 60-Hz, 2-pole synchronous motor has a synchronous reactance of 0.87 per unit. The motor achieves rated speed, rated open-circuit voltage at a field current of 27 A. For the purposes of this problem, all motor losses can be ignored.

a. With the motor operating at rated voltage and speed, calculate the field current required to achieve rated power, unity power factor operation.

b. With the motor operating at 40-Hz, 320-V, rated current and unity power factor, calculate the motor speed, motor output power and and field current.

c. With the motor operating at 75-Hz, 480-V, rated current and unity power factor, calculate the motor speed, motor output power and and field current.

10.15 A 1150-kVA, 4600-V, 60-Hz, three-phase, 4-pole synchronous motor is to be driven from a variable-frequency, three-phase, constant V/Hz inverter rated at 1250-kVA. The synchronous motor has a synchronous reactance of 1.29 per unit and achieves rated open-circuit voltage at a field current of 98 A.

a. Calculate the motor rated speed in r/min and rated current.

b. With the motor operating at rated voltage and speed and an input power of 1000-kW, calculate the field current required to achieve unity-power-factor operation.

The load power of part (b) varies as the speed to the 2.7 power. With the motor field-current held fixed, the inverter frequency is reduced such that the motor is operating at a speed of 1325 r/min.

c. Calculate the inverter frequency and the motor input power and power factor.

d. Calculate the field current required to return the motor to unity power factor.

10.16 Consider a three-phase synchronous motor for which you are given the following data:

Rated line-to-line voltage [V]
Rated [VA]
Rated frequency [Hz] and speed [r/min]
Synchronous reactance in per unit
Field current at rated open-circuit voltage (AFNL) [A]

The motor is to be operated from a variable-frequency, constant V/Hz inverter at speeds of up to 120 percent of the motor rated speed.

a. Under the assumption that the motor terminal voltage and current cannot exceed their rated values, write a MATLAB script which calculates, for a given operating speed, the motor terminal voltage, the maximum possible motor input power, and the corresponding field current required to achieve this operating condition. You may consider the effects of saturation and armature resistance to be negligible.

b. Exercise your program on the synchronous motor of Problem 10.15 for motor speeds of 1500 and 2000 r/min.

10.17 For the purposes of performing field-oriented control calculations on non-salient synchronous motors, write a MATLAB script that will calculate the synchronous inductance L_s and armature-to-field mutual inductance L_{af}, both in henries, and the rated torque in N · m, given the following data:

- Rated line-to-line voltage [V]
- Rated [VA]
- Rated frequency [Hz]
- Number of poles
- Synchronous reactance in per unit
- Field current at rated open-circuit voltage (AFNL) [A]

Exercise your program on a 460-V, 100-kW, 4-pole, 60-Hz motor with synchronous reactance of 0.932 per unit and AFNL = 15.8 A.

10.18 A 125-kVA, 540-V, 60-Hz, 4-pole, three-phase synchronous machine is to be operated as a synchronous motor under field-oriented torque control using a system such as that shown in Fig. 10.14a. The machine has a synchronous reactance of 0.882 per unit and AFNL = 17.3 A. The motor is operating at rated speed, loaded to 50 percent of its rated torque at a field current of 14.6 A with the field-oriented controller set to maintain $i_D = 0$.

a. Calculate the synchronous inductance L_s and armature-to-field mutual inductance L_{af}, both in henries.

    b. Find the quadrature-axis current i_Q and the corresponding rms magnitude of the armature current i_a.

    c. Find the motor line-to-line terminal voltage.

10.19 The synchronous motor of Problem 10.18 is operating under field-oriented torque control such that $i_D = 0$. With the field current set equal to 15.6 A and with the torque reference set equal to 0.8 times the motor rated torque, the motor speed is observed to be 1515 r/min.

    a. Calculate the motor output power.

    b. Find the quadrature-axis current i_Q and the corresponding rms magnitude of the armature current i_a.

    c. Calculate the stator electrical frequency

    d. Find the motor line-to-line terminal voltage.

10.20 Consider the case in which the load on synchronous motor in the field-oriented torque-control system of Problem 10.18 is increased and the motor begins slow down. Based upon some knowledge of the load characteristic, it is determined that it will be necessary to raise the torque set point T_{ref} from 50 percent to 85 percent of the motor rated torque in order to return the motor to its rated speed.

    a. If the field current were to be left unchanged at 14.6 A, calculate the values of quadrature-axis current, rms armature current and motor line-to-line terminal voltage (in V and in per unit) which will result in response to this change in reference torque.

    b. In order to achieve this operating condition with reasonable armature terminal voltage, the field-oriented control algorithm is changed to the unity-power-factor algorithm described in the text following Example 10.9. Based upon that algorithm, calculate

        i. the motor field current,

       ii. the direct- and quadrature-axis currents, i_D and i_Q,

      iii. the rms armature voltage, and

      iv. the motor terminal line-to-line terminal voltage (in V and in per unit).

10.21 Consider a 450-kW, 2300-V, 50-Hz, 6-pole synchronous motor with a synchronous reactance of 1.32 per unit and AFNL $= 117$ A. It is to be operated under field-oriented torque control using the unity-power-factor algorithm described in the text following Example 10.9. It will be used to drive a load whose torque varies quadratically with speed and whose torque at a speed of 1000 r/min is 4100 N · m. The complete drive system will include a speed-control loop such as that shown in Fig. 10.14b.

Write a MATLAB script whose input is the desired motor speed (up to 1000 r/min) and whose output is the motor torque, power and power factor, the field current, the direct- and quadrature-axis currents, the armature current and the line-to-line terminal voltage.

10.22 A 125-kVA, 480-V, 60-Hz, four-pole three-phase synchronous machine has a saturated synchronous reactance of 1.15 and achieves rated open-circuit voltage at a field current of 18.5 A. This machine will be operated as a motor and will be operated from an inverter with a field-oriented control algorithm. For operation at rated torque and at 1500 r/min, find the field current which results in minimum armature current and such that the terminal flux linkages do not exceed their rated value. Find the corresponding direct- and quadrature axis currents, the armature current in per-unit and Amperes, terminal voltage and power output.

10.23 Consider a field-oriented controller which limits the motor terminal current to its rated value and either the rms line-neutral flux linkage to its rated value (for operation below rated speed) or the motor terminal voltage to its rated value (for operation above rated speed). This controller is applied to the motor of Example 10.10 with the objective of producing the maximum possible torque at speeds of (a) 1000 r/min and (b) 1400 r/min. In each case, calculate the resultant motor terminal voltage and current, the direct- and quadrature-axis currents, the motor output power, and the torque in percent of rated torque and the corresponding field current.

10.24 The synchronous machine and field-controlled inverter system of Problem 10.22 is to be operated at a speed of 2000 r/min.

    a. Find the field current which results in minimum armature current such that the terminal voltage does not exceed the motor rated voltage. Find the corresponding direct- and quadrature axis currents, the armature current in per-unit and Amperes, terminal voltage, and power output.

    b. With the motor operating at 2000 r/min as in part (a), the field-oriented control algorithm is modified to deliver the maximum possible torque subject to the constraint that the terminal voltage does not exceed the motor rated voltage and the armature current does not exceed the rated value. Find the corresponding direct- and quadrature axis currents, the armature current in per-unit and Amperes, terminal voltage, power output and torque in percent of rated torque.

10.25 A 2.5-kVA, 230-V, 2-pole, three-phase permanent-magnet synchronous motor achieves rated open-circuit voltage at a speed of 3530 r/min. Its synchronous inductance is 15.6 mH.

    a. Calculate Λ_{PM} for this motor.

    b. If the motor is operating at rated voltage and rated current at a speed of 3600 r/min, calculate the motor power in kW and the peak direct- and quadrature-axis components of the armature current, i_D and i_Q respectively and the armature current in Amperes and in per-unit.

10.26 Field-oriented torque control is to be applied to the permanent-magnet synchronous motor of Problem 10.25. If the motor is to be operated at 4000 r/min at rated terminal voltage,

    a. calculate the torque and power which the motor can supply if the motor current is limited to its rated value and

    b. the corresponding values of i_D and i_Q.

10.27 A 25-kVA, 480-V, 2-pole, three-phase permanent-magnet synchronous motor has a maximum speed of 9500 r/min and produces rated open-circuit voltage at a speed of 7675 r/min. The motor has a synchronous inductance of 5.59 mH. The motor is to be operated under field-oriented torque control.

    a.   Calculate the maximum torque the motor can produce without exceeding rated armature current.

    b.   Assuming the motor to be operated with the torque controller adjusted to produce maximum torque (as found in part (a)) and $i_D = 0$, calculate the maximum speed at which it can operate without exceeding rated armature voltage.

    c.   In order to operate at speeds in excess of that found in part, flux weakening will be employed to maintain the armature voltage at its rated value. Assuming the motor to be operating at 9500 r/min with rated armature voltage and current, calculate

        i.   the motor torque,

        ii.   the motor power and power factor,

        iii.   the direct-axis current i_D, and

        iv.   the quadrature-axis current i_Q.

10.28 The permanent magnet motor of Problem 10.27 is to be operated under vector control using the following algorithm:

    ■   Terminal voltage not to exceed rated value

    ■   Terminal current not to exceed rated value

    ■ $i_D = 0$ unless flux weakening is required to avoid excessive armature voltage

Write a MATLAB script to produce plots of the maximum power and torque which this system can produce as a function of motor speed for speeds up to 9500 r/min.

10.29 A three-phase, two-pole permanent-magnet synchronous motor achieves its rated open-circuit voltage of 475 V at a speed of 19250 r/min and has a synchronous inductance of 0.36 mH. Thermal considerations limit the motor terminal current to a maximum value of 350 A. The motor is to be operated from a field-oriented controller which limits the rms terminal flux density to its rated value for speeds below 19250 r/min and which limits the motor terminal voltage to its rated value for speeds in excess of 19250 r/min. Calculate the maximum motor possible output power and the corresponding terminal current and voltage and direct- and quadrature-axis currents for operation at speeds of (a) 16000 r/min and (b) 25000 r/min.

10.30 Consider a 460-V, 50-kW, 4-pole, 60-Hz induction motor which has the following equivalent-circuit parameters in ohms per phase referred to the stator:

$$R_1 = 0.049 \quad R_2 = 0.118 \quad X_1 = 0.53 \quad X_2 = 0.55 \quad X_m = 29.6$$

The motor is to be operated from a variable frequency, constant-V/Hz drive whose output is 460-V at 60-Hz. Neglect any effects of rotational loss. The motor drive is initially adjusted to a frequency of 60 Hz.

   a. Calculate the peak torque and the corresponding slip and motor speed in r/min.
   b. Calculate the motor torque at a slip of 3.2 percent and the corresponding output power.
   c. Assuming the load torque of part (b) remains constant with speed, estimate the resultant motor speed in r/min if the drive frequency is reduced to 45 Hz by assume that R_1 is negligible. Including the effects of R_1, calculate the actual motor torque corresponding to this speed.

10.31 Consider the 460-V, 50-kW, 4-pole induction motor and drive system of Problem 10.30.

   a. Write a MATLAB script to plot the speed-torque characteristic of the motor at drive frequencies of 20, 40 and 60 Hz for speeds ranging from -200 r/min to the synchronous speed at each frequency.
   b. Determine the drive frequency required to maximize the starting torque and calculate the corresponding torque in $N \cdot m$. Plot the speed-torque characteristic for this drive frequency on the plot of part (a).

10.32 An 1100-kW, 2400-V, 8-pole, 60-Hz three-phase induction motor had the following equivalent-circuit parameters in ohms per phase Y referred to the stator:

$$R_1 = 0.054 \quad R_2 = 0.29 \quad X_1 = 0.59 \quad X_2 = 0.61 \quad X_m = 24.2$$

The motor will be driven by a constant-V/Hz drive whose voltage is 2400 V at a frequency of 60 Hz.
The motor is used to drive a load whose power is 1050 kW at a speed of 842 r/min and which varies as the cube of speed. Using MATLAB, plot the motor speed as a function of frequency as the drive frequency is varied between 15 and 60 Hz.

10.33 A 125-kW, 60-Hz, 4-pole, 480-V three-phase wound-rotor induction motor develops full-load torque at a speed of 1732 r/min with the rotor short-circuited. An external non-inductive resistance of 790 mΩ is placed in series with each phase of the rotor and the motor is observed to develop its rated torque at a speed of 1693 r/min. Calculate the rotor resistance per phase of the original motor.

10.34 The wound rotor of Problem 10.33 will be used to drive a constant-torque load equal to the rated full-load torque of the motor. Using the results of Problem 10.33, calculate the external rotor resistance required to adjust the motor speed to 1550 r/min.

10.35 A 45-kW, 400-V, three-phase, 4-pole, 50-Hz, wound-rotor induction motor develops a maximum internal torque of 237 percent at a slip of 15.7 percent when operated at rated voltage and frequency with its rotor short-circuited directly at the slip rings. Stator resistance and rotational losses may be neglected, and the rotor resistance may be assumed to be constant, independent of rotor frequency. Determine

a. the slip at full load in percent,

b. the rotor I^2R loss at full load in watts, and

c. the starting torque at rated voltage and frequency N · m.

If the rotor resistance is now doubled (by inserting external series resistance at the slip rings), determine

d. the torque in N · m when the stator current is at its full-load value and

e. the corresponding slip.

10.36 A 45-kW, three-phase, 440-V, 6-pole wound-rotor induction motor develops its rated full-load output at a speed of 1164 r/min when operated at rated voltage and frequency with its slip rings short-circuited. The maximum torque it can develop at rated voltage and frequency is 227 percent of full-load torque. The resistance of the rotor winding is 0.34 Ω/phase Y. Neglect rotational and stray-load losses and stator resistance.

a. Compute the rotor I^2R loss at full load.

b. Compute the speed at maximum torque.

c. How much resistance must be inserted in series with the rotor to produce maximum starting torque?

The motor is now run from a 50-Hz supply with the applied voltage adjusted so that, for any given torque, the air-gap flux wave has the same amplitude as it does when operated 60 Hz at the same torque level.

d. Compute the 50-Hz applied voltage.

e. Compute the speed at which the motor will develop a torque equal to its 60-Hz value with its slip rings short-circuited.

10.37 The three-phase, 2400-V, 1100-kW, 8-pole induction motor of Problem 10.32 is to be driven from a field-oriented speed-control system whose controller is programmed to set the rms line-neutral armature flux linkages $(\lambda_a)_{rms}$ equal to their rated value. The machine is operating at 850 r/min driving a load which is known to be 950 kW at this speed. Find:

a. the value of the peak direct- and quadrature-axis components of the armature currents i_D and i_Q,

b. the rms armature current under this operating condition,

c. the electrical frequency of the drive in Hz, and

d. the rms line-line armature voltage.

10.38 A field-oriented drive system will be applied to a 230-V, 15-kW, 4-pole, 60-Hz induction motor which has the following equivalent-circuit parameters in ohms per phase referred to the stator:

$$R_1 = 0.0429 \quad R_2 = 0.0937 \quad X_1 = 0.459 \quad X_2 = 0.471 \quad X_m = 24.8$$

The motor is connected to a load whose torque can be assumed proportional to speed as $T_{load} = 64(n/1800)$ N·m, where n is the motor speed in r/min. The field-oriented controller is adjusted such that the rotor flux linkages λ_{DR} are equal to the machine's rated peak flux linkages and the motor speed is 1275 r/min. Find

a. the electrical frequency in Hz,

b. the rms armature current and line-to-line voltage, and

c. the motor input kVA.

d. If the field-oriented controller is set to maintain the motor speed at 1275 r/min, plot the rms armature V/Hz as a percentage of the rated V/Hz as a function of λ_{DR} as λ_{DR} is varied between 75 and 100 percent of the machine's rated peak flux linkages. What percentage of rated peak flux linkages will result in the motor operating at rated rms armature V/Hz?

10.39 The 15-kW induction motor-drive and load of Problem 10.38 is operating at a speed of 1425 r/min with the field-oriented controller adjusted to maintain the rotor flux linkages λ_{DR} equal to the 85 percent of the machine's rated peak value.

a. Calculate the corresponding values of the direct- and quadrature-axis components of the armature current, i_D and i_Q, and the rms armature current.

b. Calculate the corresponding line-to-line terminal voltage drive electrical frequency.

The quadrature-axis current i_Q is now increased by 10 percent while the direct-axis current is held constant.

c. Calculate the resultant motor speed and power output.

d. Calculate the terminal voltage and drive frequency.

e. Calculate the total kVA input into the motor.

f. With the controller set to maintain constant speed, determine the set point for λ_{DR} as a percentage of rated peak flux linkages that sets the terminal V/Hz equal to the rated machine rated V/Hz.
(Hint: This solution is most easily found using a MATLAB script to search for the desired result.)

10.40 A three-phase, eight-pole, 60-Hz, 4160-V, 1250-kW squirrel-cage induction motor has the following equivalent-circuit parameters in ohms per phase Y referred to the stator:

$$R_1 = 0.212 \quad R_2 = 0.348 \quad X_1 = 1.87 \quad X_2 = 2.27 \quad X_m = 44.6$$

It is operating from a field-oriented drive system at a speed of 836 r/min and a power output of 1135 kW. The field-oriented controller is set to maintain the rotor flux linkages λ_{DR} equal to the machine's rated peak flux linkages.

a. Calculate the motor rms line-to-line terminal voltage, rms armature current, and electrical frequency.

b. Show that steady-state induction-motor equivalent circuit and corresponding calculations of Chapter 6 give the same output power and terminal current when the induction motor speed is 836 r/min and the terminal voltage and frequency are equal to those found in part (a).

Three-Phase Circuits

Generation, transmission, and heavy-power utilization of ac electric energy almost invariably involve a type of system or circuit called a *polyphase system* or *polyphase circuit*. In such a system, each voltage source consists of a group of voltages having related magnitudes and phase angles. Thus, a *q*-phase system employs voltage sources which typically consist of *q* voltages substantially equal in magnitude and successively displaced by a phase angle of $360°/q$. A *three-phase system* employs voltage sources which typically consist of three voltages substantially equal in magnitude and displaced by phase angles of $120°$. Because it possesses definite economic and operating advantages, the three-phase system is by far the most common, and consequently emphasis is placed on three-phase circuits in this appendix.

The three individual voltages of a three-phase source may each be connected to its own independent circuit. We would then have three separate *single-phase systems*. Alternatively, as will be shown in Section A.1, symmetrical electric connections can be made between the three voltages and the associated circuitry to form a three-phase system. It is the latter alternative that we are concerned with in this appendix. Note that the word *phase* now has two distinct meanings. It may refer to a portion of a polyphase system or circuit, or, as in the familiar steady-state circuit theory, it may be used in reference to the angular displacement between voltage or current phasors. There is very little possibility of confusing the two.

A.1 GENERATION OF THREE-PHASE VOLTAGES

Consider the elementary two-pole, three-phase generator of Fig. A.1. On the armature are three coils aa', bb', and cc' whose axes are displaced $120°$ in space from each other. This winding can be represented schematically as shown in Fig. A.2. When the field is excited and rotated, voltages will be generated in the three phases in accordance with Faraday's law. If the field structure is designed so that the flux is distributed sinusoidally over the poles, the flux linking any phase will vary sinusoidally

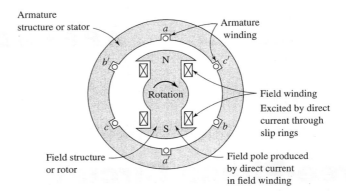

Figure A.1 Elementary two-pole, three-phase generator.

(a)   (b)

Figure A.2 Schematic representation of the windings of Fig. A.1.

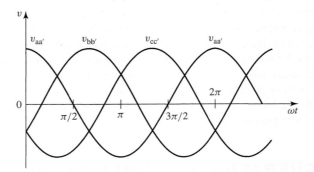

Figure A.3 Voltages generated in the windings of Figs. A.1 and A.2.

with time, and sinusoidal voltages will be induced in the three phases. As shown in Fig. A.3, these three voltages will be displaced 120° electrical degrees in time as a result of the phases being displaced 120° in space. The corresponding phasor diagram is shown in Fig. A.4. In general, the time origin and the reference axis in diagrams such as Figs. A.3 and A.4 are chosen on the basis of analytical convenience.

Figure A.4 Phasor diagram of generated voltages.

There are two possibilities for the utilization of voltages generated in this manner. The six terminals a, a', b, b', c, and c' of the three-phase winding may be connected to three independent single-phase systems, or the three phases of the winding may be interconnected and used to supply a three-phase system. The latter procedure is adopted almost universally. The three phases of the winding may be interconnected in two possible ways, as shown in Fig. A.5. Terminals a', b', and c' may be joined to form the neutral n, yielding a Y *connection,* or terminals a and b', b and c', and c and a' may be joined individually, yielding a $\triangle$ *connection.* In the Y connection, a neutral conductor, shown dashed in Fig. A.5a, may or may not be brought out. If a neutral conductor exists, the system is a four-wire, three-phase system; if not, it is a three-wire, three-phase system. In the $\triangle$ connection (Fig. A.5b), no neutral exists and only a three-wire, three-phase system can be formed.

The three-phase voltages of Figs. A.3 and A.4 are equal and displaced in phase by 120 degrees, a general characteristic of a *balanced three-phase system.* Furthermore, in a balanced three-phase system the impedance in any one phase is equal to that in either of the other two phases, so that the resulting phase currents are also equal and displaced in phase from each other by 120 degrees. Likewise, equal power and equal reactive power flow in each phase. An *unbalanced three-phase system,* however, may be unbalanced in one or more of many ways; the source voltages may be unbalanced,

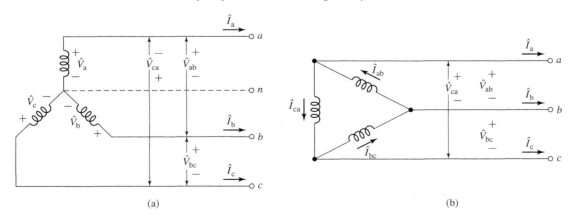

(a)   (b)

Figure A.5 Three-phase connections: (a) Y connection and (b) $\triangle$ connection.

either in magnitude or in phase, or the phase impedances may not be equal. Note that *only balanced systems are treated in this appendix, and none of the methods developed or conclusions reached apply to unbalanced systems.* Most practical analyses are conducted under the assumption of a balanced system. Many industrial loads are three-phase loads and therefore inherently balanced, and in supplying single-phase loads from a three-phase source definite efforts are made to keep the three-phase system balanced by assigning approximately equal single-phase loads to each of the three phases.

A.2 THREE-PHASE VOLTAGES, CURRENTS, AND POWER

When the three phases of the winding in Fig. A.1 are Y-connected, as in Fig. A.5a, the phasor diagram of voltages is that of Fig. A.6. The *phase order* or *phase sequence* in Fig. A.6 is abc; that is, the voltage of phase a reaches its maximum 120° before that of phase b.

The three-phase voltages $\hat{V}_a$, $\hat{V}_b$, and $\hat{V}_c$ are called *line-to-neutral voltages*. The three voltages $\hat{V}_{ab}$, $\hat{V}_{bc}$, and $\hat{V}_{ca}$ are called *line-to-line voltages*. The use of double-subscript notation in Fig. A.6 greatly simplifies the task of drawing the complete diagram. The subscripts indicate the points between which the voltage is determined; for example, the voltage $\hat{V}_{ab}$ is calculated as $\hat{V}_{ab} = \hat{V}_a - \hat{V}_b$.

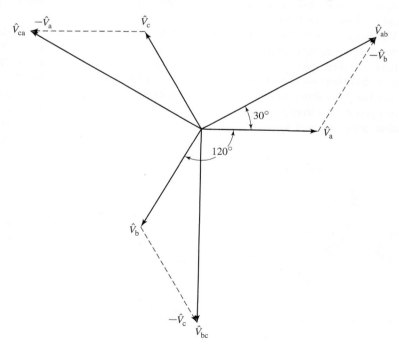

Figure A.6 Voltage phasor diagram for a Y-connected system.

By Kirchhoff's voltage law, the line-to-line voltage $\hat{V}_{ab}$ is

$$\hat{V}_{ab} = \hat{V}_a - \hat{V}_b = \sqrt{3}\,\hat{V}_a\angle 30° \tag{A.1}$$

as shown in Fig. A.6. Similarly,

$$\hat{V}_{bc} = \sqrt{3}\,\hat{V}_b\angle 30° \tag{A.2}$$

and

$$\hat{V}_{ca} = \sqrt{3}\,\hat{V}_c\angle 30° \tag{A.3}$$

These equations show that *the magnitude of the line-to-line voltage is $\sqrt{3}$ times the line-to-neutral voltage.*

When the three phases are Δ-connected, the corresponding phasor diagram of currents is given in Fig. A.7. The Δ currents are $\hat{I}_{ab}$, $\hat{I}_{bc}$, and $\hat{I}_{ca}$. By Kirchhoff's current law, the line current $\hat{I}_a$ is

$$\hat{I}_a = \hat{I}_{ab} - \hat{I}_{ca} = \sqrt{3}\,\hat{I}_{ab}\angle -30° \tag{A.4}$$

as can be seen from the phasor diagram of Fig. A.7. Similarly,

$$\hat{I}_b = \sqrt{3}\,\hat{I}_{bc}\angle -30° \tag{A.5}$$

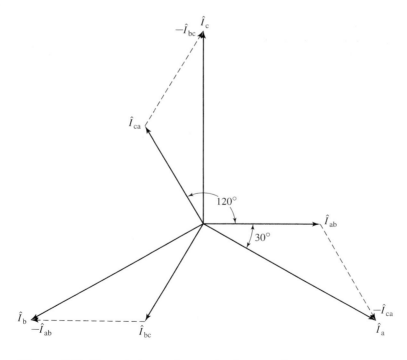

Figure A.7 Current phasor diagram for Δ connection.

and

$$\hat{I}_c = \sqrt{3}\,\hat{I}_{ca}\angle{-30°} \tag{A.6}$$

Stated in words, Eqs. A.4 to A.6 show that for a Δ connection, *the magnitude of the line current is $\sqrt{3}$ times that of the Δ current.* As we see, the relations between Δ currents and line currents of a Δ connection are similar to those between the line-to-neutral and line-to-line voltages of a Y connection.

With the time origin taken at the maximum positive point of the phase-a voltage wave, the instantaneous voltages of the three phases are

$$v_a(t) = \sqrt{2}\,V_{rms}\cos\omega t \tag{A.7}$$

$$v_b(t) = \sqrt{2}\,V_{rms}\cos(\omega t - 120°) \tag{A.8}$$

$$v_c(t) = \sqrt{2}\,V_{rms}\cos(\omega t + 120°) \tag{A.9}$$

where V_{rms} is the rms value of the phase-to-neutral voltage. When the phase currents are displaced from the corresponding phase voltages by the angle θ, the instantaneous phase currents are

$$i_a(t) = \sqrt{2}\,I_{rms}\cos(\omega t + \theta) \tag{A.10}$$

$$i_b(t) = \sqrt{2}\,I_{rms}\cos(\omega t + \theta - 120°) \tag{A.11}$$

$$i_c(t) = \sqrt{2}\,I_{rms}\cos(\omega t + \theta + 120°) \tag{A.12}$$

where I_{rms} is the rms value of the phase current.

The instantaneous power in each phase then becomes

$$p_a(t) = v_a(t)i_a(t) = V_{rms}I_{rms}[\cos(2\omega t + \theta) + \cos\theta] \tag{A.13}$$

$$p_b(t) = v_b(t)i_b(t) = V_{rms}I_{rms}[\cos(2\omega t + \theta - 240°) + \cos\theta] \tag{A.14}$$

$$p_c(t) = v_c(t)i_c(t) = V_{rms}I_{rms}[\cos(2\omega t + \theta + 240°) + \cos\theta] \tag{A.15}$$

Note that the average power of each phase is equal

$$<p_a(t)> = <p_b(t)> = <p_c(t)> = V_{rms}I_{rms}\cos\theta \tag{A.16}$$

The phase angle θ between the voltage and current is referred to as the *power-factor angle* and $\cos\theta$ is referred to as the *power factor.* If θ is negative, then the power factor is said to be *lagging;* if θ is positive, then the power factor is said to be *leading.*

The total instantaneous power for all three phases is

$$p(t) = p_a(t) + p_b(t) + p_c(t) = 3V_{rms}I_{rms}\cos\theta \tag{A.17}$$

Notice that the sum of the cosine terms which involve time in Eqs. A.13 to A.15 (the first terms in the brackets) is zero. We have shown that *the total of the instantaneous power for the three phases of a balanced three-phase circuit is constant and*

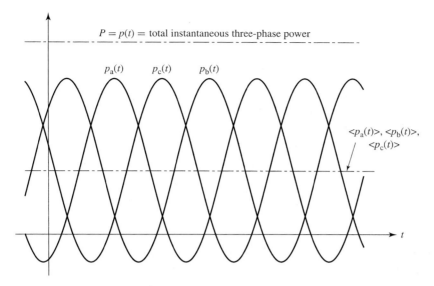

Figure A.8 Instantaneous power in a three-phase system.

does not vary with time. This situation is depicted graphically in Fig. A.8. Instantaneous powers for the three phases are plotted, together with the total instantaneous power, which is the sum of the three individual waves. *The total instantaneous power for a balanced three-phase system is equal to 3 times the average power per phase.* This is one of the outstanding advantages of polyphase systems. It is of particular advantage in the operation of polyphase motors since it means that the shaft-power output is constant and that torque pulsations, with the consequent tendency toward vibration, do not result.

On the basis of single-phase considerations, the average power per phase P_{ph} for either a Y- or Δ-connected system connected to a balanced three-phase load of impedance $Z_{ph} = R_{ph} + jX_{ph}$ Ω/phase is

$$P_{ph} = V_{rms} I_{rms} \cos \theta = I_{ph}^2 R_{ph} \qquad (A.18)$$

Here R_{ph} is the resistance per phase. The total three-phase power P is

$$P = 3P_{ph} \qquad (A.19)$$

Similarly, for reactive power per phase Q_{ph} and total three-phase reactive power Q,

$$Q_{ph} = V_{rms} I_{rms} \sin \theta = I_{ph}^2 X_{ph} \qquad (A.20)$$

and

$$Q = 3Q_{ph} \qquad (A.21)$$

where X_{ph} is the reactance per phase.

The apparent power per phase, also referred to as the voltamperes per phase, S_{ph}, and total three-phase apparent power S are

$$S_{ph} = V_{rms} I_{rms} = I_{rms}^2 Z_{ph} \tag{A.22}$$

$$S = 3 S_{ph} \tag{A.23}$$

In Eqs. A.18 and A.20, θ is the angle between phase voltage and phase current. As in the single-phase case, it is given by

$$\theta = \tan^{-1}\left(\frac{X_{ph}}{R_{ph}}\right) = \cos^{-1}\left(\frac{R_{ph}}{Z_{ph}}\right) = \sin^{-1}\left(\frac{X_{ph}}{Z_{ph}}\right) \tag{A.24}$$

The power factor of a balanced three-phase system is therefore equal to that of any one phase.

A.3 Y- AND Δ-CONNECTED CIRCUITS

Three specific examples are given to illustrate the computational details of Y- and Δ-connected circuits. Explanatory remarks which are generally applicable are incorporated into the solutions.

EXAMPLE A.1

Fig. A.9 shows an equivalent circuit for a 60-Hz transmission system consisting of a line having an impedance $Z_1 = 0.05 + j0.20\,\Omega$, at the receiving end of which is a load of equivalent impedance $Z_L = 10.0 + j3.00\,\Omega$. The impedance of the return conductor should be considered zero.

a. Compute the line current I; the load voltage V_L; the power, reactive power, and apparent power taken by the load; and the power and reactive-power loss in the line.

Suppose now that three such identical systems are to be constructed to supply three such identical loads. Instead of drawing the diagrams one below the other, let them be drawn in the fashion shown in Fig. A.10, which is, of course, the same electrically.

b. For Fig. A.10 give the current in each line; the voltage at each load; the power, reactive power, and apparent power supplied to each load; the power and reactive-power loss in

Figure A.9 Circuit for Example A.1, part (a).

Figure A.10   Circuit for Example A.1, part (b).

each of the three transmission systems; the total power, reactive power, and apparent power supplied to the loads; and the total power and reactive-power loss in the three transmission systems.

Next consider that the three return conductors are combined into one and that the phase relationship of the voltage sources is such that a balanced four-wire, three-phase system results, as in Fig. A.11.

c. For Fig. A.11 give the line current; the load voltage, both line-to-line and line-to-neutral; the power, reactive power, and apparent power taken by each phase of the load; the power and reactive-power loss in each line; the total three-phase power, reactive power, and apparent power taken by the load; and the total power and reactive-power loss in the lines.

d. In Fig. A.11 what is the current in the combined return or neutral conductor?

e. Can this conductor be dispensed with in Fig. A.11 if desired?

Assume now that this neutral conductor is omitted. This results in the three-wire, three-phase system of Fig. A.12.

f. Repeat part (c) for Fig. A.12.

Figure A.11   Circuit for Example A.1, parts (c) to (e).

Figure A.12 Circuit for Example A.1 part (f).

g. On the basis of the results of this example, outline briefly the method of reducing a balanced three-phase Y-connected circuit problem to its equivalent single-phase problem. Be careful to distinguish between the use of line-to-line and line-to-neutral voltages.

■ **Solution**

a.

$$I = \frac{120}{\sqrt{(0.05 + 10.0)^2 + (0.20 + 3.00)^2}} = 11.4 \text{ A}$$

$$V_\text{L} = I \; |Z_\text{L}| = 11.4 \sqrt{(10.0)^2 + (3.00)^2} = 119 \text{ V}$$

$$P_\text{L} = I^2 \; R_\text{L} = (11.4)^2 \; (10.00) = 1300 \text{ W}$$

$$Q_\text{L} = I^2 \; X_\text{L} = (11.4)^2 \; (3.00) = 390 \;\; \text{VAR}$$

$$S_\text{L} = I^2 \; |Z_\text{L}| = (11.4)^2 \sqrt{(10.0)^2 + (3.00)^2} = 1357 \text{ VA}$$

$$P_1 = I^2 \; R_1 = (11.4)^2 \; (0.05) = 6.5 \text{ W}$$

$$Q_1 = I^2 \; X_1 = (11.4)^2 \; (0.20) = 26 \text{ VAR}$$

b. The first four obviously have the same values as in part (a).

> Total power $= 3 \; P_\text{L} = 3 \; (1300) = 3900$ W
> Total reactive power $= 3 \; Q_\text{L} = 3 \; (390) = 1170$ VAR
> Total apparent power $= 3 \; S_\text{L} = 3 \; (1357) = 4071$ VA
> Total line power loss $= 3 \; P_1 = 3 \; (6.5) = 19.5$ W
> Total reactive-power loss $= 3 \; Q_1 = 3 \; (26) = 78$ VAR

c. The results obtained in part (b) are unaffected by this change. The voltage in parts (a) and (b) is now the line-to-neutral voltage. The line-to-line voltage is

$$\sqrt{3} \; (119) = 206 \text{ V}$$

d. By Kirchhoff's current law, the neutral current is the phasor sum of the three line currents. These line currents are equal and displaced in phase by 120°. Since the phasor sum of three equal phasors 120° apart is zero, the neutral current is zero.

e. The neutral current being zero, the neutral conductor can be dispensed with if desired.

f. Since the presence or absence of the neutral conductor does not affect conditions, the values are the same as in part (c).

g. A neutral conductor can be assumed, regardless of whether one is physically present. Since the neutral conductor in a balanced three-phase circuit carries no current and hence has no voltage drop across it, the neutral conductor should be considered to have zero impedance. Then one phase of the Y, together with the neutral conductor, can be removed for study. Since this phase is uprooted at the neutral, *line-to-neutral voltages must be used.* This procedure yields the single-phase equivalent circuit, in which all quantities correspond to those in one phase of the three-phase circuit. Conditions in the other two phases being the same (except for the 120° phase displacements in the currents and voltages), there is no need for investigating them individually. Line currents in the three-phase system are the same as in the single-phase circuit, and total three-phase power, reactive power, and apparent power are three times the corresponding quantities in the single-phase circuit. If line-to-line voltages are desired, they must be obtained by multiplying voltages in the single-phase circuit by $\sqrt{3}$.

EXAMPLE A.2

Three impedances of value $Z_Y = 4.00 + j3.00 = 5.00 \angle 36.9° \; \Omega$ are connected in Y, as shown in Fig. A.13. For balanced line-to-line voltages of 208 V, find the line current, the power factor, and the total power, reactive power, and apparent power.

■ **Solution**

The rms line-to-neutral voltage V on any one phase, such as phase a, is

$$V = \frac{208}{\sqrt{3}} = 120.1 \text{ V}$$

Hence, the line current

$$\hat{I} = \frac{V}{Z_Y} = \frac{120.1}{5.00 \angle 36.9°} = 24.02 \; \angle{-36.9°} \text{ A}$$

and the power factor is equal to

$$\text{Power factor} = \cos\theta = \cos(-36.9°) = 0.80 \text{ lagging}$$

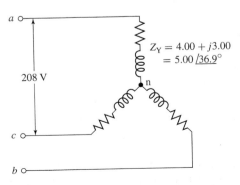

Figure A.13 Circuit for Example A.2.

Thus

$$P = 3\ I^2\ R_Y = 3\ (24.02)^2\ (4.00) = 6924\ \text{W}$$

$$Q = 3\ I^2\ X_Y = 3\ (24.02)^2\ (3.00) = 5193\ \text{VAR}$$

$$S = 3\ VI = 3\ (120.1)\ (24.02) = 8654\ \text{VA}$$

Note that phases a and c (Fig. A.13) do not form a simple series circuit. Consequently, the current cannot be found by dividing 208 V by the sum of the phase-a and phase-c impedances. To be sure, an equation can be written for voltage between points a and c by Kirchhoff's voltage law, but this must be a phasor equation taking account of the 120° phase displacement between the phase-a and phase-c currents. As a result, the method of thought outlined in Example A.1 leads to the simplest solution.

EXAMPLE A.3

Three impedances of value $Z_\Delta = 12.00 + j9.00 = 15.00\angle36.9°\ \Omega$ are connected in Δ, as shown in Fig. A.14. For balanced line-to-line voltages of 208 V, find the line current, the power factor, and the total power, reactive power, and apparent power.

■ **Solution**

The voltage across any one leg of the Δ, V_Δ is equal to the line-to-line voltage V_{l-l}, which is equal to $\sqrt{3}$ times the line-to-neutral voltage V. Consequently,

$$V = \frac{V_{l-l}}{\sqrt{3}} = \frac{208}{\sqrt{3}} = 120.1\ \text{V}$$

and the current in the Δ is given by the line-to-line voltage divided by the Δ impedance

$$\hat{I}_\Delta = \frac{V_{l-l}}{Z_\Delta} = \frac{208}{15.00\ \angle36.9°} = 13.87\ \angle-36.9°\ \text{A}$$

$$\text{Power factor} = \cos\theta = \cos(-36.9°) = 0.80\ \text{lagging}$$

From Eq. A.4 the phase current is equal to

$$I = \sqrt{3}\ I_\Delta = \sqrt{3}\ (13.87) = 24.02\ \text{A}$$

Also

$$P = 3\ P_\Delta = 3\ I_\Delta^2\ R_\Delta = 3\ (13.87)^2\ (12.00) = 6926\ \text{W}$$

$$Q = 3\ Q_\Delta = 3\ I_\Delta^2\ X_\Delta = 3\ (13.87)^2\ (9.00) = 5194\ \text{VAR}$$

Figure A.14   Circuit for Example A.3.

and

$$S = 3 \, (S_{ph})_\Delta = 3V_{l-l} \, I_\Delta = 3 \, (208) \, (13.87) = 8655 \text{ VA}$$

Note that phases ab and bc do not form a simple series circuit, nor does the path cba form a simple parallel combination with the direct path through the phase ca. Consequently, the line current cannot be found by dividing 208 V by the equivalent impedance of Z_{ca} in parallel with $Z_{ab} + Z_{bc}$. Kirchhoff's-law equations involving quantities in more than one phase can be written, but they must be phasor quantities taking account of the $120°$ phase displacement between phase currents and phase voltages. As a result, the method outlined above leads to the simplest solution.

Comparison of the results of Examples A.2 and A.3 leads to a valuable and interesting conclusion. Note that the line-to-line voltage, line current, power factor, total power, reactive power, and apparent power are equal (within round-off error) in the two cases; in other words, conditions viewed from the terminals A, B, and C are identical, and one cannot distinguish between the two circuits from their terminal quantities. It will also be seen that the impedance, resistance, and reactance per phase of the Y connection (Fig. A.13) are exactly one-third of the corresponding values per phase of the Δ connection (Fig. A.14). Consequently, a balanced Δ connection can be replaced by a balanced Y connection providing that the circuit constants per phase obey the relation

$$Z_Y = \frac{1}{3} Z_\Delta \tag{A.25}$$

Conversely, a Y connection can be replaced by a Δ connection provided Eq. A.25 is satisfied. The concept of this Y-Δ equivalence stems from the general Y-Δ transformation and is not the accidental result of a specific numerical case.

Two important corollaries follow from this equivalence: (1) A general computational scheme for balanced circuits can be based entirely on Y-connected circuits or entirely on Δ-connected circuits, whichever one prefers. Since it is frequently more convenient to handle a Y connection, the former scheme is usually adopted. (2) In the frequently occurring problems in which the connection is not specified and is not pertinent to the solution, either a Y or a Δ connection may be assumed. Again the Y connection is more commonly selected. In analyzing three-phase motor performance, for example, the actual winding connections need not be known unless the investigation must consider detailed conditions within the windings themselves. The entire analysis can then be based on an assumed Y connection.

A.4 ANALYSIS OF BALANCED THREE-PHASE CIRCUITS; SINGLE-LINE DIAGRAMS

By combining the principle of Δ-Y equivalence with the technique revealed by Example A.1, it is clear that any balanced-three-phase-circuit problem can be represented by three single-phase equivalent circuits representing the individual phases. Specifically, we have seen that in this case, the voltages and currents on each phase are

(a) Load terminals or substation bus

(b) Generator terminals or bus

Figure A.15 Examples of single-line diagrams.

identical with the exception of a 120° phase shift between phases. Thus, a solution for the voltages and currents in a single phase is sufficient to determine the voltages in currents in the remaining two phases. As a result, all of the methods of single-phase-circuit analysis can be applied. The end results of the single-phase analysis are then translated back into three-phase terms to give the final results.

Under this technique, with three-phase systems represented in terms of their Y-connection equivalent, three-phase equivalent circuits can be fully represented by the equivalent circuit of one phase, with the equivalent for the other two phases being unnecessary repetition. Similarly, a phasor representation for this system is fully represented by the phasor diagram for a single phase. In each case, the currents and voltages of the remaining phases can be easily obtained by phase shifting the single-phase values by ±120°.

Examples of such *single-line diagrams* are given in Fig. A.15, showing two three-phase generators with their associated lines or cables supplying a common substation load. Specific connections of apparatus can be indicated if desired. Thus, Fig. A.15b shows that G_1 is Y-connected and G_2 is Δ-connected. Impedances are given in ohms per phase.

When one is dealing with power, reactive power, and apparent power, it is sometimes more convenient to deal with the entire three-phase circuit at once instead of concentrating on one phase. This possibility arises because simple expressions for three-phase power, reactive power, and voltamperes can be written in terms of line-to-line voltage and line current regardless of whether the circuit is Y- or Δ-connected. Thus, from Eqs. A.18 and A.19, three-phase power is

$$P = 3\, P_{\text{ph}} = 3\, V_{\text{ph}} I_{\text{ph}} \cos \theta \tag{A.26}$$

Since $V_{1-1} = \sqrt{3} V_{\text{ph}}$, Eq. A.26 becomes

$$P = \sqrt{3}\, V_{1-1} I_{\text{ph}} \cos \theta \tag{A.27}$$

Similarly,

$$Q = \sqrt{3}\, V_{1-1}\, I_{\text{ph}} \sin \theta \tag{A.28}$$

and

$$S = \sqrt{3}\, V_{1-1}\, I_{\text{ph}} \tag{A.29}$$

It should be borne in mind, however, that the power-factor angle θ, given by Eq. A.24, is the angle between $\hat{V}_{ph}$ and $\hat{I}_{ph}$ and not that between $\hat{V}_{1-1}$ and $\hat{I}_{ph}$.

EXAMPLE A.4

Figure A.15 is the equivalent circuit of a load supplied from two three-phase generating stations over lines having the impedances per phase given on the diagram. The load requires 30 kW at 0.80 power factor lagging. Generator G_1 operates at a terminal voltage of 797 V line-to-line and supplies 15 kW at 0.80 power factor lagging. Find the load voltage and the terminal voltage and power and reactive-power output of G_2.

■ **Solution**

Let I, P, and Q, respectively, denote line current and three-phase active and reactive power. The subscripts 1 and 2 denote the respective branches of the system; the subscript r denotes a quantity measured at the receiving end of the line. We then have

$$I_1 = \frac{P_1}{\sqrt{3}\ E_1\cos\theta_1} = \frac{15,000}{\sqrt{3}\ (797)\ (0.80)} = 13.6\ \text{A}$$

$$P_{r1} = P_1 - 3\ I_1^2\ R_1 = 15,000 - 3\ (13.6)^2\ (1.4) = 14.22\ \text{kW}$$

$$Q_{r1} = Q_1 - 3\ I_1^2\ X_1 = 15,000\ \tan\ (\cos^{-1} 0.80) - 3\ (13.6)^2\ (1.6) = 10.35\ \text{kVAR}$$

The factor 3 appears before $I_1^2\ R_1$ and $I_1^2\ X_1$ in the last two equations because the current I_1 is the phase current. The load voltage is

$$V_L = \frac{S}{\sqrt{3}\ I_1} = \frac{\sqrt{(14,220)^2 + (10,350)^2}}{\sqrt{3}\ (13.6)}$$

$$= 748\ \text{V line-to-line}$$

Since the load requires 30 kW of real power and $30\tan\ (\cos^{-1} 0.80) = 22.5$ kVAR of reactive power,

$$P_{r2} = 30,000 - 14,220 = 15,780\ \text{W}$$

and

$$Q_{r2} = 22,500 - 10,350 = 12.15\ \text{kVAR}$$

$$I_2 = \frac{S}{\sqrt{3}\ V_{1-1}} = \frac{\sqrt{(15,780)^2 + (12,150)^2}}{\sqrt{3}\ (748)} = 15.4\ \text{A}$$

$$P_2 = P_{r2} + 3\ I_2^2\ R_2 = 15,780 + 3(15.4)^2(0.80) = 16.35\ \text{kW}$$

$$Q_2 = Q_{r2} + 3\ I_2^2\ X_2 = 12,150 + 3\ (15.4)^2\ (1.0) = 12.87\ \text{kVAR}$$

$$V_2 = \frac{S}{\sqrt{3}\ I_2} = \frac{\sqrt{(16,350)^2 + (12,870)^2}}{\sqrt{3}\ (15.4)}$$

$$= 780\ \text{V (l-l)}$$

A.5 APPENDIX A VARIABLES

a	Armature
base	Base quantity
d, D, DR	Direct-axis component
dc	Direct current
eq	Equivalent
f, F	Field, final
fl	Full load
i	Initial
max	Maximum
mech	Mechanical
min	Minimum
q, Q, QR	Quadrature-axis component
R	Rotor
S	Stator
ref	Reference
rms	Root mean square
ω	Electrical frequency [rad/sec]
θ	Phase angle [rad]
q	Number of phases
t	Time [sec]
i, I	Current [A]
$\hat{I}$	Current, complex amplitude [A]
p, P	Power [W]
Q	Reactive power [VAR]
R	Resistance [Ω]
S	Apparent power [VA]
v, V	Voltage [V]
$\hat{V}$	Voltage, complex amplitude [V]
X	Reactance [Ω]
Z	Impedance [Ω]

Subscripts:

Δ	Delta connection
a, b, c	Phase designations
l	Line
l-l	Line-to-line
L	Load
ph	Per phase
r	Receiving end
rms	Root mean square
Y	Y connection

B

Voltages, Magnetic Fields, and Inductances of Distributed AC Windings

Both amplitude and waveform of the generated voltage and armature mmfs in machines are determined by the winding arrangements and general machine geometry. These configurations in turn are dictated by economic use of space and materials in the machine and by suitability for the intended service. In this appendix we supplement the introductory discussion of these considerations in Chapter 4 by analytical treatment of ac voltages and mmfs in the balanced steady state. Attention is confined to the time-fundamental component of voltages and the space-fundamental component of mmfs.

B.1 GENERATED VOLTAGES

In accordance with Eq. 4.52, the rms generated voltage per phase for a concentrated winding ($k_w = 1$) having N_{ph} series turns per phase is

$$E_{rms} = \sqrt{2}\,\pi f N_{ph} \Phi_p \tag{B.1}$$

where f is the frequency and Φ_p the fundamental flux per pole.

A more complex and practical winding will have coil sides for each phase distributed in several slots per pole. Equation B.1 can then be used to compute the voltage distribution of individual coils. To determine the voltage of an entire phase group, the voltages of the component coils must be added as phasors. Such addition of fundamental-frequency voltages is the subject of this article.

B.1.1 Distributed Fractional-Pitch Windings

A simple example of a distributed winding is illustrated in Fig. B.1 for a three-phase, two-pole machine. This case retains all the features of a more general one with any integral number of phases, poles, and slots per pole per phase. At the same time, a *double-layer winding* is shown. Double-layer windings usually lead to simpler end connections and to a machine which is more economical to manufacture and are found in all machines except some small motors below 10 kW. Generally, one side of a coil, such as a_1, is placed in the bottom of a slot, and the other side, $-a_1$, is placed in the top of another slot. Coil sides such as a_1 and a_3 or a_2 and a_4 which are in adjacent slots and associated with the same phase constitute a phase belt. All phase belts are alike when an integral number of slots per pole per phase are used, and for the normal machine the peripheral angle subtended by a phase belt is 60 electrical degrees for a three-phase machine and 90 electrical degrees for a two-phase machine.

Individual coils in Fig. B.1 all span a full pole pitch, or 180 electrical degrees; accordingly, the winding is a full-pitch winding. Suppose now that all coil sides in the tops of the slots are shifted one slot counterclockwise, as in Fig. B.2. Any coil, such as $a_1, -a_1$, then spans only five-sixths of a pole pitch or $\frac{5}{6}(180) = 150$ electrical degrees, and the winding is a fractional-pitch, or chorded, winding. Similar shifting by two slots yields a $\frac{2}{3}$-pitch winding, and so forth. Phase groupings are now intermingled, for some slots contain coil sides in phases a and b, a and c, and b and c. Individual phase groups, such as that formed by a_1, a_2, a_3, a_4 on one side and $-a_1, -a_2, -a_3, -a_4$

Figure B.1 Distributed two-pole, three-phase full-pitch armature winding with voltage phasor diagram.

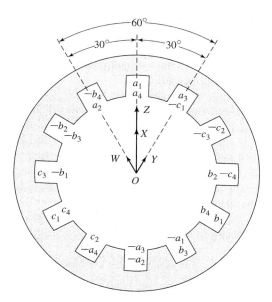

Figure B.2 Distributed two-pole, three-phase fractional-pitch armature winding with voltage phasor diagram.

on the other, are still displaced by 120 electrical degrees from the groups in other phases so that three-phase voltages are produced. Besides the minor feature of shortening the end connections, fractional-pitch windings can be shown to decrease the harmonic content of both voltage and mmf waves.

The end connections between the coil sides are normally in a region of negligible flux density, and hence altering them does not significantly affect the mutual flux linkages of the winding. Allocation of coil sides in slots is then the factor determining the generated voltages, and only that allocation need be specified in Figs. B.1 and B.2. The only requisite is that all coil sides in a phase be included in the interconnection in such a manner that individual voltages make a positive contribution to the total. The practical consequence is that end connections can be made according to the dictates of manufacturing simplicity; the theoretical consequence is that when computational advantages result, the coil sides in a phase can be combined in an arbitrary fashion to form equivalent coils.

One sacrifice is made in using the distributed and fractional-pitch windings of Figs. B.1 and B.2 compared with a concentrated full-pitch winding: for the same number of turns per phase, the fundamental-frequency generated voltage is lower. The harmonics are, in general, lowered by an appreciably greater factor, however, and the total number of turns which can be accommodated on a fixed iron geometry is increased. The effect of distributing the winding in Fig. B.1 is that the voltages of coils a_1 and a_2 are not in phase with those of coils a_3 and a_4. Thus, the voltage of coils a_1 and a_2 can be represented by phasor OX in Fig. B.1, and that of coils a_3 and a_4 by the phasor OY. The time-phase displacement between these two voltages is the same as the electrical angle between adjacent slots, so that OX and OY coincide with the centerlines of adjacent slots. The resultant phasor OZ for phase a is obviously smaller than the arithmetic sum of OX and OY.

In addition, the effect of fractional pitch in Fig. B.2 is that a coil links a smaller portion of the total pole flux than if it were a full-pitch coil. The effect can be super-imposed on that of distributing the winding by regarding coil sides a_2 and $-a_1$ as an equivalent coil with the phasor voltage OW (Fig. B.2), coil sides a_1, a_4, $-a_2$, and $-a_3$ as two equivalent coils with the phasor voltage OX (twice the length of OW), and coil sides a_3 and $-a_4$ as an equivalent coil with phasor voltage OY. The resultant phasor OZ for phase a is obviously smaller than the arithmetic sum of OW, OX, and OY and is also smaller than OZ in Fig. B.1.

The combination of these two effects can be included in a *winding factor* k_w to be used as a reduction factor in Eq. B.1. Thus, the rms generated voltage per phase is

$$E_{rms} = \sqrt{2}\pi k_w f N_{ph} \Phi_p \tag{B.2}$$

where N_{ph} is the total turns in series per phase and k_w accounts for the departure from the concentrated full-pitch case. For a three-phase machine, Eq. B.2 yields the line-to-line voltage for a Δ-connected winding and the line-to-neutral voltage for a Y-connected winding. As in any balanced Y connection, the line-to-line voltage of the latter winding is $\sqrt{3}$ times the line-to-neutral voltage.

B.1.2 Breadth and Pitch Factors

By separately considering the effects of distributing and of chording the winding, reduction factors can be obtained in generalized form convenient for quantitative analysis. The effect of distributing the winding in n slots per phase belt is to yield n voltage phasors displaced in phase by the electrical angle γ between slots, γ being equal to 180 electrical degrees divided by the number of slots per pole. Such a group of phasors is shown in Fig. B.3a and, in a more convenient form for addition, again in Fig. B.3b. Each phasor AB, BC, and CD is the chord of a circle with center at O and subtends the angle γ at the center. The phasor sum AD subtends the angle $n\gamma$, which, as noted previously, is 60 electrical degrees for the normal, uniformly distributed three-phase machine and 90 electrical degrees for the corresponding two-phase machine. From triangles OAa and OAd, respectively,

$$OA = \frac{Aa}{\sin(\gamma/2)} = \frac{AB}{2\sin(\gamma/2)} \tag{B.3}$$

$$OA = \frac{Ad}{\sin(n\gamma/2)} = \frac{AD}{2\sin(n\gamma/2)} \tag{B.4}$$

Equating these two values of OA yields

$$AD = AB\,\frac{\sin(n\gamma/2)}{\sin(\gamma/2)} \tag{B.5}$$

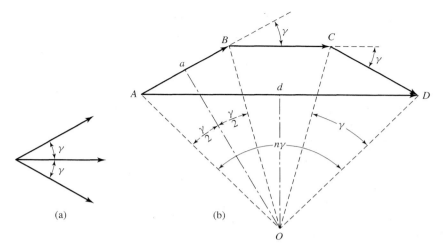

Figure B.3 (a) Coil voltage phasors and (b) phasor sum.

But the arithmetic sum of the phasors is $n(AB)$. Consequently, the reduction factor arising from distributing the winding over n slots each separated by γ electrical degrees is

$$k_b = \frac{AD}{nAB} = \frac{\sin(n\gamma/2)}{n\sin(\gamma/2)} \tag{B.6}$$

The factor k_b is called the *breadth factor* of the winding.

The effect of chording on the coil voltage can be obtained by first determining the flux linkages with the fractional-pitch coil. Since there are n coils per phase and N_{ph} total series turns per phase, each coil will have $N_c = N_{ph}/n$ turns per coil. From Fig. B.4 coil side $-a$ is only ρ electrical degrees from side a instead of the full $180°$. The flux linkage with the N_c-turn coil is

$$\lambda = N_c B_{peak} l r \left(\frac{2}{poles}\right) \int_\alpha^{\rho+\alpha} \sin\theta \, d\theta$$

$$= N_c B_{peak} l r \left(\frac{2}{poles}\right) [\cos\alpha - \cos(\alpha+\rho)] \tag{B.7}$$

where

$$l = \text{axial length of coil side}$$
$$r = \text{coil radius}$$
$$poles = \text{number of poles}$$

With α replaced by ωt to indicate rotation at ω electrical radians per second, Eq. B.7 becomes

$$\lambda = N_c B_{peak} l r \left(\frac{2}{poles}\right) [\cos\rho - \cos(\omega t + \rho)]$$

$$= -N_c B_{peak} l r \left(\frac{4}{poles}\right) \sin\left(\frac{\rho}{2}\right) \sin\left(\omega t + \left(\frac{\rho}{2}\right)\right) \tag{B.8}$$

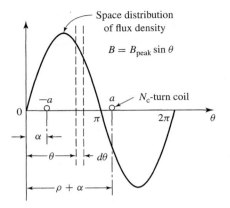

Figure B.4 Fractional-pitch coil in sinusoidal field.

and the instantaneous voltage is

$$e = \frac{d\lambda}{dt} = -\omega N_c B_{peak} lr \left(\frac{4}{poles} \right) \sin \left(\frac{\rho}{2} \right) \cos \left(\omega t + \left(\frac{\rho}{2} \right) \right) \tag{B.9}$$

The phase angle $(\rho/2)$ in Eq. B.9 merely indicates that the instantaneous voltage is no longer zero when α in Fig. B.5 is zero. The factor $\sin (\rho/2)$ is an amplitude-reduction factor, however, so that the rms voltage of Eq. B.1 is modified

$$E_{rms} = \sqrt{2}\pi k_p f N_{ph} \Phi_p \tag{B.10}$$

where the pitch factor k_p is

$$k_p = \sin \left(\frac{\rho}{2} \right) \tag{B.11}$$

When both the breadth and pitch factors apply, the rms voltage is

$$E_{rms} = \sqrt{2}\pi k_b k_p f N_{ph} \Phi_p = \sqrt{2} \pi k_w f N_{ph} \Phi_p \tag{B.12}$$

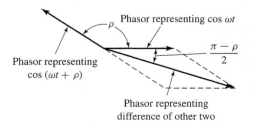

Figure B.5 Phasor addition for fractional-pitch coil.

which is an alternate form of Eq. B.2; the winding factor k_w is seen to be the product of the pitch and breadth factors.

$$k_w = k_b k_p \tag{B.13}$$

Calculate the breadth, pitch, and winding factors for the distributed fractional-pitch winding of Fig. B.2.

■ **Solution**

The winding of Fig. B.2 has two coils per phase belt, separated by an electrical angle of 30°. From Eq. B.6 the breadth factor is

$$k_b = \frac{\sin(n\gamma/2)}{n\sin(\gamma/2)} = \frac{\sin[2(30°)/2]}{2\sin(30°/2)} = 0.966$$

The fractional-pitch coils span $150° = 5\pi/6$ rad, and from Eq. B.11 pitch factor is

$$k_p = \sin\left(\frac{\rho}{2}\right) = \sin\left(\frac{5\pi}{12}\right) = 0.966$$

The winding factor is

$$k_w = k_b k_p = 0.933$$

B.2 ARMATURE MMF WAVES

Distribution of a winding in several slots per pole per phase and the use of fractional-pitch coils influence not only the emf generated in the winding but also the magnetic field produced by it. Space-fundamental components of the mmf distributions are examined in this article.

B.2.1 Concentrated Full-Pitch Windings

We have seen in Section 4.3 that a concentrated polyphase winding of N_{ph} turns per phase in a multipole machine produces a rectangular mmf wave around the air-gap circumference. With excitation by a sinusoidal current of amplitude I, the time-maximum amplitude of the space-fundamental component of the wave is, in accordance with Eq. 4.7,

$$(F_{ag1})_{peak} = \frac{4}{\pi}\frac{N_{ph}}{\text{poles}}(\sqrt{2}I) \quad \text{A·turns/pole} \tag{B.14}$$

where the winding factor k_w of Eq. 4.7 has been set equal to unity since in this case we are discussing the mmf wave of a concentrated winding.

Each phase of a polyphase concentrated winding creates such a time-varying standing mmf wave in space. This situation forms the basis of the analysis leading to

Eq. 4.41. For concentrated windings, Eq. 4.41 can be rewritten as

$$\mathcal{F}(\theta_{ae}, t) = \frac{3}{2}\left(\frac{4}{\pi}\right)\left(\frac{N_{ph}}{poles}\right)(\sqrt{2}I)\cos(\theta_{ae} - \omega t) \tag{B.15}$$

$$= \frac{6}{\pi}\left(\frac{N_{ph}}{poles}\right)(\sqrt{2}I)\cos(\theta_{ae} - \omega t) \tag{B.16}$$

The amplitude of the resultant mmf wave in a three-phase machine in ampere-turns per pole is then

$$F_A = \frac{6}{\pi}\left(\frac{N_{ph}}{poles}\right)(\sqrt{2}I) \quad \text{A} \cdot \text{turns/pole} \tag{B.17}$$

Similarly, for a q-phase machine, the amplitude is

$$F_A = \frac{2q}{\pi}\left(\frac{N_{ph}}{poles}\right)(\sqrt{2}I) \quad \text{A} \cdot \text{turns/pole} \tag{B.18}$$

In Eqs. B.17 and B.18, I is the rms current per phase. The equations include only the fundamental component of the actual distribution and apply to concentrated full-pitch windings with balanced excitation.

B.2.2 Distributed Fractional-Pitch Winding

When the coils in each phase of a winding are distributed among several slots per pole, the resultant space-fundamental mmf can be obtained by superposition from the preceding simpler considerations for a concentrated winding. The effect of distribution can be seen from Fig. B.6, which is a reproduction of the two-pole, three-phase, full-pitch winding with two slots per pole per phase given in Fig. B.1. Coils a_1 and a_2, b_1 and b_2, and c_1 and c_2 by themselves constitute the equivalent of a three-phase,

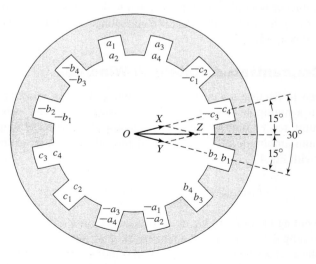

Figure B.6 Distributed two-pole, three-phase, full-pitch armature winding with mmf phasor diagram.

two-pole concentrated winding because they form three sets of coils excited by polyphase currents and mechanically displaced 120° from each other. They therefore produce a rotating space-fundamental mmf; the amplitude of this contribution is given by Eq. B.17 when N_{ph} is taken as the sum of the series turns in coils a_1 and a_2 only. Similarly, coils a_3 and a_4, b_3 and b_4, and c_3 and c_4 produce another identical mmf wave, but one which is phase-displaced in space by the slot angle $\gamma = 30°$ from the former wave. The resultant space-fundamental mmf wave for the winding can be obtained by adding these two sinusoidal contributions.

The mmf contribution from the a_1a_2, b_1b_2 and c_1c_2 coils can be represented by the phasor OX in Fig. B.6. Such phasor representation is appropriate because the waveforms concerned are sinusoidal, and phasor diagrams are simply convenient means for adding sine waves. These are space sinusoids, however, not time sinusoids. Phasor OX is drawn in the space position of the mmf peak for an instant of time when the current in phase a is a maximum. The length of OX is proportional to the number of turns in the associated coils. Similarly, the mmf contribution from the a_3a_4, b_3b_4, and c_3c_4 coils may be represented by the phasor OY. Accordingly, the phasor OZ represents the resultant mmf wave. Just as in the corresponding voltage diagram, the resultant mmf is seen to be smaller than if the same number of turns per phase were concentrated in one slot per pole.

In like manner, mmf phasors can be drawn for fractional-pitch windings as illustrated in Fig. B.7, which is a reproduction of the two-pole, three-phase, fractional-pitch winding with two slots per pole per phase given in Fig. B.2. Phasor OW represents the contribution for the equivalent coils formed by conductors a_2 and $-a_1$, b_2 and $-b_1$, and c_2 and $-c_1$; OX for a_1a_4 and $-a_3 - a_2$, b_1b_4 and $-b_3 - b_2$, and c_1c_4 and $-c_3 - c_2$; and OY for a_3 and $-a_4$, b_3 and $-b_4$, and c_3 and $-c_4$. The resultant phasor OZ is,

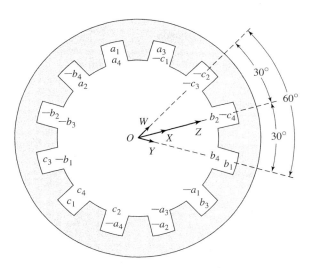

Figure B.7 Distributed two-pole, three-phase, fractional-pitch armature winding with mmf phasor diagram.

of course, smaller than the algebraic sum of the individual contributions and is also smaller than OZ in Fig. B.6.

By comparison with Figs. B.1 and B.2, these phasor diagrams can be seen to be identical with those for generated voltages. It therefore follows that pitch and breadth factors previously developed can be applied directly to the determination of resultant mmf. Thus, for a distributed, fractional-pitch, polyphase winding, the amplitude of the space-fundamental component of mmf can be obtained by using $k_b k_p N_{ph} = k_w N_{ph}$ instead of simply N_{ph} in Eqs. B.17 and B.18. These equations then become

$$F_A = \frac{6}{\pi}\left(\frac{k_b k_p N_{ph}}{poles}\right)(\sqrt{2}I) = \frac{6}{\pi}\left(\frac{k_w N_{ph}}{poles}\right)(\sqrt{2}I) \tag{B.19}$$

for a three-phase machine and

$$F_A = \frac{2q}{\pi}\left(\frac{k_b k_p N_{ph}}{poles}\right)(\sqrt{2}I) = \frac{2q}{\pi}\left(\frac{k_w N_{ph}}{poles}\right)(\sqrt{2}I) \tag{B.20}$$

for a q-phase machine, where F_A is in ampere-turns per pole.

B.3 AIR-GAP INDUCTANCES OF DISTRIBUTED WINDINGS

Figure B.8a shows an N-turn, full-pitch, concentrated armature winding in a two-pole magnetic structure with a concentric cylindrical rotor. The mmf of this configuration is shown in Fig. B.8b. Since the air-gap length g is much smaller than the average air-gap radius r, the air-gap radial magnetic field can be considered uniform and equal to the mmf divided by g. From Eq. 4.4 the space-fundamental mmf is given by

$$\mathcal{F}_{ag1} = \frac{4}{\pi}\frac{Ni}{2}\cos\theta_a \tag{B.21}$$

and the corresponding air-gap flux density is

$$B_{ag1} = \mu_0\frac{\mathcal{F}_{ag1}}{g} = \frac{2\mu_0 Ni}{\pi g}\cos\theta_a \tag{B.22}$$

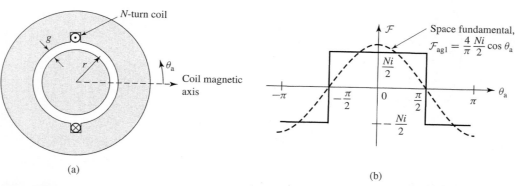

Figure B.8 (a) N-turn concentrated coil and (b) resultant mmf.

Equation B.22 can be integrated to find the fundamental air-gap flux per pole (Eq. 4.47)

$$\Phi_p = l \int_{-\pi/2}^{\pi/2} B_{ag1} r \, d\theta_a = \frac{4\mu_0 N l r}{\pi g} i \tag{B.23}$$

where l is the axial length of the air gap. The air-gap inductance of the coil can be found from Eq. 1.28

$$L = \frac{\lambda}{i} = \frac{N\Phi_p}{i} = \frac{4\mu_0 N^2 l r}{\pi g} \tag{B.24}$$

For a distributed multipole winding with N_{ph} series turns and a winding factor $k_w = k_b k_p$, the air-gap inductance can be found from Eq. B.24 by substituting for N the effective turns per pole pair ($2k_w N_{ph}/\text{poles}$)

$$L = \frac{4\mu_0 l r}{\pi g} \left(\frac{2k_w N_{ph}}{\text{poles}} \right)^2 = \frac{16\mu_0 l r}{\pi g} \left(\frac{k_w N_{ph}}{\text{poles}} \right)^2 \tag{B.25}$$

Finally, Fig. B.9 shows schematically two coils (labeled 1 and 2) with winding factors k_{w1} and k_{w2} and with $2N_1/\text{poles}$ and $2N_2/\text{poles}$ turns per pole pair, respectively; their magnetic axes are separated by an electrical angle α (equal to poles/2 times their spatial angular displacement). The mutual inductance between these two windings is given by

$$\begin{aligned} L_{12} &= \frac{4\mu_0}{\pi} \left(\frac{2k_{w1} N_1}{\text{poles}} \right) \left(\frac{2k_{w2} N_2}{\text{poles}} \right) \frac{lr}{g} \cos\alpha \\ &= \frac{16\mu_0 (k_{w1} N_1)(k_{w2} N_2) lr}{\pi g (\text{poles})^2} \cos\alpha \end{aligned} \tag{B.26}$$

Although the figure shows one winding on the rotor and the second on the stator, Eq. B.26 is equally valid for the case where both windings are on the same member.

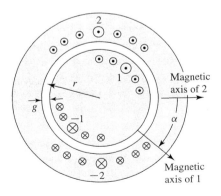

Figure B.9 Two distributed windings separated by electrical angle α.

EXAMPLE B.2

The two-pole stator-winding distribution of Fig. B.2 is found on an induction motor with an air-gap length of 0.381 mm, an average rotor radius of 6.35 cm, and an axial length of 20.3 cm. Each stator coil has 15 turns, and the coil phase connections are as shown in Fig. B.10. Calculate the phase-a air-gap inductance L_{aa0} and the phase-a to phase-b mutual inductance L_{ab}.

■ Solution

Note that the placement of the coils around the stator is such that the flux linkages of each of the two parallel paths are equal. In addition, the air-gap flux distribution is unchanged if, rather than dividing equally between the two legs, as actually occurs, one path were disconnected and all the current were to flow in the remaining path. Thus, the phase inductances can be found by calculating the inductances associated with only one of the parallel paths.

This result may appear to be somewhat puzzling because the two paths are connected in parallel, and thus it would appear that the parallel inductance should be one-half that of the single-path inductance. However, the inductances share a common magnetic circuit, and their combined inductance must reflect this fact. It should be pointed out, however, that the phase resistance is one-half that of each of the paths.

The winding factor has been calculated in Example B.1. Thus, from Eq. B.25,

$$
\begin{aligned}
L_{aa0} &= \frac{16\mu_0 lr}{\pi g} \left(\frac{k_w N_{ph}}{\text{poles}} \right)^2 \\
&= \frac{16(4\pi \times 10^{-7}) \times 0.203 \times 0.0635}{\pi(3.81 \times 10^{-4})} \left(\frac{0.933 \times 30}{2} \right)^2 \\
&= 42.4 \text{ mH}
\end{aligned}
$$

The winding axes are separated by $\alpha = 120°$, and thus from Eq. B.26

$$
L_{ab} = \frac{16\mu_0 (k_w N_{ph})^2 lr}{\pi g (\text{poles})^2} \cos \alpha = -21.2 \text{ mH}
$$

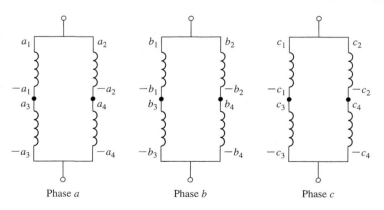

Figure B.10   Coil phase connections of Fig. B.2 for Example B.2.

B.4 APPENDIX B VARIABLES

α	Rotation angle in electrical degrees [rad]
γ	Angle between slots in electrical units [rad]
λ	Flux linkage [Wb]
μ_0	Permeability of free space $= 4\pi \times 10^{-7}$ [H/m]
Φ_p	Fundamental flux per pole [Wb]
ρ	Coil span in electrical units [rad]
θ_a	Stator spatial angle [rad]
θ_{ae}	Stator spatial angle in electrical units [rad]
ω	Electrical frequency [rad/sec]
B_{peak}	Peak magnetic flux density [T]
e, E	Generated voltage [V]
f	Electrical frequency [Hz]
$F, \mathcal{F}$	Magnetomotive force [A]
F_A	mmf amplitude [A·turns/pole]
g	aGp length [m]
i	Current [A]
l	Coil length [m]
k_b	Breadth factor
k_p	Pitch factor
k_w	Winding factor
L	Inductance [H]
n	Number of slots per phase
N	Number of turns
N_c	Number of turns per coil
N_{ph}	Number of turns per phase
poles	Number of poles
q	Number of phases
r	Radius [m]

Subscripts:

ag	Air gap
rms	Root mean square

C

APPENDIX

The dq0 Transformation

In this appendix, the direct- and quadrature-axis (dq0) theory introduced in Section 5.6 is formalized. The formal mathematical transformation from three-phase stator quantities to their direct- and quadrature-axis components is presented. These transformations are then used to express the governing equations for a synchronous machine in terms of the dq0 quantities.

C.1 TRANSFORMATION TO DIRECT- AND QUADRATURE-AXIS VARIABLES

In Section 5.6 the concept of resolving synchronous-machine armature quantities into two rotating components, one aligned with the field-winding axis, the direct-axis component, and one in quadrature with the field-winding axis, the quadrature-axis component, was introduced as a means of facilitating analysis of salient-pole machines. The usefulness of this concept stems from the fact that although each of the stator phases sees a time-varying inductance due to the saliency of the rotor, the transformed quantities rotate with the rotor and hence see constant magnetic paths. Although not discussed here, additional saliency effects are present under transient conditions, due to the different conducting paths in the rotor, rendering the concept of this transformation all the more useful.

Similarly, this transformation is useful from the point of view of analyzing the interaction of the rotor and stator flux- and mmf-waves, independent of whether or not saliency effects are present. By transforming the stator quantities into equivalent quantities which rotate in synchronism with the rotor, under steady-state conditions these interactions become those of constant mmf- and flux-waves separated by a constant spatial angle. This indeed is the point of view which corresponds to that of an observer in the rotor reference frame.

The idea behind the transformation is an old one, stemming from the work of Andre Blondel in France, and the technique is sometimes referred to as the *Blondel two-reaction method*. Much of the development in the form used here was carried out

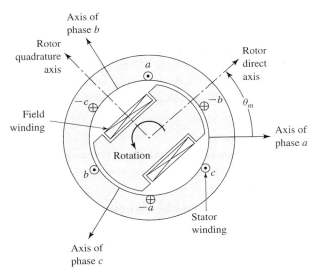

Axis of
phase b

Rotor
quadrature
axis

Rotor
direct
axis

Field
winding

Rotation

Axis of
phase a

Axis of
phase c

Stator
winding

Figure C.1 Idealized synchronous machine.

by R. E. Doherty, C. A. Nickle, R. H. Park, and their associates in the United States. The transformation itself, known as the *dq0 transformation,* can be represented in a straightforward fashion in terms of the electrical angle θ_{me} (equal to poles/2 times the spatial angle θ_{m}) between the rotor direct axis and the stator phase-a axis, as defined by Eq. 4.1 and shown in Fig. C.1.

Letting S represent a stator quantity to be transformed (current, voltage, or flux), we can write the transformation in matrix form as

$$\begin{bmatrix} S_{\text{d}} \\ S_{\text{q}} \\ S_0 \end{bmatrix} = \frac{2}{3} \begin{bmatrix} \cos(\theta_{\text{me}}) & \cos(\theta_{\text{me}} - 120°) & \cos(\theta_{\text{me}} + 120°) \\ -\sin(\theta_{\text{me}}) & -\sin(\theta_{\text{me}} - 120°) & -\sin(\theta_{\text{me}} + 120°) \\ \frac{1}{2} & \frac{1}{2} & \frac{1}{2} \end{bmatrix} \begin{bmatrix} S_{\text{a}} \\ S_{\text{b}} \\ S_{\text{c}} \end{bmatrix} \quad \text{(C.1)}$$

and the inverse transformation as

$$\begin{bmatrix} S_{\text{a}} \\ S_{\text{b}} \\ S_{\text{c}} \end{bmatrix} = \begin{bmatrix} \cos(\theta_{\text{me}}) & -\sin(\theta_{\text{me}}) & 1 \\ \cos(\theta_{\text{me}} - 120°) & -\sin(\theta_{\text{me}} - 120°) & 1 \\ \cos(\theta_{\text{me}} + 120°) & -\sin(\theta_{\text{me}} + 120°) & 1 \end{bmatrix} \begin{bmatrix} S_{\text{d}} \\ S_{\text{q}} \\ S_0 \end{bmatrix} \quad \text{(C.2)}$$

Here the subscripts d and q represent the direct and quadrature axes, respectively. A third component, the *zero-sequence component,* indicated by the subscript 0, is also included. This component is required to yield a unique transformation of the three stator-phase quantities; it corresponds to components of armature current which produce no net air-gap flux and hence no net flux linking the rotor circuits. As can be seen from Eq. C.1, under balanced-three-phase conditions, there are no zero-sequence components. Only balanced-three-phase conditions are considered in this book, and hence zero-sequence components are not discussed in any detail.

Note that the dq0 transformation applies to the instantaneous values of the quantities to be transformed, not rms values. Thus when applying the formal instantaneous transformations as presented here, one must be careful to avoid the use of rms values as are frequently used in phasor analyses such as are found in Chapter 5.

EXAMPLE C.1

A two-pole synchronous machine is carrying balanced three-phase armature currents

$$i_a = \sqrt{2}I_a \cos \omega t \qquad i_b = \sqrt{2}I_a \cos (\omega t - 120°) \qquad i_c = \sqrt{2}I_a \cos (\omega t + 120°)$$

The rotor is rotating at synchronous speed ω, and the rotor direct axis is aligned with the stator phase-a axis at time $t = 0$. Find the direct- and quadrature-axis current components.

■ Solution

The angle between the rotor direct axis and the stator phase-a axis can be expressed as

$$\theta_{me} = \omega t$$

From Eq. C.1

$$i_d = \frac{2}{3}[i_a \cos \omega t + i_b \cos (\omega t - 120°) + i_c \cos (\omega t + 120°)]$$

$$= \frac{2}{3}\sqrt{2}I_a[\cos^2 \omega t + \cos^2 (\omega t - 120°) + \cos^2 (\omega t + 120°)]$$

Using the trigonometric identity $\cos^2 \alpha = \frac{1}{2}(1 + \cos 2\alpha)$ gives

$$i_d = \sqrt{2}I_a$$

Similarly,

$$i_q = -\frac{2}{3}[i_a \sin \omega t + i_b \sin (\omega t - 120°) + i_c \sin (\omega t + 120°)]$$

$$= -\frac{2}{3}\sqrt{2}I_a[\cos \omega t \sin \omega t + \cos (\omega t - 120°) \sin (\omega t - 120°)$$

$$+ \cos (\omega t + 120°) \sin (\omega t + 120°)]$$

and using the trigonometric identity $\cos \alpha \sin \alpha = \frac{1}{2}\sin 2\alpha$ gives

$$i_q = 0$$

This result corresponds directly to our physical picture of the dq0 transformation. From the discussion of Section 4.5 we recognize that the balanced three-phase currents applied to this machine produce a synchronously rotating mmf wave which produces flux along the stator phase-a axis at time $t = 0$. This flux wave is thus aligned with the rotor direct axis at $t = 0$ and remains so since the rotor is rotating at the same speed. Hence the stator current produces only direct-axis flux and thus consists only of a direct-axis component.

C.2 BASIC SYNCHRONOUS-MACHINE RELATIONS IN dq0 VARIABLES

Equations 5.2 to 5.5 give the flux-linkage current relationships for a synchronous machine consisting of a field winding and a three-phase stator winding. This simple machine is sufficient to demonstrate the basic features of the machine representation in dq0 variables; the effects of additional rotor circuits such as damper windings can be introduced in a straightforward fashion.

The flux-linkage current relationships in terms of phase variables (Eqs. 5.2 to 5.5) are repeated here for convenience

$$
\begin{bmatrix} \lambda_a \\ \lambda_b \\ \lambda_c \\ \lambda_f \end{bmatrix} = \begin{bmatrix} \mathcal{L}_{aa} & \mathcal{L}_{ab} & \mathcal{L}_{ac} & \mathcal{L}_{af} \\ \mathcal{L}_{ba} & \mathcal{L}_{bb} & \mathcal{L}_{bc} & \mathcal{L}_{bf} \\ \mathcal{L}_{ca} & \mathcal{L}_{cb} & \mathcal{L}_{cc} & \mathcal{L}_{cf} \\ \mathcal{L}_{fa} & \mathcal{L}_{fb} & \mathcal{L}_{fc} & \mathcal{L}_{ff} \end{bmatrix} \begin{bmatrix} i_a \\ i_b \\ i_c \\ i_f \end{bmatrix} \tag{C.3}
$$

Unlike the analysis of Section 5.2, this analysis will include the effects of saliency, which causes the stator self and mutual inductances to vary with rotor position.

For the purposes of this analysis the idealized synchronous machine of Fig. C.1 is assumed to satisfy two conditions: (1) the air-gap permeance has a constant component as well as a smaller component which varies cosinusoidally with twice the rotor angle as measured (in electrical units) from the direct axis, and (2) the effects of space harmonics in the air-gap flux can be ignored. Although these approximations may appear somewhat restrictive, they form the basis of classical dq0 machine analysis and give excellent results in a wide variety of applications. Essentially they involve neglecting effects which result in time-harmonic stator voltages and currents and are thus consistent with our previous assumptions neglecting harmonics produced by discrete windings.

The various machine inductances can then be written in terms of the electrical rotor angle θ_{me} (between the rotor direct axis and the stator phase-a axis), using the notation of Section 5.2, as follows. For the stator self-inductances

$$
\mathcal{L}_{aa} = L_{al} + L_{aa0} + L_{g2} \cos 2\theta_{me} \tag{C.4}
$$

$$
\mathcal{L}_{bb} = L_{al} + L_{aa0} + L_{g2} \cos (2\theta_{me} + 120°) \tag{C.5}
$$

$$
\mathcal{L}_{cc} = L_{al} + L_{aa0} + L_{g2} \cos (2\theta_{me} - 120°) \tag{C.6}
$$

where L_{al} is the winding leakage inductance, L_{aa0} is the inductance corresponding to the constant component of the air-gap permeance and L_{g2} is the magnitude of the inductance which corresponds to the component of air-gap permeance which varies with rotor angle.

For the stator-to-stator mutual inductances

$$
\mathcal{L}_{ab} = \mathcal{L}_{ba} = -\frac{1}{2} L_{aa0} + L_{g2} \cos (2\theta_{me} - 120°) \tag{C.7}
$$

$$
\mathcal{L}_{bc} = \mathcal{L}_{cb} = -\frac{1}{2} L_{aa0} + L_{g2} \cos 2\theta_{me} \tag{C.8}
$$

$$\mathcal{L}_{ac} = \mathcal{L}_{ca} = -\frac{1}{2}L_{aa0} + L_{g2}\cos(2\theta_{me} + 120°) \tag{C.9}$$

For the field-winding self-inductance

$$\mathcal{L}_{ff} = L_{ff} \tag{C.10}$$

and for the stator-to-rotor mutual inductances

$$\mathcal{L}_{af} = \mathcal{L}_{fa} = L_{af}\cos\theta_{me} \tag{C.11}$$

$$\mathcal{L}_{bf} = \mathcal{L}_{fb} = L_{af}\cos(\theta_{me} - 120°) \tag{C.12}$$

$$\mathcal{L}_{cf} = \mathcal{L}_{fc} = L_{af}\cos(\theta_{me} + 120°) \tag{C.13}$$

Comparison with Section 5.2 shows that the effects of saliency appear only in the stator self- and mutual-inductance terms as an inductance term which varies with $2\theta_{me}$. This twice-angle variation can be understood with reference to Fig. C.1, where it can be seen that rotation of the rotor through 180° reproduces the original geometry of the magnetic circuit. Notice that the self-inductance of each stator phase is a maximum when the rotor direct axis is aligned with the axis of that phase and that the phase-phase mutual inductance is maximum when the rotor direct axis is aligned midway between the two phases. This is the expected result since the rotor direct axis is the path of lowest reluctance (maximum permeance) for air-gap flux.

The flux-linkage expressions of Eq. C.3 become much simpler when they are expressed in terms of dq0 variables. This can be done by application of the transformation of Eq. C.1 to both the flux linkages and the currents of Eq. C.3. The manipulations are somewhat laborious and are omitted here because they are simply algebraic. The results are

$$\lambda_d = L_d i_d + L_{af}i_f \tag{C.14}$$

$$\lambda_q = L_q i_q \tag{C.15}$$

$$\lambda_f = \frac{3}{2}L_{af}i_d + L_{ff}i_f \tag{C.16}$$

$$\lambda_0 = L_0 i_0 \tag{C.17}$$

In these equations, new inductance terms appear:

$$L_d = L_{al} + \frac{3}{2}(L_{aa0} + L_{g2}) \tag{C.18}$$

$$L_q = L_{al} + \frac{3}{2}(L_{aa0} - L_{g2}) \tag{C.19}$$

$$L_0 = L_{al} \tag{C.20}$$

The quantities L_d and L_q are the *direct-axis* and *quadrature-axis synchronous inductances,* respectively, corresponding directly to the direct- and quadrature-axis synchronous reactances discussed in Section 5.6 (i.e., $X_d = \omega_e L_d$ and $X_q = \omega_e L_q$). The inductance L_0 is the *zero-sequence inductance*. Notice that the transformed flux-linkage current relationships expressed in Eqs. C.14 to C.17 no longer contain inductances which are functions of rotor position. This feature is responsible for the usefulness of the dq0 transformation.

Transformation of the voltage equations

$$v_a = R_a i_a + \frac{d\lambda_a}{dt} \tag{C.21}$$

$$v_b = R_a i_b + \frac{d\lambda_b}{dt} \tag{C.22}$$

$$v_c = R_a i_c + \frac{d\lambda_c}{dt} \tag{C.23}$$

$$v_f = R_f i_f + \frac{d\lambda_f}{dt} \tag{C.24}$$

results in

$$v_d = R_a i_d + \frac{d\lambda_d}{dt} - \omega_{me}\lambda_q \tag{C.25}$$

$$v_q = R_a i_q + \frac{d\lambda_q}{dt} + \omega_{me}\lambda_d \tag{C.26}$$

$$v_f = R_f i_f + \frac{d\lambda_f}{dt} \tag{C.27}$$

$$v_0 = R_a i_0 + \frac{d\lambda_0}{dt} \tag{C.28}$$

(algebraic details are again omitted), where $\omega_{me} = d\theta_{me}/dt$ is the rotor electrical angular velocity.

In Eqs. C.25 and C.26 the terms $\omega_{me}\lambda_q$ and $\omega_{me}\lambda_d$ are speed-voltage terms which come as a result of the fact that we have chosen to define our variables in a reference frame rotating at the electrical angular velocity ω_{me}. These speed voltage terms are directly analogous to the speed-voltage terms found in the dc machine analysis of Chapter 9. In a dc machine, the commutator/brush system performs the transformation which transforms armature (rotor) voltages to the field-winding (stator) reference frame.

We now have the basic relations for analysis of our simple synchronous machine. They consist of the flux-linkage current equations C.14 to C.17, the voltage equations C.25 to C.28, and the transformation equations C.1 and C.2. When the rotor electrical angular velocity ω_{me} is constant, the differential equations are linear with constant coefficients. In addition, the transformer terms $d\lambda_d/dt$ and $d\lambda_q/dt$ in Eqs. C.25 and C.26 are often negligible with respect to the speed-voltage terms $\omega_{me}\lambda_q$ and $\omega_{me}\lambda_d$, providing further simplification. Omission of these terms corresponds to neglecting the harmonics and dc component in the transient solution for stator voltages and currents. In any case, the transformed equations are generally much easier to solve, both analytically and by computer simulation, than the equations expressed directly in terms of phase variables.

In using these equations and the corresponding equations in the machinery literature, careful note should be made of the sign convention and units employed. Here we have chosen the motor-reference convention for armature currents, with positive armature current flowing into the machine terminals. Also, SI units (volts, amperes, ohms, henrys, etc.) are used here; often in the literature one of several per-unit systems is used to provide numerical simplifications.[1]

To complete the useful set of equations, expressions for power and torque are needed. The instantaneous power into the three-phase stator is

$$p_s = v_a i_a + v_b i_b + v_c i_c \tag{C.29}$$

Phase quantities can be eliminated from Eq. C.29 by using Eq. C.2 written for voltages and currents. The result is

$$p_s = \frac{3}{2}(v_d i_d + v_q i_q + 2v_0 i_0) \tag{C.30}$$

The electromagnetic torque, T_{mech}, is readily obtained by using the techniques of Chapter 3 as the power output corresponding to the speed voltages divided by the shaft speed (in mechanical radians per second). From Eq. C.30 with the speed-voltage terms from Eqs. C.25 and C.26, and by recognizing ω_{me} as the rotor speed in electrical radians per second, we get

$$T_{mech} = \frac{3}{2}\left(\frac{poles}{2}\right)(\lambda_d i_q - \lambda_q i_d) \tag{C.31}$$

A word about sign conventions. When, as is the case in the derivation of this appendix, the motor-reference convention for currents is chosen (i.e., the positive reference direction for currents is into the machine), the torque of Eq. C.31 is the torque acting to accelerate the rotor. Alternatively, if the generator-reference convention is chosen, the torque of Eq. C.31 is the torque acting to decelerate the rotor. This result is, in general, conformity with torque production from interacting magnetic fields as expressed in Eq. 4.83. In Eq. C.31 we see the superposition of the interaction of components: the direct-axis magnetic flux produces torque via its interaction with the quadrature-axis mmf and the quadrature-axis magnetic flux produces torque via its interaction with the direct-axis mmf. Note that, for both of these interactions, the flux and interacting mmfs are 90 electrical degrees apart; hence the sine of the interacting angle (see Eq. 4.83) is unity which in turns leads to the simple form of Eq. C.31.

As a final cautionary note, the reader is again reminded that the currents, fluxes, and voltages in Eqs. C.29 through Eq. C.31 are instantaneous values. Thus, the reader

---

[1] See A. W. Rankin, "Per-Unit Impedances of Synchronous Machines," *Trans. AIEE* 64:569–573, 839–841 (1945).

is urged to avoid the use of rms values in these and the other transformation equations found in this appendix.

C.3 BASIC INDUCTION-MACHINE RELATIONS IN dq0 VARIABLES

In this derivation we will assume that the induction machine includes three-phase windings on both the rotor and the stator and that there are no saliency effects. In this case, the flux-linkage current relationships can be written as

$$
\begin{bmatrix} \lambda_a \\ \lambda_b \\ \lambda_c \\ \lambda_{aR} \\ \lambda_{bR} \\ \lambda_{cR} \end{bmatrix}
=
\begin{bmatrix}
\mathcal{L}_{aa} & \mathcal{L}_{ab} & \mathcal{L}_{ac} & \mathcal{L}_{aaR} & \mathcal{L}_{abR} & \mathcal{L}_{acR} \\
\mathcal{L}_{ba} & \mathcal{L}_{bb} & \mathcal{L}_{bc} & \mathcal{L}_{baR} & \mathcal{L}_{bbR} & \mathcal{L}_{bcR} \\
\mathcal{L}_{ca} & \mathcal{L}_{cb} & \mathcal{L}_{cc} & \mathcal{L}_{caR} & \mathcal{L}_{cbR} & \mathcal{L}_{ccR} \\
\mathcal{L}_{Aa} & \mathcal{L}_{aRb} & \mathcal{L}_{aRc} & \mathcal{L}_{aRaR} & \mathcal{L}_{aRbR} & \mathcal{L}_{aRC} \\
\mathcal{L}_{bRa} & \mathcal{L}_{bRb} & \mathcal{L}_{bRc} & \mathcal{L}_{bRaR} & \mathcal{L}_{bRbR} & \mathcal{L}_{bRcR} \\
\mathcal{L}_{cRa} & \mathcal{L}_{cRb} & \mathcal{L}_{cRc} & \mathcal{L}_{cRaR} & \mathcal{L}_{cRbR} & \mathcal{L}_{cRcR}
\end{bmatrix}
\begin{bmatrix} i_a \\ i_b \\ i_c \\ i_{aR} \\ i_{bR} \\ i_{cR} \end{bmatrix}
\tag{C.32}
$$

where the subscripts (a, b, c) refer to stator quantities while the subscripts (aR, bR, cR) refer to rotor quantities.

The various machine inductances can then be written in terms of the electrical rotor angle θ_{me} (defined in this case as between the rotor phase-aR and the stator phase-a axes), as follows. For the stator self-inductances

$$
\mathcal{L}_{aa} = \mathcal{L}_{bb} = \mathcal{L}_{cc} = L_{aa0} + L_{al} \tag{C.33}
$$

where L_{aa0} is the air-gap component of the stator self-inductance and L_{al} is the leakage component.

For the rotor self-inductances

$$
\mathcal{L}_{aRaR} = \mathcal{L}_{bRbR} = \mathcal{L}_{cRcR} = L_{aRaR0} + L_{aRl} \tag{C.34}
$$

where L_{aRaR0} is the air-gap component of the rotor self-inductance and L_{aRl} is the leakage component.

For the stator-to-stator mutual inductances

$$
\mathcal{L}_{ab} = \mathcal{L}_{ba} = \mathcal{L}_{ac} = \mathcal{L}_{ca} = \mathcal{L}_{bc} = \mathcal{L}_{cb} = -\frac{1}{2}L_{aa0} \tag{C.35}
$$

For the rotor-to-rotor mutual inductances

$$
\mathcal{L}_{aRbR} = \mathcal{L}_{bRaR} = \mathcal{L}_{aRcR} = \mathcal{L}_{cRaR} = \mathcal{L}_{bRcR} = \mathcal{L}_{cRbR} = -\frac{1}{2}L_{aRaR0} \tag{C.36}
$$

and for the stator-to-rotor mutual inductances

$$
\mathcal{L}_{aaR} = \mathcal{L}_{aRa} = \mathcal{L}_{bbR} = \mathcal{L}_{bRb} = \mathcal{L}_{ccR} = \mathcal{L}_{cRc} = L_{aaR} \cos \theta_{me} \tag{C.37}
$$

$$
\mathcal{L}_{baR} = \mathcal{L}_{aRb} = \mathcal{L}_{cbR} = \mathcal{L}_{bRc} = \mathcal{L}_{acR} = \mathcal{L}_{cRa} = L_{aaR} \cos (\theta_{me} - 120°) \tag{C.38}
$$

$$
\mathcal{L}_{caR} = \mathcal{L}_{aRc} = \mathcal{L}_{abR} = \mathcal{L}_{bRa} = \mathcal{L}_{bcR} = \mathcal{L}_{cRb} = L_{aaR} \cos (\theta_{me} + 120°) \tag{C.39}
$$

The corresponding voltage equations become

$$v_a = R_a i_a + \frac{d\lambda_a}{dt} \tag{C.40}$$

$$v_b = R_a i_b + \frac{d\lambda_b}{dt} \tag{C.41}$$

$$v_c = R_a i_c + \frac{d\lambda_c}{dt} \tag{C.42}$$

$$v_{aR} = 0 = R_{aR} i_{aR} + \frac{d\lambda_{aR}}{dt} \tag{C.43}$$

$$v_{bR} = 0 = R_{aR} i_{bR} + \frac{d\lambda_{bR}}{dt} \tag{C.44}$$

$$v_{cR} = 0 = R_{aR} i_{cR} + \frac{d\lambda_{cR}}{dt} \tag{C.45}$$

where the voltages v_{aR}, v_{bR}, and v_{cR} are set equal to zero because the rotor windings are shorted at their terminals.

In the case of a synchronous machine in which the stator flux wave and rotor rotate in synchronism (at least in the steady state), the choice of reference frame for the dq0 transformation is relatively obvious. Specifically, the most useful transformation is to a reference frame fixed to the rotor.

The choice is not so obvious in the case of an induction machine. For example, one might choose a reference frame fixed to the rotor and apply the transformation of Eqs. C.1 and C.2 directly. If this is done, because the rotor of an induction motor does not rotate at synchronous speed, the flux linkages seen in the rotor reference frame will not be constant, and hence the time derivatives in the transformed voltage equations will not be equal to zero. Correspondingly, the direct- and quadrature-axis flux linkages, currents, and voltages will be found to be time-varying, with the result that the transformation turns out to be of little practical value.

An alternative choice is to choose a reference frame rotating at the synchronous angular velocity. In this case, both the stator and rotor quantities will have to be transformed. In the case of the stator quantities, the rotor angle θ_{me} in Eqs. C.1 and C.2 would be replaced by θ_S where

$$\theta_S = \omega_e t + \theta_0 \tag{C.46}$$

is the angle between the axis of phase a and that of the synchronously rotating dq0 reference frame and θ_0.

The transformation equations for the stator quantities then become

$$\begin{bmatrix} S_d \\ S_q \\ S_0 \end{bmatrix} = \frac{2}{3} \begin{bmatrix} \cos(\theta_S) & \cos(\theta_S - 120°) & \cos(\theta_S + 120°) \\ -\sin(\theta_S) & -\sin(\theta_S - 120°) & -\sin(\theta_S + 120°) \\ \frac{1}{2} & \frac{1}{2} & \frac{1}{2} \end{bmatrix} \begin{bmatrix} S_a \\ S_b \\ S_c \end{bmatrix} \tag{C.47}$$

and the inverse transformation

$$
\begin{bmatrix} S_a \\ S_b \\ S_c \end{bmatrix} = \begin{bmatrix} \cos(\theta_S) & -\sin(\theta_S) & 1 \\ \cos(\theta_S - 120°) & -\sin(\theta_S - 120°) & 1 \\ \cos(\theta_S + 120°) & -\sin(\theta_S + 120°) & 1 \end{bmatrix} \begin{bmatrix} S_d \\ S_q \\ S_0 \end{bmatrix} \qquad (C.48)
$$

Similarly, in the case of the rotor, θ_S would be replaced by θ_R where

$$
\theta_R = (\omega_e - \omega_{me})t + \theta_0 \qquad (C.49)
$$

is the angle between the axis of rotor phase aR and that of the synchronously rotating dq0 reference frame and $(\omega_e - \omega_{me})$ is the electrical angular velocity of the synchronously rotating reference frame as seen from the rotor frame.

The transformation equations for the rotor quantities then become

$$
\begin{bmatrix} S_{dR} \\ S_{qR} \\ S_{0R} \end{bmatrix} = \frac{2}{3} \begin{bmatrix} \cos(\theta_R) & \cos(\theta_R - 120°) & \cos(\theta_R + 120°) \\ -\sin(\theta_R) & -\sin(\theta_R - 120°) & -\sin(\theta_R + 120°) \\ \frac{1}{2} & \frac{1}{2} & \frac{1}{2} \end{bmatrix} \begin{bmatrix} S_{aR} \\ S_{bR} \\ S_{cR} \end{bmatrix}
$$

$$(C.50)$$

and the inverse transformation

$$
\begin{bmatrix} S_{aR} \\ S_{bR} \\ S_{cR} \end{bmatrix} = \begin{bmatrix} \cos(\theta_R) & -\sin(\theta_R) & 1 \\ \cos(\theta_R - 120°) & -\sin(\theta_R - 120°) & 1 \\ \cos(\theta_R + 120°) & -\sin(\theta_R + 120°) & 1 \end{bmatrix} \begin{bmatrix} S_{dR} \\ S_{qR} \\ S_{0R} \end{bmatrix} \qquad (C.51)
$$

Using this set of transformations for the rotor and stator quantities, the transformed flux-linkage current relationships become

$$
\lambda_d = L_S i_d + L_m i_{dR} \qquad (C.52)
$$

$$
\lambda_q = L_S i_q + L_m i_{qR} \qquad (C.53)
$$

$$
\lambda_0 = L_0 i_0 \qquad (C.54)
$$

for the stator and

$$
\lambda_{dR} = L_m i_d + L_R i_{dR} \qquad (C.55)
$$

$$
\lambda_{qR} = L_m i_q + L_R i_{qR} \qquad (C.56)
$$

$$
\lambda_{0R} = L_{0R} i_{0R} \qquad (C.57)
$$

for the rotor.

Here we have defined a set of new inductances

$$
L_S = \frac{3}{2} L_{aa0} + L_{al} \qquad (C.58)
$$

$$
L_m = \frac{3}{2} L_{aaR0} \qquad (C.59)
$$

$$
L_0 = L_{al} \qquad (C.60)
$$

$$
L_R = \frac{3}{2} L_{aRaR0} + L_{aRl} \qquad (C.61)
$$

$$L_{0R} = L_{aRl} \tag{C.62}$$

The transformed stator-voltage equations are

$$v_d = R_a i_d + \frac{d\lambda_d}{dt} - \omega_e \lambda_q \tag{C.63}$$

$$v_q = R_a i_q + \frac{d\lambda_q}{dt} + \omega_e \lambda_d \tag{C.64}$$

$$v_0 = R_a i_0 + \frac{d\lambda_0}{dt} \tag{C.65}$$

and those for the rotor are

$$0 = R_{aR} i_{dR} + \frac{\lambda_{dR}}{dt} - (\omega_e - \omega_{me})\lambda_{qR} \tag{C.66}$$

$$0 = R_{aR} i_{qR} + \frac{d\lambda_{qR}}{dt} + (\omega_e - \omega_{me})\lambda_{dR} \tag{C.67}$$

$$0 = R_{aR} i_{0R} + \frac{d\lambda_{0R}}{dt} \tag{C.68}$$

Finally, using the techniques of Chapter 3, the torque can be expressed in a number of equivalent ways including

$$T_{mech} = \frac{3}{2}\left(\frac{poles}{2}\right)(\lambda_d i_q - \lambda_q i_d) \tag{C.69}$$

and

$$T_{mech} = \frac{3}{2}\left(\frac{poles}{2}\right)\left(\frac{L_m}{L_R}\right)(\lambda_{dR} i_q - \lambda_{qR} i_d) \tag{C.70}$$

C.4 APPENDIX C VARIABLES

λ	Flux linkage [Wb]
θ	Phase angle [rad]
θ_{me}	Rotor angle in electrical units [rad]
θ_R, θ_S	Angle to synchronously-rotating reference frame [rad]
ω, ω_e	Electrical frequency, rotor speed [rad/sec]
ω_{me}	Rotor angular velocity in electrical units [rad/sec]
i, I	Current [A]
$L, \mathcal{L}$	Inductance [H]
L_{aa0}	Inductance component corresponding to the constant component of the air-gap permeance [H]
L_{al}	Leakage inductance [H]
L_{g2}	Inductance component corresponding to the component of air-gap permeance which varies with rotor angle [H]

p	Power [W]
poles	Number of poles
R	Resistance [Ω]
S	Stator quantity
t	Time
T	Torque [N · m]
v	Voltage [V]

Subscripts:

0	Zero sequence
a, b, c	Phase designation
d	Direct Axis
f	Field winding
mech	Mechanical
q	Quadrature axis
R	Rotor

D APPENDIX

Engineering Aspects of Practical Electric Machine Performance and Operation

In this book the basic essential features of electric machinery have been discussed; this material forms the basis for understanding the behavior of electric machinery of all types. In this appendix our objective is to introduce practical issues associated with the engineering implementation of the machinery concepts which have been developed. Issues common to all electric machine types such as losses, cooling, and rating are discussed.

D.1 LOSSES

Consideration of machine losses is important for three reasons: (1) Losses determine the efficiency of the machine and appreciably influence its operating cost; (2) losses heat the machine and the corresponding temperature rise ultimately determines the maximum power output that can be obtained without undue deterioration of the motor insulation; and (3) the voltage drops or current components associated with supplying the losses must be properly accounted for in a machine representation. Machine efficiency, like that of transformers or any energy-transforming device, is given by

$$\text{Efficiency} = \frac{\text{output}}{\text{input}} \tag{D.1}$$

which can also be expressed as

$$\text{Efficiency} = \frac{\text{input} - \text{losses}}{\text{input}} = 1 - \frac{\text{losses}}{\text{input}} \tag{D.2}$$

$$\text{Efficiency} = \frac{\text{output}}{\text{output} + \text{losses}} \tag{D.3}$$

Rotating machines in general operate efficiently except at light loads. For example, the full-load efficiency of average motors ranges from 80 to 90 percent for motors on the order of 1 to 10 kW, 90 to 95 percent for motors up to a few hundred kW, and up to a few percent higher for larger motors.

The forms given by Eqs. D.2 and D.3 are often used for electric machines, since their efficiency is most commonly determined by measurement of losses instead of by directly measuring the input and output under load. Efficiencies determined from loss measurements can be used in comparing competing machines if exactly the same methods of measurement and computation are used in each case. For this reason, the various losses and the conditions for their measurement are precisely defined by the American National Standards Institute (ANSI), the Institute of Electrical and Electronics Engineers (IEEE), and the National Electrical Manufacturers Association (NEMA). The following discussion summarizes some of the various commonly-considered loss mechanisms.

Ohmic Losses *Ohmic, or I^2R losses,* are found in all windings of a machine. By convention, these losses are often computed on the basis of the dc resistances of the winding at 75°C although the calculation can typically be improved by measuring the winding temperature at each specific operating point. In addition, the ac component of the winding I^2R loss, which determines the effective (ac) resistance of the winding depends on the operating frequency and machine flux conditions. The increment in loss represented by the difference between dc and effective resistances is included with stray load losses, discussed below. In the field windings of synchronous and dc machines, only the losses in the field winding are charged against the machine efficiency; the losses in external sources supplying the excitation are charged against the plant of which the machine is a part. Closely associated with I^2R loss is the *brush-contact loss* at slip rings and commutators. By convention, this loss is normally neglected for induction and synchronous machines. For industrial-type dc machines the voltage drop at the brushes is regarded as constant at 2 V total when carbon and graphite brushes with shunts (pigtails) are used.

Mechanical Losses *Mechanical losses* consist of brush and bearing friction, windage, and the power required to circulate air through the machine and ventilating system, if one is provided, whether by self-contained or external fans (except for the power required to force air through long or restricted ducts external to the machine). Friction and windage losses can be measured by determining the input to the machine running at the proper speed but unloaded and unexcited. Frequently they are lumped with core loss and determined at the same time.

Open-Circuit, or No-Load, Core Loss *Open-circuit core loss* consists of the hysteresis and eddy-current losses arising from the time-varying flux densities in the iron of the machine with only the main exciting winding energized. In dc and synchronous machines, these losses are confined largely to the armature iron, although the flux variations arising from slot openings will cause losses in the field iron as well, particularly in the pole shoes or surfaces of the field iron. In induction machines the losses are confined largely to the stator iron. Open-circuit core loss can be found by measuring the input to the machine when it is operating unloaded at rated speed or frequency and under the appropriate flux or voltage conditions, and then deducting the friction and windage loss and, if the machine is self-driven during the test, the no-load armature I^2R loss (no-load stator I^2R loss for an induction motor). Usually, data are taken for a curve of core loss as a function of armature voltage in the neighborhood of rated voltage. The core loss under load is then considered to be the value at a voltage equal to rated voltage corrected for the armature resistance drop under load (a phasor correction for an ac machine). For induction motors, however, this correction is dispensed with, and the core loss at rated voltage is used. For efficiency determination alone, there is no need to segregate open-circuit core loss and friction and windage loss; the sum of these two losses is termed the *no-load rotational loss.*

Eddy-current loss varies with the square of the flux density, the frequency, and the thickness of laminations. Under normal machine conditions it can be expressed to a sufficiently close approximation as

$$P_e = K_e(B_{max} f \delta)^2 \tag{D.4}$$

where

$$\delta = \text{lamination thickness}$$
$$B_{max} = \text{maximum flux density}$$
$$f = \text{frequency}$$
$$K_e = \text{proportionality constant}$$

The value of K_e depends on the units used, volume of iron, and resistivity of the iron.

Variation of *hysteresis loss* can be expressed in equation form only on an empirical basis. A commonly used relation is

$$P_h = K_h f B_{max}^n \tag{D.5}$$

where K_h is a proportionality constant dependent on the characteristics and volume of iron and the units used. The exponent n ranges from 1.5 to 2.5, a value of 2.0 often being used for estimating purposes in machines. In both Eqs. D.4 and D.5, frequency can be replaced by speed and flux density by the appropriate voltage, with the proportionality constants changed accordingly.

When the machine is loaded, the space distribution of flux density is significantly changed by the mmf of the load currents. The actual core losses may increase noticeably. For example, mmf harmonics cause appreciable losses in the iron near the air-gap surfaces. The total increment in core loss is classified as part of the stray load loss.

Stray Load Loss *Stray load loss* consists of the losses arising from nonuniform current distribution in the copper and the additional core losses produced in the iron by distortion of the magnetic flux by the load current. It is a difficult loss to determine accurately. By convention it is taken as 1.0 percent of the output for dc machines. For synchronous and induction machines, stray-load loss is typically determined by various standard tests.

D.2 RATING AND HEATING

The rating of electrical devices such as machines and transformers is often determined by mechanical and thermal considerations. For example, the maximum winding current is typically determined by the maximum operating temperature which the insulation can withstand without damage or excessive loss of life. Similarly the maximum speed of a motor or generator is typically determined by mechanical considerations related to the structural integrity of the rotor or the performance of the bearings. The temperature rise resulting from the losses considered in Section D.1 is therefore a major factor in the rating of a machine.

The operating temperature of a machine is closely associated with its life expectancy because deterioration of the insulation is a function of both time and temperature. Such deterioration is a chemical phenomenon involving slow oxidation and brittle hardening leading to loss of mechanical durability and dielectric strength. In many cases the deterioration rate is such that the life of the insulation can be represented as an exponential

$$\text{Life} = A e^{B/T} \tag{D.6}$$

where A and B are constants and T is the absolute operating temperature. Thus, according to Eq. D.6, when life is plotted on a logarithmic scale against the reciprocal of absolute temperature on a uniform scale, a straight line should result. Such plots form valuable guides in the thermal evaluation of insulating materials and systems. A very rough idea of the life-temperature relation can be obtained from the old and more or less obsolete rule of thumb that the time to failure of organic insulation is halved for each 8 to 10°C rise.

The evaluation of insulating materials and insulation systems (which may include widely different materials and techniques in combination) is to a large extent based on accelerated life tests. Both normal life expectancy and service conditions will vary widely for different classes of electric equipment. Life expectancy, for example, may be a matter of minutes in some military and missile applications, may be 500 to 1000 h in certain aircraft and electronic equipment, and may range from 10 to 30 years or more in large industrial equipment. The test procedures will accordingly vary with the type of equipment. Accelerated life tests on models, called *motorettes,* are commonly used in insulation evaluation. Such tests, however, cannot be easily applied to all equipment, especially the insulation systems of large machines.

Insulation life tests generally attempt to simulate service conditions. They usually include the following elements:

- Thermal shock resulting from heating to the test temperature.
- Sustained heating at that temperature.
- Thermal shock resulting from cooling to room temperature or below.
- Vibration and mechanical stress such as may be encountered in actual service.
- Exposure to moisture.
- Dielectric testing to determine the condition of the insulation.

Enough samples must be tested to permit statistical methods to be applied in analyzing the results. The life-temperature relations obtained from these tests lead to the classification of the insulation or insulating system in the appropriate temperature class.

For the allowable temperature limits of insulating systems used commercially, the latest standards of ANSI, IEEE, and NEMA should be consulted. The three NEMA insulation-system classes of chief interest for industrial machines are class B, class F, and class H. Class B insulation includes mica, glass fiber, asbestos, and similar materials with suitable bonding substances. Class F insulation also includes mica, glass fiber, and synthetic substances similar to those in class B, but the system must be capable of withstanding higher temperatures. Class H insulation, intended for still higher temperatures, may consist of materials such as silicone elastomer and combinations including mica, glass fiber, asbestos, and so on, with bonding substances such as appropriate silicone resins. Experience and tests showing the material or system to be capable of operation at the recommended temperature form the important classifying criteria.

When the temperature class of the insulation is established, the permissible observable temperature rises for the various parts of industrial-type machines can be found by consulting the appropriate standards. Reasonably detailed distinctions are made with respect to type of machine, method of temperature measurement, machine part involved, whether the machine is enclosed, and the type of cooling (air-cooled, fan-cooled, hydrogen-cooled, etc.). Distinctions are also made between general-purpose machines and definite- or special-purpose machines. The term *general-purpose motor* refers to one of standard rating "up to 200 hp with standard operating characteristics and mechanical construction for use under usual service conditions without restriction to a particular application or type of application." In contrast a *special-purpose motor* is "designed with either operating characteristics or mechanical construction, or both, for a particular application." For the same class of insulation, the permissible rise of temperature is lower for a general-purpose motor than for a special-purpose motor, largely to allow a greater factor of safety where service conditions are unknown. Partially compensating the lower rise, however, is the fact that general-purpose motors are allowed a *service factor* of 1.15 when operated at rated voltage; the service factor is a multiplier which, applied to the rated output, indicates a permissible loading which may be carried continuously under the conditions specified for that service factor.

Examples of allowable temperature rises can be seen from Table D.1. The table applies to integral-horsepower induction motors, is based on 40°C ambient temperature, and assumes measurement of temperature rise by determining the increase of winding resistances.

The most common machine rating is the *continuous rating* defining the output (in kilowatts for dc generators, kilovoltamperes at a specified power factor for ac generators, and horsepower or kilowatts for motors) which can be carried indefinitely without exceeding established limitations. For intermittent, periodic, or varying duty, a machine may be given a short-time rating defining the load which can be carried for a specific time. Standard periods for short-time ratings are 5, 15, 30, and 60 minutes. Speeds, voltages, and frequencies are also specified in machine ratings, and provision

Table D.1 Table of allowable temperature rise, °C[†].

Motor type	Class B	Class F	Class H
1.15 service factor	90	115	
1.00 service factor, encapsulated windings	85	110	
Totally enclosed, fan-cooled	80	105	125
Totally enclosed, non-ventilated	85	110	130

[†]Excerpted from NEMA standards.

is made for possible variations in voltage and frequency. Motors, for example, must operate successfully at voltages 10 percent above and below rated voltage and, for ac motors, at frequencies 5 percent above and below rated frequency; the combined variation of voltage and frequency may not exceed 10 percent. Other performance conditions are so established that reasonable short-time overloads can be carried. Thus, the user of a motor can expect to be able to apply for a short time an overload of, say, 25 percent at 90 percent of normal voltage with an ample margin of safety.

The converse problem to the rating of machinery, that of choosing the size of machine for a particular application, is a relatively simple one when the load requirements remain substantially constant. For many motor applications, however, the load requirements vary more or less cyclically and over a wide range. The duty cycle of a typical crane or hoist motor offers a good example. From the thermal viewpoint, the average heating of the motor must be found by detailed study of the motor losses during the various parts of the cycle. Account must be taken of changes in ventilation with motor speed for open- and semi-closed motors. Judicious selection is based on a large amount of experimental data and considerable experience with the motors involved. For estimating the required size of motors operating at substantially constant speeds, it is sometimes assumed that the heating of the insulation varies as the square of the load, an assumption which obviously over-emphasizes the role of armature I^2R loss at the expense of the core loss. The rms ordinate of the power-time curve representing the duty cycle is obtained by the same technique used to find the rms value of periodically varying currents, and a motor rating is chosen on the basis of the result; i.e.,

$$\text{rms kW} = \sqrt{\frac{\Sigma(\text{kW})^2 \times \text{time}}{\text{running time} + (\text{standstill time}/k)}} \tag{D.7}$$

where the constant k accounts for the poorer ventilation at standstill and equals approximately 4 for an open motor. The time for a complete cycle must be short compared with the time for the motor to reach a steady temperature.

Although crude, the rms-kW method is used fairly often. The necessity for rounding the result to a commercially available motor size[1] obviates the need

---

[1] Commercially available motors are generally found in standard sizes as defined by NEMA. NEMA Standards on Motors and Generators specify motor rating as well as the type and dimensions of the motor frame.

for precise computations. Special consideration must be given to motors that are frequently started or reversed, for such operations are thermally equivalent to heavy overloads. Consideration must also be given to duty cycles having such high torque peaks that motors with continuous ratings chosen on purely thermal bases would be unable to furnish the torques required. It is to such duty cycles that special-purpose motors with short-time ratings are often applied. Short-time-rated motors in general have better torque-producing capability than motors rated to produce the same power output continuously, although, of course, they have a lower thermal capacity. Both these properties follow from the fact that a short-time-rated motor is designed for high flux densities in the iron and high current densities in the copper. In general, the ratio of torque capacity to thermal capacity increases as the period of the short-time rating decreases. Higher temperature rises are allowed in short-time-rated motors than for general-purpose motors. A motor with a 150-kW, 1-hr, 50°C rating, for example, may have the torque ability of a 200-kW continuously rated motor; it will be able to carry only about 0.8 times its rated output, or 120 kW continuously, however. In many cases it will be the economical solution for a drive requiring a continuous thermal capacity of 120 kW but having torque peaks which require the capability of a 200-kW continuously rated motor.

D.3 COOLING MEANS FOR ELECTRIC MACHINES

The cooling problem in electric apparatus in general increases in difficulty with increasing size. The surface area from which the heat must be carried away increases roughly as the square of the dimensions, whereas the heat developed by the losses is roughly proportional to the volume and therefore increases approximately as the cube of the dimensions. This problem is a particularly serious one in large turbine generators, where economy, mechanical requirements, shipping, and erection all demand compactness, especially for the rotor forging. Even in moderate size machines, for example, above a few thousand kVA for generators, a closed ventilating system is commonly used. Rather elaborate systems of cooling ducts must be provided to ensure that the cooling medium will effectively remove the heat arising from the losses.

For turbine generators, hydrogen is commonly used as the cooling medium in the totally enclosed ventilating system. Hydrogen has the following properties which make it well suited to the purpose:

- Its density is only about 0.07 times that of air at the same temperature and pressure, and therefore windage and ventilating losses are much less.

- Its specific heat on an equal-weight basis is about 14.5 times that of air. This means that, for the same temperature and pressure, hydrogen and air are about equally effective in their heat-storing capacity per unit volume, but the heat transfer by forced convection between the hot parts of the machine and the cooling gas is considerably greater with hydrogen than with air.

■ The life of the insulation is increased and maintenance expenses decreased because of the absence of dirt, moisture, and oxygen.

■ The fire hazard is minimized. A hydrogen-air mixture will not explode if the hydrogen content is above about 70 percent.

The result of the first two properties is that for the same operating conditions the heat which must be dissipated is reduced and at the same time the ease with which it can be carried off is increased.

The machine and its water-cooled heat exchanger for cooling the hydrogen must be sealed in a gas-tight envelope. The crux of the problem is in sealing the bearings. The system is maintained at a slight pressure (at least 0.5 psi) above atmospheric so that gas leakage is outward and an explosive mixture cannot accumulate in the machine. At this pressure, the rating of the machine can be increased by about 30 percent above its aircooled rating, and the full-load efficiency increased by about 0.5 percent. The trend is toward the use of higher pressures (15 to 60 psi). Increasing the hydrogen pressure from 0.5 to 15 psi increases the output for the same temperature rise by about 15 percent; a further increase to 30 psi provides about an additional 10 percent.

An important step which has made it possible almost to double the output of a hydrogen-cooled turbine-generator of given physical size is the development of *conductor cooling,* also called *inner cooling.* Here the coolant (liquid or gas) is forced through hollow ducts inside the conductor or conductor strands. Examples of such conductors can be seen in Fig. D.1. Thus, the thermal barrier presented by the electric insulation is largely circumvented, and the conductor losses can be absorbed directly by the coolant. Hydrogen is usually the cooling medium for the rotor conductors. Either gas or liquid cooling may be used for the stator conductors. Hydrogen is the coolant in the former case, and transit oil or water is commonly used in the latter. A large hydroelectric generator in which both stator and rotor are water-cooled is shown in Figs. 4.2 and 4.9.

(a)   (b)   (c)

Figure D.1 Cross sections of bars for two-layer stator windings of turbine-generators. Insulation system consists of synthetic resin with vacuum impregnation. (a) Indirectly cooled bar with tubular strands; (b) water-cooled bars, two-wire-wide mixed strands, (c) water-cooled bars, four-wire-wide mixed strands.

D APPENDIX

Engineering Aspects of Practical Electric Machine Performance and Operation

In this book the basic essential features of electric machinery have been discussed; this material forms the basis for understanding the behavior of electric machinery of all types. In this appendix our objective is to introduce practical issues associated with the engineering implementation of the machinery concepts which have been developed. Issues common to all electric machine types such as losses, cooling, and rating are discussed.

D.1 LOSSES

Consideration of machine losses is important for three reasons: (1) Losses determine the efficiency of the machine and appreciably influence its operating cost; (2) losses heat the machine and the corresponding temperature rise ultimately determines the maximum power output that can be obtained without undue deterioration of the motor insulation; and (3) the voltage drops or current components associated with supplying the losses must be properly accounted for in a machine representation. Machine efficiency, like that of transformers or any energy-transforming device, is given by

$$\text{Efficiency} = \frac{\text{output}}{\text{input}} \tag{D.1}$$

which can also be expressed as

$$\text{Efficiency} = \frac{\text{input} - \text{losses}}{\text{input}} = 1 - \frac{\text{losses}}{\text{input}} \tag{D.2}$$

$$\text{Efficiency} = \frac{\text{output}}{\text{output} + \text{losses}} \tag{D.3}$$

current is greater, i.e., the motor is *over-excited*, the excess mmf must be counterbalanced in the armature and a leading component of current is present; the motor then operates at a leading power factor.

Because magnetizing current must be supplied to inductive loads such as transformers and induction motors, the ability of over-excited synchronous motors to supply lagging current is a highly desirable feature which may have considerable economic importance. In effect, over-excited synchronous motors act as generators of lagging reactive kilovoltamperes and thereby relieve the power source of the necessity for supplying this component. They thus may perform the same function as a local capacitor installation. Sometimes unloaded synchronous machines are installed in power systems solely for power-factor correction or for control of reactive-kVA flow. Such machines, called *synchronous condensers*, may be more economical in the larger sizes than static capacitors.

Both synchronous and induction machines may become self-excited when a sufficiently heavy capacitive load is present in their stator circuits. The capacitive current then furnishes the excitation and may cause serious overvoltage or excessive transient torques. Because of the inherent capacitance of transmission lines, the problem may arise when synchronous generators are energizing long unloaded or lightly loaded lines. The use of shunt reactors at the sending end of the line to compensate the capacitive current is sometimes necessary. For induction motors, it is normal practice to avoid self-excitation by limiting the size of any parallel capacitor when the motor and capacitor are switched as a unit.

D.4.2 Turbine-Generator Excitation Systems

As the available ratings of turbine-generators have increased, the problems of supplying the dc field excitation (amounting to 4000 A or more in the larger units) have grown progressively more difficult. A common excitation source is a shaft-driven dc generator whose output is supplied to the alternator field through brushes and slip rings. Alternatively, excitation may be supplied from a shaft-driven alternator of conventional design as the main exciter. This alternator has a stationary armature and a rotating-field winding. Its frequency may be 180 or 240 Hz. Its output is fed to a stationary solid-state rectifier, which in turn supplies the turbine-generator field through slip rings.

Cooling and maintenance problems are inevitably associated with slip rings, commutators, and brushes. Many modern excitation systems have minimized these problems by minimizing the use of sliding contacts and brushes. As a result, some excitation systems employ shaft-driven ac alternators whose field windings are stationary and whose ac windings rotate. By the use of rotating rectifiers, dc excitation can be applied directly to the generator field winding without the use of slip rings.

Excitation systems of the latest design are being built without any sort of rotating exciter-alternator. In these systems, the excitation power is obtained from a special auxiliary transformer fed from the local power system. Alternatively it may be obtained directly from the main generator terminals; in one system a special armature winding is included in the main generator to supply the excitation power. In each of these systems the power is rectified using phase-controlled silicon-controlled recti-fiers (SCRs). These types of excitation system, which have been made possible by the development of reliable, high-power SCRs, are relatively simple in design and provide the fast response characteristics required in many modern applications.

D.5 ENERGY EFFICIENCY OF ELECTRIC MACHINERY

With increasing concern for both the supply and cost of energy comes a corresponding concern for efficiency in its use. Although electric energy can be converted to me-chanical energy with great efficiency, achieving maximum efficiency requires both careful design of the electric machinery and proper matching of machine and intended application.

Clearly, one means to maximize the efficiency of an electric machine is to min-imize its internal losses, such as those described in Section D.1. For example, the winding I^2R losses can be reduced by increasing the slot area so that more copper can be used, thus increasing the cross-sectional area of the windings and reducing the resistance.

Core loss can be reduced by decreasing the magnetic flux density in the iron of the machine. This can be done by increasing the volume of iron, but although the loss goes down in terms of watts per pound, the total volume of material (and hence the mass) is increased; depending on how the machine design is changed, there may be a point beyond which the losses actually begin to increase. Similarly, for a given flux density, eddy-current losses can be reduced by using thinner iron laminations.

One can see that there are trade-offs involved here; machines of more efficient design generally require more material and thus are bigger and more costly. Users will generally choose the "lowest-cost" solution to a particular requirement; if the increased capital cost of a high-efficiency motor can be expected to be offset by energy savings over the expected lifetime of the machine, they may select the high-efficiency machine, more costly machine. If not, users are very unlikely to select this option in spite of the increased efficiency.

Similarly, some types of electric machines are inherently more efficient than others. For example, single-phase capacitor-start induction motors (Section 9.2) are relatively inexpensive and highly reliable, finding use in all sorts of small appliances, e.g., refrigerators, air conditioners, and fans. Yet they are inherently less efficient than their three-phase counterparts. Modifications such as a capacitor-run feature can lead to greater efficiency in the single-phase induction motor, but they are expensive and often not economically justifiable.

To optimize the efficient use of electric machinery the machine must be properly matched to the application, both in terms of size and performance. Since typical induction motors tend to draw nearly constant reactive power, independent of load, and since this causes resistive losses in the supply lines, it is wise to pick the smallest-rating induction motor which can properly satisfy the requirements of a specific application. Alternatively, capacitive power-factor correction may be used. Proper application of modern solid-state control technology can also play an important role in optimizing both performance and efficiency.

There are, of course, practical limitations which affect the selection of the motor for any particular application. Chief among them is that motors are generally available only in certain standard sizes. For example, a typical manufacturer might make fractional-horsepower ac motors rated at $\frac{1}{8}$, $\frac{1}{6}$, $\frac{1}{4}$, $\frac{1}{3}$, $\frac{1}{2}$, $\frac{3}{4}$, and 1 hp (NEMA standard ratings). This discrete selection thus limits the ability to fine-tune a particular application; if the need is 0.8 hp, the user will undoubtedly end up buying a 1-hp device and settling for a somewhat lower than optimum efficiency. A custom-designed and manufactured 0.8-hp motor can be economically justified only if it is needed in large quantities.

It should be pointed out that an extremely common source of inefficiency in electric motor applications is the mismatch of the motor to its application. Even the most efficient 50-kW motors will be somewhat inefficient when driving a 20-kW load. Yet mismatches of this type often occur in practice, due in great extent to the difficulty in characterizing operating loads and a tendency on the part of application engineers to be conservative to make sure that the system in question is guaranteed to operate in the face of design uncertainties. More careful attention to this issue can go a long way toward increasing the efficiency of energy use in electric machine applications.

E APPENDIX

Table of Constants and Conversion Factors for SI Units

CONSTANTS

Permeability of free space	μ_0	$= 4\pi \times 10^{-7}$ H/m
Permittivity of free space	ϵ_0	$= 8.854 \times 10^{-12}$ F/m

CONVERSION FACTORS

Length	1 m = 3.281 ft = 39.37 in
Mass	1 kg = 0.0685 slug = 2.205 lb (mass) = 35.27 oz
Force	1 N = 0.225 lbf = 7.23 poundals
Torque	1 N $\cdot$ m = 0.738 lbf·ft = 141.6 oz·in
Pressure	1 Pa (N/m^2) = 1.45×10^{-4} lbf/in^2 = 9.86×10^{-6} atm
Energy	1 J (W·sec) = 9.48×10^{-4} BTU = 0.239 calories
Power	1 W = 1.341×10^{-3} hp = 3.412 BTU/hr
Moment of inertia	1 kg·m^2 = 0.738 slug·ft^2 = 23.7 lb·ft^2 = 141.6 oz·in·sec^2
Magnetic flux	1 Wb = 10^4 kilolines
Magnetic flux density	1 T (Wb/m^2) = 10,000 gauss = 64.5 kilolines/in^2
Magnetizing force	1 A·turn/m = 0.0254 A·turn/in = 0.0126 oersted

INDEX